I TATTI STUDIES IN
ITALIAN RENAISSANCE HISTORY

Sponsored by Villa I Tatti
Harvard University Center for Italian Renaissance Studies
Florence, Italy

quella figura va vestita tutta di Rosso co fondo doro. sotto è falsa   La testa di questa figura

Alione   N° 16 — Iacopo Peri Zazzerino.

ORPHEUS *in the* MARKETPLACE

Jacopo Peri and the Economy of
Late Renaissance Florence

Tim Carter
Richard A. Goldthwaite

HARVARD UNIVERSITY PRESS
Cambridge, Massachusetts
London, England
2013

Frontispiece:
Peri as Arion in the fifth of the 1589 *intermedi*. The text below
the image reads *Questa figura va vestita tutta di rosso con fondo
d'oro sotto e sopra; la vesta di questa figura intera e grande. Arione,
no. 16: Jacopo Peri Zazzerino* (probably a direction to a costume
maker, referring to the full-figure costume entirely in red on a
gold foundation). *Source:* Florence, Biblioteca Nazionale
Centrale, Palatina C.B.53, vol. 2, fol. 6. (With permission of the
Ministero per i Beni e le Attività Culturali della Repubblica
Italiana/Biblioteca Nazionale Centrale, Firenze; further
reproduction or duplication by whatever means is forbidden.)

Library of Congress Cataloging-in-Publication Data
Carter, Tim, 1954–
Orpheus in the marketplace : Jacopo Peri and the economy of
late renaissance Florence / Tim Carter and Richard A. Goldthwaite.
     pages   cm
Includes bibliographical references and index.
ISBN 978-0-674-72464-8 (alk. paper)
 1. Peri, Jacopo, 1561–1633.   2. Composers—Italy—Biography.
    3. Peri, Jacopo, 1561–1633—Finance, Personal.
     4. Composers—Italy—Florence—Economic
                 conditions—16th century.
 5. Composers—Italy—Florence—Economic conditions—17th
century.   6. Finance, Personal—Italy—Florence—History—
16th century.   7. Finance, Personal—Italy—Florence—
History—17th century.   8. Florence (Italy)—Economic
conditions—16th century.   9. Florence (Italy)—Economic
              conditions—17th century.
     I. Goldthwaite, Richard A.   II. Title.
          ML410.P292C43   2013
              782.1092—dc23
          [B]   2013001710

Contents

Figures and Tables

Figures

GENEALOGICAL CHARTS

GRAPH

ILLUSTRATIONS

MAPS

Tables

Preface

The immediate occasion for writing this book was Richard Goldthwaite's discovery in the Archivio di Stato, Florence (ASF) of what is here called the Peri Archive, a collection of more than two dozen account books belonging to the noted Florentine singer and composer Jacopo Peri (1561–1633) and to members of his immediate family. With these documents Jacopo Peri can claim a first in the economic historiography of this city: of the many Florentines waiting in the wings, account books in hand still to be studied, he is the first to make his appearance in the literature as a well-documented operator in the local marketplace who was neither an artisan known for his skills nor a businessman active in the forward sectors of the economy. We know much about how Florentines conducted their economic lives with respect to attitudes, practices, institutions, and opportunities; but Peri's ledgers open the door to a microhistory of the life of one fairly ordinary Florentine of middling status that offers a more focused view of the economic culture—or the culture of the market—of one of the most famous centers of early modern capitalism, and in a specific period that remains too little explored.

Tim Carter's interest in this project stemmed from musicological rather than economic concerns. In the late sixteenth and early seventeenth centuries Florence was also a center for new experiments in musical theater—not least, what we now call opera—and in songs for solo voice and instrumental accompaniment, and Peri was intimately involved in them. His *Dafne* (1598) and then *Euridice* (1600)—the latter often identified as the first opera to survive complete—brought to the stage a new form of theatrical entertainment in which a dramatic text was set entirely to music of various types. These *favole in musica*, to adopt the contemporary term, partook of a long series of discussions in Florentine academies and salons about the nature of dramatic music from classical antiquity on and how it might best be adopted in the theater of the day. They also served the agendas, and reflected the tastes, of their creators, on the one hand, and their patrons, on the other, whether the Medici grand dukes or the Florentine patricians who moved, or wished to move, in circles close to them.

This much is well known, as are the broad outlines of Peri's musical career, including his long service as a performer and composer among the Medici court musicians and in other Florentine musical institutions. The new archival material in the Peri Archive, consisting almost entirely of financial accounts, has few specific references directly related to his musical activity (they can be found in the Chronology in Appendix A). But it is precisely the new and abundant information on Peri's economic activity in Florence outside of music that has challenged us to explore whether and how his musical and other worlds intersected and interacted. These questions have tended to move beyond the scope of a single scholar, or of a single set of disciplinary methodologies, and even our collaboration, between an economic historian and a musicologist—each broad-minded in various ways—leaves plenty of room for further interpretative maneuvering. What we have found most intriguing about Peri, however, is the question of how best to characterize a life driven, like many others, by countervailing forces: the individual and the market, the specific and the general, the personal and the impersonal, art and the economy, and culture and society.

We are grateful to Mark Evan Bonds, Gian Mario Cao, Anthony Cummings, Elena Fumagalli, Brenda Preyer, Marco Spallanzani, and Sharon Strocchia for help on specific points of inquiry; to Silvia Cosi for several of the photographs; and to Graziella Coi for the graphics. Our special thanks go to Suzanne Cusick, Giuliano Pinto, Lorenzo Polizzotto, and the anonymous readers for the I Tatti Studies series and Harvard University Press, who read part or all of our manuscript and gave us invaluable suggestions for it.

A Note on Money

The Peri accounts are kept in either of the two principal monies of account long current in Florence. One is the *lira* (£); the other is variously called florin (*fl.*), ducat (*du.*), or *scudo* (*sc.*), terms used interchangeably for the same money of account. For the purpose of consistency, and to avoid confusing the reader, we use only the term "florin" in the text; but in citations we retain the terms used therein. In the original documents this money of account, whichever of the three terms is used to identify it, is almost always followed by *di moneta di £7*—indicating what is called its "price," that is, the exchange rate between it and the *lira*—to distinguish it from the *scudo d'oro*, another money of account whose price was 7½ *lire*. The *scudo d'oro*, however, was used mostly in business circles, and it is only in that context that it occasionally appears in the Peri accounts. Likewise, *fiorini di £4* were used typically for payments to servants and, again, they appear infrequently. In the sources, the symbol for the *scudo*, whether the *scudo di moneta di £7* or the *scudo d'oro*, is the inverted triangle (∇). All three of these monies of account—or all five, if one wants to distinguish between the florin, ducat, and *scudo*—were divided into 20 *soldi* (*s.*), each of which was subdivided into 12 *denari* (*d.*). In Florence the terms *soldo* and *denaro* were used generally as fractions—¹⁄₂₀ and ¹⁄₂₄₀ (¹⁄₁₂ of the *soldo*), respectively—and also for weights and measures.

All the above were, precisely, monies of account, not coins. Only rarely is a specific coin mentioned in account entries, and it is almost always the *piastra*, a large silver coin with a price of £7 or *fl.*1. By the end of the sixteenth century the silver *piastra* had replaced the gold florin as the city's major circulating coin. Other coins that occasionally appear in waste-book entries for very small transactions are the *testone* (worth £2), the *mezzo testone* (worth £1), the *giulio* (worth 13s.4d., or ⅔ of the *lira*), and the *crazia* (worth 1s.8d., or

$\frac{1}{12}$ of the *lira*). The other monetary unit mentioned in our text, the *grosso*, was not an official coin but, rather, a term used for the *soldo* ($\frac{1}{20}$ of the *lira*). The *lira*, to repeat, was not a coin.

To appreciate something of the real value of expenditures expressed in these monies, the reader might keep in mind that throughout the period an unskilled day laborer in the construction industry was paid about £1 a day, or about *fl*.35 a year—what one might consider the minimum wage. Since labor is a basic factor of production, this value is the soundest economic criterion to use.

For a guide to the evolution of the Florentine monetary system to the end of the sixteenth century, see Goldthwaite and Mandich, *Studi sulla moneta fiorentina*.

A Note on Transcriptions

Our transcriptions from primary manuscript documents adopt the following principles. Original orthographies are retained save *v* for (consonant) *u*, *i* for *j* and vice versa, *ii* for *ij* (or *y*), and *s* for long-*s*. Thus we keep *havere*, *hieri*, *hora*, *humile*, and the like; irregular doubled consonants, as in *dissegno*; and *et* for *e* or *ed*, although *&* is rendered as *et* or *e*, depending on context. Accents are added (and sometimes removed) where standard (including the *accento chiuso* on -*é*), as are apostrophes to indicate contractions (so *ne* is transcribed as *ne*, *né*, or *ne'*, depending on sense) save in common forms (*sarebbon*, *venir*). Punctuation and the use of uppercase letters is modernized. All abbreviations are expanded (including the likes of *7ᵃ* as *settimana*), as are honorifics. Insertions (whether interleaved or in the margins) are placed between > and <; deletions, where it is useful to give them, are bounded by < >; and square brackets are used for editorial additions. Transcriptions from contemporary printed documents (as distinct from such transcriptions taken from secondary sources) follow similar principles in terms of orthographies (save for ampersands) and the expansion of abbreviations, although we have tended to intervene less in matters of accents, punctuation, and the use of upper- and lowercase, "missing" apostrophes, and the styling of titles or honorifics, given that in these matters such documents tend to be more consistent internally (however inconsistent they might seem in modern Italian) and less open to interpretation.

Documents dated *stile fiorentino* (with the year beginning on 25 March) are styled in the format 23 January 1584/85, which we also adopt in other cases where confusion might arise; all dates not so styled are to be read as *stile moderno*. We translate the *e compagni* in the names of business partnership as "& Partners," the "&" indicating the formality of the organization and "Partners" avoiding the misleading organizational implications of the cognate "company."

We use the following abbreviations in citing sources: ASF, Archivio di Stato, Florence; LC, Libri di commercio (in ASF); *Herla*, Progetto Herla (<www.capitalespettacolo.it>). Churches and similar institutions are styled with the conventional S. (San, Santo, or Santa) or SS. (Santi, Santissimo, or Santissima); when "San" or "Santa" are used in a place name, they are spelled out (San Marco Vecchio). Bibliographical references use short-title forms, with full details being given in Works Cited.

ORPHEUS *in the* MARKETPLACE

Introduction

Jacopo Peri (1561–1633) may need no introduction to musicians: he is well known, by name at least, as the composer of the first opera to survive complete, *Euridice* (1600), and for his contributions to the new repertory of songs for solo voice and instrumental accompaniment that emerged in Florence around the same time. But others might wonder why an otherwise obscure Florentine in a no less obscure period of the city's history merits the attention we lavish on him here. The answer is straightforward: he left behind not just his music and a reputation as an innovative composer, but also an entire archive of personal account books heretofore completely unknown. This archive is a real treasure trove not because the documents tell us much about Peri's music (they do not), nor even because they are unique of their kind (they certainly are not), but because, quite simply, they have provided the material for this, the first economic biography of anyone—international merchant bankers for which the city is famous not excepted—operating in the completely unstudied marketplace of late Renaissance Florence, a city that a century earlier was one of the great industrial, commercial, and banking capitals of Europe. That he was a musician operating in this marketplace also gives the story a rather special twist. By bringing Peri's professional and personal spheres into sharper, more detailed focus, these account books and other new documents allow us to place him in his social and other worlds (Chapters 1 and 4)—perhaps more completely so than any other Renaissance composer— and to go beyond this to show how the life of someone of relatively modest means offers us a comprehensive view of the economic world of his time (Chapter 2) and opens up a new perspective on his musical world (Chapter 3).

First, however, it is worth setting the stage, as it were, just as did the first scene of *Euridice* prior to Peri's entrance in the role of Orpheus. He brought the famed singer of classical antiquity to musical life in the context of a court celebration, for the wedding of Maria de' Medici and Henri IV of France. But however momentous the occasion, and however significant the marriage for Florence and its grand duke in the broader terms of European power-politics, Peri afterward went home to continue his performance on the real stage of life, the local marketplace where he had to make a living finding his way through all its complex urban webs. That gave us the title for this book; now we need to explain the historiographical and documentary foundations on which it is built.

The Story So Far

Few genres in the history of music have their origins fixed so precisely as what we now call opera; few also generated such controversy at their outset that setting the record straight became a matter of historical necessity very early on. A year after Peri's death, Pietro de' Bardi—son of the Florentine patron, Giovanni de' Bardi—responded to a request from the music theorist Giovanni Battista Doni for information about the origins of the new styles of music for the stage that had emerged some forty years before. Doni, a Florentine now living in Rome, was planning to write about music in ancient Greek and Roman theater and its modern re-creation with the invention of opera. His research would underpin still more recent experiments in musical theater being undertaken by his patrons, the Barberini family, with Pope Urban VIII (Maffeo Barberini) at its head. Doni contacted for information a number of persons who had been alive at that time or were somehow related to those involved: the composer Claudio Monteverdi wrote two letters back to him in 1632–33.

Bardi's response of 16 December 1634 set down the basic facts: "There was also then in Florence Jacopo Peri, who, as the principal student of Cristofano

Malvezzi, played and composed both on the organ and keyboard instruments and in counterpoint to his [Malvezzi's?] considerable praise. And among the singers of this city he was without mistake held inferior to no one" (*Era ancora in Firenze allora Jacopo Peri, il quale, come primo scolaro di Cristofano Malvezzi, e nell'organo, e stromenti di tasto, e nel contrappunto, sonava e componeva con molto sua lode, e tra i cantori di questa città era senza fallo tenuto a nessuno inferiore*). Bardi wrote that Peri, in competition (*a competenza*) with Giulio Caccini, sweetened the roughness of earlier experiments in the new style by Vincenzo Galilei, such that they were the chief singers and inventors of this manner of composition (*acquistarono il titolo di primi cantori, e d'inventori di questo modo di comporre*). Peri had more learning, and gained great fame for his discovery of how to imitate common speech by way of a few musical notes (*Il Peri aveva più scienza, e trovato modo con ricercar poche corde, e con altra esatta diligenza, d'imitar il parlar familiare acquistò gran fama*). Caccini, on the other hand, had a lighter, more graceful touch (*più leggiadria nelle sue invenzioni*). Both, however, had found a way to move the emotions in rare ways (*muovere raramente gli affetti*).[1]

Bardi went on to describe the first opera. *Dafne*, with a libretto by "Signor" Ottavio Rinuccini (we shall see the significance of that styling), was set by Peri with few notes in short scenes (*con poco numero di sluoni* [sic], *con brevità di scene*), and was performed in a small room, and sung in private (*in piccola stanza recitata, e privatamente cantata*): Bardi was stunned by amazement (*e io restai stupido per la meraviglia*). Caccini and Peri owed a debt to Rinuccini, "but still more to Signor Jacopo Corsi, who, impassioned and content only with the excellent in this art, instructed these composers with excellent ideas and admirable doctrines, as was appropriate for something so noble" (*ma più al Signor Jacopo Corsi, che infiammatosi, e non contento, se non dell'eccellente in quest'arte, instruiva que' componitori, con pensieri eccellenti, e dottrine mirabili, come conveniva a cosa sì nobile*). They followed his lessons in all their subsequent works of this kind. After *Dafne*, many such plays (*favole*) by Rinuccini were performed, supported by his very great friend Corsi (*con*

---

1. Bardi's letter is given in Solerti, *Le origini del melodramma*, 143–47, and is translated in Strunk, *Source Readings in Music History*, 4: 15–17 (but our translation differs). Solerti and Strunk variously include numerous other prefaces and similar texts associated with early opera in Florence (including Peri's preface to *Euridice*). Relevant extracts are also presented in Kirkendale, *Court Musicians*; for Bardi, see 237–38.

l'amicissimo Corsi), and were received with much applause, including *Euridice* and *Arianna*.

There is a strong degree of Florentine pride here—for Bardi, Doni, and of course, the Barberini. The poet Andrea Salvadori had already noted in the 1620s that it brought no little glory to the Tuscan name that under the Most Serene Grand Dukes the musical practice of ancient Greek drama had been revived in Florence, although he then extended the argument to increase that glory still more, given that the court was now moving away from pagan legends in favor of more "useful" sacred ones.[2] But Pietro de' Bardi's account also elided events in somewhat confusing ways: temporal proximity to events does not guarantee accurate reporting, especially when other agendas come into play (such as Bardi's attempt to protect his father's reputation). He explicitly associated Giovanni de' Bardi's protégé, Giulio Caccini, with Corsi, and implicitly with *Dafne*, although Caccini probably had nothing to do with that opera (though he claimed in 1614 that he had); and although Caccini composed a setting of Rinuccini's *Euridice*, it was largely Peri's that was done on 6 October 1600 at the festivities celebrating the wedding of Maria de' Medici and King Henri IV (though we shall see that this was not the first performance). *Arianna* (first performed in Mantua in 1608) certainly had a libretto by Rinuccini, but Corsi was already dead, and its composer was Monteverdi (Bardi's elision was of a kind to lead at least some later historians astray). Caccini certainly had strong supporters in his camp, most notably Filippo Vitali in the preface to his opera *Aretusa* (1620) and Severo Bonini in his *Discorsi e regole sovra la musica* of the early 1650s. But so, too, did Peri, including Marco da Gagliano in the preface to the score of his own setting of Rinuccini's *Dafne* (1608).[3] And even Bonini recalled how the audience of *Euridice* had been moved to tears as Peri sang Orpheus's plea before the gates of Hades, "Funeste piagge, ombrosi orridi campi." He also called Peri, nicknamed Il Zazzerino, "a most erudite singer and composer, of excellent man-

2. Andrea Salvadori, preface to *La regina Sant'Orsola, recitata in musica nel teatro del Serenissimo Gran Duca di Toscana* (Florence: Pietro Ceconcelli, 1625), in Carter, *Jacopo Peri*, 1: 87: *Nè forse è poca gloria del nome Toscano, che si come sotto gl'auspici de' Serenissimi Gran Duchi prima in questo Teatro fù rinovato l'uso de' gl'antichi Drammi di Grecia in musica, così oggi in questo medesimo, sia stato aperto un nuovo campo, di trattare con più utile, e diletto, lasciate le vane favole de' Gentili, le vere, e sacre azzioni Cristiane.*

3. See the relevant extracts in Kirkendale, *Court Musicians*, 168–73 (Caccini), 206 (Gagliano).

ners and well born in our city of Florence, who in singing his works composed with the greatest artifice—they being in lachrymose vein, his chief talent—would have moved and disposed every stony heart to tears (*Cantore e compositor eruditissimo è stato il Sig. Jacopo Peri detto il Zazzerino d'ottimi costumi, e ben nato della nostra città di Firenze, il qual cantando le sue opere composte con sommo artifizzio, essendo di concetto lagrimevole, proprio suo talento, havrebbe mosso e disposto al pianto ogni impetrito cuore*).[4]

Far less flattering to Peri was a scurrilous sonnet by Francesco Ruspoli (1579–1625), probably written in the last years of the poet's life (see Appendix D). Ruspoli identifies his target by way of his odd physiognomy—what the poet's commentator Stefano Rosselli (1598–1664) described as big feet splayed outward and thin legs—and satirizes his mendacity, his exaggerated piety, his pompous pretensions as the Moses of counterpoint, and his arrogant tendency to wear his nobility on his ass. The commentary by Rosselli, a literary figure known today above all for his description of the tombs in Florentine churches (1657), provides further information about the composer, some of which is incorrect.[5] He says that he knew Peri in Florence (which is plausible), although internal evidence would date the commentary itself to the 1650s or early 1660s.[6] He uses a reference toward the end of Ruspoli's sonnet to claim that while Peri often said that he was born in Rome, which may or may not be true, he was raised in the orphanage of S. Caterina delle Ruote in Florence, which is false: he lived with his mother in Florence at least in the early 1580s, and anyway, S. Caterina delle Ruote probably did not become an orphanage until 1591. Rosselli explains the nickname Il Zazzerino (a reference to Peri's shock of red hair); says he was gifted with a most beautiful voice as a soprano (but he was a tenor) and was much in demand for musical performances in the city; describes his rise within the court to become the principal

4. Kirkendale, *Court Musicians*, 239. There is a modern edition and translation of the treatise in Bonini, *Severo Bonini's "Discorsi e regole,"* ed. Bonino.

5. That commentary also survives in a slightly expanded version by the Florentine chronicler Andrea Cavalcanti (1610–73). Rosselli's text (annotated to show Cavalcanti's additions) is in Ruspoli, *Poesie*, ed. Arlìa, 55–73; Cavalcanti's is in Carter, *Jacopo Peri*, 1: 284–93 (from the copy in Florence, Biblioteca Nazionale Centrale, Magl. VII.572). The birth and death dates for Ruspoli, Rosselli, and Cavalcanti given here derive from information reported by Arlìa; in some other sources they vary slightly.

6. Rosselli refers to "many years" having passed since Peri's son, Alfonso, murdered his wife (in 1642).

director of the music and the musicians (*il principal direttore della musica e de' musici*), although there was no such official position; pokes fun at the way Peri walked; and takes great pleasure in the salacious details of how Peri's son, Alfonso, murdered his wife and fled into exile. These types of stories and anecdotes had long fascinated Florentine chroniclers: it was the reverse side of the coin, as it were, of the Florentine obsession (for reasons we shall discover) with documenting family histories.

Rosselli's commentary on Ruspoli's sonnet is an interesting footnote, for all the need to take it with several grains of salt. However, it was the Bardi line that entered the musical historiography and still exerts a notable influence on accounts of Peri today. Because of his role in the rise of opera, Peri was at least a name still known in the late seventeenth and eighteenth centuries: the noted English music historian Charles Burney even went so far as to transcribe portions of *Euridice* in preparation for his compendious *A General History of Music from the Earliest Ages to the Present Period, to which is prefixed a Dissertation on the Music of the Ancients* (London, 1776–89).[7] However, he did not quite know what to make of them: "It is not difficult to discover . . . that all the patrons and artists of this new species of Music, except Monteverde, were *Dilettanti* and *shallow contrapuntists*, who, as is usual, condemned and affected to despise that which they could not understand."[8] Peri usually merited an entry in the musical dictionaries of the nineteenth century, such as the pioneering *Biographie universelle des musiciens et bibliographie générale de la musique* by François-Joseph Fétis (Brussels, 1835–44) or the first edition of George Grove's venerable *A Dictionary of Music and Musicians* (London, 1879–89). He also generated interest among such antiquarians as Adrien de la Fage, who reprinted Ruspoli's sonnet and its commentary in his quaintly titled *Essais de diphthérographie musicale* (Paris, 1864), and Giuseppe Odoardo Corazzini, whose essay "Jacopo Peri e la sua famiglia" (1895) was the result of a remarkably energetic and effective trawl through the Florentine archives. Also commonly labeled as antiquarians—although they deserve much more—are such prominent Italian scholars as Stefano Davari (1836–1909),

---

7. Burney's manuscript is in London, British Library, Additional MS 11588; see also Burney, *A General History of Music*, ed. Mercer, 2: 509–24, for an account of early opera, quoting musical passages from Peri's *Euridice*, Caccini's *Euridice*, and Monteverdi's *Orfeo*. Burney claims to have seen Peri's score in Florence in the collection of a "Marchese Rinuccini"; ibid., 2: 515.

8. Ibid., 2: 514. "Monteverde" was a standard English spelling of the composer's name.

the head of what became the Archivio di Stato in Mantua, and Angelo Solerti (1865–1907). Davari fought, quite literally, for the liberation of Italy, and his work in the Mantuan archives, in particular on Monteverdi (1884), had strongly patriotic overtones and set standards hard to beat even today. Solerti's more synthetic view of the rise of opera, on the one hand, and of Florentine court entertainments, on the other (in publications from 1903 to 1905), was also strongly rooted in archival documents—and in literary texts—if, again, with broader points to make.

The nationalist agendas of that period are clear also in the edition of Peri's *Euridice* that Luigi Torchi included in his seven-volume series transcribing into modern musical notation the "most important Italian musical works from the fourteenth to the seventeenth centuries": *L'arte musicale in Italia: Pubblicazione nazionale delle più importanti opere musicali italiane dal secolo XIV al XVII, tratte da codici, antichi manoscritti ed edizioni primitive, scelte, trascritte in notazione moderna, messe in partitura ed annotate* (Milan, 1898–1907).[9] But there were aesthetic issues in play, as well: the presumed corruption of Italian opera by the too-cosmopolitan Giacomo Puccini and his followers, and the Germanic influence of Richard Wagner's music-dramas. Both Solerti and Torchi invoke the notion of a "purer" Italian style rooted in earlier times, to which, armed with the knowledge they provided, modern composers might aspire. But the fact that Torchi's edition of *Euridice* precedes Monteverdi's *Ballo delle ingrate* and *Combattimento di Tancredi e Clorinda* (all in the sixth volume of *L'arte musicale in Italia*) raises other questions. For Davari and Solerti, too, Peri was best viewed as a precursor of the great Monteverdi. A slightly earlier Mantuan music historian, Pietro Canal, had already been misled by a series of cumulative errors (perhaps even going back to Pietro de' Bardi, we have seen) to claim that, for the Mantuan opera *Arianna* (1608), Peri wrote the recitatives and Monteverdi the arias, the latter, in the nineteenth-century Italian view, being far more important than the former. The mistake was soon corrected, but it is symptomatic.[10]

---

9. This was not the first modern edition of *Euridice*; a vocal score was published in Florence in 1863.

10. Kirkendale, *Court Musicians*, 218, traces the error back to the second quarter of the eighteenth century; it gets repeated in Alessandro Ademollo, *La bell'Adriana*, 64, and Corazzini, "Jacopo Peri e la sua famiglia," 47.

Torchi's edition of *Euridice* was in the typical early twentieth-century vein. It has a rich piano accompaniment that provides a good basis for studying late Romantic harmony but bears scant relation to Peri's original score which, save in the choruses, has just two staves, one for the voice and one for the basso continuo, the latter a "figured" bass line above which players of chordal instruments—a harpsichord, chitarrone (a large lute with a neck extension to allow for long bass strings), or the like—would add harmony according to the figures and to convention. The distinguished Italian musicologist Nino Pirrotta surely made a better job of it when he prepared *Euridice* for a performance on the newly established Terzo Programma of the RAI broadcasting network in January 1951: this Italian radio channel had been inaugurated in October 1950 with a transmission of Monteverdi's first opera, *Orfeo* (1607), which takes Peri's opera as its model even as it surpasses it.[11] But for a decent published score, we had to wait until 1981 for Howard Mayer Brown's more faithful (because literal) edition of *Euridice*—although it, too, has its quirks. A reliable edition of Peri's chamber songs, included in *Le varie musiche* issued in 1609 and a second, expanded edition in 1619, did not appear in print until 1985. By the 1980s, the so-called early-music revival of the postwar period had long been in full swing—with performers and scholars often working together—and we now have good recordings both of *Euridice* and of most of Peri's songs.[12] Yet we still have much to learn about how this music might have sounded in his time, and still more about what it might have meant, both for Peri and for his listeners. Engaging with that meaning is one of the challenges we embrace, with some trepidation, in this book, which among many other things seeks to ask—even if it can never fully answer—a simple question: how much does what we now know about Peri's life and times affect a reading of his musical works? Our conclusion—that it is both less and more than one might have thought—will be surprising.

11. The broadcast of *Euridice* and the wider issues it involves are covered in Cummings, *Nino Pirrotta*.

12. *Euridice*, directed by Anibal E. Cetrangolo, Sylva Pozzer (soprano), Luca Dordolo (tenor), La Compagnia dei Febi Armonici/Ensemble Albalonga, Pavane ADW 7372/3 (2000). *Il Zazzerino: Music of Jacopo Peri*, Ellen Hargis (soprano), Paul O'Dette (chitarrone), Andrew Lawrence-King (harp), Hille Perl (lirone), Harmonia Mundi 907234 (1999).

Sources and Documents

What has hitherto been known about Peri was already based on considerable archival research. The Archivio di Stato in Florence (ASF) is a well-known treasure house for scholars working on Tuscan history in any period. Some of its holdings have already been plumbed in prior work on Peri: the massive collection of letters in the series "Mediceo del Principato"; the documents associated with particular branches of the Medici court administration (principally the "Guardaroba medicea," i.e., the "Wardrobe," and the "Depositeria Generale" recording salaries and other payments); institutional records such as those of the Arte della Lana and Arte dei Mercantanti di Calimala (for the Duomo and S. Giovanni Battista), or of other churches in Florence (the Badia, SS. Annunziata, etc.) that became "Corporazioni religiose soppresse dal governo francese"; and *fondi* concerning confraternities ("Compagnie religiose soppresse da Pietro Leopoldo"), notaries ("Notarile moderno"), and private families. The documentation is vast, and the catalogues haphazard; and while the savvy archivist can often track through institutional records in logical ways, more general collections rely essentially on serendipity. For example, the Medici Archive Project (<www.medici.org>), the most recent attempt at producing a catalogue of the letters to the court in the *fondo* "Mediceo del Principato," currently (October 2012) identifies just two documents directly associated with Jacopo Peri—one of which refers to his son—whereas a far greater number are known already in the literature, and a few more are presented in our book for the first time.

Given Peri's connections with Mantua by way of Eleonora de' Medici (wife of Duke Vincenzo Gonzaga) and then her son, Ferdinando (who also became duke), the Archivio di Stato in Mantua contains a number of documents relevant to him. These are in the *carteggio* of the Archivio Gonzaga, although some letters were pulled out by Stefano Davari and placed in a separate collection of "Autografi," as Davari did for other well-known poets, artists, musicians, and similar figures of note. Serendipity applies here, too, save for the "Autografi": the *carteggio* is organized in files arranged geographically (by place of origin) and chronologically, most with separate fascicles grouping letters by a named sender, if an official functionary, or just lumped under "diversi" or "varie." Matters are made simpler, however, by the splendid online Progetto Herla done under the auspices of the Fondazione Mantova Capitale Europea dello Spettacolo, established in 1999 (<www.capitalespettacolo.it>).

This is a catalogue of documents in the Archivio Gonzaga (and some other Italian archives) relating to Mantuan court spectacles under the Gonzagas from 1480 to 1630. The term "court spectacles" is interpreted very broadly to include references to all manner of artists involved in such activities even when not associated with a specific theatrical or similar event. The search engine is also very efficient, and while this database's summaries of documents are no substitute for a visit to the archive, they often provide useful leads—we sometimes cite them accordingly (by reference number: e.g., *Herla* C-1828).

No such online resources were available to Corazzini or to the authors of the two most complete biographical studies of Peri to date—by Tim Carter (1980, published in 1989) and Warren Kirkendale (1993).[13] Carter's doctoral dissertation was a musicological "life and works" study typical of its time— based on archives and musical sources—if less in tune with how we might now prefer to read musicians' lives: the best recent example for Florence in our period is Suzanne Cusick's fine study of Francesca Caccini (2009). Kirkendale's work was presented as a long (fifty-five-page) entry in what is in effect a biographical dictionary (but organized chronologically) of the court musicians in Florence during the period of the Medici dukes and grand dukes, from Duke Alessandro de' Medici to Grand Duke Gian Gastone (so, 1531 to 1737). Kirkendale spent more than thirty years in archives in Florence, Mantua, and Rome (and elsewhere) in an impressively systematic search through all the types of sources noted above, and more, which must have amounted to tens of thousands of pages of documents. As some have noted, his focus on individual "court" musicians—while understandable—does not give the complete picture of music and musicians in Florence, which was as complex as in any major city in this period, and the design of his book places the emphasis on documented facts rather than interpretation.[14] But it remains an indispensable source for anyone working on the subject, and we shall refer to it often in these pages.

13. Carter, *Jacopo Peri*; Kirkendale, *Court Musicians*, 189–243.

14. The need for a broader picture is argued briefly in Carter, "Crossing the Boundaries"; for other criticisms of Kirkendale's *Court Musicians*, see the review by John Walter Hill and Kelley Harness in *Journal of the American Musicological Society* 48 (1995): 106–15, and also Annibaldi, "Sulle impertinenze della musicologia 'antropocentrica.'"

We have long known that Peri was more than just a jobbing musician: in the second quarter of the seventeenth century Pietro de' Bardi and Severo Bonini already tended to characterize him as something more. Bonini styles him *signore* and notes his good birth and fine manners, while Bardi praises his learning and invention. Although both acknowledge his role as a professional singer, they also suggest that he rose above the crowd: not quite, but almost, a noble dilettante (in the best sense of the term, rather than Burney's). Davari and Solerti were familiar enough with the archives to know that Peri had interests other than music, and Corazzini placed him in sufficiently broader social contexts to suggest that there were other stories to tell about his life in Florence. Not until now, however, have enough documents been known such that we can tell many of these stories in fuller terms.

For now we have what here is called the Peri Archive. These documents have newly surfaced in an ASF *fondo* called "Libri di commercio" (LC), a modern, heterogeneous collection consisting exclusively of private account books that probably came into the state's possession through confiscation of property and the impounding of assets for reasons such as bankruptcy or criminal condemnation. The *fondo* has existed for some time, but the previous inventory included only a fraction of its contents, without any indication that there was more, much more. However, a new inventory, produced just over a decade or so ago, lists the full collection: some 5,537 items, odds and ends of account books dating from the fourteenth to the nineteenth century and now organized alphabetically under family names. And there is Jacopo Peri, with some dozen books to his name. A relatively easy further search turned up account books of the immediate families of his first wife, the Fortunati, and of his third, the Fortini and the Monaldi (both at the end of their branches of the family line). On examination it became apparent that these books originally constituted a distinct and coherent collection of twenty-eight items, almost all account books, which we have brought together under one rubric, not just because of the family connection but also because Peri clearly had had possession of them. He himself appropriated one with many unwritten pages for recording his own accounts, and he made occasional entries or comments related to his financial interests in several of the others. All these books, including Peri's own, became a part of the patrimony he left his sons, which remained intact with its own accounting identity through three successive ledgers, down to his last surviving son, Alfonso. With Alfonso's condemnation for the murder of his wife, the Peri estate was confiscated, and hence the account books belonging to Peri, including those from the other families, came into the possession of the state in the seventeenth century as a single collection, although they were eventually separated out in the modern organization of LC (which is why the inventory numbers do not follow a single sequence, and why the Peri Archive no longer has a formal identity as such).

It is worth prefacing the details of the Peri Archive given below with some general remarks on the nature, purpose, and problems of its contents. The core of this accounting material consists of six ledgers (*libri di debitori e creditori*), two accompanied by their journals, that follow one another in succession for sixty years, from 1580 to 1640, the first two kept by Peri himself, the third, opened in the final years of his life, kept by his son Dino, and the last three kept for the administration of his estate by, first, Dino and then, after his death, by Alfonso. To explain the kind of information these ledgers yield, it is important to keep in mind the limited function of these documents. As we shall see in Chapter 2, Peri's *libri di debitori e creditori e ricordi* can be categorized as a genre that has a tradition in Florence going back to the fourteenth century. Exactly as indicated by the way Florentines identified these ledgers, accounts are opened not for all monetary transactions but for debits and credits that were not going to be settled immediately and therefore needed to be recorded. Hence account entries are few and far between and represent only a miniscule part of the writer's economic transactions. Florentines, even the very wealthy, did not keep accounts to know how much they were earning in any one year, or how much they were worth at any one time, or how much either income or net worth changed over time; and in fact, digging around in even the most detailed and voluminous private accounts does not turn up enough data to construct precise overall balances of income and expenditures, or balances of net worth. We therefore cannot expect to find in Peri's accounts a comprehensive record of his assets or of his income, including the salaries we know he was earning as a musician (all paid in cash), let alone what he might have gained from commissions and other musical services.

The *ricordi* (personal records or memoranda) in Peri's account books fall into the same Florentine tradition, for these were often to be found in the second part of a ledger containing accounts kept only for one's private affairs. They record events related to the entries in the first part of the ledger, such as investments, the purchase of properties, and dowry arrangements; but they also include marriages, births and deaths of children, nomination to public offices, and other such basic information about events in the life of the writer. However, Peri does not refer, as indeed few did, to other notable happenings in Florence, even though one might think that he would have considered them to have an impact on his career (e.g., the death of a grand duke). In almost all these aspects, Peri's *ricordi* are typical of earlier examples of the genre except for language and styling: his Tuscan reflects the vocabulary and orthographies typical of the Bembist reforms of the earlier sixteenth century, as does his careful use of punctuation, including commas, semicolons, colons, periods, and other indeterminate markings, as well as apostrophes and the like.[15] The same is true of Peri's letters, all autograph, in which the rhetoric is nuanced and carefully controlled.

While hardly being anything like a modern diary, the *ricordi* are not quite as formal and impersonal as their earlier equivalents. The writer's feelings occasionally break through, not in an explicit and direct way, yet clearly enough and certainly more so than what was typical a century before. Sometimes— rarely—Peri is explicit about strong feelings even in what should be a neutral account entry: for instance, he takes pride in one son and shows despair over another; and he does not hide his anger and distress in reporting complicated legal litigation. Elsewhere—and especially when the routine of the standard *ricordo* is broken by an entry that is different in nature and longer, if still written with detachment—only a little imagination is required: one can easily sense Peri's pride in traveling with a cardinal to Bologna and going to Rome for another, and the affection and sense of honor he feels in accompanying a daughter to a convent in Prato. With repetition over time, and considering the history of his own household, his prayers to have children take on something more than just a formula; and his goodwill toward a servant or a tenant farmer can be read into account entries that reveal a compromise over a contractual agreement. On occasion, too, one feels a strong impulse behind a *ricordo* but cannot quite decide what it was, most notably in his account of the new coffin he had made for his first two wives. In these and other instances that the reader will encounter in the course of our text, we have not hesitated to use the moment to try to penetrate through to Peri's personality, just as we have tried to engage with his music, dangerous though this strategy might seem.

15. On these developments see Maraschio, "Il secondo Cinquecento," 122–23.

But all this raises the first of several fundamental questions about these documents, whether the accounts or the *ricordi*: who did the writer expect would read them? Account books were legal documents in Florence—proof of credits and debts—and as such they could be submitted for judicial examination in cases of litigation. Moreover, with laxity about prompt payment being common during the period, accounts had to be kept on hand sometimes for years (as we shall see). Accounts, too, could figure in the settlement of estates when sons had to uncover any possible inequalities in past payments to them. As for the *ricordi*, they clearly served as a reference for all kinds of specific information about marriages, births, and offices held, useful not just for the person creating them but also for his heirs: we shall see Peri reminding his sons of future obligations that he knew would extend beyond his death. And these documents also served a higher purpose that went beyond practical matters, for they were historical records, written to future readers: hence their impersonality and formality. Florentines had nothing if not a strong historical sense: they wrote more—many more—histories and chronicles than any other Italians; and we see that historical sensitivity alive in the keeping of accounts and writing down *ricordi*, and in the enormous accumulation of these documents that makes this city stand out still today among all others in the whole of Europe. The phenomenon has often been noted for the earlier period of the republic, but the need remained acute during the century after the Medici returned to Florence as dukes and then grand dukes, indeed perhaps still more so because of the changes wrought by the *principato* in Florentines' senses of self and of place. In short, the Peri Archive bears witness not just to a deep-seated Florentine tradition of record keeping, but also to one man's attempts to fix his position in changing times.

The new evidence that we bring to the table, however, prompts further consideration of issues both specific to the materials at hand and also broader in terms of the historical enterprise. For all the richness of Peri's worlds, their relative narrowness as we present them here may seem surprising to those historians who prefer working on a larger canvas. In part, that is a result of the function of these documents, but it also raises questions about Peri's horizons beyond Florence and even within it: he certainly lived during what must count—despite the historiography—as a significant period in Florentine history, but it is not at all clear that he was aware of it, except as it affected his and his family's well-being. Then there is what the Peri Archive reveals, and what it does not: as we have suggested, the relative absence of references to music in Peri's account books—despite what we already knew of his musical career—gives significant pause for thought in terms of how books of this kind might be used, and have been used, as a documentary source for historical inquiry.

Less methodologically profound but still troublesome are matters of chronology and consistency. Peri made some of the entries later, on the basis of memory—"if I remember correctly" (*se bene mi ricordo*), he writes in one place, while in another he notes that he was making the entry on that date because he had not thought about it before (*ne ho fatto ricordo questo dì sopradetto perché non ci havevo pensato*). Elsewhere he loses track: on one occasion he starts a *ricordo* and then, realizing that he had already entered it earlier, interrupts what he was writing and adds that "it is not continued because it is written on the preceding page" (*non segue perché è scritto nella faccia indreto*), and another *ricordo* is entered twice, separated by only one folio, with no recognition of that fact. Sometimes, too, *ricordi* of the same category of events—such as election to office and purchase of government securities (*monte* credits)—are entered together although they were separated in time, and they are not always given in chronological order. Such vagaries prompt caution even in those parts of the books where greater accuracy might be expected (and was legally enforced): the account entries themselves. A few clearly postdated items, and other places where figures do not quite add up, are not in themselves sufficient to cast doubt on the overall accuracy of the accounts, at least so far as Peri was able to keep them in the best order he could (we shall see that his son Dino, a mathematician, did a more thorough job). But as with those questions of horizons and coverage, the issue requires care both by us and, we imagine, by those historians of earlier periods in Florentine history who place their trust in taking these kinds of materials at face value.

Finally, there is the perennial problem facing all committed archivists of how far one should go. Given the extraordinary completeness of the Florentine archives for the period of the grand duchy, one wonders at times whether we do not have too much material, strange though that complaint might seem. Apart from his musical activities, Peri worked on the staff of two guilds, served frequently in government office, found himself drawn into various legal problems ending up in court, invested in all the major sectors of the economy, continually drew on the services of notaries, and married three women, two of whose immediate families had serious problems of one kind or another that drew him into their vortex. All these things make his life interesting as a touchstone for his times, even without considering his fame as a musician. Yet confronting the abundance of archival documents—everything from lists of births to lists of deaths, including notarial protocols, court decisions, records of virtually all agencies from guilds to offices of the state bureaucracy, and tax assessments, not to mention the overwhelming mass of private documents of families and ecclesiastical institutions now in the public realm—anyone trawling through all these sources faces difficulties even beyond just keeping a grip on them (and accepting that other sources are still missing). While we acknowledge a need for coherence, we have tried to resist making too-easy connections between different facets of Peri's professional and personal experiences: lives are complicated, and there is no reason for them to have been any less so in the early seventeenth century than in the early twenty-first. At times, we have also had to withstand the temptation to cast our net in ever-increasing circles, instead drawing the line at a number of junctures. For instance, we have not investigated how it happened that Peri's mother-in-law by his first wife married her second husband under the assumption—incorrect, it turned out—that her first was dead (which resulted in legal problems about the legitimacy of the birth of Peri's wife); nor have we gone into the internal history of the prominent convents where he chose to send five of his daughters, who lived out their lives there. If a reader's curiosity is aroused about these and the many other tangential matters that come up in our narratives, we can only hope that the story will be taken up from where we have left it. In many instances, in fact, the documents are there, waiting to be explored.

The Peri Archive

The account books in the Peri Archive range from ledgers (*libri di debitori e creditori*) through journals, cashbooks, books of receipts, and other kinds of scrapbooks (*quadernucci, stracciafogli*, etc.). The ledgers contain accounts opened in the names of persons or sometimes categories, and often have a second section of *ricordi*; journals (*giornali*) contain a sequential record of payments and receipts, or some ordering of debits and credits or payments in and out (as in the *libro di entrata e uscita*). As is usual, these different kinds of books exist in a hierarchy (the ledger at the top), each level of which also performs a different function: thus while they are connected (entries can sometimes be tracked up the hierarchy), they do not always duplicate each other (so, not all entries in a journal will necessarily affect a ledger).

1. Peri's ledgers ("debitori e creditori") and those of his estate. In the references below we identify these sequentially as Ledgers A through F (plus Journals C and D), the system traditionally used by Florentines to indicate the sequence of account books. Peri thus designates his first ledger "A," but he did not carry through with the system, in part because when he had filled up the first ledger he chose to continue his accounts on the many unused pages in an abandoned ledger he had at hand (which we call Ledger B) rather than opening a new one. Peri's son Dino, who took over the accounts at the end of his father's life, identified the ledger he opened (Ledger C) only by the color of its binding, and he used his own labeling system in the ledgers he subsequently opened for handling the inheritance. The lettering system we have imposed on this first group of accounts avoids cryptic archival references, and also helps the reader identify the nature of the source cited:

LC 3911 (henceforth Ledger A): accounts and *ricordi* of Jacopo Peri, 1580–1626, identified by him as *libro bianco segnato A*. For the date of the opening of this ledger, see Chapter 1, note 8.

LC 3910 (Ledger B), fols. 30–71, 151–55, 171v: accounts and *ricordi* of Jacopo Peri, 1626–32, identified later by Peri's son Dino as *libro verde*. This ledger originally belonged to the Fortunati (see "4. Account books of the Fortunati family," below); finding it in his possession, Peri used the many blank pages remaining in it to continue his own accounts and *ricordi* from Ledger A (*per esser pieno il libro bianco segnato A di me, Jacopo d'Antonio Peri, mi servirò di questo*).

LC 3917 (Ledger C): accounts and *ricordi* of Jacopo Peri, 1632–33, identified as *libro giallo*; kept by his son Dino during these last two years of Peri's life.

LC 3916 (Journal C): the accompanying journal (*giornale*) to the above ledger, with *ricordi*.

LC 3919 (Ledger D): accounts of the heirs of Jacopo Peri, 1633–37, identified as *libro +*; kept by Dino Peri.

LC 3918 (Journal D): the accompanying journal (*giornale +*) to the above ledger, with *ricordi*.

LC 3909 (Ledger E): accounts of the heirs of Jacopo Peri, 1636–40, identified as *libro AB* (written as a ligature); kept by Dino Peri.

LC 3903 (Ledger F): accounts of the heirs of Jacopo Peri (identified as *libro A*), 1640; opened by Alfonso Peri after Dino's death but not continued beyond this year.

2. *Miscellaneous papers and accounts of Jacopo Peri and his estate*

LC 3912: loose documents (including copies of notarial acts), 1584–1642.

LC 3913: book (*vacchetta*) of signed receipts for payments made by Peri and his heirs, 1588–1642.

LC 2384: book of accounts, *ricordi*, and legal papers regarding Peri's inheritance of the Fortunati property at Marciano, in the Valdichiana, 1573–1605.

LC 3914: a *vacchetta* labeled *quadernuccio A* but in the incipit entitled *Quadernetto: ci terrò memoria di tutti e bestiami grossi e minuti che saranno in su li mia poderi* (Notebook: it will contain a record of all the animals large and small on my farms), 1595–1632.

LC 3902: journal of debits and credits, 1603–14, relative to the administration of the property at San Donato in Poggio on which Peri bought his first *censo* (see Table 2.2). Peri, however, had no direct involvement in managing this property; and this journal probably ended up in his possession as a result of the extensive legal problems to which this *censo* gave rise.

LC 3915: cashbook (*stracciafoglio*) kept by Peri as *camerlengo* (comptroller) of the Wool Guild, 1630–33.

LC 5239: fragmentary farm accounts, 1638–39.

3. *Account books of Jacopo's son Niccolò*

LC 3920: record of expenses kept for the manufacture of ten pairs of heddles for a silk loom, 1628–32; the book (damaged by water stains) is a mere fragment, with only a few folios written.

LC 3921: ledger (labeled *A*), 1634–36, kept primarily for administration of property in the Valdichiana inherited from Jacopo.

LC 3922: income-and-expenditures journal (labeled *A*) to the above ledger (LC 3921).

LC 3923: another accompanying journal (also labeled *A*) to the above ledger (LC 3921), 1634–37, with *ricordi*.

4. Account books of the Fortunati family

LC 3910: ledger (labeled *verde segnato A*), also with *ricordi*, of Agnolo Fortunati, continued by his son Niccolò, 1520–84 (fols. 1–28, 172–173v). The many unused folios in this book were later appropriated by Peri; see "1. Peri's ledgers ("debitori e creditori") and those of his estate" (Ledger B).

LC 2383: ledger (labeled *A*), with *ricordi*, of Niccolò di Agnolo Fortunati, 1557–94.

LC 2384: accounts regarding property of Niccolò Fortunati at Marciano, in the Valdichiana, 1573–1605; see "2. Miscellaneous papers and accounts of Jacopo Peri and his estate."

5. Account books of the Fortini family

LC 2378: collection of notarial acts regarding purchase of land in vicinity of Terranuova by the Fortini, 1441–42.

LC 2379: ledger (labeled *A*) of Giovanni di Piero Fortini, 1544–94.

LC 2380: the accompanying journal to the above ledger (LC 2379).

LC 2375: ledger (labeled *A*), with *ricordi*, of the heirs of Dino di Giovanni Fortini: fols. 1–20, 129–32 kept by his widow, Giustina Monaldi Fortini, 1596–97; fols. 21–30, 133–36 kept by Giustina's mother, Maddalena Monaldi, 1604–13; fols. 30–54 kept by Giustina's brother, Piero Monaldi, 1614–15.

LC 2376: ledger (labeled *B*) of the heirs of Dino di Giovanni Fortini, 1597–98, kept by Piero Monaldi.

LC 2377: ledger (labeled *A*), with *ricordi*, of the heirs of Dino di Giovanni Fortini, 1598–1605, kept by officials of the Magistrato dei Pupilli.

6. Account book of the Monaldi family

LC 3510: ledger and *ricordi* of Giovanni di Piero Monaldi, 1554–65, continued by his son Piero, 1565–1629

Supplementary materials not part of the Peri Archive include:

(a) *Accounts of Dino di Lorenzo Peri*. Another Peri archive exists for the line of Dino di Lorenzo, Jacopo Peri's distant cousin to whom, we shall see, he was very close. These documents contain important references to Peri, his widow, her brother Giovanni, and their son Alfonso. This archive ended up, through inheritance, in the archive of the Spinelli family (as did the archive of Giorgio Vasari, today housed in the Casa Vasariana in Arezzo). Sometime in the early twentieth century it was divided arbitrarily, without any criteria, and survives today in two collections, both of which have Peri documents that are cited here: the Spinelli Baldocci papers in ASF, and the Spinelli Archive in the Beinecke Rare Book and Manuscript Library, Yale University, GEN MSS 109, where the Peri documents are found among the Buonguglielmi family papers. (For the history of the Spinelli archive, see Goldthwaite, *Villa Spelman of The Johns Hopkins University*, 88–91, and Voci, "La vendita dei diritti per la pubblicazione delle carte di Giorgio Vasari"). In addition to this material, two income–expenditure journals of Dino's stationer's shop (1582–1609) survive in ASF, LC 3904–5.

(b) Notarial documents. In undertaking legal actions, Peri almost always gives the full reference to the relevant notarial and/or court document, and most of these can be found today in ASF (one, instead, is in the Archivio Arcivescovile in Florence). For actions he initiated, he generally used the same notary, and over most of his life he was served by only two. He usually gives the complete reference—the name of the notary and the date—for the documents he had drawn up for him; the *protocolli* of the notaries he used survive in ASF, Notarile moderno, prot. 1195–1200 (Jacopo di Ser Piermaria Lotti, 1569–94), and prot. 11155–75 (Cosimo Puccetti, 1606–48). Most of these volumes have an index of names.

The unusually long life enjoyed by Peri spanned the reigns of five Medici grand dukes (dukes until 1569): Cosimo I (1537–74), Francesco I (1574–87), his brother Ferdinando I (1587–1609), Cosimo II (1609–21), and then Ferdinando II (1621–70), the last under a regency led by Grand Duchess Christine of Lorraine (widow of Ferdinando I) and Archduchess Maria Magdalena (widow of Cosimo II) until he came of age in 1628. The genealogical chart in Figure I.1 will help keep track of these and other members of the Medici family.

In the interest of clarity, we have also presented all the now-known "facts" of Peri's life of any significance in a tabular chronology (see Appendix A): they are not recapitulated here in the narrative form typical of many biographies, although the table prompts a number of narratives, as it were, on its own behalf. The edition of Peri's known letters (Appendix B)—to which reference is made in the text by number—provides another way of reading his life, and save for a few exceptions in the *ricordi*, they are the closest we come to Peri in his own words. The list of his musical works in Appendix C, and the surviving poems about him transcribed in Appendix D, are also relevant to the following discussion.

Peri's name was styled in several ways. He signed his letters "Iacopo Perj," and the title pages of his editions have "Iacopo Peri" (see Figures 3.3, 3.5, 3.6). In other documents he appears as "Jacopino" (when he was young), "Giacomo," or "Giacoppo," or just by his nickname "(Il) Zazzerino," which was used at least from 1574. There were other Jacopo Peris active in Florence during this same period: it is a different *messer* Jacopo Peri who was in Marseilles in May–July 1600 (and perhaps until November) to prepare for the arrival of Maria de' Medici on French soil, and who meanwhile offered the house he rented in Florence to accommodate visitors to the city for her wedding.[16] The Jacopo Peri who wrote to Grand Duchess Christine from Cana (i.e., Cannes?) on 8 September 1602 (about horses) was definitely not our Jacopo; the handwriting is quite different.[17] Corazzini notes a Jacopo di Girolamo di Antonio Peri (d. 22 April 1608), and this and another Jacopo are mentioned in one of Dino di Lorenzo Peri's account books (LC 3905).[18] The latter has a *ricordo* at its end (fol. 189v) with a list—probably from the first decade of the seventeenth century—of others with the Peri family name in Florence and their property-tax (*decima*) assessments, including Jacopo di Girolamo, whose assessment (£9.5s.4d.) was only 5d. lower than that of our Jacopo, and another Jacopo (not otherwise identified) whose assessment was £2.11s.9d. We know from other sources that there was also a Jacopo di Perseo Peri (1580–1629),

16. Kirkendale, *Court Musicians*, 203, hedges the bet, but the account books and other documents confirm "our" Peri's presence in Florence at that time.

17. The letter is transcribed (on the assumption, now seen to be incorrect, that it was probably our Jacopo) in Carter, *Jacopo Peri*, 1: 309–10; it is not in Peri's hand (in contrast to all his other surviving letters), nor in that of any typical secretary.

18. For Jacopo di Girolamo, see Corazzini, "Jacopo Peri e la sua famiglia," 66 (suggesting that it was this Jacopo who married our Jacopo's second wife, Ginevra Casellesi).

COSIMO I (12 Jun 1519–21 Apr 1574)
Duke (1537–74), Grand Duke from 1569
= (29 Mar 1539) Leonora Alvarez de Toledo, Marquesa de Villafranca (ca. 1522–17 Dec 1562)
= (29 Mar 1570) Donna Camilla Martelli (1545–30 May 1590)

MARIA (3 Apr 1540–19 Nov 1557)

FRANCESCO I (25 Mar 1541–19 Oct 1587) Duke (1574–87), Grand Duke from 1576
= (18 Dec 1565) Archdss. Johanna di Austria (24 Jan 1548–11 Apr 1578)
= (5 Jun 1578) Bianca Cappello (1548–87)

ISABELLA (31 Aug 1542–75)
= (1565) Paolo Giordano Orsini, Duke of Bracciano (1537–85)

GIOVANNI (29 Sep 1543–62), Cardinal (1560)

LUCREZIA (14 Feb 1545–21 Apr 1561)
= (9 Jul 1558) Alfonso II d'Este, Duke of Ferrara and Modena (1533–97)

PIETRO (10 Aug 1546–9 Jun 1547)

GARZIA (5 Jul 1547–12 Dec 1562)

ANTONIO (1548)

FERDINANDO I (30 Jul 1549–7 Feb 1609) Cardinal (1564), then Grand Duke (1587–1609)
= (30 Apr 1589) Christine of Lorraine (16 Aug 1565–19 Dec 1637)

ANNA (1553)

PIETRO (3 Jun 1554–25 Apr 1604)
= (1571) Eleonora Alvarez de Toledo (1553–76)
= (1578/93) Brites de Lara (1560–1603)

VIRGINIA (28 May 1568–15 Jan 1615)
= (6 Feb 1586) Cesare d'Este, later Duke of Modena (8 Oct 1552–11 Dec 1628)

— BIA (1537–Feb 1542), illegitimate

— GIOVANNI (13 May 1567–19 Jul 1621), illegitimate, by Eleanora degli Albizzi

ELEONORA (28 Feb1567–19 Sep 1611) Duchess of Mantua and Marchesa of Monferrato (1587–1611)
= (29 Apr 1584) Vincenzo I Gonzaga (22 Sep 1562–9 Feb 1612)

ROMOLA (20 Nov–2 Dec 1568)

ANNA (31 Dec 1569–19 Feb 1584)

ISABELLA (30 Sep 1571–8 Aug 1572)

LUCREZIA (7 Nov 1572–14 Aug 1574)

MARIA (26 Apr 1575–3/4 Jul 1642) Queen then Regent of France (1600–17)
= (17 Dec 1600) King Henri IV of France (13 Dec 1553–14 May 1610)

FILIPPO (20 May 1577–29 Mar 1582)

ANTONIO (29 Aug 1576–2 May 1621)

COSIMO II (12 May 1590–28 Feb 1621) Grand Duke (1609–21)
= (19 Oct 1608) Archdss. Maria Magdalena of Austria (7 Oct 1587–1 Nov 1631)

ELEONORA (10 Nov 1591–22 Nov 1617)

CATERINA (2 May 1593–12 Apr 1629) Duchess of Mantua and Marchesa of Monferrato
= (7 Feb 1617) Ferdinando I Gonzaga, Duke of Mantua (26 Apr 1587–29 Oct 1626)

FRANCESCO (5 May 1594–17 Apr 1614) Prince of Capistrano

CARLO (19 Jun 1596–17 Jun 1666) Cardinal (1615), Bishop of Ostia

FILIPPO (9 Apr 1598–1 Apr 1602)

LORENZO (1 Aug 1599–15 Nov 1648)

MARIA MADDALENA (28 Jun 1600–28 Dec 1633)

CLAUDIA (4 Jun 1604–25 Dec 1648)
= (29 Apr 1621) Federigo Della Rovere, later Duke of Urbino (1605–23)
= (25 Mar 1626) Archduke Leopold of Austria (1586–32) 4 Jun 1604–25 Dec 1648)

FRANCESCO (7 May 1586–22 Dec 1612) Duke of Mantua and Monferrato (1612)
= (19 Feb 1608) Margherita of Savoy (28 Apr 1589–26 Jun 1655)

FERDINANDO (26 Apr 1587–29 Oct 1626) Duke of Mantua and Monferrato (1612–26)
= (secretly 1615; repudiated 1616) Camilla Faà di Bruno
= (17 Feb 1617) Caterina de' Medici (2 May 1593–12 Apr 1629)

(others)

MARIA CRISTINA (24 Aug 1609–9 Aug 1632)

FERDINANDO II (14 Jul 1610–24 May 1670) Grand Duke (1621–70)
= (26 Sep 1633) Vittoria Della Rovere, Duchess of Urbino (7 Feb 1622–6 Mar 1695)

GIOVANNI CARLO (13 Apr 1611–23 Jan 1663). Cardinal (1644)

MARGHERITA (31 May 1612–6 Feb 1679). Duchess of Parma (1628–46)
= (9 Oct 1628) Odoardo Farnese, Duke of Parma (28 Apr 1612–11 Sep 1646)

MATTIAS (9 May 1613–11 Oct 1667)

FRANCESCO (16 Oct 1614–25 July 1634)

ANNA (21 July 1616–12 Sep 1676)
= (10 June 1646) Archduke Ferdinand Karl of Austria (1667)

LEOPOLDO (6 Nov 1617–10 Nov 1675). Cardinal (1667)

FIGURE I.I. The Medici grand dukes. *Source:* Adapted from Gaetano Pieraccini, *La stirpe de' Medici di Cafaggiolo*, 3 vols. (Florence: Vallecchi, 1924–25), vol. 2. Birth and death dates and the like sometimes vary in later sources (such as

from Pistoia, who later (16 February 1620) became the *gran tesoriere* of the Cavalieri di Santo Stefano.[19]

We can certainly confirm that every mention in the chapters that follow is to Peri the "musician." What is yet to be revealed, however, is just how inadequate that sobriquet might be.

19. ASF, Manoscritti 132 (Francesco Settimanni's *Memorie fiorentine*, vol. 7 [1608–20]), fol. 534.

I

The Social World

With his appointment in 1573 as a singer at the Servite church of SS. Annunziata, Jacopo Peri, then just twelve years old, takes his first documented step out of a nebulous past that is almost impossible to penetrate. We do not know for sure even where he was born. A near contemporary, Stefano Rosselli, reported that Peri told him he was born in Rome of an ancient and noble Florentine family; in fact, his birth is not recorded in the usual Florentine source for this kind of information—the baptismal records in S. Giovanni Battista—nor in the obvious Roman one (S. Giovanni dei Fiorentini).[1] Only from subsequent political and guild records do we learn that he was born on 20 August 1561.[2] The picture is further confused by a loan of £50 Peri himself recorded even later, in 1598, to a local wool weaver, Costantino Mainardi,

1. Ruspoli, *Poesie*, ed. Arlìa, 67 (from Rosselli's commentary on Ruspoli's sonnet against Peri): *Jacopo Peri adunque, asseriva d'esser nato in Roma nel . . . de' Peri antichi e nobili di Firenze* (the ellipsis is present in the original).

2. ASF, Tratte 446bis, fol. 106; ASF, Arte dei Medici e Speziali 30, fol. 103; ibid., 38, fol. 145v (these are *libri dell'età*). The baptistry records for 1561 list no male names under the letter "J" (or "I") from 26 July to 14 September; the baptismal registers are now available online at <www.operaduomo.firenze.it/battesimi>.

whom he calls his godfather (*mio compare*).[3] But Rosselli's report of the rumor that Peri was an orphan raised in S. Caterina delle Ruote is clearly incorrect.[4]

Pushing back through Peri's roots does not uncover much about his father, Antonio. Born in 1517, he is recorded in 1531, at the age of fourteen, among members of the lesser guilds officially eligible (*beneficiati*) for holding public office; but his appearance along with his brother, Marco, fatherless and with no property, in the family tax return of 1534 is the only other record we have for him. Both he and his brother then slip into oblivion. What Antonio went on to do in life, besides marry and have two sons—Jacopo and Antonio Francesco—is not documented. He was certainly dead by 1569, when his brother died, as we shall see from the arrangements for the latter's children. In that year Peri was eight years old, but his filial sensibilities toward his father remained with him: he gave the name Antonio to the first of his sons by his third wife, and his preferred saint, along with S. Francesco di Paola, was St. Anthony Abbot. As to Peri's mother, Felice di Paolo dei Redditi, we know of her only by way of these newly discovered accounts kept by Peri. He was living with her in 1580, when he registered the first entry in Ledger A for the rent of their home, and subsequent entries record cash payments made by her on Peri's behalf.[5]

3. Ledger A, fol. 38 (one credit entry is for a painting on canvas of St. Sebastian). In 1602, when he was forty-one years old, Peri refers to a woman who was "formerly my wet nurse and today my maidservant" (*già mia balia et oggi mia serva*), but he may mean that she served in that capacity for one of his children; Ledger A, fol. 55.

4. For the "orphan" rumor, which stems at least in part from Francesco Ruspoli's sarcastic sonnet, and also the implausibility of S. Caterina delle Ruote, see the Introduction.

5. The basic information summarized here about Peri's father was published by Corazzini ("Jacopo Peri e la sua famiglia"); see ASF, Tratte 446 (*squittinio*, 1531), fol. 56; and ASF, Decima granducale 3589 (*campione*, 1534), fols. 137–38. His mother's full name, heretofore unknown, is revealed in a notarial document related to a dispute she had with Agnola Bonsi in 1583 (see n. 11). Is it a relevant coincidence that these two surnames—Redditi and Bonsi—are linked in a partnership in Perugia (Vincenzo di Leonardo Bonsi and Giuliano di Francesco Redditi & Partners) that just a few years earlier, in 1580, had gone bankrupt (Ricci, *Cronaca*, 300, 307)?

Corazzini's family tree includes a daughter of Ser Francesco Peri, Margherita, who married Bartolomeo di Tommaso Capponi, but nothing at all about her has emerged from our research. Furthermore, it is highly unlikely that Ser Francesco would have given a daughter the same name as his wife, who was still alive (she lived on, as we shall see, into the 1570s). It is possible that the Margherita found by Corazzini was instead Ser Francesco's wife (and Peri's

Going still further back into the history of this family, we can first identify the Peri in the fourteenth and fifteenth centuries, when two distinct branches of the family emerge, both resident in the *quartiere* of S. Croce but each with its own coat of arms: one branch located in the subdivision (*gonfalone*) called Leon Nero, the other—the branch of Jacopo—in Bue. Jacopo's forebears were modest artisans—most were leather workers (*galigai*)—and as such can occasionally be found as members of the major offices of the Florentine republic, including the Priorate, at the top of the hierarchy, held by ancestors in three successive generations of Peri's direct line down to, and including, his great-grandfather, Matteo di Lorenzo (see the genealogical chart, Figure 1.1). This Matteo was not a *galigaio* but, rather, a stationer (*cartolaio*). According to his 1480 tax return, he was then only twenty-three, unmarried, and living with his widowed mother and four younger brothers; he rented his shop and owned no property of any kind, not even his residence, for which he paid the very modest annual rent of *fl.*8. This group of brothers and their descendents continued to file a single joint tax return for the next fifty years—perhaps indicative of a family cohesion that was to last into Jacopo Peri's lifetime, tying him to distant relatives, one of the minor but continuing themes in his biography. In their 1534 return, mentioned above, the group consisted of the two brothers of Matteo still alive, two sons of a third brother, and Matteo's two teenage grandsons, Marco and Antonio (Peri's father); Matteo and the boys' father, Francesco, were dead. The only property any of them possessed consisted of two small pieces of land that had come to one of the brothers, Niccolò, as a dowry.[6]

The boys' father and Peri's grandfather, Ser Francesco (Matteo's son), became a notary (hence the title, *ser*), a profession that would have marked an economic and even social move upward; and in fact, he married the daughter of a notary. But Francesco was presumably dead by the time of the 1534 return, before he was forty years old, without having left behind any kind of patrimony to improve the economic circumstances of his heirs. Peri once

grandmother) who had remarried after her husband's early death. Bartolomeo Capponi does not show up on the extensive Capponi family tree constructed in Litta et al., *Famiglie celebri italiane*, vol. 10. The Carte Pucci in ASF (Manoscritti 595, *inserto* 18) shows a minor branch of the Capponi that used the names Bartolomeo and Tommaso in continuing sequence but provides no further information.

6. For the tax returns, see ASF, Catasto 1004, fol. 123 (1480); ASF, Decima repubblicana 13, fol. 197 (1498); and ASF, Decima granducale 3589, no. 180, fols. 137–38 (1534).

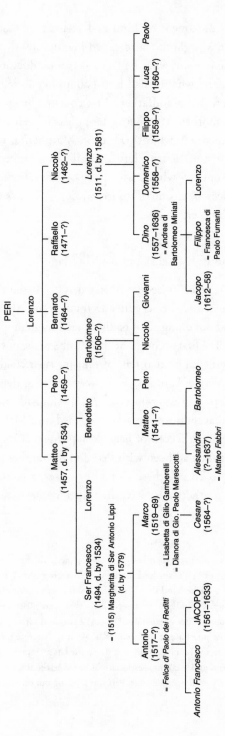

FIGURE 1.1. Genealogical chart (selective) of the Peri family. Names in italics are persons with whom Peri had a direct relation in the accounts. *Source:* Adapted from Corazzini, "Jacopo Peri e la sua famiglia," where there is a more complete genealogical tree with collateral branches; the additions here come from the Peri ledgers. Corazzini also gives Ser Francesco Peri a daughter, Margherita (who would therefore be Peri's aunt), but this is probably an error; see n. 5.

referred to a notarized document by him; and in 1600 he made a *ricordo* about his grandmother, Margherita (also called Fiammetta) di Ser Antonio di Marco Lippi, on the basis of what he learned from a document written by his father, Antonio, and what he had heard about her at first hand from Lorenzo di Niccolò Peri, his grandfather's first cousin.[7] In that document Antonio described his mother, Margherita Lippi, as the heir of her father, but Peri does not go on to say what this meant. Margherita, we shall see, outlived both her sons and in 1579 left a small inheritance to her two surviving grandsons, one of whom was Jacopo. The absence of Peri's brother, Antonio Francesco, as one of his grandmother's heirs would indicate that he was dead by then.

The Early Years before Marriage

We first hear Peri's own voice in Ledger A, dated 1580. At the time, he was just nineteen years of age, and the very first accounts record that he was living with his mother and not doing at all badly, at least by solid working-class standards of the time.[8] The first account, opened in the name of his landlord, reveals that he was paying an annual rent of *fl.*14 for their residence in Via dell'Alloro (parallel to Via dei Panzani, in the very center of the city; Figure 1.2). In addition, he was paying £16—just over *fl.*2¼—for a female servant, as we learn from the third account in the ledger, opened on 1 May 1582 for the specific purpose of keeping a record of her salary payments. Entries on this account inform us that she had been with Peri and his mother (who set her salary) since 1 May 1576. To pay these annual expenses, amounting to just over *fl.*16, he and his mother must have had an income somewhat more

7. Ledger A, fol. 109v.

8. There is a problem about the date when Ledger A was opened. The first entry on the first account, opened in the name of Peri's landlord, is dated 1 November 1580, but the extraordinary neatness and uniformity of the hand that listed the rental payments on the debit side of the account down to October 1581 indicate that very likely they were all entered at the same time. The next several accounts are not opened until almost a year and a half later, in 1582, and these include the entry for the purchase of the account book. It is therefore possible that Peri opened this ledger in 1582 with the rental account but dated the latter from November 1580. In any event, the priority of the rental account—especially if it was backdated—suggests that at the age of nineteen and legally no longer a minor, Peri was striking out on his own.

substantial than what might be considered the minimum living wage at the time, that of a manual laborer in the construction industry who, if he succeeded in finding full-time work, could expect to earn no more than about *fl.*35 a year. In any event, their employment of a servant would have ranked this widow and her son at the very beginning of adulthood in the 45 percent of households that just thirty years earlier, in the 1551 census of the city's population, had at least one servant.[9]

We have no idea, however, what their economic resources were. The ledgers provide no evidence that Peri and his mother had any land in these early years, the kind of possession that one would expect to find in private accounts, nor is any such evidence found in the records of the *decima*, a tax based on thorough surveys (extant in their entirety) of the real estate owned by Florentines. Moreover, Peri and his brother had inherited nothing from their father—or at least nothing in the Tuscan state—since their names do not show up in the records of the meetings of the Magistrato dei Pupilli, the office that oversaw the interests of all minors in the settlement of estates (and whose records are also complete for these years). Yet it is in the documents of this magistracy that we learn about one small inheritance Peri came into, for he is mentioned, if only incidentally, by the officials in their oversight of the interests of one of their wards, his first cousin Cesare di Marco di Ser Francesco Peri. Cesare, along with a sister, had come under the Pupilli's purview at the age of six, in 1569, with the death of his father, his mother having already died. Now, in 1579, the cousins' grandmother, Margherita Lippi, the mother of their fathers, had died, leaving Cesare and Jacopo, her only grandsons, as her heirs (Jacopo's brother must no longer have been alive). The problem at hand that required the Pupilli's attention was litigation undertaken by its ward's legal representative (*curatore*), a distant cousin, Lorenzo di Niccolò Peri, against members of the Federighi family regarding a credit Margherita's heirs had with them for a loan of *fl.*250 she had made to a member of that family four years earlier (the interest on the loan having in the meantime increased the credit to *fl.*292). The settlement was in Cesare and Jacopo's favor, requiring the Federighi to deposit this sum under the boys' names in the Monte di Pietà, and they did this on 4 November 1580. At 5 percent interest, this deposit paid Peri, for his half, just over *fl.*7 annually. The

9. Battara, *La popolazione di Firenze alla metà del '500*, 70.

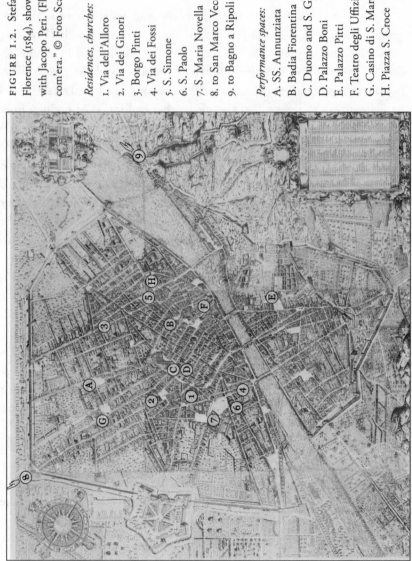

FIGURE 1.2. Stefano Bonsignori's view of Florence (1584), showing places associated with Jacopo Peri. (Florence, Museum "Firenze com'era." © Foto Scala, Florence.)

Residences, churches:

1. Via dell'Alloro
2. Via dei Ginori
3. Borgo Pinti
4. Via dei Fossi
5. S. Simone
6. S. Paolo
7. S. Maria Novella
8. to San Marco Vecchio
9. to Bagno a Ripoli

Performance spaces:

A. SS. Annunziata
B. Badia Fiorentina
C. Duomo and S. Giovanni Battista
D. Palazzo Boni
E. Palazzo Pitti
F. Teatro degli Uffizi
G. Casino di S. Marco
H. Piazza S. Croce

Pupilli officials did not deal with any other property of Margherita's, if there was any.[10]

This is the only inheritance of Peri's that we know anything about. A few years later, in 1583, Peri made *ricordi* about two court decisions regarding further litigation over inheritances in that year, one in a civil court in favor of his mother, awarding her a miniscule piece of land (which was worth only *fl.*16 when she sold it), and the other in the archbishop's court in his favor, against a claim for a small debt owed by his deceased brother of whom he was heir.[11] Judging from the accounts, however, nothing of any substance came to Peri as a result of these inheritances. We shall see that as a boy singer at SS. Annunziata he earned *fl.*6 annually from 1573 to 1577 (by which time his voice would probably have broken), and that in 1579 he took a position as organist at the Badia Fiorentina paying him *fl.*15 annually. Hence in 1580, when he dated the first entry in Ledger A, Peri had an annual income of slightly over *fl.*22 from the Badia and the interest from the Monte di Pietà, which would hardly have covered his living expenses once rent and the

10. In 1569 Margherita shows up in the Pupilli records as the guardian (*tutrice*) of the two children—Lucrezia, age eight, and Cesare, six—of her recently deceased son, Marco, Antonio's brother, who died intestate. The mother of the children was presumably also dead, since they are identified as the children of Marco's first wife; therefore their custody (*tutela*) passed by law to their father's mother. Margherita, however, recognized that the Pupilli could serve the children's interest better (*cognioscendo detti pupilli haver bisognio di maggior reggimento et ogni protectione in ogni migliore tutela*) and renounced her right in favor of the Pupilli officials, who then turned custody over to Lorenzo di Niccolò Peri, a first cousin of Margherita's late husband (and Peri's grandfather; see Figure 1.1). Presumably her financial means were limited.

The references to all the Pupilli meetings (*deliberazioni e partiti*) from 1563 to 1585 regarding Cesare, including the inheritance from his grandmother, are in ASF, Magistrato dei Pupilli del Principato 14, fol. 296; 15, fol. 44; 16, fol. 24; 17, fol. 177v; 18, fol. 189; 19, fol. 85 (Jacopo mentioned); 20, fol. 16v (Jacopo mentioned); 21, fol. 91v (where Cesare is finally freed from its guardianship on his becoming a friar). Much later, in 1610 or 1611, Peri made a *ricordo* of the problem with the Federighi in Ledger A, fol. 118; his copy of the Pupilli judgment is found in LC 3912, document dated 4 December 1579.

The deposit account, including payments of interest, opened in both the cousins' names on the books of the Monte di Pietà can be traced from 1580 to 1584 in ASF, Monte di Pietà 1364, fol. 370; 1366, fol. 221.

11. Ledger A, fols. 99v, 100, 118. For the litigation involving his mother, see ASF, Notarile moderno, prot. 4295 (Torello Conti, 1571–84), fols. 163–64; the favorable verdict of the bishop's court is found in Florence, Archivio Arcivescovile, SC 13 (*sentenze civili—notari*), fasc. 2 (1581–87), document dated 18 July 1583.

servant's salary were paid. He recorded none of this in his accounts, how-ever, and we do not know how much more was coming in from other sources to permit him and his mother to be living well above the poverty line.

In these early years Peri's ties to the extended family of his father probably counted for much, and we shall have more to say about this during his later years. His and his cousin's *curatore* in the 1579 case involving their grand-mother's inheritance, Lorenzo di Niccolò Peri, was a first cousin of their grandfather, Ser Francesco Peri. Lorenzo, a bookseller and stationer (*libraio*)—continuing the tradition of his father and uncles, including Peri's great-grandfather—was a man of some property, and his sons were also successful in business; like many *librai* in Florence, they rented a *bottega* from, and in the vicinity of, the Badia Fiorentina (where Jacopo Peri was organist from 1579 to 1605).[12] Since, we shall see, these sons later had close relations with Jacopo, to whom they were exact contemporaries, it is likely that Lorenzo in some sense supported the two distant cousins, one of whom was a minor under his charge.

Lorenzo was probably a member of the Arte dei Medici e Speziali, the one guild with which Peri was to have a long association: it was a conglomerate that took its name originally from two of its most important membership categories—doctors, and dealers in drugs and spices—but by this time, since doctors had organized themselves separately in their own Collegio, it was generally referred to, at least informally, as the Arte degli Speziali, which is the name Peri used. The guild, however, also included several other groups of artisans and shopkeepers, including *librai*. Two of the guild's *libri dell'età*, which register the birth dates of members under their family name, list Peri along with two of Lorenzo's sons (unfortunately, the entries are not dated), but the matriculation register, which records the matriculation of Lorenzo's

---

12. Lorenzo is described as a *libraio* in his sons' matriculation records (see n. 13), and the payments for the rent of his shop from 1 May 1573 are recorded in a ledger of the Badia: ASF, Corporazioni religiose soppresse dal governo francese 78 (Badia di Firenze), 91, fol. 43. The shop was taken over by Dino di Lorenzo on 1 January 1581/82 (ibid., fol. 289), and two of Dino's shop books survive, along with a journal kept by Dino for the administration of his and his brothers' patrimony, 1582–90 (see "The Peri Archive" in the Introduction). The journal has many detailed entries on the operation of several farms and rental properties in the city, and several regarding the dowry of *fl.*1,200 paid by the brothers for their sister Maria in 1583. On the wealth of the brothers, see n. 35.

five sons in 1581, does not have an entry for Peri.[13] Yet in settling Peri's estate after his death in 1633, his son Dino found that he had to pay a long-standing debt of his father's with the guild, to cover arrears on its matriculation accounts. The original debt amounted to £39 on an account dating back to 1590, and over the years Peri had only occasionally made small payments on it, leaving his estate to pay the outstanding balance of £9.13s.4d. It probably is no coincidence that in 1590, a state official confirmed to the guild Peri's presence as of 15 September 1580 on the official lists of those potentially eligible for public office, but we are not told why the guild wanted this information.[14] In any event, later in life Peri had a continuing association with the guild, for as we shall see (in Table 1.1), he served five four-month tenures as consul (he was selected four more times but did not serve), and he once took employment in it as comptroller (*camerlengo*).

Whether or not Peri did an apprenticeship in a stationer's or bookseller's shop, there is every reason to think that he followed the normal trajectory of a Florentine boy, passing through an elementary school to learn reading and writing, going on to take a course for several months in a school of commercial arithmetic (*scuola d'abaco*), and finally, around the age of twelve or so, taking up an apprenticeship in one of the city's artisan shops or places of business, where he completed what we might call his formal education by learning accounting, and business practice generally, on the job. Then at seventeen a boy presumably entered his majority—this being the age at which the Pupilli officials (who counted it as eighteen, based not on the years completed but on the year in progress) ended their tutelage of a minor—and hence was presumably able to strike out on his own. In any event, Peri's first ledger, opened when he was nineteen years old, is evidence enough that he had been brought up in the economic culture of Florence, for it reveals his mastery of the skill of accounting as it had long been practiced in the city, a subject to which we shall return in Chapter 2. We have no information, however, on what precise training Peri might have had.

It is nevertheless clear that as a boy Peri was already heading down some kind of musical path. In 1573, at the age of twelve (when most Florentine boys

13. ASF, Arte dei Medici e Speziali 38, fol. 145v; 39, fol. 103 (both *libri dell'età*); and 13 (matriculations, 1556–92), fol. 179.
14. Ledger D, fols. 34, 85 (Dino's accounts); ASF, Ospedale di S. M. Nuova 197, no. 242 (certification of Peri's registration in the state's *tratte* records).

began to go to work), he was paid to sing *laude*—i.e., spiritual songs of a type typical for Florence—with the organ (*a cantar in su l'orghano le laude*) in SS. Annunziata, at an annual salary of *fl.*6.[15] This may or may not have been a result of some prior association with SS. Annunziata in an educational context: the institution had a strong musical reputation with a succession of able Servite friar–musicians at the helm. In general, too, it made sense for a young Florentine with actual or potential talent to enter into some manner of musical training, given that it offered the potential of a stable career with some upward social mobility. Presumably, Peri began studying with the organist there, Fra Maurizio (Gianino di Giuliano Borsellini; 1530–93), who taught both organ playing and singing to the novices and also to lay outsiders: Fra Maurizio occasionally received and transmitted salary payments to Peri (including his first).[16]

It seems unlikely (if only from the salary) that the young Peri's position at SS. Annunziata was in any sense a full-time one. He held it until September 1577—presumably when his voice broke—although he may have sung at SS. Annunziata again around Christmas 1579.[17] By 1577, however, he was studying with Cristofano Malvezzi (1547–99), *maestro di cappella* of S. Giovanni Battista, who published an instrumental piece by his pupil in his *Il primo libro de recercari à quattro voci* (Perugia: Pietroiacopo Petrucci, 1577). On 1 February 1579 (after an audition on 15 January), Peri became the organist at the Badia Fiorentina at a salary of *fl.*15—about what was paid a youth his age working as an apprentice in one of the city's cloth manufactories or merchant-banking firms—and he kept this position until 1605.[18] By the time of his appointment at the Badia, he was associated with the Medici princesses (probably via Malvezzi), teaching them singing, although we do not know what remuneration he received for this, if any.[19] He also became a member of

15. ASF, Corporazioni religiose soppresse dal governo francese 119, 53 (*ricordi* of SS. Annunziata), fol. 87.

16. For music at SS. Annunziata, see D'Accone, "The Florentine Fra Mauros" (Fra Maurizio's teaching is noted on p. 100); for the salary payments, see Chapter 3.

17. Kirkendale, *Court Musicians*, 192. Peri was given a *mancia* (tip) of £2 on 24 December 1579.

18. ASF, Corporazioni religiose soppresse dal governo francese 78 (Badia Fiorentina), 265 (*ricordi*), fol. 54v.

19. For Peri's associations with Princesses Anna, Eleonora, Maria, and Virginia de' Medici from the late 1570s, see Chapter 3. He also taught a new generation of Medici princesses in the early 1600s.

the Compagnia dell'Arcangelo Raffaello, a confraternity that met in the cloisters of S. Maria Novella. Besides strengthening any religious sensibilities that prompted him to join in the first place, it offered a boy of Peri's background opportunities for future advancement. Its active musical program opened up an outlet for his talent, and associating with the many upper-class youths in the confraternity brought him into direct relations with members from the ranks of the city's most prominent families.[20] Religious devotion, musical talent, social status sound the major themes in his life, along with the keen economic sense that now also emerges in the present study.

Peri's musical career is discussed in greater detail in Chapter 3. Given his early association with the Arte degli Speziali, music may not have been his primary goal, unless he felt that joining the guild would give him some kind of fallback position, and also a base on which to build future political and other influence. But things took off for him in the 1580s, from the first major performance of his work (an *intermedio* for a comedy presented before the Medici princesses) in 1583 to his official appointment in court service by 1588. We learn very little about this aspect of his life from the extensive accounting record he himself kept for the next half century, down to his death in 1633. The accounts do not record any fees that Peri may have received as a performer, teacher, or composer. But his salaried income from music is clear enough. He continued working at the Badia as organist until 1605, earning *fl.*15 a year, and from 1586 to 1590 he received *fl.*18 a year as a singer in the choir at S. Giovanni Battista, under Malvezzi as *maestro di cappella* (holding multiple musical positions was not unusual in Florence).[21]

By 1586, Malvezzi's salary from the grand-ducal court (as teacher of the princesses) also included an allowance for his pupil, and by 1588 Peri had his own salary from the court of *fl.*6 per month, increased to *fl.*9 in September 1590, perhaps in part because of his involvement as a singer and composer in the magnificent festivities celebrating the marriage of Grand Duke Ferdinando I and Christine of Lorraine the previous year. On the eve of his marriage in 1592, Peri had a total annual income of *fl.*123 from his positions at the court and the Badia (see Table 2.5 in the next chapter), comparable to that of

20. We do not yet have a definite date for Peri's entry into the confraternity. Music there is discussed in Hill, "Oratory Music in Florence, I." For the broader issues, see Eisenbichler, *The Boys of the Archangel Raphael.*

21. For S. Giovanni Battista, see ASF, Arte dei Mercatanti di Calimala 35, fols. 22v, 33, 141.

someone solidly in the city's middling class—much higher, for instance, than the *fl*.70–75 that was the top income the best-paid craftsmen in the construction industry could hope to earn, and much higher, even, than the *fl*.60–70 salary of a manager of one of the city's cloth firms (such managers, however, usually shared in the firm's profits). On 19 May 1593, Peri's financial position, and his reputation, was also such that he could act as *mallevadore* (guarantor) for the castrato Onofrio Gualfreducci on his appointment as *sagrestano maggiore* at S. Lorenzo.[22] As we shall see in Chapter 3, it is not always clear how to interpret court salaries and the value judgments seemingly reflected therein, and therefore why Peri's, at *fl*.108 per year, was (and remained) in the middle range for the grand-ducal musicians, the best-rewarded of whom could earn *fl*.16–20 per month (see Table 3.1). But such salaries had the advantage of being, in effect, a lifetime stipend paid even into retirement: Peri received it up until his death at the age of seventy-two. A court position also brought benefits in the form of other emoluments, one-time gifts, and, probably most important, favors and access to influence. We shall see that Peri used it well.

Although Ledger A does not reveal anything about Peri's income from these and other musical sources, it provides odds and ends of evidence that he in fact enjoyed a certain economic comfort during these first dozen years of his adult life. On 2 April 1582 he opened an account in the name of Dino di Lorenzo Peri, the distant cousin who was a *libraio* (two of his shop books survive), with an entry for £3.16s. that Peri owed him for the purchase of the very account book he was using. A month later, on 12 June, he opened an account with Cosimo di Raffaello Navesi, apparently a shopkeeper, with a credit entry of £19.12s. for cloth he purchased for his mother. On 31 August he opened an account with Giovanni Fedini, *pittore* (and presumably the author of the play *Le due Persilie*, performed before the Medici princesses in February 1583 with music in part by Peri), with a debit entry of *fl*.20 for 37 *staia* of wheat sent from Figline to his home (*per la mia casa*), not an insignificant purchase inasmuch as 14–15 *staia* is considered the average annual per capita consumption in this period. At the same time—in November 1582 and in January 1583—he purchased sausages (*salsiccia fine*) and marzolino cheese that he sent to a perfumer, Antonio Porcellini, in Milan, for a total cost, in-

---

22. Kirkendale, *Court Musicians*, 194. The other *mallevadore* was the court musician Antonio Naldi.

cluding customs and shipment, of £18.10s., which Porcellini paid in part by
sending *giuli* to Florence and the rest later, in August, directly in cash (presumably in Florence)—an operation that arouses curiosity without, however,
providing enough details to stimulate speculation.[23]

In 1583 (it seems), Peri borrowed *du*.30 from the prominent businessman
and music patron Jacopo Corsi.[24] Yet at the same time he came into a modest
amount of capital through his cousin, Cesare. On 26 April 1583, in an agreement with Cesare, he withdrew in cash his half—*fl*.145 £6—of their deposit
in the Monte di Pietà.[25] Over the course of the year from June 1583 to May
1584 he spent £221 for the benefit of his cousin—medicines, repayment of
debts to their cousin Dino di Lorenzo, and, above all, expenses on Cesare's
entering the Carmine to become a friar (for a small table and a stool, cloth for
his habit, a friar's felt hat, a door lock, linens, soap, two books of rules). Peri
was eventually reimbursed for some of these expenditures, but as a present to
Cesare when the latter took orders in July 1584, he canceled the balance of
£97 due him (*gne ne fo un presente*). In fact, the "present" was more a question of keeping the books straight, although it also offers some insight into
how Peri wanted to show himself in a favorable light (if only to himself). He
got more than his money back when Cesare, as a consequence of his commitment to poverty, and after keeping *fl*.200 for himself, gave what was presumably the balance of his estate to his cousin: a "donation" of *fl*.296 in the
Monte di Pietà and all claims to any other assets that might show up.[26] Peri

23. All of these accounts appear in the first six folios of Ledger A.

24. Carter, "Music and Patronage in Late Sixteenth-Century Florence," 73. This transaction does not appear in Peri's ledger but, rather, in a list of credits on a loose piece of paper
inserted into one of Corsi's account books; ASF, Guicciardini Corsi Salviati 432, between fols.
20v and 21r. It cannot be grounded in a specific context, and while the date, 7 September,
squares with the loose leaf's position in the book, it could have come from any year.

25. Ledger A, fol. 7; ASF, Monte di Pietà 1366, fol. 221. Peri apparently did not have full
title to his half since the deposit was still legally shared by both cousins.

26. Ledger A, fols. 8, 10, 100. The official document of the donation is in ASF, Magistrato
dei Pupilli del Principato 21 (*deliberazioni*), fol. 91v; Peri's copy is LC 3912, document dated 5
July 1584. The arrangement is also documented in Dino's journal in ASF, Spinelli Baldocci
167, fol. 85 (see n. 12). Peri opened his last account in Cesare's name in 1606 (Ledger A, fol. 71).
An earlier account, however, remained open, and sometime after making the last entry on it,
on 3 August 1601 leaving a debit balance, Peri closed it with an undated note canceling the
debt on Cesare's death (*è morto, però si cancella*); Ledger A, fol. 49.

seems to have kept a place for Cesare in his affections, and even in his family pride: a portrait of the friar hung in Peri's house at the time of his death.

On the same day he withdrew his share of the deposit in the Monte di Pietà he had with Cesare, he made a two-year interest-free loan of *fl.*100 to Dino di Lorenzo Peri, along with Dino's brothers, to help finance the dowry of *fl.*1,200 for their sister (but instead the brothers began immediately to make interest payments of about 6 percent and did not pay back the loan until 1594).[27] In January 1585 he loaned *fl.*35 to a clothier; in 1587 he paid the painter Ridolfo di Giorgio £16.10s. in four installments for two small pictures (not otherwise described); also in 1587 he presumably bought some negotiable paper, for he tried, unsuccessfully, to sell three coupons (*cedole*) issued to other parties by government funds (*monti*) in Rome; in 1591–92 he tried, also unsuccessfully, to sell some jewelry—a gold ring set with an emerald surrounded by four rubies, a ring set with nine turquoise stones, a glazed pin with three rubies and an emerald, a pin set with two diamonds (where all this came from we do not know)—that he assessed at *fl.*16.[28]

The evidence is clear that things were getting better in this decade. The *fl.*296 he received from his cousin Cesare on 5 July 1584 must have enabled him, the following January, to put *fl.*300 on the exchange with the bank of Tommaso Martelli; and perhaps it was on the return of this bill that, in July 1585, he made another investment, going personally through the banker Giovambattista Michelozzi to put *fl.*300 in the wool shop of Michelozzi's nephew, Lorenzo. In 1586 he paid *fl.*76 £5.10s. for a modest property of buildings and land *nell'Alpe di Rostolena* at a place called (then and now) Maioli, above Vicchio in the Mugello, where today the paved road going up the lower slopes of the Tuscan Apennines ends. Also in 1586, he moved from the house he had been renting for *fl.*14 annually since at least 1580 in Via dell'Alloro to a new place in Via dei Ginori (behind the Medici palace) that he rented for *fl.*17, and he is documented as living there to 1591, still with his mother and one maid, on the eve of his marriage.[29] A payment toward the rent that year delivered by his mother is the last we hear of her: she was dead by 1595, when

27. Ledger A, fol. 7; Yale University, Beinecke Library, GEN MSS 109 (Spinelli Archive), Box 569, no. 8442, fols. 31, 113 (Dino's ledger, 1583–1606); ASF, Spinelli Baldocci 167, fols. 41, 78v, 82, 85, 109, 127v, 132v, 143v, 166v, 178, 192v (2), 203, 209 (the accompanying journal to Dino's ledger, 1583–90).

28. Ledger A, fols. 4, 9, 19, 22, 24.

29. Ledger A, fols. 16, 18, 20; LC 3913, fols. 1v–2v.

Peri named a newly born daughter Felice in her memory (*in buona memoria di mia madre*). But it is clear how during the 1580s, his first ten years as an adult, Peri became ever more active in the marketplace—if still modestly so—engaging in transactions with the Monte, loaning money, doing a little speculating, investing in industry and real estate, and becoming a consumer. We shall explore the consequences further in Chapter 2.

The land he bought above Rostolena in the Mugello in 1586, was to become the nucleus from which he expanded his holdings there (see Figure 2.2). Additional increments cost him *fl.*60 in 1587 and *fl.*131 for three more acquisitions from 1590 to 1592, bringing his total investment just short of *fl.*268 by the time of his first marriage (see Table 2.3). The place, however, was too far away from Florence to be readily accessible, and it is not likely that Peri was able to make frequent trips there. The situation changed in 1588, however, when he took possession of a small farm at San Marco Vecchio. As he wrote retrospectively in one of his *ricordi* in 1590, he had lacked property near Florence (*io per al presente non mi trovo poderi che sieno vicini a Fiorenza*) and felt the need to own something closer that could serve him as a *passatempo* but within an hour of the city, given his obligations to the grand duke (*sì comoda a Fiorenza, ché per stare io col Gran Duca mi trovo molto obligato, dove costì io vo in una ora e torno*).[30] This acknowledgment of the responsibilities of his new court position is striking, as is its wording (Peri proudly positions himself close to the grand duke). The property at San Marco Vecchio gave him just what he was looking for, and it came to him in the form of a prebend offered to him by his former teacher, Cristofano Malvezzi. Moreover, it was an opportunity that did not require any investment capital and yet was also to Malvezzi's advantage (*voleva pigliarne partito*). On taking this property Peri prayed "that God give to me the grace that I enjoy it a long time in good health and similarly to my children" (*che Dio mi dia grazia che io la goda lungo tempo con sanità, e così ancora e mia figliuoli*)—this latter hope sounding a continuing theme in the life of this yet-unmarried man.

This prebend, which Malvezzi had as a canon at S. Lorenzo, was the income that came from a farm at San Marco Vecchio, in the vicinity of the church of that name located at the beginning of the Via Faentina running along the Mugnone; Peri later referred to its location as being at Montui, or Montughi, the name of the wider area occupying the hillside ascending on

30. Ledger A, fols. 150v–151.

the right bank of the stream. Being just outside the Porta San Gallo (today the Piazza della Libertà), it was an easy walk from the city. Montughi was also a favored site for the country villas of Florentine patricians, including the Corsi family.[31] Malvezzi turned the complete management and income of this farm over to Peri through a traditional twenty-nine-year rental contract (*a livello*) that remained in effect for the life of the renter and two generations beyond in return for a fixed rent of *fl.*6 a year, payable in six-month install-ments. Since the prebend belonged to Malvezzi's office as canon and not to him personally, his death in 1599 had no effect on the arrangement (Peri continued to pay the rent to subsequent holders of Malvezzi's canonry). At this stage in his life, the prebend was important to Peri as an investment in-strument, and from the related accounts he opened in his ledgers we learn something about his management of the property.[32] The property, however, had no house suitable for residence, and he could not enjoy being *in villa* there.[33]

In short, during this early period Peri enjoyed considerable success. He was clearly launched on his career as a professional musician who had achieved a certain standing in Florence and the court. His economic situa-tion, too, improved: his annual income from salaried positions rose from *fl.*15 to *fl.*123 in this decade, while the increase in his rent from *fl.*14 to *fl.*17 in 1586 and the commitment taken two years later, in 1588, to a long-term annual rent of *fl.*6 for a farm, along with his modest investment in land, can be taken as indices of his improved economic security. With respect to his economic future, two pieces of information that emerge from this early period in his life, viewed retrospectively from the later years, sound notes that become other important themes in his activity as an investor. His investment in a wool shop anticipates a major economic and even professional interest in this in-dustry, and his relationship with the person through whom he made this in-vestment, Giovambattista Michelozzi, probably the most important banker on the Florentine scene at the time (and later a senator), became a continuing

31. The Corsi villa (now the Villa Finaly, Via Bolognese 134) was purchased by the brothers Jacopo and Bardo Corsi from the heirs of the bankrupt Bernardo di Niccolò Soderini in early 1587; Carter, "Music and Patronage in Late Sixteenth-Century Florence," 62.

32. *Ricordi* of the contract are in Ledger A, fols. 121v, 150v–151; the management of the property is discussed in Chapter 2.

33. The lack of a *casa da padrone* and any *masserizia* (the owner's house and its furnishings) is stated explicitly in the survey of Alfonso's properties on their confiscation; see Chapter 4.

personal contact with the rich and powerful of the city during this early period of Peri's life.

Another theme sounded in these early years is Peri's extended family (see
Figure 1.1). One gets the sense from his financial relations with the other Peri
that he was part of a tight-knit family group made up of rather distant relatives. He presumably felt close to his only first cousin, Cesare, the son of his
father's brother, Marco. They were linked together in the case they brought
against the Federighi in 1579, and Peri later financially supported Cesare's
profession as a friar. Another family member who was clearly close to the
cousins, if distant in genealogical terms, was Lorenzo di Niccolò Peri. It was
Lorenzo who, when he was "over eighty," wrote Peri, talked to him about his
grandmother.[34] Lorenzo's sons make frequent appearance in Peri's accounts.
Although on the genealogical tree they come a generation earlier than Peri—
their great-grandfather was his and Cesare's great-great-grandfather—these
distant cousins were about the same age, all born between 1557 and 1563, and
they all matriculated in the Arte degli Speziali at the same time, in 1581. Peri
bought his first ledger from Dino's shop, and Dino also took an interest in
Cesare's profession as a friar, for Peri made several of the above-mentioned
payments on Cesare's behalf through him. Of the money Peri borrowed from
the Monte di Pietà in 1583, *fl.*100 went as the interest-free loan mentioned
above to Dino and his brothers *per loro comodo*. Over the years, Peri's accounts register further dealings with these distant cousins, who appear to
have been successful in business—Domenico with a wool shop, and Luca a
silk shop—and in this capacity they will show up later in these pages. At the
turn of the century the collective tax assessment of this branch of the family,
based entirely on real-estate holdings, was the highest among all the Peri in
the city.[35]

34. See the *ricordo* cited in n. 7. There is room for a different identity of the Lorenzo in the
ricordo: it is dated 1600 but Lorenzo di Niccolò died around 1581, when he was closer to seventy than to eighty. However, no Lorenzo anywhere near eighty appears on the Peri family
tree in the Carte Pucci (ASF, Manoscritti 600, *inserto* 4), the standard genealogical source for
Florentine families. We tend to think, given the problematic chronological organization of the
ricordi, that in 1600 Peri made this *ricordo* based on earlier material.

35. The matriculation records are in ASF, Arte dei Medici e Speziali 13 (matriculations,
1556–92), fol. 179. Peri's accounts of transactions with this branch of his family are in Ledger
A, fols. 3, 7, 41, 42, 50, 53, 99v; and the loan and the interest payments on it to 1590 are recorded in Dino's journal in ASF, Spinelli Baldocci 167, fols. 41, 82, 109, 132v, 143v, 166v, 178,

Later, in 1604, Peri played a role in putting together the dowry of the daughter, Alessandra, of another, less distant relative, Matteo di Bartolomeo— *mio zio cugino*—a first cousin of Peri's father, whose circumstances left much to be desired. Peri opened an account in the name of Alessandra's husband to handle some of the arrangements for payment of her dowry, and one of the entries registers a cash payment toward the dowry to Jacopo of *fl.*192. 8*s.*7*d.* made by the Buonuomini di San Martino, a confraternity dedicated to assisting people of a certain social status who had fallen on hard times. Peri also made a *ricordo* of having given *fl.*50 of his own money to Alessandra's brother, Bartolomeo, toward her dowry, explaining that he gave this money "for the love of God" (*per amor de Dio*) and that her husband was not to know where it came from; he wrote "charity of *fl.*50" (*limosina di fi.50*) in the outer margin as a quick reference to the contents of the *ricordo*. Very much later, in 1631, toward the end of his life, Peri loaned £21 to Alessandra, now a widow.[36]

Peri grew up with no one in his immediate family except his mother and the brother he lost early on, but he had an extended family of a certain density, and he did his part—and possibly more—in keeping those ties firmly bound. Some of these relatives will make appearances during important moments in his life as recounted later in these pages. They were members in a kinship network that must have counted for much, spiritually and economically, during these early years in setting this man, fatherless and with no patrimony, on his way.

The Family

Family was important to Peri, as it was to most Florentines, not only because as a social reality rather than a mere genealogical structure a network of relatives assured a certain present and future security. The sense of family in its

---

192v, 203, 209. In the second of Dino's shop books, LC 3905, on fol. 189v, is a *ricordo* with a list of Peri family tax assessments (undated, but the first decade of the seventeenth century): in it Dino's family (including a separate listing of his mother) is at the top with *fl.*10. 18*s.*1*d.*; Jacopo follows with *fl.*9. 5*s.*9*d.* The 1632 tax report of this branch of the family, with a list of their numerous properties, is in ASF, Decima granducale 2395, no. 66, at which time the assessment on the estate of Dino and his one surviving brother was *fl.*12 11*s.*3*d.*; Jacopo's in 1633 was *fl.*18. 16*s* (ibid., 2396, no. 90).

36. Ledger A, fols. 62, 114; Ledger B, fol. 62; Ledger D, fol. 13 (notice of her death in 1637).

historical dimension as a lineage also grounded one in history and in social class, a concern that Peri felt ever more deeply as time passed. The most immediate expression of this comprehensive sense of family was the desire to set up one's own household—to amplify the network and to strengthen the tradition, and also, more simply, to have the pleasure of a wife and children, something Peri devoutly, perhaps even passionately, desired. Fortunately he did not live to see that things did not end up as he might have hoped.

Wives

CATERINA DI NICCOLÒ FORTUNATI. On 19 November 1592 Peri signed the contract for his first marriage, thereby entering a new phase in his life. Marriage, of course, meant a family, and this must have been important to him, for when he twice was left a widower he remarried in an extraordinarily short time, and he had, all together, no fewer than twenty children, the last born when he was sixty-three years old. Marriage also brought him a certain amount of wealth by way of his wife's dowry, and hence strengthened his potential as an investor—and this, too, increased with the dowries gained in his subsequent two marriages.

Peri's bride, Caterina, was the daughter, and only child, of Niccolò di Agnolo di Ser Carlo Fortunati and Oretta di Pagolo Della Casa (Figure 1.3). Born on 27 February 1578, she was not yet fifteen years old at the time of her marriage.[37] To judge from the only demographic profile we have of Florentine society, constructed on data from almost two centuries earlier (in 1427), Peri's age on his marriage (thirty-one), and the almost seventeen-year difference from that of his wife, were not particularly unusual, although that difference and her young age were closer to the extremes than to the average.[38] Men married relatively late because of the need to establish financial independence, while women did so early on the grounds of fertility and also to remove them from a father's obligations, although this presumably would have been less of a consideration in this marriage because Peri's bride was an only child. More striking are the facts that Caterina, being without brothers or sisters, was an

37. Ledger B, fol. 173v.
38. The average age at marriage for a male, based on a survey of the noble class as it was defined in 1750, had gone up to between thirty-three and thirty-four in the second half of the sixteenth century; Litchfield, "Demographic Characteristics of Florentine Patrician Families," 199.

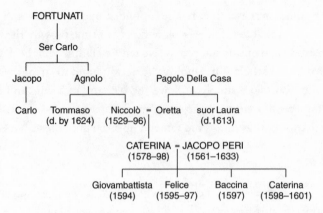

FIGURE I.3. Genealogical chart (selective) of the Fortunati family.

heiress and that Peri had virtually no patrimony—although clearly he had a degree of cultural status. It is unusual, too, that he chose not to follow many of his musician colleagues and marry within the profession. The norm among the court musicians would also have been to seek grand-ducal approval for any match.[39] We do not know whether Peri did so, but the fact that the marriage seems not to have brought any direct benefit to the court suggests that he saw—and was in a position to see—his life moving in several different spheres.

As for the bride's father, Niccolò Fortunati, little is known about his profession or economic status, despite the survival of two of his books of accounts and *ricordi*: one, scantily filled and sloppily kept, begun by his father, Agnolo, in 1520 and continued by Niccolò from 1573 to 1584; and the other his alone, also crudely written, spanning the years 1557 to 1594. He made a *ricordo* on 25 March 1570 that he was leaving his position in the shop of a shoemaker (*calzaiolo*) with whom he had been associated, but the estate he

39. Compare, for example, the request made in 1603 by the court musician Giovanni Battista Signorini that he be allowed to marry the daughter of a former dyer, Benedetto di Borgo; see Cusick, *Francesca Caccini at the Medici Court*, 36. That match did not come to fruition (because, it seems, of Benedetto's reluctance to wed his daughter to a musician wholly reliant on his court salary), and in 1607 Signorini married the singer and composer Francesca Caccini.

had at the end of his life was much larger than could have been accumulated by an ordinary artisan.[40]

The merchant banker Giovambattista Michelozzi played a central role in the match between Fortunati's daughter and Peri. He negotiated (*trattò*) the arrangements with Fortunati on 10 November 1592, and four days later he stood guarantor when, in Fortunati's house, Fortunati and Peri signed a notarized contract for the dowry of *fl.*3,200: *fl.*2,000 to be paid in cash immediately and *fl.*1,200 within a year, on the condition that this latter amount be spent on property at Marciano in the Valdichiana near Monte San Savino, where the Fortunati had long possessed property (see Figure 2.2). In January 1593 Fortunati paid the *fl.*2,000 cash component of the dowry. According to the contract, he also agreed to pay interest on the second installment of *fl.*1,200 if he could not make it on time, and in fact after a year, finding payment "not convenient," he began paying Peri the interest charge, at 5 percent, of *fl.*5 a month.[41] Meanwhile, in 1593 Peri and his wife moved into a house in Borgo Pinti rented from her father's brother, Tommaso, for *fl.*20 a year.[42]

The year after his daughter's marriage to Peri, Fortunati made a will in which, after several small bequests to others, he named her as the sole beneficiary. Moreover, he provided for the subsequent inheritance of his property by her sons and their male descendents, or by her daughter in the form of a dowry; in the absence of children, and only then, his heir was to be his cousin Carlo di Jacopo di Ser Carlo Fortunati. Fortunati died on 13 March 1596, and the presence at the moment of Peri's cousin Domenico, along with a priest, suggests another possible contact through which this marriage had been arranged. Fortunati had not paid what was to be the second installment of the dowry (although he had continued to pay the interest charge down to his death); and this credit was apparently extinguished by the transfer to Peri of

40. LC 2383, fol. 16v. See the Introduction for more on the Fortunati account books. A copy of the 1570 will of Niccolò's father is among the loose papers in LC 3912.

41. Peri's documentation of the marriage is in Ledger A, fols. 104 (*ricordo*) and 30, 39, 40, 46, 48 (the account of the dowry). Fortunati also entered *ricordi* of the event in his ledger, LC 2383, fol. 43v, and on fols. 44 and 45v therein are signed statements by Peri acknowledging receipt of what was promised him. Peri's copies of the contracts are in LC 3912, documents dated 10 and 14 November 1592.

42. LC 3913, fols. 7, 11 (receipts for payment of the rent).

the Fortunati real estate at Marciano.[43] This was Fortunati's only property; he had rented his residence in Florence.

Between the dowry and inheritance, these arrangements obviously gave Peri considerable economic security. Two thousand florins in cash was a large amount for someone of Peri's status in a society where $fl.100–150$ marked the income level of a very prosperous artisan or middle-ranking court official (although the dowries of the very rich reached as high as fifteen to twenty thousand florins). In November 1596 he bought his own house in Via dei Fossi for $fl.1,000$ (and in 1598 had work done on it amounting to just over $fl.100$). This was an area close to the edge of the built-up city, farther away from the center where Peri had formerly lived, but as respectable as any in this city where noble families had always been widely distributed throughout. The makeup of his new neighborhood, with respect to patrician households and others with servants, on the one hand, and those headed by widows and people with no surname, on the other, was very much the same as the previous one.[44] There were, however, fewer shops and, as one can see in Figure 1.4, much open space lay behind the houses that lined Peri's side of the street. His house was one of what today appears to have been a terrace of narrow houses (Figure 1.5), but it had three stories, an open court with a garden, a dovecote, and, inside, well over a dozen rooms, including an oratory (*oratorio*).[45] And he also had a prestigious neighbor, Giovanni Del Maestro (1542–1606), the grand duke's *maestro di casa*, who was living in Via dei Fossi when Peri bought the house next door.[46] One can only imagine what hopes lay behind the *ricordo* he made on the occasion of the purchase, that God

43. Ledger A, fols. 39, 40, 48, 105; LC 3912, document dated 1593 (Fortunati's will) and another related but undated document.

44. Compare the description of the general area of Via dei Fossi (squares 46, 57) with that of Via dei Ginori (squares 16, 26) in Litchfield, *Florentine Renaissance Resources: Online Gazetteer of Sixteenth-Century Florence*. In the eighteenth century, households of the nobility were still widely scattered throughout the city; Boutier and Angiolini, "Noblesses de capitales, noblesses périphériques."

45. These details come from the inventory made in 1642–44 on the occasion of the state's confiscation of the property of Peri's son Alfonso; ASF, Capitani di Parte Guelfa, numeri bianchi 311, fols. 39v–43v (and see Chapter 4). Two documents regarding the house are in LC 3912, one dated 18 November 1597 (related to the purchase), and the other dated 29 August 1612 (involving a building project of a neighbor).

46. Ledger A, fol. 107. For Del Maestro, see his family tree in ASF, Manoscritti 598 (Carte Pucci), *inserto* 25; his *memorie* and *quaderni* kept in his capacity as *maestro di casa* are now in

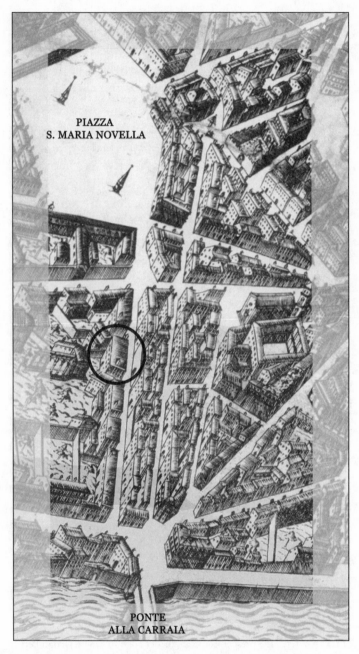

FIGURE I.4. Stefano Bonsignori's view of Florence (1584): detail (edited) showing the approximate location of the house of Jacopo Peri in Via dei Fossi. (Florence, Museum "Firenze com'era." © Foto Scala, Florence.)

FIGURE 1.5. The present house at Via dei Fossi 19, where Jacopo Peri lived from 1596 until his death. (Photo: Silvia Cosi.)

grant that the house should long be enjoyed by him, his wife, and eventually their children (*piaccia a Sua Divina Maestà ch'io la goda lungo tempo in pace e darmi figlioli che doppo me e la mia moglie la godino loro e con salute della anima*).[47] Peri lived there for the rest of his life.[48]

With respect to personal sentiments, Peri's *ricordi* are generally as opaque as the Florentine genre usually is. But during his first marriage certain sad events linked to births and deaths in his immediate family sometimes elicited an expression of his deeper sensibilities, especially for his wife, who on their marriage was less than half his age and still an adolescent. The couple lost their first child, Giovambattista (probably named after Michelozzi, who was the godfather), born on 10 February 1594, after only six weeks.[49] A second child, Felice (named *in buona memoria di mia madre*), was born on 25 June 1595.[50] And two years later, on 9 July 1597, Caterina, who had taken ill a week earlier, gave birth prematurely to a third child, another girl, born in the caul and sickly, nothing but skin and bones and half dead, such that, Peri notes, the midwife baptized her immediately. His prayers to his preferred saints, S. Francesco di Paola and St. Anthony Abbot (in memory of Peri's father and grandfather, it seems), as well as to St. Margaret (in memory of his grand-mother?), were answered: Caterina survived, and Baccina, named after a de-ceased sister of Caterina, was blessed the next day in the baptistry.[51] A little more than two months later, on 26 September, Felice died; and just two

---

ASF, Carte Strozziane I, *filze* 27, 29–30, 51. He was also *pagatore della banca militare*. His widow, Lucrezia di Lorenzo Ruspoli, became a close friend of Peri's third wife, Alessandra.

47. Ledger A, fols. 106v, 107; LC 3913, fols. 12–12v.

48. For the documentation, see Table 2.3. Corazzini located this house at Via dei Fossi 19 and surveyed its ownership to his own day: "Jacopo Peri e la sua famiglia," 43–44.

49. Ledger A, fol. 103v.

50. Ledger A, fol. 104v.

51. Ledger A, fol. 106: *naque vestita, ma tanto stentata che non era se non la pelle e l'ossa, e non ci parse che fussi al tempo; et nacque mezza morta talché la llevatrice la battezzò subito. E perchè la Caterina era stata per 8 giorni adreto assai male, mi è parso che Dio e lla Gloriosa Vergine Maria mi habbi fatto una bella grazia, poiché partorì felicemente e presto, ché tutti dubi-tavamo la creatura li fussi morta in corpo. Io mi raccomandai a S. Francesco di Pagolo e S. Anto-nio Abate, mia avvocati, che pregassino nostro Signore Dio Altissimo che volessino liberare la Caterina e che la creatura havessi l'anima, e così Santa Margherita, vergine e martire; e per loro grazia, come ho detto, fui exaudito senza mio merito. Si batezzò, cioè si benedisse, a S. Giovanni la mattina seguente a 14 hore. Li posi nome Baccina per una sorella della Caterina. E fu conpare messer Giovanni, speziale, ministro del banco de' Corsini, e non chiamai comare. Sia a laude e gloria di Dio omnipotente e del Figliuolo e Spirito Santo. Amen.*

months after that, on 26 November, so did Baccina, after what must have been four sad months of life, and sick with smallpox (*vaiuolo*) for her last twelve days.[52] Left childless, Peri prayed for other future children that might survive (*è piaciuta a Dio tormi la Baccina e tirarla a sè. . . . Prego Sua Divina Maestà sia contenta darmene degli altri, e che vivino se gli è in salute del'anima mia*).[53]

Then a year later, on 16 November 1598, Caterina died the morning after giving birth to another daughter:

> My most beloved Caterina, my companion and my dear wife, died at 17 o'clock [roughly, 11:00 A.M.] on Monday, after successfully giving birth to a daughter on Sunday night, the 15th, at 9½ o'clock [3:30 A.M.]. She was put to bed, bleeding from below; and being so weak because a fortnight before, which was All Saints' Day, she lost sleep and her appetite for food, and often [had] some fever; and she came to the aforesaid birth so weak that it did not please the Lord to return her to me in health, notwithstanding that I prayed to him with all the fervor I could. . . . The baby was born very feeble. . . . My most beloved consort was buried in S. Simone in my tomb, and at her funeral I invited five orders of friars—that is, from the Carmine, S. Francesco de' Zoccoli, S. Croce, S. Stefano, and S. Francesco di Paola—[and] twelve priests from the parish here of S. Paolo, and twelve from S. Simone, with six large candles at the altar and six around the body. *Laus Deo.*[54]

52. Ledger A, fol. 106.
53. Ledger A, fol. 106v.
54. Ledger A, fol. 107v: *mia delettissima Caterina, mia compagnia e cara mia sposa, si morì a hore 17 il lunedì, la quale partorì una bambina la domenica notte a dì 15 a hore 9½ felicemente. Si messe nel letto e lì si avviò il sangue per di sotto, e per essere lei tanto debole perché 15 dì inanzi, che fu per Ognisanti, perse il sonno e 'l gusto del mangiare e spesso qualche febbre, talché si ridusse in detto parto tanto debole che non piacque il Signiore rendermela sana nonostante che io gne ne pregassi con quanto fervore io havevo. La bambina nacque assai stenuata. . . . Si sotterrò la mia dilettissima consorte in S. Simone nella mia sepoltura, e al suo mortorio invitai 5 regole di frati—cioè il Carmine, S. Francesco de' Zoccoli, e S. Croce, S. Stefano, e S. Francesco di Pagolo—12 preti qui del popolo di S. Pagolo, e 12 di S. Simone con 6 torce alla croce e 6 al corpo. Laus Deo.*

In this period, time was reckoned on the twenty-four-hour clock, with 24 o'clock being sunset (and therefore variable during the year, although 6 P.M. is a decent average for rough reckoning). The "five orders of friars" summoned by Peri were, respectively, Carmelites, Observant Franciscans (or Zoccolanti), Franciscans, Augustinians, and Minims.

Peri named his daughter Caterina (after his wife), but she did not reach three years of age, dying of smallpox on 20 October 1601 while staying at her grandmother's villa in Montughi, where Peri had sent her while he went to the Valdichiana (presumably to look after his property there). The young child was brought back to Florence in a procession led by a cross bearer and two priests, and buried in Peri's parish church of S. Paolo (today, S. Paolino, immediately behind Peri's house in the same block), with four pairs of friars from the Carmine, four pairs of priests, and members of the Compagnia della Dottrina Cristiana di Fanciulli in attendance, and with four white candles on the altar and four around the body. The child was placed in a casket and buried near the principal door of the church, on the left-hand side, because Peri had the plan of constructing a family chapel and tomb in the building.[55] All Peri's children by Caterina had now died—the boy after only a few days and all three girls from smallpox. The extraordinarily elaborate funeral arrangements he made for his wife and later for his last child surely signal a deep sense of loss and an intense religiosity.

Meanwhile, ever since the death of his father-in-law, Niccolò Fortunati, in 1596, Peri had been confronting serious challenges to Fortunati's will from Niccolò's brother, Tommaso, and their cousin, Carlo Fortunati, on the basis of an entail (*fedecommesso*) put on some of the property at Marciano by an ancestor in the early sixteenth century, although in his will Niccolò transmitted those rights to his wife and her children. The problem came to the fore with the death of Peri's wife two years later, especially since she had not given birth to a surviving son. Things were further complicated by a lien on the property, arranged by Niccolò Fortunati, in the form of an annuity of *fl.*60 for Tommaso. The first judgments favored Peri, or rather, his daughter; in

---

55. Ledger A, fol. 110: *Ricordo questo dì, 20 d'ottobre 1601, come la mia carissima figliuola Caterina andò a paradiso mercoledì sera a una ora di notte: sia ringraziato e laudato Sua Divina Maestà. Io la mandai in villa della sua nonna a Montui sana e allegra per pigliare aria, e perché volevo andare in Valdichiana; e in capo a 10 giorni gli venne la febbre e si scoperse il vaiuolo, e in 12 giorni si morì. La feci venire in Fiorenza con 2 torce bianche accompagnata con la croce e 2 preti, e si posò qui in San Pagolo, nostra parrocchia. E a 22 hore e ½ si fece il mortorio: si chiamò e' fraticini del Carmine con 4 coppie di detti frati, 4 coppie di preti, e la Compagnia della Dottrina Cristiana di Fanciulli, con 4 torce alla croce e 4 al corpo e capanna in chiesa, tutta cera bianca. La feci formare e mettere in una cassa in un diposito acanto alla porta principale di detta chiesa a man manca, perché se piacerà a Dio voglio fare una cappella e sepoltura nuova; quanto mi sia doluta e dogga* [sic] *Iddio lo sa.*

fact, on 20 September 1601 Tommaso recognized Caterina's entail rights.[56] Just a month later, however, on 20 October the child died, and the Fortunati reopened the case. They dredged up an accusation about the legitimacy of Caterina Fortunati's birth, a complication that arose from the fact, as we learn from Peri's *ricordi*, that Oretta Della Casa had married Niccolò Fortunati, her second husband, mistakenly thinking that her first husband was dead (how this could have happened we are not told). This charge had in fact been raised by the state tax authorities earlier, in 1593, related to tax charges on her dowry, but it was rejected by the courts in Fortunati's favor.[57] We get hints from Peri's *ricordi* and account entries of how serious these legal problems were when Carlo revived the issue following Niccolò's death: Peri called the charges "impertinent, superfluous and useless, criminal, and inflammatory" (*impertinenti, superflui et inutili, criminosi, et infiamatori*), and claimed that Carlo wanted everything from Niccolò's estate (*voleva essere erede d'ogni cosa*). As a result Peri found himself, as he says, encumbered by much costly paperwork and many archival searches through documents, in addition to the mental and physical energies he expended on the case itself (*oltre al gran travaglio che ne hebbi e gran fatiche dell'anima e del corpo*).[58] For three years he had to work hard checking details of the case (*ho durato gran fatica e vigilato assai*).[59]

The final judgment came in 1605 and was not altogether in Peri's favor: he had to relinquish some land to the Fortunati and pay *fl.*600 for them to buy additional property to be included in that family's entail.[60] Nevertheless,

---

56. Ledger A, fols. 109, 109v.

57. Ledger A, fols. 103v, 108v. Oretta Della Casa's first husband, presumed dead when she married Fortunati, was Alberto di Ercole Baldovinetti, but he was still alive at Fortunati's death, and she returned to him. In 1599 Peri made five loans totaling £165.10s. to Baldovinetti and one for *fl.*6 to Baldovinetti's farm worker at Montughi, all paid back within the year; Ledger A, fols. 43, 45.

58. Ledger A, fol. 46.

59. Over these years Peri entered many *ricordi* of these problems, both in his own Ledger A, fols. 107v–109, 114–20, 157, 171, and in the Fortunati ledger in LC 2383, fol. 193. Details also emerge in the ongoing account Peri opened for payment of the dowry; Ledger A, 30, 39, 40, 46, 48. LC 3912 contains a few copies of legal documents related to settlements; see documents dated 26 November 1594, 18 August 1599, 22 March 1604/5, 1612, and the 1570 will of Agnolo di Ser Carlo Fortunati. Problems of the *fedecommesso* are noted in *ricordi* in Ledger A, fol. 119v, and LC 2384, fol. 16.

60. Ledger A, fols. 114v–115, 118, 119.

notwithstanding the death of Caterina's only surviving child in 1601, the property at Marciano remained his—probably in lieu of the outstanding debt due him in cash as part of his wife's dowry. He now had full title to the property, unbound by the dowry agreement. And with this property in the Valdichiana, Peri now had, in addition to the rented farm he could walk to at San Marco Vecchio, a place in the country where he could go to be *in villa*—as he often writes (*andare in villa*). This marriage, in short, brought him a long way toward achieving a respectable Florentine lifestyle.

Outside the household, the 1590s were in fact years of considerable success for Peri, still in his thirties. The ledgers document how he used the funds he received from Caterina's dowry to build up a comfortable patrimony for a man of his class, and later we shall analyze his investments in both real-estate holdings and business enterprises. We also know how his professional career as a musician and composer advanced during this decade, especially following the performance of his first opera, *Dafne*, during the 1597–98 Carnival season, and that of *Euridice* during the festivities celebrating the wedding of Maria de' Medici and Henri IV of France in October 1600. Although, as already mentioned, we find nothing of this success in the accounts and *ricordi*, there are other hints of his rising status in Florentine society. His "election" in December 1596 to a three-month term as one of the twelve Buonuomini di Collegio, at the top of the hierarchy of state councils, and in the next year, as one of the Capitani di Orsanmichele, could hardly have come about without (as Peri notes) the *grazia* of the grand duke, and as we shall see, he subsequently held other major state offices with some frequency. And something of his personal penetration—exactly in what guise is difficult to say—into the highest ranks of Florentine society, even into court circles, can be read in the names of the people chosen as godparents to his children—a rather special network of personal relations to be examined below.

GINEVRA DI PIERO CASELLESI. At the end of 1601, Peri was forty years old and a widower with no children. His first marriage with a young girl had lasted only six years and produced no child who reached the age of three. Within two months of his daughter Caterina's death, however, on 13 December he concluded the arrangements for marrying again, and he gave the ring to his second wife on 1 January 1602 (*il dì dello anello*, which in Florence marked the formal confirmation of marriage). She was Ginevra, the daughter of Piero di Domenico Casellesi and Baccia di Girolamo Grazini. We know virtually nothing about Piero Casellesi except that, although he had at least three sons, he was in a position to provide Peri with a dowry of, again, *fl.*2,000—a trousseau worth "about" *fl.*100, *fl.*600 in cash immediately, and *fl.*1,300 to be paid within three years (with a penalty charge for late payment of 5 percent on *fl.*900 of the *fl.*1,300).[61] In his *ricordo* of the marriage, Peri fervently prayed that "God give offspring, health, and long life to me and likewise to my most beloved wife" (*e piaccia sua Divina Maestà darmi prole, sanità e vita così alla mia dilettissima consorte*); but after only eight months, on 5 August 1602, Ginevra, too, died of a long fever that had forced the premature delivery—at only six months—of a stillborn baby (a girl) who was baptized before she had fully emerged so that she might receive her soul. Peri had the baby placed in the same tomb in S. Paolo as the daughter who had died in October 1601, while he buried Ginevra in S. Simone with the same honors given to his first wife, Caterina, and in the same casket containing Caterina's bones, all this given his plans to build a family burial place. He made careful note of the unusual arrangement so that it might be remembered, and had his actions witnessed by the priest of S. Simone, by Dino di Lorenzo Peri, and by three gravediggers.[62]

Notwithstanding his daughter's death, Piero Casellesi, and subsequently his sons—in contrast to Peri's Fortunati in-laws—kept the agreement about the dowry without creating any legal problems that merited mention in Peri's *ricordi*. In 1602–3 Peri received *fl.*600 plus six month's interest on the *fl.*900 (*fl.*22½), and from 1605 to 1614—presumably without any objections from Peri—the Casellesi stretched out their payments on the balance due, albeit with a degree of regularity. Peri's account for the dowry indicates only pay-

61. Ledger A, fol. 111.

62. Ledger A, fol. 111v: *la mia dilettissima consorte, Ginevra Casellesi, doppo una malattia di 28 giorni di febbre continua, si andò a riposare nel grembo di Sua Divina Maestà con mio grandissimo dolore e travaglio. Era gravida di 6 mesi, e in capo a 20 giorni del suo male si sconciò in una bambina che si battezzò in casa inanzi che l'uscissi tutta di corpo acciò l'havessi l'anima. Si sotterrò in S. Pagolo, e si messe nel diposito della Caterina piccina* [his last child by his previous marriage] *per potere a suo tempo mettere le ossa tutte insieme. La Ginevra la mandai a S. Simone col medessimo onore che ebbe la Caterina, mia prima moglie; e la feci mettere in una cassa e feci cavare l'ossa della Caterina, ch'erano nella solita sepoltura; e fècile mettere in detta cassa, e feci smattonare a piedi della sepoltura in terra, e vi si messe la detta cassa, e di poi si coperse e si riamattonì per poterla cavare e mettere tutte insieme nella sepoltura che, piacendo a Dio, io voglio fare; e per questo ne ho fatto il presente ricordo acciò si sappi dove è stata posta la detta cassa, presente il prete di detta chiesa e messer Dino Peri e di 3 becchini.*

ments toward reducing the balance owed, without any further interest charges.[63] Thereafter he seems to have had no continued association with the family, nor was there any reason for him to do so.

Nevertheless, Peri did not forget this woman who had been his wife such a short time and had left him with no children. Two years after her death he gave the name of Ginevra to his first daughter from his third marriage. And ten years later, finally surrounded by a wife and seven children (as we shall see in a moment), he was one day passing by S. Simone, where the two previous wives were buried, and saw that construction was under way in order to raise the floor to protect it from dampness; he enquired whether the workers had found the casket. They said they had but that it had disintegrated and they had left it untouched. Peri quickly had the bones exhumed and placed in a casket newly made by a carpenter, and the prior of S. Simone graciously allowed him to place it in the priests' tomb next to the main altar, at the threshold of the sacristy, so that he could recover it when needed, depending on whether he or his heirs decided to build a family tomb in S. Simone or elsewhere.[64] One hardly knows what to make of this decision to have the bodies of his first two wives exhumed after ten years and a single new casket made for them both—simply a problem of space? Lasting affection? A sense of possessiveness and patriarchal authority? Or perhaps even guilt, inasmuch as both died in or near childbirth?

We have nothing like a diary or letters for Peri in which he expresses his most intimate feelings about personal matters, and we can only imagine what these ten years of family life meant to him—two wives dead, one, barely beyond adolescence, dying in childbirth and the other dying when six-months pregnant; four children, all dead, none having survived for as long as three years, and a fifth not having emerged from the womb alive. Yet listening to the voice behind the brief observations he makes in the *ricordi* noting these

63. Ledger A, fol. 53.

64. Ledger A, fol. 111v: *domandando se havevano trovato la sopradetta cassa, mi dissono di sì ma ch'era fradica e che non l'havevano toccata. Io subito la feci cercare e cavare tutte le ossa, e le feci mettere in un'altra cassa, alta braccia uno e un quarto e larga circa due terzi riquadrata, ch'io feci fare subito a uno legnaiolo. E 'l priore di detto S Simone per sua cortesia la fece mettere nella sepoltura de' preti acanto a l'altar grande a pie dell'uscio della sagrestia per rendermela a mia posta quando io o mia eredi haremo fatto la nuova sepoltura in detta chiesa, o in altra dove a noi piacerà; e mi promesse farne ricordo al suo libro de' morti, nella prima faccia.* The dimensions of the new casket were approximately $67\frac{1}{2} \times 36 \times 36$ centimeters (or $28\frac{3}{4} \times 15\frac{1}{3} \times 15\frac{1}{3}$ inches).

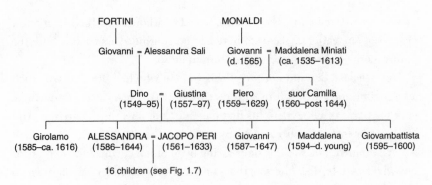

FIGURE 1.6. Genealogical chart (selective) of the Fortini and Monaldi families.

events, especially his repeated desire to have children, and knowing that he wanted his two wives buried together in the same casket and likewise the last child of each (one stillborn) in a common tomb, it is not difficult to sense that Peri was a man with deep familial and religious feelings, whether or not driven by patriarchal ambition. Clearly the short time—not quite three months—that elapsed after his second wife's death before his next marriage cannot be read as evidence of the weak affective bonds uniting husband and wife that many scholars have claimed in their effort to understand the rapid remarriage of widowers in the early modern period.[65]

ALESSANDRA DI DINO FORTINI. Widowed once again in August 1602—and two dowries richer—Peri lost no time in finding another wife, and the one he married after less than three months, Alessandra di Dino Fortini, was only sixteen years old (she was born in 1586), twenty-five years his junior.[66] She was the daughter of Dino Fortini and Giustina (Iustina) di Giovanni Monaldi, and we have considerable information about both these families, thanks to the survival (in the Peri Archive) of account books and *ricordi* of the specific members brought together by the marriage (Figure 1.6).

Dino Fortini's patrimony consisted of properties in the upper Valdarno: a farm at Castelvecchio (today, Castiglion Ubertini, about six kilometers east of Montevarchi), and, just to the north by a few kilometers, three farms at Cicogna and a *casa da padrone* in that town (see Figure 2.2).[67] In the communal

65. Calvi, "Reconstructing the Family," 275–76 (with bibliography).
66. Ledger B, fol. 152v.
67. Piero Monaldi made an inventory of this inheritance; LC 2376, fols. 137v–138v.

period, in fact, the Fortini had a lordship over the area around Castelvecchio. Dino Fortini, however, did not own a home in Florence; so on his marriage to Giustina Monaldi in 1582 the couple moved into the Monaldi home along with her widowed mother, Maddalena Monaldi, and her brother, Piero. Fortini paid *fl.*30 annually to the Monaldi for expenses, raised to *fl.*48 in 1590, by which time his family included several children.[68] Hence with his marriage to Dino's daughter, Peri was to find himself involved in two families, the Fortini and, especially, the Monaldi.

Dino Fortini died in 1595, and his widow, Giustina, assumed the guardianship of his estate and continued to live with her brother and mother, still paying them *fl.*48 a year for expenses.[69] However, she died only two years later, in 1597, leaving behind five small children. Their uncle, Piero, took over the administration of the patrimony, although after a year, in 1598, he turned everything over to the Magistrato dei Pupilli.[70] He and his mother, Maddalena, continued to care for the children, receiving *fl.*108 a year from the estate as compensation for maintenance expenses. Alessandra and her two brothers, Giovanni and Girolamo, the only children to reach maturity, thus grew up in the Monaldi household in Borgo SS. Apostoli.

The Monaldi were less well off than the Fortini.[71] Maddalena Monaldi (*née* Miniati) had brought a dowry of only *fl.*500 to Giovanni on their marriage in 1556. Nevertheless, in 1561 Giovanni Monaldi was able to buy a house in Borgo SS. Apostoli (where Peri's wife was later born) for *fl.*500 and to pay an additional *fl.*800 for improvements, though only four years later, in 1565,

68. LC 3510, fols. 165v, 167v, 168.

69. LC 2376, fol. 138v. Their expenses are recorded in Piero Monaldi's ledger, LC 3510, fols. 51, 52, 54, 58, 59.

70. The guardianship is documented by accounts kept successively by Giustina (1596–97), Piero Monaldi (1597–98), the Pupilli (1598–1605), Maddalena Monaldi (1604–13), and, again, Piero Monaldi (1614–15); see "The Peri Archive" in the Introduction. Monaldi noted the agreement with the Pupilli in LC 3510, fols. 172, 177. The administration by the Pupilli officials can also be followed in the minutes of the numerous meetings when the subject came before them; see s.v. Dino di Giovanni Fortini in the indices of their *campioni*, ASF, Magistrato dei Pupilli del Principato 28–33 (1597–1607). These latter records also include information of a financial nature about Alessandra's stay at the convent of S. Onofrio di Foligno, the deaths of the two youngest Fortini children, Alessandra's marriage to Peri, and Girolamo's problems—all subjects that come up in the following discussion.

71. Information on the Monaldi comes from LC 3510, containing accounts and *ricordi* of Giovanni, from 1554 to 1565, and his son Piero, from 1565 to 1629.

he died, leaving his widow with three small children: two daughters and a son. In 1573 Giustina, at sixteen the eldest of these children, who was to become Alessandra's mother, was sent off to the Dominican convent of S. Vincenzo d'Annalena in Via Romana; in 1580, her sister, Camilla, became a nun at the Franciscan convent of S. Onofrio di Foligno, in Via Faenza (a fashionable institution, we shall see). When, in 1582, Giustina married Dino Fortini—evidently renouncing convent life—the Monaldi provided her with a dowry of *fl.*1,000.

Giustina and Camilla's brother, Piero, the uncle of Peri's wife, followed a typical career path in the silk industry without, however, achieving much success. In 1570, at just over eleven years old, he went to work in a silk shop and subsequently advanced as an accountant, passing through jobs with seven other employers. From 1592 to 1598 he was manager of a firm, with a salary of *fl.*70 and the prospect of becoming a partner, but this did not work out, and at his next job he went back to working as an accountant for a salary of *fl.*60. He became an assistant manager (*sottoministro*) on taking his ninth job, with the Capponi firm in Pisa in 1603, and on the reorganization of this firm in 1611, Piero, now fifty-two years old, moved up to become, finally, a minor partner, contributing only *fl.*500 to the capital of *fl.*6,000 but seeing the firm change its name to Piero Monaldi & Partners, silk manufacturers in Pisa. The company was dissolved in 1613, and Monaldi "retired" from the industry and moved back to Florence. He spent the rest of his life serving frequently in government offices, mostly the better-paying ones in the territorial state, and pursuing his ambitious antiquarian interests. His historical research resulted in a treatise on the world's principal states, another on the princes of the world's major religions (both of these survive only in fragments), yet another on the city's churches (of which nothing survives), and, finally, a massive and influential survey of the Florentine nobility (which we shall have occasion to remark later on).[72] Piero, who never married, played a major role in the lives of his sister Giustina's children.

A year before turning the Fortini estate over to the Pupilli, in 1597, the Monaldi sent Alessandra, then eleven, to the convent of S. Onofrio di Foligno for her education in the virtues and piety (*accioché impari le virtù et divozioni*), presumably in preparation for her taking the veil. She had a strong

72. Monaldi's career can be traced through his *ricordi*; LC 3510, fols. 163–175v. For his antiquarian interests, see "Social Status," below, and n. 127.

tie to the place through her aunt, Camilla, who had earned so much respect that she came to be addressed as "reverend mother" (*suor madre*).[73] S. Onofrio was in fashion at the time, recently completely rebuilt with a newly dedicated church; much of the remodeling had been subsidized by Eleonora degli Albizzi (the mother of Cosimo I's illegitimate son Giovanni), who lived there from the time Francesco I put her (together with a servant and two small children) under house arrest in 1578 until her death in 1634.[74] The residential charge for Alessandra was *fl.*3 a month, or *fl.*36 a year, a not insignificant amount, but this charge ceased two years later, in October 1599, when the Monaldi paid *fl.*200 for her dowry as a prospective nun. A short time thereafter (*doppo poco tempo*), however, Alessandra, now not much older than thirteen, decided not to take the veil—just as her mother had done, it seems— although she stayed on in the community until 10 November 1602. The fee for residence was reinstated, and the dowry eventually refunded.[75]

An inventory of the furnishings of the Monaldi house drawn up in 1598 testifies to the cultural ambience into which Peri's third wife was born: it includes thirteen paintings (depicting religious figures, popes, emperors, the seasons, nature scenes), and printed books containing texts by Ovid, Dante, Petrarch, Sansovino, Bandello, Ariosto, Tasso, "Saba" (presumably Sabba da Castiglione), and Caro. While she was growing up, she may also have felt some vibrations from the research her uncle Piero Monaldi was doing in pursuit of his ambitious historical projects. The things Alessandra took along with her when she went off to the convent—a chest bearing the Fortini coat of arms, a walnut casket, a silver fork, a silver spoon, two knives with silver handles, a necklace of pearls and another of amber, and an ivory comb, along with bedding and many clothes—testify to a certain luxury in the family's lifestyle, if not also to the quality of life at S. Onofrio.[76]

---

73. LC 3510, fol. 165v. In her 1644 will, Alessandra, Peri's widow, refers to her aunt as *madre suora Camilla*; ASF, Notarile moderno, prot. 12995, no. 26.

74. Saltini, *Tragedie medicee domestiche*, 222–27.

75. This information comes from an account opened in Alessandra's name in a ledger of the convent: ASF, Corporazioni religiose soppresse dal governo francese 79 (S. Onofrio di Foligno), 133 (ledger C, 1593–1603), fol. 90. This account shows that the residential charge continued to be paid until March 1604—perhaps representing some kind of commitment until Alessandra was eighteen—although by then she was married and a mother. See also ASF, Magistrato dei Pupilli del Principato 29, fols. 124, 197v.

76. LC 2376, fols. 132v–135v, 139v–140; LC 3510, fol. 172.

Peri may have come to know of Alessandra while she was in residence there. His first wife's aunt, Laura Della Casa, was a nun at S. Onofrio, and was on a three-year term (1596–99) as the manager (*ministra*) when Alessandra arrived (later, in 1606, she is identified as *vicaria*). Peri knew *suor* Laura fairly well, for on her election as manager he loaned her *fl.*150 (which he converted to a gift to the convent two days after his first wife's death, to be used for Masses for his wife, her father, and himself), and (according to his book of receipts) he regularly and almost always personally paid the annuity of *fl.*5 bequeathed to her by Niccolò Fortunati (her brother-in-law) until her death in 1613.[77] Another notable presence at S. Onofrio was Alessandra's aunt, the highly esteemed *suor madre* Camilla, and as recounted by Peri in his *ricordi*, it was Camilla's mother (and Alessandra's grandmother), Maddalena Miniati, along with her brother, Piero Monaldi, who dominated the arrangements for Alessandra's marriage to Peri in 1602. On 26 October Peri concluded the agreement with both, and at their house three weeks later, on 17 November, just a week after Alessandra left the convent, he presented his bride with the ring and took her off to her new home. Her dowry, signed over officially to Peri on 20 December 1602, consisted of the Fortini farm at Castelvecchio, valued at *fl.*1,612, plus a claim, shared with the other heirs of her father, on an adjacent property; her trousseau was valued at *fl.*70. This, his third dowry, was thus more or less at the level of the previous two, but it took the form of a farm rather than cash. It constituted about one-fourth of the total value of the Fortini estate, which for a dowry was a relatively large portion of a patrimony to which there were also two male heirs, Alessandra's brothers.[78]

77. Ledger A, fol. 42; LC 3913, fols. 16–42. Other information about *suor* Laura comes from a book of *ricordi* (1593–1767) of the convent; ASF, Corporazioni religiose soppresse dal governo francese 79, 385, fols. 6 (her election as *ministra*), 11 (Peri's cancellation of the loan), 28v (her death). In the convent's ledger D (ibid., 332), fol. 98, an account is opened in her name as *vicaria*. Peri's loan of *fl.*150 is also recorded in an account opened in his name for this purpose in the convent's ledger C (ibid., 331), fol. 64; Peri paid cash through the Michelozzi bank.

78. The documentation for the marriage is found in Peri's Ledger A, fol. 112; in the ledger kept by the Pupilli for the administration of Dino Fortini's estate, LC 2377, fol. 163; in Piero Monaldi's ledger, LC 3510, fol. 31; and in ASF, Magistrato dei Pupilli del Principato 31, fols. 7v, 127v. Corazzini, "Jacopo Peri e la sua famiglia," 45, cites the notarial act. In 1601 the Pupilli officials put all the Fortini farms up for sale, estimating their total value at *fl.*6,225 (there was no property in the city), but they found no buyers; ASF, Magistrato dei Pupilli del Principato 30, fol. 185.

Eventually, for lack of male descendants in the immediate family of both of his wife's parents, Peri's marriage into this family complex brought more property into his hands. The surviving members of these two families—Piero Monaldi, his mother, and his deceased sister's three children (Peri's wife, Alessandra, and her two brothers, Girolamo and Giovanni Fortini)—were as one in affective terms: Monaldi wrote that they lived harmoniously in his house (*sendo stati concordi sempre in casa mia*) and exhibited clear loyalty (*chiara fedeltà*) in their relations.[79] Yet we get more than just hints of the problems they faced. On the Monaldi side there was a passive decline of economic status: Alessandra's uncle, we have seen, had an undistinguished career in business and never married, while her one aunt had become a nun. As for the Fortini, both of Alessandra's brothers—as we can perceive them through their family accounts as well as Peri's—created problems for their uncle, Piero Monaldi, some of which ended up in Peri's lap. Neither married, and it seems that Alessandra's own marriage to Peri was in some sense an expedient move to stave off the declining fortunes of her family. It may have been that she was sent to a convent to become a nun but now was plucked out of it for this purpose.

The problems these brothers, Peri's brothers-in-law, created were financial in nature and arose from two very different personalities—one irresponsible, the other of a certain incapacity. At the time the Pupilli took over the estate, in 1598, Girolamo, thirteen and therefore at an age to go to work, had instead been put out (perhaps on an apprenticeship) to Tommaso Pitti at the cost of *fl*.4 a month for his support. Two years later, in 1600, Girolamo was in Rome, where the Pupilli authorized payments for his support over the next two years (what he was doing there at age fifteen we are not told). In Rome, Girolamo ran up debts that by October 1602 landed him in jail there, and his uncle, Piero Monaldi, had to go to the city to get him out. At this point Peri, who had just contracted to marry Girolamo's sister, enters the story, having been requested by Piero Monaldi and his mother, Maddalena, with the authorization of the Pupilli officials, to execute an exchange operation through which Girolamo borrowed *fl*.100. By this time Girolamo, having reached seventeen (on entering his eighteenth year, as the Pupilli defined age), was freed from the tutelage of the Pupilli, but since his brother had not reached his

79. LC 3510, fol. 170.

maturity, and he himself was not yet twenty-one (that is, in their terms, in his twenty-second year), he still needed to appeal to the officials whenever he took out a loan on a lien against his share of the estate. In November 1603, they again authorized him to borrow *fl.*100 on the exchange, naming Peri as guarantor, this time specifying that he needed the money to get out of jail, now the Stinche in Florence (as we know from Peri's ledger). The next month he sought permission from the Pupilli to sell his share of the property at Cicogna, and so the farms were divided between the two brothers; Girolamo immediately began liquidating his portion to cover debts. These continued to mount, however, and on 17 August 1604 the Pupilli ordered that he be found, arrested, and incarcerated, this time in the Bargello.[80]

In all of this, Peri took a hand in helping the family meet some of the attendant costs. He opened an account in Girolamo's name and debited it for wine sent to him in prison, for medical assistance, and for legal fees connected to his defense and to his eventual release (many of these expenses were reimbursed to Peri by the magistracy dealing with Girolamo's debts, presumably from his assets it had seized), and over a period of six years he stood as guarantor for some of Girolamo's further exchange operations.[81] In 1607 and through a friend, Cosimo Baroncelli, Girolamo received an appointment in the service of the Florentine ambassador to Henri IV of France; when he showed up in Paris without shoes or clothes (*scalzo e nudo*), having been robbed during the trip there, Baroncelli loaned him money so he could clothe himself from head to toe (*da capo a piedi*). Girolamo never repaid Baroncelli, and after his death in Brussels in 1616, Peri, even though he himself was owed a goodly sum of money (*buona somma di denari*) by Girolamo, agreed to settle this debt by paying *fl.*70 £6 to Baroncelli or his heirs, but only after the death of Girolamo's brother, Giovanni.[82]

If Girolamo had problems running up debts, Giovanni apparently had difficulties keeping track of his finances owing to some kind of infirmity that may have involved cerebral palsy, or so one can infer from the records. The

80. For all this, see the *campioni* volumes of the Pupilli cited above in n. 70, and also the account opened in Girolamo's name in Piero's ledger, LC, 3510, fols. 61, 63, 67, 68, 75, 76, 98. Corazzini, "Jacopo Peri e la sua famiglia," 46, cites the notarial act of division between the two brothers.

81. Ledger A, fols. 61, 74 (the account); and fols. 115v, 116 (*ricordi*).

82. LC 3912, document dated 1620 (including a copy of the agreement).

Pupilli officials always referred to him as Giovannino, later actions suggest that he was in some sense disabled, and in her will of 1642, Alessandra referred to him as being sick in the mind (*malsano di mente*). But whatever Giovanni's problems were, he seems not to have been totally incapacitated. After he came into possession of his share of the inheritance from his father and reached his maturity, his grandmother, Maddalena Monaldi, took up the ledger that Giustina had kept for the administration of the Fortini inheritance until her death in 1597 and used it to keep accounts in Giovanni's name because, she wrote, he did not know how to write (*perché no sa scrivere*).[83] She kept the accounts until her death in 1613, at which time Piero took over the ledger and continued keeping accounts for Giovanni until 1615 (and he kept them as if he were in fact Giovanni, making reference to "Jacopo Peri, my brother-in-law," "Piero Monaldi, my uncle," and "Madonna Maddalena, my grandmother"—a practice further remarked in Chapter 2).[84] The debit balance on Giovanni's account with his grandmother that Piero now transferred to the new accounts amounted to *fl*.150 15*s*.3*d*., and Giovanni's signed statement of agreement about this debt to his grandmother on her death (countersigned by Peri) is written with block letters in a very simplistic and labored way, proof that he did in fact have problems writing.[85] Maddalena's death was the occasion for an agreement between Monaldi and Giovanni about his financial situation with respect to these debts, an agreement that includes a reference to Peri's intervention (*l'intervento di Jacopo d'Antonio Peri*).[86] The next year, 1614, Giovanni made a contract with his sister, Peri's wife, for transferring ownership of his farm at Cicogna to her in return for payment of debts amounting to *fl*.600—which Peri says she paid with his money—and a personal annuity of *fl*.60.[87] Giovanni resided with his uncle, Piero Monaldi, who in fact received the entirety of his nephew's annuity for his maintenance, and Piero took Giovanni with him on his numerous assignments to political office in the territorial state (having to pay extra for his carriage, since he

83. LC 2375, incipit, added note by Maddalena. Piero Monaldi also observed that Giovanni could not write; LC 3910, fol. 92.

84. LC 2375, fols. 45–54.

85. LC 2375, fol. 33.

86. LC 3510, fol. 92. Peri made *ricordi* of these debts in his Ledger A, fols. 80, 93.

87. LC 2375, fols. 52, 136; Ledger B, fol. 153 (Peri's *ricordi*). Corazzini, "Jacopo Peri e la sua famiglia," 45, cites the notarial act.

could not ride a horse).[88] At the same time, Monaldi opened an account in Peri's name showing advances Peri made to Monaldi to cover expenses related to Giovanni.[89] And Peri, too, kept a running account of credits he extended to Giovanni, much of it also to help Girolamo.[90]

Piero Monaldi died in 1629, having never married and leaving behind an estate evaluated, for tax purposes, at *fl.*1,390. In his will he left his only property, the house in Borgo SS. Apostoli, to be divided between his niece (Peri's wife) and nephew, Giovanni Fortini—*povero huomo*—adding somewhat sadly but with a sense of having fulfilled his responsibilities that they were the last of the ancient Monaldi family, and that he had done right by the remaining male heir, Giovanni (*sono l'ultimo del'antica famiglia de' Monaldi, e così mi contento compensando il bisogno di detto Giovanni, mio nipote*).[91] Giovanni, who had been living under his uncle's care, now probably went to live with his sister and the large Peri family.[92] He immediately made an agreement to cede his half of the Monaldi house to Alessandra in return for an annuity of *fl.*14 for himself and one of *fl.*6 for their aunt, the nun; given his condition, the document is careful to explain that he did not do this because of pressure, deceit, or fear, but with clear knowledge and in the best way he knew how and could (*non per forza, inganno o paura, ma di certa scienza et in ogni miglior modo che sa e può*).[93] At this point Giovanni had transferred to Peri's wife both his inheritance from their father and that from their uncle— properties burdened with annuities that now, taking all three together (two for Giovanni and one for the aunt), amounted to *fl.*80. In 1631 Peri deposited

88. In his ledger, LC 3910, Monaldi opened numerous accounts for Giovanni's expenses, and he signed some of the receipts Peri kept for payment of the annuity to Giovanni (LC 3913). Elsewhere Monaldi observed that Giovanni could not ride a horse; LC 2375, fol. 33.

89. LC 2375, fols. 36, 52; see also Monaldi's *ricordo* in LC 3510, fol. 177.

90. Ledger A, fols. 76, 79, 85; and *ricordi* in Ledger A, fols. 120, 121v, and Ledger B, fols. 153, 153v.

91. LC 3510, fols. 183v–184.

92. This would identify the eighth male (after Peri and his six sons) recorded as residents of the Peri home in the 1632 census; see Chapter 4.

93. Ledger B, fol. 153; Peri's copy of the contract is in LC 3912, document dated 6 September 1629. Peri registered the house with the Decima officials under Alessandra's name: ASF, Decima granducale 2392 (*arroti* of S. Croce), no. 97 (although in his *ricordo* he gives the wrong *gonfalone*: Chiave instead of Bue). The transfer of ownership is also registered in Piero Monaldi's account on the Decima's records; ibid., 3608 (*campione* of S. M. Novella, Vipera), fol. 269.

*fl.*100 in Giovanni's name at the Monte di Pietà with the condition that he
was to enjoy the income but that after his death the deposit was to go to his
sister, Peri's wife.[94] After Peri's death, Alessandra also made ongoing provisions for Giovanni (see Chapter 4). Clearly she was concerned about his well-
being, as were her uncle and Peri himself during their lifetimes.

It was in part genealogical chance that Peri's wife ended up with the Monaldi house in Florence as well as with the Fortini estate at Cicogna. These
properties were all that was left of the patrimony of the two families at that
point, where the particular branches to which Alessandra belonged came to
an end, and they passed to her heavily burdened with annuity claims. The
last chapter of the internal history of both families with which Peri was
joined by way of his third marriage has something of the air of decline: Piero
Monaldi's undistinguished career in the silk business, Girolamo Fortini's irresponsible behavior, and what for his brother Giovanni—if this *povero
huomo*, who converted his inherited properties into annuities, really could
not write and was *malsano di mente*—was most certainly a serious handicap
of one kind or another. But Peri's good fortune at coming into what property
they had left, notwithstanding the liens on it, cannot be dismissed as just a
lucky marriage and a quirk of genealogical fate. Rather, he entered actively
and helpfully into this Fortini–Monaldi circle and contributed significantly
to it.

Children (Until Their Father's Death)

When Peri married Alessandra Monaldi Fortini none of the children from
his previous two marriages had survived. And we have seen how fervently he
desired to have them. Presumably he saw in his third wife not just a well-
educated woman from a respectable, if declining, family but also someone
able to help him realize his hope for children: in his *ricordo* of the wedding,
he yet again expresses the hope that God, to whom all thanks and praise,
should "give us a long life and health with offspring worthy of His Divine
Majesty" (*Sua Divina Maestà sia sempre ringraziata e laudata e ci dia grazia di
lunga vita e sanità con prole degna di Sua Divina Maestà*). Given what he had
been through in his earlier marriages, he probably did not take it as a good

---

94. Ledger B, fol. 153v; ASF, Monte di Pietà 1398 (*campione di depositi condizionati*, 1628–
31), fol. 726.

omen that Alessandra's first child, born on 29 January 1604—and named Ginevra—lived only a few days. The couple went on, however, to have no fewer than fifteen more children, the last born when Peri was sixty-three (Figure 1.7).

In noting the birth of these as well as his earlier children—twenty all together (an exceptional number in a society in which four to five was normal)—Peri sometimes records why he gave them the names he did: Baccina after a sister of his first wife; Caterina after his second wife, who died giving birth to her; and of the children of his third wife, Antonio after Peri's father (and his "advocate" saint); Felice, *in buona memoria di mia madre*; Ottavia, because she was the eighth daughter. Ginevra, the first child of his third wife, was probably named after his previous wife; his first son, Giovambattista, probably after Michelozzi, who had shepherded his early investments, arranged the marriage, and served as godfather; and perhaps two others—Alfonso and Carlo—were also named after their godfathers. Of the children by his third wife, however, he conferred the same second name, Romolo (or Romola), on all but one of the sons and on three of the daughters. In this he was following a Florentine tradition going back to the late fifteenth century, for virtually every Florentine received this name along with the others with which he or she was baptized, a practice that arose around the cult of a saint considered a protector against epilepsy (*il male benedetto*), much feared as a childhood disease.[95]

Three of the sixteen children of this marriage died in early childhood, a fourth not yet in her early teens, and two as young adults. But ten were still alive when Peri died in 1633, after just over thirty years of a full—and seemingly happy—family life. His residence in Via dei Fossi became increasingly crowded, and the children brought responsibilities and costs that Peri and his wife appear to have shouldered with some equanimity. However, it seems to have been the birth of Cosimo (the tenth child, not counting their short-lived first-born, Ginevra) on 20 March 1617 that prompted Peri, just two months later, to petition the Medici for some further civic office that would ease his financial burdens (this eventually led to his appointment at the Arte della Lana); and by May 1619 the number of his children (now

95. Klapisch-Zuber, "San Romolo."

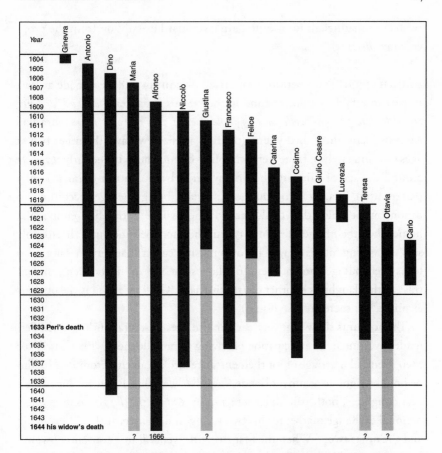

FIGURE I.7. Comparative life spans of Jacopo Peri's children by his third wife. The lighter shading indicates the years after a daughter was professed as a nun. The precise birth and death dates for the children follow (from the *ricordi* in Ledgers A–E). For the entries in the *libro dei morti* of the Arte dei Medici e Speziali, see Corazzini, "Jacopo Peri e la sua famiglia." Except for Felice, we do not have death dates for the daughters who became nuns.

Ginevra: 29 Jan–2 Feb 1604
Antonio: 12 May 1605–22 Mar 1627
Dino: 7 Jun 1606–5 May 1640
Maria: 19 Aug 1607–after 1644
Alfonso: 17 Mar 1609–18 Mar 1666
Niccolò: 14 Aug 1610–17 Nov 1637
Giustina: 22 Sep 1611–after 1644
Francesco: 5 Sep 1612–29 Nov 1635

Felice: 16 Nov 1613–29 Dec 1632
Caterina: 20 Feb 1616–19 Aug 1627
Cosimo: 20 Mar 1617–21 Aug 1636
Giulio Cesare: 25 Mar 1618–4 Oct 1635
Lucrezia: 7 May 1619–11 Nov 1621
Teresa: 26 Dec 1620–after 1644
Ottavia: 16 May 1622–after 1644
Carlo: 12 Dec 1624–1 Aug 1628

twelve) was sufficient for him to gain a standard exemption from the property tax (*decima*).[96]

DAUGHTERS. Peri's petitions for civic office in 1617–18 were made at least in part to establish a dowry fund for one of his daughters (*um poco di principio di dote per una delle mia figliuole*; Letter 21). He and Alessandra had eight of them: three died young (the first after a few days, the other two at ages two and twelve); three were sent off to became nuns in the early 1620s, at around the age of thirteen (the time when girls, in contrast to boys, legally passed from infancy into adulthood, twelve being the age, according to canon law, at which they could marry); and two were still children living at home when their father died in 1633 (but they, too, became nuns). It probably says something for his view of his own musical career that Peri does not seem to have encouraged any of them to follow somehow in his footsteps, in contrast to the daughters of other court musicians (Giulio Caccini is the obvious example, but there are also others).

The accounts show that very early in the lives of several of these girls, Peri made investments in anticipation of having to provide them with a dowry for their eventual marriage or for their entrance into a convent. From 1614 to 1616 he bought eight government bonds (*luoghi di monti*) in Rome for his two eldest daughters, both still under ten; and in 1622 he put *fl.*1,027 on the international exchange market for his two youngest daughters at the time, one six and the other two.[97] When the first two girls went off to a convent, however, he did not liquidate the bonds to pay their entrance fees or transfer them to the convent; instead, he paid the fees in cash and reassigned the name of the beneficiary to a younger daughter. In fact, the fees for each girl—described as charity and the cost for clothing and other possessions (*elemosina e fornimenti*)—did not reach the amount of a dowry that might have opened the way to what Peri would presumably have considered a suitable marriage to match his own social status, and they were certainly much lower than the dowries he had received. Such economizing was not atypical in this period of dowry inflation, which was pricing would-be upwardly mobile families out of the market: in effect, male offspring offered such families better financial

96. For the 1617 petition and its circumstances, see Letter 20; for the 1619 exemption from the *decima*, see Chapter 2.

97. Ledger A, fol. 122 (the *luoghi*), 124 (the bill of exchange).

prospects than females, given the dowries those males could attract by virtue of that mobility. The *fl.*600 that Peri paid in 1620 to the fashionable convent of S. Vincenzo at Prato for the first daughter, Maria, was by far the highest of these fees; later, in 1625, he paid only *fl.*200 for Felice's entrance into the convent of S. Onofrio di Foligno.[98] In 1631 he bought two bonds (*luoghi*) in the Monte di Pietà, the income of which was to go, after his death, to these daughters for the duration of their lives.[99]

By the time he died, Peri had sent the three daughters who had reached the appropriate age to convents, but he may have given serious thought to marriage for the last two, Teresa and Ottavia, then aged eight and ten and still at home, perhaps because by this time, with the others in convents, he felt financially more confident about being able to provide a dowry of suitable size. His relatively heavy investment in government securities seems to have been directed toward building up dowries for them. This concern comes through very clearly in his testament of 1630, a good part of which is dedicated to the necessary arrangements. He provides potential dowries for each of the youngest daughters in the form of government securities and *censi* paying an annual income of *fl.*75—equivalent to a dowry of around *fl.*1,500 invested at 5 percent (the standard basis for such calculations at the time). He further stipulated that the income from these investments, less the daughters' share of living expenses while they were still at home with the family, was to be saved in a secure place, such as the Monte di Pietà, and every two years should be used to buy *luoghi* either in Florence or Rome, to be added to this dowry fund. He does not stipulate, however, that the capital would go with them to the convent should they become nuns, and indeed his intention seems to have been to prevent that. Rather, what was to be paid was only the "usual" dowry of a nun and a charitable donation (*la dote et limosina solita et consueta*) plus an annuity of *fl.*5, and nothing more.

In January 1631, a few months after making his testament, Peri bought another *fl.*100 bond in the Monte di Pietà for each of these two youngest daughters to increase their dowries; but at the end of the next year, when (we shall see) he turned the administration of his affairs over to his son Dino, he transferred these two bonds to his two youngest sons, who had "greater need

98. Ledger A, fol. 122; Ledger B, fol. 151.
99. Ledger B, fol. 155.

and with good purpose and reason" (*più bisogno per buon fine e rispetto*).[100]
Maybe the reassignment of these last two *luoghi*, less than a year before his
death, marked second thoughts on the matter of dowries: it is not difficult to
imagine that his concerns were still felt when, just a few months after his
death, the decision was made, presumably with the agreement of his widow,
to send the two girls, now aged eleven and thirteen, to the convent of S. Caterina di Siena. They remained there for four months, and later, in 1635, they
were together under the guardianship (*per serbanza*) of the Dominican convent of S. Maria della Disciplina (later S. Maria della Neve), called *Il Portico*,
outside the city on the road to Galuzzo. Teresa took the veil (*si veste monaca*),
assuming the name of *suor* Maria Prudente, on 30 September 1635, and Ottavia followed suit sometime during the next year.[101]

Once they became nuns, the daughters disappear from their father's accounts; the cloister severed them from any formal financial relation with
their family except for the small annuities that customarily accompanied
dowry arrangements for nuns, like the ones noted above for the youngest
daughters. And this may have been the point: it would seem that Peri, with so
many sons to think about, did not want to burden his patrimony with the
expense of even a single marriage dowry. In this he was a father of his times.
The inflation of dowries and the desire to protect the patrimony and keep it
intact for male heirs were two concerns that came to the fore in Florentine
family life in the course of the sixteenth century. The dowries Peri received
corresponded, in real buying power, to those of the rich in the fifteenth century, but in his time, each was a fraction of what a rich man offered his son-
in-law. And this inflation of dowries occurred at a time when men sought to
assure the survival of their entire patrimony into the indefinite future.
Whereas a century earlier, fathers divided their wealth among all sons, by
Peri's time they were entailing their estates following the principle of primogeniture in practice, not in law, by marrying off only one of them.

Daughters suffered the consequences of these pressures on their fathers,
since a convent was much less costly than a son-in-law. Hence in early

100. Ledger B, fols. 59, 60.
101. Ledger B, fols. 59, 60; Ledger D, fols. 14, 15, 85, 97; LC 3913, fol. 76 (receipt by the
convent for the maintenance fee); LC 3918, fols. 79, 92, 93, 104. Corazzini, "Jacopo Peri e la sua
famiglia," 62, cites a letter of 1636 in which Dino Peri refers to his sister's preparation for taking vows. Since both girls were still dependents of their father's estate, the Pupilli officials
noted their decision to become nuns; see Chapter 4.

seventeenth-century Florence, daughters of some social status but limited means had only the religious life as a real alternative to marriage, and more of them ended up in convents—44 percent of those from noble families.[102] Moreover, the age at which they arrived there fell from around seventeen at the end of the fifteenth century to around thirteen (the age of Peri's daughters). Thus in the course of the sixteenth century the increasing concern on the part of fathers about these relative costs generated a dynamic that has been called a veritable "rush to convents." In Florence from the end of the fifteenth century to 1552 (when a census provides us with exact figures) the number of nuns went from around 1,200–1,300 to 3,419, or from 3 to 5.2 percent of the total population; by 1574 there were twice as many convents as there had been a century earlier (sixty-three compared with thirty), and the average population of each, moreover, had doubled; by the end of the century convents with a hundred and more residents were not unusual; and in 1622 the number of nuns had risen to 4,203, 5.5 percent of the total population of 76,023.[103] Most of these women were from families of substantial means. This might lead one to wonder, incidentally, how many Florentine boys, like Peri's sons, grew up with none of their teenage sisters at home with the family.

In going off to convents, however, Peri's daughters were not altogether cast out of the home, for something of the family went with them: Maria and Giustina were sent to the same convent in Prato; Felice went to one where her mother had been and where her great-aunt still resided; and after Peri's death the two youngest daughters went together to the convent *Il Portico*. At the time, in fact, it was not unusual for nuns to be together with a sister and other relatives in the same convent; and the presence of relatives as well as women from their own social class made conventual life something of an extension of the family.[104]

102. Litchfield, "Demographic Characteristics of Florentine Patrician Families," 203. On the aristocratization of convents in this period, see J. C. Brown, "Monache a Firenze all'inizio dell'età moderna," 130–31.

103. A survey of the dynamics behind this growth can be found in Zarri, *Recinti*, ch. 1. For the broader issues, see also Strocchia, *Nuns and Nunneries in Renaissance Florence*, and for the following centuries, the work of Silvia Evangelisti now summarized in her *Nuns: A History of Convent Life*. The 1622 population figures come from Francesco Settimanni's *Memorie fiorentine*, vol. 8 (1620–25) in ASF, Manoscritti 133, fol. 100.

104. J. C. Brown, "Monache a Firenze all'inizio dell'età moderna," 130.

Yet we must not overlook Peri's genuine religious enthusiasm in putting his daughters into convents. In this respect his choice of the Dominican convent of S. Vincenzo at Prato for his first daughter when she came of age is telling. It had recently undergone an extraordinary revival during the residence there of the Florentine nun Caterina de' Ricci (1522–90; canonized in 1746), whose fervent Counter-Reformation zeal made her famous and attracted an enormous community committed to a life of strict seclusion: in 1572, its population numbered over two hundred, between nuns, girls, and staff. The convent, although in Prato, was especially noted for the dominant presence of Florentine women from prominent families, and Peri may have been caught up in the contemporary religious devotion to the memory of Caterina de' Ricci and to the fashionable community she had founded. On 4 September 1620 he accompanied his thirteen-year-old daughter Maria there, carrying along with him, besides the appropriate clothing for her, *fl.*600 in cash, all in silver *piastre*, for her dowry; the resident nun in charge of external affairs (*sindaca*), *suor* Margherita Ricasoli (of the baronial family, Peri adds), counted it all out in the presence of the prioress and Maria. Then on 28 September (a Monday) he returned with most of his family for Maria's taking the veil (*si vestì monaca*). In his description of this trip something of his enthusiasm for placing a daughter there breaks through the usual detached and impersonal tone of the *ricordi*. Peri, Alessandra, and eight of their children (the three youngest were left at home), plus Alessandra's close friend (and their next-door neighbor), the widowed Lucrezia Del Maestro, went to Prato for the ceremony. Typically for a Florentine, Peri notes the cost of the entire enterprise, including the trip (*fl.*640). No less typical is the fact that he did so on the very day of his return (Tuesday 29 September):

> Lessandra and I left with Antonio, Dino, Niccolò, Francesco, and Alfonso, and Giustina, Felice, and Caterina—in all, eight siblings—and the maidservant. There also came Signora Lucrezia, the widow Del Maestro, our neighbor and dear to Lessandra. We took a chaise, a carriage, and a horse, and we rested for the remainder of the day. And on the following Tuesday, the 29th, at about 15 o'clock [roughly 9:00 A.M.] the aforesaid Maria, my first [surviving] daughter and first in love, was invested as a nun with great joy and contentment of us all, and of her in particular. And we returned to Florence that day after lunch. May it all be to the glory of God in the highest and of the Holy Trinity, amen. Adding up all that which I have spent between dowry, and journeys, and

[Maria's] clothing, it comes to around *fl.*640 up to this day, 29 September 1620.[105]

Peri also sent his second daughter there but did not record the occasion.[106]

His next daughter went instead to the convent of S. Onofrio di Foligno, an institution that by this time he must have known well. Felice, not quite twelve years old, was accompanied by her mother, who had formerly resided there. Peri commented that his daughter went of her own volition—a commonplace wording, although here perhaps an indication of her initiative in the matter—and to the great applause of the nuns, given that she seemed to them well brought up and of good quality (*s'accettò per monaca con sua propria volontà e con grandissimo applauso di tutte le monache, parendo loro fusse molto bene allevata e di buona qualità*).[107] He probably could not have asked for more. Felice predeceased her father, dying at S. Onofrio on 29 December 1632 at the age of nineteen.[108]

None of the convents to which Peri's daughters went was well known for its musical interests: the girls do not seem to have followed their father in this regard. Nor does he seem to have wanted to use his daughters to establish some kind of musical dynasty, as did Giulio Caccini: this was surely a matter of Peri's social ambitions. But perhaps he was also glad to keep them away from music, whether inside or outside convents, given the scandals that often emerged in those institutions that were known for it, one of which (we shall see) famously embroiled a godparent that Peri chose for his son Niccolò.

SONS. A father had more options in preparing boys for adult life, and the story of Peri's sons illustrates most of them: a court appointment following in

---

105. Ledger A, fol. 123 left: *Ci partimo la Lessandra et io con Antonio, Dino, Niccolò, Francesco, e Alfonso, la Giustina, la Felice e la Caterina—in tutto 8 fratelli—e la serva; e venne la signora Lucrezia, vedova Del Maestro, nostra vicina et cara alla Lessandra. Menamo una lettiga, carrozza e uno cavallo; ci riposamo il resto del giorno. E il martedì seguente, a dì 29, ore 15 incirca, si vestì monaca la sopraddetta Maria, mia prima figliuola e prima in amore, con grande allegrezza e contento di tutti noi, e di lei in particolare. E tornamo il giorno dopo desinare a Firenze. Sia il tutto con gloria de l'Altissimo Iddio e della Santissima Trinità, amen. Facendo il conto di tutto quello che ho speso fra dote e gite e fornimento, sono circa fi.640 sino a questo dì, 29 settembre 1620.*

106. In a *ricordo* of 1631 he refers to her at S. Vincenzo; Ledger B, fol. 155.

107. Ledger B, fol. 151.

108. ASF, Corporazioni religiose soppresse dal governo francese 79 (S. Onofrio), 385 (*ricordi*, 1593–1767), fol. 30 (list of deaths of nuns).

the father's professional footsteps, the army, the university, the church, and business. Peri had eight sons: by his death in 1633 two had died (one in childhood), four had reached adulthood, and two were at an age (fifteen and sixteen) when decisions were being made about a career. Only two sons (Dino and Alfonso) lived to an age at which one might have expected them to marry, and only Alfonso took a wife (in 1642), although with unfortunate consequences. One son became a university professor and one a priest, one may have intended to follow his father's career as a musician, one was put into the wool industry, and the two youngest were also expected to go into business of one kind or another. And one son was directed to court service but instead became something of a ne'er-do-well and a military adventurer. Peri also enrolled his sons, one after the other, in the Compagnia dell'Arcangelo Raffaello, which eventually commemorated their deaths in the customary manner.

Peri made his first two documented decisions about placing a son on a career path in response to opportunities that patrons presented to him as a composer, both in 1616 following the success of his *Euridice* outside of Florence. In April while Peri was in Bologna for a performance of the opera under the auspices of Cardinal Luigi Capponi, papal legate there, he learned that the cardinal wanted him to send one of his sons there to be put into the Jesuit Collegio dei Nobili, with the handsome annual stipend of *fl.*90. As soon as he was back in Florence, on 30 April, Peri wasted no time in sending his second son, Dino, then just ten years old, off to Bologna, since only five days later, on 5 May, he had to depart again, this time for Rome on orders from the grand duke, in the entourage of Grand Duke Cosimo II's brother, Carlo, who was formally to receive the *berretta* after having been appointed cardinal the previous December. The occasion brought Peri another opportunity to place a son, for the new Medici cardinal promised to accept Antonio, then eleven years old, into his service, and in the meantime to pay a stipend of *fl.*94 for two years for the boy's education. With this prospect, Peri sent Antonio to join his younger brother in Bologna.[109]

In retrospect, considering how they turned out, Peri's choice of his second over his first son for the position at Bologna was surely a sign of how capably he sized up these two boys, both still so young. Dino—the name of his maternal grandfather also frequently found in the distant collateral branch of

109. Ledger A, fol. 121.

the Peri family to which Peri felt close—remained in the Collegio at Bologna for many years and then went on to the university at Pisa, where he took a doctorate in law in 1628. Peri was clearly proud of this son. In 1626, in the spirit of treating his five older sons equally with respect to expenditures for them, he decided to limit each to an allowance of *fl.*20 a year for clothing (the principal expense of youths at the time) and accordingly opened an account for each; but once Dino had his degree, Peri, not unaware of favoring this son over the others, canceled some of the earlier debit entries on Dino's account for the period he was at the university, which he felt obliged to do for the honor of his house and from a sense of justice (*parendomi essere stato obligato a farlo per l'onor della casa e per buona giustizia*).[110] In his testament he refers to his son as "Dottore Dino." While still studying for his degree, however, Dino developed an interest in mathematics to the point that he regarded the course he was following in law as a mere formality. He became a student and then a personal friend of Galileo; we shall see that Dino's correspondence with the great mathematician reveals more about him. His account in his father's ledgers, given their function, tells us little more than what clothes Peri bought for him.

The eldest son, Antonio, whom Peri had passed over for the position in Bologna, turned out to be the one who created the biggest problems for his father. Whatever course his life took at the Collegio, he presumably never took up service in Cardinal Carlo's household. He was back in Florence by February 1621, now sixteen years old, when he went to work for the Torrigiani bank. Being considered "gifted with poetic ability," he was chosen at this young age to compose the Latin distichs for five paintings that formed part of the elaborate funeral decorations that the Compagnia dell'Arcangelo Raffaello organized in its oratory as part of the obsequies for Cosimo II, who died on 28 February 1621.[111]

Yet Antonio's life was also taking a turn for the worse. That same year Peri opened a debit account in his son's name to keep a record of the extraordinary expenses the boy was incurring, and these document his restless and irresponsible behavior over the next six years.[112] He left the Torrigiani bank

110. Ledger B, fol. 39.

111. Eisenbichler, *The Boys of the Archangel Raphael,* 280 (the quote is cited, but no source given).

112. Ledger A, fol. 148; Ledger B, fol. 38.

after three months because the manager had to reimburse two persons for loans made to Antonio and not paid back—and Peri, in turn, had to pay the manager *fl*.8 £5.13s.4d. In November 1624 he went to work as his father's assistant (*sotto camerlengo*) at the Arte della Lana but left that position after, again, only three months, and with a shortage in the cash box of *fl*.72 £1.9s.4d. which his father had to pay. Later that year, in September, he asked his father for money so he could go off *alla guerra* (in the Valtellina, where Venice, Savoy, and France were fighting the Spanish from 1620 to 1626). Peri gave him *fl*.30 in cash, sent another *fl*.30 through a bank order to be paid in Milan, and at his son's request paid *fl*.14 for a gold chain that Antonio could wear around his neck *per ogni suo bisogno* (presumably for quick liquidation in the currency of a given location). In December of that year Peri sent another *fl*.30 to pay a debt Antonio owed to his captain in the Valtellina; yet other payments followed.

In April 1626 Antonio was back in Florence but ready to go off again *alla guerra*, this time to Rovigo, and the ever-indulgent, if distressed, father gave him *fl*.10 "to help him, even though it was against all merit, since Antonio had asked for much more. . . . God give him help, for he has much need of it" (*per aiutarlo, se ben contro ogni suo merito, havendomi fatto ricercare di molto maggior somma. . . . Iddio lo aiuti, ché ne ha gran bisogno*). Other items followed, including a payment on 3 October of *fl*.32 £6.10s. for clothes, so that Antonio, having given up the military life, could go to Venice to do something or other (*impiegarsi in qualcosa*), which Peri again gave him at his own inconvenience, adding the wish that God grant him grace (*ch'io gne ne ho accomodati sebene con mio grande scomodo; piaccia al Signor Iddio darli la sua grazia*). On 29 November, after no fewer than nine letters from Antonio in Venice telling his father that he was penniless but was on the verge of joining the service of a Venetian nobleman (*dicendomi esser rimasto senza denari, et esser appresso accomodarsi con un nobile veneziano*), Peri finally sent only 4 scudi d'oro (equivalent to *fl*.4 £2) by post. By this time, at the end of 1626, the total of what Antonio had cost his father added up to just short of *fl*.322. Meanwhile, Peri had set up his system of clothing allowances for his sons, mentioned above, and he added one condition that clearly was directed, in desperation, to Antonio:

> I do not intend to give to any of the aforesaid sons the aforesaid sc.20 save when they stay in Florence. But whoever out of his caprice wants to wander through the world, as the aforesaid Antonio is inclined to do, let him

look to his own needs, for I will not give him credit for the aforesaid *sc.*20. For I do not want to give them money save to those who employ themselves in Florence in some business, unless they go elsewhere sent expressly by me.[113]

Antonio, in any event, was soon back in Florence, where he must have become seriously ill, for on 22 March 1627, after confessing and taking communion, he died *con grande conoscimento e devozione,* concluded Peri in a description of the impressive funeral—celebrated by Franciscan friars, the Dominicans of S. Maria Novella and the Compagnia del Sacramento—that yields not the slightest hint of a father's disappointment in a wayward son.[114]

The accounts Peri opened for the other five sons reveal little beyond the purchases of clothing Peri made on their behalf, this, in fact, being the function of the accounts. Only occasionally, and mostly by way of asides, do entries contain other information about them. As with Dino, it is from sources other than the accounts that we learn about the third son, Alfonso, for he had some public fame as a musician. In October 1618, at the age of nine, he was given clothing from the court Guardaroba, probably for his participation in a musical event. Over the next few years, while still a boy, he sang on several occasions: in December 1621, he sang a motet very well (*cantò molto bene un mottetto*) in the private chapel of the Palazzo Pitti for the visiting Duke Ferdinando Gonzaga of Mantua; and in December 1622 and again in January–February 1624 he appeared in performances organized by the Compagnia dell'Arcangelo Raffaello, with music by his father. In 1629 he participated in another performance of the Compagnia, and at his father's death in 1633 he began drawing an annual salary of *fl.*54 (half of what Peri had been earning) as a musician on the grand-ducal payroll.[115] Nothing about his musical activity, however, emerges from his father's accounts, and we do not know whether or not a musical career was for him a secondary economic activity, as it seems to have been for his father.

113. Ledger B, fol. 38: *ch'io non intendo dare a nessuno de' detti figliuoli li detti sc.20 l'anno se non mentre che gli staranno in Firenze; ma chi vorrà per suo capriccio andar per il mondo, sì come inclina il detto Antonio, pensi a fatti sua da sè, ch'io non li darò credito delli detti sc.20; ch'io non voglio darli se non a quelli che s'impiegheranno in Firenze in qualche esercitio, e almeno andranno fuori mandati espressamente da me.*

114. Ledger B, fol. 151.

115. ASF, Guardaroba medicea 391, fol. 300v (clothing, on 31 October 1618); ASF, Mediceo del Principato 6113, fol. 256 (the 1621 event); Kirkendale, *Court Musicians,* 385.

Francesco, the fifth son, became a priest. From 1628 to 1632 the debits on his account were almost all for clerical garb. On 5 July 1629 Peri arranged (at what cost we do not know) to have the Ciardi chapel in S. Ambrogio ceded to him for the purpose of eventually assigning it to Francesco once its current titular was dead; it carried an income of only *fl.*12, coming from the rent of half of a house, which Peri noted was hardly enough to pay the related expenses.[116] The next year, on 9 July 1630, Francesco, then eighteen years old, received first tonsure from the archbishop, which marked his formal entrance into the ranks of the clergy, and that very day Peri obtained a chapel in S. Frediano for him by agreeing to pay its current titular *fl.*28 per year. Peri debited Francesco's account for *fl.*98 for the expenses of this latter arrangement, adding the note that, immediately after his death, Francesco should pay back this amount to increase the dowries of his two youngest sisters, then still at home. To promote his son's career Peri apparently appealed to Cardinal Francesco Barberini, nephew of Pope Urban VIII and a prominent patron of music in Rome (as well as being a Florentine), for on 24 August 1630 he wrote a letter to thank the cardinal for his willingness to consider an unspecified benefice for his son (Letter 33). The next year he entered another debit on Francesco's account for *fl.*21, the cost of sending bulls for two benefices at Piacenza he had obtained for Francesco from the cardinal, and in 1632 the account is credited for *fl.*18 £4, the value of thirteen Venetian *zecchini* sent to Florence by Francesco's procurator for the benefices.[117] Here again is an example of the strict accounting record kept of the expenses incurred by his sons for the eventual purpose of treating each one equally, whether he be a ne'er-do-well or priest—the exception being the scholar.

Three of Peri's youngest four sons were directed into business. The year Niccolò was born, in 1610, Peri went into an informal partnership with his friend and business associate Francesco Brunacci to operate a dye shop (of which more later), and when they ceased operations the next year, Peri, in the account he opened for this occasion on 12 October 1611, referred to the firm as Niccolò di Jacopo Peri & Partners. We can only wonder why he passed

---

116. Kirkendale, *Court Musicians*, 231, notes the transaction but misconstrues its purpose.

117. Ledger B, fols 49, 58, 65 (the accounts), and fols. 151v–153v (*ricordi* of the purchase of the chapel at S. Ambrogio, the third on the right, and of the arrangement for the chapel at S. Frediano); LC 3912, document dated 18 July 1629 (copy of the contract). Kirkendale, *Court Musicians*, 231, cites the notarial document for the chapel at S. Ambrogio in ASF, Notarile moderno, prot. 11164 (Cosimo Puccetti), fols. 1v–2 (5 July 1629).

over three older sons, the eldest being only five years of age, and appropriated the name of his youngest son, barely more than one year old. In any event, at some point Niccolò went to work for Brunacci, who was in the wool business, for in 1627, when he was seventeen years old, Peri made an entry on his son's account that refers to the annual salary of *fl*.24 he was earning from his friend.[118] In December 1628 Niccolò opened a ledger with an account kept for the manufacture of ten pairs of heddles for a silk loom he had commissioned, but after two pages nothing more was written and the book remains a mere fragment.[119] There is no further evidence, however, that Niccolò pursued a career in business.

Peri assumed that his last two sons, Cosimo and Giulio Cesare, would also go into business of one kind or another. On settling his affairs in 1632, when they were still only fifteen and fourteen years old, respectively, Peri assigned some government bonds to them but stipulated they should not receive them until they were twenty,

> and that at that time they should find themselves salaried and established in a *bottega* or bank where they will have previously been for at least two consecutive years, and all this so that with greater assiduousness they attend to, and dedicate themselves to, a *bottega*. And if they do not observe what I have said, and finding themselves at the age of twenty and not salaried in a *bottega* in the aforesaid manner, I do not want them to have anything.[120]

In this last comment Peri was referring to the bonds, and not, he goes on to say, the two sons' eventual share of his estate.

In his accounts, Peri was always careful to treat his sons equally. His objective in opening separate accounts for their allowances and other payments was not to charge any one of them for overdrafts but, in the name of equity, to set up a system by which each would have a debit or credit balance to be brought into the calculations for the eventual settlement of their father's estate at his death. In applying this discipline to the keeping of these accounts

118. Ledger B, fol. 48.
119. LC 3920.
120. Ledger B, fol. 71: *et che a quel tempo si trovino salariati e provisioniati nella bottega o banco dove si troveranno almeno per due anni adreto continuati, e tutto questo acciò con maggior assiduità attendino, e badino, a bottega; e se non osserveranno quanto ò detto, e ritrovandosi d'età d'anni 20 e no' sieno a bottega salariati nel modo sopradetto, non voglio habbino cosa alcuna.*

he yielded a little to his immense pride in Dino—but not without feeling obliged to explain himself for the record—and he stiffened with disillusionment before the sad spectacle of the irresponsible Antonio—but not to the point of compromising his sense of fairness. When it came to providing for the inheritance of his estate, we shall see, Peri declared his six sons his *eredi universali* in equal measure; but then anticipating the eventuality of disagreement about how to divide everything up, he went on to do just that with great precision, given the complexity of the exercise, to make sure it would be an absolutely equitable division down to the last florin. What this concern means with respect to how he saw his family's future economic and social status is a subject to which we shall return in discussing Peri's estate after his death.

Social Status

In his satirical sonnet from the early 1620s (see Appendix D), Francesco Ruspoli attacked Peri for, among other things, "wearing his nobility on his ass" (*ha . . . la sua nobiltà sul codrione*); and another contemporary who knew Peri, Stefano Rosselli, wrote in his commentary on this poem that Peri indeed had "pretension to high nobility, passing himself off as a gentleman and wanting to be regarded as such by everyone" (*pretensione di gran nobiltà, spacciandosi per gentiluomo, e per tale da tutti voleva esser tenuto*).[121] One might get the same impression from the family portraits surviving in his household at his death, including one of Peri as a young man and another made later, it seems. Peri in fact referred to himself as *nobil fiorentino*—for example, on the title page of the printed edition of *Euridice* (which appeared in early 1601) and in his 1630 testament—and so did others, including notaries in their legal acts. It is probably no coincidence that he did so around the time of the first operas: we have seen, too, that just after *Euridice* he was looking through the family papers and also garnering information about his ancestors. Peri knew what qualified him for that social status. Florence had no officially or legally defined nobility, unlike Venice, for example, where noble status had been officially established by the legal closing of the ranks of nobility in the *Serrata* of 1297. A few Florentine families—for instance, the Ricasoli—had roots as feudal landlords in the precommunal period, but they lost that formal

---

121. Ruspoli, *Poesie*, ed. Arlìa, 55, 62; Corazzini, "Jacopo Peri e la sua famiglia," 50–56.

identity with their absorption into the city-state. Florence was not to get its *Libri d'oro* recording an official nobility until the eighteenth century, after the Medici were gone and the state was reorganized according to the foreign principles of the imperial Habsburgs.

In republican Florence there were families that long enjoyed political, economic, and hence, presumably, social status; and there was also, of course, a political elite whose power and influence went well beyond office holding. Among these families were some whose very names—such as Guicciardini and Strozzi—carried a certain prestige. The extraordinary fluidity in the ranks of these categories, however, has long defied historians' attempts to define them with much precision, even though at the time everyone knew—as we do today—what names were to be found at the top of the list.[122] With the transformation of the republic into a princely state in the sixteenth century, however, upper-class Florentines themselves became conscious of their amorphous identity. They found a certain sense of status in the hierarchy of the forms of address they used to identify one another. *Gentiluomo* emerged as a new appellation of respect, and *signore*—reinforced with *chiarissimo*—as a form of direct address, both devices by which the richest and most prominent men, who in this city had no formal titles, set themselves off not quite as an official elite but at least above the masses. The hierarchical ranking downward, however, did not stop there, for a step lower were those addressed as *messer*. The diffusion of this form of address among ordinary people represented a remarkable devaluation of the one title used in the republican period to designate men of very specific prestigious standing: doctors of law, knights, clergymen of rank, and, as a carryover from the precommunal period, the so-called magnates.

The emptying of *messer* of the specific meanings and considerable prestige it had earlier enjoyed, and its replacement by *signore* as a more general designation of status, took place in a society that was slowly assuming a more formal hierarchical structure. Tradesmen and those from whom Peri bought land tended to address him as *signore* from the very early 1600s on—suggesting that this is how Peri came to style himself in public—although those more attuned to such niceties, including court functionaries and the canon of S. Lorenzo to whom Peri paid his semi-annual rent for the farm at San Marco Vecchio continued to use *messer*, as did members of his extended

122. Padgett, "Open Elite?" discusses the broader issues.

family.[123] Not surprisingly, he was also *signore* in publications by (friendly) colleagues, as in Ottavio Rinuccini's dedication to the printed libretto of *Euridice* (1600) and Marco da Gagliano's preface to the score of his *Dafne* (1608). Peri also designates as *signore* the upper-class men—at least those who were not *cavalieri* or titled noblemen—who agreed to be godfather of his children. He used *messer*, instead, in referring to, among others, the fathers of all three of his wives, two of his landlords, the manager (*ministro*) of the Corsini bank, his business partner and *amico caro*, the wool manufacturer Francesco Brunacci, his cousin Dino Peri, and tradesmen in general.

The new forms of address, however, did not help in defining nobility, and the effort got little support from the early Medici grand dukes, all too conscious of their status as newly established princes in a city with a strong republican tradition. By Peri's time, the only Florentines who used titles were the very few to whom the grand dukes had awarded a fief on the periphery of their new territorial state, the *cavalieri* whom they appointed to their new military order of Santo Stefano, or those who had purchased or otherwise gained land and a title elsewhere. Many knights of the Cavalieri di Santo Stefano, however, came from families that had no previous distinction in Florentine society. A lifetime appointment to one of the supreme councils of state, the Consiglio dei Duecento and the Senato (the Quarantotto), carried prestige, but only the latter office lent itself to a distinct personal—but not hereditary—title. Most who aspired to noble status had to seek elsewhere to find some definition of what that meant. Wealth—although obviously an influential component of status—could not be a formal criterion, since there was no way to establish its degree with any precision, there being only surveys of landed wealth. Nor could Florentines, in a city of international merchants and bankers, circumscribe nobility's nature as did the French, for example, with their antibusiness prejudice, although Florentines clearly drew the line at those who worked with their hands, including shopkeepers (but obviously not at accountants). The rich, however, took concrete steps to protect their status from the fluidity that had characterized the distribution of private

123. The first reference to Peri as "signore" in his book of receipts (LC 3913; with entries made by those to whom he paid money) is dated 15 February 1601/2. Enea Vaini styled Peri as *messer* in a 1603 memorandum on court music, as did Malvezzi's successor at S. Lorenzo, Francesco Petrelli, and Peri's uncle-in-law (by his third wife), Piero Monaldi, both doing so well into the 1620s.

wealth in the republican period, when inheritance was partible equally among all sons. To ensure that in the future patrimonies remained intact, they restricted the alienability of family properties through the *fedecommesso*, a testamentary provision legally binding the inheritance of property, and they introduced primogeniture in practice, but not in law, by limiting the number of sons through birth control of some kind and by restricting the marriage-ability of those they did have. These measures by themselves assured the accumulation of a family patrimony through successive generations and constitute one of the dynamics that help explain how the rich became much richer from the later sixteenth century onward.[124]

In addition to the protection of their family's status in the future, these men also sought to give a time dimension to their status that extended backward into the past through concrete documentation. They therefore researched the antiquity of their families and looked for the presence of their forebears in the highest offices (the so-called Tre Maggiori) of the republican government. Some produced what were called *prioristi*— compilations, often finely embellished with coats of arms, of lists of those who had served in these offices. And if they drew on the past in the search for the proper credentials of family status, by the same token they noted, as never before, the death of the last member of a contemporary family, and hence the end of a line.[125]

This interest in family history also gave rise to a new kind of antiquarian research into the subject using archival sources. Vincenzo Borghini led the way with a projected history of the Florentine nobility that was, however, cut short by his death in 1580. About this time, Scipione Ammirato went to work on collecting the data for his *Delle famiglie nobili fiorentine* (not published until 1615), and in 1593 Paolo Mini published *Il discorso della nobiltà di Firenze, e de Fiorentini*.[126] In these same years, working away in the avant-garde

124. An especially sensitive analysis of this consciousness of nobility through the vocabulary of status is Fasano Guarini, "*Gentildonna, borghese, cittadina*." See also Litchfield, "Demographic Characteristics of Florentine Patrician Families," 202; Boutier, "Les *notizie diverse* de Niccolò Gondi," 1149.

125. See, for example, Francesco Settimanni's *Memorie fiorentine* (1532–1737), ASF, Manoscritti 125–47, which is an eighteenth-century compilation of citations from original sources (vols. 130–35 cover the period of Peri's life).

126. For Borghini, Ammirato, and Mini, see the relevant entries in the *Dizionario biografico degli italiani*; and for an evaluation of their importance for the "genealogical culture"

of this new enthusiasm for collective family history was Piero Monaldi, the uncle of Peri's third wife. Monaldi compiled an enormous manuscript on the history of Florence's families and of the Florentine nobility (*Historia delle famiglie della città di Firenze e della nobiltà de' fiorentini*). His work took the form of thumbnail sketches of well over a thousand of the city's "noble" families (this in a city with a population of about 65,000 to 75,000, or sometimes just slightly higher, during Peri's lifetime) that are little more than lists of the offices held under the republic, along with descriptions of their coats of arms. In this compilation, incidentally, the Peri and Fortini have less than a page each while the Fortunati and Casellesi are not mentioned. In 1599 Monaldi sold an elegant copy, over five hundred folios long, for *fl.*30, and had others made; and in 1607 a copy was dedicated to the grand duke. A second manuscript edition was produced in 1626, still in Monaldi's lifetime, by Monsignor Girolamo Da Sommaia, a noble himself, long-time *provveditore* of the University of Pisa, and especially well known, in his time and today, as the first passionate collector of manuscripts regarding the history of Florentine families. A number of copies of Monaldi's work, more or less contemporary, survive in the city's archives and libraries.[127] Notwithstanding the mass of data, it is completely uncritical as a historical work and of little scholarly value today, but it is a characteristic product of its time. In fact, when in 1750 the newly established Habsburg–Lorraine government decided, finally, to open *Libri d'oro* for Florence, the 268 families aspiring to noble status had to support their application with, above all, evidence that their ancestors had held high office during the republican period, prior to the Medici regime. Indeed, the families that could do this achieved the higher status of "patri-

---

of the period, see Bizzocchi, "La culture généalogique dans l'Italie du seizième siècle," 800–801.

127. Monaldi describes the copy he sold as *un libro scritto e composto da me in carta imperiale, legato in asse coverto di quoio rosso con fibbiali e borche grandi d'ottone*; LC 3510, fols. 56 (the account), 171 (the *ricordo*). Monaldi's political career, the context for his ideas of nobility, the extraordinary popularity of his treatise in the following centuries, and the manuscript tradition are treated by Boutier, "Un *Who's Who* florentin du XVIIᵉ siècle (1607)" (but the work can now be dated eight years earlier); see also Marco Cavarzere's entry on Monaldi in the *Dizionario biografico degli italiani*. Luigi Passerini, the great nineteenth-century genealogist of Florentine families, dismissed the work as useless, written *senza critica*; see Agostino Ademollo, *Marietta de' Ricci*, 5: 1797–98. For the historiographical importance of Da Sommaia (who is also known for his diary as a student at Salamanca), see Callard, *Le prince et la république*, 278–87.

cian," whereas those who got in on other grounds were designated simply as "nobles."[128]

In the spirit of his times, Peri once compiled a list of all of his ancestors who had served, all together, twenty-six terms in the highest executive office in the republic as a member of the Signoria going back to 1344.[129] Much later in life, he also commissioned a painting of his family tree, presumably for the benefit of his sons (see Chapter 4). When writing to the court secretary Andrea Cioli in early 1618 in support of his petition to Grand Duchess Christine for some civic office that would help him support his large family, he noted that since the time of his ancestors as *gonfalonieri*, his house had enjoyed all the recognition due to honored families, and had had more than twenty-five *signori* in its ranks (Letter 23). According to this criterion, he had the credentials to be considered "noble," and in fact the Peri appear on a modern compilation of "patrician houses" in this early period of the grand duchy.[130] On this list, however, the family had no other qualification (it was extinct by the time the *Libri d'oro* were opened), and it does not appear on another list compiled recently of the "Florentine ruling class" in the fifteenth century, for which the criteria are a slightly broader definition of political status and also wealth (as declared on tax reports).[131] Almost all the Peri officeholders who can be identified were leather workers (*galigai*), not a high-ranking artisan trade, but service in republican offices was open also to such artisans, inasmuch as the lesser guilds had by law a minority representation in all elected offices.[132] This distinction between major and minor guilds among earlier officeholders, however, was gradually eroded and, finally, suppressed as a legal criterion by the new Medici regime in 1532.[133] Nevertheless, by the contemporary standard of a genealogical tree that included men who

128. For the compilation of the *Libri d'oro*, see Litchfield, *Emergence of a Bureaucracy*, 52–61; and for an overview of the emergence of a Tuscan nobility from the sixteenth to the eighteenth century, see Boutier and Angiolini, "Noblesses de capitales, noblesses périphériques." At the time the *Libri d'oro* were opened, only about 20 percent of the nobles inscribed had traditional feudal titles.

129. Ledger A, fol. 192 (undated).

130. Litchfield, *Emergence of a Bureaucracy*, 378.

131. Molho, *Marriage Alliance in Late Medieval Florence*, Appendix 3.

132. See Herlihy et al., eds., *Florentine Renaissance Resources: Online* Tratte *of Office Holders*.

133. D'Addario, "Burocrazia, economia e finanze dello stato fiorentino alla metà del Cinquecento," 386–87 n. 2.

held major offices in the republican period, regardless of economic status, Peri had every right to consider his family noble.

Many of the republican magistracies survived into the grand-ducal period, but service on them was now, in effect, by appointment, not election. Office holding was, therefore, a sure sign of the favor of the grand dukes; and in this light it is surely significant that the very first office to which Peri was named, in 1596, was as one of the twelve Buonuomini di Collegio, at the top of the hierarchy of the state magistracies. Over the course of his life, from 1596 on, Peri served in a number of these offices, altogether spending, on average, about a third of his time in a salaried position plus nine four-month tenures as an unpaid consul of the Arte degli Speziali (Table 1.1). He was clearly interested in this kind of service and the benefits that ensued. For almost all the offices he held, he entered a *ricordo* noting that he had been *eletto*, usually adding that it had been by grace (*per grazia*) of the grand duke, though once, in 1620, he acknowledged the favor of *Serenissima Arciduchessa e Madama*, that is, Archduchess Maria Magdalena and Grand Duchess Christine. Moreover, on the flyleaf of Ledger A he listed the major offices, divided into categories according to the dates when their terms began (and another such list, though perhaps not in his hand, is inserted into Ledger B). In 1615 he compiled a list of the offices held since 1606, and in 1631 he again noted all the offices he had gained through the grace of his grand-ducal patrons, keeping them in one place for easier reference.[134] And tucked away out of sight inside the original wrapper of Ledger A is a small scrap of paper, undated, on which he scribbled four territorial offices, noting their salaries, the presence of a *cavaliere* and a notary on the staff, and the one-year tenure for three of them—all features that made these offices particularly attractive.

The fact that Peri held none of these offices coterminously—in contrast to the plural office holding typical in upper echelons of the Florentine patriciate—suggests that in his case they were allocated quite selectively, but this does not make them less indicative of grand-ducal beneficence.[135] Almost all the offices Peri held were among the rotating magistracies that had responsibility

---

134. Ledger A, fol. 121 left (1615); Ledger B, fols. 154–154v (1631): *tutti gli offizii che io, Jacopo Peri, ho hauto per tratta e per grazia de' Serenissimi Padroni, sebene ce n'è notati parte in questo libro per esserne fatto memoria in più luoghi. Per facilità di poterli trovare, gli ho messi tutti insieme.* The list follows.

135. Compare the discussion of pluralism in Litchfield, *Emergence of a Bureaucracy*, 190–200.

Table 1.1. State offices held by Jacopo Peri

Office	Peri's term in office[a]	Total salary in florins as declared by Peri[b]
Dodici Buonuomini di Collegio	15 Dec 1596–(5 Mar 1597)	(15)
Capitani di Orsanmichele	Jan–Dec 1598	(0)
Camerlengo, Arte degli Speziali	Dec 1601–(May 1602)	(100)
Consul, Arte degli Speziali	Sep–Dec 1602	(0)
Otto di Guardia e Balìa	Mar–Jun 1603	(24)
Consul, Arte degli Speziali	Sep–Dec 1604	(0)
Otto Conservatori di Legge	Nov 1606–Apr 1607	28½ (30)
Quattro Soprastanti delle Stinche	Jan–Jun 1610	19 £3
Nove Conservatori del Dominio	Sep 1610–(Feb 1611)	(60)
Consul, Arte degli Speziali	Sep–Dec 1612	(0)
Consul, Arte degli Speziali	May–Aug 1614	(0)
Quattro Ufficiali della Decima	Jun 1615–May 1616	142 £3.2s.4d. (150)
Podestà, Pontassieve (Diacceto)	22 Feb–22 Aug 1617	(120)
Camerlengo, Arte della Lana	28 Mar 1618, for life	120[c]
Dieci Capitani di Parte Guelfa	Mar 1619–Feb 1620[d]	73 + 166[e] (60)
Nove Conservatori del Dominio	Mar–Aug 1620	(60)
Otto di Guardia e Balìa	Mar–Jun 1621	22 £5.12s. (24)
Consiglio dei Duecento	18 Aug 1621, for life	—
Consul, Arte degli Speziali	May–Aug 1622	(0)
Sei Procuratori di Palazzo	Dec 1622–(May 1623)	(30)
Quattro Ufficiali della Decima	Jun 1623–(May 1624)	(150)
Quattro Maestri di Dogana	Sep 1625–(Aug 1626)	(144)
Sei Procuratori di Palazzo	Jun–(Nov) 1628	(30)
Podestà, Sesto (Fesulani)	Jan–Jun 1629	?
Quattro Ufficiali della Decima	Jun 1631–(May 1632)	(150)
Podestà, Montevarchi	Aug 1632, refused	

Sources: Ledger A, fols. 112v, 121, 122, 123; Ledger B, fols. 151v, 154v (here Peri lists all offices together for his convenience; *per facilità di poterli trovare, gli ho messi tutti insieme*); LC 3915, fol. 38 (refusal of the *podesteria* in 1632). He recorded only his first tenure as consul of the Arte degli Speziali; the others are found in ASF, Arte dei Medici e Speziali 46 (*Repertorio dei consoli*, year by year). He was selected on other occasions but did not serve; ibid., 42 (*Tratte dei consoli*, 1580–1623). His offices as *podestà* are confirmed by the official rosters: ASF, Tratte 992, fol. 128.

a. Peri does not always state the length of tenure; terminal dates as well as salaries indicated here in parenthesis are based on data from ASF, Manoscritti 283 (*Uffizi di Firenze*, 1604).

b. In parentheses: salary for the term in office according to ASF, Manoscritti 283 (*Uffizi di Firenze*, 1604), and ASF, Miscellanea Medicea 413 (*Teatro di grazia e di giustizia, ovvero Formulario de rescritti a tutte le cariche che conferisce il Ser. G. Duca di Toscana . . .*, 1695). "0" indicates no salary paid.

c. Peri's salary was *fl.*13 a month, out of which he had to pay an assistant *fl.*3 (and by the end of his life, *fl.*5); see LC 3915, fols. 1, 10, 13, 17, 31, 38, 42, 56.

d. According to Ledger B, fol. 154v, his term in office began in 1619, not 1620 as noted in the *ricordi*; this earlier date is confirmed by ASF, Capitani di Parte Guelfa, Numeri neri 60, fol. 91v.

e. Ledger A, fol. 123: *e per distribuzione straordinaria per conto d'incorpori, mi toccò per mia parte fi.166 incirca di moneta, cosa non seguita più per molti anni che sia toccato di gran lunga tanta somma.*

for the various departments of government. These were committees whose members served a limited term in office, with the size of the committee (seldom more than six members) and length of term (usually three, four, or six months) varying from one magistracy to the other. In the course of his time as an officeholder Peri served in every branch of government: general administration (Conservatori del Dominio), law courts (Otto di Guardia e Balìa, Conservatori di Legge, Soprastanti delle Stinche), finance (Ufficiali della Decima, Capitani di Parte Guelfa, Maestri di Dogana). Twice he was sent out of town to administer justice in a provincial city (as *podestà* at Pontassieve and at Sesto, neither far away). Carrying greater prestige was his service on two of the three councils heading these magistracies: four months as one of the twelve Buonuomini di Collegio, and twice for six months as one of the six Procuratori di Palazzo.

Peri served in these public offices with seriousness, civic-mindedness, and a sense of humanity, to judge from a document (undated, and in the end unused) that he drafted on the occasion of completing one of his terms (in June 1603 or in June 1621) as an official of the Otto di Guardia e Balìa, a panel of eight citizen-judges that functioned as a court for the most serious criminal cases, those entailing the possibility (as he wrote) of "torturing and punishing men to the point of death." The draft was presumably conceived as a joint statement with his colleagues, directed to their successors:

> We hope that they will not allow themselves to be deceived by interests and passions, and that they will hold the scales of justice fairly for the rich as for the poor, and . . . that they be given the will to be able to come down heavily on wrongdoers and lighten the penalties on the miserably afflicted according to their good conscience, committing to memory only two things: first, that they remember that they are men and that they have men to judge, and second, that it is of the greatest importance that they be in peace and unity, because from this follows every good end, just as, on the contrary, when discord arises cases do not go forward and the poor prisoners suffer the consequences, to their grave damage and universal scandal.[136]

136. Ledger A, fol. 191v: *Bozza d'alcune parole per licenziarsi da' signori Otto, quale non è servita a niente perché non mi piacque. // Noi ci siamo grandemente rallegrati che le Serenissime Altezze habbin fatto elettione delle persone loro a reggere e governare questo importantissimo magistrato, dove si tratta di tormentare e gastigare gl'huomini sino alla morte; onde essendo conosciuto benissimo da tutti noi quanto sia il lor valore, speriamo ch'elle non si lasseranno ingannare dagli*

He also concluded his statement with a typical plea for future judges to make capital of the good advice of the official in charge of the Otto which, coupled with their own prudence, would enable them to govern themselves well.

On 18 August 1621, having just come off his second tenure in this office in June, Peri received his greatest official honor from the grand duke with his appointment to the Consiglio dei Duecento, a lifetime tenure on one of the two supreme councils of state (the other was the Senato). As Peri noted proudly, "Through the grace of the Most Serene Grand Duke [Ferdinand II] and Their Highnesses [the regents Grand Duchess Christine and Archduchess Maria Magdalena], without my having asked for it, I was appointed one of the Duecento, which appointments are made by their direct action and without notice; and I was appointed in the company of one hundred persons, all from the first and principal families of the city. Laus Deo." The others included his cousin Dino di Lorenzo.[137]

---

interessi né dalle passioni, e terranno la bilancia della giustitia retta tanto per il ricco quanto per il povero. Et perché varii sono i casi e gli accidenti oltre alle buone e sante legge di questo magistrato, gli sarà dato l'arbitrio per poter aggravar la mano contro a malfattori et alleggerir le pene a' miseri afflitti, come più <piacerà> parrà alle buone coscienze loro, riducendoli a memoria solo due cose: la prima, che le si ricordino ch'elle sono huomini, et huomini hanno a giudicare; la seconda, che è di grandissima importanza, che la pace e l'unione <sia con loro per> ché da questa ne segue ogni buon fine, sì come per il contrario quando si comincia a discordare le cause non si spediscono, et i poveri prigioni ci vanno di mezzo, con lor grave danno e scandolo dell'universale. || Quanto a noi, sia gloria a Iddio, <non se> habbiamo goduto la tranquillità della pace; se ben <vero che> come huomini possiamo haver mancato in molte imperfezzioni, che di questo ce ne scusiamo appresso di loro, e ne domandiamo perdono a Dio, è ben <anco> vero che questo grave peso del giudicare ci è stato assai alleggerito dal valore e diligenza di questi honorati Cancellieri, et in particolare dal signore Segretario, huomo di grandissimo sapere e d'integra bontà, <che importa il tutto> come le vedranno con gli effetti. S'elle faranno capitale del suo consiglio ch'è accompagnato dalla lor prudenza, ci rendiamo sicuri ch'elle governeranno molto meglio di quello che habbiam fatto noi, ch'el Signore Iddio gne ne dia la grazia.

We do not know whether Peri ever presented his colleagues with a redrafted statement. These eight citizen-judges had no particularly qualifying expertise or experience, although they worked with a permanent professional staff headed by a secretary (or first chancellor), who was appointed by the grand duke and personally close to him. This magistracy under the first grand dukes has been thoroughly studied by Brackett, *Criminal Justice and Crime in Late Renaissance Florence*. Brackett observes that the comparatively low stipend, especially considering the work involved, mattered little to these men "for reasons of prestige, a sense of civic duty, and the chance to perform favors for friends and clients" (23).

137. Ledger A, fol. 124: *per grazia del Serenissimo Gran Duca e loro Altezze, senza ch'io lo domandassi, io fui fatto del numero de' Dugento, quali si son fatti di lor moto proprio*

Peri's comment is telling with respect to the social significance of government service. An appointment to a term of only a few months on a magistracy was a sop to the citizens of Florence, giving them the sense of a continuing republican tradition, whereas at the same time the Medici were building up a separate bureaucracy that generated, in turn, a distinct bureaucratic elite. Service on a magistracy, being by ducal appointment, carried with it a certain prestige, but it did not lead to entrance into the ducal officialdom. Moreover, very few senators were to be found in these rotating magistracies, and in the course of the seventeenth century the presence of patricians in general in these offices fell off notably. Peri was not likely to find himself sitting next to anyone from the elite during a committee meeting for most of the offices he held. So it is not surprising that, for all the personal relations Peri established with the rich and powerful over almost three decades, it meant something rather special to find himself, with his unexpected nomination to the Duecento, actually sitting alongside these same people on one of the two most important councils of government.

In fact, after Peri's death his sons were to learn the hard way just what the difference was between the "first and principal families" of the city (*le prime e principali famiglie*) and the amorphous and all-too-numerous class of those who claimed nobility on other grounds. The former were the real elite whose very family names evoked a long memory of high status owing to wealth and real political influence—rather than to mere office-holding in the republican period—such as the Bardi, who sprung from feudal roots, or the Corsi, who rose to wealth as recently as the fifteenth century, or even the Michelozzi, whose wealth dated from Peri's own generation. The others, instead—like the Peri—had no historical record of wealth, power, or any status at all beyond the claim to the occasional brief presence in public office as members of a guild of artisans or shopkeepers. The difference between the two classes was considerable and grew wider in the course of the sixteenth century with the establishment of the court, on the one hand, and the greater wealth of the rich, on the other. Peri's family came up against that difference when, just two years after his death, two of his youngest sons sought to participate in the historical Florentine game of *calcio*. And in a long and passionate *ricordo*

---

inaspettatamente, e sono stato fatto in compagnia di 100 persone, tutti delle prime et principali famiglie di Firenze. Laus Deo. The complete list is found in ASF, Manoscritti 131 (Francesco Settimanni, *Memorie fiorentine*, VIII), fols. 213–223v.

of the episode, Dino, their eldest brother and now head of the household, revealed how fired up he got when that difference manifested itself.[138]

The *calcio* was described as the *fior della nobiltà* by Giovanni de' Bardi, the prominent music patron who also laid down the basic rules of the game in a publication of 1580. It played to the instincts of young nobles, in particular, to show themselves off in at least two ways dear to youth: attiring themselves in the luxurious costumes that changed with every game, and throwing themselves, with a militant team spirit, into a rough and action-ridden sport that required much physical training. The game had a particular appeal, being only an occasional but very special public and courtly spectacle, and one sponsored by the grand dukes. Just a short time after Peri's death, during the games of 1635 and 1636, his sons—first Giulio Cesare and then Cosimo (both in their late teens)—several times sought to participate but were rebuffed by other youths, presumably of the elite, who challenged the Peri's qualification as nobles. And these encounters were violent and degenerated into fighting: Giulio, in fact, may eventually have died from a bad chest injury received in a brawl, from which he never fully recovered.

Dino was naturally concerned about his brothers' safety, but he was just as agitated by the challenge to the family's claim to nobility. He did not approve of the game itself, nor of the (surreptitious, it seems) actions of his younger brothers. But now it was a matter of principle, and as a consultant to the grand duke on scientific matters, he was in a position to act. He went to work "to cure the perfidy of those who, for hatred of one or other of my brothers, have stupidly sought to raise doubts about the nobility of our house" (*per fine di medicare la perfidia di alcuni che per odio contro qualche mio fratello hanno stoltamente cercato di revochar in dubbio la nobiltà di casa nostra*). He first put together documents proving the noble qualifications of the family through both his father and (he emphasized) his mother, and he gave them to two important men he knew high up in the court hierarchy, with the request that they be shown to Prince Don Lorenzo de' Medici (the present grand duke's uncle), who usually assembled players in the game for instructions and guidance. Dino had no trouble gaining the sympathy and support of these men, but that had no effect outside their circle and among the noble ruffians in the streets. So he tried another tactic "to bring to an end, finally, all silliness and

138. Journal D, fols. 106–15 (4 April 1636); ibid., fols. 119–20 (an addendum of 31 August 1636).

gossip" (*per levar via del tutto ogni sciochezza e bisbiglio*): he went directly to Grand Duke Ferdinando II, then at Poggio a Caiano with the court. There he presented the documents he had assembled, and he requested that Cosimo be put on the first team so all could see his presence among the nobility. Again, the grand duke and others present agreed, but even this did not quiet those who were determined to challenge the nobility of the Peri. So Dino took a third approach to suppress "the sinister thinking" so prejudicial to his family's origins (*il sinistro concetto pigliato da una parte di circostanti in pregiuditio della nostra nascita*). Since he had a law degree, he decided to apply for entrance to the Collegio degli Avvocati as a noble, one of the requirements being an ancestor who had been on the Signoria during the republican period: this, he felt, would be the most official way possible to establish his family's credentials beyond dispute. And he did it without saying anything to the grand duke so as to preclude any "shadow of suspicion" (*ogni ombra di sospetto*) that favoritism played a role in his admission, and therefore that his credentials might not be legitimate. The Collegio voted unanimously for Dino's appointment, and later, when he read over his *ricordo* of the affair written six months before, he commented on how he "had worked his way through the customary rigors of justice so that everyone, and Their Highnesses, may see the difference between being judged by boys and the gossip of the crowd, or by important and most judicious persons" (*ho camminato per i soliti rigori di giustitia accioché ognuno, e l'Altezze istesse, vegghino che differentia sia l'haver a essere giudicato da ragazzi e dal bisbiglio del volgo, overo da persone giuditiosissime e principali*). We do not know, however, whether the Peri boys ever managed to play their *calcio* match.

Of course, all this happened after Jacopo Peri's death. But the episode reveals the gap between the elite and the "nobility" that not even the court could close, at least not in this instance. Peri himself would never have sought to bridge it, certainly not in this way, whatever his pretensions to high nobility that aroused Rosselli's disdain. Or so we might conclude from a comment Dino made in his long *ricordo*. In describing his attempt to restrain Giulio Cesare and Cosimo, he remarked that he and the older brothers had no taste for the violence and dangers of the *calcio* and had never participated in the game, in part out of fear of their father's reaction (*per un certo timore di nostro padre*). But Peri died just as the younger brothers were arriving at their midteens, and they clearly did not feel a father's restraint. We might read the *calcio* episode in several ways: aggressive youths spoiling for a fight, a clash

between "old" and "new" Florentine families, or even the weakening authority of the grand-ducal court in regulating the social structures of the city.
Whatever the case, Peri's claims to nobility around 1600 were taking on a
somewhat different resonance in the 1630s with the second generation, which
is not an unusual phenomenon in the history of social climbing in early modern Europe.

Peri himself was probably able to fit himself into and between Florentine
class structures, but whatever social prestige he may have enjoyed derived
from the traditional worlds of commerce and civic service, and from the favor
shown him personally by select members of the elite and by the grand dukes
in the form of appointments to office and the patronage of his music. The
Peri, however, did not have the wealth or prestige to number among the elite.
Nor did the families that Peri married into have any more status. Neither the
Fortunati nor the Casellesi appears among the many hundreds of families in
Piero Monaldi's contemporary survey, and Monaldi (writing before his niece
married Peri) dismisses the Peri in a few sentences, claiming that the family
came to an end with a Lodovico di Bernardo in 1501 and an Antonio di Jacopo in 1527. The Monaldi, Fortini, and Peri are included in a 1551–52 tax
roster of the most important families in the city, but only the Fortini and the
Peri appear on the lists compiled by modern scholars.[139] The Fortini, however, do not have "high status" on one of the latter lists, and, like the Peri, they
had no qualification on them other than a record of service in one of the
republic's three highest offices—nor did they make it into the *Libri d'oro*
(whether they applied we do not know).

Nevertheless, judging from the dowries ranging from two to three thousand florins that Peri received from these families—the Fortunati, Casellesi,
Fortini, and Monaldi—they all ranked much higher, certainly, than Jacopo's
branch of the Peri.[140] Wealth obviously engendered its own social hierarchy,

139. For the 1551–52 tax roster, see D'Addario, "Burocrazia, economia e finanze dello
stato fiorentino alla metà del Cinquecento," 386–94 (the characterization of these families is
D'Addario's).

140. Only the Peri, however, appear in ASF, Carte Pucci, probably the best source (though
not the only one) for genealogical tables of leading Florentine families. The other principal
genealogical source—ASF, Ceramelli Papiani (useful, above all, for coats of arms)—has files
on both the Fortini and the Monaldi, but the information therein dates from no earlier than
the seventeenth century (nos. 2095–96, 5631–32 on the Fortini; nos. 3239–40, 7037 on the
Monaldi).

but it is important to add immediately a comment about the relevance of the nature of wealth to that hierarchy. The wealth that Peri eventually acquired put him at the level of the families into which he married, but although it was quite substantial, it was far below the level of the rich, who had become very much richer in the course of the sixteenth century. Peri arrived at what we can call a middling status, the families at his level not yet being numerous and compact enough to constitute a veritable "middle class" with all the over-tones of a modern bourgeoisie that the term brings into play. On the other hand, in notable contrast to other places, especially northern Europe (as was observed at the time by many visitors to the city from those parts to their amazement), the concept of nobility in Florence did not preclude active in-volvement in business, the classic bourgeois activity. There was no reason for Peri to have felt—and no evidence that he did—that his qualifications as a noble were in any way compromised by his investment in the cloth indus-tries, or even by the foundation of his own partnership as a wool manufac-turer, not to mention his employment as an accountant. After all, it was at the end of a career as an accountant in the silk industry that his wife's uncle, Piero Monaldi, wrote the first major historical survey of the Florentine nobil-ity, which he presented to the grand duke. And Peri fully expected some of his sons to carry on in one business or another. Music, however, may have been a different proposition, and we shall see the efforts that Peri made to distinguish himself from what might have been, and often were, perceived as the more artisanal aspects of the profession.

The solid financial status of the families Peri married into, and that which he himself achieved, did not, however, find an outlet for any of them in one of the customary manifestations of status at the time: a family chapel—although, as we have seen, Peri had aspirations toward having one construct-ed.[141] The branch of the Peri to which Jacopo belonged had traditionally been associated with the church of S. Simone, in the Gonfalone Bue of the *quar-tiere* of S. Croce, but there is no surviving monument there.[142] Peri buried his

---

141. At least, none appears in Paatz and Paatz, *Die Kirchen von Florenz*, 5: 105–16. This refer-ence work notes, however, an altar under the patronage of another branch of the Peri in the now suppressed church of S. Jacopo tra' Fossi, in the same *quartiere*; ibid., 2: 418.

142. Corazzini ("Jacopo Peri e la sua famiglia," *estratto* 3) is thus correct in identifying S. Simone as the parish church of the Peri of the Gonfalone Bue branch. He noted a shield with the Peri arms crossed with those of the Morelli in a niche above the door of the sacristy, executed in 1528 but by a Peri who was not in Jacopo's direct line of descent.

first two wives in that church, *nella mia sepoltura*, although at the time he lived across town in another *quartiere*, but he put their children and the others he had by his third wife elsewhere—and in different places. We do not know where his first child was buried; the second by his first wife, Felice, was buried in the Badia Fiesolana (in the immediate vicinity of the house of the wet nurse, where she died). After buying his own house in Via dei Fossi in 1596, Peri used the local parish church of S. Paolo for the burial of the other two children of his first wife, the premature child of his second wife, and the first child of his third wife; and in the *ricordo* of the death of the first of these he expressed his intention *fare una cappella e sepoltura nuova* in that church, although later his thoughts returned to S. Simone "or somewhere else" (see above, n. 64). Of the other four children of his third wife who predeceased him, one was buried in Ognissanti and the others in the vault of his wife's maternal family, the Monaldi, in S. Maria Novella—and he was buried with them. Despite all the deaths in his immediate family and despite his deep religiosity, Peri never got around to founding a common burial site, let alone a family chapel, and no evidence survives in his ledgers or in vestiges in the various churches mentioned above that he ever placed a prominent identifying marker on any of these tombs.

To a certain extent Peri was caught up in one of the most characteristic obsessions of Florentines: marking all their possessions with their coats of arms, from tableware, silverware, and furniture to chapels and palaces. In the inventory of his home made at his death, the items described as decorated with the Peri arms are a bed, a clothes stand, two leather door-curtains, an unspecified number of plates, and three paintings of his arms crossed with those of his wives (and the painting of the Peri family tree probably included their arms).[143] He also had a seal to mark letters with an impression of his arms (although only Letter 1 has a surviving trace of it). These arms are blazoned as azure, a mount of six coupeaux accompanied in chief by two hammers crossed in saltire (Figure 1.8). But for all his nobility, his sense of family, and his solid financial status, Peri never—so far as we know—placed his family insignia to be seen publicly anywhere in the city. One might conclude that, however pretentious his claims of nobility, however intense his effort to pass himself off as noble, and however widely he wanted it to be recognized

143. For the inventory (in ASF, Magistrato dei Pupilli del Principato 809, fols. 218–30), see Chapter 4.

FIGURE 1.8. Peri coat of arms. Palazzo Pretorio, Montecatini Alto, commemorating Jacopo di Antonio Peri's tenure as Podestà of Buggiano, 1479. This Peri was the son of the brother of Peri's great-great-grandfather. *Source:* ASF, Ceramelli Papiani 3679. (With permission of the Ministero per i Beni e le Attività Culturali; further reproduction or duplication by whatever means is forbidden.)

(to go back to Rosselli's judgment) at least in certain circles, Peri did not broadcast that status with something that all could see for themselves during his lifetime and into the future. The exception is the title page of the printed score of *Euridice* (see Figure 3.3), though even there Peri's styling as *nobil fiorentino* may, for reasons we shall see, place as much emphasis on the second word as on the first.

His music itself, however, was audibly conspicuous, if not also visibly so, and there Peri's claims to nobility did indeed come to the fore. In part, we shall see, this was to position himself in particular and advantageous ways among the court musicians, and against his competitors. It also had a significant impact, however, on his musical works and the new styles they embodied. Music, by definition, may not have had the permanence of more conventional noble attributes built or collected by Florentine patricians, but it had a kudos that demands further exploration.

Networks

As people do in any society, Florentines had long depended on networks of relatives, friends, and neighbors, and we have already seen enough to suggest that Peri was no exception: he felt close to, and acknowledged his responsibilities for, his extended family (including those of his wives); he went into business with friends such as Francesco Brunacci; and his neighbor in Via dei Fossi, Giovanni Del Maestro, was presumably helpful to Peri at court (and their wives were best of friends). Another supportive connection, it seems, was the one he had with his teacher Cristofano Malvezzi, a canon of S. Lorenzo, organist at S. Trinita from 1565 to 1570, then *maestro di cappella* of S. Giovanni Battista from 1574 until his death in 1599. Malvezzi (born in 1547) was some fourteen years older than Peri and was a reasonably active composer, with three books of madrigals and one of ricercars to his name, as well as theatrical and other occasional music. Like many teachers, he seems to have played a significant role in Peri's early musical career, facilitating his entrance into various ecclesiastical and court positions. What is perhaps more unusual in Peri's case, however, and also revealing of the changes in Florentine society under the *principato*, is the way in which he seems to have been able to extend these networks up the ranks for his own social, economic, and political benefit. He did so by way of his musical and other talents, and by forging special relations that might be viewed as aggressive social climbing were it not for Peri's probable view of them as simply a consequence of his own standing in Florentine society.

Finding Godparents

Of the various ways in which Florentines might embed themselves in the political, social, and economic networks of the city, finding godparents for one's children was among the more symbolic, in both senses of the word.[144] On the one hand, as a public display *comparaggio* variously symbolized (at least, at the moment of baptism) feudal obligations, patron–client ties, business connections, and friendship. On the other, it carried few if any responsibilities on the part of the godfather and godmother, the *compare* and *comare*, that could be enforced in any rigorous way, however seriously they might be articulated and acknowledged in the baptismal ceremony itself. Likewise, for the godchild and parents, and save for loyalties to the ruling family,

---

144. Musicians tended to make good use of the *comparaggio* (godparentage) system as a way of cultivating patronage and other networks; see, for example, Lubkin, *A Renaissance Court*, 223–26. The case of Monteverdi is discussed in Carter, "Monteverdi and Some Problems of Biography."

comparaggio does not seem to have formed permanent bonds unless they were continued in other ways.

For obvious reasons to do not least with infant mortality, baptism in this period occurred very soon after birth, and for the stillborn, immediately after being taken from the womb, as with Peri's child by his second wife. In Florence, the ritual preferably took place within the walls of S. Giovanni Battista. Hence some advance planning was necessary in choosing godparents prior to a mother's accouchement, and planning could be disrupted by a premature delivery. The *compare* and *comare* would usually attend the ceremony, either in person or, if of the highest status, by way of proxies, holding the child and presenting handsome gifts. For Peri's children, such gifts most often included a gold chain that the *compare* would place around the baby's neck; Peri was usually careful to note with some precision the gift's value (from 10 to 25 ducats). He in return would give each of the godparents a sweet (*pinocchiato*) worth, he says, around £10. Peri does not tell us whether the godparents had any influence in the selection of names for his children, although we have noted that three of his sons—Giovambattista, Alfonso, and Carlo—had the names of their godfathers, and the daughter baptized Francesca came to be called Caterina because Peri believed this to be the preference of the godfather, Cavaliere Ferdinando Saracinelli, *primo cameriere* of the grand duke, who had a son with that name.[145]

We know from Peri's *ricordi* how important the act of baptism was to him. He also chose carefully godparents from outside his family circles in ways that reflect his perceived social standing and his ambitions (Table 1.2). Of the *compari* and *comari* to his twenty children, only two came from what Peri might have considered a lower class than his: one was his business partner and *amico caro*, Francesco Brunacci, and the other, one *messer* Giovanni *spetiale*, manager (*ministro*) of the Corsini bank, who was perhaps brought in as an emergency measure for the near-stillborn Baccina. The rest of the list is impressive indeed, starting with Princess Maria de' Medici (to whom Peri had taught music, and for whose wedding to Henri IV of France he wrote

---

145. Ledger A, fol. 121 left: *gli pose nome Francesca alle fonte, se bene credo volerla chiamar Caterina per havere uno mastio col medissimo nome.* Peri wrote in the margin of this *ricordo*, *Francesca, oggi Caterina,* the name he always used for her. The masculine form of Caterina (Caterino) can in fact be found, albeit rarely.

Table 1.2.   Godparents of Jacopo Peri's children

Godparent	Child and date of birth
Giovambattista Michelozzi	Giovambattista, 10 Feb 1594
Principessa Maria de' Medici, daughter of Grand Duke Francesco I (represented by Costanza Arrighi, wife of Lesmes d'Astudillo)	
Leone de' Nerli	Felice, 25 Jun 1595
Margherita Capponi, wife of Lorenzo Michelozzi	
Giovanni, *spetiale*, manager of the Corsini bank	Baccina, 9 Jul 1597
Lorenzo Salviati	Caterina, 17 Nov 1598
Marchese Lorenzo Salviati	Ginevra, 29 Jan 1604
Contessa Martelli, wife of Giovanni Bandini	
Piero di Agnolo Guicciardini	Antonio, 12 May 1605
Bardo Corsi	Dino, 7 Jun 1606
Ottavio Rinuccini	Maria, 19 Aug 1607
Conte Alfonso Fontanella (Fontanelli; the composer), *aio* (tutor) to Archduchess Maria Magdalena	Alfonso, 17 Mar 1609
Maria Usimbardi	
Sinolfo Ottieri	Niccolò, 14 Aug 1610
Puliziana Acciaioli, wife of Cavaliere Giusti	
Niccolò Berardi	Giustina, 22 Sep 1611
Agnolo Guicciardini	Francesco, 5 Sep 1612
Francesco Brunacci, wool manufacturer and *amico caro*	Felice, 16 Nov 1613
Cavaliere Ferdinando Saracinelli, *primo cameriere* of the grand duke	Francesca (= Caterina), 20 Feb 1616
Lisabetta Guidotti, wife of Cavaliere Giovanni Del Turco	
Capitano Cesare Sabatino da Fabriano	Cosimo, 20 Mar 1617
Filippo di Nero Del Nero	Giulio Cesare, 25 Mar 1618
Niccolò di Mario Doni	Lucrezia, 7 May 1619
Ottavio Doni	Teresa, 26 Dec 1620
Alessandro Rinuccini (*depositario* of the grand duke and brother of Ottavio Rinuccini)	Ottavia, 16 May 1622
Carlo Rinuccini	Carlo, 12 Dec 1624

Source: Ledger A, fols. 103v–123v, 188. Titles and descriptions of the godparents follow Peri save where editorial (in parentheses).

and performed in *Euridice*); she was represented by Costanza Arrighi, wife of
Lesmes d'Astudillo, one of the most prominent Spanish merchant bankers
resident in Florence. It continues with Bardo Corsi (the brother of the noted
patron Jacopo Corsi), the banker Giovambattista Michelozzi, Lorenzo Michelozzi (Giovambattista's nephew) and his wife Margherita Capponi, Alessandro
Rinuccini (grand-ducal treasurer), *capitano* Cesare Sabatino da Fabriano,
and others from the Acciaioli, Del Nero, Doni, Giusti, Guicciardini, Guidotti,
Martelli, de' Nerli, and Usimbardi families. Given that few of these names appear in direct business relations with Peri—Bardo Corsi and the Michelozzi are
the obvious exceptions—it would seem that Peri was using *comparaggio* to extend his networks in other ways.

As one might expect, however, given Peri's aspirations for his musical activities, we also find a number of higher-class persons associated with other
Florentine musicians, including Niccolò Berardi, *conte* Alfonso Fontanelli,
Sinolfo Ottieri, the poet and Peri's librettist Ottavio Rinuccini (and brother
of Alessandro), *marchese* Lorenzo Salviati, *cavaliere* Ferdinando Saracinelli,
and the wife of Giovanni Del Turco. Fontanelli was a prominent noble musician and patron who was placed in authority over the court musicians from
late 1608 to early 1610; Del Turco was another nobleman with a passion for music who, along with Saracinelli, had some control over the court musicians from
the 1610s on (and Peri had just provided music for Saracinelli's *ballo rusticale*);
and Berardi was the dedicatee of Andrea Falconieri's *Il quinto libro delle musiche
a una, due, e tre voci* (Florence: Pignoni, 1619).[146] Lorenzo Salviati was the dedicatee of Giulio Caccini's first collection of songs for voice and continuo in
the new monodic style, *Le nuove musiche* (1602), and so by agreeing to support Peri in a different way, he may have been trying to maintain a balance

146. For Fontanelli, see Anthony Newcomb's entry on him in *The New Grove Dictionary
of Music and Musicians: Revised Edition.* He was primarily associated with the Este in Ferrara
and Modena; even though he was banished (1601) for the murder of his wife's lover, he remained in some kind of Este service elsewhere, save for a period in Florence (1608–10) as
maggiordomo maggiore e cavaliere d'honore of Archduchess Maria Magdalena, when he was
also placed in charge of the court musicians. He had been a frequent visitor to Florence before then, and was associated with the Accademia degli Elevati (see Chapter 3). Giovanni Del
Turco published two books of his own musical madrigals, and headed a consortium of Florentine composers in 1614 to support music printing in the city (at the press of Zanobi
Pignoni); see Carter, "Music-Printing in Late Sixteenth- and Early Seventeenth-Century
Florence," 55–56.

between the two musicians. However, Peri may eventually have regretted his choice of Sinolfo Ottieri (son-in-law of the grand-ducal secretary, Belisario Vinta), who made it a habit—or perhaps a vice—of attending the voice lessons of his favorite young female singers (he reportedly provided Peri with an organ worth *sc*.300 so he could hear Peri's pupil, Angelica Furini), and who was eventually exiled and imprisoned in Volterra for lewd behavior with the singer–nun Maria Vittoria Frescobaldi.[147] The official investigation of that affair was still ongoing when Peri took up his second term of office as one of the Otto di Guardia e Balìa in March 1621 (see Table 1.1): we do not know how he might have responded to any apparent conflict of interest.

Of course, not all these "musical" connections were necessarily, or even primarily, musical. Some of them may have arisen, rather, from the other circles in which Peri moved (or wished to move): for example, Alfonso Fontanelli, Ottavio Rinuccini, Lorenzo Salviati, and Giovanni Del Turco were well known to Jacopo Corsi, as was one of the "nonmusical" *compari*, Piero di Agnolo Guicciardini.[148] Also, the benefits gained by any such association could extend beyond Peri's musical interests: Giovanni Del Turco acted as one of the guarantors (*mallevadori*) for Peri's appointment as *camerlengo* of the Arte della Lana in March 1618. In general, there is not much evidence of Peri or his children seeking favors from these individual or collective godparents, or of their doing so precisely because they were godparents. Nor would one expect there to be: *comparaggio* was just one more element in the social glue.

And what that glue held together, at least for Peri, offers further confirmation of how much Florentine society had changed over the previous century. In the fifteenth century godparents served a much more restricted social function: they were chosen largely among neighbors but also among those who had a close personal or business relation to the father, not infrequently including those of a lower economic and social standing.[149] Peri, instead, reached much beyond his immediate circle in the attempt to cement relations with the rich and powerful. Yet just as significant as the ambitions

147. Kirkendale, *Court Musicians*, 314–16; Cusick, *Francesca Caccini at the Medici Court*, 46. Ottieri was on the court roll as a *cameriere* at a monthly salary of *fl*.16. He died in Volterra on 19 July 1622; the ledger kept by the executor of his estate survives in LC 3723.

148. Carter, "Music and Patronage in Late Sixteenth-Century Florence," 66 (Salviati), 74 (Fontanelli), 75 (Guicciardini), 78 (Del Turco).

149. Klapisch-Zuber, "Kin, Friends, Neighbors," 91–93.

godparentage served for him was the complementary function it fulfilled for the people who accepted his invitation. After all, the new kind of glue that helped hold together the emerging hierarchical structure of Florentine society worked both ways in Peri's favor, for it also included the social value of artistic connoisseurship and a new kind of noble status.

A Banker Patron (Giovambattista Michelozzi)

Giovambattista di Tommaso Michelozzi (1523–1604) is a key figure in Peri's early history as an investor. He was a remarkable entrepreneur, and it is surprising that we know hardly anything about him. Cesare Tinghi, who kept an official diary of the grand-ducal court from 1600 to 1626, occasionally commented on him in passing, and on special request from the grand duke he inserted a brief biographical note about Michelozzi on his death in 1604.[150] According to this source, Michelozzi (whose great-grandfather was the brother of the architect Michelozzo Michelozzi) started out life as a *giovanetto poverello* who left Florence to make his fortune in Venice; the chronicler Giuliano de' Ricci noted that he returned *ricchissimo*.[151] He was back in Florence by the early 1580s, when Peri first mentions him. According to Tinghi he had three wool and three silk shops, but he was primarily a banker, and he continued to have banking interests in Venice.[152] In 1594 the grand duke brought in Michelozzi to forestall the threatened failure of the great Ricci bank, which dominated the banking scene during the second half of the sixteenth century (there is hardly an account book of the period, be it for private administration, like Peri's, or for an industrial, commercial, or banking enterprise, that does not record dealings with it). The firm was reorganized with Michelozzi as a major partner under the new name Giovambattista Michelozzi, Vincenzo de' Ricci & Partners. It may not be a coincidence that the grand duke made Michelozzi a senator that very year.

150. Cesare Tinghi, "Diario primo di Sua Altezza Serenissima (1600–1615)," Florence, Biblioteca Nazionale Centrale, Fondo Gino Capponi 261/1, fols. 24–25v, 33v, 36, 42, 93, 105. ASF, Manoscritti 599 (Carte Pucci), *inserto* 2, includes genealogical trees of the family, one of which places the juncture of the banker's line with that of the architect Michelozzo Michelozzi one generation earlier.

151. Ricci, *Cronaca*, 368.

152. There are business contracts (*accomandite*) for his operations at Venice and Besançon in 1594–95: ASF, Mercanzia 10835, fols. 84, 89v.

Michelozzi built a palace on the Via Maggio, then being transformed from an industrial street to a major thoroughfare lined with imposing palaces and connecting two major victory monuments erected by Cosimo I, one in Piazza S. Felice and the other, across Bartolomeo Ammannati's new Ponte S. Trinita, in Piazza S. Trinita; and he had a villa at Montebuoni where he received the grand duke on at least one occasion. He is well remembered today for the enormous and extraordinarily expensive high altar–ciborium in *pietre dure* that dominates the crossing of the church of S. Spirito, the first work in this material created on an architectural scale. In his appeal to Grand Duke Ferdinando I for permission to build such a prominent monument, Michelozzi expressed his intention of locating a sepulcher there for himself and his descendents and marking it with his coat of arms. Although he gained patronage of this space in 1590, work on it did not begin until 1599, the principal architect being Giovanni Caccini, brother of the composer. The foundation stone was laid on 9 September, and medals were put in it depicting Pope Clement VIII (this medal in gold), Grand Duke Ferdinando, and Michelozzi (Figure 1.9). Even during construction it was a place the grand duke showed to visiting dignitaries. Michelozzi died in 1604 before it was finished. He had no children, but he enjoined his heirs, the three sons of his brother Tommaso, to continue the project, and the new altar was consecrated in 1608 (the entire project, it was said, cost *fl.*100,000). He had already brought these nephews into his business enterprises, and thereafter the bank carried their names alone.[153]

We do not know how Peri met this man: so far as we know, Michelozzi had no presence in any of the city's musical circles. But Peri established close relations with him, at least with respect to his investment interests. He first mentions Michelozzi in 1585 when he made his first long-term investment, perhaps using his earliest accumulated savings. On 6 July he put *fl.*300 in Michelozzi's hands (*messi nelle mani di . . .*) to be invested in the wool company of the latter's nephew, Lorenzo, and the two men signed a private agreement about the arrangement. Michelozzi was a major figure in the marriage

153. Acidini Luchinat, "L'altar maggiore," discusses Michelozzi's patronage of this notable monument in *pietre dure*. The information we have about it comes from ASF, Manoscritti 131 (Francesco Settimanni, *Memorie fiorentine*, vol. 6 [1596–1608]), fols. 147, 157, 365 (Michelozzi's funeral), 601, 615; and also from documents in Florence, Biblioteca Nazionale Centrale, Fondo Tordi 51 (includes his testament) and 76.

FIGURE 1.9. Portrait medal of Giovambattista Michelozzi, with the high altar of
S. Spirito on the reverse. *Left:* Inscription: IOANNES BAP[TISTA] MICHELOCTIUS
SEN[ATOR] FI[ORENTINUS]. *Right:* Inscription: TUA SIC SE[MPE]R ORO MUNERA DEUS (I
pray, O God, that your gifts be always such). (Florence, Museo Nazionale del Bargello,
Inv. 6587. Private photo.)

between Peri and his first wife in 1592, having arranged the contract for the
dowry and standing guarantor of it; and the next year Peri deposited with
him part of the cash he had from the dowry, to be put on the exchange. Michelozzi was godfather to the couple's first child, and the wife of his nephew
Lorenzo was godmother to their second. Thereafter Michelozzi, his bank,
and his nephews' businesses appear frequently in the history of Peri's investments. There is every reason to believe—although no facts to prove—that
this personal relation between the two men counted for much in Peri's decisions about where to put his money.

A Musical Patron (Jacopo Corsi)

In the next chapters we shall have something to say about the demand for
music in the private sector of the economy. In it, enlightened patrons played
a major role, no one more so than Giovanni de' Bardi (1534–1612) and Jacopo
Corsi (1561–1602), both of whom also worked closely with the court. Much of
Peri's early music was, in fact, channeled to the court through them, especially by way of his connections with Corsi.

The role of these patrons in Florence in the discussions leading to the first operas staged there is well known, and the so-called Camerata sponsored by Giovanni de' Bardi in the 1570s and '80s has gained almost mythical status in histories of the genre. Bardi was a typical soldier–courtier of the mid-century (he fought in the War of Siena in 1553–54), and also a playwright and a member of the Accademia degli Alterati and Accademia della Crusca, where he took the side of Ariosto in the well-known Tasso–Ariosto controversy of the 1580s (over the nature of epic poetry, playing off Tasso's *Gerusalemme liberata* against Ariosto's earlier *Orlando furioso*). He authored texts on a range of topics, including Roman antiquities and, we have seen, a history of the Florentine game of *calcio*. His main passion, however, seems to have been music, and he joined with Vincenzo Galilei (father of Galileo), Piero (di Matteo) Strozzi, and the philologist Girolamo Mei to examine the music of the ancients with a view to reforming the modern style of musical counterpoint that, they felt, had lost all rhetorical and emotional power. Bardi drafted several texts on the subject, including a discourse sent to Giulio Caccini on ancient music and good singing (*Discorso mandato . . . a Giulio Caccini detto Romano sopra la musica antica, e 'l cantar bene*) that advocated a drastic simplifying of musical resources, in part favoring songs for solo voice and instrumental accompaniment. Bardi also figured as an interlocutor (with Piero Strozzi) in the main manifesto to emerge from the group, Vincenzo Galilei's *Dialogo della musica antica, et della moderna* (Florence: Giorgio Marescotti, 1581).[154] Meanwhile, he remained an important patron for a number of Florentine musicians even outside what seems to have been his immediate circle: Cristofano Malvezzi dedicated to him his *Il primo libro de recercari à quattro voci* (1577), which also contains, as noted above, an instrumental ricercar by Peri (his first published work).

Bardi was heavily involved in court entertainments in the 1580s, including devising the spectacular *intermedi* associated with Medici wedding festivi-

---

154. The literature on the Camerata is large: Palisca, *Humanism in Italian Renaissance Musical Thought*, is a good place to start for the broader issues. Bardi's and other texts are edited in Palisca, *The Florentine Camerata*. Giulio Caccini sang Piero Strozzi's "Fuor de l'humido nido" in the tournament staged on 14 October 1579 during the festivities for the wedding of Grand Duke Francesco de' Medici and Bianca Cappello (Kirkendale, *Court Musicians*, 123), and Caccini called on Strozzi's support frequently thereafter; see the letters in Bacherini Bartoli, "Giulio Caccini."

ties, culminating in the grand set staged for the wedding of Grand Duke Ferdinando I and Christine of Lorraine in May 1589. This gave Peri his greatest exposure to date, presumably thanks once more to Malvezzi, who was in charge of the music for the main production presented at the festivities, Girolamo Bargagli's *La pellegrina*. The play's six *intermedi* were based on a variety of mythological themes (broadly organized around the power of music) massaged in the service of Medici propaganda. Peri sang in the chorus for several of them, and for the fifth he composed and sang a solo song (with two echoes) representing the mythical musician Arion saving himself from drowning (he is cast overboard from his ship by a mutinous crew) by charming the dolphins into coming to his aid. His virtuosic "Dunque fra torbid'onde" was also included in the publication of the music (edited by Malvezzi) that appeared as *Intermedii et concerti fatti per la commedia rappresentata in Firenze nelle nozze del serenissimo don Ferdinando Medici e madama Christiana di Lorena* (Venice: Giacomo Vincenti, 1591).[155]

By now, however, Bardi's star was on the wane: he had already in effect been superseded by the Roman Emilio de' Cavalieri (ca. 1550–1602), a composer and administrator whom Grand Duke Ferdinando I made superintendent of the court artists in September 1588. Cavalieri had been associated with Ferdinando in Rome (where the latter had spent much of his time as cardinal). But there was also another agenda in play. On his accession to the throne, Ferdinando in effect purged the old-guard administration of his predecessor (and elder brother), Grand Duke Francesco I: Bardi moved to Rome in 1592 as *maestro di camera* of Pope Clement VIII and *luogotenente generale della guardia pontificia*, and he led the papal troops in Hungary in 1594–95. The new grand duke preferred, instead, to give greater influence to younger, presumably more malleable, men. One of them was Jacopo Corsi (born on 17 July 1561), who had already joined with a group of Florentine patricians (including Piero di Agnolo Guicciardini) to provide a joust (*sbarra*) in the courtyard of the Palazzo Pitti for the 1589 wedding festivities.

Unlike Giovanni de' Bardi, Jacopo Corsi was not at all inclined toward military service: now that the territorial boundaries of Tuscany had stabilized (with the incorporation of Siena), there was scant call for it in Florence anyway. Rather, as head of the Corsi household from the age of ten—albeit under

---

155. Again the literature is large: the most recent overview is Treadwell, *Music and Wonder at the Medici Court*.

the guardianship of his uncle, Antonio—he had been groomed to run the family's businesses and to further its political, social, and economic interests. He and his younger brothers Giulio (who held a diplomatic position in the entourage of Don Pietro de' Medici in Madrid) and Bardo were ambitious. They had a wide-ranging portfolio of investments in banking, the wool and silk industries, and property; their father Giovanni (1519–71) initiated, and the sons completed, a family chapel in S. Croce; and they purchased and expanded country villas that would allow them to live the life now expected of the well-to-do in Florence.[156]

Jacopo received the education one would expect of a young Florentine patrician, not just in abacus school but also via private tutors, including music lessons with Cristofano Malvezzi, Luca Bati (who later succeeded Malvezzi as *maestro di cappella* of the Duomo and S. Giovanni Battista), and others. Clearly Corsi knew Bardi: although they were on opposite sides in the Tasso–Ariosto controversy, they were on friendly enough terms to visit Ferrara together in 1585 and 1590 along with the poet and future librettist Ottavio Rinuccini (1562–1621). Corsi also received the dedication of the second edition of Vincenzo Galilei's treatise on lute intabulation, *Fronimo* (Venice: Heirs of Girolamo Scotto, 1584), and his account books reveal a close association with Piero Strozzi. But his musical interests were no less practical than theoretical: he owned a large collection of instruments (and paintings) and regularly hosted gatherings of local and visiting musicians—as well as poets and artists—at his house. He also became Rinuccini's very close friend.

Corsi was part of a younger generation that gained significant stature and influence in the first decade of the reign of Grand Duke Ferdinando I. As his eulogist noted on his early death (in late 1602), "If he was employed in the service of his princes, he acted in such a way as to earn their eternal goodwill, and in short, everything which he did in public or in private, he carried out with such magnificence that he earned the greatest honor and well-deserved glory."[157] Corsi aggressively supported both in principle and financially the

156. For Corsi, see Carter, "Music and Patronage in Late Sixteenth-Century Florence"; Goldthwaite, "Banking in Florence at the End of the Sixteenth Century"; Pegazzano, *Committenza e collezionismo nel Cinquecento*. The family's business interests are discussed further in Chapter 2.

157. From the anonymous funeral oration in Florence, Biblioteca Nazionale Centrale, Magl. XXXXVIII.115, fol. 141v, given in Carter, "Music and Patronage in Late Sixteenth-Century Florence," 66–67: *Se in servizio de' suoi Principi era impiegato, talmente quello esercitava,*

shift in Florentine foreign policy in favor of France—culminating in the
marriage of Maria de' Medici to King Henri IV—as did Rinuccini with a
swathe of poetic propaganda. His support increased as the grand duke himself started to waver under severe pressure from both the Spanish and the
pope, who went so far (albeit somewhat improbably) as to conspire to engi-
neer the fall of the Medici and a resumption of the republic. As for the things
Corsi did "in public or in private" with "such magnificence," they included
the entertainments that he provided for the court, including the operas
Dafne and *Euridice*: these were certainly occasions for conspicuous consumption that served Corsi's strategies for family advancement by way of proximity to the Medici, but they also served broader political agendas.[158] It is not
clear, however, that Peri would have known, or needed to know, all these
machinations behind the scenes.

Corsi, Rinuccini, and Peri were more or less the same age, and while they
could never be described as coming from the same class defined by family
wealth or lineage, we have seen that the situation in Florence tended to enable and even encourage social interactions across any such divides: after all,
even Corsi's ancestors were brickmakers. Peri and Corsi had plenty of opportunities to know each other as teenagers, not least via the Compagnia
dell'Arcangelo Raffaello, and once more Malvezzi may also have oiled the
wheels. Furthermore, both their families had roots in the *quartiere* of S. Croce
(Gonfalone Bue), although in the 1590s Corsi and his family lived in the Palazzo Boni (razed in the early nineteenth century) in the current Via dei Pecori
(opposite the Monte dei Paschi di Siena, near S. Giovanni Battista but not so
far from Via dei Fossi; see Figure 1.2).[159] Peri and Corsi also had property

---

*che eternamente la benevolenza di quelli ne guadagnava, et in somma tutto quello che in privato o
in pubblico adoperava, con tal magnificentia in esecuzione il metteva, che grandissimo onore, e
meritata gloria ne riportava.*

158. For the broader political context, see De Caro, *"Euridice,"* ch. 7–8.

159. For Corsi's Florentine residence, see Carter, "Music and Patronage in Late Renaissance Florence," 63. The Palazzo Boni is discussed in Darr and Preyer, "Donatello, Desiderio
da Settignano and His Brothers, and 'Macigno' Sculpture for a Boni Palace in Florence."
Simone and Giovanni Corsi (respectively, Jacopo's uncle and father) rented the Palazzo Boni
from 1555, and Giovanni bought a third of it in 1563 (for *fl.*838) and continued to rent the rest,
an arrangement that continued for forty years, until after the death of Jacopo in 1602. The *sala
principale* at the front of the building, the main gathering place during winter months (and
presumably where *Dafne* was first performed), was richly appointed, with a fine ceiling and a
beautiful carved fireplace (now in the Victoria and Albert Museum, London) made in the

close to each other in the countryside (in Montughi). Yet there were clear social differences: something of the gap is revealed in the dowries Corsi received for his marriages to Settimia di Pierantonio Bandini in 1587 (*du*.8,000) and Laura di Lorenzo Corsini in 1595 (*du*.10,000).[160]

There is no evidence in the Corsi accounts, nor in Peri's, that they had any kind of special relations, at least in this early period, above and beyond the support Corsi gave to all Florentine musicians, few of whom did not gain some benefit from him. Indeed, apart from his loan to Peri of *du*.30 perhaps in 1583, Corsi seems to have offered greater, and more consistent, favors to Giulio Caccini (from at least 1578 onward): at various times Corsi gave him the loan of a horse and carriage, and gifts of clothes, grain, conserves, and money, and when Caccini was ill in late 1592, Corsi paid for a doctor. In August 1593, however, Antonio Salviati engineered Caccini's dismissal from court service—they had come to blows over Salviati's amorous intentions toward Caccini's voice student, La Gamberella—and Caccini was left out in the cold.[161] For his own musical plans for the mid-1590s on, Corsi may have had little choice but to turn to Peri, not just because Caccini was no longer in service but also because directly supporting him would no doubt alienate Corsi from his peers.

Only in 1600 was Caccini able to regain his position at court by way of his contributions to the festivities celebrating the wedding of Maria de' Medici and Henri IV in October (he was reinstated in service later in the year), principally by composing music for the main entertainment, Gabriello Chiabrera's *Il rapimento di Cefalo*.[162] He also inserted himself into *Euridice* by having those singers under his control sing his rather than Peri's music (we shall see in Chapter 3 why this might or might not have been reasonable). And he preempted Peri in printing the score of a complete setting of *L'Euridice composta in musica* (Florence: Giorgio Marescotti, 1600), even though it was not performed in full until December 1602 (see Figure 3.4). Caccini signed the

---

shop of Desiderio da Settignano, on the opposite side of the room from a similarly elaborate wall fountain (*acquaio*), now lost.

160. Corsi's father, Giovanni, received something closer to Peri's dowry of *du*.3,000 on marrying Alessandra Della Gherardesca in 1560. The Corsi were certainly moving upward fast.

161. Kirkendale, *Court Musicians*, 130–32. The dedication of Caccini's first collection of songs, *Le nuove musiche* (Florence: I Marescotti, 1601 [=1602]), to another Salviati, Lorenzo, may have been an attempt to heal the breach.

162. Carter, "Rediscovering *Il rapimento di Cefalo*."

dedication to Giovanni de' Bardi on 20 December 1600, while Peri's *Le musiche . . . sopra L'Euridice* (Florence: Giorgio Marescotti, 1600 [= 1601]) appeared some seven weeks later, with its dedication to Maria de' Medici dated 6 February 1600/1601 (see Figure 3.3).

Peri's printed score needed to set the record straight not just about what had been staged at the wedding (as he makes clear on his title page) but also about the background leading up to the opera. Caccini's dedication to Bardi harks back to those theoretical discussions of the 1580s, but Peri was more concerned with Corsi's role in the 1590s, and in particular, the significance of *Dafne*. Although he first politely acknowledges Emilio de' Cavalieri's precedence in bringing "our" music to the stage, he says that *Dafne* had been conceived in as early as 1594; that Corsi had composed some of the music himself before he and the librettist Ottavio Rinuccini brought Peri in on the task; and that for three successive years during Carnival it was heard with the great delight and universal applause of all present (*E per tre anni continui che nel Carnovale si rappresentò, fu udito con sommo diletto, e con applauso universale ricevuta, da chiunque vi si ritrovò*).

We shall discuss in Chapter 3 why Peri was generous to Cavalieri, and also a possible reason for his locating the inception of *Dafne* in 1594. But what else he says about it appears true. The first performance was in the 1597–98 Carnival season in Corsi's residence (the Palazzo Boni), in the presence of Don Giovanni de' Medici and other Florentine noblemen.[163] It was repeated perhaps twice in January 1599, once in Corsi's residence before 18 January (although the evidence for this is slight), and once in the Sala delle Statue of the Palazzo Pitti on 21 January, before Cardinals Del Monte and Montalto and likely also Grand Duchess Christine, given that she is mentioned in the prologue in the undated edition of the libretto that may well relate to this occasion.[164] This is a clear sign of the exalted circles in which Corsi was able

163. The modern plaque commemorating the performance of *Dafne* located at the corner of Via de' Tornabuoni and Via Corsi (see Figure 4.2) is placed on the north wall of a palace that Jacopo's brother, Bardo, bought only in 1608; see Carter, "Music and Patronage in Late Sixteenth-Century Florence," 78. However, it does refer to Jacopo's *vicine case* (neighboring houses), which is more or less true depending on how one defines *vicine*.

164. For the chronology, and the sources supporting it, see the slightly different readings in Carter, *Jacopo Peri*, 1: 29–37; and in Kirkendale, *Court Musicians*, 194–98. For the undated edition of the text, see Sternfeld, "The First Printed Opera Libretto" (and compare Kirkendale, *Court Musicians*, 197).

to move, and by association, where Peri could make a mark singing the lead role of Apollo. It is also significant that the performance in the Palazzo Pitti had some financial input from the court for a carpenter, a tailor, materials, and other expenses: these totaled some *fl.*33, a minimal sum but symbolic all the same.[165] *Dafne* was again repeated in January 1600; another edition of the libretto appeared later in the year; and it was revived in October 1604 (after Corsi's death) in honor of the visiting Duke of Parma, prompting the use of leftover copies of the 1600 printing of the libretto with a new title page.[166]

According to Peri, again in the preface to *Euridice*, *Dafne* was designed as a simple demonstration of the power of modern song (*per fare una semplice pruova di quello che potesse il canto dell'età nostra*). However, the next collaboration between Corsi, Rinuccini, and Peri raised the stakes significantly. Corsi was involved in helping to negotiate, and finance, the marriage of Maria de' Medici to Henri IV, and after the signing of the marriage contract was officially announced in Florence on 30 April 1600, the court went to celebrate at Corsi's residence. Corsi also contributed directly to the festivities for the wedding with his *Euridice*, performed on 6 October in a room of Don Antonio de' Medici's apartment in the Palazzo Pitti. So did another prominent Florentine patrician and banker, Riccardo Riccardi, by way of a *mascherata* in his famous gardens on 8 October (the music was by Piero Strozzi).[167]

The official description of the festivities, by Michelangelo Buonarroti *il giovane*, gives the impression that *Euridice* was an entirely "private" enterprise, however distinguished the result. It notes that it was Corsi who had it set to music with great learning, that Rinuccini's play was most moving and courteous, and that the actors had the most rich and beautiful costumes.[168]

---

165. The expenses are listed in ASF, Guardaroba medicea 214 (*entrata e uscita*, 1598–99), fols. 17–18v.

166. The 1600 edition (Florence: Giorgio Marescotti) almost certainly appeared after 25 March 1600, given that Marescotti normally used *stile fiorentino* dating. On 16 June 1600, the court paid him *du.*5. £6.7s.8d. *in conto saldo di libri stampati et altro*, presumably relating to the printing of *Dafne*; ASF, Guardaroba medicea 224 (*entrata e uscita*, 1599–1600), fol. 24v. Although an entry in the Corsi accounts in late August 1600 refers to *Dafne*, this is most probably a delayed payment rather than a reference to a performance then; Kirkendale, *Court Musicians*, 198.

167. Carter, *Jacopo Peri*, 1: 44 n. 116. Riccardi (1558–1612) was some three years older than Corsi.

168. See the extract from Michelangelo Buonarroti *il giovane*, *Descrizione delle felicissime nozze della Cristianissima Maestà di Madama Maria Medici, Regina di Francia e di*

In his draft of the description, Buonarroti originally identified both Peri and
Caccini as the "excellent composers" (*ottimi compositori*) of that music, but
their names were excised from the final version.[169] Similar cuts were made
elsewhere in Buonarroti's text, save for his account of *Il rapimento di Cefalo*,
which acknowledged the music by Caccini, who set the bulk of it, and (for
some choruses) by Stefano Venturi del Nibbio, Luca Bati, and Piero Strozzi.
Yet in the case of *Euridice*, despite Buonarroti's emphasis on Corsi as its pro-
vider, it is now clear that the court was significantly involved in the production and therefore in some sense supported Corsi's intentions for it. Not only
did the court allow the participation of its singers, and those invited from
outside (including Francesco Rasi from Mantua and Melchiorre Palantrotti
from Rome); it also contributed by way of the grand-ducal Guardaroba (the
Wardrobe), which among other things paid for the scenery designed and
painted by the Florentine artist Lodovico Cardi-Cigoli.[170]

Peri and Rinuccini must have completed their work on *Euridice* in or before the spring of 1600. Rumors about it were circulating in Florence in early
April: Emilio de' Cavalieri wrote from Rome to the court secretary Marcello
Accolti on 7 April that many Florentines were already being told of Corsi's
new pastoral, which all said would be something heavenly (*si è dato conto già
a molti fiorentini di una pastorale nuova che fa il Signor Jacomo Corsi, che dicono
che sarrà cosa celeste*), although Cavalieri was not impressed by the hyperbole:

Navarra (Florence: Giorgio Marescotti, 1600), in Kirkendale, *Court Musicians*, 205: *Là onde
avendo il Signor Jacopo Corsi fatta mettere in musica con grande studio la* Euridice *affettuosa, e
gentilissima favola del Signor Ottavio Rinuccini, e per li personaggi, ricchissimi, e belli vestimenti
apprestati* . . . The complete description is edited in Buonarroti *il giovane, Opere varie in versi
ed in prosa,* 403–54.

169. Florence, Casa Buonarroti, Archivio Buonarroti 88, fol. 84: *Il perché avendo il Signor
Jacopo Corsi fatta mettere in musica con grande studio la* Euridice, *affettuosa favola del Signor
Ottavio Rinuccini, parte da Jacopo Peri e parte da Giulio Caccini, ottimi compositori, e per li
personaggi ricchissimi vestimenti, e belli apprestati* . . . For the (non-)naming of musicians, see
Carter, "*Non occorre nominare tanti musici.*"

170. At least some of the costumes were provided by Corsi, however, given that an inventory of his household dated 28 June 1603 (after his death) includes one for Pluto and one for
Orpheus, as well as other *maschere* and similar items (including ten costumes for nymphs and
three for Furies); Pegazzano, *Committenza e collezionismo nel Cinquecento*, 59. For at least one
payment by Corsi linked to *Euridice* (£306.2s.9d.), and perhaps another (sc.57 £4.1s), although this may have been for hospitality during the festivities, see Carter, *Jacopo Peri*, 1: 43
n. 114.

"poor heavens and angels," he wrote (*poveri cieli et angeli*).[171] He may have softened during the October festivities—as he had to, for the sake of their smooth running—given that oil, torches, and candles to light the opera on 6 October were delivered to his rooms.[172] But the gossip circulating in April referred to something closer at hand, for it has not hitherto been known that *Euridice* was staged in the Palazzo Pitti on 28 May 1600 (a Sunday) on the order of Grand Duchess Christine.[173]

The location of that first performance was the *salone* in the apartment occupied by the Duchess of Bracciano (Flavia Peretti Orsini), which was also intended to be used for the 6 October one until *Sua Altezza* (the grand duke or grand duchess—it is unclear) decided to move it to an upper floor of the palace. The casting of those two performances must have been slightly different: Rasi and Palantrotti were not yet in Florence.[174] The switch in performance space also caused Cardi-Cigoli some problems, given that the room in Don Antonio de' Medici's apartment—directly above and roughly the same size as what is now the Sala Bianca—was wider than the original one but had a lower ceiling, forcing the painter to redo his design for the stage. He added an additional charge of *du.*25 for the inconvenience to his remarkably detailed invoice for payment for his work on *Euridice*, submitted shortly before 14 October 1600 (so, about a week after the performance on Friday, 6 October). In the invoice he broke down the costs by the various elements of the scenery (the ceiling, the flats representing the woodland scene in perspective, six movable trees, the floor of the stage) for a total of *sc.*758 £3.5s.4d. covering

171. ASF, Mediceo del Principato 1691, fol. 17; Carter, *Jacopo Peri*, 1: 301; Kirkendale, *Court Musicians*, 202–3.

172. Kirkendale, *Court Musicians*, 203 n. 79. This involvement perhaps also explains why one contemporary source attributed *Euridice* to Emilio de' Cavalieri (*messa in musica dal Signor Emilio del Cavaliere*); ibid., 204.

173. ASF, Guardaroba medicea 1152 (*affari diversi*, 1575–1739), fol. 148, contains a note, dated 9 June 1600, recording work done for this performance: *Serenissimo Gran Ducha de' dare a Camillo legniauiolo* [sic] *a Pitti per un paicho* [= *palco*] *fatto e ne Palazo de' Pitti e ne salone della Duchessa di Braciano* [sic] *con comessione di Madama Serenissima servito per recitare una comedia del Signor Jachopo Corsi sotto dì 28 di maggio sopradetto . . .* This was a month before the grand duchess gave birth to Maria Maddalena (on 29 June).

174. Compare Kirkendale, *Court Musicians*, 565–66 (Rasi traveled to Florence in August 1600, though the singers from Rome had arrived probably in early July). To forestall an obvious question, it is extremely unlikely, to say the least, that the May performance was of Caccini's score: if it were, he would surely have said something in the 1600 edition.

everything except the Underworld scene, which was painted separately by others.[175]

The Guardaroba official in charge of the 1600 festivities, Michele Caccini (no relation to Giulio, so far as we know), acknowledged that Cardi-Cigoli's statement of work done was accurate, but he queried the cost and decided to resolve the matter in a typically Florentine manner. Caccini asked five other Florentine artists (including Alessandro Allori and Bernardo Poccetti) to produce itemized estimates for the same work; he then removed one of those estimates from the reckoning and averaged the rest, offering Cardi-Cigoli *sc.*379 £3.9*s*.8*d.* (almost exactly half of his original claim), which was accepted. Caccini did, however, approve that extra charge of *du*.25 for the change of room (*mutato la sciena dalla sala da basso alla sala da alto de' Pitti*).

No doubt there were other court costs associated with *Euridice*, though the total would have been but a fraction of the *sc.*60,000 widely reported as what was spent on *Il rapimento di Cefalo*.[176] The opera was obviously also produced on a much smaller scale: *Il rapimento* involved over a hundred musicians (so it was reported), whereas *Euridice* used eleven or so principal singers and, it seems, four instrumentalists.[177] Nor did a room in the Palazzo Pitti match the impressive size of the Teatro degli Uffizi (where *Il rapimento* was performed): Cardi-Cigoli's invoice for *Euridice* measured the stage floor that

175. ASF, Guardaroba medicea 1152, fols. 445–48 (Cardi-Cigoli's invoice and subsequent comments), 463–64 (a separate list of scenery and other painting, etc., for the 1600 festivities, including references to *le muta dell'Inferno* for *Euridice*). These documents have been partially transcribed and discussed—if with some errors and misprisions—in Testaverde, "Nuovi documenti sulle scenografie di Ludovico Cigoli per l'*Euridice* di Ottavio Rinuccini," which also notes sketches by Cardi-Cigoli for the Inferno scene (even if he did not paint it).

176. Kirkendale, *Court Musicians*, 137–40. Of course, such figures can always tend to be exaggerated, as with the 3,000 gentlemen and 800 gentlewomen said to have attended the performance of *Il rapimento*.

177. See Kirkendale, *Court Musicians*, 207, for a reconstruction of the casts for two performances of *Euridice*. Kirkendale's later argument (in *Emilio de' Cavalieri*, 441) that the second cast list (from an annotated copy of the libretto printed in October), which included local singers, may be associated with Caccini's version of the opera first performed in December 1602 might need modifying in light of the presence in the list of Jacopo Giusti (Peri's pupil, we shall see), who otherwise disappears from the record after October 1600. However, it is true that there is no evidence for another performance of Peri's *Euridice* after the 6 October one, save in Bologna in 1616, and it would be odd if annotations in a libretto printed in October 1600 somehow reflected the prior May performance, although the list of singers itself would have been appropriate for it.

he painted as 104 square *braccia* (one *braccio* is some 59 cm. or just over 23 inches). However, allowing Peri to bring Orpheus to theatrical life in that smaller space almost certainly worked to his advantage. *Il rapimento* was not a success by many reckonings because the scenery was left incomplete, the stage machines did not always work properly, and, according to a diarist associated with Cardinal Pietro Aldobrandini, the music was tedious (*il modo di cantarla venne facilmente a noia*).[178] The production could not match the visual and sonic expectations created by the spectacular theatrical and musical effects of the 1589 festivities; in 1608, for the entertainments celebrating the wedding of Prince Cosimo de' Medici and Maria Magdalena of Austria, the court reverted to the pattern of a comedy with *intermedi*, as in 1589 (once more under the overall direction of Giovanni de' Bardi, who by then had returned to Florence).

To judge by its repeat performances in the years 1598–1600 (and 1604), *Dafne* had more resonance for the court than *Euridice*, but not much of its music has survived.[179] Perhaps that is because it was shorter still (445 lines of poetry, as distinct from 790) and had a smaller cast (six principal roles, including the prologue). But it may also have been because its glorification of Apollo—killing the python (a scene also represented in the 1589 *intermedi*) and eventually, after Dafne's metamorphosis, consecrating himself to art—was more easily amenable to allegorical interpretation favoring the Medici (or any other princely household, as with Marco da Gagliano's new setting of an expanded version of Rinuccini's libretto performed in Mantua in early 1608).[180] The end of *Euridice*, too, has a chorus largely in praise of Apollo (by one legend, the father of Orpheus)—and one that further allegorizes the events in *Dafne*—but its main plot is more specifically designed for a wedding, even down to the surprise happy ending as compared with the traditional myth: Orfeo descends to Hades and persuades its ruler, Plutone (Pluto), to bend the

178. Kirkendale, *Court Musicians*, 140–41.

179. In addition to the (fairly well) documented performances of *Dafne* noted above, Cardinal Del Monte suggested in June 1600 that another one might be appreciated by Cardinal Pietro Aldobrandini when he came to Florence to officiate at the forthcoming wedding; De Caro, *"Euridice,"* 166 n. 27. However, it is unlikely that this occurred (Aldobrandini arrived in Florence on 4 October 1600). For a proposed performance requested by Maria de' Medici in Paris in early 1605, to be done by Caccini, see Kirkendale, *Court Musicians*, 150; this may have some bearing on whether Caccini actually set *Dafne* to music, as he later claimed.

180. Hanning, "Glorious Apollo."

law according to royal will so that Euridice can return safely to earth (and Orfeo is not submitted to any further test). Wedding entertainments traditionally represented their female protagonists moving from one patriarchal authority to another, and Corsi and Rinuccini may also have intended Plutone's magnanimity to match the grand duke's.[181]

However, Corsi must have wanted additional, more obvious messages to be presented here. Cardi-Cigoli's painting of the proscenium framing the stage for *Euridice* included at the top Maria de' Medici's new coat of arms as Queen of France, and on either side were (painted) statues of Poetry and of Painting. There were other canvases to extend the view (once the production shifted rooms) containing images of garlands and ruins.[182] Having Poetry and Painting frame a live representation, as it were, of Music was clearly emblematic of a new union of the arts. But no less so were the ruins, representing a venerable classical antiquity now being restored to life on a new stage, and for a new queen. A similar thrust is apparent in the prologue to *Euridice*, where La Tragedia (Tragedy) announces her changed garb on so auspicious an occasion. Likewise, although Peri used the preface to *Euridice* to associate his declamatory recitative—somehow midway between speech and song, he said—with the theatrical music of the ancient Greeks and Romans, he also admitted that it was in essence a new style devised to enable "our" modern music to suit the demands of "our" modern speech.[183]

Peri's preface goes on to describe the recitative in some technical detail but then has other matters to pursue. He provides a roll call of all the nobles involved in his operatic experiments or who approved of them: *signori* Jacopo Corsi, Ottavio Rinuccini, Piero Strozzi, Francesco Cini, and Orazio Vecchi (a musician from Modena), as well as the *signor conte* Alfonso Fontanelli and *signora* Vittoria Archilei. He adds to this noble list some of the performers of *Euridice*: *signori* Francesco Rasi (who sang the role of Aminta), Antonio Brandi (Arcetro), Melchior(re) Palantrotti (Plutone), Corsi again (harpsi-

---

181. This reading of Plutone follows De Caro, *"Euridice,"* 216–22 (which also compares the Inferno scene with the one in Monteverdi's *Orfeo* of 1607).

182. Buonarroti's description confirms the statues but ignores the rest; see the extract in Kirkendale, *Court Musicians,* 205.

183. *E però (sì come io non ardirei affermare questo essere il canto nelle Greche, e nelle Romane favole usato), così ho creduto esser quello, che solo possa donarcisi dalla nostra Musica, per accomodarsi alla nostra favella.*

chord), and Don Grazìa (or Garzìa) Montalvo (chitarrone); only two of the instrumentalists, Giovanni Battista Jacomelli (playing a large *lira*) and Giovanni Lapi (a large lute), are identified as *messer*.[184] Then Peri refers to the many other most learned gentlemen who were greatly pleased by the opera, given that today, he says, music flourishes among the nobility of Florence— *altri molti intendentissimi gentilhuomini (che nella nobiltà fiorisce hoggi la Musica)*—and he notes the honor given to the "present" *Euridice* (i.e., Peri's score) by its having been performed before so great a queen and so many famous princes of Italy and France (*ad una Regina sì grande, et a tanti famosi principi d'Italia e di Francia*). Only then does Peri mention that "Giulio Caccini (detto Romano)"—"whose great worth is known to the world"—inserted some of his music into *Euridice*: the absence even of *messer* as a title is striking, as is the subsequent tart comment that Caccini composed and printed his *Euridice* after Peri's was performed before the Most Christian Queen of France.[185] And he finally remembers to acknowledge another performer, Jacopo Giusti, *fanciulletto Lucchese*, who we shall see was Peri's live-in pupil at the time. Given all those noble titles, Peri clearly felt that he was in good company.

In fact, the reception of *Euridice* was not as favorable as Peri would have us believe: some felt—so the not wholly impartial Emilio de' Cavalieri reported—that the recitative was tedious and too much like the chanting of

---

184. Peri styles Montalvo's name "Grazìa" in the preface to *Euridice*, as did others; however, in Camillo Rinuccini's *Descrizione delle feste fatte nelle reali nozze de' serenissimi principi di Toscana D. Cosimo De' Medici, e Maria Maddalena Arciduchessa d'Austria* (Florence: I Giunti, 1608), 81, he is Don Garzìa di Montalvo (directing the *mascherata* incorporated within the equestian ballet done in the Piazza S. Croce). The lutenist Giovanni Lapi was not officially on the court roll, it seems, although he had performed in the 1589 *intermedi*; he was also the leader of a *compagnia* performing Jacopo Cicognini's comedy *I morti e vivi* in May 1602 (Solerti, *Musica, ballo e drammatica alla corte medicea*, 28). It is not known whether he is related to the organist Tommaso Lapi, who we shall see may also have been associated with Peri.

185. *Non dimeno Giulio Caccini (detto Romano) il cui sommo valore è noto al Mondo, fece l'arie d'Euridice, et alcune del Pastore, e Ninfa del coro, e de' cori "Al canto, al ballo," "Sospirate," e "Poi che gli eterni imperi." E questo, perché dovevano esser cantate da persone dependenti da lui, le quali Arie si leggono nella sua composta, e stampata pur dopo, che questa mia fu rappresentata a sua Maestà Cristianissima.* In addition to the music for Euridice, the shepherd and nymph, and the three choruses mentioned here, Caccini's setting may also have been used for the prologue; McGee, "Pompeo Caccini and *Euridice*," 98.

the Passion (*che le musiche sono state tediose; et che li è parso sentire cantar la passione*).[186] Arguments over precedence in the invention of opera also ran rife in musical circles, not least as Caccini and Cavalieri made counterclaims for their own contributions to the musical styles that led to it, the latter in part because of his sacred opera, *Rappresentatione di Anima, et di Corpo*, done in Rome in February 1600 (and printed in September). Opera never established a strong foothold in the courts of early seventeenth-century Italy save under very particular circumstances: the music was often thought insufficiently varied, it went on for too long, and courtly audiences tended to prefer more active involvement in, say, dancing or jousting.[187] But this can hardly have affected the broader reputation that Corsi gained from the proceedings. Even if the new genre of opera, and the new style of recitative, had its critics, the ideals they embodied, and their fruition in Florence, redounded to Corsi's (and the city's) fame well into the 1630s, as Pietro de' Bardi and others continued to connect his name with these new forms of musical theater.

Corsi must also have felt proud of what has all the air of a family venture. Most of those involved in the production of *Euridice*—Caccini and his family, Jacomelli, Lapi, Montalvo, Peri, Rasi, and Rinuccini—had longstanding connections with him. In February 1601, he made what seems to have been a partial payment for a statue of Orpheus by the Florentine sculptor Cristoforo Stati, no doubt as a solid memento of the opera in a manner not dissimilar from Peri's printed score issued at the same time (Figure 1.10).[188]

Perhaps it was Corsi's gratitude to Peri that led him, in November 1600, to take on the composer as a partner and employee in one of his wool firms (Giulio Della Rena, Vincenzo Fiorini & Partners; see Chapter 2). But Corsi died just two years later on 29 December 1602, at the young age of forty-one.

186. Palisca, "Musical Asides in the Diplomatic Correspondence of Emilio de' Cavalieri," 351; Kirkendale, *Court Musicians*, 205. Cavalieri is speaking of both *Euridice* and *Il rapimento di Cefalo*, but the comment clearly refers to the new recitative. For a later Florentine comment on recitative generally being considered tedious, see Giulio Caccini's report from March 1618 on Domenico Belli's music for Jacopo Cicognini's *Andromeda*, given in Solerti, *Musica, ballo e drammatica alla corte medicea*, 127–28 (the original is in ASF, Mediceo del Principato 1370, document dated 10 March 1617/18).

187. Carter, "The North Italian Courts."

188. Pegazzano, *Committenza e collezionismo nel Cinquecento*, 16: on 23 February 1600/1601, Corsi paid *sc.*10 toward a statue of a triton and one of Orpheus; the latter seems to have been finished by December that year.

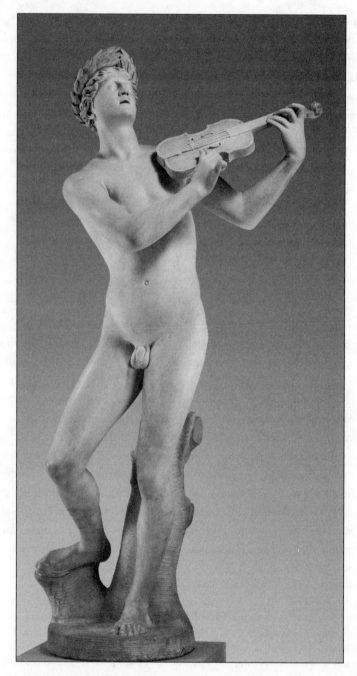

FIGURE I.IO. Cristoforo Stati, *Orfeo*. (New York, Metropolitan
Museum of Art. Image copyright © The Metropolitan Museum of Art.
Image source: Art Resource, New York.)

The loss was mourned throughout the city, elaborate obsequies were held in the Compagnia dell'Arcangelo Raffaello (with music by Marco da Gagliano, Giovanni Del Turco, and Piero Strozzi), and Bardo Corsi received letters of condolence from far and wide, including, it is said, one from King Henri IV. On his death, some of Corsi's musical instruments were in the hands of Florentine patricians or musicians—the former including Francesco Cini, whom we shall encounter in later contact with Peri—while others were sold to them or to the grand duke's Guardaroba. Over a decade later, Rinuccini was still lamenting the death of so dear a friend:

> All'hor di più gioir fuggì la spene,
> meste le Muse abbandonaro il canto,
> perdero ogni lor gloria, ogni lor vanto
> i superbi Teatri, e l'auree Scene.[189]

We have no such poignant response from Peri. But Corsi's death in December 1602, and Giovambattista Michelozzi's in May 1604, denied him in short order the ongoing support of two leading Florentines who had been, in their various ways, essential for the consolidation of his social, economic, and even musical position. One might add to this Cristofano Malvezzi's demise in 1599, and Emilio de' Cavalieri's, also in 1602. There is no sign of what Peri's reactions might have been, or what impact these deaths might have had on his actual and potential career. In principle, however, he should by now, entering his forties, have been able to stand on his own two feet, as indeed he did. This is not to say that he did not require further support at various points in his life: we shall see in subsequent chapters the impact of his ongoing relations with the Medici grand dukes, and of a new one with a Mantuan prince. But the familial and social networks into which Peri inserted himself up to

189. Rinuccini's poem "Per l'eterno sentier l'undecim'anno / fornito ha il corso, s'al contar non erro" (in *Alcune poesie sopra la morte del principe don Francesco Medici* [Florence: Giunti, 1615]) is addressed to Don Grazìa [*sic*] di Montalvo; it is given complete in De Caro, *"Euridice,"* 227. Rinuccini seems to have written it on the eleventh anniversary of Corsi's death. This fourth and final stanza translates as: "Then hope for all further enjoyment fled, / the Muses, sad, abandoned their song, / all glory and all praise was lost / by the proud Theaters and golden Stages."

and including his third marriage in December 1602 stood him in good stead as he sought to secure and strengthen his economic circumstances. Music continued to play a role in his self-fashioning, but less than we might imagine, given what the Peri ledgers and other documents now tell us about a life that was as rich, eventful, and complex as one would expect for any ambitious Florentine in the early modern period.

2

The Economic World

Growing up in Florence, Peri became fully acclimated to the market economy of one of Europe's great centers of early capitalism. Florentines knew how to make their way in a marketplace organized around the monetary nexus. Moreover, the economy had developed to the point of offering some, if limited, outlets for saving and investment even for those who had only modest amounts of disposable wealth, and more important, it had opened up plenty of opportunities for entrepreneurial initiatives, especially for skilled artisans. We know much about these issues for the fourteenth and fifteenth centuries, although they lie subsumed under business histories of industrialists, merchants, and bankers, but no study even for the earlier period brings all the information together, encapsulating it in an economic biography of a single operator trying to find his way around the local marketplace. Attention has mostly focused, instead, on the great entrepreneurs, the movers and shakers in this early capitalist society. The results are business histories that often are not much more than chronicles of investments in the forward sectors of the economy oriented to foreign markets, their ultimate focus—if there is one—usually being on the performance of the economy in general. Lacking is a study of that marketplace itself: how it functioned, what possibilities it offered, and how people dealt with one another in it—the skills and knowledge they commanded, the attitudes conditioning their initiatives, their relations with one another. Peri's accounts lend themselves to this kind of analysis. Unlike the earlier entrepreneurs who have had more success in attracting the attention of historians, he had modest resources, and his economic activity was confined within the parameters of the local market. Thus his accounts lead us away from the individual and directly into the marketplace where Florentines had to make a living, dealing with one another through monetary and credit relations for everything from consumption to investment. Rather than opening up a view from the marketplace to the overall performance of the economy, they allow us to focus instead on the market itself and the economic culture that it generated and that at the same time drove it. Indeed, in tracing his steps through the marketplace we will see Orpheus transformed into Everyman, repeatedly disappearing into the crowd that constitutes that larger picture—a picture all the more interesting because, for Peri's period, we have no other views of it.[1]

The Culture of the Marketplace

Two skills in particular served Florentines in their maneuvering about the marketplace. One was accounting, by which they kept track of their transactions; the other was banking, which facilitated the execution of the more important of those transactions through an essential institution of a capitalist economy.

Accountancy

Peri's first ledger, opened when he was nineteen years old (taking at face value the date of the first entry), is evidence that he was a product of the

1. Goldthwaite's *The Economy of Renaissance Florence* goes only to the end of the sixteenth century and gets admittedly weaker as it arrives toward that end owing to the lack of secondary literature; the specific businesses in the major sectors he covers in other studies were active only in the late sixteenth century ("Le aziende seriche e il mondo degli affari a Firenze alla fine del '500," "Banking in Florence at the End of the Sixteenth Century," and "The Florentine Wool Industry in the Late Sixteenth Century"). Malanima, *La decadenza di un'economia cittadina*, takes a long view forward but surveys only the wool and silk industries. Important statistical data on investment in the major sectors over the long period have been published in Carmona, "Aspects du capitalisme toscan." Goldberg, *Jews and Magic in Medici Florence*, a biography of a Jew almost exactly contemporary with Peri, has a chapter on the market in which Jews were active.

long-established educational system of Florence. The high professional standard of accounting practice—content, format, organization, techniques, jargon, and, above all, discipline in following the rules—as illustrated in this, his earliest ledger, had become by the later fourteenth century second nature for virtually all Florentines, from international merchant bankers down to simple craftsmen. It is generally thought that the city's children did not learn accounting in an elementary school of reading and writing or in the school of practical arithmetic (*scuola d'abaco*) that most entered thereafter, around the age of eleven or twelve. These latter schools generated the production of many manuals on arithmetical skills that survive in manuscript, and none of them, for all their orientation to practical problems, makes the slightest reference to the application of the subject to the keeping of accounts. The lack of manuals on accounting leads one to believe that the subject was not taught in a formal program of instruction but that, instead, boys learned the skill on the job. Typically they began an apprenticeship after finishing the *scuola d'abaco*, perhaps in an artisan's shop or a company office, where their first task was to keep the cashbook, the simplest form of accounts. From there, following a career pattern like that of Piero Monaldi recounted in the previous chapter, they worked their way up through the complexities of specific kinds of account books and double entry to the keeping of the ledger.

We know nothing about Peri's training in the technique, but his skill in accountancy, so characteristic of Florentine culture, is fully illustrated in his first ledger. It has the standard identification, in the usual format, that Florentines had long been using for their account books of private affairs: the cover came with the title *debitori e creditori A* at the top, the "A" indicating that this was the first book in a projected series, and the incipit, written by Peri, consists of an invocation, his name, the contents (*debitori e creditori A e ricordi*), the color of the cover of the ledger (*bianco*), and page references to the *debitori e creditori* section of the book and to that of the *ricordi*. The accounts, all opened in the names of persons, are kept in bipartite form on the two facing folio sides, or the "opening," of the book (a format called *alla veneziana*), with debits on the left and credits on the right; entries are clearly separated from one another by indentation; monetary figures are usually written out in the entry but entered in arabic numerals in a column on the right; values are in moneys of account (either the florin/ducat/*scudo* or the *lira*), with reference to real coins used in transactions being very rare; accounts are balanced by totals on both sides at the bottom and closed with a diagonal line extending from the upper right to the lower left; and the entries include all the jargon of accounting used at the time—*de' dare* and *de' havere*, *portò* and *recò contanti*, *il detto*, *per lui a*, *a buon conto*, *di contro*, *come al suo conto*, and so on. The accounts are kept in single entry, but occasionally one finds references to a cross-entry (especially when a page is filled and the balance is drawn and transferred to a new page), and the cross-reference is indicated in the usual way—*in questo* [*a*] *c*[*arta*]. Moreover, in his own private accounts Peri assumes an impersonal detachment, often using the singular third-person possessive adjective with reference to himself, and identifying holders of accounts who certainly needed no identity in a completely private document as, for example, "my wife," "my son," "my servant." Sometimes he refers to himself as *io* (or *di me*), *Jacopo Peri*, or otherwise enters his full name as one of the parties to a transaction, and in an account opened in his name he uses the third-person singular possessive with reference to himself. In other words, he, like most Florentines, kept his accounts as if consciously aware of creating a historical record likely to be consulted by unknown parties. A notable exemplification of this formality appears in the ledger (discussed in Chapter 1) kept for the estate of Dino Fortini by, in sequence, his widow, Giustina, until her death in 1597; Giustina's mother, Maddalena Monaldi, representing Giustina's son Giovanni, who had difficulty writing (and perhaps reasoning), until her death in 1613; and then her brother Piero, who kept the accounts in the name of Giovanni, his nephew. "Kept in his name" means that he kept them as if he were Giovanni in absolutely every respect, referring, for example, to himself and his relatives and using personal pronouns so that the unsuspecting reader would think that Giovanni himself had kept the accounts. It is only Piero's distinctive handwriting that gives the story away. Here the accountant has imposed impersonality on his work with a vengeance.

Further proof of Peri's training is the discipline with which he handled accounts in his first ledger: the format and the hand are uniformly neat, and cancellations and erasures are rare. Finally, in the course of keeping the ledger he makes reference to the full complement of waste-books (several of which survive) that constituted the accounting apparatus of many Florentines— *libro di uscita*, *libricciuolo di racolte*, *giornale*, *quadernuccio*, *quadernuccio lungo*, *quadernuccio delle speserelle*, *stracciafoglio*, *scartafaccio*, *quadernuccio* of signed

receipts—in which he entered data to be transferred later to the more permanent record of the *libro di debitori e creditori* or *libro grande*, what we call the
ledger. He carried the book he used for signed receipts (a small *vacchetta*, a
book in upright octavo format), which still survives, with him whenever he
made payments, as we learn from the receipt for the rent on the property at
San Marco Vecchio, where the canon at S. Lorenzo added an acknowledgment also of the rent paid the previous time, when Peri had shown up without it.[2] When the recipient of a payment was illiterate, Peri was also careful to
have the details entered in his *vacchetta* by a third party.[3]

Nevertheless, in this first ledger Peri did not always follow the rules, and
occasionally he made an error. For instance, he started off numbering pages
in his ledger in the traditional way done for texts, so that each sheet has the
same number on its recto and verso side, rather than, following standard accounting practice at the time, assigning a single number to each set of facing
pages, so that with the ledger open before the reader the verso of the sheet on
the left (with debit entries) and the recto of the sheet on the right (with credit
entries) have the same number. And when he made an error he felt obliged to
explain what had happened. At the very outset of posting the rental account,
on the ledger's second page, he realized that he had made a bit of a mess of
things (Figure 2.1). He canceled one entry he had posted on the credit side
rather than the debit side (the third in the figure) and entered it correctly,
writing in the margin that it was moved to the other side because it had originally been placed in error (*per esser questa partita posta male per errore, la ri-
pongo di qua*). Subsequently he canceled two other entries, and at the end of
the page, instead of drawing a balance and transferring the balancing entry
to a new page, he simply totaled the entries on each side and transferred
both to the new page—explaining himself in a statement squeezed into the
space at the top of the account and running across both sides: that having
erred in carrying over and indicated matters badly, he would copy things
anew and carry it over to folio 11.[4] Some years later, in 1596, when he had two

2. LC 3913, entry dated 8 November 1624.

3. One such third party, Tommaso Lapi (LC 3913, fol. 3v), may have been the Tommaso
di Agnolo Lapi *da Fiesole* (and perhaps the brother of the lutenist Giovanni Lapi who played in
the 1589 *intermedi* and in *Euridice*) who in 1605 was organist at S. Spirito; see Kirkendale,
Court Musicians, 307. It seems possible that Tommaso was Peri's pupil for a time.

4. Ledger A, fol. 5: *Per havere erato nel raccorre e segnato male, metterò tutto questo conto
inanzi, copiandolo di nuovo; e meglio lo raccorrò a carte undici.*

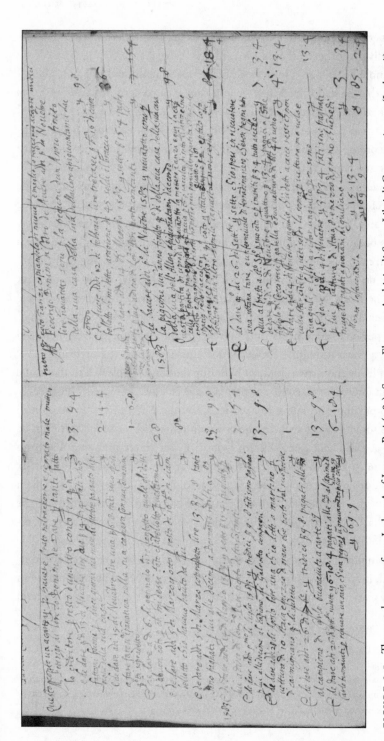

FIGURE 2.1. The rental account from Ledger A of Jacopo Peri (1582). *Source:* Florence, Archivio di Stato, Libri di Commercio 3911 (Ledger A), fol. 5 (lower account). (With permission of the Ministero per i Beni e le Attività Culturali; further reproduction or duplication by whatever means is forbidden.)

accounts opened in the name of Giovambattista Michelozzi, one in his name
personally, the other in that of his bank, he realized at one point (as we learn
from a note he squeezed into the available space at the end of one of the accounts) that he had mixed the two and thus created confusion (*ho mescolato
il mio credito del suo banco con il suo conto a parte, talché ho fatto confusione*).[5]
The next year he encountered further problems when he had to begin keeping a record of his claims on the estate his wife inherited from her father. On
the account he opened for the *Eredità di messer Niccolò Fortunati e la Caterina, sua figliuola, erede del detto quondam messer Niccolò e mia donna*, he
makes references to two earlier contracts with Fortunati for a credit advanced
to him, and then adds that until now he had only recorded matters in a *stracciafoglio* because he did not have the heart to keep a ledger—for he was not a
practical man but put his faith in God—but that now, realizing that the result was no good either for him or for anyone else, he has set up the account
as best he knew how.[6] Such explanations written into a private record are
further evidence that, in the end, these account books were conceived not as
private personal documents but, however modestly, as legal and historical
records, a motivation inherent in the accounting culture of Florentines.

Most likely the responsibility of handling the considerable wealth that came
with the dowry he received on his marriage in 1592 prompted him thence-
forth to pay more attention to keeping accounts. And in fact, he went on to
became something of a professional accountant, with recorded positions as
cashier at the Della Rena–Fiorini wool firm for thirty-nine months, from
1600 to 1603; as *camerlengo*, or comptroller, at the Arte degli Speziali for six
months during the same period, from 1601 to 1602; as cashier at his own firm
for an unspecified period beginning in 1610; and finally as *camerlengo* of the
Arte della Lana from 1618 to his death—if not also at other places not recorded in his ledgers (see Table 2.5). As cashier Peri was probably responsible
for keeping the cashbook, a task that in itself did not require much accounting skill: it was something that was done by any number of boys employed in
the city's artisan workshops and business offices. As *camerlengo*, he would

5. Ledger A, fol. 31.

6. Ledger A, fol. 39: *e perché fino a questo giorno sopradetto, di poi che morì messer Niccolò,
non ho tenuto conto se non a uno stracciafoglio, quasi non mi bastando l'animo di tenere conto al
libro per non essere io pratico ma confidato in Dio e nella verità; visto che non stava bene per me né
per altri, ho acceso questo conto nel miglior modo che ho saputo . . .*

have had more responsibilities than that of an accountant, and while these were probably not considerable at the Arte degli Speziali, it was otherwise at a major institution such as the Arte della Lana, to judge from both his much larger salary and the many books of the guild found in his possession at the time of his death.

The techniques and jargon of accountancy were well developed by the fourteenth century—very likely even earlier—and the diffusion of accounting practice among virtually all Florentines of some economic stature conditioned their behavior and attitudes in the marketplace. Accounting facilitated offsetting—the shifting of book debits and credits between debtor and creditor—as a substitute for handling cash, and as anyone who has consulted private account books of Florentines from the fourteenth century onward knows, the practice was widespread among the population. Peri's rental account open in the name of his first landlord, Federigo di Lorenzo Bonini (who lived in the Veneto), is a good example. Debit entries do not record regular periodic entries for the direct payment of rent. Instead, the landlord requested that Peri make payments in his name to third parties, and those payments then became credits toward Peri's rent. Thus on the debit side of the account Peri entered payments he made for the landlord to the fisc for taxes owed, to the peasants working the landlord's rural property, to a moneylender for redemption of a pawn, for the cost of lute songs and the shipment of them to Venice (*e de' dare, questo dì 20 di gennaio* [1583/84], *s.16 ch'io spesi in una dozina di canti da liuto e mandali a Venetia*), and for a variety of other personal expenditures of the landlord's.[7] In fact, very few rental payments were made in cash to either of his landlords. Peri continued to have relations with Bonini even after moving out of his house: in 1587 Bonini helped him procure two lutes from Padua (see Chapter 3).

These kinds of transactions required careful accounting since, as Peri's rental accounts demonstrate, payments made to third parties rarely correspond precisely to the rent owed, nor did they fit into a pattern of regular periodicity in the payment of rent. One might argue, too, that there were

---

7. Ledger A, fol. 11. It is hard to know what might have been the nature of these lute songs: 16s. would have been very cheap for even a small printed music book (compare Carter, "Music-Selling in Late Sixteenth-Century Florence") unless it was secondhand, and no *canti da liuto* were printed in Florence in this decade, so far as we know (see Carter, "Music-Printing in Late Sixteenth- and Early Seventeenth-Century Florence").

social implications of this practice, for offsetting tied Florentines together in a web of debit–credit relations that was more personal and temporally more casual than the disciplined relations we are accustomed to seeing in the classic view of the market organized around the cash nexus. Similar implications are apparent in the evident willingness of Florentines to make or receive loans within various social or other networks—we saw several examples involving Peri in Chapter 1—that also depended on trust that they would be repaid. A countervailing tendency to institutionalize the practice of shifting credits and debits at a personal level took the more impersonal form of the bank transfer, but although Peri, as we shall see, used banks for this purpose, the scope of the practice with respect to its social diffusion was still very limited.

Complementing offsetting as a form of monetary liquidity was the use of instruments that substituted for cash exchange. Probably most transactions were effected simply through oral communication between the two parties, presumably accompanied by visual inspection of their respective written records. In the absence of a direct personal encounter, however, the debtor might write out an order of payment, something like a private check, drawing on a credit he had with a third party; many such *polizze*, as they were called, survive from the fourteenth and fifteenth centuries, although no evidence for them turns up in Peri's accounts. However, paper instruments of payment, if not in the form of the private check executed in an offsetting operation, circulated in the form of the IOU. One instance of this does turn up in Peri's accounts. In April 1591 his new landlord, Honorio di Domenico Antonio Vitis, told Peri to pay £7 toward his rent by giving that amount to Giovanfrancesco *trombone* (the trombonist)—for what reason we do not know—and so Peri gave Giovanfrancesco not cash but a chit (*schrita*) for that amount he had received from one of his debtors, Angiolino Teduci.[8] Payable to the bearer, an IOU did not need to be endorsed or specifically reassigned. It was, of course, a credit instrument, one largely unknown in the earlier pe-

---

8. LC 3913, fol. 2: *Io, Giovanfrancesco sopradeto, ò ricevuto, questo dì, 3 d'aprile 1591, lire sete da messer Iacomo Peri, le quali li paga per Onorio Vitis per sua comesione per contro d'una schrita (che io, Giovanfrancesco, ò di suo, concesami) da Angiolino Teduci, il quale li era debitore.* We have added the parentheses here to explain our reading of this rather confused statement. The previous entry records a similar payment to Giovanfrancesco, if with a less clear justification, on 1 March 1590/91. Peri credited his rental account accordingly; Ledger A, fol. 20. For the trombonist (also styled *sanese*), see Kirkendale, *Court Musicians*, 118.

riod, and by Peri's time these *cedole*, as they were generally called, circulated widely as a medium of payment in the way illustrated by this example from his accounts.[9] Traffic in private debt also included the sale of credits one might have with other parties, a device we shall see Peri using in closing out his account with one of the wool companies in which he had invested. All these practices—offsetting, orders of payment, IOUs, sale of private credits—facilitated monetary exchange beyond the cash nexus and hence increased its velocity, stimulating the expansion of a financial market. In a sense, this was banking outside of banks, and it required a certain attention to keeping one's accounting records straight.

Accounting also engendered a sense of money as an abstraction. Accounts precluded transactions in cash, and in fact ledgers were kept not in real coins but in moneys of account—primarily the *lira* or the florin/ducat/*scudo* and their subdivisions in *soldi* and *denari*. Moneys of account were abstractions that for the most part did not even have an exact correspondence with real coins. For this reason one very seldom finds mention of a real coin even within the body of an entry, and some of the coins that we know were in circulation at the time are never mentioned at all. In thus inculcating a complete familiarity with moneys of account, or "ghost moneys," as they have been called, accounting brought Florentines close to the point of accepting fiduciary money in lieu of coin. Money conceived as imaginary values on paper is just one step from paper money.

Accounts as a written record gave Florentines a sense of security in this web of monetary dealings with one another, especially since private accounts had the status of legal documents. By the end of the thirteenth century Florentines had already abandoned the notary for most market transactions other than those regarding ownership of real estate. In the event of a dispute over debt or credit claims, it was enough to present the private accounting record, and the minutes of sessions of the court at the Mercanzia that dealt with such claims document how even ordinary Florentines showed up before the judges hauling their account books with them as evidence in their cases. For many operations they thus freed themselves from recourse to a notary and even to signed receipts. That personal accounts were open to inspection by the courts is one reason why Florentines—like Peri—kept them with a

9. Goldberg, *Jews and Magic in Medici Florence*, 105–11, presents many examples of these *cedole* (translated as "notes of credit") in the hands of Jewish moneylenders.

certain detachment and formality, and why errors and confusion needed to be kept to a minimum. Peri used a notary for property transactions (the purchase and sale of real estate, dowries, and *censi*), for the transmission of patronage rights over the two chapels of his son Francesco, for his last will and testament, and for other such legal arrangements, but not for any of his investments in business enterprises. Moreover, even separate written receipts for specific transactions are rare among his papers (which include the aforementioned book of signed receipts that covers, significantly, no fewer than forty-five years of his life in ninety-five pages, most of them occasioned by payments of rents and other fixed obligations).

It was therefore important, in addition to keeping one's own accounts, also to note that appropriate entries were made in the ledgers of those with whom one had dealings. Peri is very careful about this: whenever he has paid money into a bank or other business he indicates the precise place where the relevant entry was made in the firm's books—for example, "in the income journal lettered N, on folio 3"; "in the green ledger, lettered A, on folio 304"; "in their record book lettered A, on folio 3." On one occasion, 6 August 1625, he went to the Riccardi family bank, known as Giovanni Taddei, Matteo Niccolini & Partners, with an order from Carlo Rinuccini to be paid *fl.*400; but since the cashier was not on hand to count out the money and enter the transaction on the company books, Giovanni Taddei himself counted it out and made a note of the transaction to be given to Gabriello Riccardi, one of the major partners, so that the payment would be properly entered in the expenditure journal of the firm—"everything written out," Peri adds, "to all good effect for my memory."[10]

Accounting was clearly an important economic instrument for the efficient functioning of market activity, but its practices also engendered habits and attitudes that, taken all together, generated what we might call a veritable culture of accounting, a culture in which most Florentine boys like Peri were fully steeped by the time they reached their mid-teens: mastery of a technique, discipline in application, a sense of control over the flow of disparate and changing data, a degree of abstraction in the concept of money, an appreciation of a historical record, and—given the support of an appropriate legal apparatus—confidence in the marketplace.

10. Ledger A, fol. 166: *tutto scritto ad ogni buon fine per mia memoria.* On this bank, see Malanima, *I Riccardi di Firenze*, 124–25.

The use to which accounts are put is also culturally conditioned by what people consider to be their needs. Peri's accounts demonstrate that for all the antiquity, by his time, of accounting techniques, accounting functions had in fact changed little over the years. It is enough to measure the number of written pages in Peri's two ledgers against the periods they span—140 folios for the forty-five years covered in the first ledger and 31 for the six years of the second (an average, respectively, of 3 and 5 folios a year)—to realize how limited these functions were. Accounting was not used to keep track of anything like all economic activity, nor even of the most important part, let alone to impose a comprehensive order over all of one's economic life—to give even an idea of how much the income was in any given period and what its course was over time, or what the total assets were at any given moment and how net worth changed during a life. In this respect, Peri's ledgers, like those of other Florentines, including businessmen operating in the forward sectors of the economy, show how stagnant the accounting culture of the city was with respect to the functions that the technique had served since the fourteenth century.[11] Notwithstanding the centuries-long tradition of keeping accounts, the mastery of the techniques of accounting, and the enormous accumulation of account books for which the city is famous, Florentines were far from realizing what one might consider the full potential of the skill.

Banking

Peri, like most Florentines, was also steeped in the banking culture of his city. Many of his investments involved banking operations, and in the course of his career he dealt with many of the city's most prominent banks. For the early period of his life, his ledger documents two instances when he had recourse to a bank for transfer of funds, both being payments made to him by the Monte di Pietà, by this time a public savings-and-loan bank, through the Ricci bank, the city's largest private bank.[12] On 26 April 1583, the Monte gave him a check (*polizza*) on the Ricci bank for a loan he had taken out for *fl.*145 £6. A year later, on 2 November 1585, he went to the Ricci bank to withdraw the *fl.*296 that was credited to him at the Monte di Pietà thanks to the

11. See Goldthwaite, "The Florentine Wool Industry in the Late Sixteenth Century" and "Le aziende seriche e il mondo degli affari a Firenze alla fine del '500," both studies of companies contemporary with Peri.

12. Ledger A, fols. 7, 99, 100.

"donation" from his cousin Cesare on the occasion of his profession at the Carmine.

Peri's use of banks became more frequent from the 1590s on, once he found himself administering the greater wealth that in the course of a decade came to him through the successive dowries of his first two wives. On 8 January 1593 Niccolò Fortunati paid him the bulk of his first dowry at the Ricci bank, and Peri transferred the sum to the bank of Giovambattista Michelozzi.[13] In 1596 and again in 1598 he went through the Ricci bank to make payments to the convent of S. Onofrio di Foligno.[14] In 1599 he made his initial investment in a speculative wool venture with his cousin Domenico Peri by transferring credits he had with the silk company of Francesco Michelozzi to the Capponi bank, presumably the one used by his cousin; two years later the bank credited him with the profits from this operation, and he transferred some of the credit to what was by this time the Michelozzi–Ricci bank.[15] In 1602 and 1603 he stood guarantor for his brother-in-law Girolamo Fortini, who was having serious legal problems, by depositing *fl.*100 in the bank of Jacopo and Bardo Corsi and 100 *scudi d'oro* in the bank of Francesco Rinuccini; when, six years later, the fisc liquidated Girolamo's assets to pay his debts, Peri got his money back from the two banks in the form of cash payments at the Michelozzi bank.[16] On the dissolution of the wool partnership with Francesco Brunacci, in 1612, Brunacci paid *fl.*1,000 of what he owed Peri in three installments through the Scarlattini bank, two of which were paid at that bank, while the third was transferred to the Martelli bank, which paid Peri in cash.[17] On 4 August 1625 Carlo Rinuccini loaned Peri *fl.*94, which was paid to Peri at the Taddei–Niccolini bank, and on 28 November Peri paid this back at the Paganelli–Portinari bank.[18]

Peri had recourse to banks also to take out bills of exchange, the sophisticated financial instruments with which he had much familiarity. He used the bills for their basic function, as instruments for the international transfer of funds. In 1624 he personally opened an account in the name of Arcangelo

13. Ledger A, fol. 104.
14. Ledger A, fols. 12, 42.
15. Ledger A, fols. 42, 49, 50, 53.
16. Ledger A, fol. 116.
17. Ledger A, fol. 87.
18. Ledger A, fol. 166.

Innori that he used principally to record payments to Rome—probably in connection with his purchase of *monte* bonds there, as we shall see. Innori sent bills of exchange to the bank of Ottaviano Acciaioli, Marco Martelli & Partners, in Rome, as the beneficiary; on two occasions this bank sent Peri a letter acknowledging receipt of the funds. Peri made one of the cash payments to Innori through yet another local bank, Antonio and Giulio Buonaccorsi & Partners.[19] He and his heirs continued to receive interest payments on these securities in Rome from the Acciaioli–Martelli bank there.

If at this point, after the rush through all these banking operations, the reader feels a bit dizzy, that should clinch the case for Peri's comprehensive familiarity with banks and for the prominence of banks in the marketplace of late Renaissance Florence. The very number of banks recorded in his ledgers is impressive. The principal bank he dealt with was Michelozzi–Ricci & Partners (which later dropped the Ricci name), the dominant firm on the city's banking scene through the second half of the sixteenth century to the early seventeenth, but his transactions involved many other banks mentioned in the course of these pages—Alessandrini, Buonaccorsi, Capponi, Corsi, Martelli, Paganelli–Portinari, Rinuccini, Scarlattini, Segni–Medici, Taddei–Niccolini, Tempi, Torrigiani, and, in Rome, Acciaioli–Martelli. For the fifteenth century it would be virtually impossible to find a single ledger kept for the private administration of one's affairs, or even accounts kept for a business, that contains references to as many banks. The increasing recourse to banks by the general population also generated a jargon to talk about certain banking operations that more people began to use. It is surprising that, despite the sophistication of banks already in the fourteenth century, fifteenth-century Florentines had no verbs to use specifically for opening accounts or for making bank transfers, but by Peri's time, the modern vocabulary of precise technical terms had emerged: *accendere* for opening an account, *spegnere* for closing it, *voltare* for effecting a transfer (today, however, the verb is the synonym *girare*).[20]

Peri presumably had a current account in a bank, although there was no reason for him to keep a record of it in his ledgers. In the note inserted into the Giovambattista Michelozzi account (mentioned in the previous section)

19. Ledger A, fol. 163.

20. The terminology in the fifteenth century, although hardly standardized, consisted of versions of *fare buoni* and *fare creditore* (or *debitore*), or words to that effect.

he recognizes the "confusion" he had created in his own accounting by not distinguishing between transactions in the personal account of Michelozzi and those in his account with the bank. From 1605 to 1608 he in fact did keep track of his activity in his account with the bank of Giovambattista's nephews, Lorenzo and Francesco Michelozzi & Partners, bankers. In this three-year period no less than *fl.*4,314 passed through the account, almost all of it in the form of cash payments and giro operations (book transfers).[21] Peri certainly knew how to transfer funds through banks, although he never mentions the mechanism used to communicate such orders to the bank—whether an oral request made at the bank or a written order (a *polizza* or check), an instrument long familiar to most Florentines but not yet widely used. He used banks mostly for major transactions or those involving his business interests, and, of necessity in either case, with parties who had equal access to the banking system. To judge from the many accounts on his books that record his activity not as an investor but as a consumer, as an employer of servants, as a landlord, and as a seller of produce from his rural properties, he did not use banks for the myriad petty transactions he made in the local market in the ordinary course of the day. He executed many transactions of this nature through direct cash exchanges or offsetting.

Yet for all Peri's familiarity with banking practices, he sometimes handled enormous sums in cash. For example, in 1600 he paid *fl.*200 of his investment in the Della Rena–Fiorini wool company in cash; in 1605 he made two payments of *fl.*150 in cash toward his investment in the Michelozzi silk company; on 3 December 1611 he received *fl.*1,673 in cash from the Brunacci wool firm, and in July the next year he received three more payments totaling *fl.*1,000, which he collected in cash at two banks; he made two of the payments (*fl.*174. 16s.9d. and *fl.*188. 2s.10d.) mentioned above to Innori for bills drawn on Rome in cash. In these transactions he is explicit about handling cash: he uses the word *contante*, which by itself does not necessarily mean cash in a physical sense (although it usually does), but when used along with the verb *recare* or *portare*, or when those verbs are used on their own, carrying away or delivering cash in a literal sense is meant. Only once does he mention the actual coins involved: in 1620 he carried *fl.*600 in *piastre* to Prato to pay the dowry of the daughter he put in a convent there (and these were counted

21. Ledger A, fols. 67, 80.

out in the presence of the prioress, the nun who was treasurer, and the thirteen-year-old Maria).[22]

Unfortunately, no cash account survives to document movement in and out of Peri's cash box. He probably kept a cashbook or a journal where some of this activity would be recorded, but nothing survives. As *camerlengo* at the Wool Guild, however, he used its cashbox for his own personal transactions, just as businessmen used the cashbox at their place of business for their private affairs (because this reduced the necessity of handling cash personally). Such institutions thus functioned somewhat as a bank, a central place away from one's home where clients could go to pay bills or be paid. Peri's use of the guild's facilities is documented for the years 1630 to 1633 by the cash account in the one surviving *stracciafoglio*, which was the last of the many he must have gone through during his tenure at the guild.[23] On those occasions when the peasants who worked his land made sales, they sometimes deposited Peri's share of the proceeds at the guild. Thus his account records cash payments made from the sale of a calf, sheep, wine, grain, and raw silk. Likewise, people who rented one of his urban properties or owed him an annuity from a *censo* sometimes made payments in the same way. Peri himself made payments out of this account for taxes, for legal expenses, for work on his villa at Ripoli, for a doctor who treated one of his sons, for any number of things he needed for his family (a book and felt hats for his sons, ribbons for his daughters, two chickens for his son who was a priest, shares in the Monte for his daughters who were nuns), and for his home (two silver saltcellars, wool and ticking for the bolster and pillows of a new bed, black and white silk fringes for use in a new kitchen). In Chapter 4 we shall return to the *stracciafoglio* to examine the things he bought for himself. In short, the personal account kept in an official guild account book functioned something like a personal current account, giving us the one glimpse we have of this man's daily activity in the local marketplace. The account also suggests the high level of trust placed in guild and other officials to keep the books straight (we shall see in Chapter 4 an example of what could happen when they did not).

However limited Peri's use of banks may have been by modern standards, the ledgers and associated documents reveal his familiarity with major

22. Ledger A, fols. 50, 53 (1600), 68 (1605), 87 (1611 etc.), 122v (1620).
23. LC 3915, fols. 1, 10, 13, 17, 31, 38, 42, 56.

banking practices: deposits and withdrawals, bank transfers, international payments, and exchange and "rechange" for borrowing and investing funds (a practice examined in the following section). Peri, like many Florentines and not just the city's famed merchant bankers, was market wise: he knew how to use banks and how to handle his money intelligently and knowledgeably through them. But the question that now follows is how successful he was in using his money as an investor.

Investments and Employment

Peri's investment history is obviously conditioned by the amount of disposable wealth he had to invest, and it was only with the dowry that came to him on his first marriage in 1592 that he had a significant sum of money available. Yet, to go back to the opening of his first ledger, the previous ten years of his life are not uninteresting, for what he did with the little money he was able to accumulate tells us something about the opportunities available to an investor with very limited means.

Having apparently inherited nothing from his parents, Peri was nevertheless able to improve his economic status in those early years, as we have seen. He certainly did not accomplish this just through the salaries he was earning as a musician. One suspects, of course, that he occasionally received something additional by way of commissions for special performances or for his compositions, but such fees were generally not large enough to enable him to make a major investment (though we shall see some possible exceptions below). For savings, there were deposit institutions—above all, the Monte di Pietà and the state *monti*—but opportunities for investing passively in the city's enterprises were limited. Peri's first documented investments, in 1585, point to two of those outlets (the money perhaps coming from the "donation" to him made by his cousin Cesare when he became a friar). In January he took out a bill of exchange with Jacopo di Tommaso Martelli & Partners, bankers, and when it returned after three months he invested it in Lorenzo Michelozzi & Partners, wool manufacturers. The next investments we hear about are in land, but here the modest amounts of money he spent (*fl.*76 in 1586 followed by *fl.*191 over the next five years) limited his acquisitions to small parcels in a remote place—at Rostolena, far from the city in the Mugello, on the lower slopes of the Tuscan Apennines. The farm on the outskirts of the city at San Marco Vecchio of which he took possession in 1588 significantly increased the land under his personal administration, but it required no capital outlay, only a long-time commitment to pay an annual rent—itself an indication of a certain economic stability.

Then came the dowries, three in a decade, the first two consisting entirely of cash: in 1592 he received *fl.*2,000 immediately, and the second dowry, in early 1602, brought him *fl.*600 within two years (with the remaining balance of *fl.*1,320 paid in installments more or less annually over nine years). The investments following these cash influxes can be divided into three categories. The first is the cloth industry, both wool and silk, the major forward sector of the economy that directed its production to foreign markets and therefore brought wealth into the city. The second category of investments we can call financial instruments, by which are meant devices to raise capital through agreements between two parties involving a binding monetary exchange. Within Peri's portfolio these were, in the private sphere, *censi* (a type of annuity) and bills of exchange, and in the public sphere, state bonds. The final investment category is real estate, both urban and rural. Investments of this last kind were for the most part permanent, designed to create an inheritable patrimony. They were also the most substantial of Peri's investments.

In going through this survey, the reader's expectations should be tempered by the word of caution about our sources raised at the beginning of this book: Peri did not keep accounts—no Florentine did—to keep track of his investments in a systematic analytical way: to know how much they were worth at any given moment, what rate of return they yielded, how they performed over time, or what his overall patrimony looked like. And it is not easy, if indeed even possible, to know any of these things from what he recorded about his investments. Here, too, we find ourselves up against a prominent characteristic of the economic culture of this major center of premodern capitalism: its failure to recognize the full potential of double entry for drawing balances that facilitate thorough analysis of profits, losses, assets, and liabilities over any given period.

Cloth Industries

The cloth industries (wool and silk) drove the Florentine economy. They employed perhaps as much as a third of the city's workforce; they alone in the manufacturing sector directed almost all production to foreign markets; and the profits brought home from sales abroad provided the flow of wealth into the local market that fed the growth and development of the city's economy from the thirteenth century onward. The miracle of this success lay in the achievement of all this notwithstanding the complete dependence of the industries on the importation of their basic raw materials from faraway places, and on the sale of their products in equally distant but different places; behind this miracle were the city's famed merchant bankers, who went abroad to build up the international networks through which this traffic in raw materials and finished products flowed. The Florentine wool industry grew up in the thirteenth century, the silk industry at the end of the fourteenth century, and both were famed for the superior quality of their products. At the time of Peri's birth these industries were going strong, but he was to live out his life during a period when they underwent fundamental changes as a result of the extraordinary but geographically uneven expansion of the European economy during the sixteenth century. Exports of wool cloth fell off so rapidly at the end of the first decade of the seventeenth century that there is a tendency to talk about the industry's collapse. The silk industry continued to prosper, but it did so by shifting its production from the most luxurious velvets and "cloths of gold" (*drappi d'oro*, made with gold and silver threads) to simple taffetas and satins, from the topmost end of the luxury market to its bottom. Given the almost complete lack of research on these industries, however, neither development is well understood.

The structure of both industries was basically the same, and it was such that someone like Peri, of middling status with only a modest amount of money available, had a reasonably good chance of finding a manufacturing firm in which he could invest. Firms probably numbered around 150 at any one time in Florence (100 producing wool and half as many again producing silk); they were organized as partnerships that lasted three to five years; reorganization often brought a change of partners; partners included passive investors from outside the industry; and individual investments ranged from several hundred to several thousand florins—all of which added up to a class of investors whose investments ranged widely in value and whose ranks were highly fluid and not closed. Those ranks were not entered through a formal, impersonal agency such as a broker or a central institution comparable to the modern stock market. Investment openings depended, instead, on the personal initiative of the major investors who organized the partnerships, and these men worked through their own networks of relatives, friends, and neighbors (to refer to the *parenti*, *amici*, and *vicini* that Florentine historians have long seen as constituting the most basic networks in the city), but also through business associates and clients of various kinds, as well as brokers. These networks are not often discernible, but they emerge clearly enough in Peri's investment history, for as we shall see, several of the opportunities in the cloth industries that opened up to him came by way of his personal acquaintance with two of the major entrepreneurs encountered earlier, Giovambattista Michelozzi and Jacopo Corsi, as well as with his "dear friend" Francesco Brunacci. Moreover, this history reveals another characteristic of investments in cloth production: they were subject to frequent renewals, shifts, and withdrawals as a result of the kaleidoscopic partnership structure of the manufacturing sector of the economy.[24]

Peri made his first investment in the wool industry early in his career, as we have seen. On 6 July 1585 he handed over *fl*.300 to Giovambattista Michelozzi to be invested in the firm of the latter's nephew, Lorenzo Michelozzi & Partners, wool manufacturers, and Peri notes the specific place on the firm's books where he is credited for the investment. He does not tell us what form the investment in the wool company took, but it was probably a share as a partner, since his quota of the profits was to be based on his share in the total capital of the firm. Nor does he make any reference to the performance of the investment.[25]

Twelve years later, on 15 August 1596, Peri used *fl*.2,000 then in the hands of (*in mano di*) Michelozzi to invest in a silk firm that operated in the name of the latter's other nephew, Francesco. Again, both he and Michelozzi kept a signed copy of the agreement; and again, Peri notes the specific place in the firm's books where he is credited for the investment. He was a formal partner in the firm, and he opened a specific account for it in his ledger. This account shows that the firm ceased operations in 1605 and that in its liquidation, from 15 October 1605 to 26 January 1608, Peri was paid *fl*.2,368. 13*s*., all of it, except for two relatively small cash payments of *fl*.50 each, in the form of transfers of credit to his bank account (*voltatomi in banco*). These payments in cash and bank credits represent a 23.4 percent return on an investment made a decade

---

24. Notwithstanding the fundamental importance of cloth production to the Florentine economy and the controversy about its performance at this time, there is no study of the class of investors in the industries, let alone a statistical analysis of the phenomena surveyed in this paragraph.

25. Ledger A, fol. 100v.

earlier, but Peri's accounts cannot be taken at face value for this kind of detail. In any event, he probably also received his share of the other asset of the firm, silk cloth. In an arrangement made in 1602 for the settlement of a credit of *fl.*100 he had with the painter Domenico di Girolamo Salucci for having stood guarantor for him, the latter agreed that his wife would work some silk Peri had in his shop (Peri specifies *della mia bottega*); three years later, on 8 December 1605 and 22 January 1606, Peri opened accounts in the names of silk weavers, with debits for the purchase of unworked camlets he had received in the division (*spartizione*) of stock in the liquidation of the Michelozzi firm.[26]

In the meantime, Peri made two investments in the wool industry that involved him actively in the business. With the first investment, in fact, we see him as what we might call a venture capitalist, at least with respect to a single operation. On 23 January 1599, on the premises of the wool company of his cousin Domenico di Lorenzo Peri, he and Domenico agreed to speculate on the purchase and resale of a certain quantity of wool, and he opened an account in his ledger in the name of Domenico to keep track of the affair. Peri invested *fl.*200 up front in cash in the venture for a one-fourth share of the profits, but later, in July, Domenico came to Peri's house to tell him that the wool bought for Peri (*per mio conto*) had cost more than *fl.*200. So Peri immediately gave him *fl.*40 in cash, all that he had on hand at the moment (*non havevo altro che li detti fi.40, quali li detti, e li portò via di contanti*); and in December he transferred an additional *fl.*60 he had on account with Francesco Michelozzi & Partners, silk manufacturers, to the Capponi bank to be credited to Domenico. These two additional payments brought Peri's investment to *fl.*300. There is some confusion in the entries on this account, however, and it is not possible to know how this speculative venture ended.[27]

Peri was not simply a passive investor in this operation, leaving the initiative to his cousin the wool manufacturer. From the entries Peri made in his ledger recording these transactions emerges other information that indicates a certain involvement in the industry. The additional investment of *fl.*60 made in December 1599 took the form of a credit he had transferred from a firm of silk manufacturers, and the credit Domenico gave Peri for the total investment of *fl.*300 took the form of a transfer to a debit in Peri's favor on the

26. Ledger A, fols. 70, 72, 106v, 107, 111; the bank account is on fols. 67 and 80.
27. Ledger A, fol. 42 (account of Domenico Peri).

books of another wool manufacturer, Francesco and Leonardo Ganucci & Partners, which, in fact, was the buyer in the speculative venture in which Peri and his cousin had engaged. Moreover, Peri opened a separate account in the name of the Ganucci firm for this one transaction, debiting it for *fl*.473. 16*s*.—the value of the wool supplied by and purchased from Peri himself (*hauta e compra' da me*). And when Ganucci paid Peri, Peri transferred the profit to Domenico's brother, Dino di Lorenzo (with whom, we have seen, Peri had close relations).[28] The shifts in book debits and credits among these four parties, made without going through a bank, illustrate the important function of offsetting in business practice of the time.

Peri entered the closing balance on the accounts of both Domenico Peri and the Ganucci firm in October 1600. Meanwhile, in August he had taken the job of cashier in another wool firm, Giulio Della Rena, Alessandro Fiorini & Partners, which paid him *fl*.2 a month. This partnership was near the end of its contract, however; when it was renewed, on 1 November, Peri entered into it. From November 1600 to June 1601 he made payments totaling *fl*.1,000 (200 of which he borrowed from his cousin Domenico) for his share of the capital of the firm, which now took the name of Giulio Della Rena, Vincenzo Fiorini & Partners; and he opened an account for it in his ledger. The major investor in this firm was the bank of the brothers Jacopo and Bardo di Giovanni Corsi, and in fact the articles of association survive in that family's archive. The capital of the company was *fl*.7,000, to which the Corsi bank contributed *fl*.2,250; *fl*.2,000 more came from two women (Lisabetta Galilei and Maddalena Falcucci, each participating for *fl*.1,000) whose investment was most likely shepherded by the Corsi; and *fl*.750 was put in by Alessandro Fiorini, who was associated with the Corsi in other business ventures. The other investors were Peri, with *fl*.1,000, and Baccio Salomoni, for another *fl*.1,000. The partnership was to last five years (the duration of the previous contract), and the manager (*ministro*) was Giulio Della Rena, who also owned the premises out of which the firm was to operate. Although Della Rena contributed nothing to the capital, he was to have a 20 percent share in the profits, and clearly he was the professional cloth manufacturer in the venture. Of the other person who appears in the name of the firm, Vincenzo Fiorini, nothing is known except that he came from a family associated with wool companies in which the Corsi invested, as we shall see; he was

28. Ledger A, fol. 49 (account of Ganucci & Partners).

most likely a minor and a dependent (perhaps the son) of Alessandro Fiorini, who appears in the name of the previous partnership and who was still a partner in the new firm.[29]

In the organization of this firm are to be noted two other business practices of the time, alongside the offsetting mentioned above. In contrast to practice in the fourteenth and fifteenth centuries, at this later date it was not unusual for firms to carry the name of a noninvesting manager rather than the names of the principal investing partners; thus the Corsi name does not appear in the public presence of either of these firms. Moreover, firms still used the traditional way of fixing investors' shares of the profits not as percentages (which were used for other kinds of calculations) but as so many *soldi* and *denari* (and fractions thereof) for each *lira*—an extraordinarily complicated method of calculation well illustrated by the arrangements made by this firm. Peri was down for a quota of one-seventh of the profits, but only after Della Rena was paid 4 *soldi* on every *lira* (or one-fifth) for his service (*persona*) to the firm; and so Peri's share of total profits—one-seventh of four-fifths—is defined not as a fraction of the total or as a percentage but as 2 *soldi* $3^3/_7$ *denari* out of the 16 *soldi* remaining of every *lira* (which consisted of 20 *soldi*, or 240 *denari*), a fraction that works out to $^{12}/_{105}$ (we would express it as 11.41 percent).[30]

Peri's major investment in this specific business enterprise with the Corsi calls for a comment that takes the discussion much beyond his personal financial interests and into the social realm in which he moved. We have already discussed his personal relation with Jacopo Corsi, one of the city's most important patrons of musicians, outside of the grand-ducal court. Through his investment in the Corsi company, which he could hardly have made without the approval of the Corsi brothers—indeed, they very likely took the initiative in opening up this investment possibility to him—Peri plugged into one of the city's largest business complexes. Besides the bank through which the Corsi invested in the Della Rena–Fiorini firm, they also had a commercial company that operated in Sicily (a major source of raw silk for the city's industry), and a cluster of industrial firms producing both wool and

29. Ledger A, fols. 50, 66, 82 (account of the firm), and fols. 50, 53 (accounts with his cousins for the loan); ASF, Guicciardini Corsi Salviati, filza 1, no. 27 (the articles of association).

30. For the business practices mentioned above, see Goldthwaite, "Le aziende seriche e il mondo degli affari a Firenze alla fine del '500," 309–10.

silk cloth. Over the six months preceding the organization of the Della Rena–Fiorini firm, the Corsi brothers invested *fl.*13,750 in two other wool firms (one a dye house); the day the contract for the Della Rena firm was drawn up they invested *fl.*8,250 in another wool firm; and over the following year, until September 1601, they invested an additional *fl.*28,300 in two silk partnerships and a *battiloro* firm (producers of gold and silver threads and also silk fabrics)—altogether investing *fl.*52,550 in seven firms with a total capital of *fl.*73,000. In January 1602 they set up a major commercial firm in Messina for the purchase of raw silk, and meanwhile they were also operating a bank.[31] A portfolio like this one, with its cluster of so many different firms within the cloth industries, marks a significant change in investment strategy over the course of the sixteenth century, for it represented not the expansion of the sector but the increased investment in it by some investors. In other words, given the sector's structure in the preindustrial economy, men who increased their investment in it organized more, not larger, firms. It would be difficult to find investors in the fifteenth century who had more than three firms (the number in the Medici portfolio), but such clusters under the same controlling ownership had grown since then, although no others as large as that of the Corsi have yet come to light. Growth of portfolios might have meant more than just increased investment, however. Since each firm had different minor partners, like Peri, the growth of a cluster of firms brought that many more investors into the orbit of the incorporating portfolio and its owner. What implications this had for the society as well as the economy of Florence is an unexamined question. The Corsi might have thereby tightened their bonds with Peri, for instance, either assuring themselves of his loyalty to them or assuring him of their continuing support—or both.

Peri was more than a partner in the Della Rena–Fiorini firm: he was also its cashier, continuing on in his job with the earlier partnership. The articles of association charge Alessandro Fiorini with keeping the ledger, and Peri with keeping the cash account (for which he was again paid *fl.*2 per month), and go on to specify that he could not invest or loan the firm's money without

31. ASF, Guicciardini Corsi Salviati, filza 1, nos. 24–32. The cluster of Corsi firms still lacks its historian, despite the abundance of business documents in the family archive housed in ASF. Their bank has been studied in Goldthwaite, "Banking in Florence at the End of the Sixteenth Century"; and the firm in Messina, in Hoshino, "Messina e l'arte della lana fiorentina nei secoli XVI–XVII."

the approval of the partners, that cash had to be kept on hand, and that breach would invoke a penalty of 12 percent interest.[32] His task was to handle the cashbox, which involved keeping the cash accounts of the organization, not a difficult job, we have seen, but in this instance a highly sensitive one given what was at stake. Sometimes a wool firm, which with its large work-force handled considerable amounts of money, required a security deposit of several hundred florins from the father when it hired a boy just out of an abacus school to take on the job. Or instead, as with Peri, it could assign the task to one of the firm's partners. For example, in the wool firm of Cristofano di Tommaso Brandolini & Partners, operating in the 1580s, Brandolini himself, who was partner and manager, took on the additional job of cashier.[33] It is from the account for his own firm that Peri opened in Ledger A, where he enters his salary periodically, that we learn about his employment in the preceding partnership; and the salary entries continue for the next three years, until October 1603. It does not tell us what we would like to know, however: how the earlier firm came to recognize Peri's qualification for the job. In any event, this active involvement in a company in which he was just a very minor partner may have heightened his sense of ownership, for in an account he opened on his own books in the name of another dependent of the firm, who borrowed some money from him, he refers to the *bottega mia d'arte di lana*.

Peri's annual salary of *fl.*24 at the Della Rena–Fiorini firm—the only salary we have record of for his work in the private sector—was in line with the industry's standard; Brandolini's was *fl.*30. It was a good wage for a beginning apprentice, but not a living one for an adult of Brandolini's or Peri's status, for whom it represented only part-time work. For Brandolini it was an extra task for someone who was already on the scene as manager. For Peri it is impossible to know what demands were made on his time. He may have gone to the firm's quarters only on Saturdays, payday for its employees. Other than that, payments out of the cashbox of a wool firm would have been quite irregular and not frequent; accordingly, keeping account of money moving in and out of it was only a very occasional activity. Peri may have stopped by on

32. ASF, Guicciardini Corsi Salviati, filza 1, no. 27: *non possa fidare né prestare danari di detta ragione salvo che per li negoti a quella spetanti, con obbrigho di tenere pronti li danari che avessi di detta ragione in servitio e comodo di essa, e contrafacendo ne paghi l'interessi di dodici percento l'anno; e per suo salario et provisione abbi avere ducati ventiquattro di moneta l'anno.*
33. Goldthwaite, "The Florentine Wool Industry in the Late Sixteenth Century," 531.

other days long enough to bring the cashbook up to date, entering transactions effected by someone else and then reported to him. The reality of what went on within a wool shop—or the shop of any other industrial operation—during a normal workday is not something that economic historians have studied except at the most general level.

We know nothing about the performance of Della Rena, Fiorini & Partners. The articles of association specify that the accounts were to remain the property of Della Rena (although he had to make them available to any of the partners for inspection), and they do not remain in the Corsi archive, which is notable for the quantity of account books documenting the brothers' numerous business ventures. Peri's accounts, however, hint at serious problems. The last payment of Peri's salary is dated October 1603, and the firm may have shut down operations at that time, two years before the partnership was scheduled to dissolve. Credit entries continuing to 1605, taking the form of cloth, cash, and, mostly, credits in the Michelozzi–Ricci bank, brought Peri's total altogether to *fl.*1,071. 16*s.*10*d.*; but considering that these credits included payment of his salary for thirty-nine months (*fl.*78), he had not quite recouped all of his investment by that time. Subsequently he posted two small entries for his share in a further division of credits among the partners; and in 1608 he closed the account with a credit balance (representing a loss) of *fl.*37. 9*s.*11*d.* We get no information about what went wrong with this firm, but the partners seem to have held Della Rena personally responsible for some of its problems, for on 16 June 1605 Peri opened an account in Della Rena's name personally with a debit entry of *fl.*79. 7*s.*, Peri's share of the debt for which the partners were holding Della Rena liable. However, one of the partners, Baccio Salomoni, held Peri responsible for this debt and filed formal charges against him at the Mercanzia. When the court decided in his favor, Peri further debited Della Rena's account with what it had cost him—*fl.*3. 12*s.*11*d.*—in legal fees to defend himself. At this point the account showed a total debit balance of almost *fl.*83. But apparently having doubts about the possibility of collecting anything from this unreliable debtor (*non troppo buon debitore*), Peri sold the debt for *fl.*58. 18*s.*3*d.* (about two-thirds its face value) and closed the account: a transaction that offers further evidence of the free flow of negotiable paper in the Florentine marketplace.[34]

---

34. Ledger A, fols. 69 (account of Della Rena), 115 (*ricordo*). The official decision in Peri's favor is found in ASF, Mercanzia 7647 (*sentenzie*), document dated 23 December 1605; on the

On 8 June 1605, less than two years after collecting his last salary from the Della Rena–Fiorini firm, Peri opened an account for another investment as a partner in a wool firm, this time with the firm of Francesco Michelozzi (with whom Peri had already invested in a silk company), which may have been the successor to the wool firm of Francesco's bother, Lorenzo, in which Peri had invested in 1585. The company began operations on 2 January, and the manager was his cousin, Domenico di Lorenzo Peri. Peri's investment amounted to *fl.*500, made in payments extending from March to July. There are no entries on the credit side of this account, however—only a note made almost twenty years later, on 10 December 1624, stating that he still had a credit with the firm. That credit continued to be carried on the books of his heirs through to Ledger F, opened in 1640.[35] We know as little about this firm as we do about both the earlier Michelozzi firms, one wool and the other silk, in which Peri had invested: in his ledger Peri did not keep track of his investments in any of them—confirmation of the limited functions of accounting practice at the time, for all of its technical sophistication.

Nor did Peri keep much of a record of the firm he himself opened on 15 February 1609—Jacopo di Antonio Peri & Partners, wool manufacturers. He invested *fl.*2,000, and the only partner that can be identified was Francesco Michelozzi & Partners, bankers. Peri kept the cash account, but on his own books he records little about the performance of the firm. Much, if not all, of the cloth produced by this firm was sent to another wool firm, Francesco Brunacci & Partners, in what must have been a private arrangement, for Peri opened an account in the name of this firm for two major consignments of cloth produced by his own company but belonging to him personally: one for *fl.*719. 18*s.*10*d.* for cloth he received on 1 March 1610 as part of the distribution of profits, and one for *fl.*2,752. 4*s.*7*d.* on 5 March 1611 for the distribution of cloth owed to the Michelozzi bank but bought from the bank by Peri. From 3 December 1611 through to the following August the Brunacci firm paid Peri a total of *fl.*3,926 3*s.*8*d.* in cash and bank transfers. The dates of these entries would indicate that Peri's company had a short life, and that perhaps, one way

---

same day the court issued another decision in favor of Peri's claim of *fl.*79. 7*s.* owed him by Della Rena.

35. Ledger A, fol. 68; Ledger B, fol. 30; Ledger E, fol. 7.

or another, it was folded into the Brunacci firm. In any event, we do not know what his profits were from the venture.[36]

In the 1624 *ricordo* cited above, Peri notes that he still had credits with his own firm as well as with the wool and silk firms of Francesco Michelozzi. Again, on 15 October 1626, he opened a single account in Ledger B in the names of these three firms in which he still had credits, but he entered no credits and no debits on it—only a note stating that the books of all three firms remained in the hands of Margherita Michelozzi, guardian of Francesco Michelozzi's heirs, presumably because the Michelozzi had controlling interest also in Peri's firm. The firm is probably best regarded as one of those in the Michelozzi portfolio of investments that carried the name of a minor partner, just as the two Della Rena–Fiorini firms were in the Corsi portfolio; Peri goes on to say that when the books are finally closed and final balances struck, he ought to appear as a creditor of about *fl.*25, although he notes this more as an aide-mémoire (*E questo serva per notizia*) and does not go into any of the particulars. A little later, on 10 December, he made a *ricordo* to the same effect, that he was a creditor of the company operating under his name, and that none of the three companies had been completely liquidated (*son creditore nella ragione di lana che cantava in mio nome, cioè Jacopo Peri e compagni, lanaioli; e nessuna di queste tre ragioni non si son finite di saldare*).[37] In this period firms often kept their books opened for years after ending operations, punctuality in payment of debts not being a characteristic of market behavior. Of course, Peri had to keep his books for legal reasons, but after so many years he may also have been engaging in wishful thinking. In any event, that the books for his own firm, as he states, were in the hands of the Michelozzi would indicate that, yet once again, he had an important relation with this family.

On 15 February 1610, just a year after setting up his own wool firm, Peri invested *fl.*423. 14*s.*11*d.* in a partnership with Francesco Brunacci, the wool-cloth manufacturer mentioned above, for the operation of a dye shop working with madder (*guado*), the basic dye used in the wool industry. The two did not, however, draw up formal, written articles of association because they first wanted to see how things worked out (*nella qual ragione non si fece*

36. Ledger A, fols. 86–88 (accounts of Peri's firm, of the Brunacci firm, and of the Michelozzi bank).

37. Ledger B, fol. 30; Ledger A, fol. 68.

scritta per veder prima se ci tornava il conto); and since matters did not, in fact, go as well as they hoped, they ceased production twenty months later, on 12 October 1611. Nevertheless, in the single credit entry on the account for this firm in his ledger, which on 6 December 1612 balanced and closed the account, Peri registers a comprehensive total for the many payments he had received over the period for reimbursements (*per tanti rimborsatomi alla giornata in più partite*) and also a profit of "about" *fl*.180. Moreover, as he tells us in a *ricordo*, the profits from this company, together with those from his own wool company paid for the farm at Ripoli he bought in 1612 for *fl*.2,000.[38]

A detail of particular interest about this partnership is the way Peri identifies it on the account for it that he opened in his ledger: Niccolò di Jacopo Peri & Partners, woad dyers. His son Niccolò, however, was born on 14 August 1610, six months after the agreement between Peri and Brunacci in February. Peri did not open the account in his books until a year later, on 12 October 1611 (the day the company ceased production), and apparently in the meantime he had decided that the firm—which had no formal legal status as such—should carry the name of this son, whose career he perhaps planned to direct into the industry. And many years later, Niccolò did indeed find employment in the Brunacci wool firm.

Peri's complex interactions with Brunacci through his own wool firm and, at the same time, through this informal partnership for a dye house, suggests that rather than always just a passive investor, he could be something of an entrepreneur in Florence's leading industry. In these ventures, however, Peri most likely depended on personal ties to his partner, for Brunacci is the only person outside Peri's family who emerges from all this accounting material as being particularly close to him. He is described as *mio amico caro* when mentioned as the godfather to Peri's daughter Felice, born on 16 November 1613. A few years later Brunacci was one of the guarantors who backed Peri's lifetime appointment at the Arte della Lana.[39]

The dye company was Peri's last recorded investment in the wool industry. But after a break of several years, in November 1617, he put up *fl*.1,000 to become a partner in a silk firm, Arcangelo Innori & Partners (the same Innori through which he was to make payments for bond purchases in Rome).

---

38. All the information about this enterprise comes from the account in Ledger A, fol. 86.
39. Ledger A, fol. 120.

Table 2.1. Investments of Jacopo Peri in the cloth industries

Date	Investment (florins)	Company
1585, 6 Jul	300	Lorenzo Michelozzi & Partners, wool manufacturers
1596, 15 Aug	2,000	Francesco Michelozzi & Partners, silk manufacturers
1599, 23 Jan	300	speculative venture with Domenico Peri
1600, 1 Nov	1,000	Della Rena, Fiorini & Partners, wool manufacturers
1605, 8 Jun	500	Francesco Michelozzi & Partners, wool manufacturers
1609, 15 Feb	2,000	Jacopo di Antonio Peri & Partners, wool manufacturers
1610, 15 Feb	423	Niccolò di Jacopo Peri & Partners, dyers
1617, 12 Nov	1,000	Arcangelo Innori & Partners, silk manufacturers

This company began operations on 1 August 1617 and lasted five years. Peri opened an account in the name of this firm, but since the only entries on it are debits for his investment, we know nothing about its performance.

Peri's investments in the cloth industries are summarized in Table 2.1. He directed most of his investments to the wool industry, and these are concentrated in the first decade of the seventeenth century. Perhaps by 1610 he was discouraged from further investment of this kind because of the troubles he had had with the Della Rena–Fiorini manufacturing firm and with his own dye house, as well as problems that may have prevented both his and the Michelozzi wool firms from closing their books in a more timely fashion. Or perhaps his profits from this industrial sector did not meet his expectations: we shall see that whatever profits he made in these ventures do not seem to have had an impact on the overall history of his investment portfolio. All this may have been nothing more than bad luck or management problems particular to each enterprise, but the investments might also be read as signals of something going wrong in an industry that had long been the solid foundation of the Florentine economy. The situation just after the turn of the century, at the time Peri was investing, must have still seemed favorable, as it attracted investments from businessmen of the stature of the Michelozzi, the Corsi (who put fl.24,250 in the industry in 1600–1601), and the Riccardi (who had *fl.*19,000 invested in the industry in 1600).[40] Yet around 1610 the industry took a sharp turn for the worse when demand dried up in the markets abroad on which it depended. Traditional wisdom—never challenged by research into the subject—has it that costs were too high in Florence, and that Florentine products could not compete with those of the rising Venetian industry in the traditional Near Eastern markets, and with the so-called new draperies being produced in northwestern Europe.

But the Florentine silk industry, in which Peri invested in 1617, continued to prosper.[41] It had successfully survived increasing competition in foreign markets by shifting its production to lower-quality—though still luxury— fabrics that sold more easily, but it did not undergo an expansion, and its workforce, for the most part less skilled and low paid, hardly overlapped that of the wool industry. Although Peri made at least two investments in silk firms, the industry had always been less accessible than wool. There were many fewer companies and therefore fewer openings for outsiders to come in as partners, and generally firms required more substantial investments, since the raw material cost so much more than wool. Furthermore, because demand abroad was somewhat more sporadic, it seems that profits were often delayed, sometimes for many years; an investor in a silk company could not expect a steady or quick return on his capital.[42]

Active involvement in the wool industry also prepared Peri for the job he took with his appointment, on 28 March 1618, as comptroller (*camerlengo*) for the Arte della Lana. He probably owed his unusual lifetime tenure at the guild to his social standing in court circles. At the time of his appointment, in fact, he was anxious to have a government position of some kind or another in order to increase the income he needed to support a large and rapidly growing family, and he appealed to some of the most influential people he knew to

40. Malanima, *I Riccardi di Firenze*, 98.

41. The best overview of the course of the wool industry from this time forward is still that of Malanima, *La decadenza di un'economia cittadina*. For more detailed analyses of the industry in this, its last phase, see Chorley, "*Rascie* and the Florentine Cloth Industry during the Sixteenth Century," and Goldthwaite, "The Florentine Wool Industry in the Late Sixteenth Century." Malanima takes a long-term view also of the silk industry; for its adjustment to new market conditions that obtained for the later sixteenth century, see Goldthwaite, "Le aziende seriche e il mondo degli affari a Firenze alla fine del '500."

42. Goldthwaite, "Le aziende seriche e il mondo degli affari a Firenze alla fine del '500," 305.

help him. On 27 May 1617 he wrote to Duke Ferdinando Gonzaga of Mantua asking for a recommendation to the grand duke that he receive an appointment to an office in a *podesteria* or a *vicariato* (Letter 20); he must have
made the same request of his former singing pupil, Duchess Caterina de'
Medici Gonzaga, although such a letter does not survive. The duke accom-
modated him with a letter sent on 30 June, noting his desire to help Peri and
hoping that the grand duke would grant him one of the offices he had requested (the duke lists them again at the foot of his letter) so as to support his
family, both out of piety and in recognition of his abilities.[43] Peri soon realized, however, that he had made a faux pas: he was told by Grand Duchess
Christine that he had submitted his request too soon, according to a rule that
required a six-month gap between holding offices, presumably meaning two
tenures in the same category of offices, and in fact Peri at the time was *podestà*
(or chief judge) at Pontassieve. The grand duchess, however, held out a strong
hope of a positive outcome at the appropriate time. Peri explained all this in
a letter to Duchess Caterina on 8 January 1618 (Letter 21), the day on which
the six-month period expired (he said), also apologizing for having put her to
such trouble earlier when he should have known better. He repeated his request on 29 January (Letter 22), presumably because he had not received a
response in one of the past two postal deliveries from Mantua—clearly he
was impatient, and probably unreasonably so in terms of the demands of etiquette. Meanwhile, he had prepared a draft of his own new petition to the
grand duchess and showed it to her secretary, Andrea Cioli, before submit-
ting a final version on 29 January. That petition does not survive, but Peri's
cover letter to Cioli does (Letter 23). Here he asks the secretary to make additional points in his favor: he had "served" since the age of ten (he seems to
be counting from before his appointment at SS. Annunziata), he had been
appointed by Grand Duchess Johanna of Austria to teach singing to the
Medici princesses, and his family had all the qualifications for patrician status. Peri told Cioli, however, that he had decided to remove from his draft

43. There is a minute in Mantua, Archivio di Stato, Archivio Gonzaga 2292: *Il desiderio che
tengo di giovar a Giacopo Peri detto il Zazzerino mi fa pregar Vostra Altezza a compiacersi di
promoverlo a qualche d'uno degli infrascritti Ufficij, acciochè col prestar buon servigio all'Altezza
Vostra possa anco sostener la sua numerosa famiglia, assicurandomi io che la pietà di Vostra Altezza haverà non meno riguardo al bisogno che alla capacità di detto Peri per sollevarlo con qualche trattenimento conveniente a lui . . .*

petition the fact that he was currently housing and teaching a young female singer (presumably with a view to court service).[44]

In these petitions, Peri's chief argument was the number of children he had to support: six sons and five daughters, for one of whom he was trying to put together the beginnings of a dowry.[45] He then went so far as to specify the offices given to citizens and gentlemen (*che si danno a cittadini e gentil huomini*) that interested him: they were all administrative posts in the Florentine territorial state that paid better than municipal ones but at the same time required a relatively fixed presence away from Florence. When he wrote his letter to Duke Ferdinando Gonzaga, Peri was, in fact, serving in such a post at Pontassieve. But he ended up with something closer to home: on 4 February he wrote ecstatically to Cioli about the favorable response he had received from the grand duchess, also thanking the secretary in extravagant terms (Letter 24), and on 28 March 1618 he was appointed comptroller at the Lana. The letters he wrote on 23 April to both the duke and the duchess of Mantua thanking them for their support indicate that he owed this appointment to their help (Letters 25, 26); he also told the duchess that this "most noble office" had the further advantage of allowing him to stay in Florence and therefore continue to serve the court (as a musician, it is implied). And Peri presumably got even more than what he had requested, for the position carried a lifetime tenure. His predecessor had held the office for at least several years, but his position had been formally renewed every year, whereas Peri's tenure was (as he says) *a vita*, subject to annual review only with respect to the names of the guarantors who assumed surety for his performance.[46]

It can hardly be denied that Peri had the qualifications for the job, having by this time gained considerable experience working in the industry. His employment as cashier for both Della Rena, Fiorini & Partners and his own firm (and perhaps others), while not a management position, involved him in the everyday activity of the industry. Purchases of raw materials and sales of

---

44. This was Angelica Furini; see Chapter 3.

45. He actually had only ten living children, and he must have included among the five daughters he mentions his very first child by his present wife, who died after only a week.

46. ASF, Arte della Lana 308 (*Partiti, atti, sentenze*, 1615–23), fols. 60v–61: Peri's predecessor requests a discharge (*ha chiesto licentia*), and Peri is appointed. In this volume the annual renewals of the former's appointment go back two years (fols. 3v, 30v). The annual approval of Peri's guarantors are on fols. 74, 103, 137, 179, and in the following volumes (ASF, Arte della Lana 309–10).

finished products were transacted mostly through transfers on those books of the firm that a cashier did not keep. But workers and some suppliers had to be paid in cash, someone had to handle cash sales across the counter, and these movements in the cashbox needed to be tracked. An appointment at the guild, however, required considerably more attention and responsibility, since the guild was a major state institution representing the manufacturers in the city's most important industry. The comptroller's responsibilities are spelled out in great detail in a major reform of the guild, undertaken in 1589, that collapsed two older offices into one (now called the *camerlengo generale*), consolidating the mechanisms for collecting the guild's income from a large range of sources. The *camerlengo* was to collect all the income the guild had from fees charged for controlling regulated measurements of finished cloth, for marking bales with the guild's seal of approval, for cloth imports, and for matriculation in the guild; in addition he collected rents, returns from investments, and fines meted out by the guild court; and he was directly responsible for controlling the flow of income and expenditures related to the supply to the industry by the guild of woad, alum, ash, and other materials. In short, all income collected by the guild and all payments it made, at whatever level, were to go through him. He was to make payments only on receipt of official authorization, and he was to see that all income was deposited in the guild's account at the Monte di Pietà. And, of course, he had to supervise the accounting record of all this activity, and his accounts were subject to annual review. Peri's salary was set at *fl.*13 a month, out of which he was to pay one assistant *fl.*3 (which sometime before 1630 was raised to *fl.*5), and it was understood that from time to time he would also enjoy a bonus (*mancia*).[47] Finally, the reform required that the comptroller was to go to his office every day at an approved time; failure to do so would incur a fine.[48]

The guarantors who over the years put up surety for the honesty of Peri's administration were his former partner and friend Francesco di Vincenzo Brunacci, his cousins Dino and Luca di Lorenzo Peri, and three others—Cavaliere Giovanni Del Turco, Filippo di Piero Baldovini, and Bernardo di Antonio Miniati—who obviously had close relations with Peri, although we

47. He was paying his assistant *fl.*5 in 1630, when he opened the *stracciafoglio* he kept for his position at the Lana; LC 3912.

48. Cantini, *Legislazione toscana*, 12: "Riforma delle cose dell'Arte della Lana," 1589, cap. XI, 340–43.

know nothing about what they might have been save for Del Turco, a keen music patron and amateur composer who also had some kind of charge over the court musicians. Originally these guarantors assumed unlimited responsibility for Peri's financial administration, but on his request in 1621 that the liability be limited to *fl*.2,000, the guild authorities defined it for him, though not for his successors, as up to a collective *fl*.4,000. In recommending this stipulation to the grand duke, the guild purveyor (*provveditore*) emphasized Peri's "good qualities and also his sound abilities" (*le sue buone qualità, e anco ragionevoli facoltà sue*).[49]

None of the guild's accounts survives for this period to document Peri's work, but among his own documents is a waste-book (*stracciafoglio*) in which he kept records of the movement in the cashbox that he would have used in periodically updating the official cashbook of the guild.[50] This book, opened in 1630 and continuing into 1633, a few months before his death, has entries for payments related to the guild's purchase of woad and alum and to the operation of its fulling mills. The flow into the cashbox over the last fifteen months recorded in this book, from January 1632 to April 1633, amounted to, on average, *fl*.768 every month. Some idea of the nature of Peri's task in handling this level of income and expenditures and his work at it up to the very end comes in a note his son added in the final pages of the *stracciafoglio* some three months after Peri's death in August 1633. Dino listed the guild records still in the family's possession that he now, on 21 November, returned to the guild: four books of general income with accompanying documents; three income–expenditure journals for the purchase of woad and alum, also with accompanying documents; and a book of the guild's Conservadori (supervisors). The next day, on 22 November, Dino returned to the guild to make sure that these records had been correctly inventoried, and he was careful to take note of the exact reference to this effect in the guild records.

In sum, Peri's job as *camerlengo* of the Arte della Lana was close to a full-time job—even considering the rapid decline of the Florentine industry in the first decade of the century—and one requiring a degree of administrative skill besides a competence in accounting and a specialized knowledge of the

49. Corazzini, "Jacopo Peri e la sua famiglia," 50; a copy of the 1621 document is in LC 3912.

50. LC 3915.

industry. The salary of *fl.*120 a year was among the highest paid to any of the state's bureaucrats outside the court establishment. At the Monte di Pietà, the state bank with a staff of forty-two, only the general treasurer, at *fl.*144, earned more. Managers of the city's industrial firms earned much lower salaries, normally around *fl.*60–70 and rarely as much as *fl.*100 (although they usually also shared in the profits as partners).

We have seen that Peri dipped into the guild cashbox—as many businessmen at the time did through the current accounts opened in their name on the books of their businesses—for transactions, both receipts and payments, of an entirely personal nature, and in Chapter 4 we shall take another look at the *stracciafoglio* in this light.

Bills of Exchange

Among financial instruments as outlets for investment capital, the bill of exchange was traditionally the most common device at the disposal of Florentines; it had long been available through banks and was widely used as an instrument for international exchange. We have already noted how Peri used bills for this purpose. But the bill could also be manipulated as a credit instrument to circumvent the usury restriction that limited the loaning of money at explicit rates of interest. Banks used them for both loaning and borrowing money (the latter by accepting deposits, an essential banking function), and Peri at one time or another had recourse to banks for both purposes. Whatever its function, whether exchange or loan, the bank earned a small commission fee for the service.

Here is how the bill of exchange worked as a credit instrument. The bank issued a bill in Florence to exchange florins for marks, the money used at the international exchange fairs; it sent the bill to its correspondent at the international fair, usually held at Piacenza (but also elsewhere in Italy, although they were collectively called, for historical reasons, the fairs of Besançon), where the exchange was effected. Then, at the fair, the bank's agent turned around and bought florins by issuing another bill, which it sent back to Florence for collection. The difference, resulting from exchange rates varying over time, between the amount in florins of the first bill drawn in Florence and the amount of the one that returned to Florence hence payable in florins, was understood as the interest the money had gained in the ensuing interval, which one paid to the bank if it had drawn the bill for the sum of money it

had loaned, or which the bank paid if one had deposited money with the
bank for the bill. The bill, in short, was the bank's subterfuge for a direct loan
in one direction or the other: it circumvented the usury restriction by defining the interest not as a fixed rate but as the variable—and, in theory at least,
somewhat risky—play of exchange rates at the international fairs. And since
fairs were held regularly every three months, the "loans" had a fixed period
(called usance). Moreover, since the bank could renew a bill simply by drawing a new one on the return of one from abroad, it could extend a loan indefinitely, with the accumulated interest corresponding to the increase in the
value of the bills as they went back and forth (called exchange–rechange). In
the fourteenth century, however, all this apparatus became largely fictional-
ized (hence the term "fictitious exchange"): bills were no longer actually written and sent but instead simply were entries on the banker's books, and international bankers organized everything among themselves at the quarterly
so-called Besançon fairs (the term being itself a fiction). Maintaining at least
the fiction of exchange–rechange, however, was important in an economy
where the usury restriction had the moral and even legal authority of the
church behind it.[51]

Peri was fully familiar with the bill as a credit instrument. At least twice
he used it as a device to borrow money, thereby circumventing anti-usury
doctrine. In 1604, to pay the exceptionally large sum of *fl.*2,500 that he invested in his first *censo*, he borrowed the entire amount from Francesco Michelozzi, the nephew of Giovambattista. The Michelozzi–Ricci bank paid for
the *censo* and then, through a fictitious bill, put the full amount on the exchange, the arrangement being that the sum would remain on the exchange,
gaining value with each quarterly fair (representing the interest charged on
the loan), until Peri made payments to gradually reduce the amount of the
bill and eventually extinguish the balance owed. Peri had the assurance from
the bank—probably a personal favor to him, considering his long attachment
to the Michelozzi—that the total cost of the loan (i.e., the accumulated profit
earned on the exchange that increased the size of the bill with each quarterly
fair) would not exceed an annual interest rate of 6⅓ percent. He reduced what
he owed on this loan in several payments over the course of the following four
years, in the end paying an annual average of just over 5 percent interest on the

---

51. A succinct and recent survey of the European bill market for this period, complete with
bibliography, can be found in Denzel, *Handbook of World Exchange Rates*, xxiv–xliii.

loan.[52] In 1606, Peri took out another loan by putting a bill on the exchange, this time acting for his brother-in-law, Giovanni Fortini. Giovanni, wanting to loan *fl.*200 to his brother, Girolamo, to get him out of prison, where his legal problems had landed him, requested that Peri borrow the money through a bill purchased in his, Fortini's, name from any merchant banker and drawn on any fair (*piazza*) Peri chose, and to be kept on the exchange for three years. Peri stood witness to Girolamo's promise to reimburse his brother at the end of the period for the full amount accumulated during the exchange-rechange operation, including commission charges.[53] Indeed, Peri may well have initiated this operation as a way of helping Girolamo without drawing on his own funds, given that Giovanni—who, we have seen, had severe physical if not mental problems—is hardly likely to have been competent enough to execute it.

Peri, however, used bills of exchange more frequently as investment instruments by buying a bill from a bank—in other words, depositing money with the bank for a return. His record of transactions related to the various investments already mentioned reveals occasions when he drew on funds he had in bills of exchange, and at times the bills served him as a temporary way to keep money working during the gaps between his other, more long-term investments, such as those in industry, *censi*, and real estate. A bill, in fact, was the very first investment he recorded in Ledger A, and he probably was able to make the transaction thanks to the *fl.*296 he had received in July 1584 from his cousin Cesare. On 2 January 1585 Peri paid *fl.*300 to Jacopo di Tommaso Martelli & Partners, bankers, with instructions that they put it on the exchange at their discretion (*a chi pare a loro*) and for the usual commission fee; in May they paid him *fl.*301. 16s.10d. in cash through the Ricci bank (an annual rate of return of only 2.4 percent), and the following July he put *fl.*300 in the Michelozzi wool firm.[54] The large sum of *fl.*1,482. 12s. paid to him at the Ricci bank in 1593 as part of his wife's dowry was transferred by Peri to the banker Giovambattista Michelozzi to be put on the exchange.[55] In May 1595 he opened an account in Michelozzi's name with a debit entry for *fl.*1,892. 1s.5d., the amount he had put on the exchange (which may have

52. Ledger A, fol. 64.
53. Ledger A, fol. 115v.
54. Ledger A, fol. 100v.
55. Ledger A, fol. 104.

represented some of the accumulated earnings on the earlier bill), this time specifying the fair at Besançon.[56] On 2 September 1600, the very day (he emphasized) he was paid *fl.*250 at the Capponi bank as part of his profits on the speculative venture with Domenico Peri, he transferred the sum to the bank of the heirs of Francesco Rinuccini to be put on the exchange, along with additional money that he had transferred from the Michelozzi–Ricci bank. Some of the capital—*fl.*404. 3*s.*7*d.*—that later in the year he invested in the Della Rena–Fiorini wool firm came from a payment he received at the Rinuccini bank for a bill returning from Besançon (which he transferred to the wool firm through the Michelozzi–Ricci bank).[57] Likewise, on 10 March 1618 he paid *fl.*714. 4*s.*8*d.* toward his share of the capital in the Innori silk firm with money he had put on the exchange with the Alessandrini bank on the preceding 25 November.[58] The repayment of his debt of *fl.*94 to Carlo Rinuccini in 1625 through the Paganelli–Portinari bank was made with funds the Acciaioli–Martelli bank in Rome had transferred to him through the fair at Besançon.[59]

Through exchange–rechange, bills could also serve as a long-term investment instrument in the form of a bank deposit earning interest compounded quarterly. In the 1620s, when Peri was no longer active as an investor in the cloth industries, he put money on the exchange as a way to accumulate dowries for his two youngest daughters. On 9 March 1622 he transferred *fl.*1,027. 4*s.*5*d.* that had been on the exchange from the Rinuccini bank to Orazio and Piero Tempi & Partners to be put back on the exchange indefinitely at the fairs of Besançon or wherever else (*o per quelle piazze dove si facessi tal fiere*), with the intention that the deposit plus interest should accumulate to benefit the dowries (*de' cambi et ricambi vadino in aumento di tempo in tempo di dette lor dote*). Two years later he debited the Tempi account for *fl.*112. 18*s.*11*d.*, representing the increase gained from successive exchanges (*che di tanti ero stato fatto creditore da loro per li cambi e ricambi guadagnati sino a questo giorno*), an annual interest rate that works out to just over 6¼ percent). He then paid the Tempi company *fl.*400 in cash to be put on the exchange for another dowry, this time specifying the fairs at Piacenza and

56. Ledger A, fols. 31, 64, 104.
57. Ledger A, fols. 49, 50.
58. Ledger A, fol. 135.
59. Ledger A, fol. 166.

limiting what the company could charge him for the service to the standard commission fee of one-third of 1 percent.[60]

In the entries on some of these accounts Peri demonstrates his complete familiarity with the complexities of this instrument: he uses the name of the fictitious place of the fairs, he notes values in the relevant moneys of account—the mark, the money of account used at the fairs, and the *scudo d'oro* of £7½ (not the florin of £7), the money of account used by international bankers—he mentions the current exchange rate, he refers to commission charges, and he knew how to keep a bill on the exchange (exchange–rechange). In all this he displays his facility with the appropriate technical language (which included the modern term *star del credere* to indicate the banker's obligation to the investor in an operation involving variable exchange rates and commission charges).

It is clear that relatively small operators such as Peri had active interests in bills of exchange.[61] There is evidence that other musicians, for example, were familiar with this financial instrument. A receipt survives for *fl.*300 that, on 2 March 1630, Vergilio di Giuseppe Grazi, a member of the court instrumental band known as the Franciosini, deposited in cash with the bank of Bernardino Capponi & Partners to take out a bill on the fairs at Piacenza.[62] Even Giulio Caccini made money on the side as a broker in the exchange market, bringing together banker and client. In 1603, as we shall see in Chapter 3, he appealed to a court official, Enea Vaini, for assistance in brokering (*senserie del cambio*)—although Vaini felt it was not a particularly lucrative form of remuneration—and for that year and for 1609 two documents survive that are statements drawn up by banks of what they owed Caccini for services rendered as broker for exchange operations. One was for six operations amounting to *sc.*7,400 *d'oro*, the other for six amounting to *sc.*4,689; and the service (brokerage) charge, stated in *lire*, for both was the standard one-twentieth of 1 percent of the value of the bills, or to put it in contemporary terms, one *grosso* (one-twentieth of a florin) for every hundred

---

60. Ledger A, fols. 124, 150, 162.

61. Brokers in the Florentine exchange market have not been studied. Indicative of their importance at least in the Venetian market is the project of four Florentine brokers together with a Genoese broker in 1570 to organize a monopoly on the traffic there; Corazzol, "Varietà notarile," 775. Compare also De Luca, "Sensali e mercato del credito a Milano."

62. LC 2743 (loose documents belonging to Grazi), document dated 2 March 1629/30.

scudi.[63] Although his fee for these two sets of transactions was relatively small (the equivalent of some *fl.*6), a much higher payment was made by the Zecca (the Mint) to *Giulio Caccini, detto Romano, mezzano di cambi* on 5 January 1607—of *sc.*57. 17*s.*4*d. d'oro*—as part of a general settlement to the city's brokers because they had had little business yet had rendered good service.[64] Soon thereafter, in July 1607, Grand Duke Ferdinando I allocated Caccini a pension from the Mint of *fl.*70 per year—it is not clear whether any service requirements as broker were attached to it—which lasted until mid-1612. He also earned brokerage fees in 1613, 1614, and 1618, although they amounted altogether to no more than *fl.*13.[65]

Such evidence for the familiarity with bills of exchange among people of middling status, like these musicians, points to how much the market for this purely financial instrument, though long known to Florentines, had expanded. The instrument had not enjoyed this kind of popularity a century earlier, and its wider diffusion was not just the result of the shift, in the mid-sixteenth century, of the international bill market from Lyons to the more efficient fairs of Besançon, operated by the Genoese in Italy; instead, the wider market for the bill of exchange—and not only in Florence—was one of the principal reasons for the success of those fairs.

Censi

Unlike the well-established bill of exchange, the *censo* was a new financial instrument that appeared on the scene precisely at the moment when Peri entered the market: the 1580s. The *censo* was a type of annuity, for the most part derived from real estate, most often a rural property. It was an instru-

---

63. Giazotto, *Le due patrie di Giulio Caccini*, 32–34, and documents 20 and 21 (the latter with Caccini's signature acknowledging receipt of payment). These documents are published as photographs, but unfortunately they appear devoid of any context and are identified only as coming from unspecified private archives. The rates, which are not stated in the documents, have been calculated here, and they correspond to those mentioned by Davanzati's treatise on exchange (1581); see Davanzati, *"Lezione delle monete" e "Notizia de' cambi,"* ed. Ricossa, 75. There is a mistake in the addition on the second receipt mentioned above, for the correct total of the items listed is *sc.*4,289. The fee, however, was calculated on the mistaken total on the receipt.

64. ASF, Ufficiali della Moneta poi Maestri di Zecca 228, fol. 114. The payment came not from the general cash account of the Zecca but from a special cash fund of Vincenzo de' Medici, the grand duke's *depositario generale*, who ran the Mint.

65. ASF, Ufficiali della Moneta poi maestri di Zecca 231, fols. 42, 645.

ment that by this time in northern Europe—where it was known by the French word *rente*—had for a long time been used as both an investment and a source of credit. In Italy, however, the *censo* was not widely adopted until the later sixteenth century, and in fact, its existence in Tuscany has only recently been discovered.[66] It involved the purchase by the buyer, or lender, of an annuity from the seller, or borrower, who needed the capital and was prepared to pay an annual interest charge, offering as security a lien—what we might call a mortgage—on a specific property. Contracts were notarized, and the seller generally named guarantors for the transaction. The *censo* was an open-ended contract without a fixed duration, its termination being entirely the decision of the seller, who could also reduce his obligation by paying back only a part of the capital. Moreover, it could be sold by the buyer to another party or by the seller along with the sale of the encumbered property.

The advantages of this kind of loan to both buyer and seller are clear. The former had as security an official legal contract, a lien on a specific property, and the backing of guarantors; he had the promise of a steady income; and yet he did not altogether lose liquidity since he could sell the contract. The seller, or *censuario*, had maximum flexibility in handling his debt: he alone decided when, and if, the principal was to be paid back; he could reduce the principal at any time; he limited his liability to a specific property; and he was free to sell the property along with the *censo*. Moreover, other advantages emerged in practice. First, for the borrower the selling price of a *censo*—the loan—was often much larger than the maximum of the hundred-or-so florins normally available to borrowers resorting to the traditional lending institutions: the Monte di Pietà, which made direct loans, and private banks, which, to avoid the usury restriction, trafficked in bills of exchange.[67] Second, for the lender the interest rate, at 7½ to 8 percent, being fixed, was highly favorable compared with what one could get from a deposit in the Monte di Pietà (5 percent) or any one of the state *monti* (up to 7 percent), or from bills of exchange (variable, but normally 6–8 percent); in fact, by this

66. Polizzotto, "I censi consegnativi bollari nella Firenze granducale," is the first study of the topic, and the following remarks largely depend on this work. Polizzotto is continuing his research into the subject.

67. Of Polizzotto's sample of seventy-one *censi* in the period 1581–1611, only one was below *fl.*100, more than half (forty-one) were over *fl.*200, and several were above *fl.*1,000.

time (in contrast to the fourteenth and fifteenth centuries) an investment in a wool or silk firm often did not yield a much higher rate of return.

The *censo* was thus a new instrument on the Florentine scene that had its appeal to both investors and borrowers. Why this instrument caught on in Florence in the last quarter of the sixteenth century is not difficult to explain. There was much loose capital looking for outlets—hence, on the one hand, the rise in the conspicuous consumption of durable goods, which manifested itself in the flourishing of the decorative arts, and, on the other, the success of deposit institutions, above all the Monte di Pietà but also the many *monti* abroad, especially in Rome, that were successful in attracting savings from Florentines (including Peri, as we have seen). Traditional investment outlets in industry and international commerce, however, had not expanded accordingly; hence much of this newly disposable capital was available for alternative investments. At the same time, the increased earnings of agriculture as a result of the price inflation characteristic of the sixteenth century may have stimulated demand for investment capital in that sector. The *censo* opened up a new way of channeling capital that appealed to both the supply and the demand side in this market.

The ground was thus prepared, and if anything specific triggered the fairly rapid entrance of *censi* into the capital market in the 1580s, it was the papal bull issued by Pius V in 1569 that defined the *censo* as a sale and not a loan contract, thereby endowing the instrument with immunity against charges that might arise from anti-usury restrictions imposed by the church. The bull established its legitimacy as opposed to some commercial practices, such as the international exchange, and the measure of the efficacy of this official papal approval—even in a city like Florence, where several devices to circumvent the usury restriction had long been in use—can be taken in the omnipresence of explicit references to the bull in *censo* contracts. For any Florentine who felt that the church had compromised its doctrine in accepting some of the traditional practices in the money market, or who had doubts about the subterfuges behind these practices, the *censo* offered complete peace of mind—even for those who, still at this late date, questioned the legitimacy of the Monte di Pietà, approved by the papacy a century earlier.[68]

68. In response to the contemporary concern about the usurious nature of some traditional financial practices, including the bill of exchange, deposits in the Monte di Pietà, *censi*, and certain business operations, Tommaso Buoninsegni, a conservative Dominican professor of theology in Florence, published a treatise on the subject in Latin in 1587 that was immediately

Table 2.2.   Censi purchased by Jacopo Peri

No.	Date	Cost (in florins)	Interest	Property	Annuity
1	1604	2,500	8%	2 farms at San Donato in Poggio	fl.200, Jul 1604–Jun 1614
2	1604	60½+44	—	vineyard at Radda	6 then 10 barrels of wine, 1604–15
3	1604	100	7%	piece of land at Marciano	fl.7, 1605–33
4	1604	50	8%	field at Marciano	fl.4, 1605–18; fl.3, 1619–26
5	1610	100	7½%	piece of land at Marciano	fl.7½, 1611–33
6	1610	100	7%	2 pieces of land at Marciano	fl.7, 1611–33
7	1614	60	7%	piece of land at Marciano	fl.4. 4s., 1615–31
8	1632	200	6½%	house in Florence	fl.13, 1632–33

Sources: Censo no. 1, Ledger A, fols. 64, 65, 112v–113, 119v–120, 123v, 138; Ledger B, fol. 31; LC 3913, fols. 94v–95; LC 3912, documents dated 1602 and 10, 17, and 21 July 1604 (notarial acts); LC 3902 (farm accounts, 1603–14). No. 2, Ledger A, fols. 63, 113, 114. No. 3, Ledger A, fols. 113v, 126, 141, 156; Ledger B, fols. 33, 52, 53, 61, 66; LC 3915 (stracciafoglio), fols. 1, 17, 31, 42. No. 4, Ledger A, fols. 71, 113v, 127, 145. No. 5, Ledger A, fols. 97, 117. 141; Ledger B, fol. 31. No. 6, Ledger A, fols. 117v; Ledger C, fol. 29. No. 7, Ledger A, fols. 125, 139, 164; Ledger B, fol. 32; LC 3912, document dated 10 June 1615; LC 3915 (stracciafoglio), fol. 10. No. 8, Ledger B, fol. 155.

For all of its advantages, and notwithstanding its immediate popularity, the *censo* encountered some serious problems in practice, and Peri's experience in this market exposes some of them. All together, he bought eight *censi* (Table 2.2). Seven were on rural properties and earned between 7 and 8 percent, and one was on a house in the city that earned the slightly lower rate of 6½ percent, possibly because he was loaning the money to a cousin. The *censo* bought in 1604 (on a vineyard) was unusual in requiring payment in kind—barrels of wine—with no reference to a percentage rate of return, and in being limited to ten years. Except for the first *censo*, for which Peri paid the exceptionally high price of *fl.*2,500, these *censi* were very much at the low end of the market for this kind of investment. His purchase of the five *censi* on pieces of land at Marciano at a cost of *fl.*50–100 (Table 2.2, nos. 3–7) probably had as much to do with establishing his presence through loans to his neighbors in an area where he had scattered properties as with his desire for a fixed income, for the total they yielded—from *fl.*25 to *fl.*30 annually—was relatively small compared with the salary of *fl.*108 he was earning at the time as a musician at the grand-ducal court.

Taken all together, these eight *censi* that Peri bought illustrate the variability and flexibility of the instrument within its defining parameters: the value of a *censo* had a very wide range (here, *fl.*50–2,500); it could be on urban as well as rural property (no. 8); the owner of more than one property could sell separate *censi* (nos. 3, 6); the contract could take the form of an advance payment for the supply of produce for a fixed number of years (no. 2); the *censuario* could redeem the *censo* in one payment (no. 7) or in stages (no. 4); he could sell the land to pay back the capital (no. 4) or sell it encumbered with the *censo* (nos. 3, 6); he could transmit the encumbered land to heirs, who in turn could sell it (no. 3); and a *censo* as an asset of an estate could be used to satisfy credit claims (no. 7)—these latter possibilities giving rise to a lively secondary market. Of these eight *censi*, Peri sold one back to the party (not the *censuario*) that had sold it to him on the secondary market (no. 1), two were redeemed by the *censuario* (nos. 4, 7), one was self-extinguishing (no. 2), and three (nos. 1, 3, 6) ended up in the courts.

And with those three that went to court, the discussion shifts to the one serious problem that could arise with this credit instrument, notwithstanding its significant advantages: breach of contract by the *censuario*, at times in bad faith—a situation that was worsened for the buyer by the distance usually separating the two parties to the contract. Peri's experience in this respect exposes the problem better than any of the documents that have yet come to light in the study of this new investment instrument. His purchase of two *censi* (nos. 1, 2) from the fisc, and the presence of the government in the *censo* market in general, point directly to the problem. These two *censi* had already been constituted by private parties who remained in place, but the contracts had been taken over by the government as a result of claims by the owners of the *censi* against the *censuario* or his guarantors for failure of payment.

With the first *censo* Peri bought the problem continued, notwithstanding the government's intervention. Within a few years of its purchase in July 1604 (for the notable price of *fl.*2,500), he encountered difficulties collecting the annuity, which in fact was being paid not by the *censuario* but by one of the guarantors. In 1611 Peri began paying legal fees for action against the guarantors, and finally, in 1614—thanks to the intervention of the grand duke—he got his capital back from the fisc, but not without considerable legal wrangling, to the extent that

> a few days after the aforesaid judgment, I fell gravely ill and with fever, from 13 June to the end of September. During that illness, I was visited on behalf of the Most Serene Grand Duke by the Signor Cavaliere Ferdinando Saracinelli, first chamberlain to His Most Serene Highness, who brought me *sc.50* which the aforesaid Most Serene Highness sent me as a gift, so that I could better handle my affairs. This money was very dear to me, but even more so was the favor and gratitude of His Highness, for all of which praise and thanks are due to God and to the Most Holy Virgin Mother Mary.[69]

After all this Peri still had an outstanding credit of *fl.*800—for four years of the annuity—with the *censuario*, and this was extinguished only in 1621 from what the government had obtained from the estate of one of the guarantors, who in the meanwhile had gone bankrupt. Even then, the account in Peri's ledger opened in the name of the *censuario* remained unbalanced, with a small debit of *fl.*34.

Legal problems of a very different nature arose out of two of the *censi* bought on small pieces of land at Marciano, in the Valdichiana (nos. 3 and 6), where Peri had the farm that had belonged to the family of his first wife. He bought these from the same landowner, but when the *censuario* died in 1628, Peri had problems with the heirs. Believing that before his death the original *censuario* had sold both encumbered properties, he opened an account for each of the new owners; but he remained confused at this point about which property was which. The situation was complicated further by the death of one of these secondary buyers, and Peri found himself dealing with his heirs.

69. Ledger A, fol. 120: *pochi giorni doppo la detta sentenza mi ammalai gravemente e con febbre, dal dì 13 di giugno a tutto settembre; e in detta malattia fui visitato, per parte del Serenissimo Gran Duca, da il signor cavaliere Ferdinando Saracinelli, primo cameriere di Sua Altezza Serenissima, e mi recò sc.50, che mi mandò a donare la detta Altezza Serenissima acciò meglio mi potessi governare, quali mi furno molto cari, ma ancora molto più il favore e la gratitudine di Sua Altezza, che del tutto sia sempre laudato e ringratiato il Signore e la Santissima Vergine Madre Maria.* For Saracinelli, see Chapter 3; he was also godfather to Peri's daughter Caterina, *née* Francesca, in 1616 (see Table 1.2).

Looking at the names of the parties involved, one can only imagine what was going on in this rural area so far away from Florence: the buyer—Isabella Fontani—of one of the properties from the original *censuario* was the wife of a man with the same surname as the *censuario* and his heirs, and her surname was the same as that of the man who had bought the other property of the *censuario*. In 1631 Peri began legal proceedings against this woman to clarify the situation, and his numerous payments for action from the Mercanzia in Florence and from local officials extended to the time of his death in 1633. His son Dino, finding himself, as his father's executor, left with "these accursed *censi*" on his hands (*questi maladetti censi*), tried to clarify matters, anticipating, however, that he was likely to remain as confused as his father. Dino had learned from local people that Isabella Fontani had divided her encumbered land into two parts and had sold them to different people but without informing them of the encumbrance. One of these buyers was, in fact, the heir of the owner of the other encumbered property, but since he dressed as a priest (*va vestito da prete*), Dino imagined that his father had never taken action against him.

Making contracts involving land and people in the remote countryside carried its risks for investors in the city, and given the predominant use of the *censo* by owners of rural property, the instrument, for all its advantages, was particularly subject to the kind of problems that Peri and his son had to confront—the lack of precise knowledge of private arrangements within the distant and relatively isolated peasant community, and by the same token, the free range therein for deception and collusion. Large property-owners had agents who could keep a grip on the situation, but small ones like Peri were very much on their own in confronting these problems, even in an area where they had a certain presence as a local landlord.

There are still major issues to be worked out in the study of the *censo* as a credit instrument, especially with respect to the *censuario*. It might be assumed that the rates, at 7½ to 8 percent, were high relative to other popular investments because the risks were somewhat higher, and we have referred to the one risk that Peri encountered. Yet the *censuario* had to have guarantors, and while the guarantors offered some security to the investor, they themselves were prepared to take the risks involved, to the point of having to assume the burden of the loan. So in the end, the question is how serious were these risks? There is also the problem of the identity of the *censuari*. The loans were larger than what one imagines a normal peasant could possibly manage.

These were presumably property owners of some substance and some entrepreneurial talent who hoped to make improvements that would increase their
net income to the extent that they could afford to pay a high interest rate, if
not indefinitely at least until they accumulated enough capital to pay off their
debt. And following this line of reason, we arrive at one of the really large
historiographical problems yet to be confronted in the study of the economy
of early modern Tuscany: the state of the agricultural sector. Moreover, considerations about the Florentine *censi* have resonances in the historiography
of early modern Italy in general. In short, what is missing in the literature is,
above all, a study of the *censuari* themselves: who they were, what they did
with their capital, how much success they achieved, and how important they
were in the economy.

Government Securities

Also relatively new, government securities, something like modern bonds,
appeared only in the late fifteenth century, when the papacy reorganized its
debt in a more rational way to attract the capital needed to consolidate its
power over the expanding territorial state. In the course of the next century it
set up a number of *monti*, or funds built up from borrowed capital, each secured by revenues from a specific tax source, and these *monti* issued interest-
bearing certificates (*luoghi*) in a single denomination to lenders. Each of the
innumerable papal *monti* took its name from the objective in setting it up,
or from its source of revenue, or from the name of the pope under whom it
was instituted. By Peri's time investors from all over Italy were buying *luoghi*
(further evidence of the growing availability of liquid capital), and since they
could be reassigned and interest was fixed, a lively secondary market grew up
in them. In other words, they gave rise to something like a veritable bond
market. In a strict sense, *luoghi* were not bonds since they had no fixed duration, although some (called *vacabili*) took the form of a single-life annuity.
Moreover, although they and the interest claims could be reassigned, they
were not transferrable through endorsement alone; in this sense, they were
not negotiable paper of the kind that circulated in the market at Antwerp in
the later sixteenth century.

Peri seldom had recourse to this market, but his familiarity with it is indicative of its importance in attracting capital from the middling class. As we
have seen, in January 1587, still very early in his career, he tried to sell, without

success, three orders of payment (*cedole*, probably for interest payments) issued by the Monte San Giorgio in Rome to two parties (one of them a Jew,
he notes) from whom he had apparently bought them. From 1614 to 1618,
when his first two daughters were under ten years of age, he bought twelve
luoghi in papal *monti* (eight transferred from his brother-in-law Giovanni
Monaldi) almost exclusively for the purpose of establishing a secure investment for the cash component of a dowry. He bought all of these on the
secondary market—hence involving transfer of ownership—through a
company in Rome referred to only as Ticci (probably Francesco Ticci, a
banker known to have operated there), with whom he communicated through
a bank in Florence. He records what he paid for each—from *fl.*113 to *fl.*140—
and that he earned as much as 7 percent on some, but he does not indicate
their par value or the interest rate. In his testament of 1630 Peri disposed of
ten *luoghi* of two Roman *monti*—Allumiere and Cancellerie—each reportedly paying *fl.*5 annually, and the accounts of the administration of his estate
indicate that in the year he died, 1633, these *luoghi* were indeed yielding
around *fl.*50 a year.[70]

Florence was very late in instituting *monti* of this kind. Its public debt had
been consolidated in the Monte Comune in the 1340s, but that fund soon
lost its ability to attract voluntary investment capital and became, instead, a
fund consisting of credits assigned for forced loans imposed on the citizenry
in lieu of direct taxes. It was reorganized at the end of the fifteenth century in
what was called the Monte delle Graticole, designed to attract deposits earning interest rates of 3, 4, and 7 percent, depending on the length of time a
credit remained in the fund; but this *monte*, too, lost much of its investment
appeal. In 1596, when Peri liquidated credits in it for Niccolò Fortunati, he
received 42 percent of par. In 1604 he spent on the secondary market a total
of *fl.*317. 4*s.* for credits in the 7 percent category, evaluated at only 28 percent
of par because at the time the interest being paid on them amounted to only
about 2 percent of their nominal value. He bought these credits for only three
years, with the agreement that the sellers would buy them back at the price he
paid. In other words, this operation was a loan, the period being three years;
the interest, what the Monte paid in the meantime (which worked out to 6.42

70. Ledger A, fols. 18 (the *cedole*), 121v–123; Ledger D, fols. 50, 67; LC 3912, document dated
15 May 1631 (the testament).

percent return on his investment); and the security, his ownership of the credits.[71]

In the sixteenth century, the grand-ducal government had not been particularly aggressive in attracting capital because it kept its finances in order—and taxes relatively low—through personal financial initiatives, on the one hand, and limited state expenditures, on the other. In the early seventeenth century, however, its expenditures rose to the point that it, too, established *monti* on the papal model, first by instituting the practice of issuing *luoghi* by the Monte di Pietà. This organization, like many others founded throughout Italy in the later fifteenth century, was created as a charitable institution, to make loans available to the needy in return for pawns. In the course of the following century, however, it evolved into a major public savings-and-loan bank, accepting deposits and extending loans alongside its activity as a pawn bank, and it also became inseparably tied into government finance as an obligatory place of deposit for some state institutions, and as a major lender to the grand dukes.

In 1616 the government approved an initiative that permitted the Monte di Pietà to issue *luoghi* in denominations of *fl.*100 and earning 5 percent interest, payable semiannually. These were an instant success, and the officials began issuing them as printed certificates. They had to open a new series of much larger ledgers to handle the traffic, the first of these being twice the size of the previous one, and the subsequent ones very much larger still—so much so that it takes two people to lift them. Within four years deposits exceeded three million ducats, an amount equivalent to more than one-fourth of the total taxable wealth of the city 150 years earlier, when we have the only fairly reliable survey of the city's wealth, made for the *catasto* of 1427 (basing the comparison, as the others in this book, on the common denominator of the power of money to buy labor)—proof enough that there was much loose capital floating about in Florence seeking some kind of investment outlet. And this is not even to consider the money that was also flowing into the Monte del Sale—instituted in Florence in 1625 with *luoghi* of *fl.*100 paying 5 percent, deposits being guaranteed by revenue from the salt tax—and the *monti* abroad, in Rome and elsewhere. This loose cash was in the hands of people at all levels of society, from the very rich (like the Riccardi, who in 1612 had around *fl.*50,000 distributed in the Monte di Pietà, the

71. Ledger A, fols. 104v, 113v–114.

Monte del Sale, and *monti* in Rome and Naples), down to the artisans, widows, and even farmworkers whose accounts fill the ledgers of the Monte di Pietà.[72]

Peri participated in this first rush by buying three *luoghi* in 1619, two in 1620, and three more in 1624. These he liquidated in 1625; but then from 1626 down to his death he invested another *fl*.800 in *luoghi*, half of which (*fl*.400) was conditioned by designating that the interest on them, but not the capital, be paid after his death to his three daughters in convents.[73] In his 1630 testament, Peri made no reference to all these holdings, but the accounts for the administration of his estate show that in the year of his death he was receiving interest on eight *luoghi*. In his will he specified that money earned from other securities (*censi*, and *luoghi* in papal *monti*) designated as dowries for his daughters be deposited in the Monte di Pietà or some other such secure place, and that every two years these funds be used to buy additional *luoghi* in either Florence or Rome.[74] Similarly, Peri was among the first investors in the Monte del Sale: his accounts do not record any purchases, but his 1630 testament refers to no fewer than twenty-three *luoghi* he owned at the time, and the accounts for his estate show that in the year of his death these provided an annual income of *fl*.115.[75] At the time of death, therefore, Peri's portfolio of *luoghi* consisted of twenty-three in the Monte del Sale worth *fl*.2,300 yielding *fl*.115, eight in the Monte di Pietà worth *fl*.800 yielding *fl*.40, and ten in papal *monti*, of uncertain market value yielding around *fl*.50—together providing him with a relatively secure fixed annual income of *fl*.205.

Both *censi* and *luoghi di monte* offered a fixed return for an indefinite period, subject only to redemption by the seller. The buyer could not cash them

72. See Menning, *The Monte di Pietà of Florence*, 266, on the issuing of *luoghi* by the Monte; one of the *luoghi*, dated 1616, is illustrated on the back of the book's dust jacket. For the Riccardi, see Malanima, *I Riccardi di Firenze*, 102, 247.

73. His *luoghi* purchases are represented on Table 2.4, and the interest on them, in Table 2.5. His account on the Monte di Pietà books of unrestricted deposits (*depositi liberi*) runs from 1619 to his death: ASF, Monte di Pietà 816, fol. 525; 818, fol. 396; 820, fol. 312; 822, fol. 706; 825, fol. 568; 828, fol. 451. The provision for his daughters is the subject of a *ricordo* in Ledger B, fol. 155, but in his testament, as we have seen, he provided for an annuity of *fl*.5 for those in convents.

74. Ledger A, fol. 123; Ledger B, fols. 123, 154, 155; Ledger D, fol. 104; LC 3912, document dated 15 May 1631 (the testament).

75. LC 3912, document dated 15 May 1631 (the testament); Ledger D, fol. 66.

in to get his capital back, but he could sell them in a secondary market. *Censi* paid a much better return, generally around 50 percent more than *luoghi*, but they were riskier because they represented private contracts between persons usually separated by considerable distance, whereas *luoghi* were issued by governments. In the event of default, however, the buyer of *censi* could have recourse to the courts, something hardly possible if a government reneged on its obligations, as the government of Florence did during the republican period with respect to the forced loans it imposed on citizens in lieu of a direct tax. Neither of these instruments was available in Florence before the second half of the sixteenth century, about the time that Peri entered the market, and his investment history testifies to their immediate popularity. *Censi*, however, circulated only in the local market (so far as we know), whereas *luoghi* found buyers throughout Italy.

Real Estate

In the fifteenth century, real estate, especially a piece of land in the immediate countryside, was the preferred investment of Florentines of all classes, to judge from the extraordinarily high number of them—two-thirds of all households—who declared a property on their 1427 tax (*catasto*) reports. Anyone of modest economic status who had built up enough savings bought land, for fairly obvious reasons: it provided some of life's necessities; it was, for lack of any alternative, a secure and durable asset, the solid foundation of a patrimony that could be passed on to heirs; and it was a place to go to get away from the city—*stare in villa* was a famed social and even cultural tradition, at least among the better-off Florentines (such as the story-tellers in Boccaccio's *Decameron*). Someone who wanted to make his fortune, however, did not start out investing in land. Eventually Peri accumulated substantial real-estate holdings, both urban and rural (these are listed in Table 2.3, and the rural sites are located on the map in Figure 2.2), but in the early history of his investments, before he received his first dowry, land was more of a cultural interest than an economic one. When he somehow came into possession of *fl.*300 in 1585—the first capital he had to invest—he put it, first, on the exchange and then, when the bill was returned, into the wool firm of Michelozzi's nephew, whereas with that amount of money he could have bought a substantial piece of land if not, indeed, a small farm, complete with house, to support a resident sharecropper (*lavoratore*).

Table 2.3. Real-estate acquisitions by Jacopo Peri

Date	Property (see Figs. 1.2, 2.2)	Cost (in florins)	Source
1586–1600	land at Rostolena in the Mugello; sold as a farm (*podere*) for *fl.*430 in 1606	330	Ledger A, fols. 101–3, 109, 115–116v, 120 (*ricordi*); ibid., fols. 75, 144 (accounts of sale); Corazzini, "Jacopo Peri e la sua famiglia," 43, describes properties on basis of *decima* documents
1588	*farm at San Marco Vecchio* (prebend): rented for *fl.*6 annually on a 29-year rental contract, renewable for three generations	—	Ledger A, fols. 150v–153v, 107v, 121v; LC 3913 for receipts of rent payments
1596	house in Via dei Fossi, with an open court and garden	1,000	Ledger A, fols. 106v, 107; LC 3913, fols. 12–12v and loose sheet with expenses for improvements; LC 3912, documents dated 1597, 1512; Corazzini, "Jacopo Peri e la sua famiglia," 43, cites notarial purchase document
	1598: improvements	103	
1596	*farm at Marciano:* came with dowry	—	Ledger A, fols. 82, 110, 110v, 117, 117v; LC 2384 (copy of *decima* documents); LC 3912, documents dated 1583, 1603, 1609, 1620, 1629/30, 1634
	1601: land	188	
	1609: field	180	
	1609: small house	25	
	1610: land	29	

1602	*farm at Castelvecchio*: came with dowry	—	Ledger A, fol. 112; ASF, Notarile moderno, prot. 12993 (Diaceto Venterucci), nos. 129, 138 (1643 sale document)
1605–6	small farm with *casa da padrone* in Pian di Ripoli	300	Ledger A, fols. 72, 114v
1612	farm near Bagno a Ripoli	2,000	Ledger A, fols. 86, 118v; LC 3912, documents dated 1612
	1612–18: improvements	600	
1614	*farm at Cicogna*: came to his wife in exchange for an annuity of *fl*.60 plus *fl*.600 paid by Peri	600	Ledger A, fol. 120; ASF, Notarile moderno, prot. 12993, nos. 129, 138 (1643 sale document)
1624	house in Via dei Servi	501	Ledger A, fol. 188; Ledger C, fols. 27; LC 3912, document dated 18 Sep 1624
1628	house in Borgo Ognissanti	361	Ledger B, fols. 152v, 154; Ledger C, fol. 21; LC 3912, documents dated 1628, 1630
	1630: stable	64	
1629	*house in Borgo SS. Apostoli*: inherited by his wife; burdened with annuities for *fl*.6 and *fl*.14	—	Ledger B, fol. 153; LC 3510. fols. 183v-84 ; LC 3912, document dated 6 Sep 1629
TOTAL		6,281	

Notes: Properties in italics are those not acquired outright by purchase. The listed sources do not include the many accounts open in the names of sharecroppers and general farm accounts; these are scattered throughout Peri's account books, especially Ledgers A and B, and LC 3913 (receipts), 3914 (waste-book of farm accounts). Ledgers D, E, and F—kept for the administration of Peri's estate—have accounts open in the name of those properties that yielded income. References to LC 3912 indicate that in this collection of loose documents are one or more relevant to the property, usually regarding purchases and sales. A detailed description of the farms at Castelvecchio and Cicogna is found in the notarial document drawn up in 1643 when Peri's widow exchanged them for an annuity; ASF, Notarile moderno, prot. 12993 (Diaceto Venterucci), no. 129, fols. 108–11.

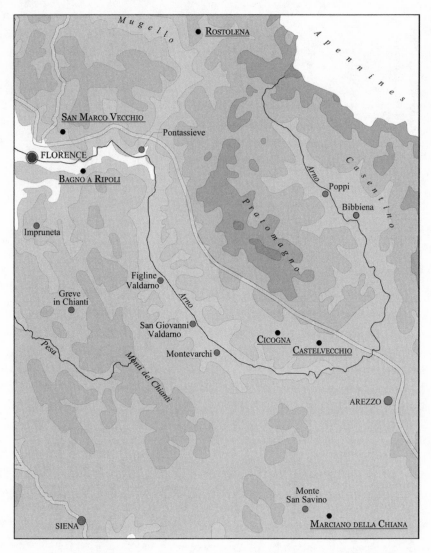

FIGURE 2.2. Map of Tuscany showing rural properties of Jacopo Peri. Places where Peri had property are underlined.

Land certainly interested Peri as an investment, but, constrained by limited funds, he approached it as a something to be accumulated in small increments. In 1586 he paid just under *fl*.77 for his first property in the Mugello, a remote area where land was probably relatively cheap, and over the next seven years he made six more purchases in the area totaling *fl*.245.[76] Together they comprised over thirty miniscule pieces of property—cultivated and wooded land, fields for pasture, a small house with an oven and barn. Most of them are described at the time of purchase as being contiguous to property he already owned, and in one instance he traded a piece of his land plus *fl*.4 for another of inferior quality because, as he explains, it was in the midst of his own properties. These purchases of small increments of land reveal a strategy directed to putting together a coherent property; and in fact in 1606 he sold them as a single unit for *fl*.430, about a third more than what he had paid out over the preceding twenty years. By this time, having come into the possession of other more significant properties, he presumably had no further interest in this land, which was of little agricultural value and in a place not easily accessible from the city.

In the early years Peri probably could not afford to buy any land closer to Florence. Yet as we have seen, he clearly wanted something nearby, a place he could walk to and so escape, at least temporarily, the demands of urban life and the court; and the prebend at S. Lorenzo offered to him by his former teacher, Cristofano Malvezzi, gave him that opportunity. So in 1588 he took out a lease on a farm at San Marco Vecchio that constituted the prebend. The farm was just outside the city gate of Porta San Gallo, located in what today is the Piazza della Libertà; Peri paid *fl*.6 a year in rent, and he assumed full responsibility for the property's management as if he were its owner. The decision to rent this farm, however, arose out of two considerations that go much beyond his desire to have a place in the country within walking distance from his home and work.

In the first place, Peri was prepared to take an active interest in running a farm. In a *ricordo* of 1590 he notes what he surely knew at the time he signed the lease just two years earlier: that the fields in this place were poor (*cattive di natura*) and had deteriorated badly (*malissimo andate*), with olive trees that produced nothing, and vines that looked like eels wanting to spread all over the place (*paiono anguille che voglino camminare*), and he adds that he was operating the farm at a loss, since it yielded him in profits only half of what he was paying in rent. He took the property, in fact, with the prospect, as he says, to plant many olive trees, fig trees, and vines, so that in time he would

76. For the first purchase, see Ledger A, fol. 192v.

improve the land and earn a profit.[77] The accounts he kept for this farm reveal his initiatives toward this end: he grafted cherry and fig trees; planted cane, wheat, vines, and mulberry trees (the last, for silkworms); dug drainage ditches; purchased lime, bricks, and tiles for the stable; built a chicken shed and dovecot; and hired oxen for work on the land. The £70 he borrowed from Malvezzi in March 1592 and paid back shortly thereafter, in May, may have been used to meet related expenses.[78] And he was successful, for some forty years later when he made a will in which he surveyed all of his assets, he noted that, notwithstanding the poor quality of the land at the farm at San Marco, he had paid much to put it right so that it was yielding him *fl.*12 a year (which would have included the value of any produce he took for his own use), *fl.*6 over what it cost him for the rent.[79]

The particular nature of this rental contract also appealed to Peri for completely different reasons: it gave him something he could pass on to his heirs. It was a traditional contract for rural property, called *a livello*: it gave the renter full control over the management of the property, its duration was twenty-nine years, and it could be renewed through three generations, two beyond the renter's life. In 1599, having lost the original document from Rome legitimizing the rental contract, Peri had a copy made, and in the *ricordo* noting this he goes on to inform his heirs of the contractual obligation to pay the rent semiannually, warning them that should they miss three consecutive payments the contract would be canceled: "So keep it in your head that every twenty-nine years the contract must be renewed, and the semiannual term begins—if I recall correctly—in April and October."[80] To further emphasize the point he drew a hand in the margin with a finger pointing to this *ricordo*. Years later, in December 1616, just as the original contract was near expiration, he made another *ricordo* of the renewal of the contract (now called a pension [*pensione*] rather than a prebend) with Malvezzi's successor to the canonry. Peri also added a warning to his heirs—he was fifty-four and knew he was unlikely to live another twenty-nine years, to eighty-three—this

77. Ledger A, fols. 150v–151.

78. Ledger A, fol. 24.

79. LC 3912, document dated 15 May 1630.

80. Ledger A, fol. 107v: *state in cervello ricordandosi che ogni 29 anni si fa uno nuovo contratto per ricognitione; e la rata de' 6 mesi comincia, se ben mi ricordo, d'aprile, e l'altra d'ottobre.* His recollection was indeed correct, to judge by the receipts written in LC 3913 by successive canons of S. Lorenzo holding Malvezzi's prebend.

time written in exceptionally large and neatly formed letters that immediately catch the attention of anyone whose eyes happen to fall on the page (and happen not to see the hand with the pointing finger he sketched in the margin here, too): "Remember every twenty-nine years to acknowledge the fact so that [the lease] does not lapse. My sons: keep it in mind. I believe, so as not to make a mistake, that it would be good to do it in the year 1644."[81] The prebend, in fact, is a very early indicator of two of the dynamics that time and time again we see driving Peri: entrepreneurial energy and a concern for family (in this instance, even before he had one).

Marriage changed Peri's stature as a landowner. The three dowries he received in the decade from 1592 to 1602 included the large farm at Marciano, in the Valdichiana between Monte San Savino and Cortona, which came to him after the death of his father-in-law, Niccolò Fortunati, in 1596, presumably in lieu of what was still owed on the dowry; and the farm at Castelvecchio (today Castiglion Ubertini), to the north of Marciano in the Arno valley a few kilometers east of Montevarchi, that constituted the dowry of Alessandra Fortini. Presumably the farm at Marciano had more investment potential, for Peri paid just over $fl.400$ for additional land, and his purchase of several small *censi* from neighbors (that is, loans to them through this instrument) suggests a strategy for further strengthening his presence in the area. Moreover, considering the farm too large for just one family of workers, and knowing that at a certain point the son of a worker would want to strike out on his own, Peri built a new house to anticipate the eventual division of the entire property into two farms, thereby rendering the property more manageable and probably more profitable, given the nature of the sharecropping system (*mezzadria*). The description of the property in the tax records at the time of its inheritance by his sons, however, indicates that there was still only one farm at Marciano, along with more than two dozen separate pieces of land divided into eighteen taxable units, obviously not yet united.[82] The property also had a residence suitable for the occasional visit by the owner, for Peri refers to the *villa* there in his 1630 testament.

Peri's other investments in real estate over the 1590s and the first decade of the next century were primarily for residential properties: $fl.1,000$ in 1596 for

---

81. Ledger A, fol. 121v: *ricordarsi ogni 29 anni fare la medessima recognizione acciò non ricaschi. Figliuoli miei: tenetelo a memoria. Credo, per non errare, sia bene farla l'anno 1644.*

82. ASF, Decima granducale 2396, no. 90.

a home in Via dei Fossi, and *fl*.300 for a lifetime lease on a villa (*casa da padrone*), called *all'Olmo*, in Pian di Ripoli, an area a few kilometers to the east of Florence upstream on the south bank of the Arno. Peri bought the lease on it from Salustio Buonguglielmi, whose family had long been landowners in those parts.[83] This villa served him as a suburban residence, and it seems to have become his preferred place to send his wife and daughters during the summer: he noted in disposing of the Marciano property in his 1630 testament that the house there was by that time only sparsely furnished.

In 1612 Peri made his one major purchase of a rural property: a farm with a house suitable for the proprietor (*casa da oste*) also in Pian di Ripoli that cost *fl*.2,000. This property, called Torricelle, was not contiguous to the Villa all'Olmo; it was farther from the river, opposite the baptismal church (*pieve*) just before the town of Bagno a Ripoli, along the principal road on the south side of the Arno leading from Florence into the upper Valdarno. Peri did not, however, take full title to the farm: he bought it from the Ospedale degli Innocenti, the prominent Florentine orphanage, in an arrangement that was to last only two generations beyond his lifetime. The contract included the obligation to pay a miniscule annual rent of £12 (probably designed as a token recognition of the real owner of the property) and to spend *fl*.300 over the following ten years for work on the farmhouse, but he ended up paying a total of *fl*.600 for improvements. He possibly accepted the limitations of his ownership on both properties because he thereby paid somewhat less than the market price for what was in effect a valuable piece of agricultural real estate, being located in the floodplain of the Arno. It consisted of a farm worked by a sharecropper, and a fruit and vegetable garden (*orto*) rented out for *fl*.25 annually, raised to *fl*.28 in 1627.

After the acquisition of the properties in Pian di Ripoli Peri bought nothing else in the countryside. In 1614, however, he paid *fl*.600 toward the settlement of his wife's arrangement with her brother Giovanni to take over his farm at Cicogna, in the Arno valley a few kilometers north of Castelvecchio, in exchange for payment of his debts and an annuity. Late in life, he also bought two houses in the city—one with a shop at street level in Via dei Servi in 1624, which he rented out on a three-generation contract for *fl*.32 per year

---

83. In the fifteenth century a *casa colonica* called *L'Olmo* along the Via di Padule crossing the valley of the Rimaggio was purchased by Sallustio Buonguglielmi; Lensi Orlandi Cardini, *Le ville di Firenze di là d'Arno*, 12.

(with the stipulation that the tenant pay *fl.*50 for improvements within two years), and another in Borgo Ognissanti in 1628, rented for *fl.*24 and then, after improvements (chiefly a stable), for *fl.*30. Peri ended his life as a substantial landowner: he had farms at San Marco Vecchio, Castelvecchio, Marciano, and in Pian di Ripoli, and three houses in Florence; and his wife had the Fortini farm at Cicogna and the family house in Borgo SS. Apostoli.

Peri administered all his rural properties through the classic sharecropping contract, or *mezzadria*, that had spread throughout much of Tuscany from the thirteenth century on with the formation of the *podere* as the basic organizational unit for working the land. The *podere* was a farm large enough to support the family of one tenant farmer. It generally included one or more buildings that provided him with a home for his family, spaces for storage and stabling, and perhaps a kiln or mill. Farming was promiscuous, that is, not specialized; the owner invested in the buildings and animals, and production was directed to a division of it between the owner and the farmer, leaving the latter with what he and his family needed to live on.

It was only in 1591, by which time he had increased his holdings above Rostolena in the Mugello to the point that they almost constituted a *podere*, that Peri began to keep accounts of farming activity, both there and at San Marco Vecchio; thereafter the administration of his rural properties is the best documented of all his investments. He opened individual accounts for his tenants; there were more than thirty of them down to the time of his death. It may be significant that, as in accounts from the earlier period, these men are each identified as *lavoratore*, or worker, and only very rarely as *contadino*, or peasant, a term—along with *mezzadro*, or sharecropper—today loaded with a specific social content that may make both words anachronistic in the context of this earlier period. (In the following discussion we shall refer to them as "tenants" or "workers.") These men, we shall see, were oriented to market exchange and frequently handled cash, sometimes large amounts; at least some were literate, or at least able to keep some kind of accounting record. More than half, incidentally, had surnames, a marked innovation in self-identification that had occurred over the course of the sixteenth century.

Peri's properties produced a bit of everything, and those in the vicinity of the city, especially the *orto* at Ripoli (which was rented out apart from the farm), sent produce to the urban market as well as to Peri's household. At Marciano workers had animals of all kinds—chickens, horses, cows, sheep, pigs—and they sold some of their production, from foodstuffs to raw wool, on the local market, but they also sent significant quantities of wheat to Peri for sale in Florence, and this constituted the chief source of his income from his possessions. In fact, when his son Dino took over the accounts toward the end of his father's life, he separated farm income into two accounts, one for wheat (*grano*) and one for forage and pulses (*biade e legumi*), the major products brought to Florence for sale. On occasion the workers at Marciano also sent some raw silk to the city.

The accounts show that expenses and profits were divided half and half, but the animals were Peri's, constituting part of the capital investment in a farm. In fact, he kept a small account book just for the transactions regarding these animals.[84] Typically, contracts between owner and workers, however, did not take a written form, and none survives for the arrangements Peri made with the men who worked his land. When he took on a new worker at San Marco Vecchio in 1606, he referred to a written agreement (*scritta*) with the previous tenant, but with the new one he had only a verbal understanding about the same conditions.[85] On the occasion of opening an account for a worker, he sometimes mentions the customary terms. In 1593, for farming one of the small pieces of land in the Mugello, the worker agreed to the usual arrangement to share profits and losses half and half.[86] Sometimes particular stipulations were added. In 1602, by which time these holdings had been transformed into a single farm, the tenant agreed to work the land according to the customary arrangements, with Peri providing half of what was needed for crops and maintenance of the animals, but in addition he was to spade a small field of Peri's once a year and to come to Florence when needed, bringing with him a pair each of capons and chickens.[87] In 1613 the arrangement with a new tenant on the farm at Castelvecchio, based on the "customary and usual pact for the working of the said farm according to the convention of an honest worker," included the obligation to give Peri two pairs of capons, four

---

84. LC 3914, which consists of separate accounts, from 1595 to 1632, for animals (*buoi, giovenchi, vacche, vitelle, porci, pecore, agnelli, cavalli, puledri, asini, muli*), farm by farm.

85. Ledger A, fol. 77.

86. Ledger A, fol. 27: *si obliga a rendermi buon conto a uso di buon lavoratore con starne a mezza perdita e mezzo il guadagno, come si usa.*

87. Ledger A, fol. 57: *si obliga a lavorare il detto podere secondo l'uso del paese, con darmi mezzo quello che vi si ricorrà e mezzo il seme e altre spese che occorressino di strami per le bestie; e più si obliga a vangare ogni anno uno staioro di terra e venire a Firenze quando bisogna con e' vantaggi soliti, cioè un paio di capponi e un paio di pollastre.*

dozen eggs (two dozen at Christmas and two at Easter), and a half barrel of grapes, and to come to Florence whenever necessary with a donkey loaded with things that belonged to Peri.[88] In 1615 a new tenant at Marciano, in addition to "the usual conditions," agreed to supply Peri annually with 300 eggs (100 at All Saints, 100 in January, 100 at Easter) plus twelve capons and ten chickens, and, in exchange for *fl.*20, he loaned Peri a mare, which Peri could use for himself, although any profit he might make from it was to go to the worker.[89] On taking on a new worker at Ripoli in 1613 he noted the agreement was the usual and customary one (*li patti soliti e consueti*): for his part the worker was to maintain a pair of oxen and a donkey suitable to deliver Peri's share of produce without any charge (these animals presumably belonged to Peri), and if Peri so wished, also a pack mule that could be saddled, for which Peri would loan the worker *sc.*30, and he was to propagate sixty vines by layering every year and to provide Peri with two pairs of capons weighing ten pounds a pair and a pair of chickens on All Saints Day and ten dozen eggs at Easter. For his part, Peri was to have half of whatever the farm produced, his only obligation being to provide half the fava beans or lupines for fertilizer.[90]

Typically, there was much fluidity in the ranks of those who worked Peri's farms: the longest any one of them stayed was eight years, and many were on the job for no more than several years. This mobility must have only complicated the problems of managing properties too far away from the city for a small landowner, like Peri, who did not have an estate manager to keep tabs on what was happening on his various and far-flung holdings. The problems he had at Marciano, the most distant of his possessions—at least a two-day trip away—must have been the most serious, since he himself probably showed up on the scene only once a year.[91] The confusion that arose with the *censuari* at Marciano, recounted earlier, illustrates the tenuousness of remote control in the administration of distant properties. Some of the workers, even those as far away as Castelvecchio and Marciano, came to Florence, but what Peri lacked was a resident agent who had management responsibilities, although

88. Ledger A, fol. 94.
89. Ledger A, fol. 99.
90. Ledger A, fol. 95.
91. The family of Peri's cousin Dino had properties in the area of Montevarchi, and in his journal (1582–90) this Dino registers the expenses for his annual trips there (usually staying the night in San Giovanni Valdarno); ASF, Spinelli Baldocci 167.

he used trusted local intermediaries who in his absence handled cash transactions with his workers for him without having, apparently, any supervisory authority.[92] Peri's son Dino took a dim view of the situation: he felt his father had been too lenient in dealing with the workers, and after his father's death he had to travel into the countryside, much to his distaste, to take care of "our several farms that are going to ruin . . . thanks to the treachery of the peasants" (*diversi nostri poderi che vanno in rovina . . . per gli assassinamenti de' contadini*).[93] The only serious problem Peri himself recorded, however, was the dismissal of a worker for having sold a donkey belonging to Peri; he never made a note of any problems that might have led him to resort to a government authority or that ended up in court.

Something of the informality of his relations with the workers, of his limited knowledge of the local situation, and hence of possible ambiguities between owner and tenant surfaces in some of the entries on the accounts he opened in the names of the workers at Marciano. When in 1602 Domenico di Piero Guerra ended his tenure, he claimed to have left behind on the property two beehives worth £21; Peri, in Florence, despite doubts about this value, credited his account accordingly but added that on his next visit he would check it out and lower the assessment to its true value.[94] On 26 April 1609, while he was at Marciano, he and his worker, Domenico di Bartolomeo Bigliazzi, drew up a list of all the transactions Bigliazzi had made over the previous months so it could be determined what he owed Peri for his half of the proceeds.[95] We are not told what evidence Bigliazzi produced for Peri, but entries in the accounts of a worker at Marciano, of another at Castelvecchio, and of a third at San Marco Vecchio refer to their own *quadernucci*.[96] In an instance after Peri's death, Dino had to accept the evidence in the *libretto* of the renter of the garden of the farm near Bagno a Ripoli that in fact

---

92. Two of these, Betto and Orazio, are not otherwise identified and appear rarely; the former is once referred to as Peri's *agente*. The other intermediary, Genevra (whom he always calls Gena) di Paolo de' Barili, appears frequently and probably had a special relation with Peri: he loaned her *fl.*80 in 1603 with the agreement that, rather than repaying it, she would, on her death, leave him a *censo* she had; he describes her as living in his house at Marciano (this is *censo* no. 8 in the discussion above of *censi*).

93. So Dino wrote to Galilei Galilei; see Galilei, *Le opere*, 15: 325.

94. Ledger A, fol. 52.

95. Ledger A, fol. 78.

96. Ledger A, fols. 59, 92; Ledger B, fol. 35.

three payments toward the rent had been made that his father had failed to enter in his accounts.[97] In a credit entry for £91 that Peri made on 25 January 1613 in the account of another worker at Marciano, he wrote that in doing this he took the word of the worker that this was the amount of cash he had received from the worker over the last year, whereas he himself had no precise memory of the payments, adding that presumably the truth would eventually come out in the final balance of the account.[98] Yet Peri trusted at least three of these workers at Marciano to handle cash for his own transactions. On 24 November 1600 Marco (not otherwise named) collected £140 from a local borrower in repayment of a loan Peri had made him.[99] On 26 May 1609 Peri authorized Domenico Bigliazzi to withdraw no less than $fl.$180 (£1,260) from the Michelozzi bank in Florence so that, once back in Marciano, he could make the payment for some land that Peri had bought, and in fact Bigliazzi represented Peri in drawing up the deed of sale.[100] In August 1630 Andrea da Rubutino made a payment of £35 toward a debt Peri had with a local notary who had done legal work for him.[101]

The accounts are not records of the half-and-half division of what the farm produced; nor were they kept to reveal Peri's eventual earnings.[102] In-stead, they record his debit and credit relations with his workers: thus an ac-count might be debited for animals turned over to a worker at the beginning of his tenure and then, and at the time he left, credited for animals returned. These worker accounts thus provide us with the kind of information about the day-to-day administration of rural properties that is lacking in most studies of the *mezzadria* system in Tuscany. It is thought that a system that resulted in production being divided between worker and owner largely left the former at the level of self-sufficiency, removing him to the margins of the marketplace and rendering his life somewhat precarious, mostly dependent on seasonal performance. In bad years he might need loans to survive, and indebtedness is generally regarded as the explanation for the considerable

97. Ledger B, fol. 46.
98. Ledger A, fol. 84.
99. Ledger A, fol. 47.
100. Ledger A, fol. 82; the deed is in LC 3912, document dated 3 June 1609.
101. Ledger A, fols. 47, 82; Ledger B, fol. 54.
102. During the 1590s he made annual lists of what he sold from his properties in the Mu-gello and the Valdichiana, but the material is sloppily organized and not always clear; Ledger A, fols. 171–80.

mobility of sharecroppers. But a somewhat different picture emerges from
Peri's accounts.

It is clear that these men operated in a market organized around a cash
nexus, even those in areas as remote as Rostolena and as distant as Marciano.
The accounts opened in the name of workers in these areas consist primarily
of debit and credit entries recording sales and purchases (*comprare* and *ven-
dere* are the verbs used): they are debited, for instance, for produce they sold
(half to be paid to Peri) and credited for purchases made for the farm (reim-
bursement for half to come from Peri). Moreover, many of the specific transactions made between them and Peri, or made locally on Peri's behalf, are
specified as being in cash (*contanti*, used together with the verbs *recò* and
portò). They usually amounted to several florins and occasionally even more:
on 27 December 1602 Domenico Guerra paid Peri £154; on 6 September 1603
Giovanni Maria di Masso, £116.16s.8d.; on 25 November 1614 Domenico Bigliazzi, £60; in May 1616 Pietro Bigliazzi, £280 (through Peri's intermediary);
in September 1617 Agnolo di Andrea, £70; on 23 January 1623 Antonio di
Luca, £69—all these workers being at Marciano, and these being only the
largest of their cash payments. And Peri made many payments in cash to
them (including his share of the cost of transporting produce to Florence).[103]

Even more impressive, especially given the notion that *mezzadri* typically
ended their tenure in debt, most of these men at Marciano, on leaving Peri's
property, paid off the debit balance on their account in cash, though not always immediately: Domenico Guerra paid £23.15s., Giovanni Maria di
Masso, £219 (sent to Florence through Peri's intermediary), and Domenico
Bigliazzi, £81.4s. On the settlement of Antonio di Luca's account, he instead
had a credit of £2.6s.4d., which Peri paid in cash.[104] The same situation obtained at Peri's property in the Mugello, much more remote: two of the four
accounts were closed with a cash payment by the worker—£24.8s.4d. and
£89.17s.8d.—and a third instead was closed with a debit entry for £63.6s.8d.,
which, it is specified, the worker owed Peri in cash (*mi doveva in denari
contanti*).[105] At the farm near Bagno a Ripoli, one worker on his departure
settled his account with Peri by paying £131.11s. 8d. in cash, and likewise another at San Marco Vecchio balanced and closed his account with two cash

103. Ledger A, fols. 52, 60, 96, 99, 127, 142.
104. Ledger A, fols. 52, 79, 96, 167.
105. Ledger A, fols. 44, 57, 62.

payments amounting to £15.4*s*.[106] These are not insignificant sums for men of this social status at a time when the unskilled urban laborer earned £1 a day. Nor were they always small sums for Peri, who in addition to whatever profit he gained from his sharecroppers also had the benefit of the fruits of their labor to feed his large household.

These "peasant sharecroppers" who worked Peri's land can perhaps be called rural proletarians, as an older historiographical tradition of *mezzadria* scholarship has it, but they were hardly victims of a "miserable system" that reduced them to indebtedness and a barely subsistence level of existence, a view influenced by the situation in nineteenth- and twentieth-century Italy. Peasants who rented the land they worked were more likely in such straitened circumstances, and while some sharecroppers did also, others did not, the difference largely being a result of the quality of the land they worked. A positive view emerges from the very few case studies that have been conducted on the basis of direct documentation, such as we have for Peri. His tenants, far from surviving as isolated self-sufficient workers of the land, were in fact active in market transactions that drew them into a cash economy, and they were not without their own resources, in their ability both to take initiatives—hence the mobility in their ranks—and to accumulate a certain surplus—hence the possibility of paying off their debts on leaving one tenure for another. And the Peri materials document situations in places far from Florence and as diverse as the remote semi-mountainous Mugello and the fertile plain of the Valdichiana. It will take a good deal more research, however, to determine just how typical these sharecroppers were and in what ways they represent changes in the *mezzadria* system from the time of its emergence in the fourteenth century as well as provide a perspective on the changes it would undergo in the following centuries.[107]

Real estate was the one kind of investment that exposed the investor to taxation. The land tax (*decima*) was, in fact, the only direct tax the grand duchy

---

106. Ledger A, fol. 160; Ledger B, fol. 35.

107. For the older view, see Jones, "From Manor to *Mezzadria*," esp. 225 (which takes the "miserable system" comment from an eighteenth-century English observer), with continuing resonances still, e.g., in Najemy, *A History of Florence*, 310. A specific study pointing to a different view is Pinto, "Contadini e proprietari nelle campagne fiorentine," 160–80; and for recent more general and balanced views, see Pinto and Tognarini, "Povertà e assistenza," 460–63, and Mucciarelli and Piccini, "Un'Italia senza rivolte?" 175–80. All these texts regard the fourteenth century.

imposed on its subjects, and it had a remarkably efficient accounting system in place to keep itself informed about landownership. Through the *decima* records one can track the detailed history of any Florentine's portfolio of real-estate holdings (less the place of residence, which was not taxable), complete with descriptions of properties, and while market values are not included, the tax imposed on each item establishes at least a criterion for their value relative to one another. Under the early grand dukes the burden of this tax was remarkably low, thanks in part to their private economic initiatives and in part to the reduction of military expenditures owing to the pacification of Italy at the time.[108] In any event, Peri eventually managed to avoid the tax altogether. In 1619, on the birth of his twelfth living child, he requested and obtained a standard exemption from the *decima* because of the size of his household. The exemption also applied to his wife's properties, and it remained in effect for his heirs, even when death reduced their number down to just his widow and the last son, Alfonso. The exemption is in fact listed in an inventory of Alfonso's assets of all kinds, taking in everything from his court stipend to cash on hand, although the corresponding space for its capitalized monetary value in the right-hand column is left blank.[109] The exemption, however, did not preclude the government's continuing interest in Peri's portfolio of real-estate holdings, and the *decima* records for his properties provide a compre-

108. Dino Fortini's father, who had the three farms and villa at Cicogna assessed at *fl.*6,225 by the Pupilli officials, paid an average tax of only *fl.*15 a year over forty-one years, from 1544 to 1585; LC 2379, fol. 232.

109. Peri's petition, officially submitted on 9 May 1619, and the official certification of its validity on 5 June 1619, are found in ASF, Auditore delle Riformagioni 32, fols. 110–11. The petition, as summarized by the court secretary Curzio Picchena, reads as follows: *Serenissimo Gran Duca // Jacopo d'Antonio Peri, humilissimo servitore di l'Altezza Serenissima, con ogni veneranza gli espone tanto in nome suo quanto in nome della Alessandra, sua legittima consorte, come essendo la verità che si trovano di presente dodici figiuoli, sette masti e cinque femmine, vivi et sani nati d'ambiduoi, perciò la supplicano si degni farli grazia che possino godere et essere exenti dalle decime del Commune di Firenze sì come hanno graziato delli altri, che metterano questa grazia in agumento di tante altre ricevute da l'Altezza Serenissima; e sempre pregheranno il Signore Iddio per ogni sua maggior felicità sì come sempre fanno.* A copy of the official act of exemption is in LC 3912, document dated 5 June 1619; see also ASF, Decima granducale 3591 (*campioni*), fol. 171. For its application to his wife's properties, see her *decima* account cited in Chapter 4. Immediately after Peri's death in 1633 his sons appealed for a continuation of the exemption; ASF, Decima granducale 1447 (*giustificazioni*), no. 554. The undated inventory of Alfonso's assets is in LC 3912.

hensive view of his holdings, and thereby a check on our survey of them constructed from his own accounts.[110]

This material, however, does not lend itself easily to an evaluation of real estate as an investment. Since almost all the rural properties Peri possessed outright had come to him by way of dowries, his accounts give us little information for calculating returns on investment. The only investment he made in land was the lease on the farm near Bagno di Ripoli: it cost him *fl.*2,600 (including the *fl.*600 spent in improvements), and in 1630 he estimated (on the basis of a five-year average) that it brought him a net income of *fl.*115 per year, a mere 4.4 percent return on his investment. He did better with the piece of land he rented at San Marco Vecchio: it initially took a good deal of attention to get it in shape, but almost a half century later, at the end of his life, it was bringing him twice as much as he was paying in rent, which is to say a net income of *fl.*6. Rents for his houses in Florence paid him returns of 6.4 and 7 percent. We know something about what he earned from his other farms, but we do not know what they represented as capital investments. In his accounts of the trust Peri set up before he died (see Chapter 4), Dino records returns over the following years that were slightly higher, if we use assessed rather than actual market value, once reaching as high as 7.3 percent. Farms, however, required attention if not direct management, and distance from the city complicated the direct administration of them, as Dino found out when he made the trip to Marciano to check up on the family properties there.

While Peri's accounts may not tell us much about the rates of return from his investments in farms, they do reveal other features of the land market in early seventeenth-century Florence. And they send signals that are contradictory. On the one hand, the appearance of the *censo* in the market, and the relatively high rate of interest it paid, would indicate that capital was flowing into the agricultural sector. This might have resulted from the interplay of new economic forces, especially on the demand side. First, the wealthy increased their landholdings and at the same time sought to consolidate what

110. The only complete survey made by the state during Peri's lifetime is that of 1618. From internal references in the records for that year (called *campioni*) one can go backward through the annual volumes (called *arroti*) to trace the history of land accumulations, and also forward to track subsequent vicissitudes. For Peri the relevant 1618 record is ASF, Decima granducale 3591 (*campione*), fol. 171. A complete survey of all his properties was made on their inheritance by his sons; ASF, Decima granducale 2396 (*arroti*), no. 90.

before had been scattered farms (*poderi*) into more compact contiguous clusters, forming veritable estates (*fattorie*)—something Peri himself did on a
very small scale first at Rostolena and then at Marciana. Second, the long-
term inflation in the course of the sixteenth century—the so-called price
revolution—which is most evident in the market for foodstuffs, made investment in the agricultural sector more attractive. And a third and final force
that had an impact on the land market arose with a redistribution of wealth
that generated the emergence of a stronger middling class of people, like
Peri, who had more money to invest at modest levels, and who considered
land the only reasonably secure investment available. All these dynamics
made the land market a somewhat different place from what it had been a
century earlier.

On the other hand, however, there were blockages in the land market that
must have impinged on fluidity on the supply side. The most serious was the
fedecommesso, or entail, that tied property to the family rather than to only
one heir, as did primogeniture. This instrument became increasingly popular
in the sixteenth century as landowners, and not just those who owned large
amounts of land, sought to extend a sense of family patrimony to their heirs
and on into the future. In his 1630 testament Peri so bound all of his properties, perhaps in the hope of establishing a solid economic foundation for
the claims to nobility that he took so seriously. The *fedecommesso* not only
impeded the free-market circulation of properties but also could lead to
contentious litigation over ownership among heirs, as we have seen with the
Fortunati. Another blockage that must have limited the circulation of properties in the marketplace was the three-generation lease, which could be obtained by outright purchase or by agreeing to pay a fixed rent for the entire
period. Peri used a purchase contract of this kind to acquire the farm near
Bagno a Ripoli, and a three-generation rental contract both to get the land at
San Marco Vecchio and to rent out his house in Via dei Servi. Through such
leases, which imposed a temporal limit on ownership, investors might have
been able to obtain properties at less cost, a consideration that may have entered into the price for Peri's properties at San Marco Vecchio and in Pian di
Ripoli, since they were so close to the city and hence likely more expensive; if
so, the three-generation lease may have expanded possibilities for investment
in real estate. Yet by the very nature of the lease, such properties were removed from the market for no insignificant length of time, and they did not,
in the end, have any lasting benefit for the family.

In bringing to light these various considerations, Peri's investment history points out the direction research needs to take to assess the performance of the agricultural sector in late sixteenth- and early seventeenth-century Tuscany. This history also reveals the particular qualities of this kind of investment that distinguish it from others a Florentine might have in his portfolio. Peri had various concerns in purchasing real estate: it was a solid investment and a sign of status, but in his accounts for the farms he also reveals himself as a hands-on landowner, a manager with clear long-term objectives and with a certain interest in farming. Moreover, he wanted property that he could pass on to his heirs. The prebend at San Marco Vecchio and the farm near Bagno a Ripoli, both subject to a three-generation lease, were the next best thing to a permanent possession for someone with limited resources to invest in valuable properties close to Florence. In his 1630 will, he warns his heirs never to rent out the property near Bagno a Ripoli because that would render the lease null and void, and he orders that all the other properties be entailed (with a *fedecommesso*). And real estate was more than just a passive investment. The desire to acquire it, unlike channeling money into other investment outlets, arose from motives informed by cultural as well as financial interests; at the same time, it was likely to draw the investor out of passivity into active engagement with his property. In this sense Peri's history as landowner encapsulates the complex meaning that real estate, more than any other investment, had for Florentines at the time.

Income and Shifting Investment Priorities

Peri's letters make occasional reference to his other affairs (presumably, including business) in ways that suggest they could be a headache at times: in March 1608 (Letter 9) he tells Cardinal Ferdinando Gonzaga that his being occupied *in altri mia affari* has been one of several things keeping him from writing music, and he makes a similar point (excuse?) to Duchess Caterina de' Medici Gonzaga in early 1620, referring to the *molti affari che mi tengono occupato* (Letter 28). One would expect Peri's accounts to reveal something of these *affari*, as indeed they do. But one must also remember that an account book is, by definition, a record of economic activity. It documents the movement of money and credit, and it sifts the relevant data through the categories that are important to the accountant, the person who posts the book. Jacopo Peri's ledgers provide an immense amount of information about his economic activities, but his categories organizing the accounts are not ours. For all of his mastery of the techniques of accounting, the function of the exercise for him—and for Florentines in general—was not eventual analysis, but instead a service to memory, a tool to help him take stock at any one time of his credit and debit relations with the people with whom he had financial dealings, and a record for eventual legal purposes and family interest. All of his accounts are opened in the name of persons: there are no accounts of total income and expenditures, of profit and loss, of the performance of investments, of overall patrimonial administration. Moreover, there is little sense of regular periodicity in the organization of the accounts. In other words, like all Florentines—for all the fame of the accounting records still surviving in the city's archives—Peri did not keep accounts to know the things that most interest us today, above all his income from musical activity—not even institutional stipends (which we know from other sources) let alone what he may have earned from commissions, performances, gifts, sales of published work, and (with just one exception) teaching. The following overview of his economic life, organized around the history of his income and the building up of a patrimony, therefore is our reconstruction, not his. It involves sifting through the data in the account books using anachronistic categories, and the ensuing analysis suffers from what is not to be found in these sources. Peri himself would probably find it little more than a curiosity.

On the basis of what we know, the discussion of Peri's life as an economic operator can be divided in three fairly distinct periods: the first takes him to his marriage in 1592 at the age of thirty-one; the second sees him successively reinforced by handsome dowries and consequently more aggressive as an investor; and the third, beginning in the mid-1610s, finds him now in his fifties, surrounded by a large family at home and assured of a highly respectable social standing in the city, settling in more passively to a stable, secure, and comfortable financial position.

The first period was surveyed in Chapter 1. It sees his affirmation not only as a musician but also as an investor, and we can fairly assume that he managed to augment his income, beyond that which is documented, by fees—or gifts—for musical activity other than the stipends that he is currently known to have held. His rising economic status is reflected in the increased rent— from *fl.*14 to *fl.*17—he was prepared to pay for the new home to which he moved in 1586, and in the somewhat risky commitment he made in 1588 to pay an additional *fl.*6 a year in taking out the twenty-nine-year lease on the

prebend at San Marco Vecchio. Meanwhile he made a few modest investments on the exchange and in cloth production, the only durable ones being
the acquisitions, beginning in 1586, of small pieces of land in the Mugello
with the conscious objective of building up the coherent property that he
later sold as a farm. In short, during these early years he was slowly gaining
respectable, if still modest, economic status in the lower ranks of the city's
middling class, thanks largely—one has to conclude on the basis of the evidence currently at our disposal—to his growing fame as a musician.

The dowry of *fl.*3,200 Peri received on his first marriage in 1592 obviously
projected him into a much higher economic class, albeit still in the middling
ranks of Florentine society, and this position was reinforced a decade later, at
the end of 1601 when he received a second dowry of *fl.*2,000, and the next
year yet a third, this time in the form of a large farm in the countryside with
a value at the level of each of the previous two dowries. With these three marriages within a decade, a new phase opens up in Peri's economic career, one
that finds him not only much better off but also propelled into the marketplace as a more aggressive investor. This second phase, along with his eventual retirement into a third phase in the mid-1610s, when he settles down as a
less active economic operator, emerges from the details of his investments
and income over the years, as shown in, respectively, Tables 2.4 and 2.5. In-
terpreting these tables, however, calls for some caution. Table 2.4 does not
include investments in bills of exchange and the value of the properties that
came to Peri through dowries. Table 2.5 does not include income from his
rural properties and returns from his investments in the cloth industries, bills
of exchange, and government securities. All these are significant items in
Peri's portfolio, and as we have seen, we know much about them, but not in
the kind of detail that goes into the construction of these tables. Remaining
completely outside our range of vision—to sound again a continuing theme
in this book—are the economic rewards of his musical activity other than his
court salary.

Taken together, the tables delineate the second and third phases in Peri's
life, the break being marked by the change that occurred roughly around 1615
in his investments and in the course of his fixed stipends. In the earlier phase
Peri was an aggressive investor. He bought a substantial house in 1596, but
otherwise he put his money into the cloth industries (1596, 1599, 1600, 1605),
taking a job with a wool firm as a salaried accountant (in 1600, if he did not
already have one), and eventually setting up his own wool company (1609)

Table 2.4.   Jacopo Peri's principal investments (in florins)

Year	Cloth industries	Real estate	*Censi*	*Monti*	TOTAL
1585	300				300
1586		76			76
1587		60			60
1588					—
1589					—
1590		21			21
1591		10			10
1592		100			100
1593		54			54
1594					—
1595					—
1596	2,000	1,000			3,000
1597					—
1598		103			103
1599	300	8			308
1600	1,000				1,000
1601		188			188
1602					—
1603					—
1604			2,754	102[a]	2,856
1605	500	200			700
1606		100			100
1607					—
1608					—
1609	2,000	205			2,205
1610	423	29	200		652
1611					—
1612		2,000			2,000
1613					—
1614		600	60	451[b]	1,111
1615				281[b]	281
1616				524[b]	524
1617	1,000				1,000
1618		600		285[b]	885
1619				300[c]	300
1620				200[c]	200
1621					—
1622					—
1623					—
1624		501		300[c]	801
1625					—
1626				200[c]	200

(continued)

Table 2.4   (*continued*)

Year	Cloth industries	Real estate	*Censi*	*Monti*	TOTAL
1627					—
1628		361			361
1629		64			64
1630					—
1631				400[c]	400
1632			200	200[c]	400
1633				2,300[d]	2,300
TOTAL	7,523	6,280	3,214	5,543	22,560

a. Monte delle Graticole; b. *monti* in Rome; c. Monte di Pietà; d. Monte del Sale

and the dye house in the name of his son (1610). In 1604 he made his single largest investment—and an extraordinarily high one by standards of the time, as well as a clearly risky one—in a single *censo* bought in the secondary market. It is significant with respect to the historiographical tradition that sees financial retrenchment among Florentines already in the sixteenth century that Peri invested heavily in the more dynamic sectors of the economy, very likely advised by the Michelozzi. During this phase he also significantly increased his landholdings in the countryside, thanks, however, to dowries that included the large farms at Marciano (1596) and Castelvecchio (1602). He paid out of his own pocket to buy more real estate: he provided the financial support for the deal his wife made with her brother to take possession of the farm at Cicogna (1614), and he purchased several small pieces of land at Marciano, as well as *censi* on a few other pieces in the vicinity, to strengthen his presence there. These, however, added up to no more than about half of his other investments. His major acquisitions were his home in Florence (1596) and the long-term leases on the villa (1605) and farm in Pian di Ripoli (1612) in the immediate countryside.

Considering all of his business activity in the first decade of the seventeenth century, it is hardly surprising that prospective patrons of his music found Peri immersed in "a thousand business affairs," as was reported to Cardinal Ferdinando Gonzaga in 1609.[111] In the mid-1610s Peri changed his investment strategy. He invested in a silk company in 1617, but otherwise he

111. So Geronimo Lenzoni wrote on 21 January 1609; see Chapter 3 also for a broader discussion of apparent clashes between Peri's business affairs and musical activities.

Table 2.5. Jacopo Peri's annual income from selected sources (in florins)

Year	Stipends					Dowries	Censi	Monte di Pietà	Rents	TOTAL
	Church posts	Medici court	State offices	Cloth industries	Total from stipends					
1579–85	15				15					15
1586	15+6				21					21
1587	15+18				33					33
1588	15+18	24			57					57
1589	15+18	72			105					105
1590	15+3	84			102					102
1591	15	108			123					123
1592	15	108			123	*(1st wife:)*				123
1593	15	108			123	2,000				2,123
1594	15	108			123	85				208
1595	15	108			123	35				158
1596	15	108			123	30				153
1597	15	108	15		138					138
1598	15	108			123					123
1599	15	108		*(firm:)*	123					123
1600	15	108		10	133					133
1601	15	108	16	24	163					163
1602	15	108	84	24	231	*(2nd wife:)* 600				831
1603	15	108	24	20	167					167
1604	15	108			123		83			206
1605	4	108			112	200	211			523
1606		108	9		117	294	211			622
1607		108	19		127	62	211			400

Year									
1608	108			108	74	211			393
1609	108			108	60	211			379
1610	108	19+40	?	167+?	260	161			588+?
1611	108	20	?	128+?	60	25			213+?
1612	108			108	60	25			193
1613	108			108	60	25			193
1614	108			108	191	25			324
1615	108	83		191		30			221
1616	108	59		167		30			197
1617	108	120	(guild:)	228		30			258
1618	108		90	198		30			228
1619	108	99	120	327		29		25	381
1620	108	40+60	120	328		29	10	25	392
1621	108	23	120	251		829	33	25	1,138
1622	108	5	120	233		29	37	25	324
1623	108	25+88	120	341		29	25	25	420
1624	108	62	120	290		29	32	25	376
1625	108	48	120	276		29	20	57	382
1626	108	96	120	324		29	8	57	418
1627	108		120	228		26	10	60	324
1628	108	30	120	258		26	10	60	354
1629	108	?	120	228+?		26	10	84	348+?
1630	108		96	204		26	10	90	330
1631	108	88	96	292		26	38	90	446
1632	108	62	96	266		35	35	90	426
1633	108		96	204		35	20	90	349

Note: Figures have been rounded to the nearest florin, and when a figure overlaps two years it has been broken down only approximately, not precisely, into separate figures for each year. The first dowry includes interest on unpaid balance due. The dowry for Peri's third wife was conveyed entirely in property. Not included are income from farms and interest from the Monte del Sale and the *monti* in Rome (see Table 2.6).

shifted out of industry into government securities, and from land in the countryside to real estate in the city: in other words, he tended to park his money rather than put it more actively to work. It is not so difficult to come up with possible reasons for this shift, but we have no way of knowing whether any of these had weight in the precise considerations that went through his mind at the time. They are not, however, mutually exclusive. He may have been burned by his more aggressive investments: precisely at the time he took an active interest in the wool industry, at the turn of the century, the international markets for the high-quality cloth that had been the foundation of the industry—and of the Florentine economy in general— since the fourteenth century began to dry up, and the decline of production for exports was rapid and permanent during the first decade of the seventeenth century. We have no record of the performance of his specific investments, but it was certainly not spectacular. As for his venture into the relatively new market for *censi* with the extraordinarily high investment he made in 1604, it caused him no end of grief, even though he eventually recovered the capital he had invested. Thereafter he bought *censi* at much lower prices on land at Marciano—possibly, as already suggested, following a strategy as landlord in the area rather than as investor. Or perhaps we ought to see his turn to the more conservative investment outlets of government securities as reflecting the concern of an aging father, now approaching sixty, for the financial stability of a rapidly growing family.

A glance at the sources of fixed income in Table 2.5 might lead one to yet another explanation for the shift in Peri's investments. His stipend as court musician must have been by this time, for a singer, something of a sinecure (though he still composed), even if it provided only a relatively small proportion of his income. In addition, he now had the very substantial salary he earned in his position, with lifetime tenure, at the Arte della Lana. Finally, from 1615 to his death in 1633 he spent almost half the time serving in a state office of one kind or another, all paying a reasonably good fee that brought him, on average, about *fl.*60 a year when in office, while his service ranged from attendance at occasional meetings to the major supervisory commitment required of the Decima officials, not to mention the full-time job of a *podestà* (see Table 1.1). During this last period Peri was earning, on average, twice as much from his various stipends as before, and often he made well over *fl.*300 a year from these sources alone, almost three times his court musician's salary.

But his total income was higher still, and much higher than what is represented in Table 2.5. The difference lies in the income from his rural properties, ranging from the small amount yielded by the prebend at San Marco Vecchio to what came in from the major farms in his possession—especially at Marciano from 1596 and near Bagno a Ripoli from 1612. Peri's accounts were not kept to provide information on what these properties yielded to their owner. Fortunately, however, at the end of his life two detailed and highly reliable assessments were made of his economic situation with respect both to the capital value of his properties and to the income they produced. One he made himself in 1630 as he prepared his testament, and the other his son Dino provided once he took over his father's accounts in the last years of the latter's life. And as a check on these estimates we have Dino's precise accounting record for these properties, broken down specifically into separate annual income accounts for each for five years after Peri's death.

In Chapter 4, we shall discuss the circumstances that led Peri to make his will three years before he died, and shall examine the specific provisions he carefully laid out therein. Here it suffices to report the detailed survey of his economic resources he made in order to assure his eight surviving children of a fair settlement. He did this with reference not to the capital value of his various investments, but to the income those investment yielded (Table 2.6). For this purpose, the rental properties and government securities presented no problem, since they yielded fixed returns. Income from farms, however, was highly variable, and to arrive at a figure for the specific purpose at hand—according to a later *ricordo* his son Niccolò made in the journal he kept for the administration of the farm at Marciano—Peri took an average of the income from these properties over the preceding five years (somewhat lower than that on Dino's subsequent accounts, as indicated in Table 2.6).[112] The total income from all sources other than salaries that he thus calculated for distribution in this settlement amounted to just short of *fl*.535. He lived for three more years, and the accounts, now kept by his son Dino, add further evidence for some of this income and allow for some adjustments, which are included in Table 2.5. To the figures here we can add *fl*.53 from two additional investments he made after dictating his will—*fl*.13 from *censo* no. 8, and *fl*.40 from the *luoghi* in the Monte di Pietà—to come up with what would seem to be an accurate assessment of his annual income from investments at the time

112. For the ricordo made by Niccolò, see LC 3923, fol. 3v.

of his death in 1633: around *fl.*600. With the additional income from his two fixed lifetime stipends—*fl.*108 from the grand-ducal court and *fl.*96 (after 1630) from the Arte della Lana—Peri was earning about *fl.*800 annually when he died. And there is even more to add, at least to the income of his household, for not included in these estimates are the farm at Castelvecchio (which was his wife's dowry), and the one at Cicogna (which she had inherited), because he did not have clear title to either. Dino included income from these properties in his accounts of the trust after his father's death, and it averaged together *fl.*309 for the years 1637–38; when in 1643 Alessandra sold them to Peri's cousins in return for an annuity of *fl.*162 (see Chapter 4), they presumably thought that the farms actually yielded much more than that annual cost. Adding this income to our calculations (even allowing for the burden of the annuity that had to be paid to his wife's brother), we can assume Peri's total income may well have amounted to over *fl.*1,000.

Table 2.6.   Jacopo Peri's income in 1630

Source of income	Amount (in florins)
Rents:	
house, Via dei Servi	32
house, Borgo Ognissanti	24
Censi (Table 2.2):	
nos. 3, 5, 6	21
no. 7	4
Monti:	
monti in Rome (10 *luoghi*)	50
Monte del Sale (23 *luoghi*)	115
Farms:	
San Marco Vecchio	6
Marciano	167
Bagno a Ripoli	115
SUBTOTAL	534
Lifetime salaries from the Arte della Lana and the court (Table 2.5)	204
TOTAL INCOME	738

Source: LC 3912, document dated 15 May 1630 (Peri's testament). Dino's accounts in Ledgers C, D, and E, covering the five years from 1634 to 1638, record an annual average income of *fl.*171 from Marciano and *fl.*160 from Bagno a Ripoli.

And it was all tax free and burdened only with annuities that death would eventually cancel.

Certainly Peri owed something of his economic status to the two salaries he had from the court and the Arte della Lana: they provided him with one-fifth to one-fourth of his total income. But they terminated with his death. Nevertheless, what he would leave his sons constituted a substantial estate that would put them solidly in the middling class of Florentines at the time (in our concluding chapter we shall try to place that ranking a little more precisely). That assessment, however, is subject to two qualifications. The first is how it would have been judged by his family. From the point of view of the immediate interest of his six surviving sons, a division of the estate into six parts (discounting any prospect of a dowry for one of the daughters) would leave all of them very much below the level of well-being at which they had grown up. From the point of view of the long-term interest of his family, a concern Peri obviously had in imposing an entail on all his property, the func-tion of his estate in offering future generations a degree of economic stability was somewhat compromised by those properties held only temporarily— namely, the villa in Pian di Ripoli (leased by Peri for his lifetime) and the farms at San Marco Vecchio and near Bagno a Ripoli (leased for three genera-tions). The properties at Ripoli were major items in Peri's portfolio: the villa, being just outside the city, served the family as a country residence, and the farm provided a good income, being perhaps the most valuable property Peri had at his disposal. But eventually these properties would pass out of the family's hands.

A second qualification to an assessment of Peri's estate regards the market value of the assets in his portfolio. His heirs might have regarded their patri-mony in these terms, since liquidity of assets facilitates the shifting of invest-ments in a portfolio, and it certainly would have been a consideration in their eventual division of the estate among themselves. That liquidity was limited by the entail (*fedecommesso*) Peri had put on all of his real estate, although by recourse to the courts it was possible to lift such restrictions. But for present purposes, liquidity is a reasonable criterion for making some assessment of Peri's success in the marketplace as an investor. This must exclude the farm at San Marco Vecchio and the farm and villa in Pian di Ripoli, since he held these properties on leases that had no marketable value (even if they re-mained available to his heirs), there being, so far as we know, no secondary market in such instruments. Moreover, the farm at Castelvecchio was legally bound by the conditions of his wife's dowry, and the farm at Cicogna and the house in Borgo SS. Apostoli belonged to her (and were, at least for the time being, burdened with annuities). His total marketable assets at the time of his death—nothing is known about possible savings and any valuable personal possessions—thus came to only around *fl.*10,000 (Table 2.7). This patrimony, separate from the properties bound one way or another to his wife, amounted to about two-and-a-half times what he had received in cash with the dowries of his first two wives, and if the farm at Marciano that came to him in lieu of cash owed on his first dowry is excluded, what he ended up with in urban real estate, government securities, and *censi*—in other words, all those assets he had purchased in the market and were in turn marketable—adds up to not much more than half again of what he had received in cash with his dowries. And inasmuch as this calculation excludes whatever profits he made from his investments in the cloth industries, it leads one to believe that he had not earned much from those ventures. This is not an impressive record, in strictly financial terms, for an investment history that extended over a period of thirty to forty years. We do not yet know how it might compare with other similar investors at the time.

This, however, is probably not the way that Peri—or any of his contemporaries, for that matter—would have considered it. Unfortunately we have no assessment of his estate at the time of his death in 1633, but data taken from two subsequent inventories, along with the prices Peri paid for the land he

Table 2.7.   Jacopo Peri's marketable assets in 1633

Property	Value (in florins)
House, Via dei Fossi	1,103
House, Via dei Servi	501
House, Borgo Ognissanti	425
Farm at Marciano	3,340
4 *censi*	500
41 *luoghi di monti*	4,100
TOTAL	9,969

Note: Figures are those of purchase price plus improvements; the value of the farm represents the capitalization at 5 percent of Peri's estimated income from it (see Table 2.6).

himself bought, allow us to estimate an approximate value of the estate (Table 2.8). The inventory made in 1640, by whom and for what purpose we do not know, appears highly exaggerated, given what other data we have, but the document is notable for including a capitalization of the leased property and even the *decima* exemption, as well as his widow's properties. The other assessment, made by the Parte Guelfa officials on confiscating Alfonso's property in 1642, presumably is more realistic, and it includes all the properties that Peri himself had accumulated (along with those that came with the dowry of Alfonso's wife). They add up to a substantial estate.

Peri, in short, ended his life having done very well for himself. His total income amounted to between twenty-five and thirty times what an unskilled day labor earned, and it was much higher, even, than what the highest paid officials at court earned in salaries. Almost all that income came from low-risk investments and from what was in effect a court sinecure, and he was far from being dependent on his one salaried job that required regular work (at the Arte della Lana). He presumably lived reasonably well, with a house in the city large enough to accommodate his numerous family and two female

Table 2.8. Estimates of the value of Jacopo Peri's properties (in florins)

Properties	Purchase price plus improvements[a]	Estimate in 1640[b]	Estimate in 1642[c]
Peri's properties:			
house, Via dei Fossi	1,103	2,000	1,650
house, Via dei Servi	501	800	700
house, Borgo Ognissanti	425	700	430
farm at Marciano	—	10,000	5,213
farm near Bagno a Ripoli	2,600	5,000	2,560
farm at San Marco Vecchio	—	500	—
TOTAL	4,629	19,000	10,553
His wife's properties:			
house in Borgo SS. Apostoli	—	1,000	—
farms at Castelvecchio and Cicogna	—	5,000	2,209

[a.] See Table 2.3.

[b.] LC 3912, document dated 1640.

[c.] ASF, Capitani di Parte Guelfa, Numeri bianchi 311, fols. 36–47v.

servants, and with a residence in the immediate vicinity of the city where he and his family could stay *in villa*. From the perspective of where he began in life, Peri, through one way or another—music, marriage, work, investment— achieved considerable economic success, and even with his estate divided into six parts, his sons would have been much better off than he had been when he started out.

3

The Musical World

The return of the Medici to Florence as dukes of Tuscany, then (from 1569) grand dukes, clearly changed the city's political landscape, and also its urban one, and had an impact on its social structure, but the Medici played their hand carefully as they consolidated their position through the second quarter of the sixteenth century. Then the victory over Siena in 1555 in effect put an end to the ambitions of pro-republican Florentines in exile, and benefited the economy by assuring the stability of the new state, reducing the pressure for direct taxation and opening up space for any number of entrepreneurial initiatives by the Medici themselves. But while their authority was no longer open to dispute, they retained enough of the civic organization of the Florentine republic to reassure—though some might say, delude—the citizenry that Medici rule was benign. Duke, later Grand Duke, Cosimo I de' Medici was also anxious not to engage in the extravagant displays of courtly consumption typical of other Italian duchies (and, for that matter, of some of his successors in Florence). Certainly he centralized artistic production, but he did so often by way of academies involving a patriciate that, while probably less able to engage in the more open-ended patronage typical of the earlier Florentine Renaissance, still had room to maneuver. The reward was proximity to the seat of power, and the prestige and profit that inevitably ensued.

Peri certainly benefited from, and regularly acknowledged, the favor of the grand-ducal family, which brought him status, a lifetime stipend, and (by way of recommendations for public offices) material wealth. Whatever his other skills, his musical talents gained his initial admission to such circles, and while his position among the court musicians was not always a happy one, he was not going to give it up. Yet Peri exercised a considerable degree of freedom within its constraints, more so than a narrow view of courtly patronage in the early modern period might suggest. Whether this was a peculiarity due to the specific nature of Florence, or whether we might better rethink the meaning of such patronage—or whatever the appropriate term might be—is something to be explored.[1] But clearly we should now seek a more nuanced view of Peri's musical work, and of his musical works, if we are to achieve some fuller understanding of this particular part of the Florentine marketplace where our Orpheus sought to negotiate his way.

The challenge, of course, is to demonstrate how his musical activities might fit within the broader frames embracing what we now know of his social and economic circumstances. Clearly, Peri saw himself as more than just a court composer and performer—even though many would have been satisfied with such a position—and music scarcely occupied center stage in his life. It is also fairly easy to demonstrate how music enabled him to extend his reach through and beyond Florentine social, civic, and commercial networks, and even to establish his noble status, though that was a tricky game to play, given the suspicions it aroused: was the musician an artist or an artisan, and was music's evident sensuality safe or dangerous? One further difficulty, however, could be turned to advantage. Music is by definition evanescent—it fully exists only in the moment of performance—and therefore is remarkably hard to pin down. While this might frustrate the scholar, Peri benefited from working within so ambiguous yet penetrating a medium. Certainly, he exploited the issue in his dealings with the Medici court.

1. For Florence, compare Cole, *Music, Spectacle and Cultural Brokerage in Early Modern Italy*; on rethinking musical patronage, see Carter, "Monteverdi and Some Problems of Biography."

Peri's Early Career

The market for music in Florence during Peri's lifetime can be divided into three sectors: the church, the court, and the private sphere. In the fifteenth century the city's major musical establishments were the *cappelle* at the cathedral, the baptistry, the Servite monastery of SS. Annunziata, and the local Benedictine abbey (the Badia Fiorentina)—the Franciscans at S. Croce and the Dominicans at S. Maria Novella, on the eastern and western edges of the city, respectively, were a separate case—and these remained active institutions through the following century and beyond. The Medici, including Lorenzo "il Magnifico," were major patrons in the private sector, but with the family's rise to ducal and grand-ducal status, a court musical establishment emerged that far overshadowed the church *cappelle* collectively. Peri seems to have gotten his start in churches but soon moved into court circles. His activity in the private sector, we shall see, is harder to discern.

To strengthen a petition submitted to Grand Duchess Christine in 1618 for an administrative office that would help him support his large family, Peri claimed to her secretary Andrea Cioli (Letter 23) that he had begun to "serve" at the age of ten (he does not say where) and then was used as a singing teacher to the Medici princesses by Grand Duchess Johanna of Austria (Francesco I's first wife, who died in April 1578). He admitted, however, that there was hardly anyone still at court able to remember so far back (some fifty years). That was probably a good thing: had Cioli checked the facts, he would no doubt have suspected Peri of gilding the lily. The first evidence we have of his service as a musician is his appointment as a boy singer at SS. Annunziata on 1 September 1573 (just short of two weeks after his twelfth birthday); he stayed there until 30 September 1577. His appointment as organist at the Badia began on 1 February 1579, when he was almost eighteen (he held the post until April 1605), and on 28 August 1586, now almost twenty-five years old, he became a singer in the choir of S. Giovanni Battista (until 21 March 1590). Until this latter appointment he was not earning very much as a musician: his annual salary at SS. Annunziata was *fl.*6 (£3.10*s.* per month) and at the Badia, *fl.*15. Yet he was already well enough known locally to catch the attention of the Florentine poet Antonfrancesco Grazzini (who died in 1584). In the late 1570s or early 1580s, Il Lasca, as he was called, wrote two *ottava rima* stanzas lamenting that even though Peri's graces in, and knowledge of, singing and playing merited the highest honors, he was unappreciated in his native city such that he did not have enough bread on which to live (see Appendix D). Matters improved with the position at S. Giovanni Battista, adding *fl.*18 per year to the income of *fl.*15 from the Badia (so, *fl.*33 in all). They did so still more after he was officially enrolled among the court musicians (by September 1588) with an annual salary of *fl.*72 (*fl.*6 per month), which increased to *fl.*108 (*fl.*9 per month) in September 1590, perhaps also in compensation for his having left S. Giovanni Battista.[2] With his positions at court and (until 1605) at the Badia, his musical salaries amounted to *fl.*123 per year (see Table 2.5), a decent sum by any Florentine standards; and as we have seen, the dowry he received for his first marriage, in 1592, put him on an even firmer financial footing. His is a quite striking musical trajectory that is worth examining in some detail.

At SS. Annunziata, Peri was one of a long series of boys appointed (one at a time) by the Servite friars "to sing to the organ": *a cantare in su l'orghano* was the usual wording on appointment and in the salary records, but Peri's appointment specified *a cantare in su l'orghano le laude* (although subsequent payment entries use the shorter form).[3] He was initially recorded as Jacopo di Antonio Peri, but subsequent listings styled him *Jacopino detto il Zazzerino* or the like (the nickname first appears in 1574). His term lasted through September 1577, presumably when his voice broke. During his time there,

2. Peri first appears in the court roll in a list dated 1 September 1588 (ASF, Depositeria Generale 389, fol. 17) but we do not know the official date of his appointment; it probably occurred around that time (when Emilio de' Cavalieri was reorganizing the court music). He is not in a similar list of 1586 save by way of an allowance that Malvezzi was receiving for him.

3. For the appointment, see ASF, Corporazioni religiose soppresse dal governo francese 119 (SS. Annunziata), filza 53, fol. 87, transcribed (with *laudi* for *laude*) in D'Accone, "The Florentine Fra Mauros," 123 (and see also 101–2). Peri's salary payments, normally bimonthly, are regularly recorded in ASF, Corporazioni religiose soppresse dal governo francese 119, filze 639–40 (the *giornale* of the *camerlengo*), and 736–37 (*entrata e uscita*); some are transcribed in D'Accone, "The Florentine Fra Mauros," 130. His last payment was on 28 September 1577 (filza 737, fol. 77) *per finito pagamento di haver cantato in su l'orghano.* He was replaced on 1 October 1577 by one Ceseri di Francesco.

For a contract for a boy singer at SS. Annunziata from 1508 (at the same monthly salary of £3.10*s.*), see D'Accone, "The Musical Chapels at the Florentine Cathedral and Baptistry during the First Half of the 16th Century," 12. This singer was to sing polyphony in the choir, in addition to the *laude*, but the performance of such polyphony at SS. Annunziata, at least by an established choir, appears to have ceased after 1527; ibid., 22–23. Some of these issues (and Peri's presence) are also discussed in Cabras, "Ricerche per la storia della cappella musicale della SS. Annunziata di Firenze."

SS. Annunziata was quite a sizable monastery, with some forty friars, plus twelve *conversi*, six *professi*, and twenty-three novices.[4] Peri's job was chiefly to perform *laude*, which were nonliturgical religious songs (either in Latin or in the vernacular) customarily sung during vigils involving prayers, readings, and homilies: the Florentine repertory had most recently been represented by Serafino Razzi's *Libro primo delle laudi spirituali* (Venice: Francesco Rampazetto, 1563). In SS. Annunziata, such exercises were normally held in the Cappella della Madonna (containing a famous miracle-working image that was an object of pilgrimage), accompanied by the church's second (small) organ.[5] Peri was a lay employee (one of the *medici, procuratori, barbieri, notai, e garzoni secolari di casa*) with a salary slightly more than the gardener's *garzone* (£3 per month) and less than that of the assistants to the head gardener and head cook (£4)—he may also have had board and lodging. He was under the direction of the monastery's organist, Fra Maurizio (Gianino di Giuliano Borsellini, 1530–93), who occasionally signed for his salary (including its first payment), personally handed the cash over to him, and presumably also acted as his music teacher; Peri probably also had lessons from the *maestro di grammatica*. His service at SS. Annunziata came at precisely the time that the church and convent were undergoing significant renovation and new building under the energetic leadership of its prior (from 1572) Michele Poccianti: Santi di Tito completed his fresco *The Feast in the House of Simon the Pharisee* in the convent's refectory in November 1573.[6] Peri may have returned there to sing for Christmas in 1579, when he received a one-time *mancia* (£2) by way of Fra Maurizio.[7]

We do not know how he initially came to the attention of SS. Annunziata. Perhaps, given his close ties to distant relatives, it was through Fra Bernardo

4. These numbers can be gauged from the semiannual lists of *vestimenti* included in the SS. Annunziata accounts, such as ASF, Corporazioni religiose soppresse dal governo francese 119, filza 123, entry for October 1579.

5. Wilson, "Lauda," in *The New Grove Dictionary of Music and Musicians: Revised Edition* (for the genre); D'Accone, "The Florentine Fra Mauros," 109 (Cappella della Madonna).

6. ASF, Corporazioni religiose soppresse dal governo francese 119, filza 45 (*ricordanze* by Michele Poccianti). Poccianti commissioned the fresco (which cost *sc.*135), added statues to the sacristy, and began the building of a new library. The library was supported by donations from leading Florentine families, and also from Grand Duke Cosimo I, Johanna of Austria, and Cardinal Ferdinando de' Medici.

7. ASF, Corporazioni religiose soppresse dal governo francese 119, filza 641, fol. 119v (24 December 1579).

Peri, who was resident in the monastery in the early 1570s.[8] The young Peri's immediate predecessor in singing *laude* to the organ was Cosimo di Giovanni del Cartolaio (son of Giovanni Benvenuti del Cartolaio, *maestro di cappella* at S. Giovanni Battista from 1571 until his death in 1574), who presumably already had some musical education from his father.[9] The source of Peri's prior training is unknown. Presumably, however, Fra Maurizio then pointed him out to Cristofano Malvezzi, who had succeeded Giovanni del Cartolaio at S. Giovanni Battista: as *maestro di cappella*, it was in Malvezzi's interest to spot young talent that might be groomed for better things. Florentine musicians moved in fairly small circles, and both Fra Maurizio and Malvezzi were organists. Certainly Peri was Malvezzi's student by 1577, when the *maestro* published a four-part instrumental ricercar by him in his *Il primo libro de recercari à quattro voci* (Perugia: Pietroiacomo Petrucci).

This publication would suggest that Malvezzi was schooling Peri in the art of counterpoint, on the one hand, and keyboard playing, on the other; there remains the as yet unanswerable question of who, if anyone, might have taught him singing at any high virtuosic level.[10] But whatever that case, one assumes that Malvezzi also recommended Peri for his next appointment, at the Badia (February 1579). His annual salary of *fl.*15 (the monastery's *maestro di grammatica* received *fl.*18) covered his playing the organ according to the custom of the church, as outlined in a (now lost) document that would be

---

8. Fra Bernardo Peri (also called Fra Bernardo and Fra Bernardo di Firenze) appears in the SS. Annunziata accounts in the regular payments for *vestimenti*, as in the *giornale* from 1572 to 1574 in ASF, Corporazioni religiose soppresse dal governo francese 119, filza 638; ASF, Monte di Pietà, 1364 (*Libro di depositi condizionati, entrata e uscita*, 1578–81), fol. 38, records a donation of *fl.*100 by Zanobi di Giovanni Barducci to Fra Bernardo di Bernardo di Antonio Peri, *professo di Santa Maria dell'Annunziata*, made on 30 August 1580. Thus this Bernardo shared the same great-great-great-grandfather as our Jacopo.

9. Kirkendale, *Court Musicians*, 182 (Giovanni di Giorgio Benvenuti del Cartolaio); D'Accone, "The Florentine Fra Mauros," 130 (Cosimo). Another of Giovanni's sons, Orazio, was in the SS. Annunziata position in 1580 (ASF, Corporazioni religiose soppresse dal governo francese 119, filza 641), and he later briefly joined the court musicians (Kirkendale, *Court Musicians*, 296, which does not quite make the connection with his father).

10. We shall see, below, that in 1630 Peri's son Dino referred to his father's musical *maestri* (plural), which might mean more than just Fra Maurizio and Malvezzi; and Malvezzi, at least, was not known as a virtuoso singer. Scipione Vecchi delle Palle, whom Caccini acknowledged as his singing teacher in his first collection of songs, *Le nuove musiche* (1602), died in 1569; it is unclear who else might have been available for Peri save Caccini himself, although in light of their future relations, he seems a very unlikely candidate.

given to him in the manner done with his predecessors (*è obbligato di sonare secondo l'ordine consueto della nostra chiesa quale gli sarà dato come hanno dato gl'altri organisti suoi antecessori*), meaning that we cannot easily gauge the extent of his duties there.[11]

Presumably Malvezzi also helped Peri gain the appointment in August 1586 in the choir of S. Giovanni Battista (until March 1590), participating in the normal round of Saturday, Sunday, and festal services. Again, it is hard to know what the workload was. In September 1586, Peri's first full month in service, the choir would have sung Mass in the Duomo on four Saturdays, Vespers in the Duomo and Mass in S. Giovanni Battista on four Sundays, and Mass or Vespers, or both, in one or the other place for five feast days (from the Nativity of the Blessed Virgin Mary on Thursday 8 September to the Feast of St. Jerome on Friday 30 September)—totaling some thirteen days in all (say, for four or five hours per day, allowing for two services and rehearsal), or fewer if only half the choir performed at any one time.[12] Peri must have been able to juggle his commitments here with those at the Badia;

11. ASF, Corporazioni religiose soppresse dal governo francese 78 (Badia Fiorentina), filza 265 (*ricordanze*), fol. 54v, dated 15 January 1578/79 (when Peri was auditioned), given in D'Accone, "The *Intavolatura di M. Alemanno Aiolli*," 154 n. 15, which also notes some other salary payments. D'Accone (154–55 n. 16) gives a similar record for the appointment of Alamanno Layolle as organist on 8 August 1570 (until 1575) that makes reference to a separate list of duties that, too, is lost. According to the salary payments in ASF, Corporazioni religiose soppresse dal governo francese 78, filza 91 (*debitori e creditori* of the Badia), Layolle was succeeded by Ser Giovanni Antonio (15 June 1575 to 15 December 1576), then Ser Lorenzo (to 15 December 1578). Peri's salary was paid in grain from May 1593 to May 1595; Kirkendale, *Court Musicians*, 192 n. 11. This was not unusual for the Badia's employees, to judge by similar entries in its books of *debitori e creditori*. This may have reflected an efficient use of the monastery's rural resources, but given the inflation in the price of grain in the second half of the sixteenth century, it was also a valuable commodity.

12. For the schedule of services after the reestablishing of the musical *cappella* in 1540, see D'Accone, "The Musical Chapels at the Florentine Cathedral and Baptistry during the First Half of the 16th Century," 25–29. It is perhaps worth noting that one Ser Ventura di Lodovico Peri was a bass singer in the newly reformed *cappella* (but no longer in 1552); see ibid., 25, 32. The estimate of the September 1586 services is drawn from the table (based on information from D'Accone's study) in Carter, *Music in Late Renaissance and Early Baroque Italy*, 76–77. It would have been a similar number of days in October, fifteen in November, and seventeen in December (because of Christmas), although these are only rough estimates: the number of days (but not services) would increase, too, if the sung Vespers were held the evening before a given feast.

given that the days and times of service were fixed, he was free, it seems, to engage in other activities as well.

Paralleling the career that Peri was following in the ecclesiastical sector of the musical market were opportunities that the court's demand for music also opened up to him. His statement in early 1618 that he had "served" since the age of ten associated him, at least implicitly, with the Medici from a very early age, which is plausible if one reckons that the Medici's direct or indirect patronage of Florentine institutions such as SS. Annunziata, S. Giovanni Battista, and the Badia meant service by association. But we shall see that from the late 1570s Peri was in contact with the Medici princesses, probably by way of Malvezzi.[13] And in 1583 the *maestro* had his student write the music for one of the *intermedi* accompanying a performance before them of the painter Giovanni Fedini's play *Le due Persilie*, mounted on 16 February.[14] Two weeks later, Malvezzi published a five-voice madrigal ("Caro dolce ben mio") by Peri in his *Il primo libro delli madrigali a cinque voci* (Venice: Heirs of Girolamo Scotto, 1583); the volume was dedicated to Grand Duke Francesco I on 1 March.

This connection with the Medici princesses placed Peri at the heart of court musical circles well before his official entrance into the roll, and clearly he was well known to the grand duke and grand duchess. If we can trust his claim that he had been employed to teach singing to the princesses as early as the reign of Grand Duchess Johanna of Austria (so, before April 1578)—when he was just seventeen—his first such pupil would have been Eleonora (b. 1566), then joined by Grand Duke Francesco I and Johanna's other daughters, Anna (b. 1569; she died in 1584) and Maria (b. 1575), as well as Virginia (b. 1568), the daughter of Grand Duke Cosimo I and his second wife (in a morganatic marriage), Camilla Martelli. Peri's first surviving letter (Letter 1) is to Virginia three years after her marriage to Cesare d'Este, the cousin (from

13. Kirkendale, *Court Musicians*, 181, noting the payment to Malvezzi of *fl.*9 per month in 1588 because *insegna alle signore principesse*. He is not listed in this capacity in the roll of 1586 (when Malvezzi was, instead, receiving *fl.*5 per month, including an allowance for Peri), but the court records are spotty in this period, and one assumes that Malvezzi had overseen the princesses' musical education for some time.

14. The composers who provided the second to sixth *intermedi* were, respectively, Stefano Rossetti, Giovanni Legati, Gostantino Arrighi, Malvezzi, and Alessandro Striggio (the elder). See also the extract from the printed edition of the play in Carter, *Jacopo Peri*, 1: 294–95. Peri bought 37 *staia* of grain from Fedini (for £140) in 1582; Ledger A, fol. 5.

an illegitimate line) of Duke Alfonso II d'Este of Ferrara: she has asked him for music (almost certainly by other composers), and he remains the most affectionate servant that he always was (*che le sono quel medesimo servitore affettuosissimo che sempre le fui*). In 1611 (Letter 18), Peri asked Cardinal Ferdinando Gonzaga, on a visit to Paris, to remember him to Maria (whose wedding festivities in 1600 had included *Euridice*).

He also wrote at least once to Eleonora after she became Duchess of Mantua (Letter 14). She had married Prince Vincenzo Gonzaga in April 1584, following the rather scandalous dissolution of his first marriage to Margherita Farnese. On 24 August that same year, she wrote to Grand Duke Francesco in support of the "great desire" (*molto desiderio*) felt by her father-in-law, Duke Guglielmo Gonzaga, that Peri should come quickly to Mantua for ten days: she styles him *Giacomo Zazzarini* and calls him "your" (i.e., Francesco's) musician (*suo musico*).[15] She went even further and sent the Mantuan court dwarf, Ambrogio, to Florence to meet Peri and accompany him on the return trip; Ambrogio arrived in a terribly bedraggled state, all hot and bothered, so Grand Duchess Bianca Cappello said. The reason for Eleonora's request may have been an imminent visit to Mantua of Alfonso II d'Este and his (third) wife, Margherita Gonzaga, with Guglielmo (or more likely, Eleonora) wishing to provide appropriate entertainment for the Duke of Ferrara, whose melomania was, and is, well known. It may also have been encouraged by Alessandro Striggio, the leading musician in Florentine service (Peri had encountered him in connection with *Le due Persilie*), who was currently spending time in Mantua after a brief visit to Ferrara.

On receipt of Eleonora's letter, Grand Duke Francesco, currently at the Medici villa in Pratolino, jumped into action, sending an order to Peri to go to Mantua. But on 29 August he had to report a state of confusion:

> For a good many years, it has never happened that Jacopo Zazzerino has gone even outside the city, let alone outside my state, as has occurred now, for just as Ambrogio arrived, he [Peri], with my permission, set off with the *maestro di cappella* [Malvezzi] to Meldola for the wedding of a

15. ASF, Mediceo del Principato 2939, document dated 24 August 1584. Although Eleonora claims that the desire is Duke Guglielmo's, it probably comes directly from her; when Guglielmo and Prince Vincenzo each wrote that same day (ASF, Mediceo del Principato 2939), the duke said that Ambrogio had been sent by Eleonora, and both Guglielmo and Vincenzo simply used the opportunity to send formal greetings.

sister of the aforesaid *maestro di cappella* who is to be married in those
parts. I immediately sent someone after him to make him return and to
send him up to you, but since I have not been told any news, I fear that
he may not have found him, for such people [Malvezzi and Peri] never
take a direct route, but go from bell-tower to bell-tower, and from music
to music. Therefore I decided, so as not to lose any more time, to send
Ambrogio himself off to Meldola, to pick up word of him and to present
to him, when he arrived, a letter by me with the express order that immediately, without any delay, he should head up to you with Ambrogio,
and although I am sorry that the desire of the Most Serene Lord Duke
has met with such a concatenation of circumstances, nevertheless it will
please me if Zazzerino is found and reaches there in time to serve His
Highness . . . [16]

That letter containing Peri's "express order," which Francesco sent with Ambrogio to Meldola, is very strongly worded: the grand duke has had fervent
letters (*lettere caldissime*) from Prince Vincenzo Gonzaga (*sic*) to have the
singer go to Mantua for fifteen or twenty days, and Peri should drop everything and go with Ambrogio back to Mantua without losing any time if he
sets any store by the grand duke's satisfaction and favor.[17]

16. Mantua, Archivio di Stato, Archivio Gonzaga 1088, fol. 121: *Sono parecchi anni, che non
è intervenuto che Jacopo Zazzerino sia uscito fuor di Fiorenza, nonché fuori de' miei stati, come è
accaduto hora, che su l'arrivo d'Ambrogio apunto con mia licentia si era incamminato con il maestro di cappella alla volta di Meldola, alle nozze d'una sorella di detto maestro di cappella, che si
debbe esser maritata in quelle parti. Et subito gli spedii uno dreto, per farlo ritornare et inviarlo
costà, ma non me n'essendo stata riportata alcuna nuova, dubito che non l'habbia trovato, perché
così fatte genti non tengono il cammino dritto, ma vanno di campanile in campanile, et di musica
in musica. Et però mi son resoluto per non perder più tempo di mandare il medesimo Ambrogio
alla volta di Meldola, per pigliar quivi lingua di lui, et per presentargli, come l'arrivi, una mia
lettera con espresso ordine, che subito senza alcuna dimora con l'istesso Ambrogio si addirizzi costà.
Et quanto mi duole che il desiderio del Serenissimo Signor Duca habbia incontrato così fatta congiuntura, altrettanto mi piacerà che il Zazzerino si trovi, et che giunga in tempo a servir Sua Altezza.* Meldola is near Forlì. The phase *di campanile in campanile* could also mean "from village to village."

17. ASF, Mediceo del Principato 264 (minutes of letters), fol. 35–35v: *Il serenissimo signor
Principe di Mantova, nostro genero, con instantia grandissima ci ha richiesto con haverci mandato
lettere caldissime, et Brogio Nano aposta, che ve gli concediamo per 15 o 20 giorni, sì che subito
all'havuta di questa vogliamo che in diligentia insieme con detto Nano vi inviate alla volta di
Mantova senza perder punto di tempo, et lasciata ogni altra cosa, per quanto stimate la satisfattione et gratia nostra.*

The very next day, however, Francesco dictated another long letter to Eleonora that more or less repeats the content of the first—although now Peri has not been out of Florence for "many years" (*non è uscito più anni sono di Fiorenza, nonché fuori dello stato*)—and then adds another chapter to the saga:

> ... But while this was going on, Zazzerino returned by another route— summoned by my first order—without meeting the dwarf. Therefore I quickly turned him in your direction, and ordered him to go with the post with as much diligence as possible, given that he is not very robust, and is not accustomed to ride a horse even slowly, let alone quickly. If he arrives in time to please the Most Serene Lord Duke, and to serve him, then I will be satisfied beyond belief. If not, I will feel even greater displeasure that His Highness's desire will have been thwarted by such a concatenation of circumstances and will not have been met by me ... [18]

Peri made it to Mantua, and fondly recalled his stay there thirty-six years later, when he noted the many signs of affection (*tante carezze*) he had received from Prince Vincenzo and Eleonora, and also from the composer Alessandro Striggio (Letter 31). It is not clear what he did there save satisfy the musical cravings of his former singing pupil Eleonora, who had just become pregnant, and he cannot have been there for long, given that Eleonora and Vincenzo, much against Duke Guglielmo's wishes given her condition, set off for a visit to Florence just after the middle of September, with the hapless Ambrogio in tow for his third trip across the Apennines in less than a month.

The grand-ducal secretary Belisario Vinta told his Mantuan counterpart, Marcello Donati (secretary to Prince Vincenzo), that all this was a very great misadventure (*una disavventura grandissima*), especially given that Peri had

---

18. Mantua, Archivio di Stato, Archivio Gonzaga 1088, fol. 123 (1 September 1584): ... *Ma in questo mentre, è avvenuto che per altro cammino il Zazzerino, raggiunto dal mio primo mandato, è venuto qua senza incontrarsi nel Nano. Ond'io subito l'ho indirizzato a cotesta volta, et impostogli che venga per la posta con la maggior diligentia che gli sia possibile, havend'egli poca complessione, et non essendo avvezzo pure a cavalcare adagio, nonché correndo. Se arriverà in tempo da contentare et da poter servire il Serenissimo Signore, ne haverò satisfattione incredibile. Se no, sentirò tanto maggior dispiacere che il desiderio di Sua Altezza si sia abbattuto a così fatta congiuntura, et da me non sarà restato* ... There is a minute of this letter in ASF, Mediceo del Principato 264, fol. 35v.

not been out of Florence for *molti lustri*.[19] The idea of a courier and a dwarf chasing across the mountains trying to find Peri is amusing, even absurd, but there are other, more striking things about this episode. Eleonora was being capricious—if also somewhat devious in using her father-in-law as leverage with her brother, the grand duke—while Guglielmo and Vincenzo were humoring her, and Francesco felt placed under obligation to benefit the Duke of Mantua (and the husband of his former wife's sister). All that is in the way of royalty. But for a grand duke, a grand duchess, a duke, a prince, and a princess to take up so much of their own and their secretaries' time—not to mention Ambrogio's—in securing the brief visit of a young singer from Florence to Mantua seems quite extraordinary. It may or may not say something about Peri's standing at court even before his official employment there; certainly Grand Duke Francesco was willing to poke fun at his (lack of) horsemanship and the tendency of musicians to be distracted from the straight and narrow, although he was careful to note that Peri was absent with permission. But it also reveals how musicians could be tokens in the exchange of courtly favors, with both honor and prestige resting on the outcome. While Peri stayed in Mantua enjoying the company of Alessandro Striggio—and perhaps discussing the music in Ferrara that Striggio had experienced during his visit there the previous month—he may also have wondered what all this meant for anyone aspiring to court service.[20] He would soon find out.

As Peri made his quick turnaround in Florence, he found a moment to ask Malvezzi for a letter of recommendation to Eleonora. The *maestro* wrote it on that busy 1 September in some haste, it seems, but blithely ignoring all the kerfuffle:

19. Mantua, Archivio di Stato, Archivio Gonzaga 1113, fol. 78 (3 September 1584). Grand Duchess Bianca Cappello also joined in the narration; see her letter to Eleonora of 29 August 1584 in Mantua, Archivio di Stato, Archivio Gonzaga 1088, fol. 383, where she says that Malvezzi and Peri have gone to Ravenna, which is not quite true, although it has entered the literature (as in Kirkendale, *Court Musicians*, 193).

20. On Striggio in Ferrara in July–August 1584, see Kirkendale, *Court Musicians*, 46. While there he had started composing music in the Ferrarese style to send back to Florence to be performed by a *concerto* on the Ferrara model, directed by Giulio Caccini. These efforts continued during Striggio's stay in Mantua for the rest of the year; see his letters from Mantua to Grand Duke Francesco in Butchart, "The Letters of Alessandro Striggio" (but the reference to the musician Giacomo Tazzarin in ibid., 77 n. 47, is incorrect: this is Peri).

> Since Zazzerino is coming, summoned by Your Most Serene Highness, I cannot, for the affection which I bear for him, fail to recommend him as much as I can, even though I know that Your Highness has always loved him. He will not fail to do Your Highness honor, and he never fails to study, such that the praises you give him will be many because of his greatness . . . [21]

Peri still counted as Malvezzi's pupil in 1586 (he was twenty-five), when the *maestro* was receiving an allowance for him from the court; it remains unclear what this covered, though temporary board and lodging would not have been unusual. Malvezzi must have been proud of his young star, for whom he also seems to have had some affection. In early 1588 he leased to Peri the property at San Marco Vecchio near Florence attached to a prebend of his at S. Lorenzo, and four years later he loaned Peri £70, presumably to help finance improvements Peri was making there. In his *ricordo* of the lease Peri comments that it would enable him to enjoy the countryside while still being within reasonable distance of the city, and he notes proudly that he needed this because his new proximity to the grand duke placed him under heavy obligations (*ché per stare io col Gran Duca mi trovo molto obligato*).

The first evidence we have in court documents of Peri's official appointment to the grand-ducal musicians—as distinct from earlier references to him being taught by Malvezzi or working with the princesses—dates from September 1588. However, the fact that the contract for his lease on the property at San Marco Vecchio was notarized on 23 February 1587/88 suggests that that appointment was made, or at least anticipated, earlier. It was a matter of some distinction. We have already seen in Chapters 1 and 2 the signs of Peri's increasing economic and social stability in the 1580s and into the early 1590s—as he moved from his twenties into his thirties—culminating in a favorable marriage match that did even more to consolidate his position. We have also seen that by the early 1580s, if not before, he was already *obligato* to

---

21. Mantua, Archivio di Stato, Archivio Gonzaga 1113, fol. 524: *Venendo il Zazzerino chiamato da Vostra Altezza Serenissima non posso mancare, per affettione ch'io li porto, di non ne lo raccomandare quanto posso, ancora che so che Vostra Altezza l'ha sempre amato. E lui non mancherà fare onore a Vostra Altezza, e del continuo non manca studiare, acciochè le laudi che lei li dà rieschino molte per grandezza sua . . .* Malvezzi concludes by asking Eleonora's favor also for himself, her longtime trusty servant.

the grand duke. But if his appointment to the court musicians was clearly a matter of pride, it also brought those obligations to a new level.

Peri's court connections before and after 1588 no doubt helped him enter the third component of the Florentine musical marketplace, the private sector, which seems to have been quite active in both the earlier and the later parts of the sixteenth century. Even during the period of the grand duchy, members of the elite were able, and even were encouraged, to exercise considerable independence within somewhat permeable social and other boundaries. For historical and other reasons, the Medici did not operate their court along the more hierarchical, segregated lines of absolute monarchies elsewhere in Europe. Rather, Florentine patricians with or without official court positions or titles moved fairly fluidly in court circles according to need, opportunity, or favor. But they also pursued their own commercial and cultural interests in the city at large, if always with an eye on the main chance: gaining proximity to the grand duke when it served their purposes to do so. This is certainly how prominent music patrons such as Giovanni de' Bardi and Jacopo Corsi used the arts, in addition to their not inconsiderable wealth, and we have already seen (in Chapter 1) how it bore fruit in works such as Peri's *Euridice*.

Antonfrancesco Grazzini's two *ottava rima* stanzas on Peri, written before 1584, sought to encourage this private sector—the many *cavalier', gentil'huomini e signori* interested in music in Florence—to pay more attention to the young musician. While there is no direct evidence of Peri's relations with Giovanni de' Bardi's Camerata in the 1580s (Bardi had closer relations with Giulio Caccini, it seems), it is difficult to imagine that they did not interact in some way. Jacopo Corsi's influence is clearer, chiefly because of what we know about *Dafne* and *Euridice*. But that reveals a problem with the sources: Peri figures as little in Corsi's financial accounts as Corsi does in Peri's. In contrast to the documentation for Peri's activity at churches and the court, reference to his performances in the private sector are thin in the archives: our knowledge of them depends on the serendipitous finding of letters in which someone happens to have described them. As another example (to which we shall return), it is only by way of such letters that we know of Peri's involvement in a performance in June 1610 at Giulio Caccini's house, where he joined Adriana Basile (the virtuoso soprano en route from Naples to service in Mantua), the castrato Giovanni Gualberto Magli, the alto Antonio Brandi, and the bass Lelio Ghirlinzoni in singing madrigals by Alfonso Fontanelli before an audience consisting of visiting dignitaries and a troop of gentlemen (*una squadra di gentilhuomini*) that also included Giovanni de' Bardi.[22] There must have been many other such occasions for music making before the elite, especially during the earlier part of Peri's career when he was most active as a performer. But here we can only proceed by inference, noting the occasional presence in the Peri accounts—if for nonmusical reasons—of other Florentine patricians associated with music, such as Pierfrancesco Bardi (the dedicatee of Girolamo Montesardo's *L'allegre notti di Fiorenza* [Venice: Angelo Gardano, 1608]) and Filippo di Antonio Salviati (the dedicatee of Raffaello Rontani's *Gl'Affettuosi: Il primo libro de madrigali a tre voci* [Florence: Cristofano Marescotti, 1610]). Peri's musical activities may or may not have encouraged such connections: historians of patronage often too quickly assume that contact in one sphere presumes familiarity in another, and for Florence, it is also clear that musical circles did not always overlap or even intersect. But this is in part the point of situating Peri in much broader socioeconomic contexts, as we do here.

Music at the Medici Court

Like all Renaissance rulers, the Medici grand dukes maintained a body of musicians—singers and instrumentalists—for the purposes of ceremony and entertainment, both on official court occasions and in more private settings for the grand-ducal family and its various strata and gendered subdivisions. But while the typical life of such a musician working for an Italian court in the late sixteenth and early seventeenth centuries seems easy to discern in general terms, it is surprisingly difficult to do so in any day-to-day (week-to-week, or even month-to-month) detail.

---

22. Ottavio Gentile to Ferdinando Gonzaga, 16 June 1610, in Mantua, Archivio di Stato, Archivio Gonzaga 1127, fol. 540, also given in part in Alessandro Ademollo, *La bell'Adriana*, 136; the passage missing in Ademollo's transcription, perhaps because he had problems reading it, is *e ve ne sono stati alcuni, che si sono falati* [sic] *da tutti ecetto che dalla signora Adriana con grandissimo stupore del detto Conte* (i.e., some of the singers got lost in reading the music, save for Basile, much to Fontanelli's amazement). Kirkendale, *Court Musicians*, 154, claims that the madrigals are by Giovanni de' Bardi, but Gentile's *alcuni madrigali scritti del Signor Conte* relates clearly to the earlier reference in the letter to *Il Signor Conte Fontanella* (sic). This occasion is also discussed later in this chapter, in "Peri's Music."

In part this difficulty is owing to the nature of the surviving archival and other sources, which usually record matters of routine as efficiently as possible, and therefore with the minimum of necessary information, and lavish the detail generally required by historians only in such exceptional occasions as when an administration needed to extend its efforts beyond the norm in some kind of special circumstance. Such circumstance would prompt the production of documents for the sake of fiscal probity (by way of detailed lists of expenditures), as proof of prestigious conspicuous consumption (printed *descrizioni* and the like), or for future reference to establish traditions and ensure consistency (in *diari d'etichetta* and similar sources).[23] Hence we know a fair amount both from the archives and from what one might call the court's publicity machine about the place of music and musicians within Medici court festivities—for example, weddings and baptisms—and state ceremonies for princely visits, the celebration of notable events, and funerals (the subjects of just about every other entry in Francesco Settimanni's *Memorie fiorentine*, the oft-cited eighteenth-century compilation of notable events in the city during the Medici grand-ducal period).

The Carnival season (from 26 December to the start of Lent)—in particular, its final week—also tended to be a busy time for musicians both within the court itself and for the civic entertainments that the Medici provided in Florence or (more often during the reign of Grand Duke Ferdinando I) in Pisa, for the dual purposes of self-promotion and public benefit. The court musicians could be required to follow the grand-ducal household on its frequent moves outside Florence—to Pisa, Livorno, or one of the Medici villas in the *contado*—though the distances were such that they were not necessarily required to take up extended residence there. For example, on 26 March 1603 (the Wednesday of Holy Week), the grand-ducal family heard Mass in S. Nicola, Pisa (listening as usual from the corridor connecting the church with the Palazzo delle Vedove), with music for three choirs done by court musicians brought specifically from Florence for the occasion (*fatti venire a*

23. For the last, the obvious example is the *diario* by Cesare Tinghi, *aiutante di camera* to successive grand dukes, which survives in three volumes (1600–1626, with a continuation after Tinghi's death to 1644) in Florence, Biblioteca Nazionale Centrale, Gino Capponi 261 (vols. 1–2), and ASF, Miscellanea medicea 11. Solerti transcribed what he considered to be the important entries in his *Musica, ballo e drammatica alla corte medicea*, although they are necessarily incomplete, and scholars should still refer to the original.

posta da Firenze); we do not know whether they included Peri.[24] Some musicians might also join the entourage of Medici family members traveling elsewhere, whether to perform or for some other reason (we shall later see an example for Peri in 1616).

But alongside these various periods of no doubt intense activity—whether according to a regular schedule or to one-time circumstance—there were quite long parts of the year when the official court calendar made fewer, if any, demands for musical performance. Likewise, and save for Holy Week as just noted, the Medici did not use their musicians to provide liturgical music for daily and weekly services on any regular basis: they celebrated the Mass and Office more modestly in private or by way of other Florentine institutions.[25] No doubt the Medici expected their musicians, in their various capacities, to serve other, more frequent and regular purposes, such as providing music at table, for passing entertainment, or in certain devotional contexts. For obvious reasons, we have less archival evidence for these kinds of domestic music making in the chambers of the Palazzo Pitti or in satellite Medici households, in part because they rarely entered the record, and in part because scholars have yet to look for it. But it would probably be a mistake to regard the court musician's job as being in any sense full-time: to give one perhaps extreme example, Aldobrando Trabocchi, a virtuoso bass, was paid *fl.*10 per month from 29 August 1602 with the obligation to serve three or four months of the year during the summer and Holy Week, wherever the court might be, but for the rest, he could stay in his house in Pienza.[26] Therefore

24. Solerti, *Musica, ballo e drammatica alla corte medicea*, 31; Carter, *Jacopo Peri*, 1: 49 n. 4. Thirteen musicians traveled to Pisa, as had occurred in other years, and were lodged for five days in the Palazzo de' Vitelli, whereafter seven returned to Florence, leaving behind Antonio and Vittoria Archilei, the *concerto de' castrati* (with Giovanni Battista Signorini), and the lutenist Pompeo Regianotti, presumably to provide music in the grand-ducal chambers.

25. In October 1628, according to the Modenese ambassador Tiburtio Masdoni, Grand Duke Ferdinando II proposed forming a separate *cappella* so as no longer to have to use the singers of the Duomo (*una Compagnia di Musici eccellenti per far cappella senza haver a servirsi più di quei del Duomo*); Harness, *Echoes of Women's Voices*, 197. Masdoni also associated this with the hiring of Girolamo Frescobaldi (as the grand duke's organist, although he was occasionally styled *maestro di cappella*). However, the separate *cappella* never materialized.

26. Kirkendale, *Court Musicians*, 296. However, Enea Vaini's report of 1603 suggested that his talents would be better used if he moved to Florence with a higher salary; Lozzi, "La musica e specialmente il melodramma alla corte medicea," 314–15. Later in September 1603, Vaini told the grand duchess of Trabocchi's wish for additional travel expenses when coming to

court musicians were free, when not prevented by commitments, to pursue other musical or nonmusical activities for financial gain or just out of personal interest, and many did. For Peri to claim that he needed a country property close to Florence to find relief from his obligations in his new court position may have been his perception, as well as a matter of pride, but while in principle he could be summoned at any time, it is not clear how often that occurred.

The Medici Musical Establishment

We now know a great deal about individual musicians working at the Medici court around 1600—in part because of the musicological impulse in favor of biography—but less about their operation as a whole.[27] The following discussion might therefore be longer and denser than one might desire, and also more speculative in its conclusions. It would also require anchoring in similar accounts (mostly lacking) of other professional groups servicing the needs of both the individual Medici and the court as an institution, whether the cooks or the upper-level administrators.

One thing is already clear, however. As with those other professional groups—but not always with other court artists (e.g., painters), who tended to be hired on an occasional, job-specific basis—the Medici kept a permanent body of musicians because their performances were needed on a permanent basis.[28] This musical establishment—documents usually speak collectively of the *musici*—seems to have been typical of its kind in some ways but not others. Grand Dukes Cosimo I and Francesco I maintained only modest forces, with twelve to fourteen *musici*.[29] Ferdinando I, however, decided to enlarge the group in 1588, presumably on the advice of Emilio de' Cavalieri, his new

Florence, also raising the question of whether court singers in holy orders were eligible to perform in secular court entertainments such as *balli*; ASF, Mediceo del Principato 5986, document dated 27 September 1603. Trabocchi certainly performed in the Holy Week music in 1604 (organized by Giulio Caccini); see Vaini's letter to the grand duchess in ibid., document dated 4 April 1604 (which also refers to the difficulty of finding altos).

27. The organization of Kirkendale's *Court Musicians* as a biographical dictionary, as it were, is emblematic.

28. For painters, see Fumagalli, "Prime indagini sui rapporti economici tra pittori e corte medicea nel Seicento." For a different group of artists and artisans, see Butters, *The Triumph of Vulcan*, though this covers a slightly earlier period.

29. D'Accone, "The Florentine Fra Mauros," 134–37.

superintendant of the Galleria dei Lavori (Gallery of Works) and therefore of the court artists (he was appointed on 3 September 1588): the number of musicians was increased, and their disposition was rationalized to allow for different performance circumstances.[30] During the span of Peri's paid service to the Medici there were some twenty-four to thirty court musicians, divided roughly equally between singers and instrumentalists, although the proportion shifted slightly in favor of the latter in the 1620s. Their constitution can be seen by way of the three sample years covered in Table 3.1, with salary costs ranging from some *fl.*2,600 per year (1588) to some *fl.*3,200 (1626). However, the court's expenditure on music was clearly higher than the sums given here because of additional disbursements: for example, salary payments for the musicians in 1643 amounted to *fl.*3,229, but a contemporary report on the court music tallied the total cost at around *fl.*4,250 (so, salaries represented some 76 percent of the total).[31] These figures exclude individual musicians listed in other capacities, and also the court trumpeters, an entirely separate group serving different ceremonial functions. Further, a few musicians might enter the roll without a salary so as to enjoy its other privileges (*per goder li privilegi del ruolo, senz'altra provisione*), although they would tend to graduate to a salary if kept in service.[32] However, almost all the musicians were gaining significantly more than the typical annual income of the most skilled construction worker in Florence (*fl.*70).

It is not always clear, however, what such a "salary" meant, since to it might be added special allowances for such things as teaching or maintaining a musical household. Emoluments could also be paid from other sources within and outside the court administration, and the monetary payment of a salary could be substituted in part, or enhanced, by the likes of dining privileges in the servants' hall (*tinello*)—which some but not all musicians had—plus clothing, provisions (wine, bread, candles, firewood, and the like), a horse with stabling rights, and so forth. Compensation could further be increased

30. The Ferrarese Resident, Ercole Cortile, reported back to Ferrara on 13 August 1588 that the grand duke was newly employing musicians and had placed them under the control of Emilio de' Cavalieri, a Roman gentleman who was very much his favorite (*Va poi Sua Altezza tuttavia stipendiando musichi di nuovo, et ha data la cura d'essi al Signor Emilio Cavalieri, gentilhuomo romano molto suo favorito*); Carter, *Jacopo Peri*, 1: 17 n. 45.

31. Kirkendale, *Court Musicians*, 43.

32. Compare Kirkendale, *Court Musicians*, 299 (Antonio di Girolamo Cinatti del Frate and Francesco Poggi).

Table 3.1. Musicians on the Medici court roll in three sample years: 1588, 1607, 1626

Name	Function	Dates of service	Monthly salary (in florins)
1588			
Bernardo di Francesco Pagani della cornetta (Il Franciosino)	wind player and head of the Franciosini	1579–22 Nov 1596 (d.)	20
Antonio Archilei	singer (?falsettist) and composer	1588–14 Nov 1612 (d.)	18
Giulio Romolo di Michelangelo Caccini	singer (tenor) and composer	1579–Aug 1593; 1 Oct 1600–10 Dec 1618 (d.)	16
Giovanni Battista Jacomelli	singer (tenor) and string player	1588–19 Jan 1608	16
Cesare del Messere *napolitano*	singer (bass)	1588–before 1599	15
Giovanfrancesco Sanese	trombonist	1579–before 3 Nov 1595	15
Onofrio Gualfreducci	singer (castrato)	1588–early 1600s (d. summer 1625)	15
Luca Marenzio	composer	1588–31 Nov 1589 (d. 22 Aug. 1599)	15
Vittoria (di Francesco Concarini) Archilei	singer, lutenist, and ?composer	1588–?1645 (d.)	10
Don Giovanni *basso*	singer (also in the Duomo)	1588–before 1599	9
Cristofano di Nicolao Malvezzi da Lucca	organist, *maestro di cappella*, and teacher of the princesses	1586–22 Jan 1599 (d.)	9
Duritio Isorelli	string player	1588–?18 Nov 1598 (d. 21 Apr 1632)	8
Zanobi Ciliani	trombonist	1579–before 23 Aug 1595	6
Niccolò Bartolini da Pistoia	singer (castrato)	1588–28 Feb 1622 (d.)	6
Mario Luchini	singer	1588–before 1599	6
Antonio di Marco Naldi *bolognese* (Il Bardella)	theorbist; *guardaroba della musica*	1588–25 Jan 1621 (d.)	6

Jacopo Peri	singer (tenor), keyboard player, and composer	1588–12 Aug 1633 (d.)	6
Baccio di Ullivieri Palibotri (also Malespina)	singer and instrumentalist	1579–? (d. 29 Oct 1610)	5
Don Cornelio di Martino de Benis da Udine	singer (in S. Giovanni Battista)	30 Mar 1546–1590	4
Antonio Francesco di Annibale Bosseni	trombonist	1586–28 Nov 1599 (d.)	4
Adriano Dalla Croce *bolognese*	cornettist and trombonist	1588–24 Apr 1595 (d.)	4
Pierino di Ullivieri Palibotri (Malespina)	singer (castrato)	1588–before 1599	4
Giovanni Piero Manenti	organist (in the Duomo)	16 Jan. 1571–1588 (d. 18 Jul 1597)	3
Cavaliere Cosimo di Mattio di Niccolò Bottegari	lutenist and composer	1588–? (d. 31 Mar 1620)	0

TOTAL MUSICIANS = 24, TOTAL ANNUAL SALARIES = *fl.*2,592

roughly divided as:

singers: 12

wind players: 5

string players: 2

keyboardists and lutenists: 4

other: 1

1607

Giulio Romolo di Michelangelo Caccini	singer (tenor) and composer	1579–Aug 1593; 1 Oct 1600–10 Dec 1618 (d.)	16
Giovanni Battista Jacomelli	singer (tenor) and string player	1588–19 Jan 1608	16
Giovanni Battista di Piero Signorini	singer (tenor) and trombonist (Franciosini)	12 May 1590–29 Dec 1626 (d.)	13

(*continued*)

Table 3.1. (continued)

Name	Function	Dates of service	Monthly salary (in florins)
Lorenzo di Bartolomeo Allegri	lutenist and composer	15 Apr 1604–15 Jul 1648 (d.)	12
Antonio Archilei	singer (?falsettist) and composer	1588–14 Nov 1612 (d.)	11
Paolo di Giuliano Grazi	organist and cornettist (Franciosini)	12 May 1590–31 Oct 1649 (d. 30 May 1652)	11
Alessandro di Andrea Mancini	cornettist (Franciosini)	12 May 1590–18 Jan 1617 (d.)	11
Antonio di Francesco Vanetti (Il Moretto)	singer and instrumentalist (Franciosini)	1 Aug 1593–after 1626	11
Vittoria (di Francesco Concarini) Archilei	singer, lutenist, and ?composer	1588–?1645 (d.)	10
Giovanni Boccherini	singer (castrato)	1 Aug 1593–before 1622	10
Francesca (di Giulio) Caccini Signorini (La Cecchina)	singer, instrumentalist, and composer	15 Nov 1607–29 May 1627, 1634–?1641 (d.)	10
Fabio Fabbri	singer (castrato)	12 Feb 1595–Jun 1623	10
Jacopo di Antonio del Franciosino	trombonist (Franciosini) and keyboard player	1 Dec 1592–31 Oct 1649 (d. 20 Sep 1657)	10
Antonio di Matteo Lassagnini (Il Biondino)	cornettist and trombonist (Franciosini), and organist	1 Aug 1593–20 Sep 1634 (d.)	10
Giuliano di Piero Samminiati	instrumentalist (Franciosini) and organist	1 Aug 1593–27 Apr 1640 (d.)	10
Aldobrando Trabocchi da Pienza	singer (bass)	29 Aug 1602–?Mar 1609 (d. 17 Mar 1641)	10
Jacopo Peri	singer (tenor), keyboard player, and composer	1588–12 Aug 1633 (d.)	9
Pompeo di Girolamo Regianotti da Modena	lutenist	1 May 1597–16 Aug 1645 (d.)	8
Niccolò Bartolini da Pistoia	singer (castrato)	1588–28 Feb 1622 (d.)	6

Giovanni Gualberto di Giovanni Battista Magli	singer (castrato)	23 Aug 1604–8 Jan 1625 (d.)	6
Antonio di Marco Naldi *bolognese* (Il Bardella)	theorbist; *guardaroba della musica*	1588–25 Jan 1621 (d.)	6
Vittorio Baldacci	instrumentalist (Franciosini)	20 Oct 1606–31 Oct 1649 (d. between Aug 1652 and Sep 1656)	5
Vergilio di Giuseppe Grazi	singer, instrumentalist (Franciosini), and composer	20 Oct 1606–12 March 1643 (d.)	5
Fra Bartolomeo Binaschi	singer (bass)	1 Jul 1589–31 Dec 1607	2
Antonio di Girolamo Cinatti del Frate (Beccafico)	singer (tenor)	Sep 1602–?Jul 1642 (d.)	0
Tommaso d'Agnolo Lapi	organist	12 Feb 1605–?after 1632	0
?Francesco Poggi *veneziano*	instrument tuner	between Oct 1602 and Jan 1603–after 1606	0

TOTAL MUSICIANS=27, TOTAL ANNUAL SALARIES=*fl.*2,736

roughly divided as:

singers: 13

wind players: 8

string players: 1

keyboardists and lutenists: 4

other: 1

1626

Francesca (di Giulio) Caccini Signorini Malaspina (La Cecchina)	singer, instrumentalist, and composer	15 Nov 1607–29 May 1627, 1634–?1641 (d.)	20
Tobbia Grünschneider	violinist (?Franzesi) and cornettist (Franciosini)	18 May 1616–after 1658	16

(continued)

Table 3.1. (continued)

Name	Function	Dates of service	Monthly salary (in florins)
Angelica (di Filippo) Furini Belli (Angelica Sciamerone)	singer	19 Sep 1618–31 Oct 1638 (d.)	16
Giovanni Battista di Piero Signorini Malaspina	singer (tenor) and trombonist (Franciosini)	12 May 1590–29 Dec 1626 (d.)	13
Paolo di Giuliano Grazi	organist and cornettist (Franciosini)	12 May 1590–31 Oct 1649 (d. 30 May 1652)	12
Antonio di Francesco Vanetti (Il Moretto)	singer and instrumentalist (Franciosini)	1 Aug 1593–after 1626	12
Jacopo di Antonio del Franciosino	trombonist (Franciosini) and keyboard player	1 Dec 1592–31 Oct 1649 (d. 20 Sep 1657)	11
Antonio di Matteo Lassagnini (Il Biondino)	cornettist and trombonist (Franciosini), and organist	1 Aug 1593–20 Sep 1634 (d.)	11
Giuliano di Piero Samminiati	instrumentalist (Franciosini) and organist	1 Aug 1593–27 Apr 1640 (d.)	11
Vittoria (di Francesco Concarini) Archilei	singer, lutenist, and ?composer	1588–?1645 (d.)	10
Pietro di Giovanni Battista Asolani	string player (Franzesi)	15 Oct 1617–27 Sep 1651 (d.)	10
Vittorio Baldacci	instrumentalist (Franciosini)	20 Oct 1606–31 Oct 1649 (d. between Aug 1652 and Sep 1656	10
Giovacchino di Stefano Biancotti *francese*	violinist (Franzesi)	1 Dec 1608–21 Oct 1648 (d.)	10
Giovanni Castor *marsigliese*	string player (Franzesi)	24 Aug 1614–31 Oct 1649	10
Giovanni Battista di Giovanni Battista dell'Auca (Il Cappellaino)	string player (Franzesi) and composer	19 Jun 1623–Dec 1648 (d.)	10
Vergilio di Giuseppe Grazi	singer, instrumentalist (Franciosini), and composer	20 Oct 1606–12 Mar 1643 (d.)	10
Lucretia di Battista detto Il Mancino	singer	20 May 1612–after 1615; 1625–26	10
Rev. Piero di Raffaello Raffaelli	singer (bass; in the Duomo)	19 Dec 1613–16 Jan 1641 (d.)	10

Jacopo Peri	singer (tenor), keyboard player, and composer	1588–12 Aug 1633 (d.)	9
Pompeo di Girolamo Regianotti da Modena	lutenist	1 May 1597–16 Aug 1645 (d.)	8
Domenico di Piero Poggi (Lo Stufaiolo)	singer (tenor)	1 Dec 1608–6 Nov 1628 (d.)	6
Rev. Domenico Sarti	singer (castrato)	1 Feb 1620–31 Oct 1649	6
Antonio di Girolamo Cinatti del Frate (Beccafico)	singer (tenor)	Sep 1602–?Jul 1642 (d.)	4
Giovanni Battista di Zanobi da Gagliano	composer and ?singer	1 Oct 1624–8 Jan 1651 (d.)	4
Francesco di Jacopo Mariani	?	26 Jan 1617–12 Jun 1635	4
Alessandro di Salvestro Tatini	singer (castrato)	13 Jan 1617–3 Sep 1637 (d. 14 Nov 1637)	4
Domenico di Matteo Belli	composer and ?singer	19 Sep 1618–5 May 1627 (d.)	0
Antonio di Francesco Brandi (Il Brandino)	singer (falsettist)	5 Oct 1611–after 1632	0
Tommaso d'Agnolo Lapi	organist	12 Feb 1605–?after 1632	0

TOTAL MUSICIANS = 30, TOTAL ANNUAL SALARIES = fl.3,180

roughly divided as:

singers: 11

wind players: 8

string players: 5

keyboardists and lutenists: 3

other: 3

Source: Kirkendale, *Court Musicians*, supplementary table (and related entries in the main text). "Function" is inevitably imprecise given the tendency of musicians to multitask; dates of service cannot always be ascertained with accuracy, and do not reflect prior contact with the court in some other capacity; and salaries do not reflect other emoluments from the court or for positions held elsewhere in the city (e.g., the Duomo, S. Giovanni Battista, S. Lorenzo), but some do include allowances for teaching, etc. The 1588 roll is somewhat confused owing to the reorganization of the *musici* on the accession of Grand Duke Ferdinando I, and also temporary appointments in anticipation of the festivities for his wedding with Christine of Lorraine in May 1589. A large number of court salaries were suspended on 31 October 1649 due to cutbacks in the court of Grand Duke Ferdinando II.

by loans or one-time gifts such as *mancie* for specific services or dowries for daughters, or (as we have seen for Peri) preferment for other salaried appointments.[33] As is typical of most courts, payments could be made from, or supported by, various sources—the *depositeria generale* (for salaries), the *dispensa* (for living allowances when not lodged in the palace), the private *camera* of the grand duke or grand duchess (the privy purse, as it were), sacred benefices and their secular equivalents—depending on custom and also on the rules for separating the costs for the grand duke's official and private households.[34]

Thus Vittoria Archilei, listed on the roll as being paid *fl.*10 per month, in fact gained *fl.*26, at least after the death of her husband, Antonio, in 1612, taking into account an additional *fl.*4 *di camera di Sua Altezza Serenissima* and *fl.*12 granted Antonio as a life pension in 1588 and rendered transferable to Vittoria in 1604. She was the leading singer of her generation, and many Florentine musicians paid homage to her, as did Peri in his preface to *Euridice* (and see Letter 6).[35] Another example is offered by Giulio Caccini, who in addition to his *fl.*16 per month (*fl.*192 per year) received a pension (*pensione*) of *fl.*70 a year from the Mint (*su la Zecca*) by decree of Grand Duke Ferdinando I from July 1607 until mid-1612.[36] Court musicians could also be musically active in positions elsewhere: thus Giovanni Battista Jacomelli (paid *fl.*16 per month from the court from 1588 to 1608) received an additional *fl.*2 per month as a tenor at the Duomo, and from 1597 another *fl.*6 per month as first organist there (so *fl.*24 in total), and his successor in the latter position in 1608, Pompeo Regianotti, also held a salaried position at court (paid *fl.*8,

---

33. For *mancie*, see, for example, the *fl.*300 that Archduke Karl of Austria presented to the musicians performing in *La regina Sant'Orsola* in October 1624, plus the gifts given on that occasion by the Medici to visiting singers; Solerti, *Musica, ballo e drammatica alla corte medicea*, 177.

34. The structure of the grand-ducal household was inevitably very complex. That and abuses of the system prompted Grand Duke Cosimo II to propose an extensive reform to rationalize matters, and to cut costs, as of 1 December 1616; see the (later) copy in ASF, Galletti 41.

35. Carter, "Finding a Voice."

36. ASF, Ufficiali della Moneta poi Maestri di Zecca 228, fol. 114; 229, fol. 19; 230, fol. 179. The pension was paid out of the Zecca's general cash account. With the payment of March 1610 (the year after Grand Duke Ferdinando I's death), the pension was terminated, but appeals made by Caccini and his two daughters resulted in its restoration, at least temporarily; ASF, Mediceo del Principato 1688, document dated 25 March 1610.

primarily as a lutenist).[37] Again, we do not always know to what extent these external positions were nominal rather than substantive.

Although the range of monthly salaries paid to the musicians, seen in Table 3.1, no doubt reflects some perception of talent, value, and heavier or lighter service requirements—as well as their bargaining power at the time of appointment—one also needs to take into account the holding of joint positions, the extent of additional benefits, and other issues. To move tangentially outside the court for a moment (and that "tangentially" will be explained in due course), the most prominent musician in Florence, the *maestro di cappella* of S. Giovanni Battista and the Duomo, was clearly valued at more than the typical monthly salary for that position (ranging from *fl.*4 to *fl.*6, which did not come from the court), given that he was also usually appointed a canon of S. Lorenzo with the customary prebends and benefices.[38]

Similar caution should be applied to comparative figures across different areas of the court. Only the highest-ranking officials had a salary of more than *fl.*50 per month: in 1588, the *maggiordomo maggiore* (Orazio Rucellai) earned *fl.*1,000 per year, but the leading administrator Belisario Vinta only *fl.*480, as did the court's chief physician and surgeon.[39] As superintendant of the court artists from 1588 until around 1602, Emilio de' Cavalieri received *fl.*25 per month (plus twenty bundles of firewood)—the same as one of the middle-ranking riding-masters or the personal servant of the princesses—which is more than the highest-paid court musician; from 1588 to 1639, Ferdinando Saracinelli, who held various titles at court but was also involved later on in supervising court entertainments, was paid only *fl.*16. The poet Battista Guarini received (as a *segretario*) *fl.*20 per month from 1 April 1599 through the early 1600s, but this may in effect have been an honorarium not requiring

---

37. Kirkendale, *Court Musicians*, 260 (Jacomelli), 262 (Archilei), 295 (Reggianotti), 340–41 (Caccini). Jacomelli's *fl.*6 as organist was supplemented by *fl.*2 from the *capitolo de' canonici* (of the Duomo), but it is not clear whether this was to replace the *fl.*2 he had previously earned as a tenor there; ibid., 185, 646.

38. Payments for the position at S. Giovanni Battista and the Duomo were complicated by various cost-sharing agreements between the Arte dei Mercatanti di Calimala, the Arte della Lana, and the Operai del Duomo; see Kirkendale, *Court Musicians*, 182 (Malvezzi as *maestro di cappella* at *fl.*5), 184 (Malvezzi receives an additional *fl.*4 as third organist at the Duomo), 185–86 (Luca Bati, Malvezzi's successor, receives *fl.*6 as *maestro di cappella*), 644–45.

39. Biagioli, *Galilei, Courtier*, 104 nn. 2–4, offers some comparisons, and for the broader issues, see Litchfield, *Emergence of a Bureaucracy*, 190–200.

formal residence. Another poet, Gabriello Chiabrera (he wrote the text of *Il rapimento di Cefalo* for the 1600 wedding), enjoyed the same arrangement. He was paid *fl.*10 per month from 1 November 1600 until his death on 14 October 1638; when he started providing texts for Medici court entertainments on a more regular basis he was allocated (on 1 October 1614) an additional *fl.*15 per month when in service (*servendo*), but received only his original *fl.*10 when not.[40] The ballet master Agnolo di Andrea Ricci had *fl.*7 per month in the 1600s and *fl.*11 in the next decade (plus an additional sum from the *dispensa* because he did not take dining privileges). From 1579 until his death in 1608, the sculptor Giambologna received *fl.*25 per month (increased from the *fl.*13 of his original appointment in 1566) plus an allowance for rent and a horse; the architect and stage designer Bernardo Buontalenti had *fl.*7 (1567–86) and then *fl.*10 (1588–1608), plus provisions valued at just under *fl.*6 per month, and a horse. In general, then, the court musicians' salaries were about what one would expect within the administration as a whole: not so different from the middle-ranking artists, architects, mathematicians, cosmographers, and so on, and for most, on a par with or higher than the dancing master. On a payroll of all court employees drawn up in early 1607 or thereabouts, the salaries of musicians amounted to 6.4 percent of the whole.[41] This might seem high, although the *musici* would have taken up a smaller proportion of the total household expenditure because unlike, say, the cooks or grooms, their day-to-day costs were mostly for personnel (reflected in salaries) rather than materials.

Again, however, one needs to be careful about the extent to which these salary figures represent one or more elements of what one might nowadays call a wage (for labor), an honorarium (a mark of distinction), a retainer (to be on call), a pension (whether or not in retirement), expenses (regular or in-

40. This did not prevent Chiabrera also being awarded (from an unknown date) a monthly salary of 25 Mantuan *scudi* by Duke Vincenzo Gonzaga, which continued at least into the early 1610s; Davari, "Notizie biografiche del distinto maestro di musica Claudio Monteverdi," 101–2.

41. ASF, Carte strozziane, Appendix 5, *inserto* 25 (*Ruolo dei provvisionati della corte di Toscana ai tempi del Granduca Ferdinando I*). This consists of only numbered folios 161–70 of an unidentified document: twenty-three musicians are listed separately on fol. 166 (the same as those given in Table 3.1 receiving salaries in 1607, save Francesca Caccini), and they are included as a group in the summary on fol. 170v: the amount paid monthly to the *musici* is *fl.*218, out of a total monthly salary bill of just over *fl.*3,411.

cidental), or fringe benefits. Presumably the majority of these payments had some rational basis—as distinct from being awarded on a whim and influenced by favoritism—inasmuch as musicians' salaries did not range as widely as one might expect, save for the obvious outliers whose circumstances can probably be explained in other ways.[42] They were also in some sense banded at various levels by virtue of specific skill sets and obligations, which was in part a matter of convenience but also, one assumes, a way to prevent disruptive rivalries within what would need to be close-knit performing groups. This seems, at least in part, to have been one aim of the reorganization of the *musici* by Emilio de' Cavalieri in 1588. Under Duke Cosimo the range of the musicians' salaries was not dissimilar to the later period—from (in 1563) *fl.*1 per month for a harpist to *fl.*20 for the singer Scipione Delle Palle (best known as Giulio Caccini's teacher) and *fl.*21 £3 for the composer Alessandro Striggio (the elder)—but there were more toward the bottom of the range than toward the top, and the gap between them was greater.[43] The notion that at least part of these salaries in some sense covered "work" is clear from the additions often made to them on the assignment of extra duties (we shall see, later in the chapter, the case of Giovanni Battista Signorini and the *concerto de' castrati* in 1603), although some such assignments did not accrue extra payments (as with Peri and the same *concerto* in 1600). Salaries constituted disposable income, for musicians regularly signed receipts of payment, which usually was in cash. That these payments seem to have been made on time testifies to the reliability of the Florentine bureaucracy and of the funding that lay behind it: plenty of Italian courts left musicians, and others, months or even years in arrears.[44]

42. Compare the comment in Goldthwaite, *The Economy of Renaissance Florence*, 364, that a two-to-one ratio in salaries for skilled construction workers (including foremen) versus unskilled ones was typical in Florence, and indeed throughout Europe, for the period 1350–1600.

43. For the musicians employed in 1563, see D'Accone, "The Florentine Fra Mauros," 134 (document 83); the picture is similar in subsequent lists given by D'Accone up to 1579, although the lower salaries gradually improve.

44. Monteverdi in Mantua is an obvious case in point; see his complaint to Duke Vincenzo Gonzaga made on 27 October 1604 in his *Lettere*, ed. Lax, 14–16 (Monteverdi, *The Letters*, trans. Stevens, 34–36). He later had great difficulty securing regular payment of a pension granted him by the duke, although the court had an ulterior motive, using the pension to keep the composer on the hook after he moved to Venice; see Carter, "Monteverdi and Some Problems of Biography."

On his succession in 1587, Grand Duke Ferdinando I conducted a court-wide purge to remove favorites (not just musicians) of his predecessor, Francesco I (Ferdinando's elder brother, who died without an heir). One of the eventual victims was Giovanni de' Bardi, who moved to Rome in 1592 in the service of Popes Clement VIII and Leo XI (he remained there until 1605). In general, however, the succession of a new ruler seems to have had less impact on the musicians in Florence than it did elsewhere (Monteverdi's discharge from Mantuan service in summer 1612 following the death of Duke Vincenzo Gonzaga is a somewhat complex example).[45] Furthermore, while the court administration was generally meticulous in noting salary payments and the addition or withdrawal of special allowances, there was also a resistance to change typical of any large-scale operation, save when (infrequent) periodic reviews prompted some kind of rationalization or reorganization. In the year after the death of Emilio de' Cavalieri on 11 March 1602 (he had already left for Rome before then), the court majordomo Enea Vaini conducted a survey of the *musici*, commenting on their individual strengths and weaknesses, on their financial situation, and on their utility.[46] In October 1649 financial exigency, and some redundancy, prompted a similar survey and then severe cutbacks in personnel.[47] For the rest, the machinery moved slowly, if at all, and with frequent breakdowns of communication: to return to Aldobrando Trabocchi da Pienza, a later addition to the court roll originally compiled in 1606 noted the singer's departure for Rome on 1 April 1609 with a rather despairing comment that this was rumored, but that no official order to remove him from the list had been given (*così è stato detto et non c'è dato ordine alcuno*).[48]

Small salary increases were possible on petition, with or without some outside help: in early 1599, members of the court wind band, the Franciosini, enlisted the support of Jacopo Corsi for pay increases from the court, which

45. Carter, *Jacopo Peri*, 1: 20–23 (purge); Carter, "Monteverdi and Some Problems of Biography."

46. Lozzi, "La musica e specialmente il melodramma alla corte medicea," 313–15. Lozzi quotes the memorandum only in part; it was in his private collection, and scholars have not yet succeeded in identifying its current location.

47. Kirkendale, *Court Musicians*, 39–40. The cuts were claimed to be temporary, although the court was also concerned to offer honorable discharges to those who wished to leave.

48. Kirkendale, *Court Musicians*, 296.

they received on 10 July.[49] But larger raises needed to be triggered by some specific situation that could be documented, such as additions to a musical household or the transfer of income from a deceased husband to a musical wife, and in general, the court preferred to offer rewards in other ways. Given that court salaries were fairly high, there was not much competition within Florence to lure the musicians from service. Nor is there a great deal of evidence to suggest that any competitiveness within the larger Italian musical marketplace allowed musicians to negotiate better terms at court (although we shall see that the argument was sometimes made in petitions for better treatment); those who wished to leave service might be pressured to stay by some argument based on loyalty or feudal obligation, but if someone could demonstrably better him- or herself elsewhere, a discharge (*licenza*) was normally granted as a sign of favor.[50] It is therefore rare to find an obvious connection between salary increases and any effort at retention in the face of a specific offer from elsewhere, although benefits to encourage retention may have been offered in other ways. It is also apparent that what one would nowadays call salary compression occurred: newer entrants to the *musici* could gain higher salaries, while those of longer-serving musicians, such as Peri, tended to remain relatively fixed.

In 1600, Emilio de' Cavalieri felt that the castratos Giovanni Boccherini and Fabio Fabbri could not live on their *fl.*6 each per month. Similarly, in 1603 Enea Vaini noted that the eight members of the Franciosini, variously paid *fl.*8 and *fl.*9 per month and some with wives and children, were *in estrema povertà*.[51] But he never put Peri in this category; either he knew of Peri's other income or he had never received any complaints from him. The

49. Carter, "Music and Patronage in Late Sixteenth-Century Florence," 72.

50. We use the term "discharge" deliberately, given that despite the modern military overtones, it best captures the notion of a *licenza*—that is, a license to leave service. A *licenza* could be imposed (i.e., a dismissal) or requested (a resignation); it also mattered whether the *licenza* was, in effect, honorable (a statement of good conduct, as it were) or dishonorable. Leaving service without a *licenza*, however, was the equivalent of desertion (to continue the military analogy) and could have serious consequences, especially for a feudal subject who might therefore be blacklisted for employment elsewhere or forced to return and pay some penalty. Whether a musician had a "clean" record was usually of some concern to those recruiting new members to their ranks, and "poaching" such recruits, although it undoubtedly occurred, was a clear breach of etiquette requiring some manner of remedy.

51. Carter, *Jacopo Peri*, 1: 307–8 (the castratos); Lozzi, "La musica e specialmente il melodramma alla corte medicea," 313 (Franciosini). The court responded to both; see Kirkendale,

castratos of course lacked one bargaining edge—any need to marry—and
the Franciosini, being heavily used at court, may not always have had the
time to extend their financial and other horizons, although we shall see an
apparent exception with Vergilio di Giuseppe Grazi, who ran a music school
and hired out himself and his students for private performances (see n. 135).
Vaini also noted that Grand Duchess Christine could help one of the Franciosini, Giovanni Battista Signorini, marry the daughter of the former dyer
Benedetto di Borgo. On making further inquiries, however (presumably because Christine was willing to favor Signorini), Vaini reported that although
Benedetto deemed the musician virtuous, he was too poor since he was entirely dependent on his court salary (*fl.*9 per month, plus an additional *fl.*2
for working with the *concerto de' castrati*); Benedetto, although willing to
bow to pressure from the grand duchess (which never came), preferred to
marry his daughter to someone with an annual income from property of
*fl.*200. But Signorini then married the singer Francesca Caccini, receiving a
dowry of *fl.*1,000 and also, it seems, additional benefit from a nonmusical
position.[52] There is no sign that Peri ever received any such advantage from
the court for his own marriages.

Compared with the typical earnings of an unskilled construction worker
in Florence (£1 per day, amounting to some *fl.*35 per year), none of these musicians was standing on the breadline; the point, rather, seems to have been
that they could not live in the manner to which they wished to become accustomed. Both Cavalieri and Vaini raised another concern, however: that
such "low" salaries would prompt some to accept offers elsewhere, or as Vaini
put it about the Franciosini, they felt, and were being recklessly told, that
they could find better opportunities in Italy or abroad (*Conoscono per loro
stessi, e da persone poco considerate sono avvertiti, che ciascun di essi troveria in
Italia e fuora vantaggiosi partiti*). On the other hand, Giulio Caccini (again
according to Vaini, in 1603) felt that his *fl.*16 per month was sufficient reward
for himself, but that he deserved some further consideration because of the
service of his family, which Caccini thought could be offered in several ways
other than by a salary increase, such as some preferment for his daughters or

---

Court Musicians, 287 (Paolo di Giuliano Grazi; the other Franciosini were treated similarly),
291–94 (Boccherini; Fabbri).

    52. Cusick, *Francesca Caccini at the Medici Court*, 36. On Signorini's receiving some (un-
known) additional position arranged by the grand duchess, see ibid., 274.

assistance in his activity brokering in the exchange market (*senserie del cambio*), although Vaini notes that, in general, such assistance had not always proven very successful for this purpose.[53] The *commodo* Caccini wanted for his daughters might have been court positions or dowries; both Francesca and Settimia Caccini received the former, and dowries were promised directly to Settimia (at least, so Giulio claimed) and indirectly, it seems, to Francesca. However, Giulio (and later, Francesca) had great difficulties receiving the dowry payments.[54]

Not all "musicians" in court service were necessarily listed (or paid) among the *musici*, especially if they were of some higher-class status: Francesco Rasi from Arezzo, a virtuoso tenor who had studied with Caccini, counted among the *diversi provisionati signori di cappa corte et veste lunghe*—the same category into which were placed the likes of Emilio de' Cavalieri, Ferdinando Saracinelli, and Battista Guarini—and was paid *fl.*2 per month from 1588 to 1595, when he entered the service of Duke Vincenzo Gonzaga of Mantua.[55] Women musicians could also be listed elsewhere. The *musici* consisted mostly of men, although a few female virtuosos were included among them after they were married to court musicians. Such marriages commonly occurred (also elsewhere in Italy) as a way of keeping women in service (for a woman, marrying outside the profession would normally mean an end to a performing career): examples include Lucia Gagnolanti (the first wife of Giulio Caccini), Vittoria Archilei, Francesca and Settimia Caccini, and Angelica Furini. But

---

53. Lozzi, "La musica e specialmente il melodramma alla corte medicea," 314: *Questo à di provisione sedici scudi il mese, che sono centonovantadue l'anno, e conosce quanto alla persona sua sola d'esser ben trattato. Ma servendo con tutta la sua famiglia le par meritare che si abbia considerazione al suo interesse, parendoli che in molti modi senza aumento ancora di provisione si possi beneficare, o nel commodo delle figlie, o con aiuto che se le potesse dare nelle senserie del cambio. Se bene par che questo modo provato non riesca molto.* For more on Caccini brokering in the exchange market in 1602–3, 1609, and thereafter, see Chapter 2.

54. Kirkendale, *Court Musicians*, 340 (Settimia); Cusick, *Francesca Caccini at the Medici Court*, 35, 274–75. Giulio Caccini had himself received a dowry (*fl.*1,000) from the court for his first marriage to Lucia Gagnolanti (or Gagnolandi); Kirkendale, *Court Musicians*, 181. Cusick notes that Francesca's dowry to Giovanni Battista Signorini (and an additional dowry promised for any daughter from the marriage) was to have been paid by the banker and sometime patron Riccardo Riccardi, although Giulio initially put Signorini's money up front; much later, Francesca entered into litigation with the Riccardi heirs. However, it is not clear whether the dowry and other money was to be paid by or through Riccardi, and either way, one detects the hand of Grand Duchess Christine behind all this.

55. Kirkendale, *Court Musicians*, 561–62.

other women musicians were recorded and paid (or not) in other capacities such as ladies-in-waiting, or as daughters or students in a musician's household. For example, Margherita di Agostino Benevoli della Scala, who became Giulio Caccini's second wife, was probably *la Margherita, che canta* listed among the *donne della Serenissima Gran Duchessa* in June 1589 (she was also *vestita, et spesata*), and earlier in the 1580s the Bolognese soprano Laura Bovia must have received some similar recompense until she was told in 1589—and probably as part of Grand Duke Ferdinando's purge—to get married, enter a convent, or return home.[56]

The court musicians formed specialized groups serving different functions and often performing in different spaces: Giulio Caccini's *concerto* (his wife, daughters, and pupils) modeled, it seems, on the Ferrarese *concerto di donne*; the *concerto de' castrati* (two castratos and a director-accompanist, the latter role taken for a while by Peri); the Franciosini, a wind band comprising cornetts and sackbuts (although its members played other instruments, including string and keyboard ones); and what became known by the second decade of the seventeenth century as the Franzesi (a string band, usually used for dancing).[57] Other male singers could contribute to a vocal ensemble covering the complete range (with castratos and falsettists on the higher parts), while the lutenists and keyboard players tended to be fairly mobile. However,

---

56. Ibid., 161 (Margherita); Carter, *Jacopo Peri*, 1: 22 (Bovia). For later examples of female musicians variously "hidden" in the court or otherwise in some sense supported by it (Arcangela Palladini, Maria Botti, Emilia Grazi, and so on, as well as Francesca Caccini's daughter Margherita), see Cusick, *Francesca Caccini at the Medici Court*, 62–66, 266–74.

57. To clarify the terminology, the *cornetto* is a wooden instrument played with a (wooden) cup mouthpiece, and therefore is a "wind" instrument and not related to the later cornet; the sackbut is an early trombone, and therefore a "brass" instrument, although it forms part of the wind band. "String" instruments can be members of either the *viola da gamba* family (what we now call viols, with instruments of different sizes reflecting the vocal ranges of soprano, alto, tenor, and bass, all played vertically and supported on or between the legs [*da gamba*]) or the *viola da braccio* one (the violin family, the smaller members of which are played on the arm [*da braccio*], although the larger ones could also be held between the legs, as with the modern violoncello). String ensembles tended not to mix *da gamba* and *da braccio* instruments save the largest viols (from which the modern double-bass descended). The softer *viole da gamba* were preferred for ensembles in chamber settings; *viole da braccio* were used for dance music, although the soprano *viola da braccio* (the violin) became the virtuoso's instrument of choice during the seventeenth century. While for acoustical reasons wind instruments were associated with outdoor use, and strings with indoor playing, the distinction was not rigidly maintained.

it was also in any court's interest for its musicians to be able to multitask, as it were, within a given instrument family or across a more comprehensive range of musical competencies. Peri was primarily a singer (tenor), but he also played the organ, harpsichord, and lute (and perhaps the chitarrone); Francesca Caccini played the lute, theorbo, keyboard, guitar, harp, and string instruments, in addition to being a singer and composer.[58] Thus the function for which musicians were registered on the rolls (e.g., as "singer")—reflected to varying degrees in Table 3.1—does not necessarily represent their sole or even principal musical activity at court: this is particularly true for the women musicians. While such versatility was useful for large-scale public events, it was even more so for the private performances provided, for example, by Peri for the princesses and, we shall see, Archduchess Maria Magdalena, and by Francesca Caccini for Grand Duchess Christine and other women of the court.

The *musici* were sufficient in number for regular needs, but when it came to special occasions more could be either brought in from other Tuscan towns or borrowed from other courts by way of reciprocal arrangements. For example, the last of the *intermedi* performed during the festivities celebrating the wedding of Prince Cosimo de' Medici and Maria Magdalena of Austria in October 1608 had thirty-six singers and thirty instrumentalists (and fifteen dancers) on stage, including two virtuosos imported from Rome, where they were associated with Cardinal Montalto: the soprano Ippolita Recupito and the bass Melchiorre Palantrotti (the latter had already sung in Peri's *Euridice* in 1600).[59] Although such borrowing of musicians may have been a necessity, it was usually cast as a favor on the part both of the lender (who thereby helped the Medici) and of the borrower (who allowed the lender's

---

58. According to the 1591 edition of the music for the 1589 *intermedi*, Peri sang the echo madrigal for Arion (fifth *intermedio*) *con maravigliosa arte sopra del chitarrone e con mirabil attenzione degli ascoltatori*. This has been read (e.g., Harness, *Echoes of Women's Voices*, 238) as suggesting that Peri himself played the chitarrone, but if he did, he is unlikely to have done it on stage at this particular moment in the *intermedio*. However, the anonymous sonnet praising Peri's singing to the lute (*al suon del tuo temprato legno*) suggests that he played this instrument; see Appendix D.

On Francesca Caccini, see Cusick, *Francesca Caccini at the Medici Court*, 61. Francesca taught Emilia Grazi to sing, play, and compose (see ibid., 84–85), even though she was on the roll as "learning to sing" (she was one of the *fanciulle che devono imparare a cantare*; Kirkendale, *Court Musicians*, 349).

59. Carter, "A Florentine Wedding of 1608."

glory to shine by displaying his musicians); the Medici adopted the same tactic in sending musicians elsewhere, such as to Mantua for the wedding of Prince Francesco Gonzaga and Margherita of Savoy earlier in 1608.

One of the musicians was placed in charge of the *guardaroba della musica*, the store of instruments and, presumably, of any manuscript or printed music needed for performance. But it is not clear to what extent the musician able to call himself the grand duke's *maestro di cappella*—Cristofano Malvezzi from 1574 to early 1599, Luca Bati to late 1608, and then Marco da Gagliano to 1643—had direct jurisdiction over the court musicians.[60] The title of *maestro* was tied to S. Giovanni Battista until the early seventeenth century, and thereafter to the Duomo—but in effect it referred to both institutions—while the *musici* instead seem to have reported to one or other court official (on the one hand, the majordomo, and on the other, someone given charge of the court artists or of court entertainments). Some confusion is apparent in the difficulty of pinning down just who had charge of the court musicians at any one time; the following were at various stages associated with a title stating or implying such authority: Emilio de' Cavalieri (1588–1602), Alfonso Fontanelli (1608–10), Giovanni Del Turco (at least in 1616–19), and Ferdinando Saracinelli (by late 1624, although he had some supervisory responsibilities for court entertainments in the preceding decade).[61] The matter clearly caused concern, however, given that the musicians seem to have been an unruly bunch: Cavalieri grew mightily tired of their squabbling during the 1600 festivities (for the marriage of Maria de' Medici and Henri IV of France), while Fontanelli, brought in to restore order after the 1608 wedding celebra-

---

60. Thus with the exception of Malvezzi (because of his other court service), the *maestri* are not given separate entries in Kirkendale, *Court Musicians*, which may seem odd but is wholly logical in Kirkendale's scheme of things, given that there was no such position within the court *musici*. It follows that frequent claims in the scholarly literature that so-and-so was *maestro di cappella* to the Grand Duke of Tuscany require careful consideration of what the title meant and of how properly, rather than just conveniently, it was used.

61. Kirkendale, *Court Musicians*, 608, disagrees on the permanence of any such position offered to Del Turco and Saracinelli (compare also Kirkendale, *Emilio de' Cavalieri*, 296) and does not mention Fontanelli in this role. For the last, see Chapter 1. Although Fontanelli was in Este service (albeit banished from Modena), he was in Florence from 1608 to 1610, when he served as *maggiordomo maggiore e cavaliere d'honore* to Archduchess Maria Magdalena. He had been a frequent visitor to the city earlier and was well known to Jacopo Corsi; he was also a member of the Accademia degli Elevati.

tions, had thrown up his hands in despair by January 1610.[62] We never hear of Peri's direct involvement in any of this squabbling—or at least, not until later in his life—and indeed any such behavior on his part would seem rather out of character for the person we now know from his own documents.

This manner of organization seems to have been something of a Florentine peculiarity: most other courts of similar size had the more conventional hierarchical model of a musical *maestro*, vice-*maestro*, and so on down some pecking order. In part, it may have reflected the Medici's strategy of appearing to continue systems and practices established during the Republic: hence the *maestro di cappella*, while appointed by the grand duke, was associated with the two main Florentine churches, the Duomo and S. Giovanni Battista, whose controlling guilds (the Arte della Lana and the Mercatanti di Calimala, respectively) officially made, and partly funded, the position. One wonders, however, to what extent some kind of typical Florentine business mentality also operated here in the desire to avoid direct management of a large workforce (compare the decentralized, semiautonomous operations to be found in the cloth industries). The *maestro* would certainly be used at court at least for musical composition, even though he was not usually included on the roll save when performing additional court-related duties (as when Cristofano Malvezzi, in 1588, was teaching the princesses). But other members of the *musici*, though by no means all, were able to compose according to their various specialisms (we shall see), even if providing music on a day-to-day basis largely consisted of performing stock repertory, usually from memory, and by way of various forms of improvisation.

The court wind and string players tended to display some manner of guild mentality, in part because of the training needed to gain technical proficiency and coverage of the repertory, and they were probably "on call" more often, given that they were needed for dancing or for the sonic accompaniment of other activities. For them, music also tended to run in the family (as is common in many periods). Vergilio di Giuseppe Grazi, one of the Franciosini, had one brother, Orazio, who was *sotto-maestro* at the Duomo and

---

62. Although Stefano Rosselli identified Jacopo Peri as *il principal direttore della musica e de' musici* (and Andrea Cavalcanti's additions to Rosselli's commentary gilded the lily still more), there is no evidence that he ever was, unless he was perceived by some to hold such a position by virtue of his seniority.

S. Giovanni Battista under Luca Bati, and another, Ottavio, who was a court trumpeter; Orazio's daughter, Emilia, was trained as a musician by Francesca Caccini; and another member of the Franciosini, Paolo di Giuliano Grazi, came from a different line of the same family.[63] The singers generally came from more diverse social backgrounds—a good voice, while it still needed training, was more a matter of luck in the first instance—and in fact the better ones tended to regard themselves as being of higher status. Here, too, musical dynasties were not uncommon (the Caccini are the obvious example). For them, music could often enable significant upward social mobility (as again is true in other periods as well). Giulio Caccini, for example, was the son of a carpenter (*legnaiolo*) from Montopoli (in the Valdarno) working in or near Rome. He gained admission as a boy soprano to the choir of the Cappella Giulia in Rome (under the Florentine Giovanni Animuccia) before being recruited to Florence on Animuccia's recommendation in 1565, specifically to perform in the festivities for the wedding of Grand Duke Francesco I and Johanna of Austria.[64] Peri, too, was upwardly mobile, as we have seen, albeit for reasons to do with more than his musical skills.

Musical talent and experience—whether or not gained through some ecclesiastical establishment—was a prerequisite for court employment, but further training could also occur on the job, as it were, by way of a formal or informal apprenticeship system, with young talent or new arrivals being tied to an existing court musician (who would usually be paid an additional allowance) until a formal appointment was judged possible or not. Thus when Caccini moved to Florence he was placed under Scipione Delle Palle, and later he took on similar responsibilities himself; Cristofano Malvezzi appears to have taken a similar role for Peri in the early stages of his career. Female musicians might come from musical households, be recruited from convents, or have their talents spotted in other ways, and, as we have seen, they would often end up marrying other musicians—as was true across Italy—in part for reasons of professional proximity but also for the possibility of remaining active after wedlock.

---

63. Carter, "Crossing the Boundaries"; Kirkendale, *Court Musicians*, 287–88 (Paolo Grazi), 507 (Vergilio), 349 (Emilia). For Emilia Grazi, see above, n. 58.

64. Carter, "Giulio Caccini"; for his family roots, see Giazotto, *Le due patrie di Giulio Caccini*.

Court service tended to be for life, and the payment of any salary continued until death (and very occasionally beyond it), even if a musician was no
longer active because of age or other incapacity.[65] Release could be granted
when someone requested a discharge to work elsewhere, or dismissal could be
imposed for inadequacy or disciplinary reasons, or for some greater difficulty
within the city. The Caccini family experienced such difficulties on more
than one occasion. Giulio was dismissed in August 1593 because of a violent
dispute with Antonio Salviati—the grand duke was reluctant to fire him (and
gave Caccini good references by way of *lettere di ben servire*) but seems to
have been put in a position where he had no choice—and he was reinstated
only after his work on the 1600 wedding festivities.[66] His daughter Settimia
and her husband, the musician Alessandro Ghivizzani, joined the *musici* on 3
November 1609 (with a monthly salary of *fl.*10 each), shortly after their marriage, but for some unknown if clearly drastic reason, Ghivizzani was banished (*bandito*) from Tuscany in mid-1611, and he moved his household back
to his native Lucca (both he and Settimia were removed from the roll), then
to Mantua, then back to Lucca, then to Parma, before Settimia reentered the
roll of Medici court musicians in 1636 (after her husband's death?).[67] Few of
the court musicians had such turbulent lives, however.

With a departure from service, a replacement would be found to fill the
gap so as to preserve the broad constitution of the *musici*. Thus it remained a
relatively stable group with respect to its makeup and even its actual membership, save for the notable increase in string players (the Franzesi) after
1610, reflecting particular trends in court entertainments under Grand Duke
Cosimo II. Most court musicians in Florence appear to have regarded the
position as in some sense the apogee of their career, and not many moved
away willingly unless to a genuinely better position (or if, being ordained in
the church, they were called elsewhere). It was a comfortable sinecure and, it
seems, not always (or at least not consistently) a very demanding one. This

65. For payments possibly continuing after death, see those of Vittoria Archilei noted in
Kirkendale, *Court Musicians*, 275–76.

66. Kirkendale, *Court Musicians*, 130–32. The dispute arose over Salviati's amorous intentions toward a singer, La Gamberella, whom Salviati had asked Caccini to teach.

67. Kirkendale, *Court Musicians*, 341–44. For their summary dismissal by Duke Ferdinando Gonzaga of Mantua in 1619, see their letters of complaint in Mantua, Archivio di Stato,
Archivio Gonzaga, 2746, docs. 299–301; they also requested *fl.*210, to be able to pay back a
moneylender.

might also indicate the provinciality, it is clear, of a court unlikely to attract significant foreign talent (although some French and German musicians ended up there), and the insertion of the Medici's musicians and their families in Florentine social and economic life in ways that may have been particular to the city because of its size, its institutional structures, and its industries. To understand the place of musicians in late sixteenth- and early seventeenth-century Florence—whether those employed by the grand-ducal family or those making a musical living in other ways—requires one to look beyond the court and what is, in the end, its rather narrow documentation. Peri becomes a particular case in point, with intriguing consequences.

But except for the rather unusual organization of the *musici* and their other opportunities in Florence, much of what has just been said about them would also apply to musicians in other courts across northern Italy and beyond. The Gonzagas in Mantua, for example, had eighteen or so court musicians in 1589–90 (so, fewer than the Medici at that time) and thirty-two to thirty-five in 1606–8 (so, perhaps more), with a slightly higher proportion of instrumentalists to singers but a similar range of performance groups: for the latter period, ten male singers, two five-part string ensembles, one five-part wind ensemble, two or three keyboard players, and one or more players of the Spanish guitar, plus female singers and a harpist.[68] The main differences were the more typical presence of a *maestro della musica* (Claudio Monteverdi) and vice-*maestro*, and the expectation that the *maestro* was meant to be a jack-of-all-trades, writing music for indoor and outdoor entertainments, the chamber, and the chapel. Florence had a similarly versatile figure in Marco da Gagliano, but also had more musician–composers who tended to specialize, one of whom was, precisely, Peri.

Within the Medici musical establishment, however, Peri was something of an anomaly. Although his entrance on the roll occurred by the normal route of service elsewhere and then apprenticeship (with Malvezzi), matters changed as he began to assert his status as a *nobil fiorentino*. Although, we shall see, he viewed himself as being of equal rank to the virtuoso tenor Francesco Rasi, for example, he remained among the *musici*—yet he married outside the profession and (so far as we can tell) without needing any manner of approval from the court, and he apparently had no interest in training any of his numerous daughters for a musical career. More work needs to be done

68. See the tables in Parisi, "Ducal Patronage of Music in Mantua," 27–36. These figures exclude the separate musical *cappella* linked to the ducal basilica of S. Barbara.

on the other lives of his musician colleagues, but it already seems clear that their social networks did not extend as far as Peri's, that they could not match his independent economic career in the business life of the city, and that none of them had a similar, continuing record of government service. That career and record may in the end be both a cause and an effect of Peri's seemingly borderline status: he had a middling position within the *musici* and did not advance therein, because of personal choice, on the one hand, and on the other, perhaps the court's sense that someone of his class, and with his ambitions, should receive preferment, if at all, in other ways.

Court Musical Entertainments

Peri's court service was closely linked to the entertainments that were a standard part of court life (see the list of his musical works in Appendix C). He had already in 1583 composed the music for the first of six *intermedi* for Giovanni Fedini's play *Le due Persilie* performed before the Medici princesses, and shortly after his appointment at court he played a leading role in the fifth of the spectacular *intermedi* accompanying Girolamo Bargagli's *La pellegrina*, staged during the festivities for the wedding of Grand Duke Ferdinando I and Christine of Lorraine in April–May 1589.[69] He was deeply involved in the emergence in Florence of what we now call opera but would at the time have been called the *favola in musica* ("play in music"), first with *Dafne*, commissioned by the prominent Florentine music patron Jacopo Corsi, and then with *Euridice*, which was Corsi's offering to the festivities for the wedding of Maria de' Medici and Henri IV of France in October 1600. In the second and third decades of the century, Peri contributed fairly regularly to Carnival and other entertainments—with *balli*, tournaments, and the like during the reign of Grand Duke Cosimo II, and other court entertainments and *sacre rappresentazioni* during the regency of Grand Duchess Christine and Archduchess Maria Magdalena in the 1620s—notwithstanding his full-time job at the Arte della Lana and his numerous family at home.

For obvious historiographical reasons, the operas have tended to loom large in accounts of Peri's musical career—and also of Florentine court entertainments—although it is clear that the novelty value of the genre soon

---

69. In this period, plays were often performed with *intermedi* before, between, and after their five acts (so, six *intermedi*, one as a prologue, one an epilogue, and four between the acts). They could be simple (a chorus) or elaborate (a mythological or similar scene) depending on the scale and purpose of the production.

wore thin: the festivities for the wedding of Cosimo de' Medici and Maria Magdalena of Austria in 1608 reverted to the well-known formula of a comedy with *intermedi* (for which Peri again composed some of the music). Those festivities harked back to the 1589 wedding, if without its luster given that Giovanni de' Bardi, recently returned to Florence, was unable to repeat the success of his role as organizer because the musicians ran riot.[70] We have seen that opera never established a secure footing in its native city: it is also clear that it was just one of a number of possible types of court entertainment, with the Florentine nobility, like many others, tending to prefer those that allowed more active participation either on the dance floor or on imaginary battlefields. Venice offered a much more secure home for opera when it was established there in 1637 (on the opening of the Teatro S. Cassiano as a "public" opera house). It was a city twice the size of Florence and an international emporium to boot (as Florence was not); in the absence of a court, opera offered, on the one hand, a fashionably new and highly visible outlet for the projection of social status and, on the other hand, myriad opportunities for entrepreneurial ventures to make money in the private market (and from what one might call the tourist trade), ranging from building theaters, renting stalls, and organizing productions to making costumes and scenery and selling librettos and refreshments.

The patterns for Florence are clear in Table 3.2, which lists musical and other entertainments at the Medici court during two sample years—one (1605) during the reign of Grand Duke Ferdinando I and the other (1615) during that of Grand Duke Cosimo II—drawn from the diary of court events compiled by Cesare Tinghi (the grand duke's *aiutante di camera*). This also gives some feel for the larger-scale rhythms of court life noted earlier: relatively short periods of intense activity focusing on Carnival, princely visits, and other court or civic occasions, amid longer interludes with nothing of note. The differences between the two years reflect the styles of two grand dukes: Ferdinando I tended to spend Carnival in Pisa whereas Cosimo II preferred Florence (perhaps because he was not generally in good health); the former tended to keep entertainments on a relatively small scale save in special circumstances; the latter made greater use of more elaborate, thematically structured entertainments, and also (in the summer months) of outdoor civic ones in the various *quartieri* of the city, which Tinghi usually explains

70. Carter, "A Florentine Wedding of 1608."

Table 3.2. Entertainments at court in two sample years: 1605, 1615

Date	Event
1605	
8 Feb (Tu)	(court in Pisa for Carnival) *festa da ballo, corsa delle oche,* and *palio*
10 Feb (Th)	*ballo*
subsequently	hunting, *corso all'anello,* quintain, and *Il giuoco del ponte*
22 Feb (Tu)	(Shrove Tuesday) *giostra al saracino, sbarra* (text by Michelangelo Buonarroti *il giovane*; music by Jacopo Peri), *festa da ballo,* and banquet
26 Jun (Su)	the grand duke gives audience to French ambassador; after lunch *si fece una bella musica tra tutti e' musici di S.A.*; at 22:00 (i.e., two hours before sunset), a *festino di ballare* arranged by the grand duchess (lasts until nightfall)
6–19 Sep	Duke of Mantua visits Florence, with *feste da ballo* at court and in residences of Florentine nobles
12–27 Oct	Virginia de' Medici d'Este (wife of Duke of Modena) visits Florence with her two sons
18 Oct (Tu)	*festa da ballo* in the Sala delle Figure in the Palazzo Pitti
22 Oct (Sa)	performance of Michelangelo Buonarroti *il giovane*'s comedy *Il natal d'Ercole* in the *casino* of Don Antonio de' Medici, 21:00–24:00
23 Oct (Su)	*ballo* at court
19 Nov (Sa)	Cardinal Zappada visits the grand duke at Poggio a Caiano; he is entertained by *una comedia recitata da un solo comediante, cosa ridicolosa*
1615	
4 Feb (We)	(court in Florence for Carnival) *Comedia a uso di zanni recitata all'improvviso da giovani fiorentini*
8, 13 Feb	the grand duke attends rehearsals of the *Veglia delle Grazie* (see 16 Feb)
16 Feb (Mo)	*Veglia delle Grazie* (text by Chiabrera; music by Peri and others) performed before visiting dignitaries in the *sala delle commedie* in the Palazzo Pitti; begins at 22:00 (i.e., two hours before sunset) and is followed by a *colazione*
17 Feb (Tu)	the grand duke attends rehearsal of the new *balletto* to be performed (see 24 Feb)
23 Feb (Mo)	the grand duke hears Mass in chambers, then attends rehearsal of the new *balletto* to be performed (see 24 Feb); after lunch, he arranges a *caccia* in the gardens of the Palazzo Pitti to entertain the archduchess and princesses

(continued)

Table 3.2. *(continued)*

Date	Event
24 Feb (Tu)	*Ballo delle zingare* (text by Ferdinando Saracinelli; music by Francesca Caccini) performed in the *sala delle commedie* in the Palazzo Pitti, partially in honor of the marriage of one of Archduchess Maria Magdalena's ladies-in-waiting; four of the *zingare* are female singers at court
25 Feb (We)	*calcio* in Piazza S. Croce done by Florentine youths
26 Feb (Th)	(Giovedì grasso) *Ballo di donne turche* (text by Alessandro Ginori; music by Marco da Gagliano), followed by dancing until 04:00
1 Mar (Su)	*calcio* in Piazza S. Croce; in the evening, a *festa da ballo* at court
2 Mar (Mo)	*giostra al saracino* in Via Larga; in the evening, a *ballo* at court
3 Mar (Tu)	(Shrove Tuesday) *calcio* in Piazza S. Croce; in the evening, a *festa da ballo* at court
25 Jul (Sa)	(Feast of S. Jacopo) *festa* on the banks of the Arno (*L'arrivo d'Amore in Toscana in grazia delle bellissime dame fiorentine*; text by Ferdinando Saracinelli), with *carri* containing singers and instrumentalists, prior to the customary *palio delle fregate*
15 Aug (Sa)	*palio* in Via Ghibellina, including a *carro* containing instrumentalists
23 Aug (Su)	*palio* ending at S. Felice in Piazza (on the theme of four seasons), including four *carri* with instrumentalists
30 Aug (Su)	*palio* in Via Larga (*Bacco con le sue baccanti*), including a *carro* containing singers and instrumentalists
6 Sep (Su)	*palio* in Via Maggio (*Villani di Licia trasformati in ranocchi*), including *carri* with singers and instrumentalists
6 Nov (Fr)	performance by the *commedia dell'arte* troupe headed by Fritellino (Pier Maria Cecchini; and on subsequent evenings in Nov and Dec)

as the grand duke's way of giving a little pleasure (*un poco di gusto*) to Archduchess Maria Magdalena and to the people of Florence.

The commonalities, however, reflect typical Florentine preferences: pseudo-military exercises (outdoor tournaments, jousts, the *calcio*, etc., or indoor hand-to-hand "combat"), usually to allow the Medici princes to demonstrate their skills and Florentine noblemen to compete for grand-ducal favor; spoken comedies (whether literary or improvised); the ubiquitous *feste da ballo* culminating in collective dancing; and, in the second decade of the century, *palii* in the city streets with pageants and horse-racing. Tournaments would usually be set in a thematic frame, anticipated by the announcement of some kind of challenge during an event at court prior to the tournament itself. The *palii* could also be given a theme, articulated by costumed characters on processional floats (*carri*). Indoor entertainments would be given in various rooms in the Palazzo Pitti, in the Teatro degli Uffizi, in other Medici locations (such as the *casino* of Don Antonio de' Medici near S. Marco), and, as a sign of favor, in the residences of (and at the expense of) prominent Florentine nobles (the Riccardi, Strozzi, Corsi, and others), or for the Medici women, in preferred convents.[71] Depending on place and protocol, audiences could be mixed, segregated, or limited by gender or rank, with the grand-ducal family present (visibly or viewing in private) or not, and with them and their principal guests identifiable or incognito.

Save for spoken comedies (which might, however, include various forms of music), any texts associated with these entertainments would normally be sung by one or more performers in character (to launch the challenge or set the stage for a tournament; to declare the theme for a *festa da ballo*)—singing gave a sense of occasion and also allowed for greater projection—and instrumentalists were necessarily involved for ceremonial purposes, to cover moments of inaction, and, of course, to accompany dancing. Therefore court musicians would be used in these entertainments in various capacities. These musicians would also be on display in other ways during the visits to Florence made by foreign dignitaries, as they were, for example, when Cardinals Del Monte and Montalto, important Medici allies in the papal Curia, were in Florence in November–December 1602 (Table 3.3). These cardinals' musical and theatrical passions were well known. In addition to the customary indoor entertainments (spoken comedies and *feste da ballo*)—it was not the season for many outdoor ones—the visitors heard the grand duke's female singers in his chambers (6 November), while during an interlude for refreshment in the final *festino di ballare* on 9 December, the court musicians sang music for three choirs.[72] In addition, and as was customary, Florentine noblemen were

71. Don Antonio de' Medici was the illegitimate son of Grand Duke Francesco I and Bianca Cappello (he was born in 1576, before they were married, and while the grand duke's first wife, Johanna of Austria, was still alive). Although Francesco I legitimized him and his succession, Ferdinando I overruled his claim to the grand-ducal throne (in part, by suggesting that Bianca Cappello had faked the pregnancy and birth), although he granted him some honors and used him for diplomatic purposes and for entertaining distinguished visitors to Florence. Ferdinando I treated his illegitimate brother, Don Giovanni de' Medici, in a similar way: he was given a leading role in arranging the 1600 wedding festivities, and later was well known for his support of *commedia dell'arte* players.

72. One should probably be suspicious of the accuracy of these kinds of reports: Tinghi was not a musician, and he was more concerned with the impressiveness of any event. In a church context, music for "three choirs" would normally imply three separate four- or five-part

given the honor (and conveniently took on the expense) of receiving distinguished guests: the cardinals spent time in the palaces of Filippo Salviati (28 November), Niccolò Berardi (3 December), and Jacopo Corsi (8 December, very shortly before his untimely death)—all three of whom had significant interest in music.

This visit also reveals one place for opera at court. On 5 December, the cardinals were given the opportunity to see a *favola in musica*: Giulio Caccini's *Euridice*, a rival setting of the same libretto by Ottavio Rinuccini composed by Jacopo Peri for the 1600 wedding (and one that Caccini had somewhat maliciously published in advance of Peri's). This seems to have been chosen to suit the cardinals' personal tastes—they had attended an early performance of Rinuccini and Peri's *Dafne* in the 1598–99 Carnival season and, of course, were present in Florence in 1600—while also, perhaps, meeting the needs of clerical propriety. Furthermore, Cardinal Montalto appears to have been an exception in not finding the new style of Florentine recitative tiresome save in small doses: he supported opera and similar entertainments in Rome during his many years as a prominent music patron there.[73]

As in many Italian courts, however, the Medici tended to prefer any dramatic presentation involving music to bring various forms of dancing into the frame—in other words, audience participation—in a manner more familiar to scholars from the French *ballet de cour* or the English masque; even the performance of *Euridice* during the 1600 wedding festivities was followed by two hours of dancing.[74] A good example is Gabriello Chiabrera's *Veglia delle Grazie*, with vocal music by Jacopo Peri and dance music by Lorenzo Allegri, performed on 16 February 1615.[75] This was done in the presence of the

---

groups (so, twelve or fifteen parts in all), but while Tinghi certainly seems to want to convey some sense of spatial separation (so, three groups of performers set apart one from the other), what he means by a "choir," and what by "sung" is less straightforward: one "choir," for example, may just have been a singer and an instrumentalist.

73. Hill, *Roman Monody, Cantata, and Opera from the Circles around Cardinal Montalto.*

74. Solerti, *Musica, ballo e drammatica alla corte medicea,* 25 n. 1.

75. The text is in Solerti, *Gli albori del melodramma,* 3: 189–99; Chiabrera styles it *Vegghia delle Gratie* (Florence: Giovanni Antonio Caneo, 1615). Although Tinghi associates Peri with the two *intermedi,* one assumes that he also set the prologue and epilogue (all the music is lost). Allegri's dances were included as the "Ottavo ballo detto *L'Iride* danzato dai Paggi, e Dame nella festa particulare fatta dalla Serenissima Arciduchessa di Toscana" at the end of his *Il primo libro delle musiche* (Venice: Bartolomeo Magni, 1618). For the *veglia* as a form of entertainment, see Carter, "Winds, Cupids, Little Zephyrs, and Sirens."

Table 3.3. Entertainments for the visit of Cardinals Del Monte and Montalto,
November–December 1602

Date	Event
5 Nov (Tu)	Cardinal Montalto arrives in Florence with his brother, Marchese Peretti (Cardinal del Monte is already there)
6 Nov (We)	after lunch, music by Vittoria Archilei, the *donne* of Giulio Caccini, and other various musicians in the grand duke's chambers; then the grand duke takes the cardinals through the city
7–21 Nov	the cardinals visit Pisa and Livorno
24 Nov (Su)	music for four choirs in the Duomo; then a *corso all'anello* in Piazza S. Trinita
25 Nov (Mo)	visit to the *casino* of Don Antonio de' Medici to view the house and gallery, and a performance (lasting two hours) of Jacopo Cicognini's comedy *I morti e vivi (con intermedi apparenti)* by young Florentines of the Compagnia del Alberto
26 Nov (Tu)	the grand duke takes the cardinals to have lunch at, and to visit, the *galleria* (in the Uffizi); they take a coach through Florence; in the evening, a *commedia di zanni*
27 Nov (We)	*caccia a leoni*
28 Nov (Th)	*festino* in the palace of Filippo Salviati
1 Dec (Su)	another *comedia recitata da giovani fiorentini con intermedi aparenti* at the *casino* of Don Antonio de' Medici, from 22:00 to 02:00 (i.e., two hours before sunset to two hours after)
2 Dec (Mo)	Lunch in the *galleria*, also with Signor Colonella of Pisa, and dancing until 23:00; then return to Palazzo Pitti for a *commedia di zanni*
3 Dec (Tu)	*festino* in the palace of Niccolò Berardi
5 Dec (Th)	Giulio Caccini's *Euridice* (libretto by Ottavio Rinuccini) performed in the *sala* of Don Antonio de' Medici in the Palazzo Pitti (lasts two hours)
7 Dec (Sa)	*festino di ballare* in the Sala delle Figure in the Palazzo Pitti, 24:00–05:00
8 Dec (Su)	*veglia* in the palace of Jacopo Corsi
9 Dec (Mo)	*festino di ballare* in the Sala Grande dei Forestieri in the Palazzo Pitti, 24:00–05:00; at 03:00 the grand duke serves a *colazione* during which the court musicians, dressed as nymphs and shepherds, sing in three choirs and perform a *balletto* (*fu da musici di Sua Altezza tutti vestiti da ninfe e pastori cantato in Musicha a 3 cori et fatto un balletto in capriole*)

Source: Solerti, *Musica, ballo e drammatica alla corte medicea*, 29–31; ASF, Guardaroba medicea, Diari d'etichetta 3, pp. 178–80; 4, fols. 28–30v (the last with some minor variations).

grand-ducal family, the papal *nuncio*, the ambassadors of Lucca and Modena, and a visiting Turkish emir with his entourage (which explains the *Ballo di donne turche* given later during this same Carnival).[76] Chiabrera framed the *veglia* as an entertainment arranged by the three Graces seeking to heal Amor of some unspecified wound. It began with a prologue for Iride (Iris, the personification of rainbows, linking the gods and mankind), who invited six ladies (masked as *ninfe di Pomona*) to dance, and then Fama did the same for six gentlemen (as *numi di Silvano*)—dancing was done by couples in this period. This character-dance by court pages and ladies-in-waiting, in seven musical sections contrasted by dance type (*gagliardo, brando, corrente*, etc.), was followed by general dancing (*senza maschera*) for an hour. Then came the first of two staged *intermedi*, with Gelosia threatening to put an end to the entertainment before being repulsed by a chorus of *amori*. This cued a return to general dancing (for another hour) in which the grand duke and archduchess participated, prior to the second *intermedio*, with Speranza announcing to Mercurio her discovery of a salve to temper the mortal wounds of Cupid's arrows so that mankind can love without dying. Iride then returned to provide the epilogue: that love had now become an immortal delight. This type of mixed-mode entertainment served the court well: it had a degree of stage spectacle (Iride appeared on a cloud descending across a stage set representing a meadow amid a forest, with a river and a bridge), appropriate mythological resonances, and some measure of dramatic coherence, but it allowed selected nobles to display particular dancing skills to specific choreography (created by the dancing-master Agnolo Ricci) without inhibiting more general dancing among the courtiers.

As already noted, the records of these particular music-theatrical events are particularly strong either because of their relatively public (even within the court) and prestigious nature, or because it was useful to keep a record for future reference of how, say, visitors of particular rank were treated in Florence in terms of hospitality, entertainment, and other activities. In turn, certain patterns emerge in the handling of such visitors according to quite strong rules of etiquette. But music must have been used far more frequently

---

76. One assumes that the Turkish visitors were there at least in part to discuss trade agreements with the Levant, a matter of regular concern for the Medici (despite the obvious religious and other problems) as a way of redirecting Florentine exports in response to changing market conditions elsewhere in Europe.

at court and in the chamber than became a matter of record, whether for entertainment or diversion, as part of civil conversation, or even, it seems, for its therapeutic benefits during pregnancy or illness. Thus as Grand Duke Cosimo II was increasingly forced to take to his bed during the last years of his reign because of gout and other maladies, musicians were often brought to his rooms in the evening.[77] Recent scholarship has also uncovered rich strata of music making associated with Medici women, whether in the chamber or in the convents that they supported (and where some of them periodically resided).[78] While the gynocentric focus—and for convents, exclusion—of these environments is clear, some male musicians could also participate in them, as with Peri and the princesses early in his career, and then with Archduchess Maria Magdalena shortly after her arrival in Florence. The theatrical and other entertainments on which Cesare Tinghi reported so assiduously in his official court diary represented only the tip of a musical iceberg.

Peri as Court Musician

Enough has been revealed thus far to suggest that Peri's situation among *musici* was not entirely typical for the court musicians as a whole: even granting the danger of expecting any of them to conform to a singular model, he appears betwixt and between their various professional and personal trajectories. Certainly, the path leading to his official appointment in his late twenties was common enough, and he was proud to note his new position close to the grand duke as cause to rent the farm at San Marco Vecchio on the outskirts of the city (*ché per stare io col Gran Duca mi trovo molto obligato*). But after *Euridice* he seems to have stepped back, for which one can try to adduce one or more of several reasons: his claims for nobility, court rivalries, Corsi's death in 1602, other (nonmusical) opportunities in Florence, family circumstances, age, ill health, a lack of ambition, the desire for one kind of lifestyle rather than another. One might just have to accept, however, that the

---

77. For two of many examples, see Solerti, *Musica, ballo e drammatica alla corte medicea*, 86 (December 1614–January 1615; the dwarfs and jesters were also summoned), 152 (January 1620; Francesca Caccini and her pupils, Arcangela Palladini, and the virtuoso bass, Giandomenico Puliaschi, visiting from Rome).

78. Cusick, *Francesca Caccini at the Medici Court*; Harness, *Echoes of Women's Voices*.

circumstances and choices determining a person's life cannot always be explained so easily, for all that one can engage with their consequences.

Peri's entrance into the roll by September 1588 was no doubt part of the reorganization and renewal of the court musicians under Emilio de' Cavalieri on the succession of Grand Duke Ferdinando I. Cavalieri had been associated with Ferdinando while the latter was a cardinal living in Rome, as were the musicians Vittoria and Antonio Archilei, and Giovanni Battista Jacomelli, and their arrival in Florence was part of what many Florentines considered somewhat grimly, if with exaggeration, a Roman invasion at court, as the new grand duke placed his favorites in high positions so as to reform the administration of his predecessor. Save for Cavalieri's presence, the impact on the musicians was not as great as elsewhere in the court; it would probably have been more so had the composer Luca Marenzio—born in Brescia but most active in Rome—been persuaded to stay in Florence after his work on the 1589 festivities. Indeed, Cavalieri made a point of noting for at least one potential hire to the court (in 1598) that the candidate was Florentine.[79] But Giulio Caccini seems to have been jumping on a bandwagon by taking advantage of the soubriquet "Romano" or "da Roma," presumably on the basis of the technicality that he was baptized there (although his father was Tuscan).[80] It did not do him much good in the end. The fact that the court musicians continued to consist mostly of Florentines, however, may not have been a result just of expediency, inertia, or even an inability to recruit from elsewhere: they, more than many Romans, were much more experienced in meeting princely demands, and once Ferdinando settled down to grand-ducal rule, he seems to have appreciated the point.

The grand duke may have been persuaded by the success of the festivities for his marriage to Christine of Lorraine in May 1589. They included Girolamo Bargagli's play, La pellegrina, with a spectacular set of six intermedi

79. Kirkendale, Court Musicians, 296 (Orazio Benvenuti).

80. When Caccini first arrived in Florence, in 1565, he was often styled "Giulio da Montopoli" in the court records (after the birthplace of his father); see Carter, "Giulio Caccini," 20 n. 21. However, the fact that "Romano" and "da Roma" were also adopted by Giulio's brother, the sculptor Giovanni, may suggest that it involved some effort to distinguish the family from the Florentine Caccini, who were patrician bankers. It is also worth noting, although the reasons and consequences are unclear, that Giulio Caccini is reported as having became a Florentine citizen only in 1600 (i.e., shortly before or after his reinstatement at court); Kirkendale, Court Musicians, 136 n. 156.

devised by Giovanni de' Bardi.[81] Thus in the first *intermedio* ("The Harmony of the Spheres"), a figure representing Dorian Harmony (played by Vittoria Archilei) descended in a cloud machine, singing the while, and was then matched by a celestial choir (representing sirens and planets), followed by an instrumental sinfonia, and a dialogue for the Fates and the Sirens (in two five-part choirs), ending with the entire body of musicians on stage singing and playing an encomium to the grand duke and the new grand duchess. The fifth *intermedio* related the story of Arion, one of the great musicians of classical myth, who used his art to charm the dolphins on being thrown off his ship by a mutinous crew. Peri played the role of Arion himself, performing a virtuoso song with double echo effects (we see him as such in the frontispiece to this book, the only representation of him that survives). He was soon to play other such mythical heroes, including Apollo in the opera *Dafne*, and Orpheus in *Euridice*.

Cristofano Malvezzi had charge of the music for the 1589 *intermedi*, and including Peri so prominently in them may have been one more favor on his part for his former student: the fifth *intermedio* was rewritten, it seems, to showcase his talents.[82] By now, however, Peri also needed to cultivate other protectors at court, and Emilio de' Cavalieri may have been one of them. Cavalieri appears to have favored Peri over Caccini, who was a decade older (and just a year younger than Cavalieri himself): presumably he supported Peri's salary increase in September 1590, and they were in close enough contact for Cavalieri to have been able to inform the court on 17 November 1598 that Peri was very afflicted (*afflittissimo*) by the death of his wife that day (in fact, the day before), although he also noted somewhat hard-heartedly that he would be in a fit state to sing in three days.[83] Matters got more tense in the

81. Saslow, *The Medici Wedding of 1589*; Treadwell, *Music and Wonder at the Medici Court.*

82. For the music (from the 1591 edition), see Walker, *Musique des intermèdes de "La pellegrina,"* 98–106. Peri's "Dunque fra torbid'onde" was a replacement for a different piece ("Ardisci, ardisci forte," to be sung by Arion to a harp accompaniment) originally intended for this part of the *intermedio*. One assumes that Malvezzi encouraged the substitution to support Peri; it may also be significant that Malvezzi excluded from the 1591 edition Giulio Caccini's contribution to the *intermedi* (the first song in the fourth *intermedio*).

83. Cavalieri to Marcello Accolti, 17 November 1598 (ASF, Mediceo del Principato 3622), given in Carter, *Jacopo Peri*, 1: 299: *Il Zazzerino faccio conto serva alla pastorale, ma per cattiva sorte, oggi se l'è morta la moglie, et sta afflittissimo. Pure in tre giorni dovrà ritornare in termine di cantare . . .* It is not clear what the *pastorale* might have been.

buildup to the next major set of Medici wedding festivities, in October 1600 for Maria de' Medici and Henri IV of France. The temperature among the court musicians rose in part because of the chaotic organization of the entertainments, but also because of the emerging claims and counterclaims for originality in the invention of new forms of theatrical entertainments involving musical recitative in the 1590s and early 1600s. Some court officials simply associated Jacopo Corsi's offering to the festivities, *Euridice*, with Cavalieri—they had no reason to know better—but those more directly involved in early opera vied over matters of precedence.[84] Cavalieri felt, after the fact, that the pastorals on which he had earlier collaborated with the poet Laura Guidiccioni de' Lucchesini—including *Il satiro* and *La disperatione di Fileno* in 1590 and *Il giuoco della cieca* (based on an episode from Guarini's *Il pastor fido*) in 1595—deserved some credit. He was particularly angry that any such precedence was ignored by the Florentine poet Ottavio Rinuccini—or *Ranocchino* ("Little Frog"), as he called him—in the preface to the printed libretto.[85] Giulio Caccini, on the other hand, had his own axes to grind as he sought to reestablish his position in Florence through the 1600 wedding festivities and therefore puffed up his own role, beating Peri to the press with his own score of *Euridice*, even though it was not performed in full until December 1602.

Peri himself tried to rise above it all: at the beginning of the preface to his printed score of *Euridice*, in explaining the nature of "this new type of song" (*questa nova maniera di canto*), he made a clear enough statement that Cavalieri was the first to bring with marvelous invention "our music" to the stage (*Benché dal signor Emilio del Cavalieri, prima che da ogni altro ch'io sappia, con maravigliosa invenzione ci fusse fatta udire la nostra musica sulle scene . . .*). However, Peri also noted that Corsi and Rinuccini had encouraged him, as early as 1594, to present that music in a different manner in *Dafne* (*piacque nondimeno a' signori Jacopo Corsi ed Ottavio Rinuccini (fin l'anno 1594), che io,*

---

84. Tinghi's diary refers to *Euridice* as *una comedia pastorale in musica fatta dal Signor Emilio del Cavaliere su alle stanze del Signor Don Antonio Medici a Pitti*; Solerti, *Musica, ballo e drammatica alla corte medicea*, 25. This kind of confusion was not untypical in such records. As far as the court was concerned, it rarely mattered anyway save when in might have affected the reputation of someone who counted.

85. See, for example, his letter to Marcello Accolti of 10 November 1600 (ASF, Mediceo del Principato, 3622), given in Palisca, "Musical Asides in the Diplomatic Correspondence of Emilio de' Cavalieri," 353–54.

adoperandola in altra guisa, mettessi sotto le note la favola di Dafne). *Dafne* was first performed in early 1598, so Peri's reference to 1594 was probably a pre-emptive strike at least against Cavalieri's *Il giuoco della cieca* (from 1595). But his opening offered a generous enough acknowledgment to Cavalieri, and one made perhaps because Peri knew he owed the Roman composer some debt. Soon afterward, however, their relations seem to have soured.

Frustrated by the difficulties over the 1600 festivities, Cavalieri developed an even dimmer view of the Florentine court musicians. On 24 November 1600, he told the court secretary Marcello Accolti that Peri's chief duty at court was the provision of (sacred) motets sung to the accompaniment of the organ (*la cura sua è del motetto del Organo*), to which Cavalieri added somewhat sarcastically that he made too big a meal of it (*et le pare gran cura*).[86] This role harks back to Peri's first position at SS. Annunziata, although it is unclear what it might mean with respect to the court. We have documentation for some of the years in which he participated in the customary music for Holy Week (1600, 1606, 1611), and he seems to have had charge of it in 1600, 1620 (see Letters 30, 31), 1622, and 1623, and perhaps at other times as well. But no doubt this was on his annual calendar: in 1611, Giulio Caccini referred to Peri singing his solos as usual (*i suoi soli al solito*).[87] No "motets" (that is, settings of religious texts in Latin) by Peri survive, however, although the collection of songs he published in 1609, *Le varie musiche*, contains two spiritual madrigals setting devotional texts in the vernacular, "O miei giorni fugaci, o breve vita" and "Anima, oimé, che pensi, oimé, che fai" (both poems are by Ottavio Rinuccini).[88]

Cavalieri's sarcasm, however, also derives from a passage earlier in this same letter to Accolti where he refers to another possible role for Peri at court, as well as to their worsening relations. He describes Peri as distinctly disgruntled,

86. Cavalieri (Rome) to Accolti, 24 November 1600 (ASF, Mediceo del Principato 3622), given in Carter, *Jacopo Peri*, 1: 307–8.

87. In Caccini's letter to Piero Strozzi, 6 April 1611 (Florence, Biblioteca Riccardiana, Ricc. 4009a), given in Bacherini Bartoli, "Giulio Caccini," 68–69 (doc. 14); but see n. 119 below.

88. More confusing is the claim on the title page of *Le varie musiche* that the greater part of its songs could be played just on the organ (*et ancora la maggior parte di esse per sonare semplicemente nel organo*). It is true that "O miei giorni fugaci, o breve vita" survives in a keyboard arrangement (see Appendix C), and the more homophonic arias could have been done similarly, but it is hard to imagine it for the more declamatory sonnet settings and madrigals.

perhaps not just because of the festivities themselves but also because his role in *Euridice* was in the process of being erased from the official description of them by Michelangelo Buonarroti *il giovane*, which appeared four days before Cavalieri's letter.[89] As he told Accolti:

> At other times, Zazzerino had the desire to perform with the castratos, so as to give me every satisfaction and to serve His Highness at whatever opportunity. Believing this, on my departure from Florence I told His Highness that, although Orazio Benvenuti was leaving, Zazzerino would perform. His Highness approved. I spoke with Zazzerino and I found him distant, saying that he did not have his former health, and that serving much or little was all the same. His reply seemed strange to me, and I spoke to him in a somewhat offended way and told him that he should not make a firm decision, but should think on it and then write to me in Rome. And from the enclosed letter from Zazzerino you will see that he is comfortable where he is, and that he does not want this bother, also feeling that I can no longer do anything as regards His Highness, and that he has better protectors than me.[90]

One of these "better protectors" was presumably Belisario Vinta, whom Peri had already approached, it seems, for help in escaping this additional duty with the castratos (Letter 2)—also citing health reasons including headaches and catarrh (*il dolore della testa che spesso mi visita, accompagnata da un catarrino salso*)—although he soon decided that discretion was the better part

---

89. For Peri and other musicians being removed from Buonarroti's *Descrizione delle felicissime nozze della Cristianissima Maestà di Madama Maria Medici, Regina di Francia e di Navarra* (Florence: Giorgio Marescotti, 1600; the dedication is dated 20 November 1600), see Carter, "*Non occorre nominare tanti musici*."

90. Cavalieri (Rome) to Accolti, 24 November 1600, in ASF Mediceo del Principato 3622 (also given, with some errors, in Carter, *Jacopo Peri*, 1: 307–8): *Altre volte il Zazzerino ha havuto desiderio di concertarsi con i castrati, dar a me ogni sodisfatione et servire a Sua Altezza in qualsivoglia occasione. Con tal credenza, al partir mio da Fiorenza dissi a Sua Altezza che se bene partiva Oratio Benvenuti, che Zazzerino havria concertato. A Sua Altezza piacque. Io parlai al Zazzerino et lo trovai alieno, dicendomi che non si trovava con quella sanità di già, et che tanto era servire molto come poco. A me parse strano la risposta, li parlai un poco resentito, et le dissi che non la pigliano per risolutione, ma che vi pensasse, et poi me ne scrivessi in Roma. Dalla inclusa del Zazzerino, la vedrà che lui si trova comodo, et non vuole questa briga, tenendo ancho che io non possi più appresso Sua Altezza, et habbia meglio protettori di me.* Cavalieri goes on to suggest that Giovanni Battista Signorini could be tried out for the position (to which he was appointed in 1603).

of valor and accepted it (Letter 3).[91] He performed with the *concerto de' castrati* (with Giovanni Boccherini and Fabio Fabbri) at least until 1603, when Giovanni Battista Signorini was given a supplement to his regular salary (*fl.*2 on top of *fl.*9) to substitute for him because, so Enea Vaini reported, Peri was going deaf (*va ingrossando l'udire*).[92] The *concerto* certainly performed in the chamber, but it could also be used, it seems, in theatrical performances.[93] The two three-voice settings—"Caro e soave legno" and "O dolce anima mia"—that Peri published in *Le varie musiche* probably relate to his work for the group. But headaches, catarrh, and deafness were an impediment to any musician, and they appear to have continued: according to Michelangelo Buonarroti *il giovane*, Peri was prevented from composing music for the poet's *Il passatempo* for the 1613–14 Carnival season *per sua indisposizione di testa.*[94]

Le varie musiche no doubt includes other music that Peri provided for consumption in courtly chambers. In early 1609, he declined an invitation from Cardinal Ferdinando Gonzaga to come to Mantua for Carnival (Letter 15) because he was in continual demand from Archduchess Maria Magdalena—recently married to Prince Cosimo—and also from a new generation of Medici princesses (a reprise of his role in the late 1570s and early 1580s): the daughters of Ferdinando I and Christine of Lorraine, including Leonora, Caterina (later Duchess of Mantua), Maria Maddalena, and Claudia (later Duchess of Urbino). Pandolfo (Della) Stufa explained the situation even more

91. Although the recipient of Letters 2 and 3 is unidentified, it is almost certainly Belisario Vinta (1542–1613), who was the First Secretary of State and therefore wielded significant influence in Florence; he also was frequently a mediator with the court for Florentine musicians. It is unclear, however, whether he was someone to whom Peri (and others) appealed in his official capacity or because he was known to have been an enthusiastic sponsor of musical performances in his residence. Of course, one does not exclude the other.

92. Lozzi, "La musica e specialmente il melodramma alla corte medicea," 314; Kirkendale, *Court Musicians*, 293.

93. In June 1603, Enea Vaini told the grand duchess about preparations for the upcoming visit of Duke Vincenzo Gonzaga (ASF, Mediceo del Principato 5986, document dated 10 June 1603): *Si seleciterà la comedia, e quando Vostra Altezza rimanderà quel concerto de' castrati, che deve cantar e recitar, si comincierà a provare.* This probably refers to Jacopo Cicognini's comedy *I morti e vivi*, performed before the duke on 25 June at Don Antonio de' Medici's *casino* near S. Marco—to judge by prior performances in 1602, this would have had music in its *intermedi*; see Solerti, *Musica, ballo e drammatica alla corte medicea*, 28–29 (1602), 31–32 (1603).

94. Carter, *Jacopo Peri*, 1: 341; Kirkendale, *Court Musicians*, 222.

clearly to the cardinal in a letter of 21 January (the day after Peri's letter): that Peri cannot get permission to leave the court because the grand duke and grand duchess want him to continue teaching the princesses, and the archduchess hears him sing every evening, given that she takes great delight in music (*poiché vogliano che seguiti d'insegnare alle Principesse, et l'Arciduchessa ancora ogni sera lo sente, et ne piglia molto gusto, poiché si diletta assai della musica*).[95] Geronimo Lenzoni also provided further information that same day:

> On receiving the letter from Your Most Illustrious and Most Reverend Lordship, I immediately found Signor Jacopo Peri, and notwithstanding a thousand business affairs which he had, he resolved to come and serve you. But he wanted me to ask permission from Madama [Grand Duchess Christine], as I did, and Her Highness was happy with the idea but wanted to have a word with His Highness the Grand Duke. But since the Lord Duke of Nevers is visiting, for whom they want to provide some kind of *festa*, and another one this Carnival for the Lady Archduchess, who also wants to hear him [Peri] sing every evening, in addition to his teaching the Lady Princesses and the Lady Archduchess—these are the reasons why His [Her?] Highness cannot give him permission. Hearing this caused me great displeasure, even if I realize that they could not do anything else given the great contentment taken in him by the Archduchess, whom it would not be right to displease. But indeed, Madama wanted me to know in particular that she had done her duty appropriately.[96]

95. Pandolfo Stufa (Florence) to Ferdinando Gonzaga, 21 January 1608/9, in Mantua, Archivio di Stato, Autografi 10, fol. 339.

96. Geronimo Lenzoni to Ferdinando Gonzaga, 21 January 1608/9, in Mantua, Archivio di Stato, Archivio Gonzaga 1126, fol. 110: *In ricevendo la [lettera] di Vostra Signoria Illustrissima e Reverendissima subito trovai il Signor Jacopo Peri, e non ostante mille negotii che haveva si risolse venire per servirla, ma volse ch'io domandasse licentia a Madama, come feci, e Sua Altezza se ne contentava, ma volse passarne parola con Sua Altezza del Gran Duca. Ma essendo sopragiunto la venuta del Signor Duca di Nivers, al quale vogliono fare non so che festa et altra questo Carnevale per la Signora Arciduchessa, qual ancora ogni sera lo vuol sentire cantare, oltre che insegnia alle Signore Principesse, et alla Signora Arciduchessa, han causato che Sua Altezza non li possa dar licentia, il che è stato sentito da me con gran disgusto, se ben conosco che non potevano far altrimenti per il gran contento che ne piglia l'Arciduchessa, la qual non conviene disgustare. Anzi Madama ha volsuto ch'io sappia particularmente che lei haveva fatto l'ofitio a modo.* The writer was probably Girolamo di Francesco Lenzoni, son of a prominent Florentine senator and diplomat, and brother of the poet Camillo Lenzoni.

The chain of communication here is revealing, if also typical: not only is Cardinal Ferdinando using brokers to gain favors, but so too is Peri. He asks Lenzoni to approach Grand Duchess Christine for permission to go to Mantua—which would clear him from any suspicion of acting out of self-interest, and insulate him from any negative response—and the grand duchess appears to agree but also prevaricates by wanting to have a word with the grand duke, or so she says: in fact, Grand Duke Ferdinando was ill (he died in February) and hardly likely to have been bothered with the matter. But the denial of Peri's request, with an appropriate explanation, comes from on high, which protects the reputations of the grand duchess and of Lenzoni, and of course Peri's as well, even if the outcome may have been what he had wanted all along. As for Maria Magdalena, we have not hitherto suspected her of having such prominent musical interests so early during her time in Florence, but perhaps her desire to hear Peri every evening was akin to Eleonora de' Medici's in Mantua in 1584, for Maria Magdalena, too, was now pregnant.

While such chamber performances may have formed a significant part of Peri's activity at court, we know more, for reasons already explained, about his contributions to court entertainments in the first two decades of the new century. *Dafne* was repeated for the visit of Duke Ranuccio Farnese of Parma in October 1604—before the libretto was revised and set anew by Marco da Gagliano for performance in Mantua in early 1608—and in February 1605 Peri provided music for a tournament in Pisa, to a text by Michelangelo Buonarroti *il giovane*, that was a customary part of Carnival celebrations (see Letters 4 and 5).[97] He also composed music for Buonarroti's play *Il giudizio di Paride*, and performed in its *intermedi*, staged during the 1608 wedding festivities for Cosimo de' Medici and Maria Magdalena: the song "Se tu parti da me, Fillide amata" in *Le varie musiche* had originally been written for the text "Poiché la notte con l'oscure piume" at the end of Act III of the play. And one of the reasons for the court's denying Ferdinando Gonzaga's request to have Peri come to Mantua in early 1609 was a forthcoming entertainment

97. Kirkendale, *Court Musicians*, 213, confuses this tournament with the one done in February 1605/6, devised by Ferdinando Gonzaga on the theme of Alexander the Great and Darius (Solerti, *Musica, ballo e drammatica alla corte medicea*, 37–38). The latter is the entertainment described in Gargiolli, "Feste fatte in Pisa l'anno 1605" (i.e., *stile fiorentino*). However, Kirkendale repeats Solerti's mistake (in *Musica, ballo e drammatica alla corte medicea*, 35 n. 2) of assuming that Gargiolli was referring to 1604/5.

for Carlo I Gonzaga, Duc de Nevers et Rethel, who arrived in Florence with his wife Catherine de Mayenne on 22 January (the day after Lenzoni's letter, given above) and who on 25 January saw a repeat performance at the behest of the grand duchess of the *veglia* that had been performed during the festivities for the wedding of Prince Cosimo de' Medici and Maria Magdalena the previous October, Francesco Cini's *Notte d'Amore* (but we do not know if Peri wrote any music for it).[98]

By the second decade of the century, Peri's main role in court theatricals involved the provision of music for one Carnival entertainment per year, usually in collaboration with one or more colleagues (often in later years, Marco da Gagliano, the *maestro di cappella*). He continued this compositional activity through his sixties—by which time he was by far the oldest court musician still in active service, but one with a full-time job outside the court—by way of contributions to *sacre rappresentazioni* chiefly for the Compagnia dell'Arcangelo Raffaello. He was also still writing the occasional song on request.[99] His last activity as a composer at court seems to have been writing the music for the role of Clori/Flora in Marco da Gagliano's opera *Flora*, performed for the wedding of Margherita de' Medici and Prince Odoardo Farnese in October 1628 (Peri was sixty-seven). It is perhaps significant that for Jacopo Cicognini's *Il trionfo di David*, performed in the Compagnia dell'Arcangelo Raffaello on 1 March 1629, Peri's son, Alfonso, sang music by Angelo Conti and not, as was customary, by his father.[100] Peri's health may have been deteriorating even before his collapse in May 1630 (see Chapter 4).

As a composer, Peri had his musical preferences. The negotiations over the opera *Le nozze di Peleo e Tetide* in 1607 are revealing: it was being considered by Ferdinando Gonzaga for the festivities in Mantua to celebrate the wedding of Prince Francesco Gonzaga and Margherita of Savoy, though it was dropped (for correspondence from Peri on the opera, see Letters 7 and 8). The librettist, Francesco Cini, was a minor Florentine poet who had some connection with Jacopo Corsi—he is also mentioned in Peri's preface to *Euridice*—and he pushed his play hard, offering Peri's services as a singer and composer

98. Solerti, *Musica, ballo e drammatica alla corte medicea*, 57.

99. See the letters from Don Pietro de' Medici (Livorno) to Michelangelo Buonarroti *il giovane*, 9 and 12 March 1625/26, concerning Peri's sending a setting of Buonarroti's poetry, in Carter, *Jacopo Peri*, 1: 343–44. Cole, *Music, Spectacle, and Cultural Brokerage in Early Modern Italy*, 2: 608, dates this as 1625.

100. Kirkendale, *Court Musicians*, 385.

as part of the package.[101] Peri would compose the parts done in recitative (*le parti che vanno recitate*) plus the prologue and some arietta among those for the nymphs or cupids (*qualche arietta di quelle delle Ninfe, o de' Cupidini*), although he was willing to consider doing all of them. This would leave to someone else only the music for the end-of-act choruses, and that for the gods who appeared at the end both singing solo and in chorus (*le musiche piene dei cori, cioè intermedii, e quelle delle deità che compariscono da ultimo, sì di quelli che cantano soli, come di quelli che cantano in coro*).[102] Cini argued that it would be a good strategy to assign the remaining music to Monteverdi or to some other Mantuan musician because they were good (*perché son valenti huomini*), because it would save trouble and expense (*briga e spesa*)—perhaps a suggestion that Peri expected some payment according to the amount of music he wrote—and because it would allow Mantuan composers to shine, thereby avoiding jealousy (*per non si tirare addosso l'invidia*). However, these specifications may also have reflected what Peri was most able to do as a composer.

Thus in court entertainments during and after the reign of Grand Duke Cosimo II, Peri's musical brief was essentially to provide his trademark recitative and perhaps some arias for himself or his musical dependents to sing, while other composers would write the choruses, the dance music, and so forth. This division of labor according to (musical) specialism was not uncommon—just as it was not unknown to have entertainments in which the separate singers each composed the parts for themselves or their pupils—but Florence seems to have established it as some kind of norm.[103] There is no doubt some merit in the traditional reading of this situation as reflecting rivalry and self-promotion between the court musicians, who, we have seen,

101. Cini had one of Corsi's harpsichords on the latter's death; see Pegazzano, *Committenza e collezionismo nel Cinquecento*, 58.

102. See Cini's letter to Ferdinando Gonzaga, 26 October 1607 (Mantua, Archivio di Stato, Autografi 10, fol. 291), given in Davari, "Notizie biografiche del distinto maestro di musica Claudio Monteverdi," 177–79.

103. Monteverdi suggested something similar for Mantua—that singers there compose their own parts—for an entertainment he had no interest in composing; see his letter to Alessandro Striggio, 9 December 1616, in *Lettere*, ed. Lax, 48–50 (Monteverdi, *The Letters*, trans. Stevens, 108–11). Monteverdi cites the precedent of *L'amor pudico* (libretto by Jacopo Cicognini), sponsored by Cardinal Montalto in Rome in 1614; compare Hill, *Roman Monody, Cantata, and Opera from the Circles around Cardinal Montalto*, 1: 279–97.

were an argumentative group: this is certainly how scholars have tended to view Caccini's insistence that "his" singers should sing his own music, not Peri's, in the performance of *Euridice* in 1600. But it also made logistical sense with respect to the way in which younger singers would learn their music, usually aurally under the guidance of their teacher. And in general there was no harm in having a specialist industry—if that is how one can view music making in Florence—differentiate and exploit the various skills of its workers.

Some examples will make the procedure clear. The 1610–11 Carnival season was the first to be celebrated during Grand Duke Cosimo II's reign (the court had been in mourning the previous year for the death of Ferdinando I), and according to Cosimo Baroncelli, it was to be filled with jousts, *sbarre*, comedies, a *balletto* (by Ottavio Rinuccini), a pastoral (by Michelangelo Buonarroti *il giovane*), and a revival of Rinuccini's *Dafne* (presumably as set by Marco da Gagliano in 1608).[104] In Rinuccini's *balletto*, done at court on the last Monday of Carnival (14 February), Peri sang the role of Nettuno (Neptune) in his customary manner and to great applause (*secondo il solito suo, con grande applauso del teatro*). He also had the task of setting to music in his "most noble" recitative style the remainder of the text, save some *ottava rima* stanzas and a madrigal (*ebbe ancora il carico di comporre musicalmente nel suo nobilissimo stile recitativo tutto il restante, toltone alcune ottave, ed un madrigale*). Those four stanzas in *ottava rima* were set to music by the same women who sang them (*composte musicalmente dall'istesse donne che le cantarono*)— Vittoria Archilei, Settimia Caccini, and Francesca Caccini (who sang two)— while the *madrigale* was composed for eight voices by Marco da Gagliano, and there was almost certainly instrumental dance music by Lorenzo Allegri.[105] The role of Nettuno was not large, given that the character delivers only the prologue (five four-line stanzas). Peri, however, set one *ottava rima*

104. Cosimo Baroncelli to Duke Vincenzo Gonzaga, 25 January 1610/11 (Mantua, Archivio di Stato, Autografi 10, fol. 254), given in Solerti, *Musica, ballo e drammatica alla corte medicea*, 60 n. 1.

105. See the account by Jacopo Cicognini (15 February 1611 [modern style]) given in Solerti, *Gli albori del melodramma*, 2: 283–94 (which dates it 15 February 1612/13), and compare Tinghi's description in Solerti, *Musica, ballo e drammatica alla corte medicea*, 61–62 (which also has Nettuno appear in the second part, but this is confused with Proteo). Kirkendale, *Court Musicians*, 219–21, clarifies the mix-up over Rinuccini's *Mascherata di ninfe di Senna* (1613) and identifies the surviving music.

stanza: his aria for Venere, "Torna, deh torna, pargoletto mio" (an *ottava rima* set strophically as two four-line stanzas, in a lyrical triple time), was included in Piero Benedetti's *Musiche* (Florence: Heirs of C. Marescotti, 1611).

Likewise, the two *balletti a cavallo* (equestrian ballets in the Piazza S. Croce) to which Peri contributed music in 1616, *Guerra d'Amore* (11 February) and *Guerra di bellezza* (16 October), also involved Paolo Grazi (and for *Guerra d'Amore*, Giovanni Battista Signorini), presumably to satisfy the need for one or more of the Franciosini to provide the necessary outdoor music for the wind band. This sense of Peri's musical specialization is also clear in what little survives of his other entertainment music from this decade (see Appendix C): the recitative-style "Queste lacrime mie, questi sospiri" (although the text is in seven six-line stanzas) for the tournament and *mascherata*, done at court in February 1613, and "Iten'omai, voi che felici ardete," an aria for Amore (although the surviving music is for two voices) at the end of the *balletto* done a year later. Yet again one is tempted to pursue a comparison with the Florentine cloth industries, with their system of "putting out" materials to pieceworkers, each skilled at only one or two of the various stages of the production process. The obvious difficulty that would arise was one of higher-level coordination, as those in charge of court entertainments—such as Giovanni de' Bardi for the 1608 wedding festivities, or Ferdinando Saracinelli for the Carnival 1624/25 production of *La regina Sant'Orsola*, as we will see—learned to their cost. This means, however, that it was quite unusual in Florence to have an entertainment in which all the music was composed by a single hand, as would tend to be the case in an opera (*Flora* notwithstanding). In other words, the types of entertainments that came to be preferred by the Medici court dictated certain modes of production that also worked recursively to regulate that preference. Not for nothing does Florentine court spectacle have a strongly formulaic quality, ringing the changes on a few basic structures, patterns, and themes, and changing only slowly over time. One corollary is that this manner, and various others, of organizing what might be called the labor market in music could account for the rather haphazard spread of single-composer operas through the north Italian courts and to Rome in the first third of the seventeenth century. But this remains just an intriguing and as yet untested hypothesis.

The centrifugal nature of the court musical establishment, with only weak line-management, was both an advantage and a disadvantage from the point of view of anyone trying to work the system. On the plus side, it allowed

those musicians who were not part of a fixed ensemble to establish and oc-
cupy their own niches with little interference, so long as the broader needs of
the court were met. Yet a market based on the aggressive pursuit of self-
interest also prompted competition both between individuals and between
camps created by strategic alliances. Again, the court may not have minded
such competition—indeed, it may have encouraged it—provided the end
result served its purpose. But Peri's fortunes at court clearly moved in inverse
proportion to those of Giulio Caccini, also a virtuoso tenor but ten years
older (he was born in 1551 and died in 1618): *Dafne* and *Euridice* were conceived during Caccini's absence from court service in 1593–1600; *Dafne* was
revived for a performance before the Duke of Parma on 26 October 1604,
after Caccini and his family had left for a nine-month tour to Paris (on 30
September); and Caccini's influence declined after the 1608 wedding festivities and into the next decade (when he was in his sixties and falling ill). That
decline was also due to the rising stature of Peri's apparent ally, Marco da
Gagliano, who was appointed *maestro di cappella* in late 1608 (after the death
of Luca Bati), following some quite bitter infighting involving Santi Orlandi,
who was supported by the Caccini camp, it seems. The 1610s saw Peri in the
ascendant once more, but in the early to mid-1620s vicious squabbling re-
emerged, this time involving Caccini's daughter, Francesca, to the point that
Ferdinando Saracinelli needed to adjudicate what he must have considered
an absurd dispute between Marco da Gagliano, Peri, Francesca Caccini, and
the playwright Andrea Salvadori over who would compose what music to be
sung by which singer for a new version of the *sacra rappresentazione, La regina
Sant'Orsola*, to be performed in the 1624–25 Carnival season.[106] Francesca
Caccini continued her battle with Salvadori through the planning stages for
the festivities to celebrate the wedding of Margherita de' Medici and Odoardo Farnese (eventually held in 1628).[107] All was not well among the court
musicians in the 1620s, if it had ever been, and Peri suffered at least some of
the consequences, if we are to believe the sonnet by Francesco Ruspoli and
other poetry of the time. But by this decade, as we now know, Peri enjoyed

106. Harness, *Echoes of Women's Voices*, 85–88; Cusick, *Francesca Caccini at the Medici
Court*, 87–88. The controversy also indirectly involved Muzio Effrem, who had composed
music for the first version of *La regina Sant'Orsola* intended for performance in 1621 but was
no longer in Florence.

107. Carter, *Jacopo Peri*, 1: 97–99.

economic autonomy outside the court, and he was doing much better on his own than many of the others were.

And he had more social status. His styling as a *nobil fiorentino* (the term appears on the title page of *Euridice*) took this self-positioning in a particular direction, suggesting that he saw himself somehow standing above his musician colleagues. There is no sign that the court viewed him differently from them in terms of the operation of the musical establishment, even if his status brought him other forms of preferment. But the image he presented to the broader public also squared with how he viewed himself in private. When he joined the entourage of the newly elevated Cardinal Carlo de' Medici in Rome in May–June 1616, he made a *ricordo* in his ledger—one of the few not concerning family events—describing matters rather proudly and in some detail (see Figure 3.1): all his expenses were paid (but he carefully recorded his outlay of *fl*.60 for the clothing he bought for the trip to honor himself and the cardinal); he traveled in a *lettiga* accompanied by a servant on horseback; in Rome he was the guest of the Florentine Resident; he had no duties at all other than to be part of the cardinal's retinue; and the cardinal promised to take his son, Antonio, into his service and first to pay an allowance for him to enter the Collegio dei Nobili in Bologna.[108] Peri was probably exaggerating as regards his duties in Rome: Cardinal Carlo de' Medici took with him three musicians (in addition to a trumpeter)—Peri, Francesca Caccini, and (her husband) Giovanni Battista Signorini—so clearly there were at least some musical expectations involved. But this makes the different story that Peri told for the record all the more significant.

108. Ledger A, fol. 121: *Ricordo il dì 5 di maggio 1616 mi partii di Firenze per ordine del Serenissimo Gran Duca per andare a Roma a servire l'Illustrissimo Signor Cardinale de' Medici, quale era partito 3 settimane inanzi incirca a pigliare il cappello. Andai a tutte loro spese in lettiga con uno servitore a cavallo; e lassù in Roma fui alloggiato dal Illustre Signor Ambasciatore, molto ben trattato et onorato. Spesi del mio in vestirmi circa sc.60 per honorare la persona mia e di chi servivo, se bene non ebbi carico di sorte alcuna, ma solo Sua Signoria Illustrissima ebbe gusto ch'io fussi numerato fra gli altri suoi servitori. Me ne tornai, et arrivai in Firenze il dì 9 giugno seguente pure in lettiga. E Sua Signoria Illustrissima per sua grazia mi promesse accettare Antonio mio figliuolo per suo servitore; e il primo di novembre 1616 seguente lo mandai ancora lui a Bologna perché 2 mesi inanzi per supplica segnata Sua Signoria Illustrissima gli assegnò sc.7 il mese <acciò che> per 2 anni acciò che io potessi mantenerlo in Bologna in compagnia de l'altro fratello, et così si fece, et come ho detto di sopra, arrivò in Bologna il dì 31 d'ottobre 1616.* For more on this trip to Rome (and other sources documenting it), see Carter, *Jacopo Peri*, 1: 80.

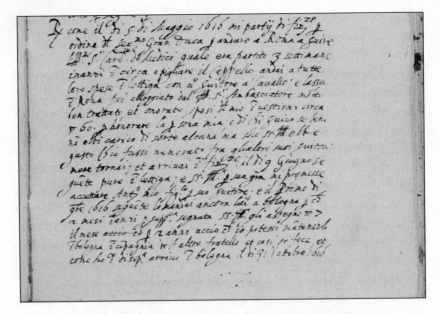

FIGURE 3.1. Jacopo Peri's *ricordo* of his trip to Rome, May–June 1616.
Source: Florence, Archivio di Stato, Libri di Commercio 3911 (Ledger A), fol. 121
(lower half). (With permission of the Ministero per i Beni e le Attività Culturali;
further reproduction or duplication by whatever means is forbidden.)

Peri left Florence for Rome on 5 May, just under a month after the others (on 9 April). The delay was caused by his trip to Bologna for a staging of
his *Euridice* (on 27 April) at the request of Cardinal Luigi Capponi, the
papal legate there: this was one of a series of entertainments (also including
a joust, a *palio*, and a play by Jacopo Cicognini) to honor Cardinals
Giovanni Battista Leni, Bonifacio Bevilacqua, and Domenico Rivarola.[109]
Also present was the Mantuan tenor Francesco Campagnolo, who was
there to sing in *Euridice* and to accompany both Peri and the librettist, Ottavio Rinuccini, onward to Mantua at the request of Duke Ferdinando
Gonzaga, although Peri had to refuse because of his forthcoming trip to

109. Ottavio Rinuccini noted the joust and the *palio* in his letter to Duke Ferdinando
Gonzaga of 20 April 1616; Mantua, Archivio di Stato, Archivio Gonzaga 1171, fol. 436. He also
said that *Euridice* was to be done *in privato*. For the Cicognini *commedia*, see Kirkendale,
Court Musicians, 208.

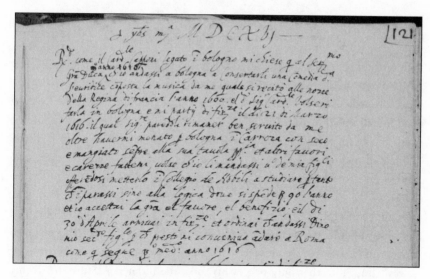

FIGURE 3.2. Jacopo Peri's *ricordo* of his trip to Bologna, April 1616. *Source:* Florence, Archivio di Stato, Libri di Commercio 3911 (Ledger A), fol. 121 (upper half). (With permission of the Ministero per i Beni e le Attività Culturali; further reproduction or duplication by whatever means is forbidden.)

Rome (Letter 19).[110] For the Bologna visit, too, Peri provided a detailed *ricordo* in his ledger (see Figure 3.2):

Cardinal Capponi, Legate in Bologna, asked the Most Serene Grand Duke in this year 1616 for me to go to Bologna to perform for him a play called *Euridice*, the music composed by me, which was staged at the wedding of the Queen of France in the year 1600. The aforesaid Lord Cardinal wanted to redo it in Bologna, and I left Florence on 21 March 1616. This lord, it seeming to him that he was well served by me—in addition to taking me with him by carriage to Bologna, and having me always eat at his very own table, and other favors and acts of endearment done for me—wanted me to send one of my sons up there, offering to put him in the Collegio dei Nobili to study up to the level of logic, where the fee is *fl.*90 a year. I accepted the grace and favor, and the benefit, and on 30 April I arrived

---

110. Campagnolo (normally styled *signore*) was a colleague of Francesco Rasi. He later sang Peri's *Canzone delle lodi d'Austria* in Florence in October 1624; see Appendix C.

[back] in Florence, and I ordered that Dino, my second son, should be sent, because I was very soon required to go to Rome . . . [111]

He did not, of course, record the disagreement he had with Rinuccini over the Bologna performance, which Peri wanted to cancel because he felt that it had too little rehearsal and weak singers.[112] But clearly he liked the carriage and fine dining. He also, and typically, used both the Bologna and the Rome trips to obtain favors for his sons: Cardinal Capponi promised to facilitate Dino's admission to the Collegio dei Nobili in Bologna, where Antonio also ended up with the support of Cardinal Carlo de' Medici in preparation for entering the cardinal's service (which he never did). Later (1630), Peri took advantage of other connections with high-placed prelates when he obtained for his son Francesco two benefices in Piacenza by way of Cardinal Francesco Barberini (Letter 33). He must have felt that he was moving in high circles. It is revealing, too, that only one of his sons, the ill-fated Alfonso, made any attempt to follow in his father's musical footsteps—the far more gifted Dino fared better as professor of mathematics at the University of Pisa (with an annual salary of *fl*.250).

This trading of service, broadly defined, for favor was typical of courtly societies, as was a reluctance, at least among certain social groups, to regard one's profession merely in professional terms. It also suggests that Peri viewed his musical activities, and the reputation accrued thereby, as a means to an-

111. Ledger A, fol. 121: *Ricordo come il Cardinale Capponi, legato in Bologna, mi chiese qui al Serenissimo Gran Duca >questo anno 1616< ch'io andassi a Bologna a consertarli una comedia detta* L'Euridice, *composta la musica da me, quale si recitò alle nozze della Regina di Francia l'anno 1600. E 'l detto Signor Cardinale volse rifarla in Bologna, e mi partii di Firenze il dì 21 di marzo 1616. Il qual signore, parendoli rimaner ben servito da me, oltre havermi menato per Bologna in carroza con seco e mangiato sempre alla sua tavola propria et altri favori e carezze fattemi, volse ch'io li mandassi uno de' mia figliuoli, offerendosi metterlo in Collegio de' Nobili a studiare per tanto ch' imparassi sino alla logica, dove si spende fi.90 l'anno. Et io accettai la grazia e 'l favore, e 'l benefizio. E il dì 30 d'aprile arrivai in Firenze, et ordinai ch'andassi Dino, mio secondo figliuolo, perché presto mi conveniva andare a Roma . . .* Cardinal Capponi had a villa in Montughi, which may explain how he and Peri traveled to Bologna together.

112. For the argument with Rinuccini, see Andrea Barbazzi's letter to Duke Ferdinando Gonzaga, 27 April 1616, in Mantua, Archivio di Stato, Archivio Gonzaga 1171, fol. 442; also given in Davari, "Notizie biografiche del distinto maestro di musica Claudio Monteverdi," 111 n. 1 (although Davari misquotes the beginning of his extract, which should properly read . . . *Questa sera si reciterà l'Euridice con l'intervento pur delli medesmi* [i.e., the cardinals and other guests], *maneggiata però dal Zazzarino et Signor Ottavio Renuzzini . . .*

other end: social and economic advancement for himself and his family. In comparison with other court musicians' salaries, his was not high, and it never increased, meaning that over time it deteriorated relative to those of his colleagues; in his last decades, we have seen, it also represented only about a sixth of his total documented annual income. Yet the fact that Enea Vaini, in his 1603 memorandum on the court musicians, did not report any particular financial or other need on Peri's part (as he did for a number of court musicians) suggests that Peri was not openly dissatisfied with his musical lot. Certainly he collected his court salary in person on a regular basis, and in cash.[113] But he may have felt that the prestige and benefits of court service—including official government appointments in Florence and other preferment—were no less important as rewards.

There is another possible factor in the equation, however. If Peri's periodic health issues were as debilitating as he claimed in 1600, and as Vaini suggested in 1603, then they did not augur well for a musician's career, especially for someone entering his forties, when the singing voice might start to decline anyway. It is striking that Peri began to take an active interest in the wool industry around this time, perhaps as some manner of security against future incapacity. One also wonders—although the ledgers do not tell us—how much additional money Peri received as one-time gifts for specific court entertainments or other services. On 23 January 1599 he invested *fl.*200 in Domenico di Lorenzo Peri's wool shop, two days after *Dafne* was performed at court; in November 1600 to June 1601, just after *Euridice*, he had liquid capital, some from prior funds, to contribute to the wool company headed by Giulio Della Rena and Vincenzo Fiorini (the Corsi bank was another investor); and on 12 March 1605, Peri invested *fl.*150 in Francesco Michelozzi & Partners, *lanaioli*, just after he had provided music for the tournament in Pisa. These coincidences are suggestive, to say the least, even if any connection remains pure speculation.

To judge by what we now know about Peri's other lives in Florence, his strategies insofar as music was concerned were relatively successful: although the salaries he gained from his musical positions were not sufficient, we have seen, to generate the quite large capital sums that he invested in property, commerce, and various financial instruments, those positions, and what he

---

113. The available salary and similar records for this period are listed in Kirkendale, *Court Musicians*, 53–57. There is nothing unusual in Peri's appearance therein.

did within them, seem to have given him some kind of access to those sums, and to ways in which they might be used. The comparison with his chief rival, Giulio Caccini, is also instructive. Although Tuscan by family, Caccini was never a complete insider in Florence; we have seen that he was commonly called "Giulio Romano" and often signed his letters "Giulio Caccini da Roma." He was also involved in frequent disputes and witting or unwitting scandals during his career, starting with his unpleasant involvement in the unhappy affair of Bernardo Antinori and Eleonora Alvarez de Toledo (wife of Pietro de' Medici) in 1575–76, and ending in 1615 with his imprisonment, converted to house arrest, for a dispute with Ottavio Archilei (son of Antonio and Vittoria).[114] He, too, engaged in commercial activity outside music as his voice declined: he was involved in the exchange market in the first two decades of the seventeenth century, and in addition he had a reputation as a cultivator of exotic plants, although there is hardly any evidence to suggest that the latter was a business activity of any importance.[115] He also left a decent inheritance on his death.[116] But neither in his other earnings nor in his estate did he rise to the level of Peri; nor did he gain civic appointments in the same way—rather, his nonmusical income was largely supplemented, it seems, by way of the honorary pension *su la Zecca* from the grand duke at least from mid-1607 to mid-1612. There are also signs that Caccini was facing financial difficulties in the second decade of the century: on 6 March 1610, his daughter Francesca wrote to Virginio Orsini, Duke of Bracciano, for financial help for her father after that pension from the Mint was dropped following the death of Grand Duke Ferdinando I (it was temporarily reinstated) and because of difficulties over retrieving Settimia Caccini's dowry, also given that his business in the exchange market was going badly (*i suoi negozi di mercato sono mancati assai*). Likewise, his house arrest in 1615 prevented him from engaging in that market, even though it supported his living costs and he paid a goodly sum to act therein (*la carcere in casa m'impedisce*

---

114. Kirkendale, *Court Musicians*, 122 (Antinori), 158 (Archilei). Around 1614, and for as yet unknown reasons, Caccini worked quite hard to establish evidence of his father's roots in Montopoli, of his own baptism at S. Giovanni dei Fiorentini in Rome, and therefore of his Florentine credentials (while also, it seems, seeking to resolve issues raised by his father's having called himself "Cacini"); see Giazotto, *Le due patrie di Giulio Caccini*, 11–13.

115. For Caccini's skills as a gardener (for which he was already known in the late 1580s), see Kirkendale, *Court Musicians*, 128, 158–59.

116. Kirkendale, *Court Musicians*, 164–66.

*il traffico de' miei negozii di mercato nuovo, i quali sono il supplimento del no-
stro vitto, e per quali io pago per poter esercitare buona somma di denari).*[117]

Caccini appears to have been much more reliant than Peri on individual
patrons in Florence to protect and advance his position—witness his long-
standing relations with Piero Strozzi that dated back at least to 1579—which
also made him vulnerable to negative actions on their part (so he discovered
in the 1590s). The same is true of his daughter, Francesca, who was heavily
dependent on the poet Michelangelo Buonarroti *il giovane*, on the one hand,
and on Grand Duchess Christine, on the other.[118] Further, Caccini seems to
have resented Peri as his younger rival; although Caccini was favored by
Giovanni de' Bardi in the 1580s, he lost ground in the 1590s, we have seen,
and in effect clawed his way back into court service in 1600. This no doubt
explains the evident antagonism between the two singer–composers that
continued through the second decade of the century: in April 1611, Caccini
was still reporting somewhat conspiratorially to Piero Strozzi on Peri's behavior during the recent Holy Week services.[119]

While Caccini's interference in the performance of *Euridice* in 1600—by
insisting that "his" singers should sing his own music and not Peri's—may
have been reasonable at the time, his preempting of the publication of Peri's
score was more aggressive. He slighted Peri in his own first collection of
songs, *Le nuove musiche* (Florence: Giorgio Marescotti, 1601 [= 1602]), both
by omission in his preface (which harks back to the glory days of the 1580s)
and, it might seem, by including an extract from his music for *Il rapimento di*

117. Kirkendale, *Court Musicians*, 158, 312, 340–41. It is not clear what Caccini meant by his
paying to participate in the market (perhaps it was a fee to operate as a broker). On 23 July
1616, the Mint gave him *fl.*140 as part of a loan, it seems (Caccini wrote an IOU for *du.*228),
and he repaid *fl.*140 on 8 June 1617; ASF, Ufficiali della Moneta poi Maestri di Zecca 231, fol.
336. This appears to have been separate from his earlier pension.

118. Cusick, *Francesca Caccini at the Medici Court.*

119. Caccini's letter of 6 April 1611 to Strozzi (Florence, Biblioteca Riccardiana, Ricc.
4009a), reporting on events the previous week (Holy Week), is given in Bacherini Bartoli,
"Giulio Caccini," 68–69 (doc. 14). It begins by claiming that Peri had come to regret what he
proposed to do and say (*Il signor Zazzerino si pentì di quanto aveva proposto di fare e dire*);
further in the letter, he writes that Peri, "our boss," did his solos as usual, but since Caccini
can only say more in person, he will hold off anything worthy of consideration for another
year (*Il Zazzerino, nostro maggiore, fece i suoi soli al solito; ma poiché non mi resterebbe che dire a
bocca, mi riserbo allora qualche cosa degna di considerazione per un altr'anno*). Both remarks are
obscure, and the reference to "solos" may or may not be to music.

Cefalo (the main entertainment of the 1600 wedding), which had been sung by Peri with different embellishments in his own manner.[120] Caccini did so again in his *Nuove musiche e nuova maniera di scriverle* (Florence: Zanobi Pignoni, 1614), again in the preface (where he claims to have set *Dafne* to music for performance at Corsi's palace, which would seem not to be true), and then in the book itself.[121] Here he includes his own settings of three texts already associated with Peri in print: "Tutto 'l dì piango, e poi la notte quando," followed immediately by "Torna, deh torna, pargoletto mio" (one of the texts set by Peri for the *balletto* done at court in February 1611 and published in Piero Benedetti's *Musiche* that same year), and, later in the collection, "Al fonte, al prato" (a tuneful strophic aria). These choices seem deliberate, and also significant, as they cover all the musical styles, save recitative, required of a composer of solo songs for the chamber and the stage in early seventeenth-century Florence.

Caccini died in early December 1618, the year before Zanobi Pignoni reissued Peri's *Le varie musiche*, and by the 1620s, Peri, in his sixties, could reasonably claim to be the most senior of the court musicians, due some deference (although he did not always get it) and more able to pick and choose his

120. Kirkendale, *Court Musicians*, 144, sees a dig even in the title of the publication, given that in the preface to *Euridice*, Peri refers to the opera as *le nuove musiche, fatte da me*. Caccini's *Le nuove musiche* includes the final chorus of *Il rapimento di Cefalo*, with separate stanzas as sung by Melchiorre Palantrotti (in the manner printed), Peri as sung with other ornaments according to his style (*con altri passaggi secondo il suo stile*), and Francesco Rasi part with the ornaments printed and part according to his taste (*parte con i propri passaggi* [i.e., as printed], *e parte à suo gusto*); see Carter, "Rediscovering *Il rapimento di Cefalo*." Of course, one might choose to read this not as an insult but, rather, as an acknowledgment. Likewise, the contrast between Caccini's styling of Peri as an excellent musician salaried by their highnesses of Florence (*Musico Eccellente stipendiato da queste Altezze Sereniss.*) and of the "famous" Rasi, nobleman from Arezzo and a very favored servant to the Duke of Mantua (*il famoso Francesco Rasi Nobile Aretino, molto grato Servitore all'Alt. Ser. di Mantova*) may be a matter of courtesy, although it keeps Peri in his place.

121. In the preface, Caccini refers to "the music which I did" for *Dafne*, performed in the house of Jacopo Corsi (*la musica che io feci nella favola della Dafne del Sig. Ottavio Rinuccini, rappresentata in casa del Sig. Jacopo Corsi*). Elsewhere, he notes a possible performance of *Dafne* (to whose music remains unclear) during his trip to Paris in 1604–5; see Kirkendale, *Court Musicians*, 150. De Caro, "*Euridice*," 185–91, is inclined to believe Caccini on the grounds that the number of actual and projected performances of *Dafne* would leave room for a setting by him (or as one might also suggest, for him to have included some of his music in one or more of them). The matter remains unresolved.

assignments. He could also look back with some pride over his career and what it had brought him and his family, and he may also have had a sense of having left at least some kind of musical legacy. Peri may not have been the most active of court musicians, nor the most cooperative if he felt (as Cavalieri put it in November 1600) that "serving much or little was all the same." But he gained significant favors from the grand-ducal family for what he managed to achieve.

Peri as Singing Teacher

Peri's claim that he taught singing to the Medici princesses from the time of Grand Duchess Johanna of Austria (Letter 23) can only refer to Eleonora de' Medici in the first instance, although he continued with Virginia, Anna, and Maria when they reached an appropriate age (probably around ten). It is not clear whether his *insegnare cantare* is to be taken literally or stretched to mean anything to do with teaching music: singing, playing lute and keyboard, reading musical notation, and basic music theory—in short, whatever a princess might need in musical skills and understanding to get by in courtly company.

On 9 February 1576/77—so perhaps just before Peri took on the job—a number of books were bought by the court from the Giunti bookshop in Florence for the use of *la Principessa* (Eleonora), including an anthology of three- and four-voice *villanelle alla napolitana* (the *Corona delle napolitane* printed in Venice by Girolamo Scotto in 1570), Philippe de Monte's First and Third books of four-voice madrigals, and a book of four-voice motets by Adriano Willaert.[122] This purchase suggests some degree of would-be musical competence, and represents a reasonably safe, relatively conservative repertory: the villanellas were simple strophic settings in a popular vein; Monte's two madrigal books contain more serious poetry, including a great deal of Petrarch; and the motets (with Latin texts) served devotional purposes. This music could have been sung in a vocal ensemble (like all music of this period,

---

122. ASF, Depositeria Generale 643; Carter, "Music-Selling in Late Sixteenth-Century Florence," 493 n. 17. Monte's *Il primo libro de madregali a quatro voci* was first published in 1562 (Venice: Antonio Gardano); his *Il terzo libro de madrigali a quattro voci* survives only in a second or subsequent edition from 1585 (Venice: heirs of Girolamo Scotto). Willaert's First and Second books of four-voice motets date back to 1539 (Venice: Girolamo Scotto), although there were subsequent editions.

it was published in partbooks) or arranged for solo voice and lute or key-board. Such arrangements were by no means unusual: Vincenzo Galilei published a treatise on how to produce them—his *Fronimo: dialogo . . . nel quale si contengono le vere, et necessarie regole del intavolare la musica nel liuto* (Venice: Girolamo Scotto, 1568), the second edition of which (1584) was dedi-cated to Jacopo Corsi. A similar performance practice is also suggested by Peri's payment, on 26 February 1587, to have two lutes sent to him from Padua (for £37, plus carriage and import duties of £16) which he gave to the princesses, his patrons (*per havermi fatto venire dua liuti per me da Padova che tanto spese che detti liuti li donai alle Illustrissime Signore Principesse mie padrone*).[123]

Peri must have adopted a similar approach when teaching the next gen-eration of princesses, and then Archduchess Maria Magdalena, toward the end of the first decade of the seventeenth century, although one assumes that the musical repertory at that point was more up-to-date, and some of it may even have been reflected in Peri's *Le varie musiche*. Indeed, that volume has a similar range of text types to those chosen for Eleonora de' Medici in 1577—Petrarch sonnets, strophic canzonettas, and two spiritual madrigals—even if they are set in a very different style. The poetry is decorous, and the music, restrained (which is not to say that it is easy to sing); further, two of the more tuneful settings—"Al fonte, al prato" (an aria) and "Con sorrisi cortesi" (a madrigal)—have texts laid under the continuo line and thus are soprano–bass duets, which would also be suitable for a female pupil and her teacher.[124]

Such music lessons were designed to lead to a modest level of accomplish-ment as a social skill. Training a professional singer was another matter alto-gether, and even if we do not know from whom Peri learned his vocal art—his silence about any of his teachers (including Malvezzi) may be another

---

123. Ledger A, fol. 18. Peri obtained these lutes by way of Federigo di Lorenzo Bonini. In 1584 Peri, who was then renting his residence from Bonini, paid to have lute songs sent to Bonini in Venice; see Chapter 2.

124. The solo songs in *Le varie musiche* variously have the vocal lines in either C1 (soprano) or C4 (tenor) clefs, but that does not force one voice type over another if one allows octave transposition, as was explicitly encouraged in some prefaces to early seventeenth-century prints. In other cases, however, there is an interesting discussion to be had about the matching (or not) of male/female poetic voices and musical voice types, even granting that male castra-tos and falsettists muddy the waters.

"noble" strategy—clearly he was willing to pass it on. While the court could avail itself of Peri's teaching for specific occasions, as was suggested for a young French girl from the convent of Montedomini proposed for a role in the 1608 *intermedi* (although in the end she refused to take part because, she said, she was a *gentildonna*), longer-term relations were more common.[125] Peri's known students include Jacopo Giusti from Lucca in the late 1590s; the young tenor Antonio di Girolamo Cinatti del Frate from about September 1602 to his official court appointment on 1 June 1609; and from December 1616 to September 1618, the soprano Angelica Furini (also known as Angelica Sciamerone), the future wife of Domenico Belli.[126] The norm would have been for the students to lodge in Peri's house—as we know for sure Giusti and Furini did—and for the court to pay Peri the costs of any of them being trained for Medici service. Here the details are more hazy: there is no record, for example, of Peri being given any money for Antonio Cinatti, who is indicated in the court roll only as being "under" Peri (*sotto messer Jacopo Peri*), while Furini's living allowance (*fl.*4 per month) was credited in her name (but it could still have ended up in Peri's pocket).[127] However, he certainly regarded his training of Furini as part of his court service and worth calling to the attention of Grand Duchess Christine in the draft of his petition early in 1618 for an office to support his family, even though he decided to omit Furini in the end for reasons of space (Letter 23).

Furini's *fl.*4 per month seems to have been a standard rate: Peri charged the same to Giovanni Giusti from Lucca when he took on his son in February 1599 to teach him singing and playing (*per insegniarli sonare e cantare*).[128] "Iacopino" resided in Peri's house until October 1600 (although he was absent for one month); as a widower with only a baby daughter, Peri had room to take him in. It is not clear what Giovanni Giusti thought he might be

125. See Curzio Picchena's letter to Michelangelo Buonarroti *il giovane*, 15 August 1608, in Carter, *Jacopo Peri*, 1: 331–32; Cole, *Music, Spectacle, and Cultural Brokerage in Early Modern Italy*, 2: 511–12. Picchena suggested Peri because Santi Orlandi did not have the necessary skill and Caccini did not want the bother.

126. Kirkendale, *Court Musicians*, 299 (Cinatti), and 316, 359 (Furini).

127. Furini's monthly payment from the *dispensa* while she was *in casa Jacopo Peri* is noted in the copy of the document detailing the reform of the grand-ducal household in 1616 in ASF, Galletti 41, paragraph 82.

128. Compare also the nonmusical example of the *fl.*4 charged by Tommaso Pitti for taking on Girolamo Fortini (later, Peri's brother-in-law) in 1598; see Chapter 1.

getting from the arrangement, save possible advancement for his son. But the boy appears to have developed some skills: he is known to have performed the fairly demanding role of Dafne in the first performance of *Euridice* on 6 October 1600.[129] Peri remembered at the last minute to give him some credit for his graceful performance (at the very end of the preface to *Euridice* comes the note that the role of Dafne was *rappresentata con molta grazia da Jacopo Giusti, fanciulletto Lucchese*). Nevertheless, Giusti did not enter court service, and he otherwise disappears from the historical record.

Having a pupil take up residence in the teacher's house was convenient—we have seen that Peri may have lodged with Malvezzi in the mid-1580s (to judge by the allowance Malvezzi received for him)—and was also, one assumes, a way of making extra money, and of gaining some kind of additional service from, in effect, a live-in apprentice. We have already noted that the Tommaso Lapi who sometimes signs receipts in the earlier layers of Peri's accounts may have been the one who was organist at S. Spirito in 1605 and, therefore, perhaps his student. Caccini refused to teach the young Roman singer Caterina Martinelli, who was being groomed for service in Mantua, unless she lived with him in Florence. The Mantuan court's refusal to accept his proposal, however, reveals the danger of such an arrangement, given that it seems to have feared for her well-being (perhaps because Caccini's son, Pompeo, had a reputation for licentious behavior).[130] Eleonora de' Medici, Duchess of Mantua, had fewer qualms, however, about a proposal to send the Ferrarese Angela Zanibelli to study with Peri for at least a year after her performance in the Mantuan festivities (in May–June 1608) celebrating the wedding of Prince Francesco Gonzaga and Margherita of Savoy. This was so that Zanibelli could refine her skills under the guidance of someone of good judgment, with natural talent being bolstered by study (*acciochè possa meglio affinare quel talento, che con la scorta di persona giudiciosa le sarà concesso dalla natura aiutata dal studio*), although she seems not to have gone to

---

129. Kirkendale, *Court Musicians*, 207. Dafne is the "messenger" who recounts the events leading up to the death of Euridice; the recitative does not demand vocal virtuosity, but it is certainly a prominent enough role.

130. Kirkendale, *Court Musicians*, 571; Martinelli eventually went straight to Mantua and lodged with Claudio Monteverdi and his wife. For Pompeo Caccini's transgressions, see ibid., 162–63, and McGee, "Pompeo Caccini and *Euridice*."

Florence in the end.[131] Perhaps the duchess had more confidence in Peri, given her own recollections of learning music from him.

Yet such arrangements always held the danger of raising suspicions. Peri's later student, Angelica Furini, was the daughter of the painter and occasional actor Filippo Furini (also nicknamed Il Sciamerone, hence the surname sometimes associated with Angelica); he performed at court in the play *La Tancia* by Michelangelo Buonarroti *il giovane* in May 1611. Angelica was born and baptized on 21 December 1601 (when Furini was living in the *popolo* of S. Simone, the former parish of the Peri family, although he later moved), making her fifteen years old when she entered Peri's household in December 1616.[132] She seems to have stayed there until her marriage to the musician Domenico Belli in September 1618. While studying with Peri, Furini came to the attention of Sinolfo Ottieri (Belisario Vinta's son-in-law), who gave Peri an organ valued at *sc.*300 in return for being allowed to observe her lessons (we have seen him in Table 1.2 as a godparent Peri chose for one of his children). Ottieri later got himself into severe difficulties in 1621 when he was found in a suspicious liaison with the nun (and virtuoso musician) Maria Vittoria Frescobaldi.[133] It is hard to imagine that any impropriety occurred, at least with Peri: Furini joined a very full household even with Peri's sons Dino and Antonio having recently been sent to Bologna. However, testimony ostensibly in support of Ottieri's melomania at his trial in 1621 suggests that Florentine nobles made something of a sport of ogling young female singers in training, and of using music lessons as a means of arranging dangerous liaisons.

On other occasions, Peri kept pupils more at a distance. In July 1608, Ottavio Rinuccini reported to Cardinal Ferdinando Gonzaga, in somewhat mysterious terms, that an unspecified *amico* had been found lodging close to Peri (for lessons, it seems) and was also studying keyboard instruments with

131. Baldassare Langosco (Mantua) to Enzo Bentivoglio (Ferrara), 18 February 1608, given in Fabris, *Mecenati e musici*, 201–2; compare also Reiner, "'La vag'Angioletta' (and Others)," 41–42. Subsequent letters (e.g., *Herla* C-3226, C-3508, C-3509) suggest that the plan changed, to send Zanibelli to Rome instead, but that she ended up returning to Ferrara.

132. Florentine baptismal records are now at <www.operaduomo.firenze.it/battesimi>. For Filippo Furini and his family, see Goldenberg Stoppato, "Proposte per Filippo Furini e documenti inediti per il figlio Francesco."

133. For Ottieri, see Chapter 1.

Alberigo Malvezzi (Cristofano's brother and the organist at the Duomo).[134] A similar arrangement operated later that same year, when Don Antonio de' Medici passed on to Peri a request from the Duchess of Mantua to audition some young girls with a view to selecting one for further training as a singer. Peri did so and made provisions for the chosen girl's lessons with a good teacher, and also checked frequently on her progress, but he did not, it seems, take her into his household (Letter 14).

This letter also gives us some sense of the qualities Peri sought in an aspiring pupil. The young student, he writes, has a more than reasonable voice (*più che ragionevol voce*), studies hard, and has a good ear (which is what matters, he says), and she reads her clefs and is beginning to sing from musical notation (*a cantare al libro*), which Peri judges necessary for a secure foundation. She also sings some ariettas to the keyboard, and has made miraculous progress in learning to play. Don Antonio de' Medici wants to send her off to Mantua straight away, but Peri advises keeping her in Florence over the winter so as to take her training still further. We do not know who this young girl was, or whether she fulfilled Peri's prediction of turning out well. But presumably she benefited from contact with someone whose vocal abilities (so Cristofano Marescotti noted in the preface to Peri's *Le varie musiche*) needed to be heard in the flesh to be understood and appreciated.

Even though Peri was one of a number of representatives of a particular style of (Florentine) singing that seems to have been widely admired across northern Italy, he did not establish a school of singers in the same way as did Giulio Caccini and then his daughter, Francesca. Nor does Peri seem to have profited from his pupils in the manner of lower-ranked musicians—such as Vergilio Grazi—who gave lessons in return for musical services from which the teacher would pocket any fees.[135] Nevertheless, Peri may have felt a simi-

---

134. See Rinuccini's letters to Ferdinando Gonzaga of 5 and 14 July 1608 (Mantua, Archivio di Stato, Autografi 10), given in Alessandro Ademollo, *La bell'Adriana*, 67–69. Ademollo suspects that the *amico* is an *amica*, and the cardinal's mistress. In a further letter to the cardinal of 12 August, Rinuccini notes how he has been asked to ensure that Malvezzi exerts diligence in teaching the *amico*, and that Peri should check on him every so often and teach him some aria or other (*di volere far ricordare a Alberigo che usassi un po' di diligenza nell'insegnare all'amico, e così al Zazzerino, che alle volte l'andassi a rivedere e gl'insegnassi qualch'aria*); Mantua, Archivio di Stato, Autografi 10, fol. 183.

135. See, for example, the contract that Vergilio Grazi drew up with Bartolomeo *calzolaio* regarding his son, Giovambattista, on 1 July 1603, in LC 2743 (a miscellany of documents re-

lar proprietary concern for those he taught: he gave Jacopo Giusti a role in *Euridice*, and later in the 1620s, he wrote the music sung by his son, Alfonso, in two or perhaps three of the *sacre rappresentazioni* performed by the Compagnia dell'Arcangelo Raffaello. In late 1624, he campaigned hard on behalf of a *castrato del Rinuccini*—a pupil, it seems, perhaps in the household of Carlo Rinuccini—whom he wished to have a role in another *sacra rappresentazione* being done at court, *La regina Sant'Orsola*.[136] Presumably, he also wrote the role of Clori in the 1628 opera *Flora* for another of "his" singers. We have already noted that this practice made it easier to mold, and teach, the music on an individual basis. As with any singer, however, once Peri's voice declined this was the only way in which it could somehow still be heard.

Altri favori e carezze

Peri greatly prized the "other favors and compliments" he received from Cardinal Luigi Capponi on the performance of *Euridice* in Bologna in the spring of 1616. There is no indication that he gained, or sought, financial payment for that performance—he was not "selling" an artwork as one might

---

garding Grazi): *Dichiarasi per la presente scritta come vera cosa è che Vergilio piglia ad insegnare cantare di musicha senza premio alcuno a Giovanbattista di Bartolomeo, calzolaio, con patto et condizione che detto Bartolomeo non possa levare detto suo figliuolo dal detto Vergilio mentre che gli dura la voce puerile, acciò detto maestro Vergilio se ne possa servire nelle sue musiche tanto fuori quanto nella scuola; et ancora volendo detto Giovanbattista andare a musiche o ad altre sorte di cantare, non possa senza licenzia del maestro, che se lui non se n'harà a servire, gli darà sempre licenzia et il guadagno sarà di Giovanbatista; et volendo detto Bartolomeo levare il suo figliuolo dal maestro Vergilio innanzi al patto et conditione senza legittima causa, il sopradetto Bartolomeo gli debba dare lire tre e mezzo il mese, et di tal danari se ne possa valere dove gli piacerà. Et contentandosi detto Bartolomeo di tal patto et conditione, si sottoscriverrà di sua propria mano questo dì et anno soprodetto* [sic] *in Firenze.* Grazi would teach Giovambattista for free, provided Bartolomeo kept the boy with him until his voice broke, in return for which Grazi could use him for musical performances either in his school or elsewhere. If the boy wished to perform independently, and Grazi had no need of him, permission would always be given, and any earnings would go straight to the boy. If Bartolomeo broke the contract, he would have to pay Grazi £3.10s. per month for the period that remained. LC 2743 also includes a letter (31 January 1615/16) from the Roman lutenist Giovanni Girolamo Kapsperger—whom the prominent Florentine scholar Cassiano dal Pozzo has asked to comment on some newly composed madrigals—and a portion of a music book containing a few keyboard pieces (some with texts) of a kind that Grazi might have used for teaching.

136. Harness, *Echoes of Women's Voices*, 102–7.

a painting—although he certainly reaped financial benefit from it by way of an allowance for his son, Dino, to study in Bologna. However, the rewards also extended in less tangible yet still powerful ways. In other words, some parts of the economy of culture did not operate in the monetary nexus. Thus the fact that so little of Peri's musical career appears in his ledgers is not just owing to the nature and purpose of the accounts; it also speaks to the nature and purpose of artistic and related activities that could not be assigned a value in accounting terms, yet could still be very valuable indeed.

Here, music might seem to be a special case. Its material objects—instruments, on the one hand, and printed music and manuscripts, on the other—certainly had value, and were also collectible in their own right. However, while they might have stood as representative of "music," they were not the music itself, which in its main medium, performance, was essentially evanescent, here one moment and gone the next. Moreover, these printed editions and manuscripts did not freeze or capture the musical work in a manner of, say, a poem, a painting, or a piece of sculpture but required some further activity to bring them to life. Nor were they transparent, save to the musically competent, and even then they embodied, by virtue of the incompleteness of their notation, various resistances that had to be overcome prior to performance. Musical work required a musical presence, which certainly benefited musicians but also placed them in some dilemmas in terms of their status. Thus Peri's resistance to the more artisanal aspects of music—his apparent preference for composing over performance, his concern for where, when, and with whom he might sing—can easily be linked to his self-perception, and self-projection, as a *nobil fiorentino*. To adopt a too-familiar term, his performance of identity by definition set limits on his musical performance.[137] Securing that identity by way of music required him to play a careful game, however, and one that demanded still more nuance, given what was, for all Peri's claims to the contrary, his borderline status between *messer* and *signore*. He could not afford to lessen his musical presence until sufficient *favori e carezze* had been placed in the bank, as it were, and even then he needed to generate periodic reminders—as he did in the second and third decades of the century—of how and why such favors had been earned in the first place, so as to ensure their renewal.

---

137. For the slightly earlier, but still potent, example of the Neapolitan bass Giulio Cesare Brancaccio and the performance of identity, see Wistreich, *Warrior, Courtier, Singer*.

The long list of civic offices occupied by Peri points to a device often used by the Medici both to give to the Florentine patriciate some sense of involvement in matters of government, and as a means of preferment (as we saw in Chapter 1). Peri's first such appointments (as one of the twelve Buonuomini di Collegio, and one of the Capitani di Orsanmichele) were made during the period of his involvement in his first opera, *Dafne* (sponsored by Jacopo Corsi), and his positions in the Arte degli Speziali in 1601–2 followed (at some distance, it must be admitted) his work for the 1600 wedding festivities and the subsequent publication of *Euridice* (again, sponsored by Corsi). Correlation is not causation, and the evident gap between the performance of *Euridice* (6 October 1600) and Peri's appointment as *camerlengo* of the Speziali (December 1601) makes one suspicious here even of some notion of correlation. The same is true of his later appointments: even when they appear closer to some particular musical service, it seems unlikely that any of them were a direct "reward" for it, or even, and more interestingly, that Peri was more inclined to perform such a service in direct response to a particular appointment. But it would be naive to expect any such direct one-for-one transactions; nor would Peri have presumed their likelihood, however much he might have hoped for them. Rather, one has a sense of two parallel trajectories in rather deft counterpoint, one musical and the other civic, with the latter, at least, culminating in some distinction with his appointment to the Consiglio dei Duecento in 1621. Although he did not receive a high salary from the court, the Medici certainly supported him in other ways enabled by, and perhaps even better suited to, his noble status.

Thus we find some quite nuanced—if wholly typical of a courtly society— webs of favor and obligation.[138] For example, the severe difficulties Peri faced in collecting the annuity from the first *censo* he purchased in 1604 led him to go to the law courts in 1611, but he retrieved his capital in 1614 thanks to the intervention of the grand duke. The stress of the court case left Peri seriously ill for the summer of 1614, a time when he was also in some financial straits, for the grand duke sent Cavaliere Ferdinando Saracinelli, his *primo cameriere*, to Peri's house with a gift of *fl.50* so that he might run his household (*acciò meglio mi potessi governare*). Almost half a year's salary was a decent "gift"—although Peri would spend more on the clothes for his trip to Rome in 1616—but his appreciation of the florins (*quali mi furno molto cari*) was

---

138. The classic texts are Elias, *Die höfische Gesellschaft*; Biagioli, *Galilei, Courtier*.

perhaps enhanced by this sign of the grand duke's favor. As for Saracinelli, he became godfather to Peri's daughter, Caterina, in early 1616 (see Table 1.2), and was the dedicatee of the second edition of his book of songs, *Le varie musiche*, of 1619.[139] The printer Zanobi Pignoni, who was also a musician, signed the typically effusive dedication (discussed in the Conclusion)—and also suggests that "a good part" of the book contained settings of poetry by Saracinelli (*buona parte delle rime qui messe in Musica sono parti del suo ingegno*)—but one assumes that Pignoni was acting in some sense on Peri's instructions, and that Peri, in turn, would in effect have been expressing his obligation to a prominent courtier who played an increasingly important role in court entertainments in the second decade of the seventeenth century and beyond.[140]

A second example suggests even longer-term transactions. Ferdinando Gonzaga (1587–1626), second son of Duke Vincenzo of Mantua, spent a great deal of time in Tuscany in the early 1600s (his mother was Eleonora de' Medici, to whom Peri had taught singing), both at the Medici court and at the university in Pisa, where he began studying in January 1604 (he would have seen the tournament for which Peri provided the music in February 1605).[141] Ferdinando was a dilettante poet and composer, and became quite closely associated with Florentine musicians, acting for a while as a patron of the musical Accademia degli Elevati, founded in June 1607 by Marco da Gagliano.[142] It was the latter who first seems to have brokered contact between Peri and Ferdinando in July 1607, leading to further negotiations during the second half of the year—by way of the Florentine poet (and patrician) Fran-

139. Saracinelli was also the dedicatee of Antonio Brunelli's *Scherzi, arie, canzonette, e madrigali a una, due, e tre voci . . . Libro terzo* (Venice: Giacomo Vincenti, 1616).

140. Saracinelli was certainly a sometime poet (and he wrote the text for Peri's "O dell'alto Appenin figlio sovrano," published in 1614), but it is not clear which of the seven songs added to the 1619 edition were set to his verse, and even if they all were, to call this a "good part" of the book is somewhat stretching a point.

141. See Ferdinando Gonzaga's (rather dismissive) comments on the Carnival entertainments in Pisa in February 1605 in his letters to his father of 8, 13, and 27 February 1605, in Mantua, Archivio di Stato, Archivio Gonzaga 1124, fols. 424–26.

142. Strainchamps, "New Light on the Accademia degli Elevati of Florence." The Elevati was preceded by a group supported by Cosimo Cini, the dedicatee of a madrigal in Santi Orlandi's *Il primo libro de madrigali a cinque voci* (Venice: Angelo Gardano, 1602), and of Marco da Gagliano's *Il terzo libro de madrigali a cinque voci* (Venice: Angelo Gardano, 1605).

cesco Cini—to have an opera performed in Mantua for the upcoming festivities celebrating the wedding of Francesco Gonzaga (heir to the ducal throne)
and Margherita of Savoy.[143] Cini proposed a subject, the wedding of Peleus
and Thetys, and wrote the libretto, and Peri set it to music.[144] Those negotiations stalled, however, as the Mantuan court opted for a different Florentine
poet, Ottavio Rinuccini, to provide the libretto for *Arianna* (set to music by
the Mantuan *maestro della musica*, Claudio Monteverdi). In the end, Ferdinando Gonzaga sided with Marco da Gagliano, whose *Dafne* (a new setting
of the libretto by Rinuccini first composed by Peri) was performed in Mantua in advance of the festivities, during Carnival in early 1608. Cini was
deeply annoyed at his waste of effort, suspecting (probably rightly) machinations on the part of Rinuccini and others. Peri accepted the outcome more
phlegmatically (Letter 8).

Peri characteristically kept himself on the sidelines of these negotiations,
using Cini as an intermediary, even though he had already prepared the
ground by sending Ferdinando Gonzaga a musical setting, probably of the
latter's poetry (Letter 6).[145] He was also very careful not to commit himself to
too much too soon, and, typically, he set conditions on the possibility of his
actually performing in the opera in Mantua: he would do so only if a singer
of well-born status, such as Francesco Rasi, were to share the stage.[146] However, the next year (1608) Peri directly approached Ferdinando, now a cardinal, to congratulate him first on *Dafne* (which had included some music by
Ferdinando) and then on the success of the 1608 Mantuan festivities (Letters
10–13). While this might have been an attempt to repair any damage caused

---

143. On 28 July, Marco da Gagliano wrote to Ferdinando Gonzaga that he would try to
satisfy him in an unspecified matter concerning Peri (*in tanto procurerò satisfarla con il Signor
Jacopo Peri*); see Vogel, "Marco da Gagliano," 551. Presumably this is what led Peri to write to
Ferdinando on 11 August 1607 (Letter 6).

144. Cini's *Le nozze di Peleo e Tetide* was proposed to Ferdinando Gonzaga by Michelangelo Buonarroti *il giovane* as a substitute for the latter's *Il giudizio di Paride*, which Ferdinando
had originally commissioned for the 1608 Mantuan festivities, although it was then coopted
for the 1608 Florentine ones; Carter, *Jacopo Peri*, 1: 56–58; Kirkendale, *Court Musicians*,
214–16.

145. For another possible identification of this setting, see below, n. 183.

146. As Francesco Cini told Ferdinando Gonzaga on 26 October 1607, *il nostro Signor Peri
presupone che il Rasi canterà anch'egli, che non cantando, non intende di farlo se non ha qualche
uno ben nato simile a lui che canti*; Davari, "Notizie biografiche del distinto maestro di musica
Claudio Monteverdi," 178 (see also Kirkendale, *Court Musicians*, 216).

by the Cini affair, or to assure the young cardinal that he did not bear any
grudge, there also seems to have been some incident in the Accademia degli
Elevati that Peri needed to remedy (Letter 10). Ferdinando then requested
that Peri come to Mantua to provide some kind of entertainment for Carnival 1609, which may have been yet another attempt to patch things up. It is
striking, too, that while the cardinal wrote to Peri to solicit this trip, he also
sent his footman (*palafreniero*) to summon him, and approached two other
intermediaries in Florence to oil the wheels: as we have seen, Pandolfo Della
Stufa and Geronimo Lenzoni worked quite hard both with Peri and with the
court to make arrangements for the trip, although they eventually failed.[147] It
would seem from these negotiations that Peri was not just another musician
on the cardinal's list.

He responded slowly, however, to Ferdinando's somewhat incessant requests for music. Although he had sent a madrigal on 11 August 1607 (Letter
6), less than two weeks later Massimiliano Gonzaga, in forwarding to Mantua music by Marco da Gagliano, wrote that Peri had nothing new because
he was busy with preparations for the wedding of Cosimo de' Medici and
Maria Magdalena of Austria (*Il Signor Jacopo Peri non si trova al presente cosa
alcuna di nuovo, per essere occupato nelle cose di queste nozze*).[148] In March and
April 1608, Peri made excuses for not responding to further requests for music on the grounds of exhaustion from the Cini opera and his other affairs
(Letter 9), and then of various personal difficulties—including a tiresome
business matter and the deaths of relatives and friends (it is unclear whom he
means)—that had caused him to drown in melancholy (Letter 11). He also
said he hoped that Ferdinando's sending him the music he had composed for
insertion in *Dafne* would cheer him up, and clearly he felt better in June
(Letter 12), not least because he had heard from Rinuccini how Ferdinando
had praised him during the recent wedding festivities in Mantua and had
even written an ode in his honor; hence in July Peri sent a sonnet setting for
three voices (originally for the *concerto de' castrati*?), and also an arietta com-

147. For the footman, see Ferdinando Gonzaga to Don Antonio de' Medici, 6 January
1609, in ASF, Mediceo del Principato 5130, fol. 462: *Spedisco un mio Palafreniero a messer Jacomo Peri invitandolo a Mantova a fare il Carnovale*. Ferdinando does not normally refer to
Peri as *messer*; it may be significant that he does so when writing to someone of rank.

148. Massimiliano Gonzaga (Florence) to Ferdinando Gonzaga, 21 August 1607; Mantua,
Archivio di Stato, Archivio Gonzaga 1125, fol. 270.

missioned by a "marescial" who had recently passed through Florence, setting a text by Cavaliere Vincenzo Panciatichi (Letter 13).[149] However, on 2
September 1608 Rinuccini told Ferdinando that Peri had still not composed
the aria to the text (by Ferdinando?) "D'un bel guardo," with the excuse that
he was so busy (as he may have been, given the imminent wedding festivities in Florence) and wanted to produce something good (*il Zazzerino non
m'ha dato l'aria sopra* D'un bel guardo; *si scusa per le tante occupazioni e per la
volontà di far qualcosa di buono*).[150] And on 29 September 1609, Santi Orlandi
reported on Peri's willingness to compose a madrigal once he was told which
text to set, although there is no sign that it was ever done.[151] It is striking how
music becomes in effect a token of exchange with the cardinal, albeit on a par
with poets sending poetry and others (including musicians) sending potted
plants and fruits.

By now, however, Ferdinando was himself getting somewhat tired of the
Florentines: he had fallen out with Marco da Gagliano over the latter's ac-
ceptance of the position of *maestro di cappella* of the Duomo (Ferdinando
seems to have hoped that he would join the household he was establishing
in Rome as cardinal). Then the severe problems facing the Accademia degli
Elevati in mid-1609 because of a rival breakaway group that petitioned for
Ferdinando's support seem to have prompted him to lose still more interest.[152] Things may have calmed down in the next few years, however: Ferdinando was in Florence in early February 1611—when he attended a performance of Marco da Gagliano's *Dafne* on 9 February (but not the *balletto*
five days later, in which Peri participated as a composer and performer)—

149. Rinuccini also mentioned the ode in his letter to Ferdinando Gonzaga, 24 June 1610;
Mantua, Archivio di Stato, Autografi 8, fol. 198.

150. Mantua, Archivio di Stato, Autografi 8, fol. 184; also given in Alessandro Ademollo,
La bell'Adriana, 60–61.

151. Santi Orlandi to Ferdinando Gonzaga, 29 September 1609, in Mantua, Archivio di
Stato, Archivio Gonzaga 990, fol. 493: *Il signor Peri la ringrazia; e prontamente la servirà, se ella
si dichiarerà qual madrigale deve fare; essendo il terzo[?] che ella diceva tutto scassato.* The letter is
hard to read, and it is not clear whether Ferdinando has sent three poems, the third of which
was missing as an enclosure or was somehow indecipherable (*essendo il terzo che ella diceva
tutto scassato*), or just a single text (*essendo il testo . . .*).

152. See Strainchamps, "Marco da Gagliano in 1608" (as *maestro di cappella*); Strainchamps, "New Light on the Accademia degli Elevati of Florence," 525–30 (the breakaway
group). The rival academy is discussed further in our Conclusion.

which perhaps encouraged their renewed correspondence in that year (Letters 16–18).[153]

Following the death of Duke Vincenzo Gonzaga in February 1612 and Francesco in December, Cardinal Ferdinando was next in line to the Mantuan throne: he resigned the cardinalate and was eventually crowned duke in early 1616. Peri remained in contact with him, although he tended to continue to seek plausible excuses not to accept invitations to visit Mantua. In early 1617, however, Duke Ferdinando married Caterina de' Medici (another of the Medici princesses to whom Peri had taught music, this time in the early 1600s), and Peri saw his chance, requesting from both the Duke and the new Duchess of Mantua recommendations to the grand duke for some civic position in Florence or the *contado* (Letters 20–22). That recommendation eventually led to Peri's lucrative appointment as *camerlengo* of the Arte della Lana on 28 March 1618, and he duly wrote to thank Ferdinando and Caterina in the following month (Letters 25, 26).

Peri had been able to find a good reason not to come to Mantua in April 1616 (because he was going to Rome), but a favor done required something in return. On 2 March 1620, Duke Ferdinando asked Peri for his *Adone* (to a libretto by Jacopo Cicognini)—it had been composed in 1611 (Letter 17)—for performance at the joint birthday celebrations for himself and the duchess in late April and early May 1620. The duke's request noted how much he esteemed Peri's works (*quanto io stimi le compositioni sue*) and also promised favors in return; it was transmitted via Pandolfo Della Stufa (who had liaised with Peri in early 1609), who was asked in a letter written the same day to reimburse Peri for any copying expenses.[154] After sending the score to Mantua (Letter 27)—very quickly, it seems—Peri also asked Marchese

153. For Ferdinando Gonzaga in Florence in February 1611, see Solerti, *Musica, ballo e drammatica alla corte medicea*, 60–61. He arrived on 8 February and left on the morning of 10 February; ASF, Guardaroba medicea, Diari d'etichetta 3, p. 349. Marco da Gagliano's *Dafne* contained some music by the cardinal, so the performance could in some sense have been in his honor; the annotations in the copy of the 1608 edition of Gagliano's score currently in Florence, Biblioteca Nazionale Centrale—which specify the cast (there is no reference to Peri) and indicate some stage directions—probably relate to this occasion.

154. The minutes of Duke Ferdinando's letters to Peri and Della Stufa (Mantua, Archivio di Stato, Archivio Gonzaga 2299, documents dated 2 March 1620) are given in Besutti, "Variar 'le prime 7 stanze della Luna'," 344–45; Besutti is the main source for our discussion of the April–May 1620 entertainments; for the broader Mantuan context in 1620, see Carter, "Monteverdi, Early Opera, and a Question of Genre." Ferdinando Gonzaga had himself begun, but

Don Giovanni Gonzaga to send a recommendation in its favor to Duke Fer-dinando's chief councillor, Alessandro Striggio (son of the composer, and the librettist of Monteverdi's 1607 opera *Orfeo*).[155] He seems to have been con-cerned that some additional support was needed to overcome any impedi-ments that might occur because, it was being said, *Adone* was a work of a type not customarily performed in Mantua.[156] He clarified that point in his own letter to Striggio (written the day before Giovanni Gonzaga's recom-mendation but presumably sent in the same post with it), where it also emerges that Peri was anxious that the performance might be held back by intrigue among the Mantuan musicians (Letter 29). The Mantuan produc-tion was indeed dropped, in part, it seems, because of a shortage of time for rehearsal; Duke Ferdinando was also contemplating a performance, for the same occasion, of Monteverdi's *Arianna* from 1608, but that never took place either. Instead, Peri composed the music for a new *ballo*, to a text sent by Duchess Caterina from Mantua (Letter 28) that was done there on 26 April (Duke Ferdinando's birthday), and repeated on 4 May to celebrate the wed-ding in Mantua of Maria Zati and Traiano Bobba the previous day (that second performance was also attended by Cardinal Leni, who had heard *Euridice* in Bologna in April 1616).[157] Caterina de' Medici took part in the *ballo*—as she had done in similar entertainments in previous years—with Princess Eleonora Gonzaga (future wife of Emperor Ferdinand II) and seven *dame*. But as had occurred in 1607, an opera by Peri proposed for Mantua

never finished, a play based on the Adonis story; see the letter to him from Marco da Gagliano, 19 August 1608, in Mantua, Archivio di Stato, Archivio Gonzaga 1124, fol. 204.

155. Peri had already set Striggio's poem "Ho visto al mio dolore" before 1608 (see Appen-dix C).

156. See the unsigned letter to Alessandro Striggio, 31 March 1620, in Mantua, Archivio di Stato, Archivio Gonzaga 1130, fol. 420 (also given in Besutti, "Variar 'le prime 7 stanze della Luna'," 349–50): *raccomando a Vostra Signoria l'Adone opera del Signor Dottor Cicognini messa però in musica dal Signor Jacopo Peri detto il Zazzerino, il quale per esser suggetto di quelle qua-lità che Vostra Signoria benissimo sa, prego che lo voglia ricevere in protettione appresso Sua Altezza Serenissima acciò col favore di Vostra Signoria venghin superati quelli impedimenti che per esser compositione non usata in codeste parti potrebbero occorrere.* Striggio asked Peri who had written the unsigned recommendation, leaving him in something of a quandary: Peri had to answer the question, but needed to soften any suggestion that he had engineered Marchese Gonzaga's letter (Letter 30).

157. Maria Zati was one of Caterina de' Medici's *dame*; see Alessandro Senesi's letters to Curzio Picchena of 6 March, 27 April, and 1 May 1620 in ASF, Mediceo del Principato 2950. Traiano Bobba was a *gentilhuomo* from Casale Monferrato.

never in the end reached the stage. Had *Adone* been performed, Peri would presumably have gone to Mantua as he did for *Euridice* in Bologna; however, he did not feel it necessary to be there for the mounting of a *ballo* (see Letter 31).

The author of the text of the *ballo* is unknown: the candidates are Striggio or, more likely (from the style), another Mantuan court secretary known for theatrical poetry, Ercole Marliani. It is quite extensive, with 289 lines of verse, and Peri must have worked very hard to set it in so short a time unless he was used only for portions of it. But he would have drawn on his experience with similar Florentine entertainments going back at least to the *balletto* done in early 1611. The prologue, delivered by Il Fato (Fate), is followed by a scene for Venere and Amore that in turn sets the stage for Luna (the Moon) to deliver seven quatrains inviting the stars to dance so as to summon her beloved Endimione (Endymion). Luna and Endimione then fall asleep, leading to a chorus of dreams, an invocation by Fama (Fame), a chorus of the gods, and a final exchange between the lovers. In reporting back to Florence on 27 April, Alessandro Senesi (the Florentine Resident in Mantua) said it was not an ordinary *ballo* (he noted *la piacevole vista d'un balletto non ordinario*), by which he might have meant its splendor or its unusual (from a Florentine point of view) structure, although it fit squarely in the tradition of Mantuan theatrical *balli* exemplified by Monteverdi's *Ballo delle ingrate* (1608), with which it shares some structural similarities.

Caterina de' Medici sent the text in at least two installments, the first of which seems to have been the Luna–Endimione section, for which Peri dispatched the music on 24 March (Letter 28). Having discovered that the Mantuans wanted Luna's seven stanzas to be varied in some manner, Peri redid them (perhaps in the same way that he varied the seven stanzas of "Queste lacrime mie, questi sospiri" for the 1613 tournament and *mascherata*), sending the new music to Alessandro Striggio on 7 April (Letter 30). He then sent on 14 April a final tranche of music (perhaps the Venere–Amore episode or the chorus of dreams and Fama's speech, both of which have the appearance of being later additions) that he had composed very quickly that same day (Letter 31). Most of the text is in *versi sciolti*, implying that it would be set as declamatory recitative: the main exceptions are the prologue's five quatrains (Peri could take as a model the prologues to *Dafne*, *Euridice*, and the 1611 *balletto*), and Luna's seven, and then the rather odd mixture of meters—lines of eight, four, and five syllables, presumably to suit varied dance patterns—in the chorus of gods toward the end. It is not clear how much of the entire text was meant to be sung and danced at the same time—not much, one suspects, except around the central dances of the stars, and then the chorus of gods—although we certainly know that there was additional instrumental dance music brought into this entertainment from elsewhere. For the most part, Peri's contribution was likely limited more or less to his traditional recitative. But having provided that, obligations were now met, and honor satisfied, on both sides, and Peri had very little further contact with the Mantuan court.

Peri's letters to Ferdinando Gonzaga and others are necessarily somewhat formal, and also reserved. He knows when and how to use the proper courtesies—as is only to be expected—reflecting nuances of rank and allegiance, although there is little of the excessive fawning that one finds in letters by other musicians of the time when writing to their "betters" (Monteverdi is a case in point). Indeed, some of Peri's letters to Ferdinando can be surprisingly direct, and are quite different from those written by, say, Marco da Gagliano, with whom the cardinal had more intense musical relations (as well as one concerning exotic flowers), but also more thorny ones. And just as Peri could rely on brokers-cum-intermediaries to ease his way through the court—Belisario Vinta, it seems, in 1600 (Letters 2 and 3), Andrea Cioli in 1618 (Letters 23 and 24), and Alessandro Striggio in Mantua in 1620 (Letters 29–32)—so could he offer his own *favori e carezze* to his friends and colleagues. He served (with Antonio Naldi) as *mallevadore* for the castrato Onofrio Gualfreducci's appointment as *sagrestano maggiore* at S. Lorenzo in 1593; he recommended a collection of poetic madrigals by Simone Finardi, whom Peri calls his *amico mio*, to Ferdinando Gonzaga in 1611 (Letter 16), and he auditioned (with Marco da Gagliano) and endorsed Giovanni Bettini for the post of organist of the Cavalieri di Santo Stefano in 1618.[158]

Peri's Music

Despite his insistence on his noble status, Peri was appointed, listed, and paid among the normal *musici*; for all his use of the title *signore*, he was no less

---

158. Finardi's letter to Ferdinando Gonzaga, 26 March 1611, is in Mantua, Archivio di Stato, Archivio Gonzaga 1128, fol. 144. On 13 May (ibid., fol. 157), he thanked the cardinal warmly for his response, including what had been communicated by *Signor Jacopo Peri mio amicissimo*.

often styled *messer*. Yet we have seen enough evidence to suggest how he saw himself as standing apart from other musicians: Francesco Cini's comment (1607) to Ferdinando Gonzaga that Peri would sing in *Le nozze di Peleo e Tetide* only if Francesco Rasi or someone of similar well-born status were also on the stage is very revealing. We have also seen that Peri used musical activities for other ends. The question now is how all this might relate to the content of his music itself, whether *Euridice* (not much of *Dafne* survives) or the songs in *Le varie musiche*.

In a sonnet written in the late 1610s or very early 1620s, the poet Ottavio Rinuccini imagines Peri pitted in a musical battle against the Neapolitan musician Muzio Effrem, who was working in Florence, both of whom appear before Ferdinando Saracinelli (see Appendix D). Effrem had formerly been in the service of the melomane Carlo Gesualdo, Prince of Venosa; his own musical works (all for more than one voice) were in Gesualdo's chromatic style; and he was a stern critic of the contrapuntal and other errors to be found in the madrigals of Marco da Gagliano.[159] Rinuccini opposes his marvelous chromaticism against Peri's more learned, restrained manner, but has Effrem claim the prize because he hears his rival make a basic music-grammatical error. It is not clear, however, whether Rinuccini views this as just a pedantic technicality irrelevant to the outcome.

The poet's stylistic preferences are more obvious in accounts of an earlier, real-life event. In June 1610, Peri was among a group of singers performing with the visiting soprano Adriana Basile at the house of Giulio Caccini, and before a noble audience (including Giovanni de' Bardi). They sang five-voice madrigals by Conte Alfonso Fontanelli (who had also been associated with Gesualdo), works in a genre and a style that for decades had marked the peak of the composer's art in the field of secular music: Monteverdi published his Fifth Book of such madrigals in 1605, and his Sixth in 1614.[160] While some such madrigals could contain virtuosic vocal writing (and still more virtuosity could be displayed by way of improvised ornamentation), the chief difficulty for the singers was usually of a different order: holding together complex contrapuntal and harmonic textures—in the June 1610 event, Fontanelli was amazed, we are told, that Basile managed to sustain her part, whereas the other performers got lost. And listeners were meant to be entranced by the expert combination of musical and poetic artifice.

Rinuccini, however, had a very different reaction, so he wrote to Ferdinando Gonzaga on 24 June. Not only did he think the male singers bad (therefore including Peri, though he does not name him). Worse still, he and all the other listeners, he said, were bored after four madrigals, with each musical beat seeming to last one year, and each word, two.[161] This marks a striking aesthetic shift in favor of the new declamatory style of solo song that certainly had its roots in Florentine thinking on music going back to Giovanni de' Bardi's Camerata in the 1570s and '80s, but that was also a sign of the taste of a new century that would eventually spread quite widely. The pattern was established by Giulio Caccini's first published collection of such songs, Le nuove musiche (Florence: I Marescotti, 1601 [= 1602]), containing music that Caccini himself traced back to the mid-1580s. The theatrical recitative may not have been popular in all camps, but the new forms of solo song clearly took off. By the mid-1630s, many commentators were noting, sometimes ruefully, how the polyphonic madrigal had declined precipitously in favor of pieces for solo voice and instrumental accompaniment: it was too complicated, old-fashioned, and unappealing.[162] Caccini's dig at counterpoint in the preface to Le nuove musiche—that he had learned more from Bardi and his Camerata than he had from thirty years of studying it—might not have been shared by Peri, who was taught it by Malvezzi. But the comment certainly reflected a trend away from complex musical structures in favor of simpler musico-poetic expression.

While Peri certainly contributed to the growth of this new repertory, it seems clear that he was operating essentially within a local musical marketplace, just as he did in other economic spheres.[163] Prominent musicians may

---

161. Ottavio Rinuccini to Ferdinando Gonzaga, 24 June 1610, in Mantua, Archivio di Stato, Autografi 8, fol. 198: *qui si trova il Signor Conte Alfonso Fontanella, fanno sì gran ragunate di cantori, ma se io ho a dire il vero a quattro madrigali vennono a noia a me, e a tutti gl'uditori, una battuta dura un anno, e una parola due, cattivi bassi, e cattivi tenori, sovrano Giovannino, in somma non fanno miracoli . . .*

162. Carter, *Music in Late Renaissance and Early Baroque Italy*, 241–42.

163. Thus it is very hard to explain the edition of Peri's *Euridice* issued in 1608 by the Venetian printer Alessandro Raverii, who also reissued Caccini's *Le nuove musiche* the previous year, and Severo Bonini's *Madrigali, e canzonette spirituali . . . à una voce sola* (Florence: Cristofano

have visited Florence but only passing through, as it were, and while there is
some evidence of their impact on Peri's music—Sigismondo d'India is the
obvious case in point—his style is too narrowly constrained to reflect the
cosmopolitan influences one finds elsewhere in early seventeenth-century
Italy.[164] The same is true of other Florentine composers. Nor did they create
dynamic intertextual worlds of musical homage or emulation, such as one
finds in, say, Mantua or (earlier) Ferrara (although we shall soon see one
example). In that same letter of 24 June 1610 Ottavio Rinuccini told Ferdinando Gonzaga how much Peri admired a duet and other arias by Monteverdi recently performed in Florence.[165] There is no evidence, however, that
his admiration translated into his own music, which in general remained
within narrow boundaries, catering to quite precise circumstances and even
tastes.

It comes as no surprise that his music for theatrical and similar entertainments was largely done on demand and in response to some specific
request. Even the unperformed *Adone* (1611) was a Medici commission and
was being slowly readied to be performed at their pleasure (Letter 17).[166]
Given that such entertainments were generally one-time events, Peri was
also willing to reuse his music if it suited him: his "Poiché la notte con

---

Marescotti, 1607) in 1608. Raverii tended to print what might be called "pirate" editions, but
it is difficult to imagine what market he thought might have any demand for Peri's opera.

164. The argument for the influence of Sigismondo d'India is in Carter, *Jacopo Peri*, 1: 214–
20. D'India was in Florence in late 1607 or early 1608 (and had also visited there before 1600).

165. Ottavio Rinuccini to Ferdinando Gonzaga, 24 June 1610, in Mantua, Archivio di
Stato, Autografi 8, fol. 198, also given in Davari, "Notizie biografiche del distinto maestro di
musica Claudio Monteverdi," 99: *quelle poche cose che sono comparse del Monteverdi com'il duo
e altr'arie sono ammirate da tutti universalmente, e dal Zazerino fuor di modo, gusto ch'io non mi
sono ingannato.* Monteverdi also visited Florence a few months later en route to Rome. We do
not know which *duo e altr'arie* by Monteverdi were performed—perhaps from *Orfeo?*—given
that he published his duets and (very few) arias much later in his career.

166. Something similar happened to the Peri–Cini *Le nozze di Peleo e Tetide*, which the
Florentine court kept in its back pocket, as it were, as we learn from Peri's letter to Ferdinando
Gonzaga of 12 November 1607 (Letter 8). The librettist of *Adone*, Jacopo Cicognini, said in
1613 that it was being held in reserve for the first wedding of the Medici princesses (Hill, *Roman Monody, Cantata, and Opera from the Circles around Cardinal Montalto*, 1: 325); on 2 April
1616 he suggested to Paolo Giordano Orsini in Rome that it might be performed on Peri's
forthcoming arrival there (Kirkendale, *Court Musicians*, 208) and suggested a possible cast,
including Francesca Caccini, Giovanni Battista Signorini, and various Roman virtuosos
(Boyer, "Les Orsini et les musiciens d'Italie au début du XVIIe siècle," 309).

l'oscure piume," a setting of the final chorus of Act III of Michelangelo Buonarroti *il giovane*'s *Il giudizio di Paride* (for the 1608 wedding), was provided with a new text by Buonarroti in honor of Archduchess Maria Magdalena ("Poiché de' Toschi al fortunato impero," although the poet marked it *non servì*).[167] The last lines of the first stanza of this second text— *e regina saluta e umil l'onora/d'Orsino eroe del bel regno di Flora*—suggest that it was almost certainly intended for Paolo Giordano Orsini (the eldest son of Virgilio Orsini, Duke of Bracciano), who acted as Prince Cosimo de' Medici's proxy at the prior wedding ceremony in Graz and then accompanied the archduchess to Florence; it may also have been commissioned by the melomane Sinolfo Ottieri, who was in Paolo Giordano's entourage on the trip to Austria.[168] The music then appeared in Peri's *Le varie musiche* (1609) with yet another text by Buonarroti, "Se tu parti da me, Fillide amata," as a more generic love lyric.

Of course, some theatrical or similar songs were themselves sufficiently generic in content as to transfer without alteration to a chamber context.[169] But there may well be other times when such retexting was done to make music designed for one context useful for another, whether out of convenience (or laziness) or because the music itself had found some favor.[170] Or perhaps it was just a rather stubborn conservatism: although Peri claimed to admire Ferdinando Gonzaga's setting of "Chi da' lacci d'Amor vive disciolto" inserted into Marco da Gagliano's *Dafne* (Letter 11)—it was so beautiful and new, he said, that he forgot his own setting of the same text (composed a decade before)—he returned precisely to, and quoted from, that former setting when composing another *ottava rima* stanza, "Torna, deh torna, pargoletto mio" for Rinuccini's *balletto* performed in February 1611.

When Peri discussed these entertainments and other music in his letters (which is not often), we see him engaging not so much with compositional

167. Carter, *Jacopo Peri*, 1: 251.

168. According to the list in the official account of the 1608 festivities, Camillo Rinuccini's *Descrizione delle feste fatte nelle reali nozze de' Serenissimi Principi di Toscana D. Cosimo de Medici e Maria Maddalena Arciduchessa d'Austria* (Florence: I Giunti, 1608), 73 (where he is identified as Sinolfo Otterio).

169. For "Queste lagrime mie, questi sospiri" (probably by Peri), see Carter, *Jacopo Peri*, 1: 264–66; Peri, *"Le varie musiche" and Other Songs*, ed. Carter, 101–7.

170. Kelley Harness builds on this idea to recover Florentine theatrical music from the 1620s that now survives with other texts; see, for example, Harness, *Echoes of Women's Voices*, 75.

issues—which in any event one would not expect in this kind of correspondence—but with more pragmatic ones concerning performance. For the tournament held in Pisa in February 1605, for example, Peri carefully noted the singers to whom the chorus parts might be allocated, and also the instruments to be used (Letter 4). His naming of singers was presumably in large part a matter of pragmatism, unless he was hoping thereby to support those to whom he felt closer than others—the castratos and Giovanni Battista Signorini (with whom he had worked previously in the *concerto de' castrati*) and Antonio Brandi (associated with Marco da Gagliano). For the Cini–Peri *Le nozze di Peleo e Tetide* in 1607, he made precise suggestions for the continuo ensemble (Letter 7): a harpsichord, chitarroni, a large lyra-viol, and a harp, which is close to what he had used in *Euridice* in 1600 (but with a *liuto grosso* instead of a harp). Both the 1605 specifications and the 1607 ones evoke a rich sonic world going far beyond how this relatively simple music might have looked on the page. It also made sense to comment on such practical matters for those planning a performance. That Peri did so, however, also suggests that he viewed his job as done once the music was written down and sent to the court, and that he was not necessarily going to become somehow involved in the performance or its direction: he probably did not go to Pisa himself for the tournament.

Such matters clearly concerned the would-be performer of Peri's music, but probably not many of its listeners. So long as the music served its purpose, however defined, they were not concerned with how it came about. The conceptual distinction between musical function and content meant that judgments of the one did not necessarily involve assessment, or even awareness, of the other: if the music did its job, the court was happy. This distinction could also work on other aesthetic levels. *Euridice* was clearly intended to symbolize a cultural and even political renewal in Florence: there was a precedent (Catherine de Médicis) for marrying a Medici princess to French royalty, but it was no small thing in 1600. Opera may not have been particularly popular at the time, it may not have flourished at the Medici court, and (we have seen) not everyone liked the recitative style and its proximity to heightened declamation. But its "invention" in Florence remained a matter of some courtly and civic pride, if we are to believe subsequent propagandists (see the Introduction). When Peri wrote to Ferdinando Gonzaga congratulating him on the performance of Marco da Gagliano's *Dafne* (Letter 10), he noted that the opera was in a style that came closer to dramatic speech than that of any other composer (*tal modo di canto è stato conosciuto più proprio, e più vicino al parlare, che quello di qualcun'altro valent'huomo*). The reference is clearly to the recitative, and the context, the well-known arguments over precedence in its invention among the Florentines around 1600. Clearly Peri felt some ownership of the recitative style, as Marco da Gagliano himself generously and extensively acknowledged in the preface to the score of *Dafne* published in Florence in October 1608.

We have seen that in early 1611, Jacopo Cicognini could refer to Peri's providing music *nel suo nobilissimo stile recitativo*—another sign of his proprietary rights—and the composer associated it with a noble manner of singing, and one that also had impeccable Humanist credentials. Nor did it require—or display—great compositional skill, at least in the sense of writing complex counterpoint: Peri's earlier contrapuntal exercises (the four-part ricercar and five-voice madrigal published by Malvezzi) demonstrate basic proficiency but no major accomplishment.[171] Likewise, the songs published in *Le varie musiche* do not exhibit great compositional ingenuity in conventional technical terms, although they are certainly very good of their kind, and although Pietro de' Bardi and others referred to Peri's *scienza* in music, they seem to have been referring to something other than how he understood the handling of musical notes.[172] When Marco da Gagliano was in Mantua in March 1608 (for the performance of his *Dafne*) and needed to ensure proper rehearsal of his music in Florence for the forthcoming wedding of Prince Cosimo de' Medici and Maria Magdalena of Austria, he asked that Peri supervise his music for one, two, and three voices, but he wanted Antonio Francesco Benci to take care of an eight-voice madrigal.[173] Not for nothing did Peri's style change little during his career: his recitatives for the role of

171. The same is true of the polyphonic choruses in *Euridice*, and the two three-part settings in *Le varie musiche*: they are fairly simple, although (for the most part) effective. This makes one slightly suspicious of Cesare Tinghi's report that Peri composed the music for three choirs performed in S. Nicola in Pisa during Holy Week 1622, and for four choirs in 1623 (*pace* Kirkendale, *Court Musicians*, 229), although there is some question about what Tinghi meant by *cori*; see above, n. 72.

172. For Bardi, see the Introduction; for other comments on Peri's *scienza*, see the poems in Appendix D.

173. See Gagliano's letter to Michelangelo Buonarroti *il giovane*, 8 March 1608, in Cole, *Music, Spectacle, and Cultural Brokerage in Early Modern Italy*, 2: 505. Gagliano had Cardinal Ferdinando Gonzaga write to Peri on his behalf (and compare Appendix B, Letter 9). Benci was a member of the Accademia degli Elevati.

Clori in *Flora* (1628) differ little from those he wrote for *Euridice* in 1600. But if the simplicity of writing for solo voice meant that its various styles were denigrated in some professional musical circles, it clearly worked to Peri's advantage as regards the image of himself he evidently sought to project.

The title page of the printed edition of Peri's *Euridice* is revealing in this light, especially in comparison with the one by Caccini that beat Peri to the press (Figures 3.3, 3.4). For the Peri, the typographical layout is simple, the only decoration a coat of arms representing the merging of the Medici with the French royal family. Yet we gain all the necessary information: why the work was performed (at a wedding) and for whom (Maria de' Medici, Queen of France and of Navarre). Peri also makes it clear that he is a *nobil fiorentino*, and Ottavio Rinuccini gets his due as *signore*. The elaborate title page that graces at least some copies of Caccini's *Euridice* is more complex.[174] The main blocks comprising the engraving—an elaborate frame around a representation of ancient ruins, with a river god (Tiber or Arno?) at the front—date back at least to the mid-1550s, and had been used for the title page of Vincenzo Galilei's *Dialogo della musica antica, et della moderna* (1581). They overwhelm the typography, which presents very little information indeed (of course, there was none to present about the performance), and Rinuccini is ignored. Yet Giulio Caccini takes the care to style himself *detto Romano*, which casts Peri's *nobil fiorentino* in an even stronger light.

One of Peri's motives for publishing his score was no doubt to set the record straight, as it were, given Caccini's preemptive strike: Peri signed the dedication to Maria de' Medici on 6 February 1600/1601 (Caccini's to Giovanni de' Bardi was dated 20 December 1600). One assumes that the production of the edition was a private venture, with costs paid by Peri (or by the court), rather than a commercial enterprise on the part of the printer.[175] It

174. For the background to this title page, see Carter, "Giulio Caccini," 22–24. Some surviving copies of the edition have a simpler one.

175. This seems implied by the fact that on 13 December 1601 (LC 3913, fol. 18v), Giorgio Marescotti signed a receipt for £2.10s. paid by Peri via Salvestro Magliani as the final payment of what was due to him for printing *Euridice* (*sono per le mie fatiche delle musiche di detto Peri vendute a [i]stanzia sua, et per ogni resto di tutto quello habiamo havuto da fare insieme insino dì detto*). Magliani was a *libraio* in Florence also associated with the Giunti press in 1589; see Carter, "Music-Printing in Late Sixteenth- and Early Seventeenth-Century Florence," 55 n. 52; Carter, "Music-Selling in Late Sixteenth-Century Florence," 484. The wording of this receipt is not entirely straightforward, but it suggests that Marescotti sold (and therefore also

LE MVSICHE
DI IACOPO P'ERI
NOBIL FIORENTINO
Sopra L'Euridice

DEL SIG· OTTAVIO RINVCCINI
Rappresentate Nello Sponsalizio
della Cristianissima

MARIA MEDICI
REGINA DI FRANCIA
E DI NAVARRA.

IN FIORENZA
APPRESSO GIORGIO MARESCOTTI·
M D C·

FIGURE 3.3. Title page of Jacopo Peri's *Euridice* (Florence: Giorgio Marescotti, 1600 [= 1601]). (Florence, Biblioteca Nazionale Centrale. With permission of the Ministero per i Beni e le Attività Culturali/Biblioteca Nazionale Centrale, Firenze; further reproduction or duplication by whatever means is forbidden.)

FIGURE 3.4. Title page of Giulio Caccini's *Euridice* (Florence: Giorgio Marescotti, 1600). (Florence, Biblioteca Nazionale Centrale. With permission of the Ministero per i Beni e le Attività Culturali/Biblioteca Nazionale Centrale, Firenze; further reproduction or duplication by whatever means is forbidden.)

also served as some kind of monument to his contribution to the 1600 festivities—just as Jacopo Corsi paid for a statue of Orpheus from the sculptor Cristoforo Stati around the same time as that edition appeared (see Figure 1.10)—but it seems to be an understated one. The two editions of Peri's *Le varie musiche* (1609, 1619) give a similar impression (Figures 3.5, 3.6). Peri, styled *signor*, certainly appears on their title pages, but otherwise he is distanced from these editions: the printer Cristofano Marescotti provided a preface in 1609, and Zanobi Pignoni signed the dedication to Ferdinando Saracinelli in 1619. Why Peri chose to publish these songs—if he did (a caveat to be explained shortly)—remains unclear. It is striking that *Le varie musiche* appeared only after the death of Grand Duke Ferdinando I, who may have placed some kind of actual or implied hold over its contents.[176] Perhaps Peri sought to use its publication as a way of securing his position in the eyes of Grand Duke Cosimo II, to support his side in the squabbles still going on in Florence in the aftermath of the 1608 wedding festivities and Marco da Gagliano's appointment as *maestro di cappella* of the Duomo, or to assert his preeminence in the face of the notable increase in publications of solo songs around this time.[177] Ten years later—the normal period marking the lapse of copyright in this period—the volume was reissued, with two songs removed and seven added.[178] Pignoni claimed in his preface that the new edition was

---

printed?) *Euridice* at Peri's expense (*a stanzia sua*), and also that this payment was final settlement for a debt associated with *Euridice*, and not linked to the sale of one or more copies of it.

176. For Ferdinando I's reluctance to have his musicians gain credit for their work, see Carter, "*Non occorre nominare tanti musici.*" Cusick, *Francesca Caccini at the Medici Court*, 104, builds on this to suggest that it was a gambit so that the grand duke might better sustain and display his own prestige. Whatever that case, it is certainly true that the court musicians projected themselves more aggressively, and their roles in court entertainments were better acknowledged, during the reign of Grand Duke Cosimo II.

177. For the publication rate of solo-song collections, see Carter, *Jacopo Peri*, 1: 213–14: an unprecedented five (including Peri's) appeared in 1609, including one by Sigismondo d'India (whom Peri seems to have admired) and, closer to home, one by the Florentine Severo Bonini, who was very much in the Caccini camp. Peri may also have been motivated by Francesco Rasi's decision to publish his own first collection of songs, *Vaghezze di musica*, in 1608, and also, perhaps, by the Venetian reissues of *Le nuove musiche* in 1607 (by Alessandro Raverii) and of nine arias from the same collection in 1608 (by Giacomo Vincenti).

178. The term "copyright" is anachronistic, but it describes the situation well enough. Neither edition of *Le varie musiche* had a formal privilege from the Medici administration (nor did *Euridice*)—such a *privilegio* would (for a fee) have protected the contents from unlicensed reproduction in Tuscany for a standard ten years—but this was typical of Florentine music

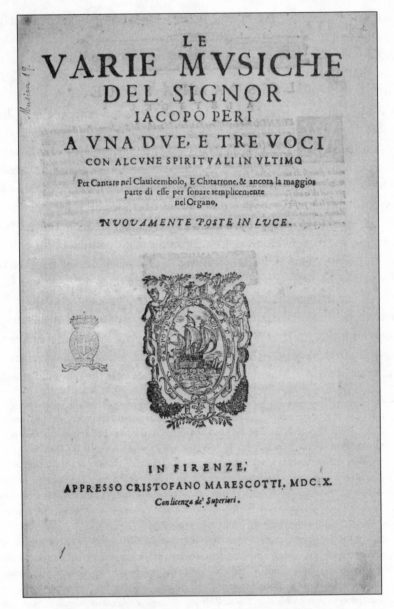

FIGURE 3.5. Title page of Jacopo Peri's *Le varie musiche* (Florence:
Cristofano Marescotti, 1609). (Florence, Biblioteca Nazionale Centrale. With
permission of the Ministero per i Beni e le Attività Culturali/Biblioteca
Nazionale Centrale, Firenze; further reproduction or duplication by whatever
means is forbidden.)

FIGURE 3.6. Title page of Jacopo Peri's *Le varie musiche* (Florence: Zanobi Pignoni, 1619). (Paris, Bibliothèque nationale de France. Reproduced by permission.)

done to satisfy the continual demands made of him for Peri's songs, and given that new works by the composer had fallen into his hands, he was using them to enrich the book.[179] On Peri's part, this could again be self-projection in the musical sphere to match his newly strengthened position in Florentine civic life after his appointment at the Arte della Lana, to cement his reputation after Caccini's death, or to anticipate likely changes at court owing to the extended illnesses of Grand Duke Cosimo II.

On 8 June 1630 Peri's son Dino claimed to Galileo Galilei that his father kept his music very close to his chest (*perché in questo genere egli è stato un huomo trascuratissimo*), that nothing remained either by him or by his teachers (*trova residuo nessuno d'intavolature, nè di suo nè de' suoi maestri*), and that what little he had collected in a book had been stolen twenty years before (*e quel poco che si trovava haver raccolto in un libro gli fu rubato già 20 anni sono*).[180] Dino's use of the past tense makes it clear that, so far as he was concerned, Peri's musical career was now over, which was true: he was almost sixty-nine years old and had just suffered a serious collapse. But the idea that he had been "robbed" of a book of songs twenty years before is more troublesome. While this might refer to some manuscript collection filched by a competitor, the timing seems suspiciously close to the publication of *Le varie musiche* by Cristofano Marescotti in 1609. If so, was Dino suggesting that the edition appeared without Peri's approval? This seems very unlikely in the small world in which Marescotti operated, and given that in the case of music he largely produced what seem to have been "vanity" editions in which he had little or no financial interest once he was paid for his materials and his work, so he could not afford to alienate Florentine composers by following

---

prints, given that there was just one main music printer in the city; for the broader issues, see Carter, "Music-Printing in Late Sixteenth- and Early Seventeenth-Century Florence." Absent a privilege, there was no legal standing for any ten-year rule of copyright, even if there may have been some customary expectation of it.

179. *A' Benigni Lettori / Per soddisfare alla continue dimande che mi erano fatte delle Musiche del Signor Jacopo Peri, mi disposi di nuovo a ristamparle; con la quale occasione essendomi capitate alle mani altre opere dell'istesso autore, ne ho arrichito il presente libro. Godete Benigni Lettori, e le nuove, e le vecchie Arie, e gradite il desiderio che ho hauto di servirvi.*

180. Galilei, *Le opere*, 14: 116. Dino was responding to a request from Galilei for *intavolature* (literally, lute intabulations, but Dino may just mean scores) of *arie antiche*, meaning older music. It is unclear to what extent the chest *piena di scritture di musica* inventoried among the property of Alfonso Peri confiscated after his murder of his wife (in 1642) contained material deriving from his father; see Chapter 4.

unscrupulous practices. Or perhaps Dino was just confused by the fact that Marescotti himself wrote the preface to the volume (there is no dedication)—even though this was not uncommon in the case of "noble" authors who wished to give the dignified appearance of reticence.

Or maybe Dino captured something that Peri felt himself, that once these songs were published, he somehow lost possession of them. The anxieties are typical of print culture: publishing one's work was in principle good for one's reputation (and perhaps even one's income), but the material thus published moved outside the author's control and entered common currency. This was even more of an issue for music because its notation was both imprecise and incomplete in terms of the performance issues that brought it to full effect.[181] Not for nothing did Marescotti suggest in his preface that so far as he had been told, one really needed to hear these songs performed in the flesh as played and sung by the composer to gain a better appreciation of their perfection (*ma per quel ch'io odo sarebbe necessario sentirle sonare e cantare da lui medesimo per conoscere maggiormente la lor perfezzione*). When Ottaviano Lotti, the Medici Resident in London, received a copy of Peri's *Le varie musiche* in 1612, he thought it a very noteworthy gift but he could not report that hearing the music had brought pleasure, because it needed study and because the only one of the English court's musicians who could sing it was currently away in the country. He said, however, that it would certainly be heard and would bring pleasure at some point.[182]

It was impossible for musical notation to capture what an unknown poet praised as Peri's singing to the lute in the manner of a new Orpheus, a worthy heir of David, and one able to make heard on earth the angelic harmonies of heaven (see the anonymous sonnet in Appendix D). The unstated corollary of Marescotti's comment was that although the songs might not look much on the page, there was more in them to meet the ear than the eye. While the remark might seem defensive of the music's apparent simplicity, it was also, of

---

181. Carter, "Printing the 'New Music'."

182. Lotti to an unidentified recipient, 4 October 1612 (ASF, Mediceo del Principato 4190, fol. 54v), given in Kirkendale, *Emilio de' Cavalieri*, 441: *Il libro di musiche del Signor Jacopo Peri è un regalo segnalatissimo, ma perché gli ha bisogno di studio per noi altri di qua, et anche s'è incontrato che quel solo servitore di Sua Altezza che può cantarlo è in campagna, non si può dire non si essendo sentito egli è piaciuto, ma si sentirà et piacerà al certo.* The *solo servitore* was probably Angelo Notari, a Paduan singer who was in the service of Prince Henry of England from 1610 or 1611, and who published his *Prime musiche nuove* in 1613 (London: William Hole).

course, a cunning marketing tool if one additional function of *Le varie musiche* was to encourage consumers somehow to "buy" a performance by Peri himself, or to take lessons from him so that a proper performance might be achieved.

But however distant the image of Peri's songs in print might have been from their performance, clearly that image was still carefully crafted. The book offers an appropriate, and typical, mix of lyrical–declamatory settings (for the sonnets and poetic madrigals) with tuneful triple-time arias (for the strophic canzonettas), and two settings of devout spiritual madrigals at the end. Some of them clearly reflected work done specifically at court—the three-voice settings probably for the *concerto de' castrati*, or "Se tu parti da me, Fillide amata" deriving from theatrical music he wrote in 1608—while others could equally have served some purpose there: we have already suggested their utility for Peri's relations with the younger Medici princesses and with Archduchess Maria Magdalena. The poets are mostly contemporary Florentines (Buonarroti *il giovane*, Cini, Rinuccini) or those associated with the court (Chiabrera, Guarini); the exception is a poem ("Ho visto al mio dolore") by Alessandro Striggio (the younger) that Peri may have received by way of his connections with Ferdinando Gonzaga.[183] More surprising, however, is the presence of no fewer than four settings of sonnets by Petrarch. This, too, suggests Peri's local horizons: Petrarch was, after all, the quintessential Tuscan poet and still a subject of regular discussion in Florentine academies. But it also gives *Le varie musiche* a surprisingly literary and also serious flavor that makes it stand apart from most other such collections of the time.

Moreover, there appears to be another underlying agenda here. Peri's through-composed setting of Petrarch's "Tutto 'l dì piango, e poi la notte quando" displays a fine, understated sensibility toward the poetry, a strong sense of line, a careful manipulation of short- and long-range harmonic processes, and a certain melancholic frame of mind that may be characteristic of

---

183. Striggio's poem was published in Pietro Petracci (ed.), *Ghilranda* [sic] *dell'Aurora: scelta di madrigali de' più famosi autori di questo secolo* (Venice: Bernardo Giunti and G. B. Ciotti, 1609), although Peri received it sooner, given that his setting was first published in Girolamo Montesardo's *L'allegre notti di Fiorenza*, which appeared at the very beginning of 1608. It is possible that this setting is the "madrigal" that Peri sent to Ferdinando Gonzaga on 11 August 1607 (Letter 6), although the context and content of that letter suggests that the setting sent then was to poetry by Ferdinando himself.

Peri himself or may just be a pose. Peri seems to draw here on the songs of Sigismondo d'India, a visitor to Florence who also proclaimed noble status (as a *nobile palermitano*) on his title pages around this time. One might further detect in Peri's music a kind of precise accounting of the words in ways to match the careful way he kept his own financial records. In the case of "Tutto 'l dì piango," however, it is also worth focusing on the differences with Giulio Caccini's very different setting of the same text in his second book of songs, *Nuove musiche e nuova maniera di scriverle* (1614).

As he did with many Florentine musicians, we have seen, Ferdinando Gonzaga also asked Caccini for his songs: on 1 May 1606, Caccini sent a setting of "I tuoi capelli, o Filli, in una cistula" (an old text by Jacopo Sanazzaro), which he says Ferdinando had asked him to put to music using an unusual range of notes (*che mi comandò che io facesse in musica di corde non ordinarie*), perhaps a reference to the style that Caccini displayed in two pieces in his 1614 volume with an extraordinary range from low bass to high tenor. As for "I tuoi capelli" and a *madrigaletto* he also sent at the same time, he told the cardinal that if they were sung with the emotion required by the words and by Caccini's style, then they would be pleasing (*le quali musiche se saranno cantate con quello affetto che ricercano le parole et insieme il mio stile, credo che potranno essere di qualche gusto a Vostra Altezza com'io desidererei*).[184] On 5 October 1609, Caccini also sent an unspecified sonnet setting.[185] This was a poetic form unusual for him, but the idea may have been triggered precisely by the four sonnet settings in Peri's *Le varie musiche* published that same year. There are no sonnets in Caccini's first collection of songs, *Le nuove musiche* (1602), but two in his second volume of 1614, "Tutto 'l dì piango, e poi la notte quando" and "Io che l'età solea viver nel fango" (the latter text by Giovanni Della Casa); of course, we do not know if either was the one sent to Mantua in 1609. "Io che l'età solea" is one of the two wide-ranging bass–tenor songs. In "Tutto 'l dì piango," however, the *corde non ordinarie*, as it were, are represented by the extraordinarily detailed level of vocal ornamentation notated in the score.

The contrast with Peri's setting could not be greater. Caccini opts for a set of strophic variations (broadly speaking, the same musical framework for the

---

184. Caccini's 1606 letter (Mantua, Archivio di Stato, Autografi 6, fol. 4) is given in Alessandro Ademollo, *La bell'Adriana*, 63.

185. Mantua, Archivio di Stato, Autografi 6, fol. 6, given in ibid., 63–64.

sonnet's two quatrains and two tercets) with a simpler harmonic structure but a more flamboyant, highly virtuosic vocal line rich in the embellishments and ornamentation typical of what Caccini claimed was his new singing technique. Peri was certainly familiar with this kind of florid writing: we see it in his "Dunque fra torbid'onde" for the 1589 *intermedi*. But that is the last time that such writing appears in Peri's published output. In effect, Caccini represents the singer as singer, fully engaging with the craft of vocal technique—even if the result was meant to sound effortless in performance— whereas Peri is the singer as poet. Or to put the same point in terms more consonant with the broader themes of the present book, Caccini's setting is artisanal—which is not to say it is not of high quality—whereas Peri's is self-consciously artistic.[186]

While Caccini's life was primarily grounded in music with some lesser involvement in commerce, Peri's, it seems, was the reverse, and with business interests much more in keeping with Florence's traditional industries. Certainly he worked in those industries, but never as a *lavoratore* and most often as an investor. One can view his musical publications, and their contents, in a similar light, as projecting a particular *bella figura*, both as a matter of personal pride—such as one also finds in the *ricordi* in the ledgers—and in order to sustain a reputation and honor that would aid him in other spheres. However, this does not prevent his songs from also being seen as some kind of personal reflection on, and response to, his worldly and spiritual environments. Just as one might hear Peri's singing voice in a setting such as "O miei giorni fugaci," the first of the two spiritual madrigals in *Le varie musiche*, one can also, perhaps, sense in it the deep religious feelings we have traced elsewhere in his life. He would probably have been proud to know that even in the 1650s, other of his songs were still being sung to devotional texts in the *lauda* tradition, bringing things back full circle to his first musical position in Florence.[187]

---

186. For the two settings, see Peri, *"Le varie musiche" and Other Songs*, ed. Carter, 5–8; Caccini, *Nuove musiche e nuova maniera di scriverle*, ed. Hitchcock, 51–59. Although Caccini's setting—his only one of Petrarch—was published later than Peri's, this is no strong indication of which came first, but clearly one was written in competition with the other. For a discussion of them in a slightly different context (how to represent the lyric "I"), but with similar conclusions, see Carter, "*Tutto 'l dì piango . . .*"

187. Kirkendale, *Court Musicians*, 241, notes that the collection *Laude e canzoni spirituali* (Rome: Ignatio de' Lazzeri, 1654) contains spiritual texts associated, it seems, with Peri's pro-

Peri certainly gained some reputation from his music. In 1605 Monteverdi included him (and Caccini) among the composers associated with his new *seconda pratica*—although he grouped him with the regular musicians in his list rather than the noble ones—and in 1620 he paid him another compliment, if in a slightly detached way, in connection with the *ballo* that Peri had provided for performance at Mantua.[188] He also clearly knew *Euridice* and made musical references to it in his opera *Orfeo* (1607) even as he sought to outshine it. Peri was included among the celebrated musicians of Florence that the Neapolitan Girolamo Montesardo anthologized in his collection *L'allegre notti di Fiorenza* (1608)—so was Caccini—and other Tuscan composers of the time sought to include music by him in their own printed collections (Piero Benedetti in 1611, and Antonio Brunelli in 1614), in effect claiming his support for their individual musical endeavors.[189] The network spread further: on 28 July 1608 Peri told Ferdinando Gonzaga of writing music for an unnamed *marescial* in Florence (Letter 13), and the

---

logue to *Dafne*, with an aria in *Euridice* (Tirsi's "Nel pur ardor della più bella stella"), and with "Bellissima regina" in *Le varie musiche*.

188. For Monteverdi and the *seconda pratica*, see most recently Carter, "*E in rileggendo poi le proprie note.*" For his letter to Alessandro Striggio of 10 May 1620, see Monteverdi, *Lettere*, ed. Lax, 105–7; Monteverdi, *The Letters*, trans. Stevens, 212–13. He commends the Mantuan court's decision to drop *Arianna* and *Adone*, and to perform just Peri's *ballo*: *Che puoi abbi datto occasione al Signor Zazzarini che anch'egli si possa mostrare servitore di merito de la grazia di Sua Altezza Serenissima* [= Duchess Caterina], *ha tutti li requesiti che Ella mi scrive, non tanto, ma la dolce e virtuosa emulazione darà occasione maggiore di far altra cosa a li altri per mettersi in grazia, ché senza la cognizione de la via non si può arivare a posto determinato.* Monteverdi's remarks here on Peri—that he has all the requisites that Striggio has described, and that "sweet and virtuous emulation" of his example will inspire others to even greater things—seem very carefully nuanced, avoiding any direct comment on his actual music.

189. Benedetti sang in the 1608 Mantuan wedding festivities, and Ferdinando Gonzaga tried to recruit him into his service in the second half of 1610 but he refused, partly, he claimed, because he had a large household to support, but also because he felt that his service in 1608 had not properly been recognized; see his letters to Ferdinando Gonzaga of 4 and 18 September and 16 October 1610 in Mantua, Archivio di Stato, Archivio Gonzaga 1127, fols. 573, 585, 597. His 1611 volume also includes music by Marco da Gagliano. By 1618 he was a chaplain to the Medici court, and in 1630 he was made a canon of S. Lorenzo. Brunelli was *maestro di cappella* at the Duomo of S. Miniato (near Pisa), then of Prato, ending up (in March 1613) as *maestro* for the Cavalieri di Santo Stefano in Pisa; he also seems to have been closely associated with Caccini, who appears, in addition to Peri, in his 1614 volume (as do Lorenzo Allegri and Vincenzo Calestani).

song in the Brunelli collection ("O dell'alto Appenin, figlio sovrano," to a
text by Ferdinando Saracinelli) was written in honor of the wedding of one
Conte Francesco Torelli. What, if anything, the count appreciated in the
music thus presented to him remains an interesting question, but presumably at least part of it was the sense of what it meant to be a cultivated *nobil
fiorentino.*

4

Last Years, Death, and the End of the Line

Peri must have faced his final years with considerable equanimity. Music was not going to figure much in them, given that he was too old to perform, and probably even more disinclined to compose (see the list of works in Appendix C). He also ran up against typical rivalries among the court musicians, resulting in the disputes over *La regina Sant'Orsola* in 1624–25 and what appears to have been a feud between Francesca Caccini and the poet Andrea Salvadori that led to the dropping of the opera proposed for the forthcoming wedding of Margherita de' Medici and Odoardo Farnese, *Iole ed Ercole* (for which Peri seems to have composed a recitative lament for Iole).[1] The *sacre rappresentazioni*—plays on religious themes—performed at court and in the Compagnia dell'Arcangelo Raffaello were part of a trend in the 1620s during the regency of Grand Duchess Christine and Archduchess Maria Magdalena: we have seen Salvadori claim that the glory of Florence was enhanced by this move away from the vain fables of the Gentiles typical of early opera in favor of representing true and holy Christian acts, bringing greater profit and delight (citing Horace; *di trattare con più utile, e diletto, lasciate le vane favole de*

---

1. Kirkendale, *Court Musicians*, 324–26.

Gentili, le vere, e sacre azzioni Cristiane).[2] Peri's musical contributions to them (often in collaboration with Marco da Gagliano's brother, Giovanni Battista) were generally in connection with singers trained by him, including his son Alfonso. He wrote some other occasional pieces for court entertainments probably in his trademark recitative—to be sung by the Mantuan tenor Francesco Campagnolo (who sang in the performance of *Euridice* in Bologna in 1616)—and also for private patrons (e.g., Don Pietro de' Medici in Livorno). Peri's last commission, so far as we know, was to provide the music for the role of Clori (who becomes Flora) in Marco da Gagliano's opera *Flora, o vero Il natal de' fiori* (to a libretto by Salvadori), performed in the Uffizi Theatre on 14 October 1628 as part of the Medici–Farnese wedding festivities.[3]

Although he assiduously collected his salary as a court musician, it was looking more and more like an honorarium. But he also had a good job at the Arte della Lana that required actual work from him, and he was a property owner of some substance, certainly ranking him solidly in the middling class. At home he was served (since 1621) by two female servants and surrounded by a large family, undoubtedly much enlivened by two young daughters and two teenage sons, and it surely gave him considerable satisfaction that of his adult sons, one was an intimate member of Galileo's circle, another a priest, a third perhaps a budding musician, and a fourth getting established in business, and that four of his daughters were comfortably settled in local convents of some prestige. Moreover, in the public sphere he was a frequent officeholder and had unquestionable noble status. And he must have been something of a presence on the local scene to have become one of the targets of Francesco Ruspoli, popular in the tavern life of the city for delivering bitingly satirical and salacious sonnets against prominent men about town (most of which he destroyed before he died).

Peri's social standing emerges clearly out of the bureaucratic impersonality of a census the grand-ducal government made of the city's households and population in 1632, just a year before his death. In that document, organized street by street, his house was one of thirty-two in Via dei Fossi. As on any

<hr/>

2. Andrea Salvadori, preface to *La regina Sant'Orsola, recitata in musica nel teatro del Serenissimo Gran Duca di Toscana* (Florence: Pietro Ceconcelli, 1625).

3. Marco da Gagliano scrupulously acknowledged Peri's contribution in his edition of the opera (Florence: Zanobi Pignoni, 1628) both in the prefatory materials and in the score itself. One wonders whether Peri was again involved also because one of his pupils (or perhaps Angelica Furini?) sang the role.

street in Florence at the time, many of his neighbors were modest artisans and people at lower levels in the service sector, although the list also included a *notaio* and an official (*cancelliere*) of the Arte dei Cuoiai, as well as a number of widows of unknown status. But of the twelve households at his end of the street, nine had, all together, twenty-six servants, seven of them male. And amid all the statistical information in this official document written out in cursive, his name stands out from the others in roman uppercase letters: *Jacopo Peri, musico eccellentissimo.*[4]

Peri's was a large house, but it had to accommodate an exceptionally large family. From the inventory made just after Peri's death and another done eight years later, we know that it had some twenty-four spaces, going from the basement probably through three stories to a terrace. About one-fourth of them were service and storage rooms, including the kitchen. The living rooms (in the somewhat ambivalent terminology of the time) consisted of four *sale*, six *camere* plus two *anticamere*, three *stanze*, and a *scrittoio*, in addition to an *oratorio* listed in the later inventory. The principal bedroom had a bed with columns and silk hangings and spread, and one of the *sale* had what were then fashionable leather hangings. There were a good number of pictures (none with attributions or dimensions) both in the house in Florence and in the villa in Pian di Ripoli: half represented religious subjects—two Madonnas, St. John the Baptist, St. Margaret, St. Jerome, the Good Samaritan, the Annunciation, the Nativity, the Crucifixion—and the others included four landscapes, a view of the world (*il circuito della terra in tela*), two portraits of Peri (one *quando era giovane*), another of his cousin Fra Cesare, and four of unnamed *donne*, perhaps including Peri's wives and daughters (the later inventory lists a portrait of his wife Alessandra). In addition there were those family items mentioned in Chapter 1: the painted Peri family tree that he commissioned, the three panels with his arms crossed with those of his wives, and the other items bearing the Peri coat of arms (a bed, a clothes stand, leather door hangings, plates). The only musical item mentioned in the earlier inventory is what it first described as a harpsichord (*buon accordo*), then corrected to a spinet attached to its case (*anzi una spinetta attaccata alla cassa*). There is no reference here to printed or manuscript music—we shall see one later—but this inventory does not include any books at all, suggesting that such material was ignored for present purposes. For the rest, how-

4. Florence, Biblioteca Nazionale Centrale, Magliabechiana EB 15.2 (*Descrizione de' fuochi et delle persone della città di Firenze . . . , 1632*).

ever, Peri must have found himself comfortably settled in this large and fashionably furnished home.[5]

His health was another matter. To judge from scattered comments here and there in the letters, Peri had always suffered problems with it. As early as 1584 Grand Duke Francesco described him as "not very robust." In 1600, at the age of thirty-nine, Peri complained about his weakened condition, with headaches and catarrh, and about not having his former health (Appendix B: Letter 2). In 1603 it was reported that he was going deaf, and in 1610 that he was suffering from problems in his head. At the age of fifty, in 1611, he complained about feeling his age (Letter 18). Then in 1614 he suffered the serious collapse resulting from the legal problems with his first *censo*, described in Chapter 2. In 1620, now fifty-nine years old, he wrote that he felt "the weight of years" (Letter 28). Yet he went on, apparently not slowed down. By the late 1620s, however, he was an old man by any reckoning, and still more so considering the life expectancy of the times; at some point he must have begun to think about putting his affairs in order in anticipation of his demise, notwithstanding what must have been the very lively scene in a home crowded with children, some of whom were still quite small.

A Final Reckoning

In 1626, at the age of sixty-five, Peri took the first recorded step toward imposing some order on his accounts in the effort to assure an equitable division

---

5. For the two inventories of the Peri home, see ASF, Magistrato dei Pupilli del Principato 809 (*Atti e sentenzie*, January–March 1633/34), fols. 218–30, made by the Pupilli officials around 19 January 1633/34 in the presence of Alessandra and Dino (fols. 219–26 cover the house in Via dei Fossi, and fols. 227–29 the villa in Pian di Ripoli); and ASF, Capitani di Parte Guelfa, Numeri bianchi 311, fols. 39v–43v, made on the confiscation of Alfonso's property in 1642. The former is patently not a complete inventory: it does not list enough rooms and beds to house Peri's numerous family. It was probably made as a mere formality, since the officials did not assume any role in the administration of the estate. In a signed statement added at the end of the inventory Peri's widow acknowledges that the officials have consigned all the contents of the house to her, and in fact the document does not appear in the several books of official Pupilli inventories but in a miscellany of hundreds of documents dating from the same time, today all bound together. We can assume that, given the occasion, the second inventory is accurate, although in its current state it is very difficult to read; for extracts (also including paintings), see Kirkendale, *Court Musicians*, 387. Here we have used the second inventory to describe the rooms in the house, but our description of the furnishings comes exclusively from the first and is therefore probably incomplete.

of his estate among his sons, perhaps prompted by the irresponsible and expensive behavior of the eldest, Antonio, then just twenty-one. On 1 September Peri inserted in Antonio's account—the source cited earlier for the report
of the wayward life of this son, who had run up a debit balance of *fl*.284—a
long, undated note about his plan to give credit (not cash) allowances to his
sons in order to impose some order on his own accounts of the expenses they
were beginning to incur as they grew up, and also to generate debit–credit
balances for each of them to assure their equitable treatment in the eventual
settlement of his estate:

> and since I find myself short of income and profits, so as not to touch capi-
> tal I therefore assign to the five older sons *sc*.20 a year for each, and with
> this and with their own earnings they should think about clothing them-
> selves each in his own way. And therefore I will debit each one for what I
> will give them, and will credit them every year for the said *sc*.20 . . . [6]

He then went on to open, for the first time, individual accounts in the names
of the four next-oldest of his seven sons—Dino (then twenty years old), Alfonso (seventeen), Niccolò (sixteen), and Francesco (fourteen)—in each of
which he repeated the above explanation; six years later, in 1632, he added
accounts for his two youngest sons, Cosimo and Giulio Cesare, then fifteen
and fourteen years old.[7]

For a man earning close to *fl*.1,000 a year, Peri's lament in 1626 at finding
himself "short of income and profits" sounds a bit hollow. Six years later, in
the last year of his life, the basic expenses for his household of some dozen
persons (for food, wine, fuel, and two full-time servants, plus the clothing
allowances for his sons) added up to little more than half that amount.[8]
Moreover, in his last decade Peri was investing regularly: *fl*.501 for the house
in Via dei Servi and *fl*.300 in government securities invested in 1624; *fl*.200
more for government securities in 1626; *fl*.361 for the house in Borgo Ognis-

6. Ledger B, fol. 38: *e perché mi trovo scarso d'entrate e di guadagni, per non intaccare el capitale, perciò assegno a 5 figliuoli maggiori sc.20 l'anno per uno, e con questo e con i lor guadagni
pensino a vestirsi ogniun di loro a lor modo; e perciò farò debitore ciascuno di quanto li darò e
creditore ogni anno delli detti sc.20 . . .*

7. Ledger B, fols. 38, 39, 47, 48, 49.

8. The accounts for this last year, from September 1632 through August 1633—now kept by
Peri's son Dino with great precision—show itemized household expenditures of £2,740 (Ledger C, fol. 33), to which has to be added the allowance of *fl*.20 for each of the six sons. At this
rate of expenditure, however (and excluding the allowances)—some *fl*.30 per month—one can
see why court musicians earning *fl*.6–9 per month claimed poverty (see Chapter 3).

santi in 1628, plus *fl.*64 for improvements the next year; and no less than *fl.*3,100 between a *censo* and more government securities in the last three years of his life (see Table 2.4)—all this in income-yielding properties or instruments. Yet with seven sons (in 1626) to send on their way in life, and two daughters to be provided with a dowry, he had to think about the patrimony he would soon be leaving them. With such a *numerosa famiglia,* as he wrote in 1630 in thanking Cardinal Francesco Barberini for the benefice awarded to his son Francesco (Letter 33), he claimed not to be in a position to give this one of his six sons the help he needed. But "needed" is the key word here, its meaning dependent on expectations.

This patrimonial concern must have come home to Peri on 8 May 1630 (a Wednesday), when he suddenly suffered a major attack on his health. Ten days later, on 18 May, his son Dino described what happened in a letter sent to his teacher, Galileo Galilei, in Rome (Galileo having just made his ill-fated last trip there with the manuscript of the *Dialogue*):

> I come to give you some good news: my father was dead and now he is revived. See, Your Lordship, if I have reason to rejoice!
>
> Three or four days after you left here, he began to feel sickly. The fever came and sent him to bed without respite. Tuesday night last week he seemed to be better and to have had a bit of rest. And the next morning, given that he had in his heart some monetary business for the Depositeria which pressed him, he gets up very slowly, tells the servant that he is fine, and goes out about his business. After he had finished it, and tired his head for a good while in counting out money, the desire to go to Mass came upon him, and to requite this desire he got down on his knees. But he was not to get much satisfaction, because at around the Elevation of the Host he felt a growing sickness in his stomach, and he decided to get up to go and sit on some bench. At this moment of moving himself comes a sudden fainting spell that makes him fall on the floor, hitting his head so hard that the noise alone makes everyone who was in the church think he was dead. Help and comfort came quickly, and some gentlemen put him in a sedan chair and accompanied him home, where I had just heard from her [the servant] the news of him leaving his bed and the house. And part of me was glad, and part scandalized, and I was angry when I saw him being carried here, sweating, freezing, lacking all strength, and, one might say, completely beyond himself, and, in sum, in such a state that I feared that he might die in my arms before I finished undressing him. His shirt was totally drenched, and he continued to sweat even in the bed itself; he

could hardly form a word, and nothing was found that could revive his spirits.

May Your Lordship judge what trouble and torment I had, in seeing myself deprived of all hope that I would not lose him. Here, to be sure, there was no sign of life for two hours. . . . [9]

Contar di denari and *desio d'una messa*—money and God: both major themes in Peri's life—were foremost in the mind of this sixty-nine-year-old man when confronted with what might have been death.

But he also thought about his family, another theme repeatedly sounded in the accounts. On 15 May—a week after this event—Peri, Florentine noble, sound in reasoning, feeling, sight, hearing, and intellect but infirm of body and lying in bed (*nobil fiorentino, sano, per gratia di Dio, di menti, senso, vedere, udire et intelletto, benché del corpo infermo et nel letto iacente*) dictated his last will and testament to his notary, and called in no fewer than six Carmelites from his parish church of S. Paolo to stand as witnesses.[10] The document sets

9. Galilei, *Le opere*, 14: 100–102 (the styling here follows this edition, as in all subsequent quotations): *Signor Galileo, // vengo a darle una buona nuova: mio padre era morto e hora è resuscitato. Guardi V. S. s'i' ho cagione di rallegrarmi // Tre o quattro giorni dopo ch'Ella si fu partita di qua, cominciò a sentirsi ammalaticcio: venne via la febbre, lo messe nel letto senza lasciarli requie. Martedì notte poi della settimana passata gli parve d'esserne netto e d'haver preso un po' di riposo; e la mattina, perch'egli haveva nel cuore un negotio di denari per la Depositeria, che gli premeva, si leva cheto cheto, dice a una serva ch'egli sta bene, e se ne va fuora intorno a quella sua faccenda. Dopo che l'hebbe spedita, e affaticata la testa per un buon pezzo in quel contar di denari, gli venne desio d'una messa, e per cavarsi questa voglia si messe in ginocchioni; ma non gli fu fatta la gratia di gustarla tutta, perchè intorno al levar del Signore si sentì venir travaglio allo stomaco, e si risolvette a rizzarsi per andar su qualche panca a sedere. In questo muoversi viene uno svenimento repentino che lo precipita in terra con una percossa della testa tanto grande che il rumor solo fece stimarlo per morto a chiunque era in chiesa. Venne subito soccorso e conforto, e alcuni gentilhuomini lo messero in seggiola e l'accompagnorno a casa, dove a punto io intendevo da colei la nuova dell'esser uscito del letto e di casa. E parte mi rallegravo, parte mi scandalizavo; e andavo in collera quand'i' me lo veggo portar avanti sudato, agghiacciato, privo d'ogni forza, e, si può dir, affatto d'intendimento, e in somma in grado tale, ch'io dubitavo che m'havesse a spirar tra le braccia innanzi ch'io finissi di spogliarlo. La camicia era molle fradicia, seguitava pur nel letto medesimo a sudare, non poteva quasi formar parola, non si trovava cosa che gli ravvivassi gli spiriti. // Giudichi V. S. che travaglio e che tormento era il mio, nel vedermi tolta ogni speranza di non l'haver a perdere. Quivi sicuramente: non appariva vita per du' hore.* The letter was written on 18 May, which in 1630 was a Saturday, so the reference to the Tuesday of the preceding week is to 7 May.

10. Peri made a *ricordo* of the testament in Ledger B, fol. 153v; the document itself survives in two copies, one among the miscellaneous collection of family papers (LC 3912, dated 15

out sufficiently complex arrangements to lead one to think that Peri had been studying the situation with much care, perhaps from the very moment he recovered from his collapse a week earlier. In it he left £50 to each of the servants, carefully provided for dowries for his two daughters remaining at home, put an entail (*fedecommesso*) on all his property (imposing inalienability but not primogeniture on it), and named his six sons as "universal heirs" (*eredi universali*)—all standard procedures at the time. But then he went on to anticipate the separation of the brothers, and this led him to a careful survey of the income his various investments yielded (the basis of the discussion in Chapter 2), and accordingly, to the partition of these assets in such a way as to ensure an absolutely equal division of income so that each of his sons would have *fl.*68 annually plus a share of the Peri property. In his preoccupation with income rather than capital value, and in the intricacy and precision of his calculations, the testament reveals what we might call an accountant's mentality. The complexity of the arrangements almost compel any reader of the document to take pencil in hand and work things out on paper—as we have done here in Table 4.1.

With respect to the real estate, if a division were to be effected, Niccolò and Francesco would have the farm at Marciano, Giulio Cesare and Cosimo the one at Ripoli, Alfonso the two rental houses in the city, and Dino the family home in Via dei Fossi. Three particulars of these arrangements, however, call for explanation. First, since the farm at Marciano yielded more than their fair share of the estate's total income, Niccolò and Francesco were to make annual payments to their four brothers to equalize their shares of that income. Second, the home in Via dei Fossi, which made up the bulk of the share of the eldest son, Dino, was rented out not on the market but to his brothers, who continued to live there. Finally, *fl.*80 from the annual yield of the government securities that were to constitute the dowries of the two daughters would go to their maintenance expenses until they married, with the rest to be reinvested in securities to increase their dowries; but if they became nuns, these securities were to be used to pay the usual convent entrance costs, with the rest to be divided among the brothers.[11] And income from the remaining securities was to be used to top up their shares.

May 1630), and the notarial copy in ASF, Notarile moderno 11173, no. 9. Corazzini, in a rare slip, read the date of the will as 15 March and therefore as 1630/31, putting it a year ahead.

11. Later, Niccolò made a *ricordo* summarizing these arrangements; LC 3923, fol. 3v.

Table 4.1. Jacopo Peri's partition of income among his children in 1630 (in florins)

Property	Dino	Alfonso	Niccolò	Francesco	Cosimo	Giulio Cesare	Teresa	Ottavia	TOTAL
Farm at Marciano	23	7	63	63	5½	5½			167
Farm near Bagno a Ripoli					57½	57½			115
Monti in Rome							25	25	50
Monte del Sale	5	5	5	5	5	5	50	35	115
Censi								25	25
House, Borgo Ognissanti		24							24
House, Via dei Servi		32							32
House, Via dei Fossi	40								40
TOTAL	68	68	68	68	68	68	75	85	568

Note: Although Peri mentions the prebend at San Marco Vecchio in the testament, he does not include the income from it in these arrangements; the small profit it yielded after paying the rent was to go to the son who kept the accounts. The income from the house in Via dei Fossi is a hypothetical rent. Peri correctly calculates the total income of the two daughters, Teresa and Ottavia, together but overlooks the discrepancy between them; his elder daughters in convents are excluded from this partition, presumably because they had already been provided for.

Dino's letter to Galileo, quoted above, was written three days after Peri drew up this will, and in it he goes on to say that his father had recovered from whatever it was that had hit him:

... But in fact now he is alive, and in such a state of health that one can call him cured. There was no cut on his head, because to his good fortune in falling he first fell on his behind and then his head, for if he had fallen straight down the poor man would have stayed there forever. The pain he had has passed, and the fever did not worsen, but starting not many days ago it began to decline, and at present there is nothing remaining of it. He has been left with no ill effects, and I am only a little bit frightened because of knowing from the doctors that blows to the head do very great and strange things, such that persons have been found well twenty, thirty, or forty days after a blow, and then they suddenly die.

But in truth, I would never believe this to be such a case. My mind is very calm, and it seems to me that I am revived, too, because it would have fallen to me to take care of everything, and to be always involved in a thousand kinds of problems very alien to my temperament. I have even had to become a lawyer and tire myself with a hundred details in the testament which he wanted to finish. And then there are the continual ups and downs of the mind, and the awareness of being forced, on his leaving us, to set myself up as the father [*babbo*, the familiar Tuscan form] of a large family, when I myself still need to stay with the wards—all this kept me in perpetual torment and anxiety.[12]

---

12. Galilei, *Le opere*, 14: 100–102: *Ma in fatti e' si trova adesso vivo, e in tale stato di salute che si può chiamare franco. Nella testa non ci hebbe rottura, chè la sua minor disgratia volse che nel cadere dessi prima delle natiche in terra e poi della memoria; chè se il colpo veniva a tutto piombo, il poveretto restava quivi per sempre. Il dolore che ci haveva è passato; la febbre ancora non malignò, ma in capo a non molti giorni si messe in declinatione, e di presente non ce n'è più residuo. Non ci è rimasto cattivo segno nessuno, e non mi tiene con un po' di timore se non il sapere da' medici, che le percosse della testa fanno delle stravaganze grandissime, sì che si sien trovate persone star bene venti, 30 e 40 giorni dopo il colpo, e poi morirsene presto presto. / Ma veramente questo non crederei mai che fusse per essere un caso simile. Me ne sto con l'animo assai quieto, e mi par proprio d'esser resuscitato anch'io, perché mi toccava a riparar per tutto, esser sempre in mille sorte di brighe alienissime dal mio genio. M'è bisognato fare insin da legista, e affaticarmi per cento versi intorno al testamento ch'egli ha volsuto finire; e poi la compassione e il sollevamento dell'animo continuo, e quel conoscermi astretto nel suo partirsi da noi a mettermi a far da babbo d'una gran famiglia, quand'i' ho bisogno di star ancor ne' pupilli, mi teneva in perpetuo tormento e batticuore.*

On 8 June Dino wrote again to Galileo to report that after "that very strange incident" (*quello stranissimo accidente*) his father, now out of bed and able to leave the house, "was continually regaining strength and energy" (*e va di continuo prendendo ristoro e vigore*).[13] Peri, in fact, was able to write to Cardinal Francesco Barberini in August (Letter 33)—although his handwriting shows signs of age—to thank the cardinal for his help in securing the benefice for his son Francesco. He also went back to work at the Arte della Lana: in October 1630, just five months after the attack in May, he opened the one surviving waste-book (*stracciafoglio*) that he kept on the job there.

That fall the plague struck Florence, the worst outbreak since the Black Death in 1348; on 19 January 1631, to escape it, Peri took his three youngest sons, along with a servant, to the villa at Ripoli, leaving his wife and the other children quarantined (*serrati*) in the house in Florence; he remained there as long as the Ufficiali di Sanità advised.[14] In June he was chosen for a year's appointment as one of the Decima officials (see Table 1.1). But from the beginning of 1632, entries in Ledger B become less frequent. In August he turned down an appointment as *podestà* at Montevarchi (which would have taken him within a few kilometers of the farms at Castelvecchio, Cicogna, and, only slightly farther away, Marciano). He made his last entry in Ledger B—for payment of a servant—on 5 October, while *in villa;* but there is a yet later entry, dated 18 November, in the *quadernetto* kept for transactions involving the animals on his farms.[15] On 28 December the individual accounts for his two youngest sons were opened, but the hand seems to be his son Dino's, not his.[16]

Four months earlier, on 31 August 1632, Peri did what Dino told Galileo he most feared: he made his reluctant but ever-loyal son *babbo d'una gran famiglia* by turning over to him the full administration of the family's affairs. Hence Dino took up a new ledger—Ledger C: *libro di debitori e creditori tenuto per la famiglia del Signor Jacopo Peri da me, Dino, suo figliuolo*—and he opened the first account in the name of "signor Jacopo Peri, our father, for

---

13. Galilei, *Le opere*, 14: 116–17.
14. Ledger B, fol. 154.
15. Ledger B, fol. 69; LC 3914, fol. 63 (but unpaginated).
16. Ledger B, fol. 71.

the settlement he made to go into effect on the first day of September 1632 as
he has it written down" (*Signor Jacopo Peri, nostro padre, per la risoluzione da
lui fatta e cominciata ad effettuarsi a dì primo di settembre 1632, come per sua
scrittura*).[17] The written convention does not survive, but in a note inserted
into the account opened in the name of his son Francesco, Peri stated his
intention to assign the income from all his properties to his sons, "reserving
for me what I earn personally for my work and for my living from 1 September 1632 on into the future" (*riservatomi quel ch'io guadagno con la persona
per mio servizio e per mio vivere, dal primo di settembre che viene 1632 in là per
l'avvenire*).[18]

The essential elements of this arrangement emerge from Dino's extraordinarily well organized, detailed, and comprehensive accounts. Peri turned all
the income from his investments over to his sons, and they were to administer everything and maintain the household. Since they now had designated
shares of that income, Peri no longer wanted any problems (*io non voglio più
brighe*) over the clothing allowance he had given them six years earlier, and so
he closed out these accounts, adding (on Dino's) "and if it happens that I am
compelled to give them money out of necessity, some more and some less, all
of that for which they are debtors is to be calculated into the equal division
among them all, as I affirmed in my testament" (*e se occorrerà per necessità
ch'io sia forzato a darli de' quattrini a chi più e a chi meno, tutto quello che saranno debitori devino stare a calculo e pareggiarsi fra di loro sì come ho fermo nel
mio testamento*).[19] Whichever of the sons served as administrator and kept the
books was to be paid *fl*.30 a year for his labor, with each of the six brothers
contributing *fl*.5. Peri kept what he earned in salaries for himself but agreed to
pay *fl*.12 a month out of his own pocket for the further support of the family.
He specified that during the time his wife and daughters were *in villa* this
allowance was to be divided into two parts: *fl*.10 for their support, and *fl*.2 for
the sons remaining in town. Finally, he agreed to pay *fl*.10 a year as a rent
charge (*pigione*)—presumably his contribution to household expenses. After paying a total of *fl*.154 for his family's maintenance out of the *fl*.264 he
was earning from salaries at that time, Peri was left with *fl*.110 for his personal expenses. With these arrangements Peri hoped to set up a centralized

17. Ledger C, fol. 1.
18. Ledger B, fol. 65.
19. Ledger B, fol. 39 (Dino's account); see also fol. 65 (Francesco's account).

accounting control over income and expenditures to assure an equitable division of it among his heirs.

What Peri did here was, in effect, to set up what one would call a trust—an entirely personal arrangement made through an informal written convention that had, however, no legal personality. Peri assigned to this trust all of his assets, including the family residence, and in addition agreed to make an annual contribution to its operation. Its beneficiaries were his wife and children. The trust paid an accountant (one of the children) to manage its affairs and deal with the expenses of running the household. Since Peri himself did not number among the beneficiaries but lived with them in the same house, he paid an annual rent to the trust for the added expenses related to his presence—in effect, a fee for living in his own house with his own family. These arrangements reveal, yet again, something of an accountant's detachment and instinct to impose order on the matter at hand. But whatever he thought about how to bring all this under accounting control, he was wise to turn this task over to his son Dino, as we shall see.

When Peri thus withdrew from looking after his assets—and perhaps from running his household—he was a very old man in the eyes of his contemporaries. Yet the documents reveal a hand that is still strong. Indeed, he did not retire altogether but remained hard at work on the job as comptroller at the Arte della Lana. The *stracciafoglio*—the one account book that survives from his administration—dates from these last years (1630–33) and documents just how much work was involved, and we have Dino's testimony for the apparatus of account books he had to return to the guild after his father's death (see Chapter 2). Moreover, there were personal matters to attend to. In the very first entry on the initial account in Ledger C opened in Peri's name, Dino notes that oversight of his father's waste-book of petty expenditures for various things left in the home (*quadernuccio delle speserelle per diverse robe lasciate alla casa non comprese nell'obligo della sua risolutione*) was excluded from the responsibilities imposed on him by the settlement. Unfortunately, this *quadernuccio* does not survive; but since Peri used his account at the guild also as a cash account for personal expenditures—normal practice at the time for businessmen with respect to their business accounts—the *stracciafoglio* records some of the things he bought for himself during the last two years of his life: a hat not otherwise described (*fl.2*) and two more of felt (*fl.2. 4s.*); hosiery (*calzette; fl.2. £5*); two pairs of footwear (£8.10s.); clothes made of camlet (*casacca, calzone e maniche di ciambelotto; fl.2 £6.6s.8d.*);

chestnut-colored silk for a suit to wear *in villa* (*vestito da villa*) that cost him *fl*.1 £4 to have made; chestnut-colored taffeta for his laces (*legacci*; £2); two small silver salt cellars (£4.8s.4d.); a Peri family tree done by the painter Alberto di Bartolomeo (*fl*.1 £2); his share (£4.2s.4d.) of the cost of a banquet held at Fiesole on 13 March 1632; and various things for his house—horsehair for his mattress, pillows for a new bed, white and black silk fringes for a new kitchen, and canvas for a new armoire.[20] And all this time, for almost three years through to the fall of 1633, the plague was raging in the city, eventually taking the lives of perhaps one-tenth of the population.

By January 1633 Peri may have shifted more responsibilities of his job at the Arte della Lana to his assistant, Domenico Catastini, since he raised Catastini's salary from *fl*.5 (where it had been at least since 1630) to *fl*.6½ a month, with the increase coming out of his own pocket.[21] In April he made his last general balance of the activity in the cashbox over the preceding fifteen months. On 8 June he made his last entry in the *stracciafoglio*, registering a debit on the account of the *sotto camerlengo* for cash consigned to him by Catastini, the cashier (the few subsequent closing entries are in a different hand, probably that of Dino). Meanwhile, during this last year of his life Peri took on the part-time services of a third female servant (the family had long had two), calling back a woman who had worked for him some ten years earlier. Down to August 1633, when Dino closed his father's accounts at the time of his death, this woman was paid for occasional service (*aiuto di servitù in più volte circa un anno*), perhaps to assist an elderly if not also ailing man.[22]

Peri died on 10 August 1633—maybe from old age, maybe from the plague—and he was buried three days later, on 13 August, in S. Maria Novella.[23] In his

20. These expenditures appear on his personal account in the *stracciafoglio*; LC 3915, fol. 1 et seq.

21. LC 3915, fols. 3, 8, 15, 18, 30, 36, 54, 58 (Catastini's account in the *stracciafoglio*).

22. Ledger C, fol. 32; over the course of a year, she was paid for about six months of work.

23. Corazzini, "Jacopo Peri e la sua famiglia," 59 n. 3, cites the reference in the city's *Libro dei morti* for the date of Peri's death as 12 August, but this is probably when his funeral took place, before his burial the next day; see ASF, Decima granducale 1447 (*giustificazioni*), no. 554 (and Corazzini, "Jacopo Peri e la sua famiglia," 59 n. 8). We now have his son Dino's word that his father died on 10 August: in Ledger D, fol. 67, on an account opened for income from Peri's holdings in the *monti* of Rome, Dino made a debit entry for the interest paid down to his father's death on that specific day (*resto di frutti maturi di detti dieci luoghi sino al dì della morte di nostro padre seguita a dì 10 d'agosto 1633*). This entry is discussed further below. The

testament of 1630 he expressed the wish that he be laid out flat on the floor there—at the most with no more than a rug under him, warning that any other arrangement would weigh heavily on the conscience of his wife and children, this being his will and desire (*che sia messo in chiesa in piana terra, et al più con un tappeto sotto il suo corpo, altrimenti facendo aggrava la conscienza di sua moglie e figli perché questa è la sua volontà e il suo desiderio*)—and that the church priests sing the usual Requiem and Office of the Dead according to custom, and say twenty low Masses (*cantare da padre del detto convento la messa grande de' morti con l'offitio secondo l'uso et dire venti messe piane di requiem da celebrarsi parte di loro all'altare privelegiata*). He was to be interred in the Monaldi family tomb along with the deceased children of his third marriage, and a hundred Masses were to be said in his memory. The accounts, now continued by Dino, document some of the funeral expenses: 13*s*.4*d*. for the certificate from the health authorities permitting his burial, £4 for washing and dressing his body, *fl*.75 for wax (*cere per il suo corpo*), *fl*.100 £5.6*s*.4*d*. for 54 meters (92½ *braccia*) of black twill plus £10.3*s*.4*d*. for working this cloth, £33.15*s*.4*d*. to the friars for the funeral possession, £8 for three gravediggers (*becchini*).[24] Nine days later, on Sunday 21 August, the members of the Compagnia dell'Arcangelo Raffaello said (*si disse*) the Office of the Dead for the soul of *nostro fratello et benefattore*.[25]

Once or twice on entering a *ricordo* of the death of someone in his immediate family, Peri thought about a family tomb, perhaps a chapel, but he

plague raged from July 1632 to September 1633; Corradi, *Annali delle epidemie occorse in Italia*, 2: 65.

24. LC 3913 (book of receipts), fols. 74–74v; Ledger D, fol. 35 and Journal D, fols. 124–25 (account of funeral expenses).

25. ASF, Compagnie religiose soppresse da Pietro Leopoldo A CXLVII, 162/23 (*ricordanze*), fol. 61 (mistranscribed as *si desse* in Kirkendale, *Court Musicians*, 232); the same was done for Jacopo Cicognini, the librettist of *Adone*, on 30 October (ASF, Compagnie religiose soppresse da Pietro Leopoldo A CXLVII, 162/23, fol. 62v). The members of the Compagnia dell'Arcangelo Raffaello would either say (*si disse*) or, less often, sing (*si cantò*—in chant, one assumes) an Office of the Dead for each of its members when possible during its regular Sunday morning or Wednesday evening meetings: the Office for Peri's son Antonio (d. 22 March 1627) was sung on 28 March 1627; ibid., 162/22, fol. 143. We shall see other examples later in this chapter. Singing rather than saying the Office might imply some special respect (presumably Peri was there for Antonio's service), or conversely, some request for simplicity (Peri's own Office was said), though this is not always clear. However, the wording *fratello et benefattore* (applied to Peri but not to his sons) does suggest some kind of honor.

never got around to doing anything about it, nor even to providing grave markers, so far as we know. We have already recounted how, in burying so many—between wives and children—he moved from one church to another, early on abandoning the church of the ancestors who testified to the nobility of which he was so proud. The family tomb of his third wife gave him, finally, a place he could settle on without further concern. The Monaldi had had a prominent monument in the choir of S. Maria Novella, but with the destruction of the rood screen (*tramezzo*) as a result of the Counter-Reformation reforms, it no longer existed at the time Peri began using the family's burial site; today all that remains of the Monaldi's presence in the church is a simple burial slab in the floor inscribed to an earlier member of the family and deco-

FIGURE 4.1. The modern plaque in S. Maria Novella, Florence, commemorating Jacopo Peri. (Photo: Silvia Cosi.)

FIGURE 4.2. The modern plaque on the Palazzo Corsi (Via Tornabuoni, on the north side facing Via Corsi) commemorating the performance of *Dafne* in Jacopo Corsi's *vicine case* (nearby houses). (Photo: Silvia Cosi.)

rated with a heraldic shield—left, however, completely blank.[26] Not even a family coat of arms marks the burial site of Peri, his wife, and their many children, while the modern plaque (in the floor of the nave before the left transept, under the organ) is only approximately located in the general area of his burial site (see Figure 4.1). Nor is Peri well served by the only other public recognition of him in this city of commemorative plaques: the one noting the gatherings promoted by Jacopo Corsi that led to the first performance of *Dafne* (with an incorrect date) is placed on the palace that Jacopo Corsi's brother, Bardo, did not buy until 1608 (see Figure 4.2).

26. In his *Historia delle famiglie della città di Firenze e della nobiltà de' fiorentini*, Piero Monaldi, who must have seen the original monument, calls it a *magnifico sepolcro*, destroyed with the elimination of the rood screen (*tramezzo*) and replaced by a tomb slab in the floor; ASF, Manoscritti 423, fols. 336–37. Corazzini, "Jacopo Peri e la sua famiglia," 59–60, describes the destruction of ancient tombs resulting from restoration work on the church in his own time.

A Widow and Her Sons

At Peri's death the Magistrato dei Pupilli stepped in as usual to oversee the interests of the minors of the family in the execution of his testament. This magistracy, notwithstanding a rich archive that goes back to its foundation at the end of the fourteenth century, has never been studied in detail, but the record of its dealings with the Peri family testify to the seriousness with which it took its charge.[27] When the officials met on 12 November 1633 they recognized Peri's widow, Alessandra, as *tutrice* of the children but without the responsibility for the administration of the estate, which instead was assumed by Dino, the eldest son, and they identified the four heirs not yet eighteen years old for whom they were responsible—Cosimo (seventeen), Giulio Cesare (sixteen), Teresa (thirteen) and Ottavia (twelve), determining their age not, as we do, by the years completed but by the year they were in. They also decided to send a staff member to the Peri house to make an inventory of the entire patrimony (described above). On 9 December 1633 the Pupilli officials noted that the two girls were sent off *in osservanza* at the convent of S. Caterina di Siena and that the usual fees had been paid. On 13 April 1635 they went to the Peri home to assure themselves that Teresa's decision to become a nun had been made freely by her, and to learn what convent she intended to join (by this time she and her sister were at the convent *Il Portico* on the road to Galuzzo). On 14 September Dino took Teresa, along with their mother, Ottavia, and a servant, off to Prato to see her sisters in the convent there, traveling in a coach-and-four put at their disposal by the grand duke's son Don Lorenzo; Teresa took the habit two weeks later at *Il Portico*. Since this decision affected the execution of Peri's will, the Pupilli officials subsequently verified the observance of its provisions regarding the girls. Then at three meetings in November of the following year they similarly followed Ottavia's decision to become a nun. Finally, on 4 March 1637 they noted the earlier deaths of the two youngest uncles, and hence the termination of their tutelage. They had had no reason to interfere in the administration of the estate, for the trust had remained intact, administered by Dino and unchallenged by any of the brothers.[28]

---

27. A notable exception is Giulia Calvi's study of the Magistrato dei Pupilli's policy toward the remarriage of widows with children, "Reconstructing the Family."

28. ASF, Magistrato dei Pupilli del Principato 46 (*deliberazioni e partiti*, 1632–34), fol. 314; 47 (1634–35), fol. 295; 48 (1636–37), fol. 179v (their last meeting about the Peri

Meanwhile Dino, Peri's eldest living son, had been keeping the accounts of the trust for more than a year (in Ledger C); now, at his father's death, finding himself fully in charge of the patrimony and responsible to his family for it in accordance with Peri's testament, he immediately opened another new ledger, Ledger D, dating all the opening entries 11 August, the day after his father died. Dino took over responsibility for the administration of the estate until his own death just a few years later, in 1640. During that time he filled up Ledger D and opened a new one, Ledger E.

At the time he took over the ledgers Dino was well on his way to a career as a professional mathematician. As we have seen, at the age of ten he went off to study at the Jesuit Collegio dei Nobili at Bologna, thanks to the opportunity that Cardinal Luigi Capponi offered his father and to the cardinal's "generous allowance of several hundreds of *scudi*" (*dispendio di parecchi centinaia di scudi*), as Dino wrote to Galileo on 24 September 1633.[29] He went on to take a degree in jurisprudence at the University of Pisa in 1628, the event that induced his proud father to make an exception to the equal-handed treatment with which he had planned to handle his sons' clothing allowances. Dino, however, had no interest in law: he found it alien to his nature (*me ne trovo alieno*)—as he wrote in a long *ricordo* entered in Journal D many years later, on 4 April 1636—and he never practiced it.[30] He enrolled in the Collegio degli Avvocati (after his father's death) not for professional reasons but only because, given the entrance requirements, it was the surest way he could think of to establish a formal recognition of his and his family's nobility (as we have seen). Instead, as he wrote in the 1636 *ricordo*, when he was seventeen he "tasted the poison of all this chit-chat about geometry and the free pursuit of philosophic truth" (*assaporai il veleno di tutte le ciancie dico la geometria e la libera verità filosofica*). Somewhere along the line he got to know Galileo, probably at the university in Pisa but perhaps even earlier through his father, who was just three years older (Galileo was born in 1564) and who almost certainly knew Vincenzo Galilei (Galileo's father, who died in 1591), if only by way of Jacopo Corsi. By 1627, while Dino was still studying

---

estate). For the inventory, see n. 5 above. Teresa's profession is recorded in Journal D, fols. 79, 89v, 92.

29. Galilei, *Le opere*, 15: 278.

30. Journal D, fols. 106–15. Compare also his comment to Galileo (in his letter of 18 May 1630) about having to tire himself over Peri's testament.

law at the university, he had entered into the spirited circle of young scholars bound by close friendship in their dedication to the great mathematician.[31] Galileo's correspondence includes a number of letters from Dino as well as many references to him in other letters, and this material, along with the *ricordi*, provides us with much biographical information about him.[32]

In the spring and early summer of 1633, while Galileo's clash with the papacy was coming to a head, Dino was in residence in the villa at Montughi of Cardinal Luigi Capponi, his old patron, where he assisted the cardinal in his reading of Galileo's work, and on 4 June he wrote to Galileo to tell him how much the cardinal appreciated it. He had enough status as a scholar to be included among the mathematicians the local inquisitor summoned on 27 August, just two weeks after the death of his father, for a reading of the Inquisition's sentence against Galileo. On 26 November 1635 Dino wrote to his teacher, now under house arrest in Arcetri, profusely expressing his willingness to accompany this "superhuman intellect" (*sovr'humano intelletto*) in "accumulating further riches in research and new trophies meriting immortality" (*accumular nuove ricchezze di speculationi e nuovi trofei per l'immortalità*). Meanwhile Galileo, who even in confinement did not lose his influence in placing his students in university posts throughout Italy, interested himself in finding one for Dino; it was on his recommendation that on 22 January 1636 Grand Duke Ferdinando II named Dino, then just thirty years old, to the chair of mathematics at the University of Pisa, with an annual stipend of sc.250. On 12 May the rector of the university reported to Galileo the great success with which Dino had begun his teaching to the glory of Galileo's fame (*Nella virtù e sapere eminente del Signor Dino risplende la gloria e trionfa il nome di V. S. Eccellentissima*), and in a letter Galileo wrote on 18 October he mentions this appointment, referring to Dino as "a noble of this city, mathematician of the university at Pisa, of wondrous intellect and angelic nature, very much respected and loved by me" (*nobile di questa città, matematico dello Studio di Pisa, d'ingegno mirabile, di costumi angelici, da me stimatissimo e amatissimo*). During the next several years numerous correspondents of Galileo make reference to Dino's presence at the side of his former teacher, now confined to Arcetri and going blind, helping him in his relations with the

31. Galilei, *Le opere*, 13: 358, 386.

32. All the letters cited here are in Galilei, *Le opere*, vols. 15–17, and can be found by date or via the index s.v. Dino Peri.

scientific community abroad, and Galileo selected him to be one of the witnesses of the testament he made on 21 August 1638. During these years the grand duke also kept Dino very busy in satisfying his own curiosity about matters scientific: Dino wrote to Galileo on 24 October 1637 that he was *occupatissimo in varie curiosità del Gran Duca*.

With these intellectual interests and his dedication to Galileo, it is hardly surprising that the responsibilities he had to assume when his father set up the trust fell heavily on his shoulders. The *perpetuo tormento e batticuore* that he most feared when his father made his testament became a reality—and a repeated theme in his letters to Galileo. And his life became more complicated with his father's death in August 1633 just at the time the Inquisition issued its condemnation of Galileo and the great scientist began his return from Rome. Writing to Galileo in Siena in autumn 1633 Dino complains about all the problems of settling his father's affairs. On 24 September he recounts how his father's death has caused him the greatest troubles (*m'ha messo in fastidi grandissimi*), given that he has to carry all the weight on his shoulders and is greatly tormented to see himself submerged in horrible matters very alien to his temperament (*mi trovo tutto il peso addosso, con tanto tormento per vedermi immerso in cosacce alienissime dal mio genio*); on 1 October he refers to "so many domestic troubles" (*tanti fastidi domestici*); on 12 November complains about having to leave Florence to go to the Valdichiana to inspect various of the family's *poderi* going to ruin because of the destructive doings of the peasants, adding "I find that my father was too sweet in temperament . . . and it is continual torment to have my brain always embroiled in this hogwash of mercantile trafficking, and to be totally banished from all philosophical speculation" (*Trovo che mio padre era di sangue troppo dolce . . . ed è un tormento continuo, nell'havere il cervello sempre rinvolto in queste porcherie di traffichi mercantili, e bandito affatto da ogni filosofica speculatione*). And on 26 November he reports on how he found his domestic responsibilities far more laborious than he believed they would be (*mia cura domestica . . . veramente piu laboriosa ch'i' non credevo*).

Yet despite these complaints, Dino could not have been more scrupulous and precise in his administration of the trust. The extraordinary care with which he kept its accounts goes somewhat beyond the demands of accountancy and leads one to see them as a reflection of the mind of the mathematician that he was. In this sense they are not only a historical record of the estate but also an expression of the personality of Peri's most notable son. In

Ledger C, before Peri's death, he had already brought all his father's economic activities—as his father never had—under complete and comprehensive accounting control by imposing on it the rigor of formal double-entry. Every transaction is entered twice, on both the debit and credit sides of the ledger, complete with cross-references; there is a cash account and a profit-and-loss account; and the transfer from one ledger to another occasioned the drawing up of a balance—in short, all those features that constitute true double-entry bookkeeping. Moreover, he opened separate accounts not only for specific persons—his father, mother, each of his brothers, each of the servants, each of the workers (*lavoratori*) on the farms—but also (as his father never had) for impersonal things and activities. Thus there are separate accounts for the income (*entrata*) from each of the several properties, and separate accounts for each major category of household expenditures: food (one for *vitto*, another for *camangiare*), wine, oil, fuel, furnishings (*masserizie e arnesi*), salaries of servants, and a "general" account (*spese generali*) to take in everything else.[33] Each servant, for example, has a separate account opened in her name: it is debited for cash payments made to her (with cross-reference to the cash account) and credited for what was due to her as salary (with cross-reference as a debit to a salary account, where credits have cross-entries as a loss on the profit–loss account). Expenditures for clothing, not falling into the category of the collective family expenses, are debited instead on the separate accounts of individual members. And to make sure he got everything right from the start, especially with respect to the complicated arrangements of the *censi*, Dino went back over his father's accounts, occasionally leaving traces of the fact by inserting comments in his minute and very neat hand. And he even traveled into the countryside to check things out for himself. Moreover, in addition to imposing accounting order and an articulated organization on economic activity, Dino introduced periodicity, taking stock of these activities at the end of every year—a feature that allows a reading of the ledgers for annual income and expenditures. Finally, he assured the formality of the

---

33. The difference between the two food categories is not altogether clear, but the contents of the two accounts are somewhat distinct. The *vitto* account consists of entries for what would seem to be the basic foods: wheat (along with the costs of its milling and gate duties on bringing it into the city), pulses, salt, pepper, saffron. The *camangiare* account consists of animals and fowl brought into the city for meat, and other things described only generally as *spese minute*, presumably all the other expenses for the table; it is by far the larger of the two accounts.

ledger as an accounting record by entering his own *ricordi* not there but in the accompanying journal (those for Ledgers C and D survive).

The accounts Dino opened in his father's name in Ledger C, covering the last year of Peri's life, encapsulate the quality of his accounting ability. He handles his father with the complete impersonality of an accountant even though the document is, after all, a record kept for the sole purpose of satisfying a single nuclear family. The accounts recording his father's transactions with the trust are opened in the name of *signor* Jacopo Peri. On one such account Dino debits Peri for what he had agreed to pay toward the maintenance of his family—*fl.*12 monthly for general support and *fl.*5 semiannually for his share of the hypothetical rent of the house where they all lived—and credits it for the cash payments Peri made. When his father died, Dino had to separate Peri's affairs from those of the heirs, and he did so (as one might expect) with absolute mathematical accuracy. For instance, since Peri had designated his two daughters as heiresses of the income from the ten *luoghi di monti* in Rome, Dino divided the semiannual payments of the interest due for the period in which Peri died into two parts: one for the amount due Peri from the beginning of the semester, 1 July, to the time of his death on 10 August; the other due the sisters from 11 August for the rest of the semester. Dino does the calculation down to the day, explaining his procedure: he calculates his father's share of the *fl.*25 £2.19s.4d. paid for the first semester along with two-ninths (1⅓ out of six months) of the *fl.*25 £1.9s.8d. paid for the second semester as totaling £217.3s.8d. (off by 0.4528 of a *denaro* as worked out on a modern calculator). Thus he credits the separate account opened only for this income (*frutti di 10 luoghi di monte di Roma*) with this amount and debits it for one payment to Peri's account and two others for each of his two daughters, all three payments accompanied by references to the appropriate cross-entry on the separate accounts of his father and sisters.[34]

It is worth dwelling a bit more on these accounts in Dino's ledgers, for while the technique with which they are kept is his, the ultimate function the accounts were meant to serve was imposed by Peri. The task of the accountant was to administer what we have called the trust for the purpose of distributing its income according to Peri's specifications. In other words, the estate remained intact. So, for example, Dino opened an account in Ledger D for the urban rental properties—the houses in Via dei Servi and Borgo

34. Ledger D, fol. 67. This calculation by Dino confirms the specific day of Peri's death.

Ognissanti—and the income entered on it is transferred not as a credit on the profit–loss account of the trust but as a credit on the account opened in the name of Alfonso, in accordance with Peri's will. On the account for the management of the farms at Marciano, the net income is transferred to the general profit–loss account of the trust, along with income from the other properties. This account is then debited for expenses, and the resulting net income divided into shares for each of the beneficiaries, again according to Peri's testament, with cross-references to the credit side of their individual accounts.

Dino's ledgers, in short, come as close to representing the perfection of double entry, in its rules and professionalism as well as in its intellectual function, as was practiced at the time even in the most sophisticated business circles. While his accounting records are neither innovative nor unique, few of the hundreds and hundreds of private accounts we have down to this time meet this standard; Dino's can stand up against comparison with any ledger one is likely to find in the archives of this city so famous in the history of accounting for the enormous quantity of surviving private account books and for the technical quality of accountancy. His accounts are a far cry from the private ledgers of his father, who was—among other things—a sometime professional accountant.

Nothing very much emerges from Dino's accounts and *ricordi* about any of his brothers except for their deaths. Several of Niccolò's account books survive. He was twenty-three when his father died, and as we have seen, he had started off his career in the wool industry, but there is no further evidence of his employment therein. In 1632 he was appointed—thanks, he wrote, to the recommendation of his father—to a low-paying position (probably as an accountant) in the lower division (3–4 percent funds) in the administration of the Monte delle Graticole, the major fund handling the public debt, and after three years, in 1635, he advanced to the upper division (7 percent funds).[35] Meanwhile, Francesco, the priest, decided that he wanted to dedicate himself to study and make a career in the field of learning (*intende e vuol seguire gli studi et tirarsi avanti nelle scienze con speranza di fare in esse buon profitto*), and since to this end he felt he had to go abroad (*fuora della sua patria*), the trust was modified to give him a fixed annuity. Inas-

---

35. LC 3923, fols. 5–5v, 76v. His starting salary was £25½ a month; he describes the new position in 1635 as *guardiano de' libri*.

much as his and Niccolò's share of the income from the trust was to come almost entirely from the property at Marciano (Table 4.1), the brothers made an agreement in a notarized document of 1634 according to which Niccolò would manage the farm and out of its proceeds pay Francesco *fl.*60 a year.[36] The ledger Niccolò kept for this purpose survives, along with the accompanying income–expenditure journal and day- and record-books. On 1 July 1637 Dino made a note in Journal D that he was handing over to Niccolò most of the future accounting responsibility of the trust; perhaps the burdens he so often complained about to Galileo had finally become too much.[37] But when he opened Ledger E, Dino added to the incipit a note that although the ledger was to be kept by Niccolò, the latter had been ill all through the summer of 1637 and died on 17 November.

Niccolò was the fourth brother to die in the course of just two years, from October 1635 to November 1637. Giulio Cesare died on 4 October 1635 at the age of seventeen;[38] Francesco, the priest, several weeks later, on 29 November 1635;[39] Cosimo nine months later, on 21 August 1636;[40] Niccolò at the end of the next year.[41] All of them were honored with an Office of the Dead in the

36. LC 3923, fol. 4; a copy of the agreement, dated 20 September 1634, is in LC 3912, where Francesco's motivation for it is cited.

37. Journal D, fol. 124.

38. Journal D, fols. 97–98 (death from complications, described at great length, from an injury to the chest); Ledger D, fol. 87 (funeral expenses). The genealogical table in Corazzini, "Jacopo Peri e la sua famiglia," has his death on 3 November 1635.

39. Journal D, fol. 100 (death); Ledger D, fol. 89 (funeral expenses and his estate). Francesco died (Journal D) "after two months of putrid fever, after having much earlier begun to lose a lot of weight and to pine away" (*dopo due mesi di infermità con febbre putrida; haveva cominciato molto tempo innanzi a smagrare e intristire*).

40. Journal D, fol. 118 (death); Ledger D, fols. 91 (funeral expenses), 95 (estate). Cosimo died (Journal D) "after a hundred days of putrid fever that in the end became also hectic fever . . . At the beginning of May, and still looking healthy, he committed himself to the care of Dr. Maccanti to protect himself from sickness; but before finishing this cure he contracted a very intense fever that then subsided slowly, but so very slowly that he lost weight, vitality and his usual robustness" (*doppo cento giorni di febbre putrida, che in ultimo si accoppiò con etica . . . Si messe al principio di maggio con buona cera in purga nelle mani del medico Maccanti per preservarsi da mali; e innanzi che finissi la purga gli venne una febbre grandissima che andò poi calmando, ma così lenta lenta l'ha disfatto di grasso e fresco e robustissimo ch'egli era*).

41. Ledger E, incipit (death); LC 3913, fols, 79–79v (funeral expenses). According to Ledger E, for almost all the summer of 1637 Niccolò was indisposed with catarrh and violent coughing (*è stato quasi tutta la prossima 'state 1637 indisposto per catarro e violenza di tossa*). He went to the country and returned at the beginning of October "with a much improved complexion.

Compagnia dell'Arcangelo Raffaello.[42] Dino made *ricordi* about the deaths of these four brothers, adding some detail about how they died, and he opened accounts for funeral expenses and for the settlement of their estates, which consisted of no more than the inheritance from their father and which were divided equally among the surviving brothers in each instance with no further complications.

It may, in the end, not be hard to explain the rapid sequence of deaths of these four brothers. They were all young adults, and with the possible exception of Giulio Cesare, who (according to Dino) may have died as a result of injuries suffered in a *calcio* game, the brothers seemed to have died in similar ways. The cause was not likely the plague, which had long subsided after striking Florence severely in the early years of the decade (Peri may have died from it), or any aftereffects it may have left in its wake. It is difficult to believe that these brothers suffered from a congenital disease: their mother died at fifty-eight, and their father at seventy-two, and they were survived by four of the five sisters who had reached adulthood. But living together, these brothers, unlike their sisters in the relative isolation of convents, would have all been precariously exposed to any highly contagious disease circulating through the general population that hit any one of them. Stefano Rosselli gave one such disease as the cause of their deaths, tuberculosis (*morirono tisichi*), which fits the various symptoms Dino recorded.[43] Yet his mention of "putrid fever" in his descriptions might also make one wonder whether his brothers had died instead from typhus.

But in fact in the evening of 17 October he suffered the loss of a large amount of blood from the mouth, the likes of which had never been seen. Then came a fever that the doctors considered putrid; he suffered one or two violent losses of blood that stopped him completely; but the sickness went on to end with asthma and hydropsy. And on 17 November he yielded his soul to God" (*con cera molto migliorata. Ma infatti la sera de' 17 di ottobre fece gran perdita di sangue per bocca, donde mai per l'innanzi se n'era visto. Gli venne la febbre battechata da' medici per putrida; hebbe uno o due altri sgorghi di sangue che ben si fermò totalmente; ma il male andò poi a terminare in asma et idropisia. E il dì 17 di novembre ha reso lo spirito a Dio*).

42. ASF, Compagnie religiose soppresse da Pietro Leopoldo A CXLVII, 162/23, fols. 92v (for Francesco, on 2 December 1635), 103 (Cosimo, on 27 August 1636), 121r (Niccolò, on 22 November 1637). Giulio Cesare was probably included in the Office for several (unnamed) members on 14 October 1635 (ibid., fols. 91v). For Cosimo's Office, the heirs donated ten pounds of candles *per limosina*.

43. Ruspoli, *Poesie*, ed. Arlìa, 69.

Dino himself suffered ill health, very likely also from tuberculosis. In his long *ricordo* of 1636 on the *calcio* episode he describes in great detail a lengthy illness that struck him in the late winter and spring of that year, and the chief symptoms were not unlike those suffered by the two brothers who had died the previous fall: namely chest pains and coughing up blood. Since as a result he could not get to Pisa to teach, he suffered a cut in salary (despite an appeal to the grand duke).[44] Two years later Galileo, in a letter of 25 July 1638 written to a former student and professor at Rome, reported that Dino had been in bed for five days, and that although the doctors did not consider this illness serious, the fact that no fewer than four of Dino's brothers had died in the previous two years made his friends, and Galileo himself in particular, worry about his prospects. But Galileo, ever attentive to possibilities for placing his students, immediately followed this concern with the question about the measures the university would likely take should Dino die: think about it a little bit, he says to his correspondent, and let me know (*ci applichi un poco il pensiero, e me ne accenni qualche cosa*).[45] In letters written in Pisa to Galileo in Florence, dated in September 1639 and January and February 1640, Dino referred to problems of ill health.[46] The situation worsened to the point that this thirty-four-year-old man felt compelled, on 3 May, to make a testament; he died two days later, on 5 May.[47] Dino had not lived long enough to have produced any results of his scientific research, his only surviving text being comments inaugurating his university course.[48] Hence we have no direct testimony of his intellectual talents other than the ledgers and journals he kept for the trust Peri had charged him to administer for the sake of the family. He, too, was honored in the Compagnia dell'Arcangelo Raffaello, with a sung Office of the Dead on Sunday 13 May. But given all his efforts to document the nobility of his family, he would not have been

44. Journal D, fols. 111–15. Corazzini, "Jacopo Peri e la sua famiglia," 62, cites the appeal to the grand duke.

45. Galilei, *Le opere*, 17: 359.

46. Ibid., 18: 108, 136, 155.

47. Dino's testament is in ASF, Notarile moderno, prot. 11174 (Cosimo Pucetti, testaments 1635–43), fols. 68–69.

48. The very brief biographical note on Dino in Galilei, *Le opere*, 20: 505, mentions the *prelezione* without citing a reference. Corazzini, "Jacopo Peri e la sua famiglia," 63, cites Dino's testament.

pleased with the entry in the confraternity's book of *ricordanze*—as *messer* Dino Peri.[49]

At the time of Dino's death in 1640 Peri's estate remained intact.[50] The entail on it (a *fedecommesso*) did not preclude division, but only alienation from the family. However, none of the children made any liens on it since none had married and had children. Nothing had been sold and nothing added. So the trust essentially dissolved when everything passed to the single ownership of the last son, Alfonso, the only lien remaining the obligation to pay a small annuity to his sisters, who were nuns. Alfonso closed out Dino's Ledger E and transferred all open accounts to a new ledger that he identified with the letter A (here called Ledger F). The accounts, however, were posted for only about a year, entries becoming ever more infrequent, and the ledger remains incomplete.[51]

Alfonso had gone on the court payroll as a musician after his father's death, at half his father's salary of *fl*.9 a month. He had already gained something of a reputation for singing in *sacre rappresentazioni* (often to his father's music) in the Compagnia dell'Arcangelo Raffaello in the 1620s, but little is known about a continuing musical career, or any other professional activity.[52] For almost four months of the year his father died, from the late spring into the summer, Alfonso kept the day journal for household accounts while Dino was in residence with Cardinal Capponi and preoccupied with Galileo's trial.[53] Otherwise he appears in Dino's ledger only as a beneficiary of the trust. Andrea Cavalcanti, who knew Alfonso, accused him of social "pretentions" in wanting to participate in the *calcio* games and in seeking a high-born wife well above his station. He had many upper-class "protectors" (*protettori*) and especially frequented the household of Barone Alessandro Del Nero (*in casa di cui egli era domestichissimo*), a fairly prominent music patron at the time and a notable sponsor of the *calcio* to whom Dino had appealed when defend-

49. ASF, Compagnie religiose soppresse da Pietro Leopoldo A CXLVII, 162/23, fol. 168v. The family (so, Alfonso?) gave the confraternity four pounds of candles *per limosina*.

50. The passage of the estate from Peri to Dino and then to Alfonso is recorded in ASF, Decima granducale 3590 (*campione* of S. Croce, Bue, 1618), fols. 33, 422.

51. Alfonso may have paid a professional to keep the accounts: entries are in an extraordinarily neat hand, and there is an account opened in the name of a salaried *scrivano* (who was paid *fl*.2 a month), but entries for payments stop at November 1640.

52. Kirkendale, *Court Musicians*, 385–87.

53. Ledger C, fol. 24.

ing his younger brothers against the prejudice of the youth of the elite.[54] On 9 January 1642, now the sole proprietor of the estate Peri had left his sons, Alfonso married Maddalena, daughter of Lorenzo di Leonardo Lioni. We know nothing more about her father than what Rosselli says about him: he was a *galantuomo* and very honorable. The Lioni, however, had no better claim to "nobility" than did the Peri, although Maddalena's dowry of *fl*.2,250, more or less at the level of the three dowries Peri had received, would indicate that her father had substantial if middling economic status, about that of Alfonso at the time.[55]

As a result of a growing dissatisfaction with the size of the dowry, it was said, Alfonso had never been able to show much affection for his wife, and his obsession eventually reached the breaking point in the heinous act that dramatically brought this branch of the Peri to a calamitous end. On 20 June, less than half a year into his marriage, and with Maddalena now several months pregnant, Alfonso led his wife to bed for a rest after dining, and while she was undressing he took a table knife and repeatedly stabbed her, making particularly bloody strikes in the neck that perforated her throat and esophagus and killed her.[56] In part on the basis of testimony by two servants, Alfonso was condemned to death by hanging. He was given a month to appear and to justify his actions. However, he managed to flee Florence, ending up in Rome never to return so far as is known, although he will reappear shortly in our story.

---

54. Ruspoli, *Poesie*, ed. Arlìa, 70 n. 1: Alfonso had *pretensione di giocare al Calcio . . . e di conseguire per moglie fanciulle di nascita e di ricchezze molto superiori alla di lui condizione e sustanze*. This is an addition by Cavalcanti to Stefano Rosselli's commentary on Ruspoli's sonnet against Peri. Alessandro Del Nero was the dedicatee of Domenico Visconti's *Il primo libro de arie a una e due voci* (Venice: Ricciardo Amadino, 1616), and of a similar collection of songs by Raffaello Rontani (a musician earlier associated with Don Antonio de' Medici), *Le varie musiche . . . a una, et due voci . . . Libro sesto* (Rome: G. B. Robletti, 1622). In both dedications, Del Nero is styled *Signore di Porcigliano*.

55. A copy of the marriage contract is in LC 3912, document dated 9 January 1642. The dowry amounted to *fl*.1,850 in cash, a trousseau, and a farm at the time of the marriage, plus *fl*.400 after the death of Lioni. For the comparative status of the family, see Litchfield's list of patrician families in *Emergence of a Bureaucracy*, 362–82.

56. All this comes from the official description of the murder in ASF, Otto di Guardia e Balìa del Principato, 332 (*partiti*), fols. 8–9; given in Kirkendale, *Court Musicians*, 386–87. None of the other contemporary commentators on Peri's life, however, advances an explanation for this sudden outbreak of violence.

Since he was a condemned murderer, the Capitani di Parte Guelfa, the magistracy charged with handling the property of condemned criminals, confiscated all of Alfonso's possessions. The magistracy's inventory of it has served us at several points in the course of our story in providing information about Peri not otherwise available, including the value of his real-estate holdings and the size of his house in Via dei Fossi. As for music, the inventory contains only the "harpsichord" (*un buonaccordo con quattro piedi di albero per sonare*) that is probably what the Pupilli officials in early 1634 had eventually decided was a spinet, and a painted wooden chest full of music (*una cassa di albero dipinta piena di scritture di musica*). The latter may suggest that Jacopo Peri kept far more of his music than was published—which is also what one would expect given what we know of his musical works that are now lost—although we should remember that in 1630, Dino Peri said that nothing of his father's music survived.[57]

The dénouement of our story begins with Peri's widow, Alessandra Fortini. This woman, who at the age of sixteen had married a man twenty-five years her senior, who had lost her husband and eleven of her sixteen children, who had seen her last son condemned to death for an atrocious crime and disappear forever in his flight from justice, was now left at home, separated from her only surviving children—the four daughters enclosed in convents—living alone with her only other relative still alive, a brother who was, in her own words, *malsano di mente*.

Alessandra has hardly any presence in her husband's ledgers, but that is only because few occasions arose for him to enter her name in the kind of accounts he opened. Apart from the lien she had on the farm at Castelvecchio, which had constituted her dowry, she had full title to the property that came to her from what was left of the Fortini and Monaldi estates: the farm at Cicogna, obtained in 1614 (with Peri's financial help) from her brother in exchange for an annuity of *fl.*60, and the Monaldi house in Borgo SS. Apostoli, half of which she inherited from her uncle in 1629 and the other half she gained on that occasion in another exchange with her brother for an annuity, this one of *fl.*14. These properties were thus burdened with the annuities owed to her brother, eventually amounting to *fl.*74, and another of *fl.*6 to an aunt on the Monaldi side, who was a nun. But they were hers, managed apart

---

57. The term *scritture di musica* would imply manuscripts, although it is not clear that those doing the inventory would have articulated any difference from printed music.

from her husband's property—even the property that constituted her dowry—and registered under her maiden name, not under Peri's, in the tax records (the *decima*).[58] We know nothing about who administered Alessandra's properties and how much they brought her in net income, whether she or Peri kept the accounts or paid an accountant to do the job, or how she used her own money. In keeping his accounts Peri did not in any way consider her property a part of his own estate: it does not figure into his accounts or in his testament or in his trust.

What appears to be Alessandra's economic autonomy, at least in these matters, throws another light on how much women's position had changed since the fifteenth century. Although many more, like Peri's six daughters, were sent off to be enclosed in convents, at least a few, like Alessandra, emerge with considerably more status. Earlier women generally did not have direct control even over their dowries, unless it was so delegated to them as widows; now they did, and dowries were very much larger. Earlier, few women inherited real estate or in any other way had a large amount of capital at their disposal, so women of property do not show up in the *catasto* records of the republic.[59] They do, instead, appear in the *decima* records of the grand duchy, as does Alessandra, found under her maiden name in the *gonfalone* of her family, not Peri's. We have also noticed, in contrast to the earlier period, two women who appear as investing partners alongside Peri in the Della Rena wool firm. In fact, to judge from many references to Peri's wife as Alessandra Fortini, women were now often identified in personal and official documents, as they had not been a century early, by their maiden name alone; *signora Alessandra Fortini, nostra madre*, is how Dino entitled the account he opened in his mother's name in Ledger C, while Peri was still alive. Alessandra, in short, signals a subject in the social, if not also economic, history of this city that merits scholarly attention, a subject that may not be unrelated to the impressive role women played in the cultural life of the grand-ducal court.[60]

58. ASF, Decima granducale 3590 (*campione* of S. Croce, Bue, 1618), fol. 1.

59. Chabot, *La dette des familles*, 88–89; compare Goldthwaite, *L'economia della Firenze rinascimentale* (which contains an addendum to Goldthwaite, *The Economy of Renaissance Florence*, regarding the role of women in the economy).

60. The new cultural roles of women are the subject of Cusick, *Francesca Caccini at the Medici Court*; Harness, *Echoes of Women's Voices*. See also Cole, *Music, Spectacle and Cultural Brokerage in Early Modern Italy*, 306–12.

After her husband's death there was a fusion of the two estates, his and hers, presumably because the children were heirs to both and they had now come into their own. Thus her farms at Castelvecchio and Cicogna became part of the trust that Dino administered, and they show up in Ledgers D and E—the only evidence we have for their operation. The property at Cicogna apparently suffered from bad management: in 1632 Dino made an entry for expenses sustained by his mother "at the ruins of Cicogna" (*nelle rovine dela Cicogna*); and ten years later when Alessandra put it up for sale, the notarial act describes the property as having badly deteriorated under the care of her husband and sons.[61]

Peri would seem to have been scrupulously correct about this separation of his affairs from hers. On 16 June 1627, for instance, he opened a rare account in her name with a credit for *fl.*50 she had loaned him in cash to be paid back in four months (*prestatimi contanti di sua denari avanzatosi in più tempo per rendergnene fra mesi 4*), and closed it the next year on 17 September—long after the due date—with a single balancing debit entry for repayment of the loan in cash (*in tante piastre*).[62] It was very likely because of her financial autonomy that he saw no reason to make any provision for her in setting up the trust, except for the stipulation for the monthly allowance that should go for expenses when she and her daughters were *in villa*. In his testament Peri clearly manifests complete confidence in his wife, for in designating the officials of the Magistrato dei Pupilli as official overseers (*tutori e curatori*) of his sons who were still minors, he makes it clear that nevertheless his wife was to be their legal guardian and to all effects administratrix of his estate (*la signora Alessandra . . . sia attrice et amministratrice de' tutti gl'effetti dell'eredità di detto testatore mentre detti sua figli eredi staranno insieme*).

Indeed, if we had any of Peri's waste-books, and especially the daybook (*giornale*) in which he would have entered monetary transactions daily for later posting in the more generalized format of the ledger, we would probably know how important Alessandra's role was in managing their extraordinarily large household. In fact the journals that survive for Ledgers C and D kept by Dino show just this. There Dino made many entries regarding money she

61. Ledger C, fol. 19; ASF, Notarile moderno, prot. 12993 (Diaceto Venterucci, 1638–49), no. 129, fols. 108–11 (11 November 1643).

62. Ledger B, fol. 45.

turned over to him that she had received from such things as rents and sales of produce owed to the trust but paid to her personally, and from the sale of possessions of his father, as well as entries for money paid to her in compensation for what she had spent for sake of the household, such as food, furnishings, medical expenses, and servants, and for money owed to the daughters that she took to them in the convent. Some of these entries refer to her own account books (*scartafaccio*, *libricciuolo*) where she kept a record of what she owed to the trust and what it owed her. These transactions in the journals reveal how active she was in running the household, but they do not show up on an account opened in her name in the ledgers.

Alessandra was fortunate to have her own properties, because with the condemnation of Alfonso, all those belonging to him, inherited from his father, were subject to confiscation by the state. There were certain complications in the handling of this problem, but eventually she took full possession of the farm at Castelvecchio, which had been her dowry, as well as the one at Cicogna, and following her petition, the grand duke allowed her to stay in the family home in Via dei Fossi.[63] On 9 July 1642, within a month of Alfonso's condemnation, she made a will in which she names her brother, Giovanni, her principal universal heir, adding a provision in the event of his death before recovering his faculties (*prima di ritornare in buona dispositione*). Among her few small bequests are *fl*.25 to each of the four daughters who were nuns, *fl*.10 to her aunt, *madre suora* Camilla at S. Onofrio di Foligno, and a mere £25 to Alfonso. She went on to make him her principal heir should he return in the good graces of the state, but we have no idea what contacts she may have had with him in Rome. A year later, on 11 November 1643, finding herself alone, old, and in poor health (*rimasta sola, et in età grave e con poco sanità*), and knowing that her brother would never have any heirs, she sold both farms to Jacopo and Filippo di Dino di Lorenzo Peri in return for an annuity of *fl*.162 payable to her and after her death to her brother Giovanni, after whose death a smaller annuity was to go to Alfonso. In March 1644 she became gravely ill and made a second will in which she changed the bequests to her brother and her aunt to reflect the annuities arranged with her husband's cousins, but left that of Alfonso at £25, and named her four daughters (whom she identifies by their conventual not baptismal names) as heiresses and Jacopo di Dino Peri as one of the executors. In

---

63. Corazzini, "Jacopo Peri e la sua famiglia," 66, summarizes the documentary evidence.

all these arrangements, as we observed in Chapter 1, she showed how concerned she was about her brother and also how close the ties were that Peri had always had with this distant branch of his family. In contrast to her husband, whose will was drawn up in the presence of six Carmelite friars, Alessandra called in two servants, a coachman, a baker, a gardener, and a plumber to witness hers.[64] She died less than three weeks later, on 26 March, and was buried alongside her husband in her family tomb in S. Maria Novella.

With Jacopo and Alessandra's four daughters enclosed in convents, the only dangling thread in the story is the fugitive son, Alfonso. What his mother, or anyone, knew about him in exile is undocumented, although her testament indicates that at least she thought he might still be alive, but Alfonso resurfaces with Giovanni Fortini's demise in 1647. The fiscal authorities had taken possession of the Peri house on Alessandra's death and sold it a month later, and—in yet another gesture of goodwill among the Peri cousins—Filippo and Jacopo di Dino Peri took in her brother, continuing to pay the annuity to him until his death on 8 July 1647 (he was buried in S. Remigio). Giovanni, however, bequeathed to his nephew Alfonso an annuity of fl.60 (perhaps the fl.60 he had been receiving since 1614 from Alessandra—and then her estate—for his share of the farm at Cicogna). This took the form of a lien on the properties of Alessandra, and since the Monaldi patrimony was now in the hands of the sons of Dino di Lorenzo Peri, it is thanks to the survival of the archive of Filippo di Dino (see the Introduction) that we can wind up the story with a postscript on this last son of Jacopo's, now living in Rome.[65]

64. The two testaments are in ASF, Notarile moderno, prot. 12995 (Diaceto Venterucci, testaments, 1617–56), no. 22, fols. 25v–27v (1642), and no. 26, fols. 31–32v (1644). The sale document of 1643 and a subsequent clarification of it are in ibid., prot. 12993 (Diaceto Venterucci, 1638–49), no. 129, fols. 108–11, and ibid., no. 138, fols. 116–116v. The acquisition of the property at Cicogna by Filippo and Jacopo di Dino Peri and their accounts for the payment of the annuity to Alessandra and then to Giovanni, along with memoranda of their deaths, are found in their ledgers and accompanying journals: ASF, Spinelli Baldocci 169 (ledger), fols. 112, 117; 170 (ledger), fols. 57, 61 (the deaths of both Alessandra and Giovanni); 173 (ledger), fol. 36; 168 (journal), fols. 105–6 (Alessandra's death), 108v (Giovanni's death). For the subsequent history of the house in Via dei Fossi, see Chapter 1.

65. Filippo and Jacopo di Dino Peri's ledgers have accounts opened specifically in Alfonso's name, and this material is complemented in the accompanying journals: ASF, Spinelli Baldocci 169 (ledger), fol. 218; 170 (ledger), fols. 23, 127; 173 (ledger), fol. 55; 168 (journal), fol. 147; 171 (journal), fols. 106–33 (Alfonso's death is noted on fol. 129v); 172 (journal), fols. 32, 83,

Although Alfonso had lost all benefit of his father's property and income in Florence, it seems that he still had access to the *monti* investments in Rome, while any income from his mother's side remained unencumbered. Filippo di Dino Peri's accounts record the dutiful payment of the annuity left by Giovanni Fortini for the next twenty years, until Alfonso's death on 18 March 1666, while other papers include a few letters regarding Alfonso, and some half dozen from Alfonso himself. Those to Filippo complain quite bitterly about his not receiving regular installments of the annuity (and about his general financial situation), even though Filippo's own records suggest otherwise. Moreover, the account in Alfonso's name on Filippo's books shows debit entries for payments made for Alfonso to third parties in Florence, including a legal representative (*procuratore*) and his former patron, Alessandro Del Nero, while in the correspondence Alfonso refers to investments he made in Florence through his cousin. These contacts would suggest that Alfonso's legal position as a fugitive from Florentine justice had been somewhat tempered.

Especially interesting are Alfonso's close ties to the relatively new organization of the Oratorians at the Chiesa Nuova in Rome, and it may be that he found some kind of sanctuary in their community. Filippo di Dino Peri received one letter written on Alfonso's behalf from Pietro Giacomo Bacci (1575–1656), sometime head of the Roman congregation and author of an authoritative and extraordinarily popular biography of the founder, S. Filippo Neri (1515–95); another prominent Oratorian, Francesco Cerretani (1608?–66), a cofounder of the congregation in Florence (1632), served Alfonso as a local go-between in his dealings with Filippo. Since the order had been founded by a Florentine patrician who had become a saint (in 1622), the city's elite enthusiastically embraced it, and it was most likely through some of his acquaintances from the better days of his youth—who would have been first-generation enthusiasts—that Alfonso had recourse to it, perhaps

---

106, 130, 168, 172v. Relevant letters are found scattered through the Peri papers in Yale University, Beinecke Library, GEN MSS 109 (Spinelli Archive), Buonguglielmi Family Papers, Box 490, folders 7669–78.

For further details see Corazzini, "Jacopo Peri e la sua famiglia," 63–67, who cites Rosselli's claim that Alfonso was allowed to escape so that the property at Ripoli would not return immediately to the Ospedale degli Innocenti and therefore become exempt from taxation by the state. Corazzini then adds that Alfonso lived in Rome on income from *luoghi di monte* that could not be confiscated.

aided by the Oratorians' well-known musical interests. He may not have been as prominent a singer as his father, but he probably used his connections generated by the art in similar nonmusical ways.

Alfonso was also in touch with his sisters. In a letter to him written in 1655 from the convent *Il Portico* (presumably sent to Filippo Peri for forwarding to Rome but perhaps never sent on) *suor* Maria Prudente (Teresa) complained that Alfonso had not been answering her letters and threatened not to write him anymore. In a letter of 1660, this time addressed to Filippo, she asks her cousin to forward an enclosed letter to Alfonso, who had informed her of not being well. Filippo's accounts, moreover, show that Alfonso drew on credits to make payments to the convents where his sisters were (*Il Portico* and S. Vincenzo at Prato), and he seemingly left a small annuity at least to his sisters at the former institution. Presumably this represented in some sense a continuation of the obligations imposed in Jacopo Peri's testament of 1630.

With Alfonso's death in 1666, and with his surviving sisters all in convents, the branch of the Peri family that went back to Jacopo's grandfather in effect came to an end. Peri's numerous family of sixteen children, twelve of whom reached adulthood (with ten alive when he died), did not proliferate into various branches. Rather, it simply withered away. One might find this remarkable enough given how many sons there were, and it is still more so for having occurred over so short a time. And that end came just at the juncture in its history when the family was on the rise. Peri himself was, we might say, a self-made man who raised his family out of artisan status and gave it a solid economic foundation in the middling ranks of a newly defined nobility. His sons collectively represented the next step in the stereotypical ascent. Dino had originally been directed into the legal profession, the clearest path for a new family into the bureaucracy of the ruling class, and Francesco headed into the church, another institution of the establishment. Both professions, in principle at least, had a higher and more solid status than that of musician. And these two sons each had intellectual aspirations, fully realized in an institutional sense by Dino. The youngest sons, instead, were attracted to the games of the elite, and it was seemingly Alfonso's social climbing that led to his disastrous fall, even if in the end it may also have given him something of a personal safety net. For all the family's attempted ascent through the ranks of the nobility, it did not survive.

Conclusion

An early seventeenth-century Venetian treatise on accountancy makes a comparison as extravagant in its way as the aim of this book:

> Who can deny that double-entry bookkeeping is akin to music? To that music, I say, of which consist the heavens, the spheres, the elements: all things created and the creator himself, God? Because just as in music, to limit the argument to the art as regards song, so many varied things and diverse voices, such as the alto, the bass, the soprano, the upper, the lower, the middle, the tenor and whatever have between them so well ordered a relation that not only do they not create tedium for the listeners but they also bring with them pleasing, sweet, and suave melody. So in double-entry bookkeeping is there such variety of debit and credit, journal and ledger, large entries and small, perfect and imperfect, primary and secondary in beautiful correspondence and sympathy that in them one realizes that not only does it not render business matters obscure and perplexing to the mind, but also it causes peace and tranquility in the spirits of their masters. And just as in music all the aforesaid voices and their ensemble are governed by the clef and by the beat, so, and not otherwise, do all those affairs, transactions, and dealings in the double-entry account

book concern these two purposes: capital and profit–loss. And to conclude, just as the great Themistocles, as described by the divine Plato in his
Timaeus, was judged totally ignorant and an idiot because he confessed
himself inexperienced in music, so, equally, will any merchant of whatever
kind lacking this graceful skill be deemed unworthy of weighty operations, and even if he were a second Argus [i.e., with a hundred eyes], he
will necessarily in the course of time remain mocked and deluded in the
judgment of his agents.[1]

That commonplace account of Themistocles will return in another context
related to Peri. But we suspect that as a musician and an accountant, he would
have appreciated a metaphor that he might have understood as making sense
of his life, just as we see it encapsulating what, in the final analysis, this book
is all about: bringing together the social, economic, and musical worlds of one
late Renaissance Florentine—whether harmoniously or not—in an effort to
envision a whole greater than the sum of its parts.

All history is about continuity and change, and which dynamic gets emphasized depends on the objective of the historian. The decision about where
to put the emphasis, however, is not always such a simple matter. We have
chosen to place Peri in the context of the Renaissance, a period that in its
classic moment extended from the late fourteenth to the early sixteenth century, but we hedge a bit by throwing in the qualifying "late." What does this

---

1. Giovanni Antonio Moschetti, *Dell'universal trattato di libri doppii* (Venice: Luca Valen-
tini, 1610), fols. IV–2 (keeping the original orthography): *Chi mi negherà, che'l Libro doppio non
sia simile alla Musica? a quella Musica dico, della quale consistono i Cieli, le Sfere, gli Elementi:
tutte le cose create, & lo stesso lor Creatore Iddio? poiche si come nella Musica, per star nei confini
dell'arte propria del canto, tante cosi varie, e diverse voci com'è l'alto, il Basso, il Soprano, l'Acuto,
il Grave, il Medio, il Tenore, & che so io hanno tra di loro una relatione cosi ben ordinata, che non
solo non recano fastidio à gli ascoltanti, ma anchora apportano seco grata, dolce, & soave melodia:
cosi nel libro doppio tanta varietà di dare, & havere; Giornale, & libro Maestro: partide grandi,
& partide piccole: perfette, & imperfette, prime, & secondarie con la bella corrispondenza, & sim-
patia, che in esse si scorge non solamente, non rende gli negotij oscuri, & perplessi gli animi: ma
cagiona ancora quiete, & tranquillità nelle menti de' loro padroni, & si come nella Musica tutte le
dette voci, & il lor concerto si reggono per la chiave, & per la battuda, cosi, & non altrimenti tutti
li negotij, trafichi, & facende nel libro doppio à quelli duoi termini risguardano. Capitale, & Pro,
e danno, & per finirla si come il gran Themistocle, come narra il Divino Platone nel Timeo per
essersi confessato imperito dalla Musica fu stimato per totalmente ignorante, & idiota, cosi pari-
mente qual si voglia mercante senza questa gratiosa arte sarà riputato indegno di gravi maneggi, &
ancorch'egli fosse un secondo Argo, resterà necesariamente in processo di tempo ad arbitrio de suoi
agenti burlato, e deluso.*

mean for the study of a man whose documented life straddles the turn from the sixteenth to the seventeenth century?—rather different things for the economic historian and the musicologist. The former is burdened by the weight of a historiography that has put all the emphasis on the earlier "classic" period to the almost total neglect of what happened thereafter. Thus the study of an economic operator such as Peri is also necessarily a process of looking backward in the attempt to measure performance and structural transformations in the economy through comparisons with the earlier period, and one has to resist the natural tendency to charge the word "late" with decline, not just change. The music historian faces a different historiographical problem. Peri's time marks the beginning of what is customarily called the musical Baroque (and opera is often regarded as a quintessential Baroque genre), yet he was a leader in the (attempted) rebirth of the theatrical music of classical antiquity, and in that sense he can be placed squarely in a Renaissance that does not even require a qualifying "late." Moreover, save in the eyes of the harshest contemporary critics, decline is hardly a theme in the direction the history of music took thereafter.

These problems stem from different historiographical, and also disciplinary, perspectives. Perhaps some other perils of cross-disciplinary engagement have also been apparent in the previous chapters of this book, where methodological particularities may seem to have skewed our picture of Jacopo Peri first one way then the other. So how might we best sum up the various strands of Peri's life discerned by way of the documents uncovered in this study, and how might we best tie them together?

The Economic Scene ca. 1600

In the end what the Peri Archive has most revealed is that in entering the marketplace, Jacopo Peri steps out of his historiographical role as a new Orpheus to take on the identity of one who lived and worked in a complex economic and social world, one heretofore virtually terra incognita but which we now know better thanks to his own documentation of it. We have seen how that documentary record constitutes a microhistory through which opens up a broad view of how that economy functioned. And so with Peri unmasked as Orpheus and exposed as Everyman, now lost in the crowd, we can conclude his story by setting this, its final scene, within a wider temporal perspective that throws new light on the economy of Renaissance Florence. For the many things that we found going on in Peri's marketplace invite a comparison with the situation a century earlier that is, instead, so well known in its details. Although Peri's ledgers have little to tell us directly about the performance of the leading sectors of the economy, we can nevertheless read into such a comparison something about how one of Europe's most advanced capitalist economies was doing during a period generally seen as one of contraction if not decline.[2]

One initial difference that strikes anyone looking at the marketplace revealed by the Peri materials lies in the level of private wealth and its social distribution. These materials throw no light on the lowest end of the wealth spectrum, although we know from other sources how much poorer the poor became in the course of the sixteenth century.[3] At the upper ranges of that spectrum, however, we see how much richer the rich had become in the meantime, and more important, as we learn from Peri's history, how much more prominent on the scene was a middling class of men with substantial wealth. For this period statistical data for constructing a social profile of wealth like that derived from the 1427 *catasto* do not exist, but what we know about wealth distribution in 1427 provides a background for making at least one comparison. The value of Peri's marketable assets—about *fl*.10,000 (see Table 2.7)—was 285 times the annual salary of an unskilled worker; with this power to buy labor, the basic factor of production, he would have ranked in the upper 1.23 percent of taxpayers in 1427, with the richest man in the city having eleven times that wealth.[4] We do not have enough information to

2. For the background of the following discussion, see Goldthwaite, *The Economy of Renaissance Florence.*

3. Studies of workers' wages across time are based on data from the construction industry, the minimum wage being considered that of an unskilled day laborer (the criterion used in this book). None of Peri's accounts records information of this kind. However, his ledgers include separate accounts for sixteen female servants, and their wages, ranging from £16 to £48 per annum (never as high as *fl*.7) were no higher than what they had been in the fifteenth century, notwithstanding the doubling of the cost-of-living index in the meantime. As in the earlier period, Peri always stated the salary of a female servant in *fiorini di* £4 per annum, i.e., in a specific florin of account priced at £4, not at £7. But despite the quotation of such a salary as an annual figure with the expectation that servants would stay on the job for at least a year, the turnover among them was high, as was typical also for earlier periods. Of the sixteen Peri employed, seven served less than a year; the longest any served was eight and a half years.

4. In the early seventeenth century, *fl*.10,000 could purchase 70,000 man-days of labor (at £1 per day and £7 per florin); in 1427 it took *fl*.8,750 (at 10*s*., or £½, per day and £4 per

identify Peri's percentile among taxpayers in 1633, but the multiple separating him from the rich was certainly very much greater—by between sixty and seventy times, to make a comparison with the Riccardi, perhaps the city's richest family, who in the early seventeenth century had a patrimony of well over *fl.*600,000 and an annual income alone averaging *fl.*22,000.[5] The distance that the wealthiest had come by Peri's time can also be measured by such benchmarks as the *fl.*34,000 Averardo Salviati paid for his chapel in S. Marco in the 1580s, the *fl.*52,550 Peri's patron Jacopo Corsi and his brother invested in the cloth industry alone in less than two years, or the more than *sc.*100,000 *d'oro* Peri's financial advisor Giovambattista Michelozzi had on the exchange in a private account (plus *fl.*7,000 to *fl.*8,000 in cash at home) at the time of his death—all sums that leave the fifteenth century far behind.[6] On this yardstick, Peri hardly ranks with the wealthy. Yet he was very well off, with an annual income that (according to our estimate) was twenty-five to thirty times that of an unskilled manual laborer.

Peri was able to enter the market as an active investor thanks to the dowries he received—three in a decade, the first two in cash—and the increase in the size of dowries is one index of how much wealthier some people were. His dowries would have been, in real buying power, well within the range of top dowries a century earlier, but in his day the spread was very much wider, reaching up to ten times that amount (factoring the rate of inflation into the calculation) with the *fl.*15,000–20,000 that the very rich paid to get their daughters married.[7] More significantly, dowries not only followed the inflationary trend but, in a market inflated with money, they also lent themselves more easily to settlement in cash. Hence, in contrast to the typical fifteenth-century dowry, we find much smaller trousseaus, no more depreciated paper credits in an unstable dowry *monte*, no more expensive counterdowries in the form of the *camera* on which the fifteenth-century husband spent so much to

---

florin). In the 1427 *catasto*, 120 out of 9,780 households had this amount of taxable wealth; the wealthiest had *fl.*100,000.

5. Malanima, *I Riccardi*, 250 (patrimony), 253 (income).

6. So Giovambattista Michelozzi said in his testament, drawn up shortly before his death; Florence, Biblioteca Nazionale Centrale, Fondo Tordi 51, insert 3.

7. In a study of ninety-three dowries from the fifteenth century, only one reached *fl.*3,000 and no other was higher than *fl.*2,500; Chabot, *La dette des familles*, 147. The median for dowries in the seventeenth century was *fl.*10,000; Litchfield, "Demographic Characteristics of Florentine Patrician Families," 203.

furnish in preparation for reception of his bride. A father could now pay a
dowry entirely in cash, and as Peri discovered, it was cash up front, with a
strict percentage penalty charge for any delay in payment. This had not been
much of a possibility a century earlier. But now large cash payments made
physically in specie seem not to have been unusual, to judge from some of
Peri's transactions we have cited.

An increase in the quantity of money in an economy, and its greater fluidity, should, in theory at least, result in the lower cost of money, and indeed
the Peri ledgers reveal just this. Virtually all the monetary transactions he
engaged in that involved a specified cost of money reveal an annual interest
rate of 5 percent. This is the rate he received in depositing money in a *monte*,
whether in Florence or Rome; the rate he himself charged for the delayed
payment of two of the three dowries owed to him and for the schedule of
payments for the farm he sold at Maioli; and the rate he used in calculating
the rental value of his house in setting up his trust. The annual earnings from
censi were higher, around 7 percent of the capital invested; and the range of 5–7
percent was what at the time one might have expected as a return on an investment in the wool industry or in the international exchange market, although
we have very little evidence for what Peri earned on either. The cost of money
was generally higher in the fifteenth century: the *catasto* assessments were
based on a capitalization of income at 7 percent; six-month time deposits, the
standard instrument then used by an outside investor in the city's industries,
ranged from 7 to 10 percent; and partners in an industrial, commercial, or
financial firm expected a much higher rate of return from their enterprise.
This drop in interest rates echoes a general theme in this history of sixteenth-
century Europe, and the reason is everywhere the same: more disposable
wealth in the form of liquid capital. The standardization of a fixed rate of 5 percent, however, suggests that the usury doctrine may also have been a factor in
the money market, that rate being the one authorized for the Monte di Pietà.

More disposable wealth, the rich ever richer, and a larger middling class
made a big difference on the demand side of the marketplace, where people
spend money for consumption and seek outlets for savings and investment;
and the uses of wealth were less restrained because of exceptionally low taxes
on capital investments. Consumption, especially of durable goods, is another
index of greater wealth, conspicuous to some extent still today in the survival
of so many of those goods in our museums. The extensive documentary evidence, however, is only now beginning to attract historians of Renaissance

Italy. Unfortunately Peri's ledgers tell us hardly anything about his expenditures of this kind. He opened accounts only in the names of persons, not things, unlike his son Dino, who kept separate accounts for furnishings (*masserizia e arnesi*), for heating (*fuoco*), and for comestibles (categorized separately as *vino, olio, vitto, camangiare*). Peri would have kept any record of expenditures of this kind in waste-books, which no longer survive. However, the two inventories we have of his house (discussed in Chapter 4) signal how much the material culture of Florentines had changed over the previous century. The Peri furniture falls into a complex typology (including *buffetti, stipetti*, a *studiolo intarsiato* with drawers and little doors, a bookcase, a small chest of drawers, several kinds of chairs with arms decorated with leather and silk upholstering and brass studs, and beds with columns and canopies); some of the walls were covered, in the new fashion, with hangings in both gold-embossed leather and luxurious damascene silks with gold trim; scattered throughout the house were well over a dozen paintings; and the later inventory lists an *oratorio*. In contrast, the houses of the very rich a century earlier—for example, Francesco di Antonio Nori and Giovanni di Francesco Tornabuoni, both among the city's richest bankers and associates of the Medici—had a picture or two, no silk hangings, and furniture that, though highly worked with inlay and carving, falls into a limited typology of simpler forms.[8] The transformation of the domestic interior into more specialized spaces filled with a greater variety of furnishings was a manifestation of the growth of the consumer sector and the enlargement of material culture within an economy stimulated by more disposable income.

This material culture included the sound of music, and music, too, was a growth industry at Peri's time. Traditionally demand for his products came from the church, and this, in fact, gave Peri his start in the market. He then found a major client in the form of the court, whose policy of welfare economics (generally referred to as "patronage") generated a growing and more diversified demand for music. Outside these spheres, in the private market, demand was also growing. In surveying the Peri materials we have found hints of how he may have exploited the options: performance, composition (also for amateurs), publication, teaching, and even, perhaps, trading in scores and instruments. He also found clients outside the court, and above all he was on

8. ASF, Magistrato dei Pupilli avanti il Principato 174, fols. 228–233v (Nori), and 181, fols. 146v–150 (Tornabuoni).

the cutting edge in shaping new taste and thus renewing demand, a major dynamic in modern economies. The evidence does not indicate how much headway he made in the private market, but we do not yet know how far anyone at the time could have done so as an entrepreneur. But there were plenty of opportunities here, of various and different kinds. On entering the market Peri may have thrown aside his guise as Orpheus to work for bigger economic returns, but his musical career calls attention to what was becoming a growth industry in Europe generally. And that process of growth went beyond increased production to generate a continual renewal of its products, improved and new technologies, an appeal to patrons and hence further investment, and above all the increase of human capital involved in both production and use of its products—all these were dynamics that constituted a veritable creative industry in the economic and not just artistic sense of the term. This is a story yet to be told.

While the growth of material culture is suggestive of more wealth circulating among more people, the clearest evidence of it lies in the financial sector. This sector comes into the picture as never before with instruments designed to attract such wealth, a development hardly noted in the historiography and one that Peri's investment history illuminates. These instruments were three: the bill of exchange, the *censo*, and government securities. The first, as we have noted, had long been utilized by Florentines, although Peri's familiarity with, and frequent use of, it indicates how much more popular it was than it had ever been in the past. Government securities and *censi* were new to the Florentine market, having appeared during Peri's lifetime, and both took precedence over bills of exchange in popularity. They had the advantage over the bill in paying a specified dividend, in being fixed rather than subject to periodic renewal, and perhaps also in inspiring greater confidence by not being tied to a mysteriously complex financial instrument oriented to a market abroad—not to bring into the argument also the relevance of any concern about usury. The market for government securities in the form of *luoghi di monte* reached pan-Italian dimensions, whereas *censi* were a more purely local phenomenon, being based on specific pieces of real estate.

The frequency of usage of these three instruments—government securities, *censi*, bills of exchange—by a large segment of the population, as indicated in Peri's familiarity with them, signals something new in the history of the Florentine economy: an impressive growth of a capital market. This market had long been operative in Florence, secured by a strong institutional framework protective of private contracts, lubricated by a high degree of liquidity in the form of credit instruments, and frequented by operators fully acclimated to the culture of "ghost monies" (as Carlo Cipolla called monies of account). Operations in the market, however, were limited in an earlier period by instruments that depended on highly personal networks and functioned for short-term arrangements. By Peri's time the instruments had become more institutionalized and hence impersonal. The state stood behind government securities as never before, land provided a basic security for *censi*, and the greater number of banks tied into the international fairs of Besançon offered a reasonably objective private structure for dealing in bills. Moreover, these instruments, unlike those of the fourteenth and fifteenth centuries, offered outlets for long-term, even lifetime and beyond, investments. Finally, this capital market, strengthened by its long tradition of practice, was more immune to penetration by the negative moral and religious ideologies that so contorted arrangements between earlier borrowers and lenders in their attempts to work within usury restrictions.

Luoghi di monti and *censi* are not to be regarded simply as technical innovations in the category of financial instruments. Together they are also symptomatic of a profound change in the economic culture of Florentines: a veritable savings revolution in both economic practice and expectation. What people like Peri very likely wanted when they purchased these things was a permanent, steady, and fixed income—in other words, an annuity—although they did not yet have a word for it (it is variously referred to as a *provvisione, salario,* and *usufrutto*).[9] None of the transactions of the kind we have encountered in this survey of Peri's investment history is characteristic of the earlier period: the exchange of an annuity for ownership of a property, the burdening of a property with a lien of an annuity, the assignment of an annuity to a nun enclosed in a convent, the testamentary bequests of an annuity. We have encountered these practices in Peri's concern for his daughters, in his three-generation rental contracts (one as renter, one as landlord), in his wife's settlements with her brother, in his son Niccolò's settlement with his brother Francesco, and along the way, in several other arrangements among his relatives. And this, with no reference to capital values, was the way Peri thought about the value of his estate when he set up what we have called—and here

9. The modern term *vitalizio*, however, does appear in Filippo and Jacopo di Dino Peri's Ledger B (1650–57): ASF, Spinelli Baldocci 173, fols. 4, 36.

the term does not seem anachronistic—a trust. This idea extended also into the grand-ducal financial administration of the court *musici* (and others) to whom it offered a permanent lifetime stipend. What was new, in short, was the very idea of an annuity as a financial arrangement, and by Peri's time it had become deeply embedded in Florentine economic practice and culture.[10]

Peri's investment history thus suggests that the economy had entered into a different phase following a modernizing trend in accord with much that was happening throughout the European economy at the time. Yet in revealing the range of investment possibilities in the early seventeenth century, that history, as modest as it was, exposes an essential weakness of the economy, or better, a serious weakening of an economy that had shown considerable vitality a century earlier: the narrowing of outlets for investment in the forward sectors of the economy, and more generally, in productive enterprise of any kind. The wool industry—or at least that part of it oriented to foreign markets—was gone, and the silk industry was limited to a relatively small number of firms, while artisan enterprise for the most part continued to operate on a small scale without outside capital. To the extent that *censi* attracted investment, agriculture would seem to have been the one growth sector of the economy, but little is known about it. Land, however, required administration of distant properties and generally a certain minimum investment; *censi* paid well but were risky. This left government securities, exactly the sector that attracted Peri and presumably so many of those people, like him, who owned much of the increased disposable wealth in the economy. Government securities, represented by the various *monti* in Florence and elsewhere, were clearly a growth sector. In fact the clearest evidence for greater wealth and its social diffusion is the extraordinary increase, in Florence, of the funds the Monte di Pietà had on its hands and the number of foreign *monti* (especially in Rome) now available on the local market.

As an economic phenomenon as distinct from a financial one, however, this growth points to a major problem in the economy: the channeling of dis-

---

10. In northwestern Europe, instead, the annuity was a well-developed instrument by the fourteenth century. The difference in Italy emerges in various essays on the subject collected in Boone, Davids, and Janssens, *Urban Public Debts*. For the contemporary popularity of the *livello* in Venice, a slightly different annuity instrument, see Corazzol, "Varietà notarile."

posable wealth into savings in the form of government securities rather than into investment in productive enterprise. The question that comes to the fore, therefore, regards the importance of government spending for social service, on the one hand, and for economic growth, on the other. The redistribution of some of that wealth can be an economic stimulus, although the increased wealth in the hands of the Florentine government did not come from the appropriation of it, via taxes, from the ever-richer rich except to the extent they were landowners. In some significant ways, the early Medici grand dukes used these resources to strengthen the economy—for instance, the development of the port of Livorno, projects for Pisa, mining enterprises, land reclamation in the lower Arno valley and in the Valdichiana, promotion of sericulture throughout the countryside—in ways the republican government never had. They also set up a vast, varied, and superior-quality artisan workshop—the famous Gallery of Works, perhaps the first of its kind, at least in its scale—but they did this more to promote their prestige than to bolster the economy.

Expanding the ranks of the state's employees to bring in artisans and artists of all kinds, including musicians, had the effect of enlarging the middling class so often mentioned in these pages with reference to Peri's economic status. Of the salaried persons on the grand-ducal payroll from 1610 to 1620, twenty-six of the forty-four musicians and twenty-six of the thirty-three artists earned at least as much as the $fl.$108 paid to Peri, and stipends went as high as $fl.$240 for musicians and $fl.$360 for artists. This spending represents a redistribution of wealth through the government into the hands of some fifty people who earned more than three times what an unskilled day laborer earned; given what these people were paid to do, this redistribution was in effect an investment in human capital of the kind that the republican government had never made. In fact, in 1607 the total of musicians' salaries under the grand dukes was from one-sixth to one-fifth of what the republic paid for its entire bureaucracy in the capital city (*uffici intrinsici*) in 1487; to extend the comparison, taken all together the total spent by the grand duke for court employees alone—$fl.$40,941 annually—amounted to half of what the republic paid for its entire bureaucratic apparatus, both urban and territorial (and 143 of these employees earned more than Peri). All this was a further stimulus to the economy to the extent that these same people spent their earnings in the marketplace, thereby recycling their court salaries into the productive and service sectors of the economy. But it will take a good deal more research to formulate a hypothesis about the economic role, positive or negative, that the government played in the redistribution and hence recycling of wealth.[11]

Clearly Peri, in the historiography of the Renaissance no less innovative as Everyman than as Orpheus, opens up new vistas on the changing economic scene in Florence—at least for the moment, until the historiographical record is filled in with more research bringing other players into the marketplace so that we can get a better idea of what went on there. The wider perspective on the earlier period that will open up as a result will put into high relief the dynamic of change that has been notably absent in the historiography of the economy of one of the major centers of early capitalism.

The Musical Scene ca. 1600

Florence around 1600 has always held more interest for music and theater historians than for scholars in other fields. The reasons are obvious enough, given the spectacular *intermedi* celebrating the wedding of Grand Duke Ferdinando I and Christine of Lorraine in 1589, and then, at the turn of the century, the rise of opera and other new forms of court entertainment: by this reckoning, the Medici court was one of the more exciting of those in central and northern Italy during the period. Yet the relative weight of the various historical disciplines in the modern academic world inhibits such revisionist thinking: music and theater history are usually low down in the pecking order even for those who place any value on the arts in general as figuring within—nay, helping to define—political, social, and economic structures. And even granting these disciplines a larger place in the broader schemes of historical inquiry, it is easy to view *intermedi* and opera in the manner of bread and circuses offered up to a weak-willed Florentine populace becoming lulled into courtly decline.

---

11. In 1487 fewer than fifty employees in the central administration of the state earned more than Peri, and fewer than ten earned more than the highest-paid musician on the grand-ducal payroll. Calculations for the comparison are based on the 1607 court payroll cited in Chapter 3, n. 41, and on the 1487 payroll of the republic discussed in A. Brown, "Offices of Honour and Profit," 150, 173–76. Here as elsewhere in the present book, the basis of comparisons of monetary values across time is the purchase power of the *lira* in the respective labor market.

How, then, does Peri's biography fit into this scene? The fact that music figured in his portfolio—if less prominently than we might expect—poses additional challenges. Here the Peri Archive might seem cause for disappointment: it scarcely provides the kind of information on his musical activities as a composer and performer that the eager archivist might hope for or expect. While this is owing, at least in part, to the nature and purpose of his financial accounts, it also poses some intriguing questions about where music might sit within the economy of culture in this period, and indeed where one might best look to find its traces.

The art and architecture that Florentines individually and collectively used to embody and project power, even during the republic, have left their permanent trace in the city as we know it today. Music, on the contrary, and by virtue of its performative nature, is hardly an indelible marker: instead we have only its residue in more or less vague musical and textual sources, or even just the silence we find in Peri's account books. Yet musicians may have had more "power" in the marketplace than other artists, precisely because their physical presence was essential to the enterprise: a madrigal may not last long in performance, but while it does, one has little choice but to listen to the musicians singing it. Add to that the role of music as a sign of education and good breeding, so Castiglione tells us, and its prominent role in the culture (and cultivation) of classical antiquity—plus, one might suggest, its potential for amateur participation in ways not possible for the other arts—and one can see why it might have become a valuable commodity in Peri's period, even if that value was not measured or traded in financial terms. As we have suggested already, we can thus speak fairly of some kind of cultural capital invested in, and deriving from, the art. There were, of course, other options for civic and courtly advancement for those with different talents or interests. But while music's shift during the Renaissance from the quadrivium (with arithmetic, geometry, and astronomy) to the trivium (with grammar, logic, and rhetoric) certainly reflected a changing worldview embracing the new sciences, it also opened the door to musical performance and appreciation as a mark of culture, and as an instrument of eloquence. This, at least in part, is how music served Peri's broader purpose of projecting an air of nobility.

There were dangers in this strategy because music could easily be accused of representing frivolity, on the one hand, or a perilous sensuality, on the other. The dedication to Ferdinando Saracinelli of the 1619 edition of Peri's *Le varie musiche* engages with the challenge.[12] Here the printer Zanobi Pignoni, or his authorial proxy, writes that according to the "prince of moral philosophers" (i.e., Seneca, *De beneficiis*, I.11), gifts to friends or patrons should be appropriate to their physical or intellectual abilities—so one should not give hunting weapons to women and old men, books to the ignorant, or nets (to catch wild animals) to literati—and says that he has not fallen into this trap in presenting musical works to Saracinelli because the latter is most knowledgeable about, and takes wondrous delight in, the art of music.[13] This understanding of music can bring Saracinelli nothing but honor and profit because, so Aristotle says (*Politics*, VIII), it is as useful in rendering the spirit well composed by way of honest pleasure as gymnastics is for keeping the body fit. Moreover, the wise Greeks understood that music was extremely necessary for the perfection of the knight (Saracinelli was a knight of the Cavalieri di Santo Stefano), for we read that Epaminondas, equally skilled in the arts of war and peace, sang and played with much grace, whereas Themistocles, however valorous in arms, was considered lacking in some way in

12. *Illustrissimo Signore mio Colendissimo / il Signor Cavaliere Ferdinando / Saracinelli. / Balì di Volterra, e cameriere segreto / del Serenissimo Gran Duca di Toscana. // Saggiamente ne consiglia il Principe de' Morali Filosofi, che volendo noi Amici, o Padroni nostri presentare, habbiamo tale avvertenza, che i doni da noi fatti sieno proporzionati, ò all'uso del corpo, ò al diletto dell'animo di chi gli riceve: essendo errore (dice egli) farebbe colui, che alle femmine, ò a gli huomini vecchi donasse armi da Cacciatori, libri a gli Ignoranti, e reti a' Letterati; Tale errore senz'alcun dubbio credo d'havere schivato mentre per testimonio della mia obligata servitù porgo à Vostra Signoria Illustrissima in dono Opere di Musica, della qual professione ella è intendentissima, e solita di prenderne meraviglioso diletto, nè puote à lei arrecare altro che onore, e giovamento la cognizione di essa, e 'l diletto che ne prende, perché, come dice il famoso Peripatetico, tanto vale la Musica à render ben composto l'animo con l'uso d'uno onesto piacere, quanto la Ginnastica con l'esercizio delle membra à render gagliardo il corpo; intesero ancora i saggi Greci, che alla perfettione del Cavaliero era l'uso della Musica sommamente necessario; onde si legge, che Epaminonda nell'arti della Guerra, e in quelle della Pace egualmente perfetto, con molta grazia cantava, e sonava, e Temistocle per altro nell'armi valorosissimo, fu notato di mancare in qualche parte nella civil conversazione, posciaché in un convito di nobili, e virtuosi Cavalieri confessò di essere affatto della Musica ignorante. Credo per queste cagioni, che non le sia per esser discaro il dono, tanto più che buona parte delle rime quì messe in Musica sono parti del suo ingegno: l'eccellenza poi dell'Opera, e 'l nome dell'Autore possono ancora appresso à Vostra Signoria Illustrissima far più grata la mia fatica; Le fo umil riverenza, e la supplico à mantenermi nella solita protezione. // Di Vostra Signoria Illustrissima / Obligatissimo Servitore / Zanobi Pignoni.*

13. The fact that Pignoni "signs" the dedication does not necessarily mean that he was its author. For composers, etc., using proxies in writing such texts, see Carter, "Printing the 'New Music'," 6 (and n. 12).

civil conversation because he once confessed to a gathering of noble and virtuous knights that he was wholly ignorant of music.[14] For these reasons, Pignoni says, his gift will not be displeasing to Saracinelli, not to mention the fact that a good number of the poems set to music here come from his pen, while he will also appreciate the excellence of the results and the name of the composer. These are conventional tropes in dedications, and they present typical defenses of music, but it is revealing that they still needed to be said.

The role of prominent patrons in late sixteenth-century Florence— Giovanni de' Bardi, Jacopo Corsi, and others—has long been recognized as central to the emergence of opera. Scholars have also examined the place of music in feminine, and feminized, environments, whether the chambers and beyond of Medici wives and daughters, or the convents that they patronized: here music even offered women advantages denied them in other spheres, given the performance opportunities made available to them at least in certain contexts, and the virtues of music's slippery semiotics.[15] One should not exaggerate: no doubt there were as many tone-deaf men and women in Florence as in any society. Yet when Sebastiano Ximenes informed Cardinal Ferdinando Gonzaga on 1 September 1609 of the formation in Florence of a new musical academy (breaking away from Marco da Gagliano's Accademia degli Elevati), he claimed that it was supported by no fewer than eighty of the "most principal lords and gentlemen" of the city, with Don Giovanni and Don Antonio de' Medici at their head: these *principalissimi signori e gentil'huomini* included the likes of Antonio Antinori, Alessandro Del Nero, Giovanni Del Turco, Piero Gianfigliazzi, Bartolomeo Panciatichi, Giuliano Ricasoli, Ottavio Rinuccini, and Piero Strozzi—in other words, men from the leading Florentine families.[16] The rise of music printing in Florence from

14. Castiglione compares Epaminondas and Themistocles in *Il libro del cortegiano*, I, though Cicero (*Tusculanae disputationes*, I.4) had already established the commonplace, and we have already seen Themistocles at the start of this present Conclusion.

15. See Harness, *Echoes of Women's Voices*; Cusick, *Francesca Caccini at the Medici Court*.

16. For Ximenes's letter announcing the new academy (Mantua, Archivio di Stato, Archivio Gonzaga 1127, fol. 249), see Strainchamps, "New Light on the Accademia degli Elevati of Florence," 526–27. The names of at least some of its members (as given above) can be deduced from Santi Orlandi's letter to Cardinal Ferdinando, 1 September 1609, passing on greetings from various Florentine noblemen; Mantua, Archivio di Stato, Autografi 6, fol. 65. Some of these names, plus Cosimo Cini, appear in a similar letter from Orlandi of 29 September 1609;

1581, while marginal compared with Venice, and then the formation in 1614 of a formal company to support it—Zanobi Pignoni & Partners (the latter including two noblemen and a musician)—also suggest that there was some kind of musical market among local patrons and consumers: some forty-five music prints appeared from Florentine presses from 1581 to 1641.[17] This market was strong enough to sustain not just private music teachers for the nobility or for boys seeking to enter the profession, but also a de facto music school: the Florentine composer Filippo Vitali rented rooms for this purpose at least in the early 1620s, and they were then taken over by Vergilio Grazi (whom we have already seen profiting from his apprentice singers in Chapter 3).[18] For a brief period, at least, Florence was by all accounts a musical city, and one that could appreciate the value of bringing a singing Orpheus to modern musical life.

In 1634, Pietro de' Bardi claimed that one of the virtues of his father's Camerata, a delightful and continuous academy, was that it brought a benefit (*guadagno*) to the noble Florentine youth by enabling them to avoid vice, and in particular all forms of gambling, through engagement not only in music but also in poetry, astrology, and other sciences, all of which brought reciprocal profit (*utile vicendevole*) to so fine a gathering.[19] The mercantile terminol-

---

Mantua, Archivio di Stato, Archivio Gonzaga 990, fol. 493 (*Herla* C-4917). To this list one should probably also add Giovanni Battista Strozzi *il giovane* and Raffaello Cavalcanti; Strainchamps, "New Light on the Accademia degli Elevati of Florence," 528. However, it would seem that Ottavio Rinuccini remained faithful to the Elevati, to judge by his letter of 5 August 1609 given in Alessandro Ademollo, *La bell'Adriana*, 57.

17. Carter, "Music-Printing in Late Sixteenth- and Early Seventeenth-Century Florence," 55–56 (partnership), 68–72 (music prints from Florentine presses). For the company, Pignoni was the printer (he was also a musician); the partners were Giovanni Del Turco, Lodovico di Francesco Arrighetti, and the composer Giovanni Battista da Gagliano (brother of Marco), each of whom invested the relatively small sum of *sc.*100 in an *accomandita* arrangement intended to last three years. Four music prints attributed to the partnership appeared in 1614, and one in 1615, although Pignoni also issued editions under his own name during these years, and continued to do so thereafter.

18. A document dated 2 January 1623/24 in LC 2743 (the Grazi miscellany) refers to Vergilio Grazi renting two rooms from Domenico Testi currently occupied by Filippo Vitali's music school (*dove di presente tiene scuola il Signor Filippo Vitali*). Vitali was in Rome in 1618–20 but back in Florence from 1621 to 1631; Grazi was to rent the rooms (at *sc.*10 per year) from May 1624 to April 1625.

19. For Bardi's letter to Doni, see the Introduction. He writes (Solerti, *Le origini del melodramma*, 144) of *una dilettevole e continua academia, dalla quale stando lontano il vizio, e in*

ogy is striking—and typically Florentine—as is the notion that it could operate in the abstract rather than in financial terms. Bardi's statement also
reflects a strong degree of wishful thinking: Florentines were always ready to
gamble on anything and everything—dice, card and ball games, and even
the outcome of a papal conclave—despite regular grand-ducal prohibitions
against it. We have also seen a number of the other vices in which they engaged (viz. Sinolfo Ottieri), and how Peri's sons discovered that the "noble
Florentine youth" could be boorish ruffians when it came to matters such as
the *calcio*.[20] While civilized conversations certainly took place in Florence—
and we shall find Peri partaking in a discussion of the work of Galileo
Galilei—one should probably treat Bardi's idealization of them with a grain
of salt.

Yet one might reasonably ask what these musical consumers, in particular,
were actually consuming. It is hardly likely that Ximenes's eighty *signori e
gentil'huomini* were all actively performing music in the manner often
claimed typical of "amateur" music making in the earlier Renaissance: a
group of friends sitting around a table singing madrigals or playing viols.
While so pleasant an image might itself, at least to some degree, be a historiographical fiction—there have always been professional musicians paid to
perform before an audience—we have seen (in Chapter 3) that contemporaries noted its decline even at the time, in the face of newer musical styles
and genres, and also of their musical demands, which threatened to margin-
alize the amateur performer from modern musical developments save where
they could be modified for easier use. The latter certainly occurred even in
the case of Peri's songs: one of the additions to *Le varie musiche* in its 1619 edition, "Hor che gli augelli," survives in at least two other sources, one notated
in much simpler rhythms and the other (in manuscript) pared to the bones
by way of giving just the text and letter-tablature for the Spanish guitar (obviat-
ing the need to read musical notation at all).[21] For more complex repertories,

---

*particolare ogni sorta di giuoco, la nobile gioventù fiorentina veniva allettata con molto suo gua-
dagno, trattenendosi non solo nella musica, ma ancora in discorsi e insegnamenti di poesia,
d'astrologia, e d'altre scienze, che portavano utile vicendevole a sì bella conversazione.*

20. For Corsi and gambling, see Carter, "Music and Patronage in Late Sixteenth-Century
Florence," 65.

21. For the additional sources, see Appendix C. By the late 1610s there was a vogue for
prints and manuscripts containing "popular" solo songs in versions just with text and so-
called guitar letters (where A, B, C, etc., above the words cued particular chords learned as

however, there was a marked shift in musical consumption in favor of what one might call connoisseurship in terms of listening to, and paying for, performers and performances.[22] While this now made music little different from the other arts—where connoisseurship had long been embedded in the market—it brought clear benefits to the musical profession not just because music needed musicians, but also because there was less canonic resistance to innovation in music given the absence, precisely, of a canon. In the contemporary art market, "old" masters of prior generations at times held higher value than new ones, but music of those same generations commanded scant respect—if indeed it was known at all beyond very narrow professional circles. Jacopo Corsi may have been willing to pay a premium for a Madonna that he thought to be by Pontormo (*fl.*30), far more than he did for new portraits of his daughters by Santi di Tito (£35 and £42), but he was not going to do the same for music from Pontormo's era.[23]

A musical market based on the new would by definition be fragile and mercurial, but it would also be full of opportunities to be taken or missed. While we do not yet have enough evidence to state it as anything more than a hypothesis, it would seem that musicians of Peri's time fared better in status and economic achievement than, say, contemporary painters and sculptors: in part these musicians had greater access to salaried positions, and in part, we have seen, they had more room to maneuver in other professional and economic spheres because, save at the moment of performance, their art need not always have been particularly time-consuming. They were also protected, at least to a degree, by a market that was not particularly international in scope nor highly competitive (save in the case of personal antagonism), and by minimal immediate production costs for the individual music producer

---

finger patterns) and therefore lacking any form of musical notation; see Veneziano, *Rime e suoni alla spagnola*. This is similar to modern-day guitar shorthand (G, Dm, F[7], etc.), though the early seventeenth-century letters do not themselves indicate harmonic content. The method required prior knowledge of the melodies, and also relates to some manner of oral transmission.

22. For the broader issues, see Dell'Antonio, *Listening as Spiritual Practice in Early Modern Italy*.

23. Carter, "Music and Patronage in Late Sixteenth-Century Florence," 69 (Pontormo), 64 (Santi di Tito). For Corsi's purchases of printed music, see ibid., 71–72. While Corsi's buying of music by Dominique Phinot (ca. 1510–ca. 1556)—comprising a setting of the Lamentations of Jeremiah—might seem to be an exception to our remark about "old masters," this music was still current in the repertory.

(the performer or composer) even if there were longer term "costs" for the time and training needed to achieve high professional standards.[24]

We have long known that Jacopo Peri became a somewhat reluctant musician, and this book has shown even more clearly the defined and limited place his art had in his life. Perhaps one should turn the argument around, however: the surprising aspect of his biography is not so much his sometime reticence as a performer and composer, but that he ended up being a musician at all. His widowed mother's strategy for her son (if the strategy was hers) might have been logical enough at the outset: it made sense to put a youngster with actual or potential talent into some manner of musical education because—should talent and training come to fruition—it offered a stable career with some upward social mobility. The wisdom is clear from Peri's early musical appointments up to and including his entrance to the court *musici*: he established himself in significant Florentine institutions and gained a decent set of salaries on which he could have lived if not in comfort, then at least without too much hardship. A few other musicians in Florence may have done better in overall financial terms: Antonio Naldi, for example, left *fl.*24,000 on his death in early 1621, most to *luoghi pii* according to Francesco Rasi.[25] But Peri eventually reached a position not dissimilar to that of Emilio de' Cavalieri, despite starting from a much lower base: when he died in 1602, Cavalieri's assets included *fl.*8,600 in shares of offices and in *censi*, *fl.*6,400 in *luoghi di monte*, a villa worth *fl.*3,000, and an annual income of *fl.*150 from fishing rights.[26] And certainly Peri did not live in disrepute (*più presto sordidamente che altro*), as Rasi reported of Naldi; nor did he have to pay off debts of *fl.*12,000 during his lifetime, as Cavalieri complained on his return to Rome in April 1601, when he also found his "house" (i.e., family) half ruined (*mezza rovinata*).[27] Given what we now know about the capital and other income Peri gained over time, his court salary provided an ever smaller proportion of his total annual income; this may have been true of a few other

24. Of course the big question, which can hardly be answered here, is how these general, and somewhat tentative, remarks might square with a broader comparative view of the art market in this period along lines suggested by Goldthwaite, "The Painting Industry in Early Modern Italy."

25. Kirkendale, *Court Musicians*, 280, citing a letter from Rasi reporting Naldi's death, written on 26 January 1621.

26. Kirkendale, *Emilio de' Cavalieri*, 82.

27. Ibid., 83 (Cavalieri), 280 (Rasi on Naldi).

court musicians as well. But clearly Peri judged it in some way better to stay in court service than not, which one might interpret as a need for security, a resistance to change, or even, perhaps, the view that it was easy money. However, this Orpheus, so well aware of the values beyond the marketplace that he knew so well, may also have felt that his court service was a price worth paying for the range of benefits that ensued: preferment via civic appointments in Florence, contacts and associations with influential persons within and outside the city, and even just the chance to sit at a cardinal's table for dinner.

Behind the Scenes

When Peri took the stage as Orpheus in his opera *Euridice* on 28 May and then 6 October 1600, he must have felt it to be the height of his career. Here he was, at the age of thirty-nine, singing his own music before the grand duke and grand duchess, visiting princes and prelates, and even the new Queen of France. According to his opening lines, those caves that echoed the mythical musician's laments, and the trees that bowed their heads when he did sing, should no longer weep at his mournful song, for it is now a time for celebration.[28] It is a cathartic moment for Orfeo—about to marry his beloved Euridice—but it may have been one for Peri, too, given the not-so-distant events in his personal life that certainly were cause enough for tears: the death of his wife and their children. Or perhaps he enjoyed a moment of personal pride when Plutone, ruler of the Underworld, announced his decision to release Orfeo's bride—allowing mercy and pity to overrule the law—because of the power of the musician's tears and his beautiful singing.[29] What emotions did Peri feel, rather than represent, on so princely a stage? Did he somehow identify himself with Orpheus, a liminal figure able to cross various boundaries by virtue of his art? Alas, we have no way of knowing.

Nor do we have any way of knowing what the real man looked like behind the stage costume he wore in his role as the mythical musician Arion in 1589,

---

28. Orfeo's first speech in *Euridice* begins: *Antri, ch'ai miei lamenti / rimbombaste dolenti, amiche piagge, / e voi, piante selvaggie, / ch'a le dogliose rime / piegaste per pietà l'altere cime, / non fia più no che la mia nobil cetra / con flebil canto a lagrimar v'alletti: / ineffabil mercede, almi diletti, / Amore cortese oggi al mio pianto impetra.*

29. As Plutone says, *Trionfi oggi pietà ne' campi inferni / e sia la gloria e 'l vanto / de le lagrime tue, del tuo bel canto.*

an illustration of which, the frontispiece to this book, is the only representation we have of Peri. No likeness of him survives, although two portraits of Peri, one as a young man, were in his house at the time of his death (a *ritratto del padre di detti erede senza cornice* and a *quadrino ritrattovi il padre di dette erede quando era giovane*), and one of him and another of his wife are listed in the inventory of the house eight years later when Alfonso was living there (*dua quadri dove è dipinto il padre e la madre di Alfonso Peri*). What we know about his appearance comes from Ruspoli's deprecatory poem (see Appendix D) and Rosselli's more measured commentary on it. According to Rosselli, Peri was slender and of medium build and made a handsome presence (*una bonissima presenza*), with a head of notably long hair (hence his nickname Zazzerino) of a color somewhere between blond and red that was especially attractive and remained so well into his old age (when Rosselli knew him). Rosselli adds, however, that the older Peri had thin, splayed legs and large feet that pointed outward so that his manner of walking was open to ridicule.

And what can we tell about Peri's personality? On the face of it, not much seems to emerge from our new material documenting him—most of it generated by Peri himself. He left behind letters, which we publish here, but they were all written on formal occasions, and his *ricordi*, here brought to light for the first time, are firmly rooted in the grand Florentine tradition of recording facts rather than expressions of feeling, a long way from being entries in what we would consider a diary. Yet something still comes through. In his letters one gets a quite strong sense of Peri's character. He emphasizes the demands on his time made by his business affairs (Letters 9, 11, 28) and by his family situation (Letters 11, 17, 20–22), and also mentions what may have been a recurring illness that seems more than just an excuse for not composing or performing (Letter 2). Despite the inevitable formality of courtly correspondence, there are other moments, too, when his personality comes through. It may be hard to tell whether he is annoyed or embarrassed by his blunder in making excuses for not accompanying the *concerto de' castrati* (Letter 3), but one can almost hear his voice out loud in his calls for *pazienza* (Letters 11, 12). In his fifties he could even start making fun of himself, as he imagines an absurdly impulsive trip to Paris (Letter 18). He is not frightened of making his feelings known to Prince, then Cardinal Ferdinando Gonzaga—although the tone changes when Ferdinando becomes duke—and one would never find "messer" Marco da Gagliano, for example, writing to him in the way

Peri does over *Le nozze di Peleo e Tetide* (Letters 8, 12, 17).[30] Ferdinando, too, seems to acknowledge the difference, trying to make peace over the *Tetide* affair by praising Peri in public, by writing poetry in his honor (Letters 12 and 13), and by referring to him in courteous terms.[31] Peri appears to feel genuine affection for his former singing pupil Maria de' Medici, now Queen of France, and even nostalgia for the good old days when he taught the young princesses singing (Letter 18). Such nostalgia comes through still more strongly in Peri's comments to Alessandro Striggio about the latter's musician-father (also Alessandro), whom he praises to the skies and regards as something of a saint (Letters 29–32, the last in particular). These are more than just conventional platitudes: as Peri says when offering to return the younger Striggio's favors (Letter 32), "I swear to you in truth that this is not out of ceremony but for genuine love" (*et le giuro in verità che queste non son cirimonie ma vero amore*).

Likewise, something of the man also emerges in the *ricordi* that Peri made of notable events in his life. Even when they are described without any particular personal comment, something occasionally comes through that lends itself to interpretation. In the course of this narrative of his life, we have recorded occasions that evoked some expression of emotion: the desire to find peace and quiet away from the city; immense satisfaction with any recognition from the grand dukes; frustration and even anger over endless litigation in the courts (to the point of sending him to bed); deeply felt religious sentiments, ranging from his refusal to prosecute one of his delinquent *censuari* because he went about dressed as a priest (as the suspicious Dino wrote) to the severity of the way he wanted to be laid out on the floor of the church for his funeral. Above all emerges a strong personal sense of family: affection expressed on the death of his first two wives; a desire to have children and many of them; pride in Dino but disappointment and distress with Antonio; determination to treat his sons equally; love for his daughter Maria, and joy in accompanying her to a convent; pride in the nuns' recognition of Felice's qualities. This sense of family, moreover, extended beyond his immediate

30. The differences are clear in the letters transcribed in, for example, Strainchamps, "The Unknown Letters of Marco da Gagliano."

31. Ferdinando addresses his letter of 2 March 1620 (on the proposed performance of the Peri–Cicognini *Adone* in Mantua) *Al Signor Giacomo Peri*; Mantua, Archivio di Stato, Archivio Gonzaga 2299. Yet he was also sensitive to the nuances, using *messer* when referring to Peri in a letter to Don Antonio de' Medici of 6 January 1609; see Chapter 3, n. 147.

household to take in distant relatives and in-laws, and dominating it was his explicit and repeated insistence on its nobility. Yet there were limits to whatever patriarchal ambitions he had: he disliked the violence of the *calcio*, notwithstanding its social credentials; he had many sons at a time when noble families sought to protect the future of their patrimony by limiting their male offspring, and hence their inheritance, to just one; and although he took a step toward that protection in imposing a *fedecommesso* on his properties, he invested in temporal leases instead of outright purchases.

Another characteristic of the private man was his dedication to his business affairs. This comes out in the letters when he explains why he has not been able to do anything with music, or why he could not accept commissions (Letters 9, 11, 28); this compulsion to tend to business even when struck by a possibly fatal attack on his health in 1630 is what so distressed Dino. And what he did on the job as a salaried employee in the private sphere suggests that behind this work ethos was the somewhat plodding banality of the accountant. Yet his remarks about being too distracted by other matters to compose music, while convenient, also seem tinged with the occasional note of regret. Presumably he enjoyed his art, at least when it was not an obligation.

Peri was self-effacing about his own work—save when he needed to make a statement—even if he was proud of his accomplishments. He tended to support his musical colleagues, whether a castrato needing a guarantor for the post of *sagrestano maggiore* at S. Lorenzo (Onofrio Gualfreducci in 1593), a fellow composer needing assurances that his music would be properly prepared in his absence (Marco da Gagliano in 1608), or an organist seeking professional advancement (Giovanni Bettini for the post of organist to the Cavalieri di Santo Stefano in 1618).[32] He used his connections to do favors for his friends (Simone Finardi in 1611; see Letter 16), but not to excess, or to the extent of overplaying his hand. He kept himself somewhat aloof from the arguments surrounding the rise of opera, giving credit where it was due (in the preface to *Euridice*) and allowing the record to speak for itself. He generally avoided the controversies and scandals that embroiled other musicians in Florence even if they had some impact on him. And only in the 1620s—when he was in his sixties—does he seem to have become somewhat crotchety in dealing with other court musicians.

32. See Chapter 3 (and Letter 9).

He certainly had his social pretentions: he was attuned to the hierarchical distinctions being made in his day, and in certain spheres, at least, he made it clear how he fit into the scheme of things. By virtue of being a *nobil fiorentino* he claimed the title *signore*, by which he was addressed by many (though not all) of his contemporaries, whether the tradespeople writing in his book of receipts or those of higher status than Peri, such as Ferdinando Gonzaga in his letters. He certainly had higher social aspirations, as we have seen in his connections with Jacopo Corsi, in his choices of godparents for his children, in the professional paths chosen for some of his sons, and in his insistence on the nobility of his family. But his pretensions had limits—he assumed that other of his sons would go to work in one of the city's businesses—as did his family pride: he had no attachment to his family's traditional church after burying his first two wives there (but not their children), and he showed no serious interest in founding a family burial monument or chapel there or elsewhere (although the thought occurred to him on occasion) or in putting his coat of arms in any public place. The three figures that Peri identifies most strongly as his particular friends—although he must have had more— are his business associate "messer" Francesco Brunacci, Don Simone Finardi (prior of S. Pancrazio), and his fellow composer "messer" Marco da Gagliano.[33] These three *amici* well define the various circles in which Peri moved— industry, the church, and music—and while none of them was a *signore*, they perhaps were those with whom he felt most comfortable in his day-to-day life.

On the whole, these impressions somehow come together to form a view of the man that was widely shared at the time: that he was a "nice" person— *di sangue troppo dolce* (as Dino wrote to Galileo, referring to what he considered the casual way his father managed workers on the farms) and *d'ottimi costumi* (as Severo Bonini noted after his death)—not eccentric, and with no exaggerated characteristics, certainly none that generally antagonized other people except for those, like his rival Caccini and the poet Ruspoli, who had their axes to grind. Seen in a wider social perspective, as a citizen-judge of the city's worst criminals, Peri reveals himself a man of fairness and considerable

33. For other of Peri's "friends" (the poet Francesco Cini, the son [Ottavio] of Vittoria Archilei, and Giovanni Battista Signorini), see Letter 11. However, Peri's emphasis here on *amici mia* may be, rather, to reassure Cardinal Ferdinando Gonzaga that he has adhered to etiquette by keeping the cardinal's music within a small circle.

humanity. And clearly he was also devout: it is probably no coincidence that the last two songs in *Le varie musiche* are settings of devotional texts, and we have already imagined him singing "O miei giorni fugaci" as he considered the nature of growing old, just as, when he could sing it no more, he might have played the surviving keyboard arrangement on the spinet in his house to offer some manner of spiritual consolation.

Of course, the relatively benign impression that has emerged from our study could just be the result of the surviving documents, and something murkier may lie beneath their surface (as we have suggested with Sinolfo Ottieri). Much about Peri also still remains hidden from us. We know virtually nothing, for instance, about his intellectual interests. Yet his household may have enjoyed a certain cultural ambience: his third wife came from a refined family (as we know from the inventory of her childhood home and from the interests of her uncle), and at least two of their sons pursued careers as intellectuals. Consider also the image of Peri that emerges in the Galileo correspondence—not in letters between the two men (there are none that survive, if there ever were any) but in comments the correspondents make about him. Galileo (1564–1642) was an almost exact contemporary of Peri's and most likely knew him through his father Vincenzo's musical activity: Galileo himself played the lute and keyboard instruments, and as one would expect of any scientist–mathematician in this period, he had at least a passing interest in experiments involving the acoustic properties of music, as well as taking enjoyment in it as an art.[34] His letters point to more than just a personal acquaintance, or even friendship, with Peri. Niccolò Aggiunti (1600–35), one of the bright young protégés with whom Galileo surrounded himself (Dino was another), adds to a letter he wrote to his mentor on 29 April 1624 a postscript in which he sends affectionate greetings from Peri (*saluta Vostra Signoria affettuosissimamente*), with whom, adds this young man forty years Peri's junior, he had spent a couple of hours the other day talking about the great mathematician's work.[35] At the time, Aggiunti was tutor to the young Grand Duke Ferdinando II, and only two years later he was named to a professorship at Pisa, the post that, after his premature death, passed to Dino. Later, in 1628, when Galileo was getting ready for the graduation of his son, Vincenzo,

---

34. Walker, "Some Aspects of the Musical Theory of Vincenzo Galilei and Galileo Galilei."

35. Galilei, *Le opere*, 13: 176.

from the university at Pisa, he asked Peri to write to the rector there about the attendant costs, rather than making a direct enquiry on his own behalf.[36] Galileo's keen personal interest in Peri was certainly the reason that Dino wrote him the long letter—cited in Chapter 4 almost in its entirety—in which he recounts the details of the collapse his father suffered in May 1630. And perhaps fearful of Peri's death, Galileo a few days later wrote to Dino asking for some of his father's music, to which Dino responded, in the letter we have also cited, bringing his mentor up to date on his father's recovery.

And then there is Peri's literary culture. Here, too, the documents reveal nothing about this, and we do not have an inventory of any of the books he may have possessed. Yet Peri is without doubt a "literary" composer, both in his poetic choices and in his sensitivities to language and to rhetoric. These sensitivities are apparent also in his *ricordi* and letters, with their nuanced vocabulary, careful spelling, and graduated system of punctuation signs quite different from what one finds in earlier Florentine writing. This is not unusual for the later sixteenth century in the context of the language reforms promoted by Pietro Bembo and then the Accademia della Crusca. But of all his contemporaries, Peri perhaps came closest to finding an appropriate musical means to convey and express what he called (in the preface to *Euridice*) *la nostra favella*.[37] The poems that he set in his chamber songs also tend to exhibit a literary taste beyond the norm, and a desire to set them (for example, the Petrarch sonnets) in a nonformulaic manner with respect to structure and to individual musical-rhetorical gestures that, we have seen, avoid the flashier virtuosity typical of a good number of his contemporaries. His careful accounting of the text and his evident preference for some kind of musical moderation suggest that here, perhaps, the man and his music are of a piece.

But that "perhaps" lets slip the perils of any biographical enterprise. However extensive the documentation we now have for Peri, it will never be enough. His account books are limited by scope and purpose; his letters, however revealing, remain constrained by formality and convention; and while at least a decent part of his music survives and can be read in various ways, we cannot hear him sing it himself. The biographer relies on, and must be faithful to, the documents, but the inferences drawn from them, and the

36. This we learn from the letter the rector then wrote to Galileo; ibid., 13: 224–25.

37. This is also the conclusion drawn, on detailed technical grounds, in Hill, "Beyond Isomorphism toward a Better Theory of Recitative."

speculations made upon them, are hazardous at best, and always prone to wishful thinking. Is there more to be found about Peri in the archives? Undoubtedly, yes. Are there other stories to be told about him? Answer: the same.

Nevertheless, he has already illuminated much about the worlds in which he moved. We have concentrated on the economic and musical contexts, but Peri has also presented us with enough material about the social scene to inspire further research into the profound changes that Florentine society underwent under the first Medici grand dukes, with the ever-poorer poor, the ever-richer rich, and an ever-growing class of people, like Peri, in between, all subsumed under an increasingly hierarchical structure. We have seen how his economic, musical, and domestic spheres intersected in various ways—for example, in his networking to gain favor, and in his appeal to business and family concerns to explain a lack of music or its defects. Especially when he goes so far as to think about how an exchange (*senseria*) of notes in a musical passage will produce a good profit (*buon guadagno*), and how it is important to make capital of good advice, he is revealing hints of how deeply rooted he was in the culture of the marketplace.[38] If it has been his account books that for us have now brought Peri into the marketplace for the first time, they have shown us that in fact he had been there all the while.

38. For the exchange of musical notes, see Letter 11 (by one reading). Peri advocates making capital of good advice in his draft statement to the Otto di Guardia e Balìa; see Chapter 1, n. 136.

APPENDIX A

Chronology

Note: Entries related to Peri's musical activities are *italicized*; an asterisk indicates that these music-related entries are recorded in Ledger A.

1561	
Aug 20	birth of Jacopo di Antonio di Francesco Peri (in Rome?).
1573	
Sep 1 (–1577)	*hired to sing* laude *to the organ at SS. Annunziata at monthly salary of £3.10s. (until 30 Sep 1577).*
1576	
May 1	earliest date for payment of a servant (by his mother).
1577	
—	*Cristofano Malvezzi includes Peri's* Ricercar del primo tuono *in his* Il primo libro de recercari à quattro voci;
Sep 30	*ends service at SS. Annunziata.*
1579	
—	heir, with his cousin Cesare, of their grandmother, her only known asset being a credit for a loan of *fl.*250 made several years earlier;
Feb 1 (–1605)	*hired as organist at the Badia at annual salary of sc.15 (until April 1605);*
Dec 24	*receives mancia of £2 from SS. Annunziata.*
Late 1570s?	*becomes member of the Compagnia dell'Arcangelo Raffaello (S. Maria Novella).*
1580	
Nov 1	first entry on rental account for house in Via dell'Alloro;
Nov 4	*fl.*292 deposited in the Monte di Pietà from the estate of his grandmother, to be shared with his cousin Cesare.

(continued)

1582

—   opens his first ledger.

1583

Feb 16   *Giovanni Fedini's* Le due Persilie *performed before the Medici*
                             princesses, with music in part by Peri;

Mar 1   *Cristofano Malvezzi includes Peri's "Caro dolce ben mio" in his* Il
                             primo libro delli madrigali a cinque voci;

Sep 7?   lent *du.*30 by Jacopo Corsi.

1584

Jan 20   **sends* canti da liuto *to Venice;*

Jul 5   received *fl.*296 from his cousin Cesare on the latter's profession
                             as a friar;

late Aug–Sep   *Eleonora de' Medici (who married Prince Vincenzo Gonzaga in*
                             April), requests Peri's presence in Mantua, but he is in Meldola
                             with Malvezzi for wedding of latter's sister. On his return to
                             Florence, however, Peri goes to Mantua and renews contact
                             with Alessandro Striggio (the elder).

1585

Jul 6   invests *fl.*300 in Lorenzo Michelozzi & Partners, *lanaioli.*

1586

—   *Cristofano Malvezzi's court salary includes allowance for his pupil,*
                             Peri;

May 1   rents house in Via dei Ginori;

Aug 28 (–1590)   *hired as singer at S. Giovanni Battista at six-monthly salary of sc.9*
                             (until 21 Mar 1590);

Sep 12   purchases first piece of land above Rostolena, Val di Sieve, for
                             *fl.*76; down to 1600 buys other properties there for *fl.*254 to
                             build up a *podere.*

1587

Feb   **orders two lutes from Padua for the use of the princesses;*

Oct 19   Grand Duke Francesco I de' Medici dies; succeeded by Grand
                             Duke Ferdinando I de' Medici.

1588

Feb 23   contracts for Malvezzi's prebend on farm at San Marco
                             Vecchio;

Sep   *appears on list of court musicians at monthly wage of sc.6;*

Sep 16   *Letter 1 to Virginia de' Medici d'Este (who married Cesare d'Este,*
                             later Duke of Modena, in February 1586) about sending music
                             to Ferrara.

1589

May 2 — *performance of Girolamo Bargagli's* La pellegrina *and* intermedi *in Teatro degli Uffizi at wedding festivities for Grand Duke Ferdinando I and Christine of Lorraine, with music in part by Peri (who also sings);* the intermedi *are repeated on 6, 13, 15 May, and 9 June.*

1590

Mar 21 — *ends service at S. Giovanni Battista;*

Sep 21 — *his monthly salary at court is increased to* sc.9.

1591

Mar 1 — **pays monthly rent through Giovanni Francesco Trombone;*

Apr 3 — **pays monthly rent through Giovanni Francesco Trombone;*

Dec 20 — **borrows £70 from Cristofano Malvezzi (paid back by 12 May 1592).*

1592

Nov 10 — contracts first marriage with Caterina di Niccolò Fortunati (arranged by Giovambattista Michelozzi).

1593

May 19 — *serves as guarantor for the castrato Onofrio Gualfreducci's appointment as* sagrestano maggiore *of S. Lorenzo.*

1594

Feb 10 — birth of son Giovambattista;

Mar 24 — death of son Giovambattista.

1594–95

— — *Jacopo Corsi approaches Peri to set to music* Dafne *(text by Ottavio Rinuccini).*

1595

Jun 25 — birth of daughter Felice.

1596

Mar 13 — gains farm at Marciano as consequence of death of wife's father, Niccolò Fortunati, as balance owed on dowry (pays *fl.*422 for other contiguous properties down to 1610);

Aug 15 — invests *fl.*2,000 in Francesco Michelozzi & Partners, *setaioli*;

Nov 1 — buys house in Via dei Fossi for *fl.*1,000, and subsequently pays *fl.*103 for improvements;

Dec 15 (–1597) — appointed one of the twelve Buonuomini di Collegio (until 5 Mar 1597).

1597

Jul 9 — birth of daughter, Baccina;

Sep 26 — death of daughter Felice (buried in the Badia Fiesolana);

Nov 26 — death of daughter Baccina (buried in S. Paolino).

(continued)

1597–98

Carnival   *first performance of* Dafne *in presence of Don Giovanni de'*
                  Medici; Peri sings role of Apollo.

1598

Jan–Dec   appointed one of the Capitani di Orsanmichele;

Nov 16   birth of daughter Caterina; death of wife Caterina in childbirth
                  (buried in S. Simone).

1599

Jan 21   *performance of* Dafne *in Palazzo Pitti in presence of Cardinals*
                  Del Monte and Montalto and probably Grand Duchess
                  Christine (may have been preceded by a private performance in
                  Corsi's palace just before 18 Jan); libretto printed;

Jan 23   invests *fl.*200 in wool venture with Domenico Peri (plus *fl.*100
                  later in year);

Feb 1   *takes in Jacopo Giusti to teach him singing and playing.*

1599–1600

Carnival   *performance of* Dafne *(unclear where); libretto printed in second*
                  edition (but after 25 March?).

1600

Mar 14   *Vittoria Archilei refers to Peri preparing music for Holy Week in*
                  Pisa;

May 28   *first performance of* Euridice *(text by Ottavio Rinuccini) in*
                  Palazzo Pitti; Peri sings role of Orfeo;

Aug (–1603)   employed as cashier in the firm of Della Rena, Fiorini &
                  Partners, *lanaioli* (until Oct 1603);

Oct 6   *performance of* Euridice *in Palazzo Pitti as part of the wedding*
                  festivities for Maria de' Medici and Henri IV of France; Peri
                  sings role of Orfeo;

Oct 9   *sings in* Il rapimento di Cefalo *(text by Gabriello Chiabrera;*
                  music by Giulio Caccini and others) in Teatro degli Uffizi as
                  part of wedding festivities;

Nov 1   invests *fl.*1,000 as partner in Della Rena, Fiorini & Partners,
                  lanaioli;

Nov 18   *Letter 2 (probably to Belisario Vinta) seeking to excuse himself*
                  from working with the concerto de' castrati;

Nov 21   *Letter 3 (probably to Belisario Vinta) noting his agreement to work*
                  with the concerto de' castrati.

1601

Feb 6   *dedicates to Maria de' Medici the printed score of* Euridice;

Oct 20   death of daughter Caterina (last child by first marriage; buried
                  in S. Paolino);

Dec (–1602)   appointed *camerlengo*, Arte dei Medici e Speziali (until May
                  1602);

Dec 13	*settles accounts with Giorgio Marescotti for printing of* Euridice; makes dowry arrangements for second marriage to Ginevra di Piero Casellesi.

1602

Aug 5	death of wife Ginevra (buried in S. Simone);
Sep–Dec	appointed consul, Arte dei Medici e Speziali;
Oct 26	concludes marriage arrangements with Alessandra di Dino Fortini; gains farm at Castelvecchio from dowry.

1603

Mar–Jun	appointed one of the Otto di Guardia e Balìa;
Apr 15	*accompanies princesses to Villa di Castello with a dancing master;*
Aug?	*Enea Vaini reports on the court music, noting that Peri is still performing with castratos but may be replaced because he is having problems with his hearing.*

1604

Jan 29	birth of daughter Ginevra;
Feb 2	death of Ginevra (buried in S Paolino);
Jul 21	buys a *censo* for *fl*.2,500 (other *censi* purchases for *fl*.254 follow in this year);
Sep–Dec	appointed consul, Arte dei Medici e Speziali;
Oct 26	Dafne *performed in Palazzo Pitti before Duke Ranuccio Farnese of Parma; libretto (1600 edition) survives with new 1604 title page and revised prologue;*
Nov 6	invests *fl*.102 in Monte delle Graticole.

1605

Feb 10, 12	*Letters 4 and 5 to Grand Duchess Christine about a* sbarra *by Michelangelo Buonarroti il giovane with music by Peri;*
Feb 22	*performance of the* sbarra *in Pisa;*
Mar–Jul	invests *fl*.500 in Francesco Michelozzi & Partners, *lanaioli;*
Apr	*ends service at the Badia;*
May 12	birth of son Antonio;
Jul 23	buys lifetime lease on a *poderetto* with a *casa da padrone* in Pian di Ripoli for *fl*.300.

1606

Mar 22	*performs Holy Week music arranged by Ferdinando Gonzaga in S. Nicola, Pisa;*
Jun 7	birth of son Dino;
Nov (–1607)	appointed one of the eight Conservatori di Legge (until Apr 1607).

1607

Jun	*Marco da Gagliano establishes the Accademia degli Elevati (under protection of Ferdinando Gonzaga), with Peri as a member;*

(continued)

Aug–Nov	*Francesco Cini negotiates with Ferdinando Gonzaga to have his* Le nozze di Peleo e Tetide *(music by Peri) performed in Mantua for the forthcoming festivities celebrating the wedding of Prince Francesco Gonzaga and Margherita of Savoy;*
Aug 11	*Letter 6 to Prince Ferdinando Gonzaga sending music;*
Aug 19	birth of daughter Maria;
Oct 26	*Letter 7 to Prince Ferdinando Gonzaga about* Le nozze di Peleo e Tetide;
Nov 12	*Letter 8 to Prince Ferdinando Gonzaga about* Le nozze di Peleo e Tetide.

1608

Jan 1	*Girolamo Montesardo includes Peri's "Ho visto al mio dolore" (text by Alessandro Striggio [the younger]) in his* L'allegre notti di Fiorenza;
Mar 10	*Letter 9 to Cardinal Ferdinando Gonzaga agreeing to rehearse Marco da Gagliano's songs for one, two, and three voices;*
Apr 8	*Letter 10 to Cardinal Ferdinando Gonzaga congratulating him on his contributions to Marco da Gagliano's* Dafne *(performed in Mantua in late February or early March);*
Apr 23	*Letter 11 to Cardinal Ferdinando Gonzaga saying he has not composed anything recently because of other business and the death of relatives and friends;*
Jun 30	*Letter 12 to Cardinal Ferdinando Gonzaga congratulating him on the recent wedding festivities in Mantua;*
Jul 28	*Letter 13 to Cardinal Ferdinando Gonzaga sending a sonnet setting and an aria;*
Oct 25	*performance of Michelangelo Buonarroti il giovane's* Il giudizio di Paride *and intermedi in Teatro degli Uffizi at wedding festivities for Prince Cosimo de' Medici and Maria Magdalena of Austria, with music in part by Peri (who also sings);*
Nov 19	*repeat performance of Michelangelo Buonarroti il giovane's* Il giudizio di Paride *and intermedi;*
Dec 15	*Letter 14 to Duchess Eleonora de' Medici Gonzaga about training a female singer for Mantua.*

1609

—	*publishes* Le varie musiche;
Jan 20	*Letter 15 to Cardinal Ferdinando Gonzaga declining his request to come to Mantua for Carnival;*
Feb 7	Grand Duke Ferdinando I de' Medici dies; succeeded by Grand Duke Cosimo II de' Medici;
Feb 15	invests *fl.*2,000 as partner in his own wool partnership;
Mar 17	birth of son Alfonso.

1610

Jan–Jun	appointed one of the four Soprastanti delle Stinche;
Feb 15	invests *fl*.423 in Niccolò Peri & Partners, dyers;
Jun	*sings with Adriana Basile in Caccini's house, and is said (by Rinuccini) to admire Monteverdi's music;*
Jul 2	buys a *censo* for *fl*.100 at Marciano;
Aug 14	birth of son Niccolò;
Sep (–1611)	appointed one of the Nove Conservatori del Dominio (until Feb 1611);
Dec 19	buys a *censo* for *fl*.100 at Marciano.

1611

Feb 14	*performance of a* balletto *(text by Ottavio Rinuccini) in Palazzo Pitti, with music in part by Peri (who sings role of Nettuno); one of his songs, "Torna, deh torna, pargoletto mio," is later published in Piero Benedetti's* Musiche *(1611);*
Mar 26	Letter 16 to Cardinal Ferdinando Gonzaga recommending poetry by Simone Finardi;
May 14	*Letter 17 to Cardinal Ferdinando Gonzaga about having set Cicognini's* Adone *to music;*
Sep 22	birth of daughter Giustina;
Nov 12	Letter 18 to Cardinal Ferdinando Gonzaga about his wish to visit the court of Maria de' Medici in Paris;
Dec 12	*Piero Benedetti includes Peri's "Torna, deh torna, pargoletto mio" (from Feb 1611 balletto) in his* Musiche.

1612

Aug 22	buys three-generation lease on farm near Bagno a Ripoli for *fl*.2,000 (pays *fl*.600 for improvements until 1618);
Sep–Dec	appointed consul, Arte dei Medici e Speziali;
Sep 5	birth of son Francesco.

1613

Feb 17, 19	*performance of a tournament and* mascherata *in honor of Prince Federigo Della Rovere of Urbino (betrothed to Princess Claudia de' Medici), perhaps with music by Peri;*
May 5	*performance of* Mascherata di ninfe di Senna *(text by Ottavio Rinuccini revising 1611 balletto with new first part) in Palazzo Pitti, probably with music by Peri;*
Nov 16	birth of daughter Felice.

1614

Feb 9	*performance of a* balletto *ending with* Marte ed Amore *(devised by Ferdinando Saracinelli) for baptism of Prince Mattias de' Medici, with music in part by Peri (who was also to have written music for Michelangelo Buonarroti il giovane's Balletto della cortesia performed on 11 Feb, but he was indisposed);*

(continued)

May–Aug	appointed consul, Arte dei Medici e Speziali;
Jul 25	*Antonio Brunelli includes Peri's "O dell'alto Appenin figlio sovrano" (for wedding of Conte Francesco Torelli) in his* Scherzi . . . libro secondo;
Aug 18	gains a *censo* for *fl*.60 at Marciano (in settlement with a debtor);
Sep 12	invests *fl*.451 in *monti* in Rome;
Sep 29	pays *fl*.600 toward the agreement his wife made with her brother to take possession of farm at Cicogna in exchange for an annuity.

1615

Feb 16	*performance of* Veglia delle Grazie *(text by Gabriello Chiabrera), with music for two* intermedi *by Peri;*
Jun (–1616)	appointed one of the four Ufficiali della Decima (until May 1616);
Nov 6	invests *du*.281 in *monti* in Rome.

1616

Feb 11	*performance of the equestrian ballet* Guerra d'Amore *(text by Andrea Salvadori) in Piazza S. Croce, with music in part by Peri;*
Feb 16	*performance of a* ballo rusticale *(devised by Ferdinando Saracinelli) in Palazzo Pitti, with music by Lorenzo Allegri and Peri;*
Feb 20	birth of daughter Caterina;
Mar 21–Apr 30	**in Bologna for performance of* Euridice *at request of Cardinal Luigi Capponi;*
Apr 2	*Jacopo Cicognini suggests to Paolo Giordano Orsini that Peri would be willing to perform* Adone *during his forthcoming trip to Rome;*
Apr 20	*Letter 19 to Duke Ferdinando Gonzaga declining invitation to go to Mantua because of impending trip to Rome;*
Apr 27	*performance of* Euridice *in Bologna;*
May 5–Jun 9	**in Rome in the service of Cardinal Carlo de' Medici;*
Sep–Nov	invests *fl*.524 in *monti* in Rome;
Oct 16	*performance of the equestrian ballet* Guerra di bellezza *(text by Andrea Salvadori) in Piazza S. Croce in honor of Prince Federigo Della Rovere of Urbino, with music by Paolo Grazi and Peri;*
Dec	*Angelica Furini lodges with Peri to learn singing.*

1617

Feb 6	*performance of* veglia, La liberazione di Tirreno ed Arnea *(text by Andrea Salvadori) at festivities for wedding of Caterina de' Medici and Ferdinando Gonzaga, with music by Marco da Gagliano and perhaps in part by Peri (but probably not);*
Feb 22–Aug 22	appointed Podestà, Pontassieve;
Mar 20	birth of son Cosimo;
May 27	Letter 20 to Duke Ferdinando Gonzaga requesting recommendation for offices in Tuscany to support his large family;
Nov 12	invests *fl*.1,000 as partner in Arcangelo Innori & Partners, *setaioli*.

1618

Jan 8	Letter 21 to Duchess Caterina de' Medici Gonzaga requesting recommendation for offices in Tuscany;
Jan 29	Letter 22 to Duchess Caterina de' Medici Gonzaga repeating request for recommendation for offices in Tuscany; Letter 23 to Andrea Cioli enclosing petition to grand duchess for these offices;
Feb 4	Letter 24 to Andrea Cioli thanking him for his help with the petition;
Mar 25	birth of son Giulio Cesare;
Mar 28	appointed *camerlengo generale* of Arte della Lana for life with monthly salary of *fl*.10;
Apr 23	Letters 25 and 26 to Duke Ferdinando Gonzaga and Duchess Caterina de' Medici Gonzaga thanking them for their recommendations;
Jun 22	invests *fl*.285 in *monti* in Rome;
Aug	*auditions (with Marco da Gagliano) Giovanni Bettini for post of organist of Cavalieri di Santo Stefano.*

1619

—	*new edition of* Le varie musiche *dedicated to Ferdinando Saracinelli;*
Mar (–1620)	appointed one of the ten Capitani di Parte Guelfa (until Feb 1620);
May 7	birth of daughter Lucrezia;
Sep 25	*performance of opera* Lo sposalizio di Medoro ed Angelica *(text by Andrea Salvadori) in Palazzo Pitti in honor of succession of Emperor Ferdinand II, with music by Marco da Gagliano and Peri;*
Oct 26	invests *fl*.300 in Monte di Pietà.

1620

—	*Giovanni Stefani includes Peri's "Hor che gli augelli" in the second edition of his* Scherzi amorosi . . . Libro secondo *(the first edition, probably from 1619, is lost);*
Mar–Aug	appointed one of the nine Conservatori del Dominio;
Mar	*Letter 27 to Duke Ferdinando Gonzaga about possible performance of* Adone *(text by Jacopo Cicognini) in Mantua in late April/early May;*
Mar 24	*Letter 28 to Duchess Caterina de' Medici Gonzaga about a* ballo *for performance in Mantua in late April/early May;*
Mar 30	*Letter 29 to Alessandro Striggio (the younger), about the Mantuan performances;*
Apr 7, 14	*Letters 30 and 31 to Alessandro Striggio about the Mantuan performances (although* Adone *has been dropped);*
Easter	*directs (and composes?) music for Holy Week (in S. Nicola in Pisa?);*

(*continued*)

Apr 26	*performance of Peri's* ballo *in Mantua (repeated on 4 May);*
Apr 28	*Letter 32 to Alessandro Striggio about the Mantuan* ballo;
May 4	*repeat performance of Peri's* ballo *in Mantua;*
Sep 28	travels to Prato for daughter Maria's investiture as nun;
Nov 27	invests *fl.*200 in Monte di Pietà;
Dec 26	birth of daughter Teresa.

1621

Feb 28	Grand Duke Cosimo II de' Medici dies; succeeded by a minor, Ferdinando II, under a regency;
Mar–Jun	appointed one of the Otto di Guardia e Balìa;
Apr 29	Claudia de' Medici marries Prince (soon to be Duke) Federigo Della Rovere of Urbino;
Aug 18	appointed a member of Consiglio dei Duecento for life;
Nov 11	death of daughter Lucrezia (buried in Ognissanti).

1622

Mar 24	*directs (and composes?) music for Holy Week in S. Nicola, Pisa;*
May–Aug	appointed consul, Arte dei Medici e Speziali;
May 16	birth of daughter Ottavia;
Sep 11–26	*five performances of a* sacra rappresentazione, La benedittione di Jacob *(text by Giovan Maria Cecchi, revised by Jacopo Cicognini), in Compagnia dell'Arcangelo Raffaello (S. Maria Novella), with music by Giovanni Battista da Gagliano and Peri;*
Dec (–1623)	appointed one of the six Procuratori di Palazzo (until May 1623);
Dec 25, 27, 31	*three performances of a* sacra rappresentazione, Il gran natale di Christo salvator nostro *(text by Jacopo Cicognini), in Compagnia dell'Arcangelo Raffaello, with music by Giovanni Battista da Gagliano and Peri.*

1623

Apr 12	*composes and directs music for Holy Week in S. Nicola, Pisa;*
Jun (–1624)	appointed one of the four Ufficiali della Decima (until May 1624).

1624

—	first documented contacts with Galileo Galilei;
Jan 5	*performance of a* sacra rappresentazione, La celeste guida, o vero L'arcangelo Raffaello *(text by Jacopo Cicognini), in Compagnia dell'Arcangelo Raffaello, with music by Giovanni Battista da Gagliano and Peri;*
Jul 1	invests *fl.*300 in Monte di Pietà;
Sep 18	buys a house in the Via dei Servi for *fl.*501;
Oct 7	*performance by Francesca Campagnolo and ?Francesca Caccini of Peri's* Canzone delle lodi d'Austria *in honor of visit of Archduke Karl of Austria;*

Nov	*involved in disputes over the music for a forthcoming (January 1625) performance of the* sacra rappresentazione, La regina Sant'Orsola *(text by Andrea Salvadori);*
Dec 12	birth of son Carlo.

1625

Feb 10	*performance of a tournament,* La precedenza delle dame *(text by Andrea Salvadori), sponsored by Cardinal Carlo de' Medici in honor of visit of Prince Władisław of Poland, with music by Peri;*
Sep (–1626)	appointed one of the four Maestri di Dogana (until Aug 1626).

1626

Mar	*(or Mar 1625?) sets text(s) by Michelangelo Buonarroti il giovane for Don Pietro de' Medici;*
Mar 16	invests *fl.*200 in the Monte di Pietà;
Mar 25	Claudia de' Medici marries (by proxy) Archduke Leopold of Austria.

1627

Mar 22	death of son Antonio (buried in S. Maria Novella);
Aug 19	death of daughter Caterina (buried in S. Maria Novella).
1627–28	*sets to music (part of?)* Iole ed Ercole *(text by Andrea Salvadori) for forthcoming festivities for the wedding of Margherita de' Medici and Odoardo Farnese, but the opera is dropped.*

1628

Mar 28	buys a house in Borgo Ognissanti for *fl.*361, and subsequently pays *fl.*64 for improvements;
May 17	rector of University of Pisa writes to Galileo Galilei about university fees in response to a request by Peri;
Jun–Nov	appointed one of the six Procuratori di Palazzo;
Aug 1	death of son Carlo (buried in S. Maria Novella);
Oct 14	*performance of the opera* Flora *(text by Andrea Salvadori) in Teatro degli Uffizi at festivities for Medici–Farnese wedding, with music by Marco da Gagliano and Peri.*

1629

Jan–Jun	appointed Podestà, Sesto;
Jul 5	procures chapel in S. Ambrogio as future benefice for his son Francesco;
Jul 17	his wife inherits half of her family house in Borgo SS. Apostoli, and in September gains the other half through an exchange with her brother for an annuity.

1630

May 8	suffers a serious attack on his health;
May 15	makes his will;

(continued)

Jul 9	obtains chapel in S. Frediano as benefice for his son Francesco;
Aug 24	Letter 33 to Cardinal Francesco Barberini thanking him for his willingness to consider an unnamed benefice for his son Francesco.

1631

Jan 8	invests *fl.*200 in Monte di Pietà;
Jun (–1632)	appointed one of the four Ufficiali della Decima (until May 1632);
Nov 13	invests *fl.*200 in Monte di Pietà.

1632

Feb 16	invests *fl.*200 in Monte di Pietà;
May 28	buys *censo* on house in Florence for *fl.*200;
Aug	appointed Podestà at Montevarchi but declines;
Dec 29	death of daughter Felice.

1633

Jun–Jul	invests *fl.*2,300 in Monte del Sale;
Aug 10	dies;
Aug 13	buried in S. Maria Novella;
Aug 21	memorial service for Peri held in Compagnia dell'Arcangelo Raffaello.

APPENDIX B

Letters from Jacopo Peri

1   To Virginia de' Medici d'Este (Ferrara), 16 September 1588
2   To ?Belisario Vinta (Florence), 18 November 1600
3   To ?Belisario Vinta (Florence), 21 November 1600
4   To Grand Duchess Christine of Lorraine (?Pisa), 10 February 1604/5
5   To Grand Duchess Christine of Lorraine (?Pisa), 12 February 1604/5
6   To Prince Ferdinando Gonzaga (Mantua), 11 August 1607
7   To Prince Ferdinando Gonzaga (Mantua), 26 October 1607
8   To Prince Ferdinando Gonzaga (Mantua), 12 November 1607
9   To Cardinal Ferdinando Gonzaga (Mantua), 10 March 1607/8
10   To Cardinal Ferdinando Gonzaga (Mantua), 8 April 1608
11   To Cardinal Ferdinando Gonzaga (Mantua), 23 April 1608
12   To Cardinal Ferdinando Gonzaga (Mantua), 30 June 1608
13   To Cardinal Ferdinando Gonzaga (Mantua), 28 July 1608
14   To Duchess Eleonora de' Medici Gonzaga (Mantua), 15 December 1608
15   To Cardinal Ferdinando Gonzaga (Mantua), 20 January 1608/9
16   To Cardinal Ferdinando Gonzaga (Mantua), 26 March 1611
17   To Cardinal Ferdinando Gonzaga (Mantua), 14 May 1611
18   To Cardinal Ferdinando Gonzaga (?Paris), 12 November 1611
19   To Duke Ferdinando Gonzaga (Mantua), 20 April 1616
20   To Duke Ferdinando Gonzaga (Mantua), 27 May 1617
21   To Duchess Caterina de' Medici Gonzaga (Mantua), 8 January 1617/18
22   To Duchess Caterina de' Medici Gonzaga (Mantua), 29 January 1617/18
23   To Andrea Cioli (Florence), 29 January 1617/18
24   To Andrea Cioli (Florence), 4 February 1617/18
25   To Duke Ferdinando Gonzaga (Mantua), 23 April 1618
26   To Duchess Caterina de' Medici Gonzaga (Mantua), 23 April 1618
27   To Duke Ferdinando Gonzaga (Mantua), March 1619/20
28   To Duchess Caterina de' Medici Gonzaga (Mantua), 24 March 1619/20
29   To Alessandro Striggio (the younger; Mantua), 30 March 1620
30   To Alessandro Striggio (the younger; Mantua), 7 April 1620
31   To Alessandro Striggio (the younger; Mantua), 14 April 1620
32   To Alessandro Striggio (the younger; Mantua), 28 April 1620
33   To Cardinal Francesco Barberini (Rome), 24 August 1630

We have thirty-three letters written by the musician Jacopo Peri, spanning the period from 1588 to 1630. As one might expect—whether because of the nature of the correspondence (and its recipients) or because of the types of archival searches undertaken by scholars—these letters largely concern Peri's musical work. The main exceptions are the sequence in 1617–18 that he wrote to persons in Florence and Mantua seeking support for his petition to the Medici to be given an office that would provide additional income to help support his family (Letters 20–26), which resulted in his appointment as *camerlengo* of the Arte della Lana in April 1618, and Letter 33, written in 1630 in the hope of gaining an ecclesiastical benefice for his son Francesco. We have relatively few letters from Peri to the Medici or their officials; he would have needed to write to them only when he felt that something more formal than a direct conversation was required (see Letters 2, 3, 24, and 25), or when the court was elsewhere (Letters 4 and 5). The bulk of his surviving letters are addressed, rather, to Prince (then Cardinal, then Duke) Ferdinando Gonzaga of Mantua, with whom Peri had a long-term, if sporadic, relationship (see Chapter 3). It would be foolish to claim, however, that the present collection of Peri's letters is in any way complete, and that there are not others still to be found in libraries and archives not yet mined by scholars working on this period.

Nothing written to Peri survives, so far as we know; apparently such letters, if they were kept at all, were not of interest to the state when it confiscated his son Alfonso's property. However, for Letter 27 we do have a minute (a secretary's summary) of the letter to which Peri was replying. Having only one side of the correspondence creates typical problems: the letters are clear enough when Peri was writing on his own initiative, but when he was responding directly to something previously sent or communicated to him, his points are sometimes obscure (see Letters 10 and 11).

All thirty-three letters are in Peri's own (very readable) hand: clearly he did not see a need to pay a scribe for elegant copperplate (see Figures A.1–A.3). Most of them were written on a single side of a half-bifolium: the other half would typically have been folded over and used to write the address—with the whole usually folded again—although this half has often been removed from the surviving letters, and there is rarely any indication of how a letter was sealed (Letter 1 is a useful exception). As Peri got older, he was sometimes willing to leave minor corrections and additions in place rather than starting a letter anew; in his last surviving letter (Letter 33), written when he was sixty-nine, he shows other signs of age as well in his handwriting. He tended to write without great ceremony, apart from the conventional openings and closings, plus commonplace politenesses that only occasionally tend toward the extreme; the letters are straightforward and direct—save when Peri got into an awkward situation—which surely reflects his sense of status. In his letters and *ricordi* he was very careful with spelling, and only a few characteristics of the Florentine dialect have crept in, such as the placing of the aspirate *h* after a hard *c* or the confusion of liquid consonants—*chreda* (once in Letter 11), *um poco* for *un poco* (Letters 14, 21), *im particolare* (Letters 2, 11), *el* for *il* (more often)—and a not atypical (for Tuscans) tendency to use the first-person feminine singular possessive pronoun as a feminine and masculine plural (e.g., *per molte mia imperfettioni* in Letter 2), and to suppress the *v* in conjugating *(h)avere* (*harò, hauto,* etc.). Peri uses diacriticals very carefully, and also has a strikingly nuanced and consistent system of punctuation, with weak and strong commas (it seems), semicolons, colons, and periods (this, of course, disappears in the transcriptions). Here is someone who appears to care about language.

These letters were written on a Monday (Letters 8, 9, 12–14, 21–23, 25, 26, 29), Saturday (Letters 2, 5, 6, 16–18, 20, 33), Tuesday (Letters 3, 10, 15, 28, 30–32), Wednesday (Letters 11, 19), Friday (Letters 1, 7), Thursday (Letter 4), and Sunday (Letter 24). The days on which he wrote letters to recipients outside of Florence will have been determined at least to some degree by the schedule for the post: thus a good number of the letters to Mantua were written on either a Monday or, if Peri was rushing to catch the courier (compare Letter 31), a Tuesday.

Most of the letters presented here have been published in some form before, although almost none complete; however, we reexamined all of them in the archives. They are transcribed according to the principles adopted for this book as a whole. As elsewhere, too, insertions (whether interleaved or in the margins) are placed between > and <; deletions, where it is useful to give them, are bounded by < >; and square brackets are used for editorial additions. The commentary preceding each letter consists of: (1) a first paragraph with a fairly complete summary (material in parentheses is editorial, added for clarification); (2) where needed, a second and subsequent paragraphs providing further information or comment useful for any reading of the letter; and (3) details of the archival source and of those secondary sources where almost all (or significant parts) of a given letter is transcribed in a coherent form.

1 To Virginia de' Medici d'Este (Ferrara), 16 September 1588

Peri has heard from Madama Margherita (Gonzaga d'Este?) that Virginia (wife of Cesare d'Este) wants some music, whether arias or madrigals, but he does not know whether they are for singing or playing. He reminds her of his faithful service, and asks for clarification about the genre and also about likely performers, even though there are so many "rare" (highly talented) musicians in Ferrara that he would be sending water to the sea.

The letter is addressed (on its reverse) "All'Illustrissima et Eccellentissima Signora e Patrona mia Colendissima La Signora Donna Virginia Medici D'Est[e]." Unlike all the other surviving letters, this one still bears—on the paper tab originally attached to it—some of the red wax with which it was closed, and in the faint impression of the seal that remains on the wax one can discern a heraldic shield with the mount of six coupeaux that formed the lower portion of Peri's coat of arms. Virginia de' Medici was one of the Medici princesses to whom Peri taught singing, prior to her marriage in 1586. The "Madama Margherita" to which the letter refers is very probably Margherita Gonzaga d'Este, wife of Duke Alfonso II d'Este. Peri seems to have been fond of the proverbial redundancy of sending water to the sea; it reappears in Letter 11.

> Modena, Archivio di Stato, Letterati 55; also given in Catelani, "Una lettera inedita di Jacopo Peri"; and in Kirkendale, *Court Musicians*, 193 (but for the location, see Kirkendale, *Emilio de' Cavalieri*, 441). Catelani assumed that "Madama Margherita" was the daughter of Emperor Charles V and wife of Alessandro de' Medici (and then of Ottavio Farnese); Kirkendale followed, but later made the correction (*Emilio de' Cavalieri*, 441).

L'Illustrissima et Eccellentissima Signora mia Colendissima

Da Madama Margherita intesi come Vostra Eccellenza Illustrissima voleva ch'io le mand[ass]i non so che arie, o madrigali, ma non sapendo se havevano da servire per cantare o per sonare, con questa occasione mi son mosso a scriverle questi quattro mal composti versi, con baciarle humilmente la veste e ricordarle che li sono quel medesimo servitore affettuosissimo che sempre le fui. Imperò mi facci gratia d'avisarmi quello che la vuole ch'io facci, e per chi hanno da servire, che se bene sarà un voler mandar l'aqua al mare, sendo costì homini tanto rari, nondimeno per ubbidire a Vostra Eccellenza Illustrissima subito la servirò con tutto mio sapere. E con questa humilmente li bacio la veste pregandola a tenermi in sua buona gratia. Che nostro Signore Dio li conceda ogni maggior felicità. Di Fiorenza il dì 16 di settembre 1588.

Di Vostra Eccellenza Illustrissima

Humilissimo et affettuosissimo servitore

Jacopo Peri

2 To ?Belisario Vinta (Florence), 18 November 1600

Giovanni Boccherini (one of the court castratos) has come to Peri on behalf of the recipient of the present letter, seeking an answer to what they discussed in person (Peri's accompanying the *concerto de' castrati*). Peri wishes to be excused on the grounds of ill health, given his headaches and catarrh, which prevents him from working and singing. He hopes that the recipient will make his excuses to the grand duke (or grand duchess?).

The letter has no indication of its recipient, but Belisario Vinta is likely, and the mode of address is appropriate for him, if also for other court secretaries.

> Archivio di Stato, Florence (ASF), Mediceo del Principato 900, fol. 142; also given in Carter, *Jacopo Peri*, 1: 306–7; and (in part) in Kirkendale, *Court Musicians*, 211.

Molto Illustre Signore e Padrone mio Colendissimo
Giovannino venne a trovarmi per parte di Vostra Signoria dicendomi li dovessi dare la resoluzione di quello che a bocca m'haveva ragionato. Ma con mio gran travaglio, sono forzato dirle ch'io conosco per la mia indebolita complessione non poter pigliare questo carico, e particolarmente il dolore della testa che spesso mi visita, accompagnata da un catarrino salso, che per forza mi bisogna astenere dallo studio, et im particolare del cantare, che desidero pur vivere. Imperò la prego volermi havere per scusato, e non si sdegnare con meco, supplicandola che per sua solita humanità vogli anco scusarmi appresso Sua Altezza Serenissima della mia impotenza, che nel restante mi sforzerò con ogni diligenza servire a Sua Altezza come è mio debito. E di nuovo la prego farmi questo favore, che lo metterò nel numero fra gli altri benefitij ricevuti da lei, alla quale mi conosco molto ubligato. E facendo fine con ogni reverenza li bacio le mani. Di Fiorenza il dì 18 di novembre 1600.

Di Vostra Signoria Molto Illustre
Affettuosissimo servitore
Jacopo Peri

3 To ?Belisario Vinta (Florence), 21 November 1600

After Peri wrote his previous letter, Vincenzo Giugni (in charge of the Wardrobe) told him that the grand duke (grand duchess?) did indeed wish him to accompany the *concerto de' castrati*, even though he had made his excuses as best he could. Therefore Peri quickly went to speak with the grand duke (grand duchess?) stating his readiness to obey. He explains this to the recipient so that he will not press the case for Peri's being relieved of this task; he says he will work hard at it; and he asks for the recipient's protection, which he thinks he will need more than ever.

The letter has no indication of its recipient, but Belisario Vinta is likely (following Letter 2).

> ASF, Mediceo del Principato 900, fol. 171; also given in Carter, *Jacopo Peri*, 1: 308–9; and (in part; also misconstrued) in Kirkendale, *Court Musicians*, 211.

Molto Illustre Signore e Padrone mio Colendissimo

Di poi scritto a Vostra Signoria, Sua Altezza mi fece dire dal Signor Vincenzio Giugni che la mente sua era ch'io mi contentassi di concertarmi con li detti giovani nonostante ch'io gli havessi fatto fare mia scusa nel miglior modo ch'io potevo, del che subito parlai a Sua Altezza offerendomi pronto all'ubbidienza. Imperò ne ho voluto subito dar conto a Vostra Signoria acciò non segua più inanzi con Sua Altezza. E se bene conosco per molte mia imperfettioni e brighe essere poco atto a questa impresa, con tutto ciò non mancherò d'ogni diligenza per quanto potranno le mia deboli forze acciò Sua Altezza venga servita. Prego bene Vostra Signoria a tenere la mia protettione perché credo ne harò bisogno più che mai. E con questa facendole riverenza le prego dal Signore Dio ogni contento. Di Fiorenza li 21 di novembre 1600.

> Di Vostra Signoria Molto Illustre
> Affettuosissimo servitore
> Jacopo Peri

4 To Grand Duchess Christine of Lorraine (?Pisa), 10 February 1604/5

Peri provides music for a tournament (between "Tuscans" and "foreigners") for Carnival, to a text by Michelangelo Buonarroti *il giovane* and as commissioned by the court majordomo (Enea Vaini). He is waiting to try it out. The Tuscans should be performed by Giovanni Boccherini (a castrato), Antonio Brandi (alto), Giovanni Battista Signorini (tenor), and a bass, with two chitarroni, at least one lute, and a violin; a chitarrone player and a violinist can be found among the Franciosini. For the foreigners, Peri suggests Fabio Fabbri (another castrato) and three other voices, plus bass and tenor trombones, a *cornetto muto*, and a flute, which are all instruments that are easy to carry. Even though the music is written for four parts, Peri has repeated the last verse for eight, since it seemed appropriate to him.

The tournament was performed in Pisa on 22 February 1604/5; the text survives in Florence, Casa Buonarroti, Archivio Buonarroti 84, fols. 151–152v. It alternates verses for a Tuscan and a foreign herald, prior to a chorus for all the Tuscan heralds; however, Peri appears to have set the text for two groups of four singers each.

ASF, Mediceo del Principato 5987, fol. 308; also given in Carter, *Jacopo Peri*, 1: 312–13; in Barocchi and Gaeta Bertelà, *Collezionismo mediceo*, 1: 603; and (in part) in Kirkendale, *Court Musicians*, 212–13 (which, however, confuses the tournament with the one done in early 1606).

Serenissima Gran Duchessa

Ho fatto con ogni diligenza, e copiato la musica sopra le incluse parole del Signor Buonarroti, come mi ordinò il Signor Maiord'homo, quale non mando per hora perché oggi non ho possuto metter insieme tanti ch'io le provi se ci fussi [*sic*] errori. Intanto la comandi quello devo fare.

Circa al conserto a me parrebbe che li Toscani dovessino essere Giovannino, il Brandino, Giovanni Battista Franzosino et un basso chi parrà a Vostra Altezza Serenissima, consertati con due chitarroni, un leuto almeno, senza diminuire, et un violino. Quanto a chitarroni tra i franzosini vi è chi ne sonerà uno, et il simile il violino.

Li 4 stranieri bisogna oltre a Fabio tre voci chi piacerà a lei, accompagnati con dua tromboni basso et tenore, un cornetto muto per contralto, et una traversa, che sono tutti strumenti facili a portare. E se bene l'opera è a quattro sì come lei comandò, l'ultimo verso l'ho fatto replicare a 8 parendomi approposito. Questo è quanto a me parebbe, rimettendomi a sua comandamenti. E con questa con ogni debita reverenza et humiltà me le inchino, e le bacio la veste pregando sempre il Signore Iddio per ogni sua maggior felicità. Di Fiorenza li x di febbraro 1604.

> Di Vostra Altezza Serenissima
> Humilissimo e devotissimo servo
> Jacopo Peri

5 To Grand Duchess Christine of Lorraine (?Pisa), 12 February 1604/5

Given that the majordomo is ill, Peri is sending the music for the tournament directly to the grand duchess. He has now tried it out and there are no errors in it; he has also written to Giovanni Battista Signorini (one of the Franciosini) telling him what is necessary for the performance.

ASF, Mediceo del Principato 5987, fol. 309; also given in Carter, *Jacopo Peri*, 1: 313;
in Barocchi and Gaeta Bertelà, *Collezionismo mediceo*, 1: 604; and (in part) in
Kirkendale, *Court Musicians*, 213.

Serenissima Gran Duchessa

Ritrovandosi el Signor Maiord'homo indisposto non ho volsuto darli fastidio. E però ho preso ardire di nuovo scrivere a Vostra Altezza Serenissima
questi dua versi, e mandarli l'opera fatta nella quale non ci è errori ch'io sappi
e l'ho provata. Et per altra mia le dissi come mi pareva si dovessi consertare,
et ho scritto a Giovanni Battista Franzosino quanto debba fare in questo servizio. Hora l'Altezza Vostra Serenissima facci quanto le piace, et io con ogni
debita reverenza me le inchino, baciandoli humilmente la veste. Le prego dal
Signore Iddio ogni felicità maggiore. Di Firenze li 12 di febbraio 1604.

> Di Vostra Altezza Serenissima
> Humilissimo et ubbientissimo [*sic*] servo
> Jacopo Peri

6 To Prince Ferdinando Gonzaga (Mantua), 11 August 1607

Peri sends a madrigal (setting poetry by Ferdinando Gonzaga, it seems); he is
grateful for the opportunity to compose it, given that there are so many excellent musicians in Mantua. He sang it to Vittoria Archilei, and since it seemed
suitable for her voice, she begged him for a copy; Peri hopes that Ferdinando
will not mind his having given her one. He has conveyed Ferdinando's greetings to the "Camerata" (= the Accademia degli Elevati) and they reciprocate.

One assumes that this letter, Peri's first to Ferdinando Gonzaga, has to do
with the poet Francesco Cini's attempts to secure the commission of the opera
Le nozze di Peleo e Tetide (with music by Peri) for performance at the upcoming
festivities in Mantua for the marriage of Prince Francesco Gonzaga and Margherita of Savoy (eventually held in May–June 1608); Peri inserts himself into
this affair more directly in his next letter. Discussions over *Tetide* had begun in
July 1607, with Cini making contact with Ferdinando Gonzaga in August (see
Kirkendale, *Court Musicians*, 214–16); however, the negotiations did not bear
fruit. It is possible that the madrigal sent with this letter was "Ho visto al mio
dolore," to a text by Alessandro Striggio (the younger), although the context
and content of this letter suggests that it was to poetry by Ferdinando himself
(and see Chapter 3, n. 183).

Mantua, Archivio di Stato, Autografi 6, fol. 45 (*Herla* C-1829); also given in Kirkendale, *Court Musicians*, 214. The right-hand edge of the letter is quite badly frayed.

Illustrissimo et Eccellentissimo Signore e Padrone mio Singularissimo
Rimando a Vostra Eccellenza Illustrissima el madrigale con la musica composta da me con amore. E se sarà di poco valore, ne incolpi la debolezza
dell'ingegno mio, ma non già la prontezza dell'animo, che invero non ho mai
fatto musica sopra parole più volentieri che queste, perché da lei mi vien co-
mandato. E benissimo conosco che havendo appresso di sé huomini eccellentissimi oltre che lei medesima lo poteva fare perfettamente in ogni modo si sia
degnata farmi questo favore, e se qualche volta mi darà da far qualcosa, lo
riceverò per grazia particolare, poiché non desidero altro che havere occasione
di mostrarmele vero e devoto suo servitore, si per mio debito come per inclina-
zione particolare che ho di servirla, e questo lo dico sinceramente. Trovan-
domi a sorte ieri con la Signora Vittoria gne ne fece sentire; e perché gli parve
a proposito per la sua voce, facendomene instanzia non potei mancare dar-
gnene copia, sperando sia con buona grazia di Vostra Eccellenza Illustrissima.
Feci anco le raccomandazioni alla camerata, e gli rendon mille grazie. Et io
con loro con ogni affetto e reverenza gli baciamo la veste, pregando il Signore
Dio gli conceda il colmo delle sue grazie. Di Firenze li xi d'agosto 1607.

> Di Vostra Eccellenza Illustrissima
> Affettuosissimo et obligatissimo servitore
> Jacopo Peri

7 To Prince Ferdinando Gonzaga (Mantua), 26 October 1607

Peri is grateful for Ferdinando's memory of him, and for the opportunity to compose *Le nozze di Peleo e Tetide*. He and Francesco Cini (the librettist) have spoken
at length, and Peri asks what kinds of instruments are available in Mantua for the
accompaniment: in addition to a harpsichord and several chitarroni, he would
like a large lyra-viol and a harp. He also wants matters to remain confidential.

Mantua, Archivio di Stato, Autografi 6, fol. 46 (*Herla* C-1830); see Figure A.1; also
given in Davari, "Notizie biografiche del distinto maestro di musica Claudio
Monteverdi," 179–80; and in Solerti, *Gli albori del melodramma*, 1: 84–85.

Illustrissimo et Eccellentissimo Signore e Padrone mio Singularissimo
Io devo infinite grazie alla memoria che Vostra Eccellenza tien di me, e particolarmente hora che la mi comanda ch'io la serva in una cosa che di già per mio
gusto havevo cominciata. Onde tanto maggiormente hora m'apparecchio con
ogni mio studio e diligenza a far quanto saprò, perché ella resti pienamente

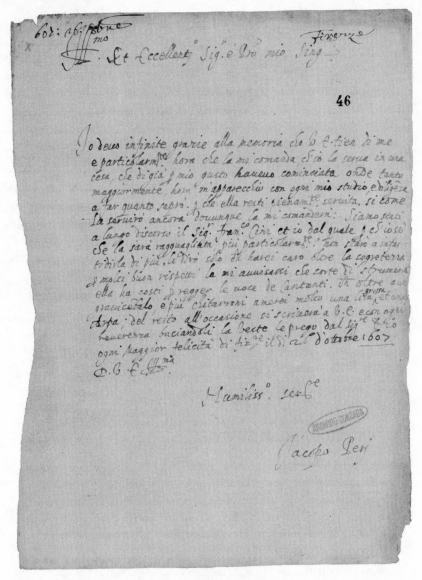

FIGURE A.I.   Jacopo Peri, letter to Prince Ferdinando Gonzaga, 26 October 1607
(Letter 7). *Source:* Mantua, Archivio di Stato, Autografi 6, fol. 46. (Reproduced by
permission of Archivio di Stato, Mantua.)

servita, sì come la servirò ancora dovunque la mi comanderà. Siamo stati a
lungo discorso il Signor Francesco Cini et io, dal quale perch'io so che la sarà
ragguagliata più particolarmente, non starò a infastidirla di più. Le dirò solo
che havrei caro, oltre la segretezza per molti buon rispetti, la mi avvisassi che
sorte di strumenti ella ha costì per regger le voce [*sic*] de cantanti, ché oltre a
un gravicembalo e più chitarroni, amerei molto una lira >grossa< et una arpa.
Del resto all'occasione si scriverà a Vostra Eccellenza, e con ogni reverenza
baciandoli la veste le prego dal Signore Dio ogni maggior felicità. Di Firenze
il dì 26 d'ottobre 1607.

> Di Vostra Eccellenza Illustrissima
> Humilissimo servitore
> Jacopo Peri

8 To Prince Ferdinando Gonzaga (Mantua), 12 November 1607

Peri has shown to Cini the latest letter from Ferdinando; the poet has not re-
ceived any letters from the prince. Both Peri and Cini accept the decision that
Le nozze di Peleo e Tetide is to be dropped, but they have agreed to ask for it to
be returned, as Peri does, so that it can be available for performance elsewhere.
Peri thanks Ferdinando for the favors recently done him with the Duke and
Duchess of Mantua (it is unclear what these favors might have been).

> Mantua, Archivio di Stato, Autografi 6, fol. 47 (*Herla* C-1831); also given in Davari,
> "Notizie biografiche del distinto maestro di musica Claudio Monteverdi," 180; and
> in Solerti, *Gli albori del melodramma*, 1: 85.

Illustrissimo et Eccellentissimo. Signore e Padrone mio Colendissimo
Ho mostrato la mia ultima di Vostra Eccellenza al Signor Francesco Cini,
quale m'ha risposto che non ha ricevuto sue lettere, e circa alla favola resta
contento e sadisfatto di quanto piace a Vostra Eccellenza purché la si degni
rimandargnene, sì come sono rimasti insieme. Et io ancora per mio interesse
a ciò fare la prego, poiché ho durato la fatica a comporla, sperando che presto
si reciterà qui ogni volta che non sia in altre mani. Rendo infinite grazie a
Vostra Eccellenza delli favori fattomi con Loro Altezze Serenissime, alle quali
di nuovo con ogni reverenza m'inchino, et a Vostra Eccellenza insieme, rendendomi sempre prontissimo ad ogni loro comandamenti, che nostro Signore
Iddio gli conceda il colmo d'ogni felicità. Di Firenze li 12 di Novembre 1607.

> Di Vostra Eccellenza Illustrissima
> Affettuosissimo e devotissimo servitore
> Jacopo Peri

9 To Cardinal Ferdinando Gonzaga (Mantua), 10 March 1607/8

Peri agrees to rehearse Marco da Gagliano's music for solo voices (for the forth-coming festivities for the wedding of Prince Cosimo de' Medici and Archduchess Maria Magdalena of Austria) as Ferdinando requests, and says that Gagliano has no more affectionate a supporter than him (Peri). He congratulates Ferdinando on the performance of Gagliano's opera *Dafne* (sponsored by the cardinal in Mantua in late February or early March 1608). He says that he has not composed any music for a long while because he is busy in other affairs (see also the letter of 23 April 1608) and spent so much time on *Le nozze di Peleo e Tetide*, but will meet the cardinal's requests for music when his inspiration returns.

Ferdinando Gonzaga was named cardinal on 10 December 1607; Peri ac-knowledges the elevation in his initial and closing salutations, but not in the internal honorifics (*Vostra Eccellenza Illustrissima*). For the request to rehearse Ga-gliano's music, see also the latter's more specific letter to Michelangelo Buonarroti *il giovane*, 8 March 1608, in Strainchamps, "The Unknown Letters of Marco da Gagliano," 90, 111; and in Cole, *Music, Spectacle, and Cultural Brokerage in Early Modern Italy*, 2: 505. This refers to Peri's rehearsing the music for one, two, and three voices (and Antonio Francesco Benci doing the same for an eight-voice madrigal); it also specifies the occasion for which this music has been written.

> Mantua, Archivio di Stato, Autografi 6, fol. 44 (*Herla* C-1828); also given in Davari, "Notizie biografiche del distinto maestro di musica Claudio Monteverdi," 181; in Solerti, *Gli albori del melodramma*, 1: 85–86 n., 87, 92 n.; and (in part) in Kirken-dale, *Court Musicians*, 217.

Illustrissimo et Reverendissimo Signore e Padrone mio Colendissimo

Poiché Vostra Eccellenza Illustrissima mi comanda ch'io eserciti le musiche del Signor Marco da Gagliano, et in particolare quelle che cantano soli, stia pur sicura ch'io non mancherò d'ogni diligenza, e le custodirò come le mie proprie. E dica pure al Signor Marco che se ne stia con l'animo quieto, che qui el suo servizio non patirà, et invero che Vostra Eccellenza Illustrissima non poteva raccomandarle a suggetto che vedessi le cose del Signor Marco con più affezzione di me, e che più desiderassi servir lei. Ho inteso che si son fatte cose bellissime, e quanto honore si sia fatto el Signor Marco nella nuova *Dafne* fatta recitar da Vostra Eccellenza Illustrissima, del che sommamente me ne rallegro. Quanto a musiche nuove non ho fatto niente e un gran pezzo, per essermi impiegato in altri mia affari, oltre che messi in musica l'opera del S. Cini con molta caldezza et assiduità, e perché l'opera era assai lunga, ne restai stracco di maniera che ancor me ne sento. Imperò mi scusi se per ora in questo non la obedisco, che quando la vena mi ritornerà non mancherò del

mio debito. E intanto la prego conservarmi vivo in sua grazia, e con ogni affetto e reverenza baciandoli la veste, e prego el Signore Dio gli conceda ogni
felicita maggiore. Di Firenze il dì X di Marzo 1607.

> Di Vostra Eccellenza Illustrissima e
> Reverendissima
> Devotissimo Servitore
> Jacopo Peri

10 To Cardinal Ferdinando Gonzaga (Mantua), 8 April 1608

Peri once more congratulates Ferdinando Gonzaga on the two musical entertainments done in Mantua to universal applause, including *Dafne*, enriched by
Ottavio Rinuccini and composed by Marco da Gagliano. The style is the most
appropriate, and the one closest to speech, ever devised by man. Gagliano has
told Peri that some arias in the opera were done by Ferdinando, and his com-
mendation has moved Peri to ask to see some of them so that he can sing them
for his pleasure. He also complains that Ferdinando is speaking ill of him and
he urges caution, for truth will out. After his customary closing sentiments,
Peri asks once more for the arias.

We know from the preface to Marco da Gagliano's *Dafne* (Florence: Cristofano Marescotti, 1608) that Ferdinando Gonzaga wrote three "arias" for the
opera. Two were for Apollo: "Pur giacque estinto al fine" (pp. 11–12 of the 1608
score) and "Un guardo, un guard'appena" (p. 48). One was for Amore (or Venere): "Chi da' lacci d'Amor vive disciolto" (pp. 19–20). As for Ferdinando
"speaking ill" of Peri, the matter appears to concern an election held in the
Accademia degli Elevati in which Ferdinand counted on Peri but which instead went against him, notwithstanding the presence of Peri at the voting.
However, the meaning of this part of the letter is obscure.

> Mantua, Archivio di Stato, Autografi 6, fol. 49 (*Herla* C-1833); also given in Solerti,
> *Gli albori del melodramma*, 1: 88; and (in part) in Alessandro Ademollo, *La
> bell'Adriana*, 58–59; Kirkendale, *Court Musicians*, 217.

Illustrissimo et Reverendissimo Signore e Padrone mio Colendissimo
Essendo universalmente volato el grido a Firenze quanto allegramente e vir-
tuosamente Loro Altezze Serenissime habbin' passato e' giorni carnevaleschi
con le due feste recitate in musica con aplauso [*sic*] di tutta Mantova, et in
particolare la *Dafne* fatta recitare da Vostra Eccellenza Illustrissima arricchita
dallo stesso Signor Rinuccini di nuove invenzioni, e composta dal Signor
Marco, con infinito gusto al pari d'ogn'altra, e da vantaggio, poiché tal modo

di canto è stato conosciuto più proprio, e più vicino al parlare, che quello di qualcun'altro valent'huomo, come mio debito vengo a rallegrarmi con Vostra Eccellenza Illustrissima, sì come feci col Signor Marco, quale in risposta m'ha detto che Vostra Eccellenza Illustrissima ha composto in detta favola alcune arie in somma eccellenza, e tanto l'ha commendate che m'è venuto desiderio grandissimo di vederle. Imperò se la mia non fosse prosunzione, ardirei pregarla mi favorisse mandarmene qualche d'una per cantarla per mio gusto, e per reverenza che porto alle cose sue, poiché tanto onora questa professione. Harei bene da querelarmi con seco per il male che ella va dicendo di me, ma guardi a non dir tanto che sia troppo perché la verita harà il suo luogo; e tanto più me ne sono accertato poiché si guardò da me quando per sua grazia volse favorire d'entrare nella nostra accademia, ma non gli valse perché mi ritrovai presente, e gli detti un favore grande, e 'l maggior che fussi. Nel piatto se fu bianca o nera Dio lo sa, sì che ogni huomo è buono a qualche cosa. E di nuovo ricordandomele suo devotissimo servitore con ogni debita reverenza gli bacio la veste, pregando el Signore Dio gli conceda el colmo d'ogni felicità, purché l'arie venghino. Di Firenze il dì 8 di aprile 1608.

> Di Vostra Eccellenza Illustrissima e
> Reverendissima
> Devotissimo servitore
> Jacopo Peri

11 To Cardinal Ferdinando Gonzaga (Mantua), 23 April 1608

Peri thanks Ferdinando for sending the cardinal's music for *Dafne* (which he had requested on 8 April). The aria for Apollo is very affecting and beautiful, and to Peri's taste, and "Chi da' lacci d'Amor vive disciolto" is so delightful and new that it makes him forget his own setting even though it had something worthwhile in it and had been often praised. He has had these arias performed for Francesco Cini, for the son of Vittoria Archilei (Ottavio), and for other friends, including Giovanni Battista Signorini, the husband of Francesca Caccini, to whom Peri also read the cardinal's letter written in his own hand. (The next passage in the letter is obscure.) Peri repeats that he has not composed anything for a long while (compare the letter of 10 March 1608)—and that if he had, it would be sending water to the sea—but he hopes that singing the cardinal's songs will arouse him from his sleep, and drag him out of his current melancholy caused by the death of relatives and friends (we do not know who). He asks that the cardinal at least remember him as a most devoted servant.

For Ferdinando Gonzaga's contributions to *Dafne*, see the commentary to
the previous letter: Gagliano also noted when writing to the cardinal on 15 July
1608 that "Chi da' lacci d'Amor vive disciolto" and a separate piece by Ferdinando, "Dolce cor," were very popular in Florence, with every music student
singing them with great delight (*gli giuro da servitore non è rimasto scolare che
non le canti e con gran gusto*); Mantua, Archivio di Stato, Autografi 6, fol. 19
(*Herla* C-1589), given in Vogel, "Marco da Gagliano," 553. As for the "obscure"
central section of the present letter, it gives the impression that the cardinal has
queried one measure in one of the arias—suggesting a change, which he indicates by solmization syllables (using *li* for *la* sung as *mi*)—and Peri seems to
agree, also bringing in a curious mixture of business terminology: the exchange will produce a good profit. However, it is very hard to identify the *cassetta* (bar or measure) to which Peri refers, and it is also possible that this is instead a coded reference to an attempt to recruit musicians, including Signorini,
to Mantua. For Peri's fondness for the proverbial redundancy of sending water
to the sea, see also Letter 1.

Mantua, Archivio di Stato, Autografi 6, fol. 50 (*Herla* C-1834); also given in Davari,
"Notizie biografiche del distinto maestro di musica Claudio Monteverdi," 181–82;
in Solerti, *Gli albori del melodramma*, 1: 88–89; and (in part) in Kirkendale, *Court
Musicians*, 217.

Illustrissimo e Reverendissimo Signore e Padrone mio Colendissimo
Rendo infinite grazie a Vostra Eccellenza Illustrissima e Reverendissima
dell'arie che m'ha mandato, tutte due bellissime. E l'aria d'Apollo è molto
affettuosa e bella, et è secondo el mio gusto, e le giuro in verità, che quella
Chi da' lacci d'Amor mi è parsa tanto vaga e nuova che m'ha fatto sdimenti-
car la mia, che pur ci havevo dentro qualche affetto, sendomi stata più volte
assai commendata; ma spogliato d'interesse, giudico e confesso esser questa
di Vostra Eccellenza Illustrissima assai più bella. L'ho fatte sentire al Signor
Cini, al figliuolo della Signora Vittoria, et ad'altri amici mia con molta lor
meraviglia, et im particolare al Signorini, marita [*sic*] della Signora Francesca,
al quale lessi la lettera che Vostra Eccellenza Illustrissima m'ha favorito scrivere di suo pugno. E sentì el desiderio che l'ha della cassetta de' *re mi fa sol li*,
per rendere in contracambio, *e-mi mi re mi mi*, che a questo tacque, ma come
prossimo di chi ne ha gran quantità, non dubito punto farà tal senseria, e per
lui non è da lassar tal occasione se andrà ben considerando perché ci sarà da
far buon guadagno, nonché altro mescolandoli insieme si farà buon composto. Quanto a me s'io havessi cosa alcuna di nuovo (se ben conosco mandar
l'acqua al mare) non mancherei mandargnene <sì> per obbedirla e ricevere il

favore. Ma mi chreda in verità, come ho detto altre volte, è gran pezzo ch'io non ho fatto niente, per qualche negozio fastidioso in che mi trovo involto, come per non havere hauto molta occasione, e questa è la verità. Sì che Vostra Eccellenza Illustrissima che ha del fatto non resti favorirmene che forse sarà cagione cantandole di svegliarmi dal sonno in ch'io mi trovo, e cavarmi della malinconia per parenti et amici persi che sono andati a riposarsi a miglior vita per le petechie che qui si fanno sentire, sì che godino felicemente in sanità, e faccino le feste gloriosamente. Con mio martello pazienza, almeno si degni tener memoria di me, suo devotissimo servitore, che l'amo e reverisco con tutto el quore. E con ogni reverenza inchinandomi, gli bacio la veste. Di Firenze li 23 d'aprile 1608.

> Di Vostra Eccellenza Illustrissima
> Affettuosissimo e devotissimo servitore
> Jacopo Peri

12 To Cardinal Ferdinando Gonzaga (Mantua), 30 June 1608

Peri notes the favorable opinion held by all those returning from the recent festivities in Mantua celebrating the wedding of Prince Francesco Gonzaga and Margherita of Savoy (May–June 1608), and is moved by the high praise Ferdinando bestowed on him in public among so many lords and most excellent virtuosos. Rinuccini has also told him that Ferdinando has written verse in Peri's honor; he is so grateful that he does not know how to respond. He is sorry not to have been able to serve in the Mantuan festivities, especially after the fruitless work he did on *Le nozze di Peleo e Tetide* (not mentioned, but clearly implied), which has been placed in a drawer and has not been heard by anyone. Peri hopes that if Ferdinando visits Florence, he will deign to hear the piece if only as sung by Peri himself, for then it will have its perfect conclusion.

The verse (other sources call it an ode) in praise of Peri by Ferdinando is lost, although there are several references to it in other documents, such as Rinuccini's letter to Ferdinando Gonzaga, 24 June 1610; Mantua, Archivio di Stato, Autografi 8, fol. 198.

Mantua, Archivio di Stato, Autografi 6, fol. 51 (*Herla* C-1835); also given (in part) in Davari, "Notizie biografiche del distinto maestro di musica Claudio Monteverdi," 93. Kirkendale, *Court Musicians*, 236 n. 249, identifies the recipient as Alessandro Striggio, but this is impossible given the closing salutation (and note that Peri refers to this letter in his next one to the cardinal). Rather, Peri mistakenly returned to an older style of referring to Ferdinando Gonzaga in his opening address.

Illustrissimo et Eccellentissimo Signore e Padrone mio Colendissimo
Son tornati tutti questi signori mia amici et padroni dalle lor felicissime
nozze, i quali non posson' saziarsi di raccontare i favori e gl'honori che
hanno ricevuto da Loro Altezze Serenissime, con tanta splendidezza che
maggiore non harebbon' saputo immaginarsi, e con grido universale che
tutte le feste son riuscite in ogni parte mirabilmente. E questo sia detto da
me per la sincera verità, perché così vien detto pubblicamente da tutti, et
io come suo devotissimo servitore vengo con questa a darle il buon pro, e
rallegrarmi con Vostra Eccellenza Illustrissima, et insieme renderle infinite grazie di tanto honore ch'ella m'ha fatto in tale occasione, poiché
tutti per una bocca mi dicono quanto Vostra Eccellenza Illustrissima mi
habbia mille volte il giorno ricordato con mia gloria alla presenza di tanti
signori e virtuosi eccellentissimi, e di più fatto versi in mia lode bellissimi
come dal Signor Rinuccini ancora mi sono stati lodati in somma eccellenza, talché non ho possuto contenermi di non mi commovere più volte
per tenerezza. Illustrissimo et Eccellentissimo Signor mio, che poss'io of-
frirle in contracambio, altro ch'una eterna memoria scrivendo nel mio
cuore l'amore e l'affetto ch'ella mi porta, ché questo rendasi certa ch'io lo
farò? Mi duol bene e grandemente non havere hauto occasione di poterla
servire in tale allegrezze. Durai qualche fatica, sì, per lei; non ebbe effetto,
pazienza. Io l'ho riposta in un cantone, e nessuno l'ha da sentire, e sta
aspettando che Vostra Eccellenza Illustrissima passi di quà, che s'ella si
degnerà sentirla solo una volta dalla mia bocca, gli parrà haver ricevuto
perfettissimo fine. E con questo io me le ricordo devotissimo servitore di
poco merito ma di grandissimo affetto, e le fo humilmente reverenza,
pregando nostro Signore Dio per quella felicità che merita el suo valore.
Di Firenze il dì 30 di giugno 1608.

> Di Vostra Eccellenza Illustrissima e
> Reverendissima
> Devotissimo servitore
> Jacopo Peri

13 To Cardinal Ferdinando Gonzaga (Mantua), 28 July 1608

Peri repeats his congratulations on the Mantuan festivities, worried that
his previous letter on the matter (30 June) had been lost in the mail (and

perhaps also that he had been too harsh in his remarks about *Le nozze di Peleo e Tetide*). He also reiterates his thanks for Ferdinando's kind words, and for the verse in his honor. He sends a sonnet setting for three voices, and also an arietta commissioned by a *marescial* who had recently passed through Florence; the text is by Cavaliere (Vincenzo) Panciatichi.

For other settings by Peri of texts by or associated with Ferdinando Gonzaga in this period, see Chapter 3.

> Mantua, Archivio di Stato, Autografi 6, fol. 52 (*Herla* C-1836); also given in Alessandro Ademollo, *La bell'Adriana*, 64–65; and in Solerti, *Gli albori del melodramma*, 1: 102–3.

Illustrissimo e Reverendissimo Signore e Padrone mio Colendissimo
Alla tornata di questi signori intesi con allegrezza grande le nuove delle loro felicissime feste riuscite tutte ammirabilmente e con tanta pompa che non sanno ancor saziarsi di comendarle, sì come fanno delle gran carezze et onori ricevuti, che più non si può dire. Et io come suo devotissimo servitore gli detti el buon pro, ma havendo circa otto giorni sono ricevuto una di Vostra Eccellenza Illustrissima e Reverendissima, e per quella non m'havendo detto niente, ho creduto sia mal capitata. Imperò vengo di nuovo con questa a rallegrarmi, e ringraziarla infinitamente di tanto onore ch'ella mi ha fatto trattando di me in tale occasione, con tanta mia reputazione, e di più fatto versi bellissimi in mia lode, ch'io non so altro che mi dire, se non che terrò memoria eterna de' favori e grazie che del continuo mi fa. E per ubbidire a quanto mi comanda gli mando un sonetto a tre voce [*sic*], et una arietta fatta a requisizione d'un Marescial che pochi giorno passò di quà, e le parole son del Cavalier Panciatichi. Accetti el buon animo mio, e mi conservi vivo in sua memoria., E con questa humilmente facendole reverenza, me le inchino e li bacio la veste, pregando sempre il Signore Dio la exalti a maggior felicità. Di Firenze li 28 di luglio 1608.

> Di Vostra Eccellenza Illustrissima e
> Reverendissima
> Devotissimo servitore
> Jacopo Peri

14 To Duchess Eleonora de' Medici Gonzaga (Mantua), 15 December 1608

Peri was asked by Eleonora, Duchess of Mantua, via Don Antonio de' Medici, to audition some girls and select one for training and recruitment to Mantua.

He has done so; he has found the girl a good teacher; and he will monitor her training. She has a more than reasonable voice, studies hard, and has a good ear, which is what matters. She reads music in all the clefs, and is beginning to sing from musical notation, which Peri regards as essential for a good foundation. She also sings ariettas to the harpsichord and is learning to play that instrument so fast that it seems she is performing miracles. Don Antonio wishes to send her to Mantua immediately, but Peri recommends keeping her in Florence over the winter to solidify her lessons. However, he will do whatever Duchess Eleonora commands.

Mantua, Archivio di Stato, Autografi 6, fol. 53 (*Herla* C-1837); also given in Alessandro Ademollo, *La bell'Adriana*, 82; and (in part) in Kirkendale, *Court Musicians*, 219 (but Kirkendale is incorrect that this concerns young girls sent to Peri from Mantua).

Serenissima Signora e Padrona mia Colendissima

Dall'Illustrissimo Signor Don Antonio Medici mi fu fatto vedere e sentire da parte di Vostra Altezza Serenissima alcune fanciullette piccole, acciò se ne cappassi una per impararli a cantare, e così feci, la quale si è sollecitata al possibile. Et io non ho mancato provederli buon maestro, e l'ho visitata spesso tendendoli diligente cura, e spero farà buonissima riuscita. Ha più che ragionevol voce, studia volentieri, et ha buonissimo orecchio, che è quel' che importa. Legge sicurissima per tutte le chiave, e comincia a cantare al libro, qual giudico necessario per far buon fondamento. Canta ancora alcune ariette sopra lo strumento di tasti, et impara a sonarle, che invero per il tempo che l'ha imparato si può dire quasi che facci miracoli. Sua Eccellenza Illustrissima che disedera servire l'Altezza Vostra Serenissima harebbe volsuto mandargnene quanto prima. Io tutto lodo, ma giudicherei fussi bene tenerla qui ancora questo inverno per assodarla um poco più, se bene a Vostra Altezza Serenissima non mancano huomini eccellentissimi che posson fare il medesimo, ma quanto più sarà digrossata, manco fatica dureranno a condurla a perfezzione. Rimettendomi del tutto al suo volere, intanto non mancherò tenerli l'occhio adosso perché da me resti servita. E con ogni reverenza inchinandomi, humilmente li bacio la vesta [sic], pregandole dal Signore Iddio il colmo d'ogni maggior felicità. Di Firenze li 15 di dicembre 1608.

Di Vostra Altezza Serenissima
Humilissimo e devotissimo servo
Jacopo Peri

15 To Cardinal Ferdinando Gonzaga (Mantua),
20 January 1608/9

Peri thanks Ferdinando for the invitation to come to Mantua, but he must decline because the grand duke has placed him in the service of the princesses and of Archduchess Maria Magdalena, all of whom make use of him continuously and also need him for upcoming Carnival entertainments. Peri asks the cardinal to remind the Duchess of Mantua (Eleonora de' Medici) of his service long ago.

The Carnival entertainments included the repeat performance of Francesco Cini's *Notte d'Amore* (from the 1608 wedding festivities) on 25 January. For other letters relating to Ferdinando Gonzaga's request for Peri to come to Mantua at this time, see Chapter 3.

> Mantua, Archivio di Stato, Autografi 6, fol. 48 (*Herla* C-1832); also given (with significant errors) in Solerti, *Musica, ballo e drammatica alla corte medicea*, 39 n. 1.

Illustrissimo et Reverendissimo Signore e Padrone mio Colendissimo
Tanto quanto fu grande l'allegrezza quando lessi la lettera di Vostra Signoria Illustrissima e Reverendissima, vedendo con quanto affetto mi desiderava, sperand'io sicuramente poter venire a ricevere sì segnalato favore, con altrettanto dolore gli rispondo che non m'è concesso di venire a servirla poiché il Gran Duca mio Signore havendomi destinato non solo al servizio delle Illustrissime Signore Principesse, ma della Serenissima Arciduchessa, le quali del continuo si servon' di me, et particolarmente in questo Carnevale per loro trattenimenti. Imperò la supplico e prego a scusarmi e non si sdegnar verso di me, poiché mi trovo legato, accertandola vivamente che maggior contento non potevo ricevere che venire a servirla e goderla, e con tale occasione rinfrescare la mia antica servitù con Madama Serenissima. Et inchinandomi con ogni debita reverenza, gli bacio la veste, pregando il Signore Dio che gli conceda il colmo d'ogni maggior felicità. Di Firenze li 20 di gennaio 1608.

Di Vostra Eccellenza Illustrissima e

Reverendissima

Obligatissimo servitore

Jacopo Peri

16 To Cardinal Ferdinando Gonzaga (Mantua), 26 March 1611

Peri recommends his friend Don Simone Finardi, prior of the monks of S. Pancrazio, who has printed some poetic madrigals dedicated to the cardinal (his

Affettuosi accenti [Florence: Cristofano Marescotti, 1611]) and has many good qualities, as well as profound admiration for Ferdinando. Peri will not say whether the poems are bad or good, for fear of offending the cardinal's judgment, but he thinks that they are good, and they please Peri enormously. He would like them even more if they did not include verse in praise of Peri, but he was glad that Finardi has shown him to the world as grateful to the cardinal.

For the identification of the book, see Kirkendale, *Court Musicians*, 221 n. 164. When Finardi was the prior of S. Trinita in Florence—and also, it seems, the founder of an academy there—he himself was the dedicatee of Severo Bonini's *Madrigali, e canzonette spirituali . . . a una voce sola* (Florence: Cristofano Marescotti, 1607); see also Finardi's letter at *Herla* C-1394.

Mantua, Archivio di Stato, Autografi 6, fol. 54 (*Herla* C-1838); also given in Alessandro Ademollo, *La bell'Adriana*, 190–91.

Illustrissimo et Reverendissimo Signore et Padrone mio sempre Colendissimo Havendo il Molto Reverendo Padre Don Simone Finardi Priore delli Reverendi Monaci di S. Pancrazio messo alla stampa alcuni sui madrigali, et dedicatogli a Vostra Signoria Illustrissima et Reverendissima, ne ho sentito estremo contento, perché essendo il suddetto Padre amico mio, non potevo sentir cosa più grata che egli havessi, con occasione sì honorata, cercato d'acquistar la grazia e servitù di Vostra Signoria Illustrissima. Et come tale, con questa mia gne ne vengo a raccomandare caldamente per quella servitù che con lei tengo, pregandola che ne voglia tenere particolar protezzione, perché invero, oltre alla Musica, è persona di gran lettere e molto stimato nella sua religione; e per la fame delle rare virtù di Vostra Signoria Illustrissima è innamorato talmente di lei, che quando ci troviamo insieme non sa ragionar d'altro. E per palesargli questo suo affetto, non havendo altra occasione più pronta, ha preso ardire di dedicarle questi sua Madrigali, i quali se sien buoni o cattivi non ne tratterò perché farei troppo ingiuria all'ottimo giudizio di Vostra Signoria Illustrissima. Son ben certo che lei conoscerà che sono de' buoni che sieno usciti fuora, et a me piacciono sommamente, e più mi sarebbon piaciuti se con molto mio disgusto e contro ogni mio merito non si fusse lasciato tanto trasportare dall'amore in lodarmi. Ho bene hauto caro che egli m'habbia palesato al mondo per molto grato a Vostra Signoria Illustrissima perché da segnalati favori ch'ella m'ha sempre fatti non posso persuadermi altro. Sì che Illustrissimo Signore, se per amor mio piglierà a favorir questo mio amico mi sarà favor singulare che me e lui renderà eternamente obligati a Vostra Signoria Illustrissima, alla quale baciandole humilmente la

veste, le prego dal Signore Iddio ogni maggior felicità. Di Firenze li 26 di
marzo 1611.

Di Vostra Signoria Illustrissima et

Reverendissima

Devotissimo servitore

Jacopo Peri

17 To Cardinal Ferdinando Gonzaga (Mantua), 14 May 1611

Peri has thanked Finardi on Ferdinando's behalf and has made the offers as he
was asked to do. Finardi is delighted with the cardinal's satisfaction with his
little gift (the book) and wants no other reward than to be counted among the
cardinal's servants, for he has an incredible love and reverence for him. (In the
second paragraph Peri moves on to theatrical works he has on hand, seemingly
in response to a request from Ferdinando.) As for *Le nozze di Peleo e Tetide*, it is
true that four years ago he hurriedly set it to music, but he never finished it
because Ferdinando's commission had lapsed. Then Francesco Cini (the librettist) put *Tetide* to one side on the order of the grand duchess, and Peri has not
thought about it since. He has also set to music a libretto by Jacopo Cicognini
(*Adone*), and this is slowly being prepared with the intention of performing it at
the request of the grand duke.

For *Adone*, see also Hill, *Roman Monody, Cantata, and Opera from the Circles
around Cardinal Montalto*, 1: 325 (Cicognini sends the libretto to Cardinal
Montalto, 30 March 1613, saying that it is being held in reserve for the first wedding of the Medici princesses); Kirkendale, *Court Musicians*, 208; and Boyer,
"Les Orsini et les musiciens d'Italie au début du XVIIᵉ siècle," 309 (on Cicognini proposing to Paolo Giordano Orsini a performance in Rome in 1616).

> Mantua, Archivio di Stato, Autografi 6, fol. 55 (*Herla* C-1839); also given (in part) in
> Davari, "Notizie biografiche del distinto maestro di musica Claudio Monteverdi,"
> 183; and in Solerti, *Gli albori del melodramma*, 1: 86 n.

Illustrissimo et Reverendissimo Signore et Padrone mio Colendissimo

Non ho mancato di ringraziare il Padre Don Simone Finardi per parte di
Vostra Signoria Illustrissima e fattoli quelle offerte sì come da lei mi viene
ordinato. E con tale occasione, ancor lui m'ha letto la cortesissima sua con
grandissima allegrezza. E fo fede a Vostra Signoria Illustrissima che 'l detto
Padre riman tanto sadisfatto che l'habbi gradito il suo piccolo dono che non
si puo dir più, e non desiderà altra grazia da lei, se non che lo tenga vivo nel
numero de' sua sviscerati servitori, che invero per quel che sempre ò visto da

qualche anno in qua, ch'io ho sua conoscenza, gli porta tanto amore e reverenza che è cosa incredibile. Et io ancora resto ogni giorno più obligato a favori e grazie ch'ella per sua benignità mi concede.

Circa alla *Tetide*, è vero che circa quattro anni sono, se bene in fretta, ne messi in musica gran parte, ma raffreddandosi il comandamento di Vostra Signoria Illustrissima rimase da me imperfetta. E poco doppo il Signor Francesco Cini si ripigliò la sua favola, e mi disse per ordine di Madama Serenissima ch'io non dessi l'arie fatte ad alcuno, ché Loro Altezze se ne volevan servire. E d'allora in qua io non ci ho più pensato. È ben vero ch'io ne composi un'altra fatta dal Cicognino, che per ordine di Sua Altezza si va da me mettendo in pratica pian piano per recitarsi al lor beneplacito, e questo è quanto le posso dir. E resto del tutto al suo comando, pregandola caldissimamente a conservarmi nella sua dolce grazia, che il Signore Iddio l'exalti al colmo d'ogni maggior gloria. E con ogni debita reverenza me le inchino, e le bacio la veste. Di Firenze li 14 di maggio 1611.

> Di Vostra Signoria Illustrissima et
> Reverendissima
> Humilissimo et obedientissimo servitore
> Jacopo Peri

18 To Cardinal Ferdinando Gonzaga (?Paris), 12 November 1611

Peri hopes that Ferdinando has arrived safe and well at the French court. He reminds the cardinal that he is his servant, and would be tempted to be there himself were he not prevented by some family problem and age, so powerful is his urge to see the Queen of France (Maria de' Medici), his lady from long ago, one last time before he dies. Indeed, he is almost inclined to drop everything and take the post to Paris, which would no doubt make the cardinal laugh. He asks Ferdinando to tell him whether the queen has any memory of his ancient service, and to remember him to her, and he reasserts his confidence that Ferdinando will do so on his behalf.

Mantua, Archivio di Stato, Autografi 6, fol. 56 (*Herla* C-1840); also given in Alessandro Ademollo, *La bell'Adriana*, 189–90.

Illustrissimo et Reverendissimo Signore e Padrone mio Singularissimo
Se Vostra Signoria Illustrissima è arrivata sana e lieta come desidero, et così si mantiene in cotesta regia et allegra corte, me ne rallegro infinitamente. Io me le ricordo servitore devotissimo, e ben volentieri lo farei di presenza se qualche

travaglio familiare e l'età non mi spaventassi, ché 'l desiderio ch'io ho di servire Vostra Signoria Illustrissima e di riveder una volta prima ch'io muoia la
Maestà della Regina, mia antica signora, è tanto ardente ch'io non lo posso
più soffrire; e dubito ch'una volta lasciato ogni rispetto non mi venga preso la
posta e correndo arrivarmene fino a Parigi. So che Vostra Signoria Illustrissima si riderebbe di me s'io le comparissi inanzi così all'improviso, ma chi sa?
Intanto la prego e supplico per quella cosa che Vostra Signoria Illustrissima
più ama farmi degno di avisarmi se la Maestà della Regina ha punto di memoria dell'antica mia servitù. E sapendo che l'occasione non gli mancherà, la
prego a ricordarmele servitore e farli un humilissima e devotissima reverenza
in mio nome. So che per sua benignità non le sarà se non caro, rendendomi
sicuro che Vostra Signoria Illustrissima per sua bontà non mancherà far questa
grazia a un suo servitore che tanto l'ama et osserva, e però con fiducia starò
aspettando da lei la desiderata risposta. E per più non tediarla, con ogni humiltà baciandole la veste le prego dal Signore Iddio somma felicità. Di Firenze li
12 novembre 1611.

> Di Vostra Signoria Illustrissima e
> Reverendissima
> Devotissimo et obbedientissimo servitore
> Jacopo Peri

19 To Duke Ferdinando Gonzaga (Mantua), 20 April 1616

Peri (writing from Bologna) is greatly honored by Duke Ferdinando's invitation to come to Mantua and assures him that he has requested a *licenza* from
the grand duke to do so, the *licenza* being necessary because he should be going
to Rome with Cardinal Carlo de' Medici.

Ferdinando Gonzaga became ruler of Mantua following the death of his
elder brother, Francesco, in December 1612; yet he remained a cardinal for a
while and was not formally crowned duke until 6 January 1616. Peri was in
Bologna for the performance of *Euridice*. Rinuccini was also invited to
Mantua at the same time; see his letter to Duke Ferdinando, 26 April 1616,
in Mantua, Archivio di Stato, Archivio Gonzaga 1171, fols. 436–37 (*Herla*
C-1142).

> Mantua, Archivio di Stato, Archivio Gonzaga 1171, fols. 434–35 (*Herla* C-1141);
> also given in Davari, "Notizie biografiche del distinto maestro di musica Claudio
> Monteverdi," 111; and (in part) in Kirkendale, *Court Musicians*, 224.

Serenissimo Signore mio Colendissimo

Non mi poteva arrivar grazia magiore, né più da me desiderata, che occasione di servire Vostra Altezza Serenissima, e però la ringrazio per mille volte dell'onore fattomi di chiamarmi a Mantova, dove verrò prontissimo a ricevere i sua comandamenti come il Serenissimo Gran Duca mio Signore, al quale ho di già fatto domandar licenza, me la conceda. Se non fusse ch'io sono in obligo di andare a Roma a servire l'Illustrissimo Cardinale Medici per il tempo ch'egli dimora là, harei preso sicurtà di venir subito senza altra licenza, ma in simile occasione dubiterei d'errare. Ottenuta la licenza, subito mi metterò in viaggio per servirla come è mio debito. E con ogni humiltà facendole reverenza, le prego dal Signore Iddio il colmo d'ogni felicità e grandezza. Di Bologna li 20 aprile 1616.

Di Vostra Altezza Serenissima

Humilissimo e devotissimo servitore

Jacopo Peri

20 To Duke Ferdinando Gonzaga (Mantua), 27 May 1617

Because of his large family of ten children, Peri requests a recommendation from Duke Ferdinando for one of the offices that are given to citizens and gentlemen of Florence, a qualification he meets. His wish list includes the Podesteria di Prato, the Capitanato delle Montagne di Pistoia, the Vicariato delle Chiane, and the Vicariato della Pieve a Santo Stefano.

Peri's latest child, Cosimo (his tenth with his third wife, discounting the short-lived first-born, Ginevra), had been born just two months before. It is unclear who added to this letter the identification "il Zazzerino" under Peri's name, and when, although it appears to have been done at the time the letter was received, presumably by a court secretary. See also the minute of Duke Ferdinando's letter to Grand Duke Cosimo II of 30 June 1617 asking him to favor Peri so that he can support his family, and identifying possible positions (the same ones as on Peri's list); Mantua, Archivio di Stato, Archivio Gonzaga 2292 (*Herla* C-2611).

Mantua, Archivio di Stato, Archivio Gonzaga 1129, fol. 560. The letter is wrongly dated 27 March 1617 in Kirkendale, *Court Musicians*, 224–25.

Serenissimo Signore

Ritrovandomi oggi in necessità per la famiglia grave di dieci figliuoli, sono astretto chiedere aiuto al Serenissimo Gran Duca mio Signore, che mi conceda alcuno delli offizii che si danno a cittadini e gentil'huomini de' quali io son capace, e presto. Si negozieranno li quattro qui a piede annotati, ché ogniuno di essi sarebbono buoni per me. Ma perché molti sono li pretendenti, confidato nella benevolenza di Vostra Altezza Serenissima ho preso ardire supplicarla si degni, non per mio merito ma per carità, farmi degno d'una lettera al Serenissimo Gran Duca in mia raccomandazione che mi conceda uno delli detti offizii. Sì come ancora supplico alla Serenissima Signora Duchessa d'un'altra simile per Madama Serenissima, che s'io l'otterrò mi sarà di qualche sollevamento. E tutto riconoscerò dall'Altezza Vostra, alla quale humilmente inchinandomi, bacio la veste e prego il Signore Iddio le conceda il colmo d'ogni felicità. Di Firenze il dì 27 maggio 1617.

Di Vostra Altezza Serenissima

Podesteria di Prato
Capitanato delle Montagne di Pistoia
Vicariato delle Chiane
Vicariato della Pieve a Santo Stefano

Humilissimo et devotissimo servitore

Jacopo Peri

[in another hand] >il Zazzerino<

21 To Duchess Caterina de' Medici Gonzaga (Mantua), 8 January 1617/18

Peri requests a recommendation to Grand Duchess Christine (compare Letter 20, to Duke Ferdinando Gonzaga); Duchess Caterina had provided one for him before, but his petition had been denied because six months had not elapsed since holding a prior office of this kind. That time is now up on the very day of writing this letter, and two offices are now in play: in Pieve Santo Stefano (also mentioned in Letter 20) and in Anghiari. Because Peri is burdened with five daughters and six sons, he needs additional financial support to establish funds for a dowry.

Peri had acted as music tutor to Caterina de' Medici when she was in Florence (just as he did for an older generation of Medici princesses in the early 1580s); she married Duke Ferdinando Gonzaga on 6 February 1617. The "prior office" was presumably Peri's tenure as *podestà* of Pontassieve, which had ended on 22 August 1617 (see Table 1.1); by the six-month rule, this would have allowed Peri to assume a new position in late February 1618, so presumably Peri's remark about six months having elapsed on the day of writing means that 8 January was the day on which he could declare his candidacy for an office with effect from a future date. But he is not entirely honest with Duchess Caterina: he has only four daughters still alive (although he did know that his wife was expecting another child, a son born in March).

Mantua, Archivio di Stato, Archivio Gonzaga 1129, fol. 501. This letter is incorrectly dated 8 January 1617 (modern style) in Kirkendale, *Court Musicians*, 224.

Serenissima Signora

La lettera che per benignità e grazia di Vostra Altezza Serenissima ella scrisse a mio favore alla Serenissima Madama per ottenere uno delli offizii ch'io domandavo, quando gne ne presentai, mi rispose ch'io havevo divieto per sei mesi, atteso che ero tornato allora da un altro offizio, e mi dette buona speranza per al tempo debito. Et perché oggi è spirato il divieto, et in breve s'hanno da negoziare due altri offizii, cioè *la Pieve a Santo Stefano* et *Anghiari*, di nuovo reverentemente supplico l'Altezza Vostra farmi grazia di rinfrescare le raccomandazioni a Madama Serenissima con un'altra lettera acciò per mezzo suo possa ottenere uno delli sopradetti offizii, con il quale potrei mettere insieme um poco di principio di dote per una delle mia figliuole, ché ne ho cinque, e sei masti, peso grandissimo alle mia forze, ché tutti insieme le resteremo in perpetuo obligatissimi. Et humilmente inchinandomi prego il Signore Iddio la conservi, et la renda ogni giorno più felice, et reverentemente le bacio la veste. Di Firenze li 8 gennaro 1617.

> Di Vostra Altezza Serenissima
> Humilissimo et devotissimo servitore
> Jacopo Peri

22 To Duchess Caterina de' Medici Gonzaga (Mantua), 29 January 1617/18

Peri repeats, and presses, his request for Duchess Caterina to refresh her recommendation to Grand Duchess Christine. If he had known about the six-month rule before, he would not have bothered the duchess earlier, but he has great need of a new, and warm, recommendation to the grand duchess, or even the grand duke, for which he will remain in perpetual obligation. He seeks an office either in Pieve Santo Stefano or in Anghiari.

Mantua, Archivio di Stato, Archivio Gonzaga 1129, fol. 510. The letter is incorrectly dated 27 January 1617 (modern style) in Kirkendale, *Court Musicians*, 224.

Serenissima Signora

Più giorni sono, scrissi una simile à Vostra Altezza Serenissima supplicandola mi volesse far grazia rinfrescar le raccomandazioni a Madama Serenisima con una lettera in mia raccomandazione per ottenere uno offizio, quale non potetti conseguire perché allora ero tornato da un'altro offizio che mi dava divieto, e per spazio di 6 mesi non potevo haverne. E s'io havessi saputo questa legge, harei rispiarmato [sic] il favore di Vostra Altezza al tempo debito. Et hora ch'io ho finito il divieto, di nuovo la supplico si degni per sua benignità farmi grazia di nuova et calda raccomandazione a Madama Serenissima, o vero al Serenissimo Gran Duca, acciò ch'io conseguisca questo benefizio per suo mezzo, ché ne ho grandissimo bisogno, ché io con tutti i miei figliuoli le resteremo perpetuamente obligati, pregando il Signore Iddio le conceda ogni maggior felicità, et humilmente inchinandomi le bacio la veste. Di Firenze li 29 gennaro 1617.

Di Vostra Altezza Serenissima

Uno delli offizii ch'io desidero è

* la Pieve a Santo Stefano, o vero

* Anghiari.

Humilissimo et devotissimo servitore

Jacopo Peri

23 To Andrea Cioli (Florence), 29 January 1617/18

Peri submits a petition to Grand Duchess Christine (now lost) with the present cover letter, asking Cioli to make additional points in support of his request for one of several government offices. He notes his service since the age of ten, and his appointment by Grand Duchess Johanna of Austria to teach singing to the princesses (so, before her death on 11 April 1578); however, there is only one lady-in-waiting, Cesia Vecchia, who might remember the fact, since it was so long ago. His family line has enjoyed all the honors, from *gonfaloniere* up, conferred on honorable families, and has had more than twenty-five Signori (the highest office in the republic). Peri has already shown Cioli a draft of his petition to the grand duchess, but now, for the sake of brevity, he has decided to omit the mention of the young girl (Angelica Furini) currently lodging with him (to learn singing).

ASF, Mediceo del Principato 1370, unpaginated. Cusick, *Francesca Caccini at the Medici Court*, 369 n. 24, cites this letter, but locates it incorrectly as in ASF, Mediceo del Principato 1371. The letter has no address, but it is filed among those sent to Cioli.

Illustrissimo Signore et Padrone mio Colendissimo

Confidato nella gentilezza e bontà di Vostra Signoria Illustrissima, le mando la inclusa per Madama Serenissima, e la supplico soggiungerle due parole in mio favore, conoscendo mi saranno di grandissimo aiuto per ottenere uno delli domandati offizij. Et perché Vostra Signoria habbia qualche informazione de' fatti mia, sappia ch'io cominciai a servire d'anni X mentre viveva il Gran Duca Cosimo, et dalla Gran Duchessa Giovanna d'Austria fui messo ad insegnare cantare alle Principesse sue figliuole, e son tanti anni che di donne non ci è chi se ne possa ricordare altri che la Signora Cesia Vecchia. Et ho sempre servito et ubbidito. Et la casa mia ha goduto da Gonfalonieri in poi tutti gli onori che godono le famiglie onorate, et ha hauto più di 25 Signori. Quanto alla fanciulla ch'io tengo in casa che nella bozza ch'io mostrai a Vostra Signoria facevo menzione, mi è parso meglio non ne trattare per più brevità, oltre che a loro Altezze sta il comandare et a me ubbidire. Et con questa baciandole le onoratissime mani, prego il Signore Iddio le renda il merito di quanto farà per me, et che ogni giorno la renda più felice. Di Firenze il dì 29 gennaro 1617.

> Di Vostra Signoria Illustrissima
> Devotissimo servitore
> Jacopo Peri

24 To Andrea Cioli (Florence), 4 February 1617/18

Peri has received a favorable reply from the grand duchess and expresses his gratitude to Cioli, while also hoping that he can call on him for future favors. He is Cioli's slave, but given that he is neither able nor good enough to do anything for him, all he can offer are his prayers.

ASF, Mediceo del Principato 1370, unpaginated. The letter has no address but is filed among those sent to Cioli.

Illustrissimo Signore et Padrone mio Osservandissimo

Ho preso tanto contento della amorevolissima sua che maggiore non saprei dire, visto che senza ch'io habbia con Vostra Signoria Illustrissima merito né servitù, ella per sua bontà con tanta cortesia m'ha favorito appresso Madama Serenissima che dalla risposta di Sua Altezza ho preso speranza mi sortisca la mia domanda. Et per guidardone del fastidio dato a Vostra Signoria di nuovo mi dà animo che in altri miei bisogni possa pigliar ardire di ricercarla del suo aiuto. Giuro a Dio ch'io le resto schiavo, et poich'io non posso né son buono per lei a cosa alcuna, prego il Signore Iddio che la rimeriti per me, et del continuo la metterò a parte delle mie fredde orazioni pregando sempre per il mantenimento di sua sanità et prosperità come mio benefattore. Et con ogni affetto le bacio le onoratissime mani. Di Firenze li 4 febbraio 1617.

> Di Vostra Signoria Illustrissima
> Affettuosissimo et devotissimo servitore
> Jacopo Peri

25 To Duke Ferdinando Gonzaga (Mantua), 23 April 1618

Peri thanks Duke Ferdinando for the letter of recommendation to the grand duke, which, together with the one from Duchess Caterina, has enabled him to receive a very honorable permanent position in Florence (with the Arte della Lana) earning him *sc.*10 per month. He is all the more grateful because no one else can help him gain favor from the grand duke and grand duchess.

Mantua, Archivio di Stato, Autografi 6, fol. 57 (*Herla* C-1841); also given in Alessandro Ademollo, *La bell'Adriana*, 138–39.

Serenissimo Signore

Rendo quelle grazie maggiori a Vostra Altezza Serenissima ch'io so et posso delle raccomandazioni che per sua benignità ella fece più mesi sono con la sua lettera al Serenissimo Gran Duca a mio favore, le quali hanno operato talmente insieme con quelle della Serenissima Signora Duchessa sua Consorte, che queste Altezze m'hanno fatto degno d'uno offizio onoratissimo qui in Firenze perpetuo, del quale ne caverò *sc.*10 il mese, che mi sarà di qualche sollevamento. Tutto riconosco dall'Altezza Vostra et dalla sua Serenissima, et me le riconosco infinitamente obligato, et la supplico con tutto il core si degni tenermi nella sua protettione, non havend'altri a chi ricorrere ne' miei bisogni per ottener qualche grazia da queste Altezze. Et con ogni humiltà inchinandomi, le bacio la veste e prego il Signore Iddio le conceda ogni maggior felicità. Di Firenze li 23 aprile 1618.

> Di Vostra Altezza Serenissima
> Humilissimo et obligatissimo servitore
> Jacopo Peri

26 To Duchess Caterina de' Medici Gonzaga (Mantua), 23 April 1618

Peri thanks Duchess Caterina for the letter of recommendation to the grand duchess, which has enabled him to receive a very noble permanent position in Florence as *camerlengo* of the Arte della Lana, earning him *sc.*10 per month, while also leaving him able to serve the grand duke (presumably, as musician), which would not have been possible had he moved away.

> Mantua, Archivio di Stato, Autografi 6, fol. 58 (*Herla* C-1842); also given in Alessandro Ademollo, *La bell'Adriana*, 138.

Serenissima Signora

Rendo quelle grazie maggiori ch'io posso et so a Vostra Altezza Serenissima delle raccomandazioni fatte alla Serenissima Madama Madre a mio favore, le quali hanno operato talmente che 'l Serenissimo Gran Duca mio Signore m'ha fatto grazia di eleggermi Camarlingo dell'Arte della Lana, offizio nobilissimo ed è durante mia vita, dove ne caverò *sc.*10 il mese, et potrò in un tempo medesimo servire a Sua Altezza, il che non sarebbe seguito andando fuora. Tutto riconosco dall'Altezza Vostra et dalla sua Serenissima, et me le riconosco principalmente dalla benignità di Vostra Altezza, et perciò vivo e le resto con perpetuo obligo. Et prego il Signore Iddio che le conceda ogni maggior allegrezza et felicità, alla quale humilmente inchinandomi, le bacio la veste. Di Firenze il dì 23 d'aprile 1618.

> Di Vostra Altezza Serenissima
>
> Humilissimo et obligatissimo servitore
>
> Jacopo Peri

27 To Duke Ferdinando Gonzaga (Mantua), March 1619/20

Peri is sure that his *Adone* will have a happy outcome in its Mantuan performance, where it will be sung exquisitely, especially given that Duke Ferdinando can make up for its weaknesses by revising, cutting, and adding anything that might be needed, something that the poet (Jacopo Cicognini) also approves.

The plan was to perform Peri's *Adone* (on which he had been working in 1611; see Letter 17) and a newly composed *ballo*, as well as Monteverdi's opera *Arianna* (first performed in 1608) during the birthday festivities for Duke Ferdinando Gonzaga and Duchess Caterina de' Medici Gonzaga in late April and early May 1620. In the end, only the *ballo* was performed.

The letter leaves the date blank, noting only the month and year. However, Duke Ferdinando wrote to Peri on 2 March 1620 about staging *Adone* for the birthday of his wife on 2 May: a minute of his letter survives in Mantua, Archivio di Stato, Archivio Gonzaga 2299 (*Herla* C-2099; partly given in Davari, "Notizie biografiche del distinto maestro di musica Claudio Monteverdi," 123; Kirkendale, *Court Musicians*, 226; Besutti, "Variar 'le prime 7 stanze della Luna'," 344). Here the duke also notes that this request demonstrates how much he values Peri's music (*Puo perciò Vostra Signoria conoscer da questo desiderio mio quanto io stimi le compositioni sue*). On the same day (Mantua, Archivio di Stato, Archivio Gonzaga 2299; *Herla* C-2100), the duke wrote to Abbate Stufa asking him to convey the letter to Peri and to reimburse him for any copying costs (Besutti, "Variar 'le prime 7 stanze della Luna'," 344–45).

> Mantua, Archivio di Stato, Autografi 6, fol. 59 (*Herla* C-1843; which, however, dates this March 1619 [modern style]); also given in Kirkendale, *Court Musicians*, 226–27; and in Besutti, "Variar 'le prime 7 stanze della Luna'," 345.

Serenissimo Signore

Bene avventurato sarà il mio *Adone* arrivando in mano di Vostra Altezza Serenissima, poiché per sua benignità si compiace volermi onorare di farlo cantare, e farlo degno di comparire, nel suo Real Teatro. Ché maggior allegrezza non posso sentire che ricever questa gloria, rendendomi sicuro che sotto la sua ombra non mi sarà attraversato, et sarà cantato exquisitamente. Solo temo che non le sia per riuscire a gran pezzo quanto Vostra Altezza crede, ma a questo ci è rimedio ché, essendo padrona di me et dell'opera, potrà lei medesima perfezionarla con rifare, levare et aggiugnere quanto farà bisogno, che di tanto si contenta anco il poeta. Et humilmente inchinandomi, con ogni reverenza le bacio la veste, et prego il Signore Iddio le conceda il colmo d'ogni maggior felicità. Di Firenze il dì [blank] di marzo 1619.

Di Vostra Altezza Serenissima

Humilissimo et devotissimo servitore

Jacopo Peri

28 To Duchess Caterina de' Medici Gonzaga (Mantua), 24 March 1619/20

Peri encloses music (now lost) to the words previously sent to him (for the *ballo*) according to the instructions he received, and if he has not understood them well, he is willing to revise it. He will also set any further text Duchess Caterina may send him, as she has suggested might occur. It is true that since he is old and occupied by his many affairs, he is somewhat out of practice, so if he has not done well, he asks for forgiveness, and begs the duchess to accept his goodwill. But there is no greater favor and grace that he can receive than her commands.

Presumably, Duchess Caterina intended the *ballo* as her birthday present to Duke Ferdinando (whereas *Adone* was his to her).

Mantua, Archivio di Stato, Autografi 6, fol. 60 (*Herla* C-1844, which, however, dates this 24 March 1619 [modern style] and identifies the recipient as the Duke of Mantua); also given in Alessandro Ademollo, *La bell'Adriana*, 238; in Besutti, "Variar 'le prime 7 stanze della Luna'," 348; and (in part) in Kirkendale, *Court Musicians*, 227.

Serenissima Signora

Ho fatto le musiche sopra le parole che Vostra Altezza Serenissima s'è compiacuta mandarmi, le quali sono con questa alligate. Et ho cercato osservar' l'ordine scrittomi, ma se per disgrazia io non l'havessi bene inteso, eccomi pronto all'emenda. Et se Vostra Altezza mi manderà altre parole sì come mi accenna, subito la servirò con ogni diligenza come mio debito. È ben vero che essendo aggravato dagli anni, oltre a molti affari che mi tengono occupato, mi tengono anco raffreddato nell'esercitio, però s'ella non verrà così ben servita, la supplico a scusarmi et accettare la buona volontà, accertandola che maggior favore e grazia non posso ricevere che d'esser fatto degno de' suoi comandamenti. Et con questa con ogni reverenza inchinandomi, humilmente le bacio la veste, et prego il Signore Iddio le conceda il colmo d'ogni maggior felicità. Di Firenze li 24 marzo 1619.

> Di Vostra Altezza Serenissima
> Humilissimo et devotissimo servitore
> Jacopo Peri

29 To Alessandro Striggio (the younger; Mantua), 30 March 1620

Peri tells Striggio how the Duke of Mantua had requested his *Adone* about a fortnight before (in fact, earlier), and asks him—if only for the love Striggio's father bore Peri—to become the protector of the work, especially from mischievous musicians. He is also ready to come to Mantua for the performance provided he can get permission from the grand duke and grand duchess. Peri then refers to having sent the music for a *ballo* for the Duchess of Mantua, and notes again that he is happy to be making this connection with him.

Although the addressee is not identified, it is clearly Striggio, given the reference to his father—Alessandro Striggio (the elder)—whom Peri had known in the 1580s. Peri had asked at least one person to reinforce his current request; see Letter 30.

Mantua, Archivio di Stato, Autografi 6, fol. 61 (*Herla* C-1845); also given in Besutti, "Variar 'le prime 7 stanze della Luna'," 349; and (in part) in Kirkendale, *Court Musicians*, 227. For the first line of the letter, Besutti transcribes "15" as "25" (which in fact is closer to the actual date of the duke's commission, written on 2 March), but Peri's "2" is quite different from his "1."

Illustrissimo Signore et Padrone mio Colendissimo

Il Serenissimo Signor Duca circa 15 giorni sono per huomo a posta mandò per il mio *Adone*, favola composta dal Cicognino e messa in musica da me con qualche diligenza, scrivendomi volerla far rappresentare queste feste di maggio, cosa che mi sarebbe di gran favore. Ma considerato ch'ella è comparsa costì orfana, conosco che ha bisogno d'un padre che la favorisca e regga. Et perciò ho preso ardire scrivere a Vostra Signoria Illustrissima et supplicarla almeno per l'amor che mi portava il suo Signor Padre, si degni esserne protettore in tutti e sua bisogni, e tenerla raccomandata ancora a cotesti signori musici, acciò per qualche interesse non mi sia tenuta indreto. Et sapendo quanto >sia< l'autorità sua in cotesta corte, son sicurissimo che appoggiata al suo favore si condurrà a felice porto. Et anco quando paressi a Sua Altezza ci fussi bisogno della persona mia, non mi parrà fatica quando sia con buona grazia delli mia Serenissimi Padroni venire a servir coteste Altezze. Similmente la Serenissima Signora Duchessa mi mandò alcune parole perch'io vi facessi sopra la musica, dicendomi dover servire per un suo ballo, la qual subito feci, e gne ne mandai la settimana passata, et per ogni buon fine prego Vostra Signoria Illustrissima fargnene sapere. E intanto con questa occasione desidero rinovare la servitù seco, offerendomi prontissimo a servirla in tutto quello che possono le mia deboli forze. Et con ogni affetto baciandoli la mano, prego il Signore Iddio li conceda il colmo d'ogni felicità. Di Firenze il dì 30 di marzo 1620.

Di Vostra Signoria Illustrissima

Affettuosissimo servitore

Jacopo Peri

30 To Alessandro Striggio (the younger; Mantua), 7 April 1620

Peri much appreciates Striggio's kind response and willingness to favor both *Adone* and the *ballo*, and now he breathes more easily. He is willing to drop *Adone*, given that it is not a work to be done in a fortnight, so long as it is not replaced by something equivalent. On Friday morning (3 April) he received the remainder of the words for the *ballo*, and he has sent the music back by the present post, having tried to compose it according to the instructions given. However, he has also been very busy with Holy Week celebrations in Florence (Easter Sunday was on 19 April). He has revised the seven stanzas for the Moon because the court wanted them varied somewhat, and rightly so. He asks that they be shown to the singers and players in advance. As for the unsigned letter of recommendation for *Adone* (which Striggio has clearly asked about), it probably came from Marchese Gonzaga. Once more, Peri recognizes in Striggio his father, who loved Peri more than he deserved, and whose fame lives on.

The recommendation for *Adone*, which Peri identifies as probably coming from Marchese Gonzaga (probably Don Giovanni Gonzaga), is at Mantua, Archivio di Stato, Archivio Gonzaga 1130, fol. 420 (*Herla* C-3331; unsigned letter to Striggio, 31 March 1620); given in Besutti, "Variar 'le prime 7 stanze della Luna'," 349–50.

Mantua, Archivio di Stato, Archivio Gonzaga 1130, fol. 423 (*Herla* C-3332); also given in Alessandro Ademollo, *La bell'Adriana*, 238–39; in Besutti, "Variar 'le prime 7 stanze della Luna'," 352–53; and (in part) in Kirkendale, *Court Musicians*, 227–28.

Illustrissimo Signore et Padrone Colendissimo

Grandissimo contento ho ricevuto dalla lettera di Vostra Signoria Illustrissima poiché ho trovato in lei tanta benignità et cortesia che prontamente ha preso a favorirmi, non solo nell'*Adone* ma nel ballo da farsi di presente, che sommamente la ringrazio, et ora starò con l'animo posato havendo tal protettore. Quanto all'*Adone*, Sua Altezza faccia il suo piacere, et invero non è opera da condursi bene in 15 dì, et a me basta non mi sia stata ritenuta indreto per altra opera simile. Venerdì mattina ricevei il restante delle parole del ballo et subito vi messi mano, et per il presente ordinario l'ho mandate a Sua Altezza, le quali mi sono ingegnato comporle secondo l'instruzzione. Et se saranno cosa debole, la prego tenermi scusato in parte per la brevità del tempo, et anco perché ho il capo nelle malinconie delli offizii di questa Settimana Santa. Mi viene accennato che le prime 7 stanze della Luna si sarebbon desiderate alquanto variate, et con buona ragione, però l'ho rifatte tutte variate. Ma per grazia Vostra Signoria si degni prima che Sua Altezza le senta, farle dare una vista a chi le deve cantare e sonare, et a lei dò piena cura di rassettere [*sic*] e far quanto farà bisogno. La lettera senza sottoscrizione, credo sia del Signor Marchese Gonzaga, che a mia richiesta disse volere raccomandare l'*Adone* alla sua protezzione. Et per fine, con allegrezza interna la ringrazio di nuovo, parendomi haver ritrovato il suo Signor Padre, quale invero mi amava

molto sopra i miei meriti, e qui continuamente ancor risuona la sua gran
fama. Et con ogni affetto baciandoli le onoratissime mani, prego il Signore
Iddio li conceda il colmo delle sue grazie. Di Firenze li 7 d'aprile 1620.

> Di Vostra Signoria Illustrissima
>
> Affettuosissimo et devotissimo servitore
>
> Jacopo Peri

31 To Alessandro Striggio (the younger; Mantua), 14 April 1620

Peri sends more music for the *ballo* set to words that he received this same day
after lunch, and he is rushing to catch the post. He asks Striggio to pay his re-
spects to the duke and duchess. As for coming to Mantua, there is no need in
the case of the *ballo*, and he would not get permission anyway, given that he
has the responsibility for music for Holy Week and Easter. However, some
other time he would very much like to revisit Mantua, because it is thirty-six
years since he was there, when he received many signs of affection from Striggio's father and from the father and mother of the present duke (i.e., Vincenzo
and Eleonora).

> Mantua, Archivio di Stato, Archivio Gonzaga 1130, fol. 424 (*Herla* C-3333); also
> given in Alessandro Ademollo, *La bell'Adriana*, 239–40 (dated 12 April 1620); in
> Besutti, "Variar 'le prime 7 stanze della Luna'," 353; and (in part) in Kirkendale,
> *Court Musicians*, 228.

Illustrissimo Signore et Padrone mio Colendissimo
Oggi dopo desinare ho ricevuto una di Madama Serenissima et una di Vostra
Signoria Illustrissima entrovi le parole aggiunte, le quali mando in questa alligate con l'aria, et perché ho paura che 'l corriere non parta in questo mezzo,
sarò piu breve ch'io posso. Et prima mi facci grazia far reverenza a Sua Altezza Serenissima >da mia parte< con quelle affettuose <che> parole che
Vostra Signoria saprà molto meglio di me, ringraziandola del grato affetto
che tiene verso di me. Et circa il venir costì adesso, per conto del ballo non ci
è bisogno di me, oltre che già queste Altezze m'hanno dato carico d'alcune
musiche in questi giorni santi e feste di Pasqua che non posso lassare. Ma con
altra occasione <del> più opportuna spero ricevere questo onore di far reverenza a cotesti Principi e riveder Mantova, che sono circa 36 anni ch'io ci fui,
et dal Signor Padre di Vostra Signoria ricevei tante carezze che più non potrei
dire, sì come dal Serenissimo Padre e Madre del Signor Duca, et so sicuramente che anco adesso riceverei ogni honore appoggiato al suo favore. Et le

resto obligatissimo per la protettione che per sua benignità e grazia ha preso della mia persona, e baciandoli le honoratissime mani prego il Signore Iddio li conceda ogni vero bene. Di Firenze li 14 aprile 1620.

> Di Vostra Signoria Illustrissima
> Affettuosissimo et devotissimo servitore
> Jacopo Peri

32 To Alessandro Striggio (the younger; Mantua), 28 April 1620

Peri is grateful for having decided to entrust his music to Striggio, because it has gained his favor and refreshed an old friendship. He notes again how Striggio reminds him of his (Striggio's) father, and he offers him any kind of service in return—not out of ceremony but for genuine love—especially given how readily Striggio has acted in his favor.

Mantua, Archivio di Stato, Autografi 6, fol. 62 (*Herla* C-1846); see Figure A.2; also given in Besutti, "Variar 'le prime 7 stanze della Luna'," 357–58.

Illustrissimo Signore et Padrone mio Colendissimo
Ringrazio sommamente il Signore Iddio che m'inspirò a raccomandar le mie musiche a Vostra Signoria Illustrissima le quali mi sono state mezzane di acquistarmi la sua grazia, e rinfrescar l'amicizia antica. Et nuove grazie le rendo delli amorevoli offizii fatti a coteste Serenissime Altezze a mio favore, et io ad ogni lor cenno sarò sempre prontissimo et obedientissimo a servirle. Et la prego si degni mantenermi vivo nella lor grazia, et anco in grazia di lei medesima. Et sia certa che mentre le scrivo mi par di scrivere all'istesso suo Signor Padre felicissima memoria, e mi son sempre ricordato, né mai mi sdimenticherò, della affezzione et amore che mi portava, et conseguentemente delli oblighi ch'io le tengo, quali vanno moltiplicando <nella> verso la persona di Vostra Signoria Illustrissima. Et altro non desidero che d'havere occasione di poterla servire, et le giuro in verità che queste non son cirimonie ma vero amore, et tanto maggiore quanto ho visto per la prontezza de' fatti usati da lei verso di me, che ben somiglia in virtù e bontà il suo santo e felice padre io non finirei mai. Il Signore Iddio <Dio> li doni il colmo delle sue grazie. Di Firenze li 28 aprile 1620.

> Di Vostra Signoria Illustrissima
> Affettuosissimo et devotissimo servitore
> Jacopo Peri

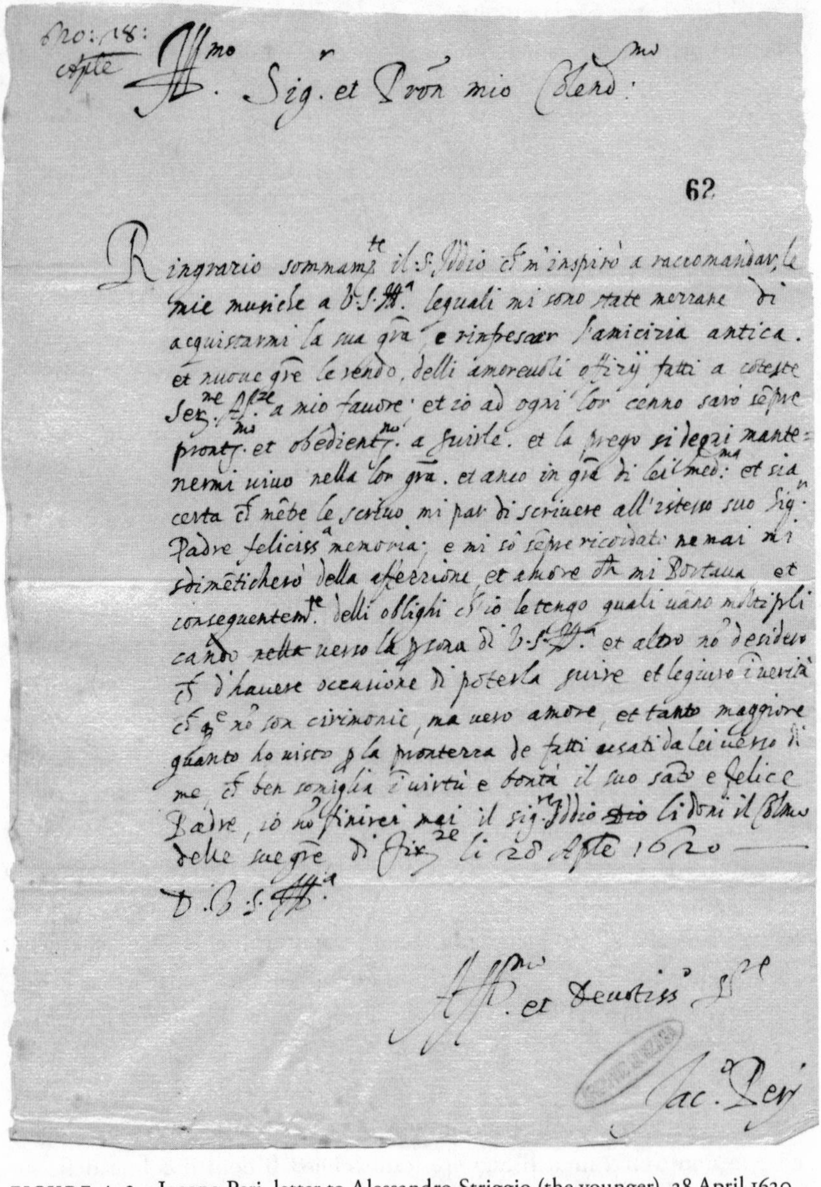

FIGURE A.2. Jacopo Peri, letter to Alessandro Striggio (the younger), 28 April 1620 (Letter 32). *Source:* Mantua, Archivio di Stato, Autografi 6, fol. 62. (Reproduced by permission of Archivio di Stato, Mantua.)

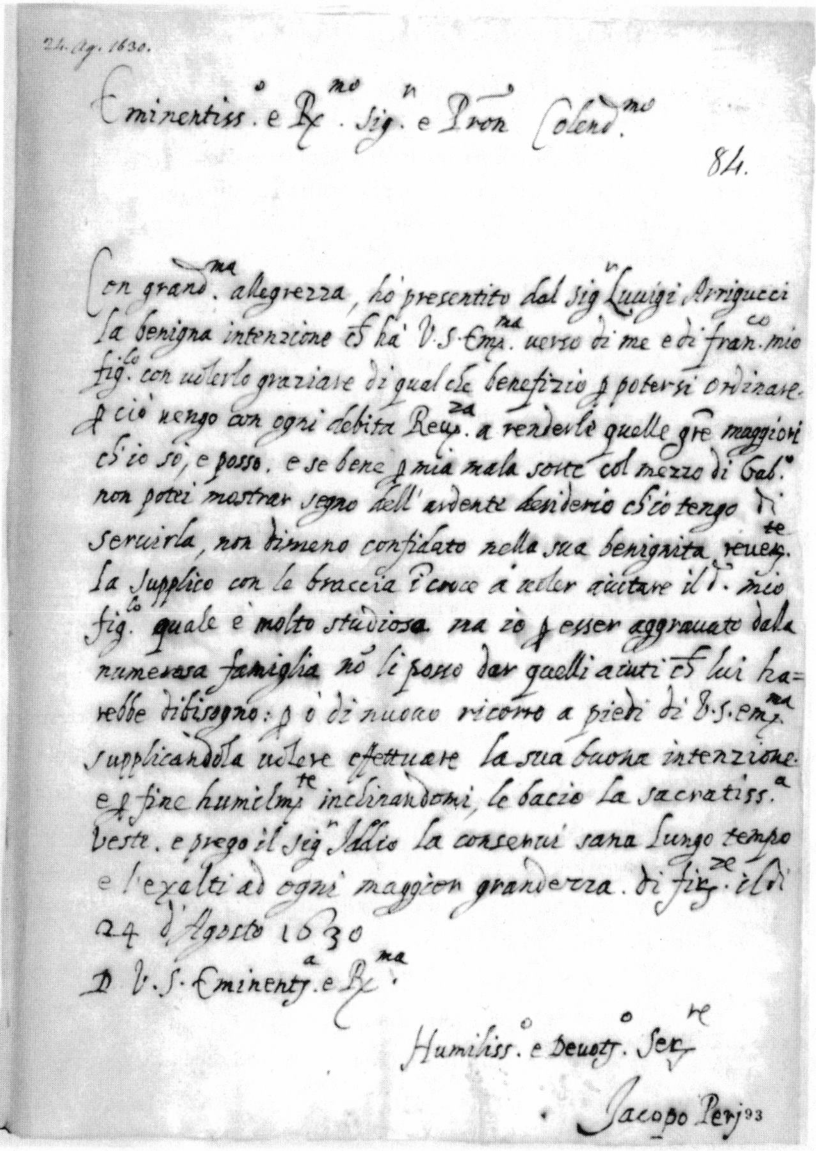

FIGURE A.3. Jacopo Peri, letter to Cardinal Francesco Barberini, 24 August 1630 (Letter 33). *Source:* Rome, Biblioteca Apostolica Vaticana, Barb. lat. 6474, fol. 93. (© 2013 Biblioteca Apostolica Vaticana. Reproduced by permission of Biblioteca Apostolica Vaticana, with all rights reserved.)

33 To Cardinal Francesco Barberini (Rome), 24 August 1630

Peri thanks the cardinal for his willingness to consider a benefice for his son Francesco—so he has learned from Luigi Arrigucci—so that he can be ordained. He apologizes for not having been able to serve the cardinal by way of "Gab.o" (Gabriello?); nonetheless he hopes that the cardinal will aid his son, who is very studious, given that Peri cannot give him all the help he needs because he is burdened by his large family.

> Rome, Biblioteca Apostolica Vaticana, Barb. lat. 6474, fol. 93; see Figure A.3; also given in Morelli, "Saggio di lettere di musicisti dalle raccolte di autografi della Biblioteca Apostolica Vaticana," 452–53.

Eminentissimo e Reverendissimo Signore e Padrone Colendissimo

Con grandissima allegrezza ho presentito dal Signor Luuigi [*sic*] Arrigucci la benigna intenzione che ha Vostra Signoria Eminentissima verso di me e di Francesco mio figliuolo con volerlo graziare di qualche benefizio per potersi ordinare. Perciò vengo con ogni debita reverenza a renderle quelle grazie maggiori ch'io so e posso. E se bene per mia mala sorte col mezzo di Gab.o non potei mostrar segno dell'ardente desiderio ch'io tengo di servirla, nondimeno confidato nella sua benignità, reverentemente la supplico con le braccia in croce a voler aiutare il detto mio figliuolo, quale è molto studioso, ma io per esser aggravato dalla numerosa famiglia non li posso dar quelli aiuti che lui harebbe di bisogno. Però di nuovo ricorro a' piedi di Vostra Signoria Eminentissima supplicandola volere effettuare la sua buona intenzione. E per fine humilmente inchinandomi, le bacio la sacratissima veste, e prego il Signore Iddio la conservi sana lungo tempo e l'exalti ad ogni maggior grandezza. Di Firenze il dì 24 d'agosto 1630.

> Di Vostra Signoria Eminentissima e
> Reverendissima
> Humilissimo e devotissimo servitore
> Jacopo Peri

Catalogue of Peri's Musical Works

Works are listed by category, and in chronological order therein, save those only in manuscript that cannot otherwise be dated. Known poets are included in parentheses after the title. The sections "Chamber Songs" and "Instrumental Music" include only those works that survive, and not others mentioned in letters and other documents (e.g., Letters 6, 13); nor does this catalogue include Peri's compositions for Holy Week celebrations—for example, in 1623—or similar uncorroborated works (some are noted in Appendix A: Chronology). "Theatrical Music" is defined broadly to include works that might somehow be staged outside of a theater; "Chamber Songs" also include pieces for more than one voice which therefore are not "songs" by any narrow definition of that term.

Vocal works have details of voice type where indicated by clef (S, A, T, B = soprano, alto, tenor, bass); instrumental parts are indicated by clef or function (C1 = a C clef on the first line of the stave counting up, and likewise for G2, C2, C3, C4, F4; Bc = Basso continuo). A vocal work for, say, soprano and basso continuo will normally be presented on two staves in C1 clef (S) and F4 clef (Bc), while alto, tenor, and bass voice parts are normally in the C3, C4, and F4 clefs, respectively; Peri does not use so-called high clefs (*chiavette*) in any systematic way (nor the F3 clef associated with them), although the G2 clef sometimes appears in his instrumental writing (e.g., in the *Ricercar del primo tuono* and in the final ritornello of *Euridice*), and one four-part chorus in *Euridice* ("Poiché gl'eterni imperi") is notated in C2, C3, C4, and F4 clefs (C2 also appears in the *Ricercar del primo tuono*). Note, however, that vocal lines for soprano and alto do not necessarily imply female voices, and that a song notated for soprano voice could be sung by a tenor (transposing down an octave) or vice versa.

Theatrical Music

Intermedio I for Giovanni Fedini, *Le due Persilie*. Performed: Florence, 16 February 1582/83. Text published 1583 (Florence: Giunti) as *Le due Persilie, commedia . . .*

fatta recitare da gli Illustri Signori, il Signore Girolamo e 'l Signor Giulio Rossi, de'
Conti di San Secondo, alla presenza delle Gran Principesse di Toscana, il dì 16 di
febbraio 1582, in Firenze; for relevant extracts, see Carter, *Jacopo Peri*, 1: 294–95.
Music lost.

"Dunque fra torbid'onde," T(TT), 4 instruments (C1, C3, C4, F4): echo song for
Arion in *Intermedio* V for Girolamo Bargagli, *La pellegrina*. First performed:
Florence, Teatro degli Uffizi, 2 May 1589, as part of the festivities celebrating the
wedding of Grand Duke Ferdinando I de' Medici and Christine of Lorraine.
Repeated: 6, 13, 15 May, and 9 June 1589 (not always with *La pellegrina*). For the
(unknown) author of the text, see Kirkendale, *Court Musicians*, 240. Music
published in Cristofano Malvezzi (ed.), *Intermedii et concerti, fatti per la*
commedia rappresentata in Firenze nelle nozze del Serenissimo Don Ferdinando
Medici, e Madama Christiana di Loreno, Gran Duchi di Toscana (Venice:
Giacomo Vincenti, 1591); for a modern edition, see Walker, *Musique des*
intermèdes de "La pellegrina," 98–106. Despite the presentation of the accompaniment in four separate instrumental parts, a note in the 1591 edition suggests
that the song was accompanied by a single chitarrone.

Dafne (Ottavio Rinuccini): *favola in musica*. First performed: Florence, Palazzo
Boni (residence of Jacopo Corsi), in 1597–98 Carnival season. Repeated:
Florence, Palazzo Pitti, 21 January 1598/99 (perhaps preceded by another
performance in Palazzo Boni before 18 January 1598/99), in 1599–1600 Carnival
season (before 26 January 1599/1600), and on 26 October 1604. Included some
music by Jacopo Corsi. Libretto survives in manuscript in Florence, Biblioteca
Nazionale Centrale, Magl. VII.562, and was published in ?1599 (Florence:
Giorgio Marescotti, but there are no publication details on the title page; see
Sternfeld, "The First Printed Opera Libretto"), 1600 (Florence: Giorgio
Marescotti), 1604 (Florence: Cristofano Marescotti; using leftover copies of 1600
edition with new title page and prologue); for a modern edition, see Solerti, *Gli*
albori del melodramma, 2: 65–104. Portions of the music survive variously in
Brussels, Conservatoire Royal/Koninklijk Conservatorium, Bibliothèque/
Bibliotheek, Codex 704, and Florence, Biblioteca Nazionale Centrale, Magl.
XIX.66; see Porter, "Peri and Corsi's *Dafne*." These include: the prologue ("Da
fortunati campi, ove immortali"); the scene 1 chorus "Almo dio, che 'l carro
ardente"; Amore's scene 2 aria "Chi da' lacci d'Amor vive disciolto"; the Nunzio's
narration in scene 5, "Qual nova meraviglia"; Apollo's scene 6 aria "Non curi la
mia pianta o fiamma o gelo"; and the scene 6 chorus "Bella ninfa fuggitiva." The
last two are attributed to Corsi in the Brussels manuscript; the others are
unattributed in both sources.

Euridice (Ottavio Rinuccini): *favola in musica*. First performed: Florence, Palazzo
Pitti, 28 May 1600. Repeated: 6 October 1600, as part of the festivities celebrating the wedding of Maria de' Medici and Henri IV of France. Repeated:

Bologna, 27 April 1616. There may have been a second performance shortly after the 6 October 1600 one; see the two cast lists in Kirkendale, *Court Musicians*, 207 (but note the comments in Chapter 1). Libretto published 1600 (Florence: Cosimo Giunti), with various subsequent editions; for a modern edition, see Solerti, *Gli albori del melodramma*, 2: 105–42. Music published as *Le musiche di Iacopo Peri nobil fiorentino sopra L'Euridice del Sig. Ottavio Rinuccini rappresentate nello sponsalizio della Cristianissima Maria Medici Regina di Francia e di Navarra* (Florence: Giorgio Marescotti, 1600; dedicated to Maria de' Medici, 6 February 1600/1601); reissued in 1608 (Venice: Alessandro Raverii). For the 1600 title page, see Figure 3.3; for portions surviving in diverse manuscripts, see Kirkendale, *Court Musicians*, 241–43; for a modern edition, see Peri, *"Euridice,"* ed. Brown.

Tournament (Michelangelo Buonarroti *il giovane*). Performed: Pisa, 22 February 1604/5. Text (beginning "O di barbari fregi / e di barbaro ardire") is in Florence, Casa Buonarroti, Archivio Buonarroti 84, fols. 151–152v. Music lost.

Le nozze di Peleo e Tetide (Francesco Cini): *favola in musica*. Composed summer–autumn 1607; proposed for performance in Mantua, 1608. Text and music lost.

"Poiché la notte con l'oscure piume": final chorus of Act III of Michelangelo Buonarroti *il giovane, Il giudizio di Paride*. First performed: Florence, Teatro degli Uffizi, 25 October 1608, as part of the festivities celebrating the wedding of Cosimo de' Medici and Maria Magdalena of Austria. Repeated: 19 November 1608, in honor of Duke Vincenzo Gonzaga. Text published 1608 (Florence: Sermatelli), 1609 (Rome: Guglielmo Facciotto); for a modern edition, see Buonarroti *il giovane, Opere varie in versi ed in prosa*, ed. Fanfani, 43–111. Music for the chorus survives in Florence, Conservatorio Statale di Musica Luigi Cherubini, Codex Barbera (unattributed); for a facsimile, see Ghisi, "Ballet Entertainments in Pitti Palace," after p. 424. Music published with text "Se tu parti da me, Fillide amata" in Peri, *Le varie musiche* (1609); see below under "Chamber Songs."

Balletto (Ottavio Rinuccini). Composed in collaboration with Marco da Gagliano, Vittoria Archilei, Francesca and Settimia Caccini, and probably Lorenzo Allegri (Peri composed music sung by himself as Nettuno, and other sections of the text). Performed: Florence, Palazzo Pitti, 14 February 1610/11. Text given in a letter by Jacopo Cicognini to an unknown recipient, 15 February 1610/11, in Solerti, *Gli albori del melodramma*, 2: 283–94 (but with incorrect date). A portion of Peri's music, "Torna, deh torna, pargoletto mio" (for Venere [S, Bc]), was published in Piero Benedetti, *Musiche* (Florence: Heirs of Cristofano Marescotti, 1611), and also survives in Venice, Biblioteca Nazionale Marciana, MS 10317 (It. IV.743) and MS 10318 (It. IV.742); for a modern edition, see Peri, *"Le varie musiche" and Other Songs*, ed. Carter, 68–69. The following passage (for Proteo [T, Bc] and Venere [S, Bc]) survives as a fragment in Florence,

Conservatorio Statale di Musica Luigi Cherubini, Codex Barbera (unattributed); for a facsimile, see Ghisi, "An Early Seventeenth Century MS with Unpublished Italian Monodic Music by Peri, Giulio Romano and Marco da Gagliano," 51.

Adone (Jacopo Cicognini): *favola in musica*. Composed 1611; proposed for performance in Mantua, May 1620, but canceled; see also Hill, *Roman Monody, Cantata, and Opera from the Circles around Cardinal Montalto*, 1: 325 (Cicognini saying in 1613 that the opera was being held in reserve for the first wedding of the Medici princesses); Kirkendale, *Court Musicians*, 208 (Cicognini proposing to Paolo Giordano Orsini a performance in Rome in 1616); and Boyer, "Les Orsini et les musiciens d'Italie au début du XVIIᵉ siècle," 309 (Cicognini suggesting a possible cast for that Rome performance). Text and music lost.

Tournament and *mascherata* (Giovanni Villifranchi). Composed in collaboration with Marco da Gagliano and Lorenzo Allegri (Peri's involvement is not documented but can perhaps be deduced from the surviving musical setting). Performed: Florence, Teatro degli Uffizi, 17 and 19 February 1612/13, in honor of Prince Federigo Della Rovere of Urbino (now betrothed to Grand Duke Cosimo II's sister, Claudia de' Medici; he was seven years old and she, eight). Text published (probably by Villifranchi) as *Descrizione della barriera, e della mascherata, fatte in Firenze a' XVII et a' XIX di febbraio MDCXII al Serenissimo Signor Prencipe d'Urbino* (Florence: B. Sermatelli, 1613). A portion probably by Peri, "Queste lacrime mie, questi sospiri" (T, Bc), survives in Florence, Biblioteca Nazionale Centrale, Banco raro 238 (Magl. XIX.114); for a modern edition, see Peri, *"Le varie musiche" and Other Songs*, ed. Carter, 101–7.

Mascherata di ninfe di Senna (Rinuccini). A revision of the 1610/11 *balletto* (with a new prologue for Nettuno and new first part). Performed: Florence, Palazzo Pitti, 5 May 1613, to celebrate the wedding of Mario Sforza and Renata d'Umena. Text published 1613 (Florence: Heirs of Marescotti); for a modern edition, see Solerti, *Gli albori del melodramma*, 2: 261–82. Music lost, save what survives of 1610/11 version.

Marte ed Amore (Ferdinando Saracinelli): end of a *balletto*. Performed: Florence, Palazzo Pitti, 9 February 1613/14, in honor of the baptism of Prince Mattias de' Medici. Text published as *Balletto fatto nel battesimo del terzo genito delle Serenissime Altezze di Toscana da signori paggi di S.A.S.* (Florence: Zanobi Pignoni, 1613); for a modern edition, see Solerti, *Musica, ballo e drammatica alla corte medicea*, 347–54. Final aria for Amore, "Iten'omai, voi che felici ardete," survives as a duet (SS, Bc; first stanza only) probably by Peri, in Florence, Biblioteca Nazionale Centrale, Banco raro 238 (Magl. XIX.114; unattributed); for a modern edition (as "Iten'omai, voi che felice ardete"), see Peri, *"Le varie musiche" and Other Songs*, ed. Carter, 108–9.

?*Balletto della cortesia* (Michelangelo Buonarroti *il giovane*). Associated with Buonarroti *il giovane*'s *Il passatempo*; perhaps composed in collaboration with

Antonio Brunelli (according to Cesare Tinghi's court diary), although Buonarroti *il giovane* says it was done entirely by Francesca Caccini. Performed: Florence, Palazzo Pitti, 11 February 1613/14. Text and music lost.

Gelosia scacciata da gli Amori and *La Speranza guidata da Mercurio* (Gabriello Chiabrera): two *intermedi* for Chiabrera's *Veglia delle Grazie*. Performed: Florence, Palazzo Pitti, 16 February 1614/15. Text published 1615 (Florence: Giovanni Antonio Caneo); for a modern edition, see Solerti, *Gli albori del melodramma*, 3: 189–99. Music lost.

Guerra d'Amore (Andrea Salvadori): *balletto a cavallo*. Composed in collaboration with Paolo Grazi and Giovanni Battista Signorini. Performed: Florence, Piazza S. Croce, 11 February 1615/16. Text published 1616 (Florence: Zanobi Pignoni, 1615 [*stile fiorentino*]); for an edition, see Salvadori, *Poesie*, 1: 316–58. Music lost.

Ballo rusticale (Ferdinando Saracinelli). Composed in collaboration with Lorenzo Allegri. Performed: Florence, Palazzo Pitti, 16 February 1615/16. Text and music lost.

Guerra di bellezza (Andrea Salvadori): *balletto a cavallo*. Composed in collaboration with Paolo Grazi. Performed: Florence, Piazza S. Croce, 16 October 1616, in honor of Prince Federigo Della Rovere of Urbino. Text published 1616 (Florence: Zanobi Pignoni); for an edition, see Salvadori, *Poesie*, 1: 372–93. Music lost.

?*La liberazione di Tirreno ed Arnea* (Andrea Salvadori): *veglia*. Peri is associated with the entertainment in Cesare Tinghi's court diary, but his name is then canceled; music probably entirely by Marco da Gagliano. Performed: Florence, Teatro degli Uffizi, 6 February 1616/17, to celebrate the wedding of Caterina de' Medici and Ferdinando Gonzaga, Duke of Mantua. Text survives in Florence, Biblioteca Nazionale Centrale, Palat. 251; for an edition, see Salvadori, *Poesie*, 1: 300–315. Music lost.

Lo sposalizio di Medoro ed Angelica (Andrea Salvadori): *favola in musica*. Composed in collaboration with Marco da Gagliano. First performed: Florence, Palazzo Pitti, 25 September 1619, to celebrate the accession of Emperor Ferdinand II. Proposed for performance in Mantua, January 1622, but canceled (see Strainchamps, "The Unknown Letters of Marco da Gagliano," 98–100). Repeated: 29 January 1625/26 (without music). Text published 1623 (Florence: Pietro Ceconcelli); for an edition, see Salvadori, *Poesie*, 1: 129–66. Music lost.

Ballo (?Ercole Marliani or Alessandro Striggio [the younger]). Performed: Mantua, 26 April 1620, for the birthday celebrations of Duke Ferdinando Gonzaga. Repeated: 4 May 1620, to celebrate the wedding of Traiano Bobba and Maria Zati. Text published as *Versi cantati nel ballo fatto dalla Sereniss. Sig. Duchessa di Mantova, per celebrare il giorno natale del Sereniss. Sig. Duca suo consorte, à i 26 d'aprile 1620* (Mantua: Aurelio and Lodovico Osanna [1620]); for a modern edition, see Besutti, "Variar 'le prime 7 stanze della Luna'," 365–74. Music lost.

?*La regina Sant'Orsola* (Andrea Salvadori): *sacra rappresentazione*. Composed mostly
   by Marco da Gagliano and with music also by Francesca Caccini and Muzio
   Effrem, but may at some stage have had one or more pieces by Peri (for role of
   St. Michael) to be sung by a castrato in the household of (Carlo?) Rinuccini
   whom he seems to have been teaching. Planned for performance for wedding of
   Claudia de' Medici and Federigo of Urbino in April 1621 but canceled after
   death of Grand Duke Cosimo II. First performed: 6 October 1624, Teatro degli
   Uffizi, in honor of Archduke Karl of Styria. Repeated: 28 January 1624/25
   (revised), in honor of Prince Władisław of Poland. For Peri's involvement in the
   early 1625 version, see the documents in Harness, *Echoes of Women's Voices*,
   102–7. Libretto published in 1625 (Florence: Pietro Ceconcelli); for an edition,
   see Salvadori, *Poesie*, 1: 1–90. Music lost.

La benedittione di Jacob (Giovan Maria Cecchi, revised by Jacopo Cicognini): *sacra
   rappresentazione*. Composed in collaboration with Giovanni Battista da
   Gagliano (Peri wrote the music for the roles of Archangel Raphael and God the
   Father, probably to be sung by his son Alfonso). First performed: Florence,
   Compagnia dell'Arcangelo Raffaello (S. Maria Novella), 11 September 1622.
   Repeated: four times up to 26 September 1622, with the court in attendance on
   23 September. Text and music lost.

Il gran natale di Christo salvator nostro (Jacopo Cicognini): *sacra rappresentazione*.
   Composed in collaboration with Giovanni Battista da Gagliano (Peri wrote the
   music sung by his son Alfonso). First performed: Florence, Compagnia
   dell'Arcangelo Raffaello (S. Maria Novella), 25 December 1622. Repeated: 27
   December (with the court in attendance) and 31 December. Text and music lost.

La celeste guida, o vero L'arcangelo Raffaello (Jacopo Cicognini): *sacra rappresentazione*. Composed in collaboration with Giovanni Battista da Gagliano (Peri wrote
   the music sung by his son Alfonso). First(?) performed: Florence, Compagnia
   dell'Arcangelo Raffaello (S. Maria Novella), 5 January 1623/24. Text and music
   lost.

?*La regina Sant'Orsola* (Andrea Salvadori): *sacra rappresentazione*. For the performance on 6 October 1624 (which may have included music by Peri), see above
   (1621).

*Canzone delle lodi d'Austria cantata al Serenissimo Arciduca Carlo doppo il banchetto
   in Villa Imperiale* (Andrea Salvadori). Music by Peri, sung by Francesco
   Campagnolo (and perhaps Francesca Caccini). Performed: Poggio Imperiale, 7
   October 1624, in honor of Archduke Karl of Styria. For the date, see Harness,
   Echoes of Women's Voices, 145; for the singers, see Kirkendale, *Court Musicians*,
   229–30 (but only Campagnolo is mentioned in the 1624 edition of the text). Text
   published 1624 (Florence: Pietro Ceconcelli). Music lost.

La precedenza delle dame (Andrea Salvadori): tournament. Music by Peri, sung by
   Francesco Campagnolo. Performed: Florence, Casino di S. Marco, 10 February

1624/25, in honor of Prince Władisław of Poland. Text published 1625 (Florence: Pietro Ceconcelli); for an edition, see Salvadori, *Poesie*, 1: 422–31. Music lost.

Iole ed Ercole (Andrea Salvadori): *favola in musica*. Planned for the festivities celebrating the wedding of Margherita de' Medici and Odoardo Farnese, Florence, 1628, but dropped. For the text, see Salvadori, *Poesie*, 1: 471–76. A possible portion, "Uccidimi, dolore, e qui mi veggia," survives in Bologna, Civico Museo Bibliografico Musicale, Q49, and Prague, Národní Muzeum, Lobkowitz MS II.La.2 (both attributed to Peri); for a modern edition, see Peri, *"Le varie musiche" and Other Songs*, ed. Carter, 92–100.

Flora, o vero Il natal de' fiori (Andrea Salvadori): *favola in musica*. Composed in collaboration with Marco da Gagliano (Peri wrote the music for the role of Clori/Flora). Performed: Florence, Teatro degli Uffizi, 14 October 1628, as part of the festivities celebrating the wedding of Margherita de' Medici and Odoardo Farnese. Libretto published twice in 1628 (Florence: Pietro Ceconcelli; Florence: Zanobi Pignoni); for an edition, see Salvadori, *Poesie*, 1: 167–249. Music published as *La Flora . . . rappresentata nel teatro del Serenissimo Gran Duca nelle reali nozze del Serenissimo Odoardo Farnese Duca di Parma, e di Piacenza; e della Serenissima Principessa Margherita di Toscana* (Florence: Zanobi Pignoni, 1628); for a modern edition, see Gagliano, *La Flora*, ed. Court.

Chamber Songs

PRINTED

"Caro dolce ben mio, perché fuggire" (Livio Celiano), SATTB; included in Cristofano Malvezzi, *Il primo libro delli madrigali a cinque voci* (Venice: Heirs of Girolamo Scotto, 1583; dedicated to Grand Duke Francesco I de' Medici, 1 March 1583); for a modern edition, see Peri, *"Le varie musiche" and Other Songs*, ed. Carter, 63–67.

"Ho visto al mio dolore" (Alessandro Striggio [the younger]), S, Bc; included in Girolamo Montesardo, *L'allegre notti di Fiorenza . . . dove intervengono i più eccellenti musici di detta città: Musiche a una, due, tre, quattro, e cinque voci* (Venice: Angelo Gardano, 1608; dedicated to Pier Francesco Bardi, 1 January 1608); see Carter, *"Serate musicali" in Early Seventeenth-Century Florence*." Also published in Peri, *Le varie musiche* (1609/1619); see below.

Le varie musiche del signor Iacopo Peri a una, due, e tre voci con alcune spirituali in ultimo per cantare nel clavicembalo, e chitarrone, et ancora la maggior parte di esse per sonare semplicemente nel organo, nuovamente poste in luce (Florence: Cristofano Marescotti, 1609). For the title page, see Figure 3.5; for a modern edition, see Peri, *"Le varie musiche" and Other Songs*, ed. Carter, 1–49. Contains:

"In qual parte del ciel, in qual idea" (Petrarch), S, Bc. Also survives in
Brussels, Conservatoire Royal/Koninklijk Conservatorium, Bibliothèque/
Bibliotheek, Codex 704 (unattributed).

"Al fonte, al prato" (Francesco Cini), SB, Bc.

"Tutto 'l dì piango, e poi la notte, quando" (Petrarch), S, Bc.

"Tra le donne onde s'onora" (?Ottavio Rinuccini), S, Bc. Also survives in
Florence, Conservatorio Statale di Musica Luigi Cherubini, Codex Barbera
(with text "Fra le donne ond'il bel Arno" [?Rinuccini]; unattributed).

"Quest'humil fera, un cor di tigre o d'orsa" (Petrarch), S, Bc.

"Bellissima regina" (Ottavio Rinuccini or Gabriello Chiabrera), S, Bc. Also
survives in Florence, Conservatorio Statale di Musica Luigi Cherubini, Codex
Barbera (unattributed).

"Lasso, ch'i' ardo, et altri non mel crede" (Petrarch), S, Bc.

"Ho visto al mio dolore" (Alessandro Striggio [the younger]), S, Bc. First
published in Girolamo Montesardo, *L'allegre notti di Fiorenza . . . dove intervengono i più eccellenti musici di detta città: Musiche a una, due, tre, quattro, e cinque
voci* (Venice: Angelo Gardano, 1608); see above.

"O durezza di ferro e di diamante," T, Bc.

"Lungi dal vostro lume," S, Bc.

"Solitario augellino," T, Bc.

"Se tu parti da me, Fillide amata" (Michelangelo Buonarroti *il giovane*), T,
Bc. Also survives in Florence, Conservatorio Statale di Musica Luigi Cherubini,
Codex Barbera (with text "Poiché la notte con l'oscure piume" from Buonarroti
il giovane, Il giudizio di Paride); see under "Theatrical Music," above (25 October
1608). A third text by Buonarroti *il giovane* for the music survives, "Poiché de'
Toschi al fortunato impero"; Florence, Casa Buonarroti, Archivio Buonarroti 84,
fols. 180v–181r (and see Chapter 3). However, an annotation there says that it was
not used (*non servì*).

"Con sorrisi cortesi" (Gabriello Chiabrera), SB, Bc.

"Caro e soave legno" (Ottavio Rinuccini), SSB, Bc.

"Un dì soletto" (Gabriello Chiabrera), S, Bc. A fragment also survives in
Florence, Conservatorio Statale di Musica Luigi Cherubini, Codex Barbera
(unattributed).

"O dolce anima mia, dunque è pur vero" (Battista Guarini), SSB, Bc.

"O miei giorni fugaci, o breve vita" (Ottavio Rinuccini), S, Bc. An arrangement for keyboard survives in Florence, Biblioteca Nazionale Centrale, Magl.
XIX.115 (unattributed).

"Anima, oimé, che pensi, oimé, che fai" (Ottavio Rinuccini), S, Bc.

"Torna, deh torna, pargoletto mio" (Ottavio Rinuccini), S, Bc; included in Piero
Benedetti, *Musiche* (Florence: Heirs of Cristofano Marescotti, 1611; dedicated to
Conte Cosimo Della Gherardesca, 12 December 1611); for a modern edition, see

Peri, *"Le varie musiche" and Other Songs*, ed. Carter, 68–69. See under "Theatrical Music," above (14 February 1610/11).

"O dell'alto Appenin figlio sovrano" (Ferdinando Saracinelli), T, Bc; included in
Antonio Brunelli, *Scherzi, arie, canzonette, e madrigali a una, due, e tre voci per
sonare, e cantare con ogni sorte di stromenti . . . Libro secondo* (Venice: Giacomo
Vincenti, 1614; dedicated to Grand Duke Cosimo II, 25 July 1614), with heading
"Nelle nozze del Signor Conte Francesco Torelli"; for a modern edition, see Peri,
"Le varie musiche" and Other Songs, ed. Carter, 70–74.

Le varie musiche . . . con aggiunta d'arie nuove (Florence: Zanobi Pignoni, 1619;
dedicated by Pignoni to Ferdinando Saracinelli [no date]). This is a second
edition of *Le varie musiche* (1609), with all its songs except "Se tu parti da me,
Fillide amata" and "Con sorrisi cortesi." For the title page, see Figure 3.6; for a
modern edition of the added songs, see Peri, *"Le varie musiche" and Other Songs*,
ed. Carter, 50–62. The new songs include (at the beginning of the volume):

   "Qual cadavero spirante," T, Bc.

   "Hor che gli augelli," S, Bc. Also survives in Florence, Biblioteca Nazionale
Centrale, Magl. VII.1222bis (text and letter-tablature for guitar). Also published
in Giovanni Stefani, ed., *Scherzi amorosi: Canzonette ad una voce sola poste in
musica da diversi . . . libro secondo, nuovamente corretti et ristampati* (2nd? ed.,
Venice: Alessandro Vincenti, 1620).

   "Che veggio, ohimé, che sento," T, Bc. Stanzas 1 and 6 also survive in
Florence, Biblioteca Nazionale Centrale, Banco raro 238 (Magl. XIX.114;
unattributed).

   "Tra le lagrime e i sospiri," S, Bc.

   "O core infiammato," SB, Bc. Also survives in Florence, Biblioteca Nazionale
Centrale, Banco raro 238 (Magl. XIX.114; unattributed).

   "Freddo core che in amore," S, Bc.

   "Care stelle," S, Bc.

"Hor che gli augelli," S, Bc; included in Giovanni Stefani, ed., *Scherzi amorosi:
Canzonette ad una voce sola poste in musica da diversi . . . libro secondo, nuovamente corretti et ristampati* (2nd? ed., Venice: Alessandro Vincenti, 1620). The
first edition (now lost) probably dates from 1619. Also published in Peri, *Le varie
musiche* (1619); see above.

OTHER SONGS IN MANUSCRIPT

"Intenerite voi, lacrime mie" (Ottavio Rinuccini), TT, Bc; in Brussels, Conservatoire Royal/Koninklijk Conservatorium, Bibliothèque/Bibliotheek, Codex 704
(attributed to Peri), and Florence, Biblioteca Nazionale Centrale, Magl. XIX.66
(unattributed); for a modern edition, see Peri, *"Le varie musiche" and Other
Songs*, ed. Carter, 74–76.

?"Iten'omai, voi che felice [felici] ardete" (Ferdinando Saracinelli), SS, Bc; in
Florence, Biblioteca Nazionale Centrale, Banco raro 238 (Magl. XIX.114;
unattributed); for a modern edition, see Peri, *"Le varie musiche" and Other Songs*,
ed. Carter, 108–9. See under "Theatrical Music," above (9 February 1613/14).

?"Occhi, fonti del core, occhi piangete," T, Bc; in Florence, Biblioteca Nazionale
Centrale, Banco raro 238 (Magl. XIX.114; unattributed); for a modern edition,
see Peri, *"Le varie musiche" and Other Songs*, ed. Carter, 110–12.

?"Queste lacrime mie, questi sospiri" (Giovanni Villifranchi), T, Bc; in Florence,
Biblioteca Nazionale Centrale, Banco raro 238 (Magl. XIX.114; unattributed);
for a modern edition, see Peri, *"Le varie musiche" and Other Songs*, ed. Carter,
101–7. See under "Theatrical Music," above (17 February 1612/13).

"Se da l'aspro martire," S, Bc; in Prague, Národní Muzeum, Lobkowitz MS II.La.2
(attributed to Peri); for a modern edition, see Peri, *"Le varie musiche" and Other
Songs*, ed. Carter, 83–91.

?"Tu dormi, e 'l dolce sonno," T, Bc; in Florence, Conservatorio Statale di Musica
Luigi Cherubini, Codex Barbera (unattributed; first stanza only); London,
British Library, Additional MS 30491 (attributed to Peri; in the hand of Luigi
Rossi); Prague, Národní Muzeum, Lobkowitz MS II.La.2 (attributed to Peri);
Rome, Biblioteca Universitaria Alessandrina, MS 279 (attributed to Cesare
Marotta). For modern editions, see Peri, *"Le varie musiche" and Other Songs*, ed.
Carter, 77–82; Hill, *Roman Monody, Cantata, and Opera from the Circles around
Cardinal Montalto*, 2: 239–44 (and for the irresolvable conflict in attribution, see
ibid., 1: 218).

"Uccidimi, dolore, e qui mi veggia" (Andrea Salvadori, *Iole ed Ercole*), S, Bc; in
Bologna, Civico Museo Bibliografico Musicale, Q49 (attributed to Peri), and
Prague, Národní Muzeum, Lobkowitz MS II.La.2 (attributed to Peri); for a
modern edition, see Peri, *"Le varie musiche" and Other Songs*, ed. Carter, 92–100.
See under "Theatrical Music," above (1628).

Instrumental Music

Ricercar del primo tuono, 4 instruments (G2, C2, C3, F4); included in Cristofano
Malvezzi, *Il primo libro de recercari à quattro voci* (Perugia: Pietroiacomo
Petrucci, 1577; dedicated to Giovanni de' Bardi [no date]). Also survives in
Florence, Biblioteca Nazionale Centrale, MS Mus. II.I.295 (Magl. XIX.107). For
a modern edition, see Malvezzi, Peri, and Padovano, *Ensemble Ricercars*, ed.
Swenson, 36–39.

Four Poems concerning Jacopo Peri

Although the four known contemporary poems that mention Peri are familiar to scholars working in the field, we republish them here for the references they make to his economic circumstances in his early years (no. 1), his musical skills and learning as a singer and instrumentalist (nos. 1, 2, 3), his rivalries with other Florentine musicians (no. 3), and a famously negative, and probably unjustified, opinion of his purported arrogance and exaggerated piety (no. 4). The texts have been lightly edited to conform to the principles adopted elsewhere in this book.

1 Antonfrancesco Grazzini ("Il Lasca")

Grazzini (1504–84) wrote a great deal of occasional poetry (sonnets, *canzoni*, madrigals, *ottave rime*, *capitoli*) often addressed to specific Florentines or on subject matter of interest to them, many cast in a humorous vein (for example, he wrote a 100-line *capitolo* addressed to the musician Giovanni Animuccia in praise of spinach). The present two *ottava rima* stanzas have no heading, but their subject is clear; they may have been commissioned by Peri or someone close to him. The biblical reference is to Luke 4:24.

> Lucca, Biblioteca Statale, MS 1513, fol. 179, edited in Grazzini, *Le rime burlesche*, ed. Verzone, 395; also given in Ruspoli, *Poesie*, ed. Arlìa, 58 n., and in Kirkendale, *Court Musicians*, 235–36. Line 9: Verzone and Arlìa give it as *Ma quando mi ricorda . . .* (the reading here follows Kirkendale). Line 14: Kirkendale gives it as *in cui si fa prova.*

> Com'esser può fra tanti hoggi in Fiorenza
> cavalier', gentil'huomini e signori,
> non sia chi abbia tanta coscienza,

che di costui, ch'io parlo, s'innamori?
La grazia, il canto, il suono e la scienza
sua mertan premio grande e sommi onori;
ma temo, ohimé! ch'al vostro Zazzerino
non nuoca l'esser nato Fiorentino.

Ma quando mi ricordo aver già letto
nell'Evangelio, ove scritto si trova
"Nessun profeta alla sua patria accetto,"
non mi par cosa inusitata e nuova;
ma ben crepo di rabbia e di dispetto,
quand'un gentil spirto, in cui fa prova
e mostra la natura ogni sua possa,
non abbia tanto pan che viver possa.

How can it be that today in Florence among so many / knights, gentlemen, and lords / there is not one with a good enough conscience / to take into his affections him of whom I speak? / His grace, his song, his playing, and his learning / deserve great reward and highest honors. / But I fear, alas, that for your Zazzerino / it harms him to have been born a Florentine. // But when I recall having already read / in the Evangelist, where one finds it written / "No prophet is accepted in his own country," / it does not seem to me anything unusual or new. / But I burst with rage and scorn / when a gentle spirit, in whom Nature offers proof / and reveals all her power, / does not have enough bread that he can live.

2 Anonymous

This sonnet adopts all the tropes common in praising singers at the time, including the reference to Orpheus (also the role that Peri took in his *Euridice*). *Legno* is a frequent metonym for a lute (compare Peri's trio "Caro e soave legno" in *Le varie musiche*). The "Theban singer" is Pindar.

> Florence, Biblioteca Riccardiana 2833, fol. 475; also given in Ruspoli, *Poesie*, ed. Arlìa, 56–57 n.; Kirkendale, *Court Musicians*, 236. Line 2: *rapito* is conjectural (there is an ink blot in the manuscript). Line 3: Ruspoli gives *novello Orfeo, novel Teban cantore*; Kirkendale gives *novello Orfeo, nuovo Teban cantore*.

O Peri, al suon del tuo temprato legno
mancan gli spirti altrui [rap]ito il core:
novell'Orfeo, nuovo Teban cantore,

unico cigno del celeste regno.
Ti fanno di Davidde erede degno
l'arpa e la cetra sino al ciel sonore,
però dell'universo il gran motore
simile a quel di lui ti diè l'ingegno.
A' tua concenti a que' de' cieli uguali
ciascun s'arresta, e 'l cor ratto s'invia
là dove il valor tuo gl'impenna l'ali.
La leggiadra tua man quell'armonia
degli angelici cori, che i mortali
non ponno udir, ne fa sentir qual sia.

O Peri, at the sound of your well-tuned lute / others' spirits fall weak, the heart transported: / a new Orpheus, a new Theban singer, / a unique swan of the heavenly kingdom. // You are made a worthy heir of David / by the harp and lyre sounding up to heaven, / nay the prime mover of the universe / akin to that of Him who gave you your talent. // At your concents equal to those of the heavens / everyone stops, and the heart, stolen, flies / where your valor gives it wings. // Your graceful touch that harmony / of angelic choirs, which mortals / cannot hear, makes heard as what it [the harmony] might be.

3 Ottavio Rinuccini

This *sonetto caudato* by Rinuccini (1562–1621) pits Peri against Muzio Effrem (1549–after 1626). Effrem, formerly in the service of Carlo Gesualdo, Prince of Venosa, was known in Florence in the second half of the 1610s, if not before; he then entered court service from 1619 to 1622. He engaged in a vicious controversy with Marco da Gagliano over the musical solecisms he claimed to find in the latter's *Sesto libro de madrigali a cinque voci* (Venice: Bartolomeo Magni, 1617); see Kirkendale, *Court Musicians*, 362–65. The onlookers in the present musical duel include Ferdinando Saracinelli (the dedicatee of the second edition of Peri's *Le varie musiche*) and the singer Antonio Brandi (who took the role of Arcetro in the first performance of Peri's *Euridice* and later entered court service).

It is not clear what instruments are being played in the contest (lute or keyboard). But Rinuccini invokes (if not entirely accurately) a range of musical terms—Effrem's *fa*s generated by *musica ficta* (lowering a note by a semitone), and B naturals in the *durus* hexachord, and Peri's B flats in the *mollis* hexachord—and as a result paints Effrem as a modern chromaticist (as was Gesualdo), whereas Peri is more learned and restrained. Effrem claims the prize, however, because he hears two consecutive (parallel) octaves in Peri's performance: this, like consecutive fifths, is a basic music-grammatical error, almost the first one learns to avoid when studying counterpoint and harmony. We do not have the "other poem" (or is it another song?) to which this sonnet refers.

Solerti, *Gli albori del melodramma*, 1: 90 n. (from a manuscript formerly associated with the Biblioteca Trivulziana, Milan).

> Discese in campo il Flemma e 'l Zazzerino
> avanti il cavalier Saracinello,
> venendo incontro a 'l musical duello
> fêr prova ciaschedun da paladino.
>
> Di *fa* finti o *b* duri un suon divino
> temprando Muzio disusato e bello,
> empié di maraviglia ogni cervello:
> così racconta il battitor Brandino.
>
> Indi l'altro con man pronta e soave
> desta fugando le più dotte corde,
> or di *b* molle, or di natura grave.
>
> Ma 'l Flemma, che l'orecchie non ha sorde,
> udito il risonar di doppie ottave,
> chiede la palma, e lo rampogna e morde.
>
> Il partir fu discorde:
> incerta la vittoria, eguale il vanto,
> il resto s'udirà nell'altro canto.

Effrem stepped down to the battlefield, and Zazzarino, / before Cavaliere Saracinelli, / and coming together for a musical duel, / each made a test in the manner of a paladin. // Tempering a divine sound of feigned *fa*s or *b-duri*, / unusual and beautiful, Muzio / filled every head with marvel: / so recounts Brandino, the umpire. // Then the other [Peri], with hand prompt and sweet, / stirs up in his fuguing the most learned strings, / now in *b molle*, now in grave manner. // But Effrem, who does not have deaf ears, / having heard the sound of double octaves, / asks for the victory palm, and he derides and insults him. // The outcome was discordant; / uncertain the victory, equal the merit, / and the rest will be heard in the other poem.

4 Francesco Ruspoli

Some thirty satirical sonnets by Francesco Ruspoli (1579–1625) survive. They take to an extreme the burlesque vein cultivated by Antonfrancesco Grazzini earlier in the sixteenth century (see no. 1, above). Eleven of his sonnets received an explanatory commentary by Stefano Rosselli (1598–1664), later slightly expanded by Andrea Cavalcanti (1610–73); Rosselli identified the specific persons attacked in six sonnets, including the present *sonetto caudato*, which, according to Rosselli, had Peri as its target. Kirkendale, *Court Musicians*, 190, tentatively suggests that the poem was commissioned by the composer Muzio Effrem (see no. 3, above), although it could have been any of Peri's rivals in Florence.

The reference to St. Hilarion is probably to the anchorite (291–371) famous for his ascetic diet. Rosselli used the mention of S. Caterina delle Ruote (St. Catherine of Alexandria, martyred on a saw-toothed wheel) to claim that Peri was brought up in the Florentine orphanage of that name, but this is incorrect (see Chapter 1). As for singing to the organ, this was Peri's first job at SS. Annunziata in 1573, and he continued to do it at court (see Chapter 3). *Berlingaccio* is *Giovedí grasso*, the day of Carnival devoted to ribald feasting.

Florence, Biblioteca Nazionale Centrale, Magl. VII.572, fol. 11v; edited in Ruspoli, *Poesie*, ed. Arlìa, 55–56 (with Roselli's commentary following); also given in Carter, *Jacopo Peri*, 1: 284–93 (with Cavalcanti's commentary), and in Kirkendale, *Court Musicians*, 189–90 (poem only). For other sources, see ibid., 694.

Un c'ha le gambe a faccelline storte,
e la sua nobiltà sul codrione,
se par nel viso un sant'Ilarione,
più tristo è poi d'un birro delle porte.

Le sue bugie son peggio della morte,
ma le porge con tanta divozione
ch'io ne disgrado il miglior bacchettone
quando si disciplina e batte forte.

Quest'è quel Moisè del contrappunto,
che i virtuosi sbalza e ripercuote,
né gli sovvien ch'ei mendicò 'l panunto.

O santa Caterina delle Ruote,
mandate una saetta per l'appunto
che lo fenda nel mezzo delle gote;

acciò che in su le note
possa cantar questo mio sonettaccio
in sull'organo il dì di Berlingaccio.

One who has legs like twisted torches, / and [wears] his nobility on his ass, / if in his face he looks like a Saint Hilarion, / he is even more miserable than a guard standing at the gate. // His lies are worse than death, / but he delivers them with such devotion / that I rank lower the best flagellant / when he disciplines and hits himself hard. // This is that Moses of counterpoint, / who overthrows and batters virtuosos, / and he does not remember that he once begged for oiled-bread. // O Saint Catherine of the Wheel, / send down a lightning bolt for the purpose / of splitting his cheeks down the middle; // so that to the [musical] notes / he might sing this my mischievous sonnet / to the organ on the last Thursday of Carnival.

Works Cited

Acidini Luchinat, Cristina, "L'altar maggiore," in *La chiesa e il convento di Santo Spirito a Firenze*, ed. Cristina Acidini Luchinat (Florence: Giunti, 1996), 337–56.

Ademollo, Agostino, *Marietta de' Ricci, ovvero Firenze al tempo dell'assedio: Racconto storico*, 2nd ed. rev. Luigi Passerini, 6 vols. (Florence: Chiari, 1845).

Ademollo, Alessandro, *La bell'Adriana ed altre virtuose del suo tempo alla corte di Mantova: Contributo di documenti per la storia della musica in Italia nel primo quarto del Seicento* (Città di Castello: S. Lapi, 1888).

Annibaldi, Claudio, "Sulle impertinenze della musicologia 'antropocentrica'," *Il saggiatore musicale* 3 (1996): 361–91.

Bacherini Bartoli, Maria Adelaide, "Giulio Caccini: Nuove fonti biografiche e lettere inedite," *Studi musicali* 9 (1980): 59–71.

Barocchi, Paola, and Giovanna Gaeta Bertelà, eds., *Collezionismo mediceo e storia artistica*, 4 vols. (Florence: SPES, 2002–11).

Battara, Piero, *La popolazione di Firenze alla metà del '500* (Florence: Rinascimento del Libro, 1935).

Besutti, Paola, "Variar 'le prime 7 stanze della Luna': Ritrovati versi di ballo per Jacopo Peri," *Studi musicali* 34 (2005): 319–74.

Biagioli, Mario, *Galilei, Courtier: The Practice of Science in the Culture of Absolutism* (Chicago: University of Chicago Press, 1993).

Bizzocchi, Roberto, "La culture généalogique dans l'Italie du seizième siècle," *Annales ESC* 46 (1991): 789–805.

Bonini, Severo, *Severo Bonini's "Discorsi e regole": A Bilingual Edition*, trans. and ed. MaryAnn Bonino (Provo, UT: Brigham Young University Press, 1979).

Boone, Marc, C. A. Davids, and Paul Janssens, eds., *Urban Public Debts: Urban Government and the Market for Annuities in Western Europe (14th–15th Centuries)* (Turnhout, Belgium: Brepols, 2003).

Boutier, Jean, "Les *notizie diverse* de Niccolò Gondi (1652–1720): À propos de la mémoire et des strategies familiales d'un noble florentin," *Mélanges de l'École Française de Rome* 98 (1986): 1097–151.

————, "Un *Who's Who* florentin du XVIIe siècle (1607)," in *Société et idéologies des temps modernes: Hommage à Arlette Jouanna*, ed. Joël Fouilleron et al., 2 vols. (Montpellier: Université de Montpellier III, 1996), 1: 79–100.

Boutier, Jean, and Franco Angiolini, "Noblesses de capitales, noblesses périphériques: Les dynamiques des élites urbaines dans le Grand-duché de Toscane, XVIe–XVIIIe siècles," in *Le nobiltà delle città capitali*, ed. Martine Boiteux et al. (Rome: Roma Tre-CROMA, 2009), 51–75.

Boyer, Ferdinand, "Les Orsini et les musiciens d'Italie au début du XVIIe siècle," in *Mélanges de philologie, d'histoire et de littérature offerts à Henri Hauvette* (Paris: Les Presses Françaises, 1934), 301–10.

Brackett, John K., *Criminal Justice and Crime in Late Renaissance Florence, 1537–1609* (Cambridge: Cambridge University Press, 1992).

Brown, Alison, "Offices of Honour and Profit: The Crisis of Republicanism in Florence," in Brown, *Medicean and Savonarolan Florence: The Interplay of Politics, Humanism, and Religion* (Turnhout, Belgium: Brepols, 2011), 139–76.

Brown, Judith C., "Monache a Firenze all'inizio dell'età moderna: Un'analisi demografica," *Quaderni storici* 85 (1994): 117–52.

Buonarroti, Michelangelo *il giovane*, *Opere varie in versi ed in prosa*, ed. Pietro Fanfani (Florence: Le Monnier, 1863).

Burney, Charles, *A General History of Music, from the Earliest Ages to the Present Period (1789)*, ed. Frank Mercer, 2 vols. (New York: Dover, 1957).

Butchart, David, "The Letters of Alessandro Striggio: An Edition with Translation and Commentary," *Royal Musical Association Research Chronicle* 23 (1990): 1–78.

Butters, Suzanne B., *The Triumph of Vulcan: Sculptors' Tools, Porphyry, and the Prince in Ducal Florence*, 2 vols. (Florence: Olschki, 1996).

Cabras, Maria Giuseppina, "Ricerche per la storia della cappella musicale della SS. Annunziata di Firenze (1576–1713)" (tesi di laurea, Università di Firenze, 1972).

Caccini, Giulio, *Nuove musiche e nuova maniera di scriverle (1614)*, ed. H. Wiley Hitchcock, "Recent Researches in the Music of the Baroque Era" 28 (Madison, WI: A-R Editions, 1970).

Callard, Caroline, *Le prince et la république: Histoire, pouvoir et société dans la Florence des Médicis au XVIIe siècle* (Paris: PUPS, 2007).

Calvi, Giulia, "Reconstructing the Family: Widowhood and Remarriage in Tuscany in the Early Modern Period," in *Marriage in Italy, 1300–1650*, ed. Trevor Dean et al. (Cambridge: Cambridge University Press, 1998), 275–96.

Cantini, Lorenzo, *Legislazione toscana*, 32 vols. (Florence: P. Fantosini, 1800–1808).

Carmona, Maurice, "Aspects du capitalisme toscan au XVIe et au XVIIe siècles: Les sociétés en comandite à Florence et à Lucque," *Revue d'histoire moderne et contemporaine* 11 (1964): 81–108.

Carter, Tim, "Crossing the Boundaries: Sacred, Civic and Ceremonial Space in Late Sixteenth- and Early Seventeenth-Century Florence," in *Atti del VII centenario del Duomo di Firenze*, vol. 3: *"Cantate domino": Musica nei secoli per il Duomo di Firenze; atti del convegno internazionale di studi (Firenze, 23–25 maggio 1997)*, ed. Piero Gargiulo et al. (Florence: Edizioni Firenze, 2001), 139–46.

———, *"E in rileggendo poi le proprie note:* Monteverdi Responds to Artusi?" *Renaissance Studies* 26 (2012): 138–55.

———, "Finding a Voice: Vittoria Archilei and the Florentine 'New Music'," in *Feminism and Renaissance Studies*, ed. Lorna Hutson, "Oxford Readings in Feminism" (Oxford: Clarendon Press, 1999), 450–67.

———, "A Florentine Wedding of 1608," *Acta musicologica* 55 (1983): 89–107; reprinted in Carter, *Music, Patronage and Printing in Late Renaissance Florence.*

———, "Giulio Caccini (1551–1618): New Facts, New Music," *Studi musicali* 16 (1987): 13–31; reprinted in Carter, *Music, Patronage and Printing in Late Renaissance Florence.*

———, *Jacopo Peri (1561–1633): His Life and Works*, 2 vols. (New York: Garland, 1989; modified reprint of Ph.D. diss., University of Birmingham, 1980).

———, "Monteverdi and Some Problems of Biography," *Journal of Seventeenth-Century Music,* forthcoming.

———, "Monteverdi, Early Opera, and a Question of Genre: The Case of *Andromeda* (1620)," *Journal of the Royal Musical Association* 137 (2012): 1–34.

———, "Music and Patronage in Late Sixteenth-Century Florence: The Case of Jacopo Corsi (1561–1602)," *I Tatti Studies: Essays in the Renaissance* 1 (1985): 57–104; reprinted in Carter, *Music, Patronage and Printing in Late Renaissance Florence.*

———, *Music in Late Renaissance and Early Baroque Italy* (London: Batsford, 1992).

———, *Music, Patronage and Printing in Late Renaissance Florence*, "Variorum Collected Studies Series" CS682 (Aldershot, UK: Ashgate, 2000).

———, "Music-Printing in Late Sixteenth- and Early Seventeenth-Century Florence: Giorgio Marescotti, Cristofano Marescotti and Zanobi Pignoni," *Early Music History* 9 (1989): 27–72; reprinted in Carter, *Music, Patronage and Printing in Late Renaissance Florence.*

———, "Music-Selling in Late Sixteenth-Century Florence: The Bookshop of Piero di Giuliano Morosi," *Music and Letters* 70 (1989): 483–504; reprinted in Carter, *Music, Patronage and Printing in Late Renaissance Florence.*

———, *"Non occorre nominare tanti musici*: Private Patronage and Public Ceremony in Late Sixteenth-Century Florence," *I Tatti Studies: Essays in the Renaissance* 4 (1991): 89–104; reprinted in Carter, *Music, Patronage and Printing in Late Renaissance Florence.*

———, "The North Italian Courts," in *Man and Music: The Early Baroque Era; from the Late 16th Century to the 1660s*, ed. Curtis Price (London: Macmillan, 1993), 23–48.

———, "Printing the 'New Music'," in *Music and the Cultures of Print*, ed. Kate van Orden (New York and London: Garland, 2000), 3–37.

————, "Rediscovering *Il rapimento di Cefalo*," *Journal of Seventeenth-Century Music* 9 (2003), <www.sscm-jscm.org/v9no1.html>.

————, "*Serate musicali* in Early Seventeenth-Century Florence: Girolamo Montesardo's *L'allegre notti di Fiorenza* (1608)," in *Renaissance Studies in Honor of Craig Hugh Smyth*, ed. Andrew Morrogh et al., 2 vols. (Florence: Giunti Barbèra, 1985), 1: 555–68; reprinted in Carter, *Music, Patronage and Printing in Late Renaissance Florence*.

————, "*Tutto 'l dì piango* . . . : Petrarch and the 'New Music' in Early Seventeenth-Century Italy," in *Il Petrarchismo: Un modello di poesia per l'Europa*, ed. Loredana Chines, 2 vols. (Rome: Bulzoni, 2006), 1: 391–404.

————, "Winds, Cupids, Little Zephyrs, and Sirens: Monteverdi and *Le nozze di Tetide* (1616–17)," *Early Music* 39 (2011): 489–502.

Catelani, A., "Una lettera inedita di Jacopo Peri," *Boccherini* 3 (1864): 22–23.

Cavarzere, Marco, "Monaldi, Piero," in *Dizionario biografico degli italiani* (Rome: Istituto della Enciclopedia italiana, 1960–), 75: 561–63.

Chabot, Isabelle, *La dette des familles: Femmes, lignage et patrimonie à Florence aux XIVᵉ et XVᵉ siècles* (Rome: École Française de Rome, 2011).

Chorley, Patrick, "*Rascie* and the Florentine Cloth Industry during the Sixteenth Century," *Journal of European Economic History* 32 (2003): 487–526.

Cole, Janie, *Music, Spectacle and Cultural Brokerage in Early Modern Italy: Michelangelo Buonarroti il Giovane*, 2 vols., "Fondazione Carlo Marchi: Quaderni" 44 (Florence: Olschki, 2012).

Corazzini, Giuseppe Odoardo, "Jacopo Peri e la sua famiglia," *Atti dell'Accademia del R. Istituto Musicale di Firenze* 33 (1895): 33–87.

Corazzol, Gigi, "Varietà notarile: Scorci di vita economica e sociale," in *Storia di Venezia dalle origini alla caduta della Serenissima*, vol. 6: *Dal Rinascimento al Barocco*, ed. Gaetano Cozzi et al. (Rome: Istituto della Enciclopedia italiana, 1994), 775–91.

Corradi, Alfonso, *Annali delle epidemie occorse in Italia dalle prime memorie fino al 1850*, 5 vols. (Bologna: Gamberini, 1865; repr. Bologna: Forni, 1972–73).

Cummings, Anthony M., *Nino Pirrotta: An Intellectual Biography*, "Memoirs of the American Philosophical Society" (Philadelphia: American Philosophical Society, 2013).

Cusick, Suzanne, *Francesca Caccini at the Medici Court: Music and the Circulation of Power* (Chicago: University of Chicago Press, 2009).

D'Accone, Frank, "The Florentine Fra Mauros: A Dynasty of Musical Friars," *Musica disciplina* 33 (1979): 77–137; reprinted in D'Accone, *Music and Musicians in Sixteenth-Century Florence*.

————, "The *Intavolatura di M. Alemanno Aiolli*," *Musica disciplina* 20 (1966): 151–74.

————, "The Musical Chapels at the Florentine Cathedral and Baptistry during the First Half of the 16th Century," *Journal of the American Musicological Society*

24 (1971): 1–50; reprinted in D'Accone, *Music and Musicians in Sixteenth-Century Florence.*

———, *Music and Musicians in Sixteenth-Century Florence,* "Variorum Collected Studies Series" CS857 (Aldershot, UK: Ashgate, 2007).

D'Addario, Arnaldo, "Burocrazia, economia e finanze dello stato fiorentino alla metà del Cinquecento," *Archivio storico italiano* 121 (1963): 362–456.

Darr, Alan Phipps, and Brenda Preyer, "Donatello, Desiderio da Settignano and His Brothers, and 'Macigno' Sculpture for a Boni Palace in Florence," *Burlington Magazine* 141, no. 1161 (December 1999): 720–31.

Davanzati, Bernardo, *"Lezione delle monete" e "Notizia de' cambi,"* ed. Sergio Ricossa (Turin: Fògola, 1988).

Davari, Stefano, "Notizie biografiche del distinto maestro di musica Claudio Monteverdi, desunte dai documenti dell'Archivio storico Gonzaga," *Atti e memorie della R. Accademia Virgiliana di Mantova* 10 (1884–85): 79–183.

De Caro, Gaspare, *"Euridice": Momenti dell'umanesimo civile fiorentino* (Bologna: Ut Orpheus Edizioni, 2006).

Dell'Antonio, Andrew, *Listening as Spiritual Practice in Early Modern Italy* (Berkeley: University of California Press, 2011).

De Luca, Giuseppe, "Sensali e mercato del credito a Milano tra XVI e XVII secolo," in *Il mercato del credito in età moderna,* ed. Elena María García Guerra et al. (Milan: FrancoAngeli, 2010), 239–57.

Denzel, Markus A., *Handbook of World Exchange Rates, 1590–1914* (Farnham, UK: Ashgate, 2010).

Eisenbichler, Konrad, *The Boys of the Archangel Raphael: A Youth Confraternity in Florence, 1411–1785* (Toronto: University of Toronto Press, 1998).

Elias, Norbert, *Die höfische Gesellschaft: Untersuchungen zur Soziologie des Königtums und der höfischen Aristokratie mit einer Einleitung: Soziologie und Geschichtswissenschaft,* "Soziologische Texte" 54 (Berlin: H. Luchterhand, 1969); trans. Edmund Jephcott as *The Court Society* (New York: Pantheon Books, 1983).

Evangelisti, Silvia, *Nuns: A History of Convent Life* (Oxford: Oxford University Press, 2007).

Fabris, Dinko, *Mecenati e musici: Documenti sul patronato artistico dei Bentivoglio di Ferrara nell'epoca di Monteverdi (1585–1645),* "ConNotazioni" 4 (Lucca: Libreria Musicale Italiana, 1999).

Fasano Guarini, Elena, *"Gentildonna, borghese, cittadina*: Problèmes de traduction entre la cour d'Henry IV et la cour des Médicis," in *Société et idéologies des temps modernes: Hommage à Arlette Jouanna,* ed. Joël Fouilleron et al., 2 vols. (Montpellier: Université de Montpellier III, 1996), 1: 163–78.

Fumagalli, Elena, "Prime indagini sui rapporti economici tra pittori e corte medicea nel Seicento," in *Vivere d'arte: Carriere e finanze nell'Italia moderna,* ed.

Raffaella Morselli, "Annali del Dipartimento di Scienze della Comunicazione dell'Università degli Studi di Teramo" 2 (Rome: Carocci, 2007), 135–66.

Gagliano, Marco da, *La Flora,* ed. Suzanne Court, "Recent Researches in the Music of the Baroque Era" 171 (Middleton, WI: A-R Editions, 2011).

Galilei, Galileo, *Le opere,* 20 vols. (repr. Florence: Barbèra, 1968).

Gargiolli, Carlo, "Feste fatte in Pisa l'anno 1605 [= 1606]," *Propugnatore* 15 (1882): 425–30.

Ghisi, Federico, "Ballet Entertainments in Pitti Palace, Florence, 1608–1625," *Musical Quarterly* 35 (1949): 421–36.

——, "An Early Seventeenth Century MS with Unpublished Italian Monodic Music by Peri, Giulio Romano and Marco da Gagliano," *Acta musicologica* 20 (1948): 46–60.

Giazotto, Remo, *Le due patrie di Giulio Caccini, musico medices (1551–1618): Nuovi contributi anagrafici e d'archivio sulla sua vita e la sua famiglia,* " 'Historiae musicae cultores' biblioteca" 38 (Florence: Olschki, 1984).

Goldberg, Edward, *Jews and Magic in Medici Florence: The Secret World of Benedetto Blanis* (Toronto: University of Toronto Press, 2011).

Goldenberg Stoppato, Lisa, "Proposte per Filippo Furini e documenti inediti per il figlio Francesco," *Paragone/Arte* 60, nos. 87–88 (September–November 2009): 3–24.

Goldthwaite, Richard A., "Le aziende seriche e il mondo degli affari a Firenze alla fine del '500," *Archivio storico italiano* 169 (2011): 281–341.

——, "Banking in Florence at the End of the Sixteenth Century," *Journal of European Economic History* 27 (1998): 471–536.

——, *The Economy of Renaissance Florence* (Baltimore: Johns Hopkins University Press, 2009); rev. and trans. as *L'economia della Firenze rinascimentale* (Bologna: Il Mulino, 2013).

——, "The Florentine Wool Industry in the Late Sixteenth Century: A Case Study," *Journal of European Economic History* 32 (2003): 527–54.

——, "The Painting Industry in Early Modern Italy," in *Painting for Profit: The Economic Lives of Seventeenth-Century Italian Painters,* ed. Richard E. Spear et al. (New Haven: Yale University Press, 2010), 275–301.

——, *Villa Spelman of The Johns Hopkins University: An Early History* (Florence: SPES, 2000).

Goldthwaite, Richard A., and Giulio Mandich, *Studi sulla moneta fiorentina (secoli XIII–XVI)* (Florence: Olschki, 1994).

Grazzini, Antonfrancesco (Il Lasca), *Le rime burlesche edite e inedite,* ed. Carlo Verzone (Florence: G. C. Sansoni, 1882).

Hanning, Barbara Russano, "Glorious Apollo: Poetic and Political Themes in the First Opera," *Renaissance Quarterly* 32 (1979): 485–513.

Harness, Kelley, *Echoes of Women's Voices: Music, Art, and Female Patronage in Early Modern Florence* (Chicago: University of Chicago Press, 2006).

Herlihy, David, R. Burr Litchfield, Anthony Molho, et al., eds., *Florentine Renaissance Resources: Online* Tratte *of Office Holders, 1282–1532*, <www.stg.brown.edu/projects/tratte>.

Hill, John Walter, "Beyond Isomorphism toward a Better Theory of Recitative," *Journal of Seventeenth-Century Music* 9 (2003), <www.sscm-jscm.org/v9no1.html>.

———, "Oratory Music in Florence, I: 'Recitar Cantando,' 1583–1655," *Acta musicologica* 51 (1979): 108–36.

———, *Roman Monody, Cantata, and Opera from the Circles around Cardinal Montalto*, 2 vols. (Oxford: Clarendon Press, 1997).

Hill, John Walter, and Kelley Harness, review of Warren Kirkendale, *The Court Musicians in Florence during the Principate of the Medici*, in *Journal of the American Musicological Society* 48 (1995): 106–15.

Hoshino, Hidetoshi, "Messina e l'arte della lana fiorentina nei secoli XVI–XVII," in *Studi dedicati a Carmelo Trasselli*, ed. Giovanni Motta (Soveria Mannelli [Catanzaro]: Rubbettino, 1983), 427–46.

Jones, P. J., "From Manor to *Mezzadria*: A Tuscan Case-study in the Medieval Origins of Modern Agrarian Society," in *Florentine Studies: Politics and Society in Renaissance Florence*, ed. Nicolai Rubinstein (London: Faber and Faber, 1968), 193–241.

Kirkendale, Warren, *The Court Musicians in Florence during the Principate of the Medici, with a Reconstruction of the Artistic Establishment*, "'Historiae musicae cultores' biblioteca" 61 (Florence: Olschki, 1993).

———, *Emilio de' Cavalieri, "gentiluomo romano": His Life and Letters, His Role as Superintendent of All the Arts at the Medici Court, and His Musical Compositions* (Florence: Olschki, 2001).

Klapisch-Zuber, Christiane, "Parenti, amici, vicini," *Quaderni storici* 33 (1976): 953–83; trans. as "Kin, Friends, Neighbors: The Urban Territory of a Merchant Family in 1400," in Klapisch-Zuber, *Women, Family, and Ritual in Renaissance Italy* (Chicago: University of Chicago Press, 1985), 68–93.

———, "San Romolo: Un vescovo, un lupo, un nome alle origini dello stato moderno," *Archivio storico italiano* 155 (1997): 3–48.

Lensi Orlandi Cardini, Giulio Cesare, *Le ville di Firenze di là d'Arno*, 2nd rev. ed. (Florence: Vallecchi, 1965).

Litchfield, R. Burr, "Demographic Characteristics of Florentine Patrician Families, Sixteenth to Nineteenth Centuries," *Journal of Economic History* 29 (1969): 191–205.

———, *Emergence of a Bureaucracy: The Florentine Patricians, 1530–1790* (Princeton: Princeton University Press, 1986).

———, *Florentine Renaissance Resources: Online Gazetteer of Sixteenth-Century Florence*, <www.stg.brown.edu/projects/florentine_gazetteer>.

Litta, Pompeo, et al., *Famiglie celebri italiane* (Milan: Giusti et al., 1819–74).

Lozzi, C., "La musica e specialmente il melodramma alla corte medicea," *Rivista musicale italiana* 9 (1902): 297–338.

Lubkin, Gregory, *A Renaissance Court: Milan under Galeazzo Maria Sforza* (Berkeley: University of California Press, 1994).

Malanima, Paolo, *La decadenza di un'economia cittadina: L'industria di Firenze nei secoli XVI–XVIII* (Bologna: Il Mulino, 1982).

————, *I Riccardi di Firenze: Una famiglia e un patrimonio nella Toscana dei Medici* (Florence: Olschki, 1977).

Malvezzi, Cristofano, Jacopo Peri, and Annibale Padovano, *Ensemble Ricercars*, ed. Milton A. Swenson, "Recent Researches in the Music of the Renaissance" 27 (Madison, WI: A-R Editions, 1978).

Maraschio, Nicoletta, "Il secondo Cinquecento," in *Storia della punteggiatura in Europa*, ed. Giuseppe Antonelli et al. (Rome: Laterza, 2008), 122–37.

McGee, Timothy, "Pompeo Caccini and *Euridice:* New Biographical Notes," *Renaissance and Reformation* 26 (1990): 81–99.

Menning, Carol Bresnahan, *The Monte di Pietà of Florence: Charity and State in Late Renaissance Italy* (Ithaca: Cornell University Press, 1993).

Molho, Anthony, *Marriage Alliance in Late Medieval Florence* (Cambridge, MA: Harvard University Press, 1994).

Monteverdi, Claudio, *Lettere*, ed. Éva Lax, "Studi e testi per la storia della musica" 10 (Florence: Olschki, 1994).

————, *The Letters,* trans. Denis Stevens, 2nd ed. (Oxford: Clarendon Press, 1995).

Morelli, Giorgio, "Saggio di lettere di musicisti dalle raccolte di autografi della Biblioteca Apostolica Vaticana," *Nuova rivista musicale italiana* 31 (1997): 367–485.

Mucciarelli, Roberta, and Gabriella Piccinni, "Un'Italia senza rivolte? Il conflitto sociale nelle aree mezzadrili," in *Protesta e rivolta contadina nell'Italia medievale*, ed. Giovanni Cherubini, *Annali dell'Istituto "Alcide Cervi,"* 16 (1994): 173–205.

Najemy, John M., *A History of Florence, 1200–1575* (Oxford: Blackwell, 2006).

Newcomb, Anthony, "Alfonso Fontanelli," in *The New Grove Dictionary of Music and Musicians: Revised Edition*, ed. Stanley Sadie, 29 vols. (London: Macmillan, 2001), 9: 76–78.

————, "Alfonso Fontanelli and the Ancestry of the *seconda pratica* Madrigal," in *Studies in Renaissance and Baroque Music in Honor of Arthur Mendel*, ed. Robert L. Marshall (Kassel: Bärenreiter, 1974), 47–68.

Paatz, Walter, and Elisabeth Valentiner Paatz, *Die Kirchen von Florenz: Ein kunstgeschichtliches Handbuch*, 5 vols. (Frankfurt am Main: Klostermann, 1952–55).

Padgett, John F., "Open Elite? Social Mobility, Marriage, and Family in Florence, 1282–1494," *Renaissance Quarterly* 63 (2010): 357–411.

Palisca, Claude V., *The Florentine Camerata: Documentary Studies and Translations* (New Haven: Yale University Press, 1989).

————, *Humanism in Italian Renaissance Musical Thought* (New Haven: Yale University Press, 1985).

————, "Musical Asides in the Diplomatic Correspondence of Emilio de' Cavalieri," *Musical Quarterly* 49 (1963): 339–55.

Parisi, Susan, "Ducal Patronage of Music in Mantua, 1587–1627: An Archival Study" (Ph.D. diss., University of Illinois at Urbana–Champaign, 1989).

Pegazzano, Donatella, *Committenza e collezionismo nel Cinquecento: La famiglia Corsi a Firenze tra musica e scultura*, "Le voci del museo" 22 (Florence: Edifir, 2010).

Peri, Jacopo, *"Euridice": An Opera in One Act, Five Scenes*, ed. Howard Mayer Brown, "Recent Researches in the Music of the Baroque Era" 36–37 (Madison, WI: A-R Editions, 1981).

————, *"Le varie musiche" and Other Songs*, ed. Tim Carter, "Recent Researches in the Music of the Baroque Era" 50 (Madison, WI: A-R Editions, 1985).

Pinto, Giuliano, "Contadini e proprietari nelle campagne fiorentine: Il piviere dell'Impruneta," in Pinto, *Toscana medievale: Paesaggi e realtà sociali* (Florence: Le Lettere, 1993), 153–80.

Pinto, Giuliano, and Ivan Tognarini, "Povertà e assistenza," in *Prato, storia di una città*, ed. Elena Fasano Guarini, 4 vols. (Florence: Le Monnier, 1986), 1: 429–500.

Polizzotto, Lorenzo, "I censi consegnativi bollari nella Firenze granducale: Storia di uno strumento di credito trascurato," *Archivio storico italiano* 168 (2010): 263–323.

Porter, William V., "Peri and Corsi's *Dafne:* Some New Discoveries and Observations," *Journal of the American Musicological Society* 18 (1965): 170–96.

Reiner, Stuart, " 'La vag'Angioletta' (and Others): 1," *Analecta musicologica* 14 (1974): 26–88.

Ricci, Giuliano de', *Cronaca (1532–1606)*, ed. Giuliana Sapori (Milan: Ricciardi, 1972).

Ruspoli, Francesco, *Poesie . . . commentate da Stefano Rosselli,* ed. C. Arlìa (Livorno: Francesco Vigo, 1882).

Saltini, Guglielmo Enrico, *Tragedie medicee domestiche (1557–87)* (Florence: Barbèra, 1898).

Salvadori, Andrea, *Poesie,* 2 vols. (Rome: Michele Ercole, 1668).

Saslow, James M., *The Medici Wedding of 1589: Florentine Festival as "theatrum mundi"* (New Haven: Yale University Press, 1996).

Solerti, Angelo, *Gli albori del melodramma*, 3 vols. (Turin: Bocca, 1903; repr. Hildesheim: G. Olms, 1969).

————, *Musica, ballo e drammatica alla corte medicea dal 1600 al 1637: Notizie tratte da un diario con appendice di testi inediti e rari* (Florence, 1905; repr. New York: Broude, 1968; repr. Bologna: Forni, 1989).

————, *Le origini del melodramma: Testimonianze dei contemporanei* (Turin: Bocca, 1903; repr. Bologna: Forni, 1969).

Sternfeld, Frederick W., "The First Printed Opera Libretto," *Music and Letters* 69 (1978): 121–38.

Strainchamps, Edmond, "Marco da Gagliano in 1608: Choices, Decisions, and Consequences," *Journal of Seventeenth-Century Music* 6/1 (2000), <www.sscm -jscm.org/v6no1.html>.

————, "New Light on the Accademia degli Elevati of Florence," *Musical Quarterly* 62 (1976): 507–35.

————, "The Unknown Letters of Marco da Gagliano," in *Music in the Theater, Church, and Villa: Essays in Honor of Robert Lamar Weaver and Norma Wright Weaver*, ed. Susan Parisi (Warren, MI: Harmonie Park Press, 2000), 89–111.

Strocchia, Sharon T., *Nuns and Nunneries in Renaissance Florence* (Baltimore: Johns Hopkins University Press, 2009).

Strunk, Oliver, *Source Readings in Music History*, rev. ed., vol. 4: *The Baroque Era*, ed. Margaret Murata (New York: Norton, 1998).

Testaverde, Anna Maria, "Nuovi documenti sulle scenografie di Ludovico Cigoli per l'*Euridice* di Ottavio Rinuccini," *Medioevo e Rinascimento* 17/n.s. 14 (2003): 307–21.

Treadwell, Nina, *Music and Wonder at the Medici Court: The 1589 Interludes for "La pellegrina"* (Bloomington: Indiana University Press, 2009).

Veneziano, Giulia, ed., *Rime e suoni alla spagnola: Atti della giornata internazionale di studi sulla chitarra barocca, Firenze, Biblioteca Riccardiana, 7 febbraio 2002* (Florence: Alinea, 2003).

Voci, Anna Maria, "La vendita dei diritti per la pubblicazione delle carte di Giorgio Vasari (1909/10): Un caso di competizione scientifica in un'epoca di forti suscettibilità nazionali," *Quellen und Forschungen aus italienischen Archiven und Bibliotheken* 83 (2003): 207–63.

Vogel, Emil, "Marco da Gagliano: Zur Geschichte des Florentiner Musiklebens von 1570–1650," *Vierteljahrsschrift für Musikwissenschaft* 5 (1889): 396–442, 509–68.

Walker, D. P., "Some Aspects of the Musical Theory of Vincenzo Galilei and Galileo Galilei," *Proceedings of the Royal Musical Association* 100 (1973–74): 33–47.

Walker, D. P., ed., *Musique des intermèdes de "La pellegrina": Les fêtes de Florence, 1589* (Paris: CNRS, 1963; repr. 1986).

Wilson, Blake, "Lauda," in *The New Grove Dictionary of Music and Musicians: Revised Edition*, ed. Stanley Sadie, 29 vols. (London: Macmillan, 2001), 14: 367–74.

Wistreich, Richard, *Warrior, Courtier, Singer: Giulio Cesare Brancaccio and the Performance of Identity in the Late Renaissance* (Aldershot, UK: Ashgate, 2007).

Zarri, Gabriella, *Recinti: Donne, clausura e matrimonio nella prima età moderna* (Bologna: Il Mulino, 2000).

Index

Striggio, Alessandro (the elder), 212n14,
    213, 215, 216, 233, 368, 376, 419, 421,
    422, 423
Striggio, Alessandro (the younger), 263n103,
    289, 309n188, 402; and Peri (1620),
    289–90, 291, 368, 419–23; poetry set by
    Peri, 289n155, 306, 380, 383–84, 394,
    431, 433, 434
Strozzi (family), 81; palace as performance
    space, 249
Strozzi, Giovanni Battista *il giovane*, 362n16
Strozzi, Piero di Matteo, 361; and the
    Camerata, 105; as composer, 105n154,
    111, 112, 120; and *Euridice*, 116; and
    Giulio Caccini, 105n154, 112, 257n87,
    273; and Jacopo Corsi, 107, 116, 120

Taddei, Giovanni, 132; bank with Matteo
    Niccolini, 132, 134
Tasso, Torquato, 59, 105, 107
Tatini, Alessandro di Salvestro, 229
taxation, taxes. *See* Florence, economy of
Teatro degli Uffizi, 30, 114, 249, 312, 377,
    378, 380, 385, 428, 429, 430, 431, 432,
    433
Teduci, Angiolino, 130
Tempi, Orazio and Piero: bank of, 160
Testi, Domenico, 362n18
Themistocles, 348, 360
Ticci, Francesco: bank in Rome, 170
time: reckoning of, 50n54
Tinghi, Cesare, 102, 220n23, 246, 249n72,
    250n75, 253, 256n84, 264n105, 297n171,
    431
titles, 81–82; forms of address (see *messer*;
    signore). *See also* Ser; *gentilhuomo*
Torchi, Luigi, 7–8
Torelli, Francesco, 310, 382, 435
Tornabuoni, Giovanni di Francesco, 353
Torricelle. *See* PERI 5 (farms and farmland)
Torrigiani bank, 75
tournaments (jousts, *sbarre*, etc.), 105n154,
    106, 118, 245, 246–49, 264, 268; Peri's

music for, 247, 261, 265, 271, 284, 290,
    296, 379, 381, 385, 392–94, 429, 430,
    432–33
Trabocchi (da Pienza), Aldobrando, 221,
    226, 234
trivium, 359
trombone (sackbut). *See* musical instruments
tuberculosis, 336, 337
typhus, 336

Ufficiali di Sanità, 321
Uffizi Theatre. *See* Teatro degli Uffizi
Urban VIII (pope), 2, 4, 78
Usimbardi, Maria, 99, 100
usury. *See* capital market

Vaini, Enea, 161, 221n26, 234, 235, 236, 237,
    259, 271, 379, 392
Vanetti, Antonio di Francesco (*Il Moretto*),
    226, 228
Vasari, Giorgio, 20
Vecchi, Orazio, 116
Vecchi Delle Palle, Scipione, 210n10, 233, 242
veglie, 250n75, 262; Peri's music for, 247,
    250–52
Venice, 76, 80, 102, 129, 246, 275, 276n123,
    362
Venterucci, Diaceto, 175, 342n61, 344n64
Venturi del Nibbio, Stefano, 112
villa (as social phenomenon). *See* Florence,
    aspects of social life
Villa all'Olmo. *See* PERI 5
Villa di Castello, 379
Villifranchi, Giovanni, 430, 436
Vinta, Belisario, 101, 215, 231, 258, 279, 291,
    378, 391–92
viola da braccio (violin, etc). *See* musical
    instruments
viola da gamba (viol). *See* musical
    instruments
Visconti, Domenico, 339n54
Vitali, Filippo, 4, 362
Vitis, Honorio di Domenico Antonio, 130